Business Policy and Strategy

Text and Cases

The Goodyear Series in
Administration and Business Management

Lyman W. Porter
Joseph W. McGuire
Series Editors

MICHAEL BEER, *Organization Change and Development: A Systems View* (1980)

Y. N. CHANG, FILEMON CAMPO-FLORES, *Business Policy and Strategy: Text and Cases* (1980)

Business Policy and Strategy (soft-cover version—text only) (1980)

G. JAMES FRANCIS, GENE MILBOURN, JR., *Human Behavior in the Work Environment* (1980)

ROBERT H. MILES, *Macro Organizational Behavior* (1980)

Resourcebook in Macro Organizational Behavior (1980)

Business Policy and Strategy

Text and Cases

Y. N. Chang
California State University, Fullerton

Filemon Campo-Flores
California State University, Long Beach

GOODYEAR PUBLISHING COMPANY, INC.
Santa Monica, California

Library of Congress Cataloging in Publication Data

CHANG, Y N
Business policy and strategy.
(Goodyear series in administration and business management)
Includes index.
1. Management. 2. Corporate planning.
3. Industrial management—United States—Case studies. I. Campo-Flores, F., joint author.
II. Title. III. Series.
HD31.C4579 658.4'01 79-22714
ISBN 0-87620-127-3

ISBN: 0-87620-127-3

Y-1273-5

Current printing (last number):
10 9 8 7 6 5 4 3 2 1

Printed in the United States of America

To members of our families:
Jean, Gary, Andrew, and Audrey Chang,
and
Laura and Arian Campo-Flores.

Contributors

John A. Pearce II
Sexton Adams and Adelaide Griffin
Roger M. Atherton and Dennis M. Crites
John E. Grob under the supervision of Y. N. Chang
Charles F. Hoitash
Charles C. Snow
R. W. Allen
F. Campo-Flores
Kelvin M. Teeven
Dharmendra T. Verma
Jerome L. Youderian and Jack Van Haaster under the supervision of Y. N. Chang
Zoe-Vonna Milligan under the supervision of D. J. Piehl
Forrest W. Price and Albert Winkler
Barry Richman
Susanne Franklin and Margaret Krasnick under the supervision of Y. N. Chang
Thomas Wheelen, J. David Hunger, and C. Allan Foster
Lawrence D. Chrzanowski and Charles S. Wilson under the supervision of Ram Charan
Ephaim Smith and Eleanor Schwartz
Melvin J. Stanford
Patrick Manterer under the supervision of Y. N. Chang
Robert Jechart, Francis J. MacBride, and Steven M. Elliott under the supervision of Y. N. Chang
William Naumes
Edward B. Beckerley and Reginald J. Brown under the supervision of Y. N. Chang
James Hillquist under the supervision of Y. N. Chang
Jeremy F. Plant under the supervision of Donald Axelrod, Renneselaer Wallace, and William Wallace
Leete A. Thompson
W. Harvey Hegarty and Harry Kelsey
Robert D. Hay
David Sprinkgate
C. E. Ferguson and L. Dandurand

Contents

ILLUSTRATION CAPSULES

Preface

In the study of business policy and strategy, there is a trend toward greater emphasis on text material and its integration with case analysis. Teachers as well as students are searching for innovative ways to pursue this method of study because it fulfills the requirement of a capstone course in the business curriculum and also reflects the increasing attention that the business world is giving to policy and strategy.

This book has been prepared to meet this challenge. Specifically, it fulfills three objectives. First, it provides a comprehensive and logically structured body of knowledge as a framework for teaching the policy course. Second, it provides a group of carefully selected cases to illustrate text materials and develop the student's ability to analyze complex problems. Third, it bridges, for the student, that puzzling gap between academic theory and actual business practice.

There are eighteen chapters of original text material, plus thirty case studies. Cases are introduced at the end of each part in order to facilitate their meaningful integration with text material. Our text section is comprehensive but structured for easy understanding.

A simplified conceptual model governs the design of the book. We present policy-strategy as an integrated concept embedded in the end-means chain. We present strategy-making as a function to encompass three distinct but closely related activities: strategic planning, which is confined to policy deliberation and objective-setting (that is, what the company is and desires to be); strategic formulation, which deals with the exploring and selecting of strategic alternatives (that is, how the company will meet its present and future challenges); and strategic management, which focuses on the implementing, adjusting, and recycling of strategies (that is, how strategies can be put to work consistently well). By accepting such hypotheses, this complex subject can be presented simply. To this end, we have conscientiously avoided the common faults of ambiguity and information overkill, which often cause text material to lose focus. Our presentation balances theoretical exposition with practical treatment of how strategic issues are dealt with and how strategies are made and implemented.

The thrust of this book is to disclose the ways in which business policy and strategy can be studied as an organized body of knowledge, an analytical skill, and an attitude for learning and management. Part One, The Conceptual Framework of Business Policy and Strategy, explains the rationale for studying business policy and strategy and defines a conceptual model that guides the logical development of the book. The main body of the text—Parts Two, Three, and Four—contains thirteen chapters that discuss strategy-making as an organized whole.

In Part Two (strategic planning), we discuss organizing and administering the strategic function, analyzing external and internal factors, deliberating policy issues, and setting objectives.

In Part Three (strategic formulation), we zero in on corporate and functional strategies. A matrix of strategic alternatives is constructed to describe the three situations of growth, profit instability, and financial insolvency. Typical problems to be encountered in each of these stages and the likely approaches to be followed in each of the three situations are described. The three basic strategies of growth, stability, and survival thus form a logically constructed framework for studying and analyzing cases. Functional strategies are discussed as the driving forces of corporate strategy and as a linkage between strategies and tactics. Three chapters are devoted to this important subject. Chapters 10 and 11 offer discussions on marketing and finance, respectively; in chapter 12, research and development (R&D) and production strategies are studied.

The three chapters in Part Four discuss strategic management—strategy-structure-process, tactical planning and execution, strategic control, and recycling strategies.

Part Five (strategies in special situations) offers a unique treatment of business strategies for small business and international business. Chapter 18 summarizes the text and assesses the future outlook.

Extensive research was undertaken in the preparation of this book. We reviewed the most recent writings both in the United States and abroad and incorporated relevant citations from the policy and strategy books, research papers, and periodicals. Important studies made by business executives have been included, and other writings of benefit to the student are cited in notes at the end of each chapter. In our research, we found that certain topics of importance are missing from most textbooks. Hence, there are treatments of newly developed materials on social responsibility (Chapter 6), corporate strategies (Chapters 8 and 9), and functional strategies (Chapters 10, 11, and 12), tactical planning and execution (Chapter 13), small business strategy (Chapter 16), and international business strategy (Chapter 17).

Throughout the book, company cases are used for illustration. Especially significant examples are presented as Illustration Capsules. Illustration Capsules also highlight techniques for review, such as ratio analysis, planning models, and useful analytical techniques.

Case instruction is an integral part of the policy course. When properly used, it provides one of the best learning methods. It stimulates independent thinking, self-discovery, and learning from peers. The cases in this book have been carefully selected to represent a variety of industries, business sizes, and situations. To facilitate quick reference, there is a matrix (Table A, p. 40) presenting pertinent data for each case. There is also a discussion of our case selection criteria.

We, the authors, have a combined industrial experience of more than 23 years and policy teaching experience of 16 years. We have long appreciated the challenge of teaching the policy course, and we believe that our collaboration has added a new dimension to the study of business policy.

In undertaking this project, the authors are indebted to many individuals for their encouragement, stimulation, and constructive critiques. We wish to express special thanks to Professors Joseph W. McGuire and Lyman W. Porter of the University of California, Irvine, series editors for the Goodyear Series in Administration and Business Management, for their support and invaluable suggestions. Roger Holloway and Hal Humphrey, Goodyear Publishing Company, have meticulously executed the project from the beginning to the end. Professors Charles C. Snow of Pennsylvania State University, Geoffrey R. King of California State University, Fullerton, and David B. Jemison of the University of Indiana, Bloomington, also read the complete manuscript and offered suggestions that materially increased the quality and usefulness of the book.

Sincere appreciation is due our colleagues who generously granted permission to include their cases in the book. Our thanks also go to our students at California State University, Fullerton who have in various ways helped prepare several cases that are contained in the book.

PART I

The Conceptual Framework of Business Policy and Strategy

The conceptual framework of business policy and strategy will be examined from two perspectives: the theoretical perspective of studying the policy course, and the practical perspective of applications in the business world. Strategy is a crucial element in war. Depending upon its application, battles are won or lost, generals and statesmen glorified or condemned. In politics, strategic concepts are employed in foreign affairs and in election campaigns. In business, strategy plays a central role in sustaining a viable present and a promising future for the company. As it is in war and politics, strategy making in business is an art of general management, a game of competition, and a technique of managing in times of rapid change and uncertainty. Strategy making is an attitude, a mode of thinking and of action, and a style of managing. Strategy is a concept of great complexity and a discipline of considerable rigor.

In the first two chapters, we provide a rationale for studying policy and strategy and explain what the study has to offer to business students. In chapter 1, the basic framework and nature of the concept of business strategy are discussed at length. In chapter 2, the concept is examined from a broader perspective, studying its application in war, politics, and business. Our object in this chapter is to present business strategy as the central thrust of contemporary management and to stress competence in strategy making as a prerequisite for and necessary attribute of aspiring business executives. The study of strategy to this end meets the challenge of a capstone, integrative course and exposes students to a field vital to their pursuit of a profession.

CHAPTER ONE

The Concept and Its Generic Nature

Business policy is fast becoming one of the most challenging and rewarding courses in the business curriculum. This course offers students various benefits: (1) the opportunity to review what they have learned in the past and to pull all that knowledge together in the present policy course; (2) the chance to develop skills for analyzing and solving complex business problems; (3) the chance to learn a new discipline—that is, the application of strategic concepts in business management; and (4) the opportunity to develop an awareness of the relationship between classroom study and the application of strategy in the business world.

In this chapter, we examine business policy and strategy as a field of study and discuss the concept in great detail. It is here that we introduce definitions of key terms, the conceptual model, and the rationale for the structure of the book. We then discuss the various facets and characteristics of business strategy.

THE STUDY AND RESEARCH OF BUSINESS POLICY AND STRATEGY

During the past two decades, business policy and strategy as a discipline has rapidly matured, and study in this field has become more rewarding. There are two reasons for this development: (1) the increasing realization of the importance of strategy in the policy course; and (2) the accelerated pace of research.

Emphasis on Strategy

The dual concept of policy and strategy is becoming more integrated. Business policy, which defines a company's purpose, mission, and objectives, fully complements strategy, which specifies critical courses of action and means of deploying resources to achieve company objectives. They are tied together through the end-and-means linkage. Both in concept and in practice, however, business strategy is the underlying theme of the policy course. It provides much of the substance and dynamism of the course and mirrors the practice of strategy in corporate management. In the classroom, the early and more confined approach to studying policy as an aspect of general management has now greatly expanded to include the treatment of strategy. Thus, in more recently published books on policy, we witness the frequent linking of policy and strategy in book titles and a more comprehensive treatment of both.[1] In the business world, the early emphasis on long-range planning, basically a policy activity, has long undergone changes toward the adoption of the total concept of strategy management. Thus, recent wide discussion on corporate strategies in business literature reflects the evolution of this trend.[2]

Studying business strategy serves multiple functions in the policy course:

1. Students learn the substantive and behavioral aspects of strategy making. Strategy making follows the methodical development that centers on substantial analysis of the contending forces and their dynamics. This involves systematic examination of external and internal factors and exhaustive exploration of options and alternatives. Of equal importance is the behavioral significance implicit in decision making; it affects personal values, ethics, interpersonal relationships, and organizational behavior at large.
2. Students learn the skill of identifying strategic issues, those limiting and crucial issues confronting an organization in a given situation. Strategic thinking enables students to differentiate the major issues from the trivial and to search for solutions to resolve short-term and long-term problems simultaneously.
3. Students learn to deal with specific issues of functional importance. Hence, their past learning in economics, management, marketing, finance, production, and other disciplines is brought to bear.
4. Students learn that strategy is a subtle concept, a skill, and an attitude. They learn to apply strategy to achieve established objectives, develop skills to formulate and execute strategies, and adopt an attitude of analyzing and resolving problems strategically. Possessing a high level of strategy-making capability enhances the graduate's chance to advance professionally.

Research in Policy and Strategy

A substantial increase in the amount of published research work in the past few years has played an important part in facilitating the study of business policy and strategy. The research studies can be divided into two areas: conceptual development, and empirical research.

CONCEPTUAL DEVELOPMENT There have been important advances made in the exploration of the dual concept of policy and strategy itself. The initial works on the subject are those of Alfred D. Chandler, Jr., Kenneth Andrews, and H. Igor Ansoff.[3] Chandler's book is a pioneering work on corporate strategic development; Andrews concentrates on the role of top management in policy and strategy, viewing the role as that of architect of strategic development and implementor of strategic execution. Ansoff makes a serious inquiry into the rationale, theory, and processes of corporate growth strategy. Recent writers, notably C. Roland Christensen, William E. Glueck, Thomas J. McNichols, and Charles W. Hofer, have made significant contributions through their textbooks and research findings, and their works provide broader interpretations of the framework.[4]

A number of studies have shown that strategy has a positive impact on a firm's performance. Thus, the suggestion of Stanley Thune and Robert House that companies using formal planning outperform the nonplanners has been substantiated by other studies (see illustration capsule 1). Still others have suggested that the concept of strategic planning should be broadened to one of strategic management.[5] In a conference organized in May 1973 at the Graduate School of Management of Vanderbilt University, the concept of strategy management was explained. Here, strategy management was presented as a chosen system of management that conceives, selects, and implements "strategic programmes."[6] Underlining the concept of strategy management is the emphasis on the interplay of external and internal forces, the dynamic relationship of policy and strategy, and the development of "strategic management systems." In essence, strategy management must be viewed as encompassing the three activities of planning, formulation, and implementation.

Illustration Capsule 1

RESEARCH STUDIES ON THE IMPACT OF STRATEGIC PLANNING UPON PROFITABILITY

Thune and House Study

The authors attempted to calibrate the success of companies engaged in formal planning as opposed to those in informal planning on the basis of an economic performance criterion. The authors analyzed individual company performance as well as industry-by-industry comparisons among thirty-six firms engaged in the drug, chemical, machinery, oil, food, and steel industries. It was found that the greatest success among long-range planners occurred in rapidly changing industries and among medium-sized companies. The conclusion derived from the study's data indicates that a strong correlation exists between impressive economic performance and the use of long-range planning.

Source: Stanley S. Thune and Robert J. House, "Where Long-Range Planning Pays Off," *Business Horizons,* August 1970, pp. 81–87.

The Herold Report

The author conducted a seven-year study of firms employing formal planning and firms employing informal planning methods in the drug and chemical industries. In all cases, those firms whose management utilized formal planning techniques, reinforced by above-average R&D expenditures, significantly outperformed those firms that did not rely on formal planning. He concluded that formal planning should be considered a strong indicator of a firm's future success.

Source: David M. Herold, "Long-Range Planning and Organizational Performance: A Cross Valuation Study," *Academy of Management Journal,* March 1972, pp. 91–102.

The PIMS Study

The Profit Impact of Market Strategies (PIMS) is being developed to measure the effects of strategic decisions upon a company's return on investment. PIMS is a profit model comprising thirty-seven distinct variables that reflect the profitability of a company in the context of its competitive position. The three most significant factors determining return on investment were market share, investment intensity, and unique company factors, such as diversification or specialization. The PIMS model provides management with a useful tool for the realistic assessment of corporate and divisional objectives and strategic choices.

Source: Stanley Schoeffler, Robert D. Buzzell, and Donal F. Hearny, "Impact of Strategic Planning on Profit Performance," *Harvard Business Review,* March/April 1974, pp. 137–45.

The Karger and Malik Report

The authors proposed to determine the success of long-range planning efforts. The success of these efforts were compiled on the basis of generally accepted financial performance measurements. Ninety U.S. companies in five industry categories participated. Results illustrated the superior performance of those firms employing long-range planning methods over those firms that did not. The researchers concluded that management is either delinquent or grossly negligent if long-range planning is not implemented.

Source: Delmar W. Karger and Zafar A. Malik, "Long Range Planning and Organizational Performance," *Long Range Planning,* December 1975, pp. 60–4.

EMPIRICAL RESEARCH In the area of empirical research, a large amount of literature exists. One of the major sources of material comes from the Academy of Management, which discusses policies and strategies at its annual meetings.

In recent years, studies have been focusing on strategic behavior. Several researchers made the initial inquiries into how business firms perceive strategic problems and how they select and pursue appropriate types of strategies for a set of environmental conditions. In addition, there are research studies on methods of teaching and studying the policy course. These studies are summarized in illustration capsule 2. Policy literature is also extensively reported in journals in the United States and in Europe.[7]

Illustration Capsule 2

REPRESENTATIVE EMPIRICAL STUDIES REPORTED AT THE ACADEMY OF MANAGEMENT ANNUAL MEETINGS

Hofer Study

The focus of this study was on the content of strategy in contrast with prior concentration on processes. The author suggested that "it is now feasible to develop a series of conditional propositions about the most appropriate types of strategic behavior for a given set of environmental conditions." To this end, the author summarized studies up to that time and listed hypotheses and propositions of the early writers. He then presented a list of strategically significant environmental and organizational variables and proposed a four-step research towards the construction of a framework to guide the development of a contingency theory of business strategy.

Source: Charles W. Hofer, "Toward a Contingency Theory of Business Strategy," *Academy of Management Journal*, December 1975, pp. 784–810. First reported in *Proceedings of the Academy of Management, 1974*, p. 5.

Schendel and Patton Study

In this study, the authors attempted to answer the question of why some firms are able to recover from decline or stagnation, although others seem unable to do so. By using thirty-five match-pair samples drawn from twenty-four SEC classes, the authors showed that under similar circumstances the recovered firms and nonrecovered firms displayed varying behavior in the choice of strategy and its implementation, thus, resulting in different outcomes. This paper will be followed by another one examining specific strategic and tactical moves.

Source: Dan Schendel and G. R. Patton, "An Empirical Study of Corporate Stagnation and Turnaround," *Proceedings of the Academy of Management, 1975*, pp. 49–51.

Godiwalla, Meinhart, and Warde Study

Focusing on a different area of investigation, these authors reported findings derived from questionnaire replies from 195 U.S. chief executive officers. The authors attempted to show how strategic configurations and influence mixes (or priority mixes) affect chief executive officers' perception in different organizational environments. By classifying a firm's organizational environment into four types, a contingency framework indicating the nature and composition of the effective strategic configurations and influence mixes can be constructed. The researchers showed the different sets of perceptions under each of the environmental conditions.

Source: Yezdi M. Godiwalla, Wayne A. Meinhart, and William D. Warde, "The Strategic Configurations and Influence Mixes of Organizational Functions for Overall Corporate Strategy," *Proceedings of the Academy of Management, 1978*, pp. 111–15.

Richards Report

In this study of 150 graduate and undergraduate policy courses, aided by personal interviews and examinations of syllabuses and teaching materials, Richards found that diversity in teaching policy was "not only understandable and expected but desirable at this stage." Twenty-two separate objectives were examined and related to appropriate teaching vehicles. The author showed that there is a complementary relationship between classroom teaching and empirical research. He considered this to be an encouraging sign pointing toward better teaching and learning.

Source: Max D. Richards, "Diversity in Teaching," *Proceedings of the Academy of Management, 1976*, pp. 155–59.

Definition of Key Terms

For a meaningful discourse, it is important that some of the key terms used in this book be defined before we set forth our conceptual model. Clear definition reduces semantic difficulties and clarifies the logical structure of a theory.

Business policy: A basic framework defining the fundamental issues of a company, its purpose, mission, and broad business objectives, and a set of guidelines governing the company's conduct of business within its total perspective.

Strategy: A master plan that delineates critical courses of action toward the attainment of company objectives, and a blueprint that defines the means of deploying resources to exploit present and future opportunities and to counteract present and future threats.

Strategy making: An integrated activity composed of a series of decisions and actions that include strategic planning, strategic formulation, and strategic management.

Purpose, mission, goals, and objectives: Purpose refers to a company's statement on the basic characteristics of its enterprise; *mission* refers to the scope and direction of business endeavors. *Goals* are general in nature; *objectives* are specific statements of achievements targeted for a certain time frame. *Goals* and *objectives* are used interchangeably.

Functional strategies: Strategies confined to a critical functional area, but nevertheless designed to substantiate and support the firm's total strategy. Functional strategies may include plans for marketing, finance, R&D, manufacturing, and management.

Tactics: An organized but ceaseless stream of specific actions designed to execute strategic decisions.

THE FRAMEWORK OF THE BOOK

The Conceptual Model

Figure 1.1 depicts the conceptual model we will use in guiding the development of our study. The model is based on three premises: (1) strategy making is an integrated activity made up of three distinct activities; (2) policy and strategy are related in the ends-and-means relationship; and (3) strategy and tactics are considered as a unified concept. To attain consistent performance, the organization cannot depend solely upon the actions of top management but must rely as well on the efforts of the lower ranks in implementing the supporting strategies and tactics.

The model is constructed of four blocks:

1. *Business policy* constitutes the ends—the deliberation of the company's purpose, mission, and objectives by the board of directors and the chief executive officer (CEO)/president.
2. *Strategy* sets forth the means—the delineation of courses of action and resource allocation in a plan, formulated at the general-management level.[8]

FIGURE 1.1 A SIMPLIFIED CONCEPTUAL MODEL

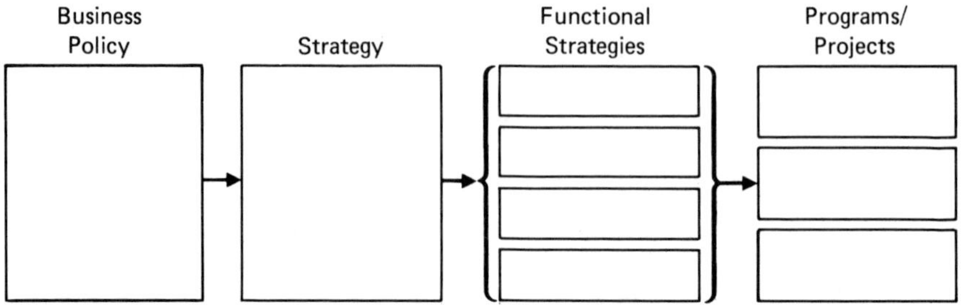

Ends: "WHAT" • Purpose • Mission • Goals/objectives	Means: "HOW" • Courses of action • Resource allocation • Strategic guidelines	Submeans • Functionally based • Support to strategy • Basis for tactics	Submeans • Tactically oriented • Functional programs • Special projects
Board of Directors/ CEO/President	CEO/President/ Group Presidents/ Division General Managers	Functional Managers	Functional/Program/ Project Managers

3. *Functional strategies* are submeans—the explorations of strategic/tactical actions to support company strategy, and a linkage between strategies and tactics.

4. *Programs and projects* are submeans—the planning of tactical actions at functional and supervisory levels.

Strategy Making as an Integrated Function

The first premise on which we based our conceptual model is that strategy making is an integrated function consisting of three distinct but closely related activities: strategic planning, strategic formulation, and strategic management (see figure 1.2). A brief discussion of the strategy-making concept is in order here not only because it elaborates on our conceptual model, but also because these three activities form the core of our structural model.

Strategic planning is viewed as a policy-making function. It is concerned with defining the company's basic characteristics (purpose), the composition of its business mix (mission), and the qualitative and quantitative projection of its achievement (short- and long-term business objectives). Included in strategic planning activities are the environmental analysis made to assess opportunities and threats, the position audit of internal capabilities, and the setting of business objectives. In substance, strategic planning articulates goals, deliberates policy issues, and assumes the company's capacity to achieve.

Strategic formulation encompasses all the activities related to the development of strategies at general-management and functional levels. The total organization is considered in exploring viable means to deploy resources, mobilize organizational forces, and prescribe a program of strategic actions to achieve the

FIGURE 1.2 THE THREE PHASES OF STRATEGY MAKING

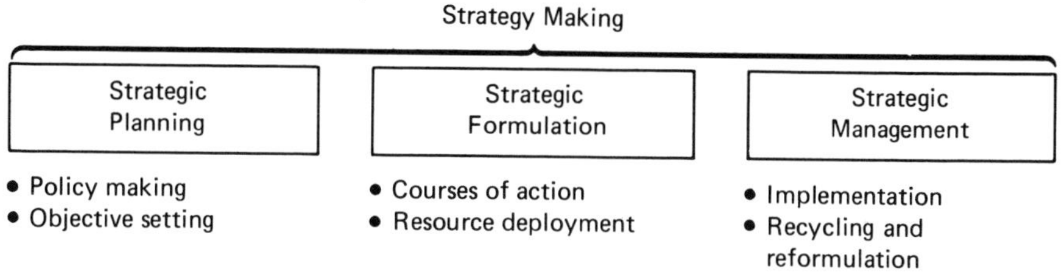

company's established objectives. Strategic planning defines the ends and visualizes the perspective; strategic formulation explores alternative means and generates directional and programmed activities to overcome constraints and explore opportunities. Strategic formulation includes developing strategic guidelines, conducting situation studies, and formulating strategic plans.

Strategic management, the third phase of the integrated function, covers all activities involving implementing, recycling, and reformulating strategies. Implementation is the operating aspect of strategy making—the initiation of strategic and tactical actions and the institution of the control mechanisms to measure and take corrective actions. As strategic assumptions evolve simultaneously with new information and coming events, the validity of the strategy must be tested, updated, modified. Effective strategic management converts a sound strategy into action. Indeed, a brilliantly conceived strategy would be only an abstract idea if it incited no action. A fully developed strategy would be rendered ineffective if it lacked provision for adjusting and recycling.

The Structure of the Book

The structure of the book, depicted in figure 1.3, is an outgrowth of the conceptual models presented in figures 1.1 and 1.2. Because we have based our conceptual model on a logical analysis of strategy making, the course material is presented in a logical, integrated manner. Each of the five parts follows in turn our conceptual progression.

Part One, The Conceptual Framework of Business Policy and Strategy, focuses on why business strategy is relevant to students' learning.

Part Two, Policy Making and Strategy Planning, centers on how policy issues are studied and strategic planning is accomplished.

Part Three, Strategy Formulation, emphasizes what types of strategies are formulated to meet varying situations at both corporate and functional levels.

Part Four, Strategy Management, discusses how strategies are converted into tactics and actions.

Part Five, Business Strategies in Special Situations, explains how strategies are formulated in small firms and international operations, thus applying the previous parts of the text.

FIGURE 1.3 THE STRUCTURAL MODEL

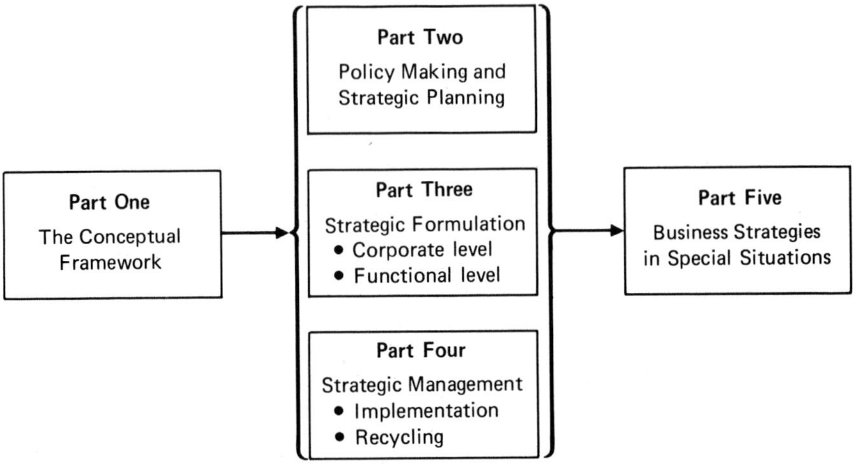

THE NATURE OF BUSINESS STRATEGY

A Concept of Management

Business strategy is a management concept in that it affords a fundamental method for solving complex business problems. Strategy making is an attitude and a dedication that evolves around the intelligent and deliberate contemplation of the present and future, the economical use of resources, and the development of means for achieving objectives. It should not be abstract, mechanistic, or totally quantitative because quantitative, formalistic thinking is no substitute for seasoned human intuition and judgment.[9] Strategy making demands discipline, creativity, and the total management of the process. In particular, company executives find it difficult to grasp the fine points. Causes of strategy malfunction include lack of conceptual guidance, inadequate staff support, insufficient commitment by supervisors, and separation of tactical management from operational authority.[10]

A proper understanding of strategy making requires that we review the objective-strategy-implementation linkage and the external-strategy-internal decision framework. In both cases, strategy serves as the pivotal link. It is generally assumed that individual and organizational actions are goal oriented. When a person is hungry, he or she initiates action to satisfy the desire for food, and when an organization has discovered a purpose, it strives for achievement of that purpose. For business organizations, however, goal setting is more complex than it is for individuals. Business objectives must be identified in specific terms—rate of growth or recovery, sales dollars, profit margin, and return on investment, to name a few. They must be both realistic and achievable. For example, if a company set its objectives far above the industry average and beyond what the company had ever achieved in the past, such objectives would not be willingly supported by the people who are supposed to work toward their realization.

A good strategy is set forth without generalization; it specifies who does what, when they do it, and how. Strategy critically evaluates objectives to determine if they are realistic and achievable and at the same time defines a course of action or method of implementation. Without such careful definition, strategy is no more than an expression of aspiration and a futile exercise in intellectual vanity. If it provides anything less than a master plan or blueprint, it gives no sense of direction to the implementation process and no incentive for intelligent actions.

The Meaning of Matching and Calculating

The decision framework in which strategy is the pivotal link between the external environment and internal organization centers on choice—thc matching of capabilities and opportunities. Matching suggests two essential ingredients: estimation, and calculation.

Estimation, or forecasting, requires a company to make forecasts concerning the economy, the industry, and technology. A business firm that projects a straight-line increase of sales year after year defies the facts of modern economic life. An industry's probable future trends, changing characteristics, and prospects of being the target for government regulations offer opportunities and place restrictions on a business firm's future possibilities. The marketplace—its size, demand, and changing characteristics—also affects a company's probability of success. In modern times, technology can create or displace an industry or a market. Competition poses threats as well as opportunities, demanding the serious consideration of options. Intelligent consultation of published forecasts and specialists and judgment of probabilities, and objective assessment of the market that the company is serving and that which will develop are prerequisites of sound strategic formulation.

Calculation is the key element in matching external opportunities with internal capabilities. It is an art of comparing and risk taking. It requires objectivity, cold calculation, and preparatory action, aimed at building a readiness for action and a posture for decision. Company capabilities can be expressed in quantitative and qualitative terms concerning strengths and weaknesses. Such evaluation reflects the substantive parts of a company's present and future capacities. Future capabilities, either expanded or consolidated, must be objectively specified, quantitatively stated, and realistically projected. Exaggeration or underestimation of these capabilities often leads to faulty calculation. In the 1960s, when growth was the accepted theme, few companies took sufficient note of the difficulties that would be inherent in managing greatly enlarged operations. The miscalculation of RCA's projected capabilities in its computer venture negatively affected the outcome. Likewise, the correct assessment of the market opportunities by Ford in its Mustang project was a classic example of bold, on-target calculation. A wise executive makes an attempt at calculating chances of success *before* he or she sets company objectives and explores the development of a strategy. Assessment and appreciation of capacity, strengths, and weaknesses are the prerequisites of strategy selection.

The Art of Strategy Making

In the study of military strategy, principles are drawn from past wars and battles because certain patterns of conduct are considered decisive in affecting the outcome of military engagements. Likewise, in business strategy making, certain rules can be deduced that, when properly applied, increase the grasp of the art.

TOTAL MANAGEMENT VIEW Business strategy must be formulated from the point of view of general management. The interests and purposes of the total enterprise take precedence over departmental claims in determining objectives, priorities, and resource allocation. In developing company strategy, a general manager should not be prejudiced by a natural preoccupation with past specializations, biased by a preoccupation with one issue at the expense of all others, or restricted to a limited course of action.

FULL IMPACT The deployment of a company's resources must exert its full impact in the marketplace. As in war, all forces must be coordinated to deliver their total impact upon the opponent. Marketing, technology, finance, and management have a combined force in business strategy. Full impact can be achieved by exploiting company strengths while developing counteractions to conceal company weaknesses. Polaroid Corp.'s action in developing and launching the SX-70 camera is a good example of a well-conceived and executed strategy achieving full impact. Developed under guarded secrecy for several years, the SX-70 was the first completely self-developing color picture camera and represented an important technological advance. When it was launched in October 1972, Polaroid staged such a complete advertising and marketing program that the product received an enthusiastic reception far beyond normal anticipation.[11]

CONTENDING FORCES In the business world, the company must contend with three primary forces—the customer, competitors, and the government—each decisively affecting a company's posture. Sound strategy requires accurate and thorough assessment of the role, impact, and behavior of these forces. Sensitivity to changes in customer attitudes and needs is fundamental to a company's success. Options are limited by the competitive alignment in the industry, by the strengths and weaknesses of the company and its various competitors, by past behavior, and by probable behavior in the future. Likewise, government and community actions not only affect the company's position but greatly narrow the selection of strategies and tactics.

TIMING, FLEXIBILITY, CONCENTRATION, AND CONTINGENCY PLANNING Timing is of the essence in business strategy. Time of entry into a market, time of acquisition, and time of marketing actions are a few examples. IBM's timely introduction of several generations of computers has been a highly significant factor in the company's business success. Poorly timed acquisitions can bring disasters. Rockwell International's acquisition of Admiral Corp. in April 1974, at the time of a recession, brought the company into financial crisis.[12]

Flexibility of posture has a special meaning in a dynamic business environment. Sudden turns of economic activity, quick counteractive thrusts by competitors, and changing customer attitudes all require strategic adjustments. Quick regrouping of resources, modification of objectives, and changes in the timetable are necessary actions. Concentration of effort is a difficult rule to follow. In industries such as aerospace and engineering construction, for which the primary method of realizing sales is bidding, careful selection of bidding opportunities is a crucial task of management. Such selection economizes resources, sustains engineering and marketing efforts over the long term, and generally increases the firm's probability of success. A rifle-shot approach is always preferable to a shotgun approach. Contingency planning is a preventive action that facilitates quick shifts of position in anticipation of unlikely but foreseeable changes.

REALISM, RELEVANCY, AND CONSTRAINTS Realism in forecasting future opportunities and threats and in assessing the company's competitive position and resource capabilities can prevent undue procrastination and purely paper theorizing. Relevancy in identifying issues of importance and in stimulating top management to assume the prime responsibility for strategic problems is a prerequisite to sound strategy making.

In formulating strategy, there are certain constraints that, if not properly understood, will adversely affect the outcome of a strategy. Constraints caused by future uncertainty, resource limitations, management inadequacy, and external threats imposed by sociopolitical factors and competition are realities of business life. They must be studied, appraised, and dealt with.

SUMMARY

From our brief overview, a few concluding remarks are in order. First, the study of policy and strategy serves a distinct purpose and offers benefits to students.

Second, conceptual clarity is important. To this end, we introduced a conceptual model and the concept of strategy making. Together, they form the framework for the structure of our book. Third, conciseness in thought increases comprehension. In our discourse on the nature of business strategy, we have identified a few key concepts. We agree with most of the contemporary writers that strategy is a management concept; its effectiveness, however, depends on its total acceptance on the part of top management. We also stressed the matching and calculating process, and the factors involved in the art of strategy making. The grasp of these simple, yet subtle, concepts are imperative in the study of business policy and strategy. We will now turn to a review of strategy in action—how the concept has been applied in the business world.

NOTES

1. For example, see William E. Glueck, *Business Policy: Strategy Formulation and Management Action* (New York: McGraw-Hill, 1976); George A. Steiner and John B. Miner, *Management Policy and Strategy: Text, Readings, and Cases* (New York: Macmillan, 1977); Hugo E. R. Uyterhoeven, Robert W. Ackerman, and John W. Rosenblum, *Strategy and Organization: Text and Cases in General Management* (Homewood, Ill.: Irwin, 1973); and Arthur A. Thompson, Jr., and A. J. Strickland III, *Strategy and Policy: Concepts and Cases* (Dallas, Texas: Business Publications, 1978).
2. For a notable example, see the weekly section on corporate strategies in *Business Week*.
3. Chandler, *Strategy and Structure: A Chapter in the History of Industrial Enterprises* (Cambridge, Mass.: MIT Press, 1962); Andrews, *The Concept of Corporate Strategy* (Homewood, Ill.: Dow Jones-Irwin, 1974); and Ansoff, *Corporate Strategy* (New York: McGraw-Hill, 1965).

4. See C. Roland Christensen, Kenneth R. Andrews, and Joseph L. Bower, *Business Policy: Text and Cases* (Homewood, Ill.: Irwin, 1978); Glueck, *Business Policy;* McNichols, *Policy Making and Executive Action* (New York: McGraw-Hill, 1978); and Charles W. Hofer and Dan Schendel, *Strategy Formulation: Analytical Concepts* (St. Paul, Minnesota: West Publishing, 1978).
5. Dan Schendel and Kenneth J. Hatton, "Business Policy of Strategic Management: A Broader View for an Emerging Discipline," *Proceedings of the Academy of Management, 1972,* pp. 99–107.
6. H. Igor Ansoff, R. P. Declerck, and R. L. Hayes, eds., *From Strategic Planning to Strategic Management* (New York: Wiley, 1977), pp. 29–33. In another article in the same book, strategic management is also conceived as a methodology for planning the transformation of a firm's strategy in the postindustrial era (pp. 39–77).
7. Journals in the United States reporting this literature include: *Academy of Management Journal, Harvard Business Review, Business Horizons, California Management Review,* and *Sloan Management Review,* among others. For European sources, see *Long Range Planning,* and Bernard Taylor and John R. Sharkee, eds., *Corporate Strategy and Planning* (New York: Wiley, 1976).
8. Different authors make varied suggestions. For example, J. Thomas Cannon refers to result strategy, action strategy, and commitment strategy in *Business Strategy and Policy* (New York: Harcourt, Brace and World, 1968), fig. 2. McNichols classifies strategies as root strategy, operating strategy, organizational control strategy, and recovery strategy in *Policy Making and Executive Action,* pp. 11–13. Hofer and Schendel suggest three levels of strategies—corporate strategy, business strategy, and functional area strategy—in *Strategy Formulation.*
9. Long-range planning in the United States during the 1960s was criticized for being too formal, mechanistic, and heavily quantitative. For discussion, see Seymour Titler, "Corporate Strategic Planning—The American Experience," in *A Hand Book of Strategy Planning,* ed. Bernard Taylor and Kevin Hawkins (London: Longman, 1972), p. 380.
10. George A. Steiner gives twenty-five reasons for faulty long-range planning, in *California Management Review* 3, no. 4 (1965), pp. 93–94. D. E. Hussey provides a checklist of reasons why planning may fail, in *Introducing Corporate Planning* (Oxford: Pergamon Press, 1971), p. 24.
11. Initial report in *Wall Street Journal,* 23 October 1972, p. 1.
12. *Business Week,* 3 November 1975, pp. 92–94.

CHAPTER TWO

Business Strategy In Action—A Perspective

The study of business strategy cannot be confined to a theoretical discussion. Its relevance to the practice of business must be given full recognition because not only does its practical application provide important insight into the very value of strategy, but the growing significance given strategy by business firms renders the study a critical part of the student's business training. In this chapter, we provide such a perspective. We will study briefly the roots of the concept from which business strategy derives its guidelines. We will then review the development of business strategy in the United States in the past two decades. The discussion of the early application of strategy in war and politics and its more recent application in business place the present difficulty and future concerns of business in perspective and demonstrate the specific benefits that strategy can provide contemporary management.

THE ROOTS OF THE CONCEPT

Strategy is one of the oldest and most subtle of concepts. Throughout history, strategy has been applied in war and politics. Our purpose in making a concise but cautious inquiry into the roots of the concept is twofold: (1) to identify certain key concepts common to all strategies; and (2) to achieve a broad perspective on the concept in its application to business competition.

Military Strategy

Military strategy is a subject that concerns the darker side of human nature; it deals with methods of deploying national power for violent ends. War, unfortunately, is a human reality. In all ages, societies have fought countless wars for conquest or survival. Yet, despite its purposes, military strategy offers a rich field of study because all great military minds understood the need for a master plan with which they could set their actions, inspire their troops, and gauge their success. With such a plan, the major objectives were kept in clear view, and daily tactics could be adjusted on a contingency basis to keep the overall action moving toward the ultimate goals.

Throughout history, great thinkers have written about war.[1] Books on strategy were written setting forth full analyses of battles and wars of historical importance. These works contain wisdom that can be applied to practically every competitive activity in which crucial contests decide important consequences.

From the richness of these voluminous historical accounts, invaluable strategic concepts have emerged. The more important concepts are as follows:

1. Policy is paramount in the success of military campaigns. National policy, which articulates the political *ends* of a nation, and strategy, which applies the *means* to accomplish the political ends, together comprise a single, integrated concept. However, means must serve the ends, not the other way around.
2. The success of a military strategy depends on sound calculation of external and internal factors influencing the strengths and weaknesses of the opponent vis-à-vis those of the strategist and on the skillful deployment of military forces.
3. Successful planning and management of military strategy become increasingly more rigorous and systematic as the complexity of military affairs and the volume of the resources employed increase.
4. Strategy depends on tactics for implementation. Without tactical actions at operational levels, strategy can be only partially effective.

Political Strategy

In politics, strategy plays a less conspicuous role, at least in verbal usage. In foreign policy, the term *strategy* is not widely used, perhaps due to its strong military connotation. In practice, however, the strategic concept of balance of power, for example, has indeed dominated modern political thinking. Today, because of a sharpened conflict in world politics and the ever-present danger of nuclear war, strategy plays a central role in preventing war and securing peace.

In domestic politics, strategic concepts are applied in the formulation of so-called game plans and large-scale programs to solve complex problems. Hence, we note references to "housing strategy," "anti-inflation strategy," and so forth. Strategy operates well in domestic politics in allocating resources, overcoming administrative difficulties, and organizing efforts aimed at resolving major political issues. In recent years, due to the increasingly competitive nature of political campaigns, campaign strategy has received more attention.[2] A political candidate, trying to win a political campaign despite severe time and money constraints, uses strategy to maximize the chances of winning.

From this extensive practice, we can readily delineate certain strategic concepts in politics that have equal importance in business strategy.

1. The formulation of policy and strategy in international politics is a vital activity of the state. The determination of national policy depends largely on the nation's orientation to the world and the aspirations of its people and government. A country may espouse a variety of national goals. Realistically, however, it is the pursuit of national power that provides substance to these goals.[3] Therefore, strategy for foreign policy is also dictated by the nature and intensity of the competition, and planners must estimate the opposing powers' intentions, capabilities, and competitive responses.

2. In foreign policy, identifying the number of adversaries, their spheres of influence, and their combined instruments demands accurate analysis and subtle calculations. Diplomacy, political alliance and subjugation, trade and economic exploitation, displays of military force, and direct or orchestrated encroachment are instruments of political strategy. Their artful deployment involves yet another aspect of strategy.
3. In domestic politics, strategy is used in solving complex problems, in finding solutions to allocation of scarce resources, and in overcoming constraints. Strategy is thus an art of general management.

Through our brief discussion, we have identified the policy-strategy relationship, the strategy-tactics linkage, the need for the artful deployment of instruments, and the management nature of the total strategy process as concepts that apply in war, politics, and business.

THE DEVELOPMENT OF BUSINESS STRATEGY IN THE UNITED STATES

The evolution of the concept of strategy in business can be traced to the early concept of planning. Since the end of World War II, a strong trend toward long-range planning has occurred. The initiation of long-range planning in the early 1950s, and the practice of economic planning with an emphasis on resource allocation in the 1960s, led ultimately to the present interest in strategic planning. A concise review of this development will place subsequent discussions of business strategy in the proper perspective.[4]

Early Thought on Planning

Planning, one of the basic managerial functions, is the process of forecasting, innovating, and initiating actions. Early management writers gave full recognition to planning, although it was initially confined to the functional areas of production, sales, and finance.[5] Frederick W. Taylor (1856–1917) emphasized the need to select, train, and organize workers in an effort to increase production through planning. Henri Fayol (1841–1925) spoke of planning as one of the five management processes. He focused on planning at the level of general management. Fayol, whose maxim was "managing means looking ahead," conceived the idea of long-range planning for the whole company based on yearly and ten-year forecasts in all areas of management. His concept of planning was not introduced in the United States until 1949; its value did not become apparent until that time. In the meantime, functional planning in production, finance, sales, and administration had long been accepted in business firms. Production control and planning, capital and administrative budgeting, cash and sales forecasting, and personnel loading are familiar practices in all industrial organizations. In essence, functional planning is a traditional method of management.

Long-Range Planning

In the 1950s, rapid changes in economic and social life took place in the United States. Increases in consumer purchases and buying power, fueled by technological advances, created new demands and new business opportunities. The earnest quest for a new perspective, more aggressive goals, and an expanded ability to forecast future events gave rise to long-range planning. In the first years, even as they began developing long-range plans and emphasized goal setting, planners simultaneously attempted to resolve the basic problems of their "new" profession—its methodology, its professional status, and its very rationale in the world of business. Indeed, planners in the late 1950s searched desperately for an improved discipline and methodology to which they could refer.[6]

The acceptance of planning was slow but enthusiastic, as evidenced by the increasing number of staff engaged full-time in long-range planning. By the mid-1950s, only 8 percent of the companies surveyed had one or more persons engaged in long-range planning. A few years later, the number rose to 18 percent. In 1963, another study reported that among the 500 largest industrial companies in the United States, 60 percent had organized corporate-planning departments, and another 20 percent intended to develop them.[7] Most companies prepared long-range plans annually. Organizationally, long-range planning units were formed in the functional departments, mostly in marketing and finance, with a few exceptional units reporting to the chief executive officer or the president himself.

Economic Planning

In the early 1960s, economic planning, with its emphasis on resource allocation, became an important concern. On the one hand, there were industry-wide movements toward accelerated R&D, diversification, and international business, all of which demanded large capital. Thus, in a large company, whose expanding interests might have multiplied into an unmanageable number of business units, the allocation of limited resources among conflicting and competing units posed a complex problem for management. On the other hand, there were the emerging concepts and techniques made available by the Department of Defense in its effort to allocate funds among various services and a large number of weapons systems. Economic planning was the central theme of military planning. Program structures based on mission (objectives) and on resource allocation judged by systems analysis techniques dominated planning thought. In industry, company after company moved to focus on the forecasting of national economic trends, government policies, and the availability of capital and raw materials in the marketplace. Economic and financial concepts and techniques were applied to study cost of capital, company valuations, and profitability determinants. Financial planning and control added a new dimension to long-range planning.

Aided by a general strengthening of the planning function, and equipped with newly developed quantitative methods, long-range planning had reached a new threshold. However, severe business setbacks for certain companies were brought about when overly ambitious growth and heavy borrowing overstretched their capabilities. These disappointments, in turn, highlighted the need for a change in business planning.

Strategic Planning

The emphasis on strategic planning in the late 1960s was indicative of the inadequacies of long-range planning as it had been developed so far. Strategic planning, as defined by George A. Steiner, is "the process of determining the major objectives of an organization and the policies and strategies that will govern the operation, use, and disposition of resources to achieve those objectives."[8] The central thrust of the statement concerns the determination of policy and strategy.

In the 1950s, when long-range planning was deeply involved with goal setting, it ignored the *means* for implementing the plans. As a result, the long-range plans of that decade were excessively burdened with projections and business data. They contained either too few strategic statements or were completely devoid of them. Such plans lacked substance and were often treated lightly by management, thus offering insufficient incentive for action. In the 1960s, when economic planning overemphasized resource allocation, long-range plans became inward-looking and heavily quantitative. Strategy—the core of planning—was again overlooked.

By the early 1970s, it was quite common to find strategic planning as a vital part of company organization. As a function, strategic planning, focusing on strategy as its central theme, began to replace the traditional long-range planning. Along with the change in concept were noticeable changes in organizational practice. Within the corporation, business units were consolidated. Operating divisions were reorganized into integrated business units based on criteria such as mission, competition, and the ability of the units to perform integrated planning and control over their component subunits. For example, GE consolidated its 170 or more departments into fewer than 50 clearly identified Strategic Business Units (SBUs)—a positive step towards the efficient allocation of scarce resources.[9] (See chapter 3 for further discussion.)

Corporate participation in long-range planning became more direct. In the process of planning, which increasingly involved group executive officers, operating divisions, and functional departments, a much more formal and well-monitored procedure was evolved. Another significant improvement was found in the area of organization and administration. More planning staff were taken out of functional departments to report to the chief executive officer or the president. Standing committees on policy and strategy began to appear at top-management levels to deliberate long-range strategic decisions. Planning organizations were further strengthened in status and importance; responsibilities were generally enlarged to include merger, acquisition, and divestiture programs.[10] The initial enthusiasm provided a fresh inspiration toward the total adoption of business strategy in management.

BUSINESS STRATEGY IN ACTION—AN EXPERIENCE

Business strategy had become a serious concern in the mid-1970s. With the dual stress of the energy crisis and the economic recession of the early 1970s, American business failures skyrocketed. Business difficulties resulting from the earlier growth syndrome, that is, the single-minded pursuit of growth of the 1960s with its vicious cycle of growth, profit decline, and financial distress, signaled the coming changes in rules of the business game. The search for a new, more effective concept and technique has begun. Let us examine the growth syndrome, the vicious cycle, and the cost of growth. Such a discussion will describe business activities in the 1950s and 1960s and focus on strategic application in the business world.

The Growth Syndrome

In the past two decades, the U.S. economy has experienced a more prolonged and rapid growth than in any other period of its history. From a level of $211.9 billion in 1945, at the end of the second World War, the nation's GNP expanded 4.5 times to $976.4 billion in 1970.[11] U.S. industry by itself had grown at a much higher rate, however, from roughly 6 percent to nearly 10 percent per year during the period between 1955 and 1973.[12] A large number of corporations had achieved a still higher rate of annual growth. High-technology companies, such as IBM, Xerox, Texas Instruments, 3M, and Polaroid, registered a growth rate of 16.5 percent in sales from 1945 to 1974.[13] For many U.S. corporations, "growth" had been a magic word, almost an obsession.

THE POSITIVE GAINS OF GROWTH No one can deny that economic growth yields many positive results. An increase in the output of goods and services enlarges the tax revenues of the government, stimulates the investment of business firms, and increases the wages and real income of households. The enlargement of government revenue contributes significantly to the solution of social and national security problems, and business investment in technology ensures future production possibilities. The general increase in the wages and real income of the American worker is a positive sign of an affluent society that has abundant materials and the potential for still-larger consumption. Moreover, the economic growth of the past two decades has minimized the effect of business cycles. In contrast to the U.S. economy in the late nineteenth and early twentieth centuries, which was marked by prolonged periods of recession and occasionally full-scale depression, the postwar economy has suffered from much shorter and milder recessions—a total of six up to 1975.

TECHNOLOGY Technology is an important driving force behind economic growth. The postwar pursuit of technology has been phenomenal. Benefited by the arduous push for war production in the early 1940s and by heavy government financing of close to 50 percent of R&D expenditure in the postwar period, technological advancement in the United States steadily accelerated. Total R&D expenditure, including that of public and private sectors, advanced from $5 billion in 1953 to a level of about $27 billion toward the end of 1970. Throughout this period, business firms spent on an average of between 3 and 9 percent of their annual sales dollars for research and development. As a result, there emerged a number of new industries and new materials, and a general increase of productivity was achieved through automation and the use of advanced machines. Technological advancement provided positive benefits to all industries and particularly to the chemical, pharmaceutical, material, and aerospace industries.[14]

The rapid rise of the electronics industry, a child of technological wonder, repeated the success story of the burgeoning auto industry in the early twentieth century. In a short twenty years, the electronics industry grew from the embryonic size of $1.1 billion in 1950 to a gigantic $34 billion in 1970.[15] Companies such as GE, RCA, and Texas Instruments in the electronics industry and IBM, Burroughs, and Control Data Corporation in the computer industry had become billion dollar companies. Their products—televisions, transistor radios, digital watches, and computers of all types—have profoundly changed our life style and business operations. Equally significant is the fact that the greatly advanced state of postwar technology gave the United States a dominant role in the world market.

CONSUMPTION AND WORLD ECONOMIC RECOVERY The population explosion, capital accumulation, and economic recovery in Europe and Asia during the postwar period added further impetus to growth. In the United States, the postwar "baby boom" enlarged the consumer market. Yearly population growth peaked at over 4 million in 1957 and stayed at that level for several years, until a gradual decline began in 1964. Personal consumption, however, increased year after year, from $199.7 billion in 1945 to $616.8 billion in 1970, an increase larger than that of the nation's GNP. The wants of consumers and the producers' will to satisfy their demands acted upon each other to generate the highest level of consumption and production ever attained in the United States. Between 1955 and 1964, the U.S. economy recorded $750.0 billion worth of capital investment; in the next ten years, the figure doubled to $1.6 trillion.[16]

Economic recovery in the war-torn countries created an enormous demand for American goods and services. U.S. exports jumped from $13.9 billion in 1945 to $43.2 billion in 1970. U.S. direct investment abroad was valued at $166.9 billion for the same year. Foreign investments returned a large and rapidly growing share of total U.S. corporate profits, and a large number of U.S. firms received more than half their total income from overseas. In certain industries, such as computers, the U.S. supplied 90 percent of the world market. Indeed, the combination of technology, population increase, capital accumulation, and the emergence of a world market had directly contributed to the expansion of American business.

THE LIABILITIES OF THE GROWTH SYNDROME Economic growth inevitably produced side effects. In recent years, the goal of economic growth has been subject to severe criticism and public debate. Indeed, the antigrowth movement has gained a strong following and has advanced some philosophically convincing arguments.[17] There have been, in the main, three arguments behind the movement. The "quality of life" proponents assert that the single-minded pursuit of material production has created immense human suffering. Poor education, inadequate health care, poverty, urban disturbances, and a general deterioration of social morality in industrial nations are definite signs of an uneasy society. The second group of critics asserts that the emission of poisonous pollutants, if it remains unchecked, will make the physical environment extremely harmful to human life. The third argument, concerned with the depletion of natural resources, forecasts a doomsday economy. According to this model, economic growth would reach its limits within the next one hundred years, if prevailing trends of population growth, food production, and excessive natural resource utilization were sustained.[18]

The debate, although centering around economics and public issues, has brought to light some pressing challenges to business. In his 1958 book *The Affluent Society,* John Kenneth Galbraith challenged what he called the "conventional wisdom" and its opinions on production.[19] He alleged that demand was created by business firms through mass advertising, mass selling, and a deliberate quickening of product obsolescence. The wants created or contrived by producers were engineered waste, and a disservice to the public. Companies engulfed in the growth syndrome—the pursuit of growth at any cost—are thus inefficient, and their growth unsustainable in the long run. In the mid-1960s, noted economists, environmental forecasters, and scientists alike pronounced an even stronger verdict against corporate irresponsibility for raising high-level spillover costs and endangering human and natural life.

CONSTRAINTS TO GROWTH Society's concern for quality of life, pollution, and resource scarcity imposes high costs of doing business and will no doubt restrict economic growth. The resource needs and employment considerations involved may become a deterrent to corporate growth. Large corporations possess power that, when unchecked, breeds economic monopoly and sociopolitical irresponsibility. ITT, Lockheed Aircraft, and some large oil companies may have gone beyond their legitimate use of power. Still, bigness is biologically limited. A very large company may grow to a point beyond which diseconomies will set in. A very sizable company may expand to a point beyond which it is no longer manageable. These side effects offer rather convincing arguments against economic growth. They can help us focus on some important strategic issues that will be discussed throughout this book.

The Vicious Cycle

As the country entered the 1970s, the economy began to show signs of stress. The merger movement, which peaked at 2,400 mergers in 1968, started to level off. Declining earnings and heavy borrowing among several conglomerates showed evidence of serious trouble. On May 22, 1970, the Dow Jones average dropped twenty points to a low of 640.[20] The economy was deeply strained, and industry helpless, exhausted. The 1973–1974 energy crisis delivered the final blow. The economic boom of the past two decades came to a screeching halt.

CONDITION In the next year or so, a large number of American companies experienced the severe effects of the vicious cycle. *Vicious cycle* is defined as a situation in which certain external threats and internal weaknesses drive a company from one stage to the next in a successive movement of deterioration. Thus, poorly conceived growth inevitably leads to financial losses; financial losses bring on insolvency or bankruptcy (see figure 2.1).

The three phases of *growth, instability,* and *survival* constitute the vicious cycle, a cycle that can inflict great losses and that, in the early 1970s, toppled many chief executive officers. Every company, no matter how successful, must live through one or more of these three distinctive phases. The first phase of the cycle may occur at any time, leading in turn to the second phase, which, if not skillfully managed, may lead to the third phase. The severity of each phase and the time it takes to complete it vary, however. One company may experience a much sharper fluctuation than does another. A new company may quickly pass through its business life cycle into demise. Even large companies may sink into bankruptcy after a prolonged growth. On the other hand, within a large, widely diversified company, each division may face different fluctuations.

BEHAVIOR The vicious cycle is a slow-moving but inevitable process, demonstrating a variety of shapes and forms. It takes its most spectacular form among the conglomerates, some of which have risen quickly and failed miserably. Most conventional growth companies, by contrast, complete the cycle quickly but without detriment to the company. Still another (and fairly large) group of well-managed companies operate in between the growth and instability phases. Considering the conglomerates as a group, a complete cycle could take as long as twenty years, as in the case of Litton Industries and Boise Cascade, or be completed in as

FIGURE 2.1 THE VICIOUS CYCLE

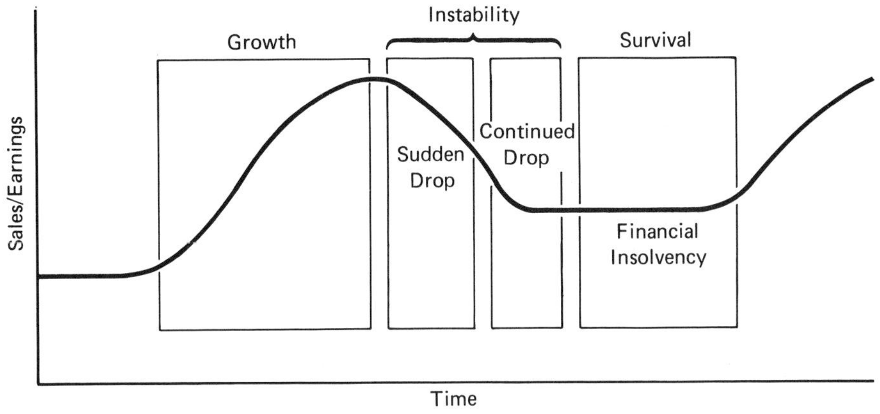

few as ten years, as in the case of Whittaker Corp. A typical cycle might consist of several years spent in the first phase of growth, two to three years in the second phase of profits decline, and then a longer period of survival that could last for several years before the company reached a stabilized position for the resumption of growth.

To graphically illustrate the varying forms of the vicious cycle, figure 2.2 shows the configurations commonly observed among business firms. Configuration 1 shows a company's quick growth and sudden demise, typical of young, overly aggressive companies, such as KDI Corp. (see illustration capsule 4). Configuration 2 depicts a company that sustains a prolonged, high rate of growth and then quickly deteriorates through the remaining two phases of the cycle, struggling to survive. Boise Cascade and Whittaker Corp. experienced this pattern. Configuration 3 illustrates the mild impact of the cycle when well-managed companies ex-

FIGURE 2.2 VARYING FORMS OF THE VICIOUS CYCLE

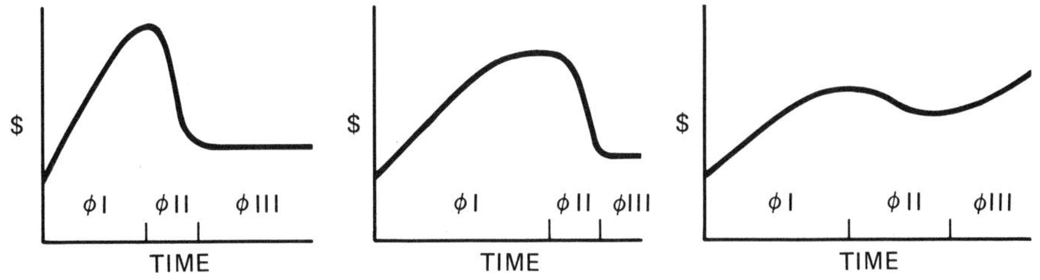

Configuration 1
Fast rise—sudden demise

Configuration 2
Prolonged growth—sharp deterioration

Configuration 3
Prolonged growth—brief pause

perience a brief pause in the second phase, but avoid the financial insolvency stage of the third phase altogether. Such is the case of Avon Products, Inc.

To illustrate the varied forms of the vicious cycle, let us cite three cases of companies that experienced the impact of the cycle in the period between 1955 and 1976.[21] Boise Cascade is cited to show the adverse effects of the cycle upon a large corporation. Chrysler Corp. is cited for its cyclical crises. Avon is noted to illustrate how a leader in an industry experienced the cycle in a milder way. Illustration capsules 3 and 4 present more-detailed reports on two other companies, which plunged into the vicious cycle with severe consequences.

Boise Cascade. Boise Cascade was originally a forest products company, but it launched into a supergrowth path in 1957. By 1968, its sales had passed $1 billion, an increase from $35 million in 1957. This spectacular twelve-year annual growth represented a compounded rate of 33 percent. Over the next three years, the company made still-larger acquisitions—Ebasco Industries, and land investments in California. In all, it made thirty-five acquisitions. By 1970, compounded by the recession, losses in land investments, and high interest payments, profits began to decline; in the next two years, losses climbed to $255 million. The president was ousted, and the company battled against bankruptcy.

Chrysler Corp. Chrysler, the third-largest auto manufacturer in the United States, had a chronic management crisis, and it completed three cycles in fifteen years. The year 1960 was one of financial crisis, in which the company faced profit and liquidity problems. Within four years, the company managed to achieve full recovery. Between 1963 and 1968, it resumed growth, moving aggressively in the marketplace and enforcing tightened internal controls. Market share was restored from a disastrous low of 8.6 percent in 1962 to a high of 18.1 percent in 1968. Then, an earnings decline and heavy borrowing for product development and foreign operations brought on a financial crunch. By 1970, the company suffered a loss of $7.6 million, following a sharp decline in 1969. At the same time, its debt shot up to $800 million. Chrysler survived the second crisis, and fully recovered in 1973. However, the company was doomed to a still-larger crisis in 1974. In two years, 1974 to 1975, Chrysler once again reported a loss of $324.5 million. The company managed to survive the latest crisis during the recent boom of auto sales in 1976.

Avon Products. Avon Products experienced spectacular growth throughout the past two decades. Yearly increases in sales and earnings were maintained at 17 to 19 percent. Seizing upon the explosive growth of disposal income, increasing urbanization, and formation of large families during these years, Avon fully exploited the consumer market. Avon's aggressive product development and its employment of thousands of housewives in door-to-door sales were the key approaches that facilitated growth. Changing times in the early 1970s, characterized by rising costs, raw material scarcity, and cautious, inflation-weary consumers, forced Avon to reassess its marketing approach. The company's growth rate began to fall. By 1974, earnings dropped sharply to $111.74 million, from $135.75 million the previous year. Within a year, the company's profits rebounded, and it thus safely avoided financial difficulties.

Illustration Capsule 3

WHITTAKER CORP.

In 1965, Whittaker's sales were approximately $40 to $45 million. Earnings were relatively small, and the company was involved almost exclusively in aerospace. Then Whittaker began to pursue growth through acquisition.

In 1966, Whittaker's sales were $84 million. About half of this was generated in aerospace business. However, during 1967, twenty acquisitions were made. Whittaker made purchases in such widely diversified fields as sailboat making, plasma physics research, titanium forming, industrial chemicals, and many others. Throughout these purchases, the president at that time, Dr. William M. Duke, maintained that these purchases were part of a product-oriented growth. Throughout 1967, Whittaker's sales climbed to $200 million. Whittaker left the aerospace field and became a "complex of companies that turn out basic materials and end products in 120 separate lines." Materials was the thread that tied these companies together. The intent was to develop or supply any materials needs by a user and acquire companies that were both producers and users of materials.

In 1967, Duke said the company's goal was to be between $800 million and $1 billion in sales for 1972. The method was acquisition. Duke made thirty-two acquisitions himself in 1968, continuing to purchase companies capable of materials technology infusion. Whittaker was trying to avoid the conglomerate image, and the related legal complications.

Acquisitions in the first quarter of 1969 included Universal Athletic Sales Co., Trojan Boat Co., Kettenburg Marine, Precision Forge Co., Arcadia Machine & Tool Co., Aircraft Hydro-Forming, Hol-Gar Mfg. Corp., American Finishing Co., and Bishop Tube Co. Whittaker's earnings per share in 1963 to 1968 topped 500 of the largest U.S. corporations.

In total, through 1969, over 135 separate acquisitions were made by Whittaker. In 1970, Whittaker began to experience difficulties. Prior to 1970, Whittaker's resources had been stretched thin. Some errors in purchasing companies were made. In 1970, the company had a new president, Joseph F. Alibrandi. During 1970, an after-tax loss of approximately $7 million was experienced, due to the sale or discontinuance of unprofitable businesses. Units scheduled for divestiture in 1971 caused Whittaker a $7 million loss in 1970. Also in 1970, a good-will write-off related to the divested companies caused an additional $10 million write-off.

In 1971, to bolster the financial position of the firm, a program of debt reduction through improving operations, controlling capital expenditures, more effective asset management, and the sale of assets peripheral to Whittaker's main business thrust was enacted. This plan was intended to clearly define the business areas to be pursued. The plan was centered around four business areas: materials; housing and urban development; recreation; and transportation.

For 1972, an additional twenty or so units were to be divested, with an expected yield of $15 to $40 million in cash. At least $52 million was available to pay $38 million of maturing debt. Whittaker was still regrouping and tightening up their sales centers. New acquisitions were nil in this period.

Divestitures in 1973 largely encompassed various construction operations. These units unfavorably impacted the 1973 after-tax profit by $21 million. However, in 1973, the company did reshape its debt maturity schedule into one the company could meet reasonably without additional external financing. In 1973, the company realized that rebuilding the foundation and structure of the company would take longer than originally anticipated.

Source: "The Threat That Ties Diversity Together," *Business Week,* 2 December 1967, pp. 74–78; "Bringing Sanity to a 140-Company Conglomerate," *Business Week,* 15 March 1976, pp. 66–68; and *Whittaker Annual Report,* 1970 through 1973.

Illustration Capsule 4

KDI CORP.

"As a company that moved from obscurity to moderate popularity—and then crumbled with astonishing speed—KDI is in many ways typical of the companies that were thrown together through rapid-fire acquisition during the wild days of the conglomerate craze." This era was the middle to late 1960s. However, this company has amazed those who remember the time. It has survived the fall and come back to a profitable position.

History

KDI, originally founded as Kraus Design Inc., manufactured products varying from mechanical-drawing instruments to electric motors, until 1965, when it converted to fuses for the military. In 1966, Mr. Cox and Mr. Akers took control, and in two years, KDI acquired ninety-seven widely diversified companies. Sales went from $858,451 to $139.6 million. Profits went from a loss of $281,790 to a profit of $5.2 million.

Problems

However, the firm had many problems. The company expanded too quickly without taking time to fit the new companies in or sometimes even properly evaluate their profitability. New companies requiring tremendous cash flow were purchased. Corporate staffers were added too fast. Nonconservative accounting practices, such as capitalizing R&D expenditures, made the company look better than it was.

When the 1970 crunch hit, KDI was cash depleted, owed $30 million to banks, and needed more. After failing to find additional outside financing, KDI went to their own bank, who suggested an outside consultant be brought in.

Why KDI Did Not Go Down

With all these problems, how did KDI survive? First, among the 107 acquisitions, 25 or 30 were solid companies, still run by former owners. These companies went on generating profits. Also, banks and insurance lenders wanted KDI to stay active. Finally, KDI was not looted. No one sold their stock in large blocks, so the market was not undercut.

Changes

However, the banks did insist on a change in top management. Mr. Taylor replaced Mr. Akers as chairman, and Louis D. Matthey, from the consulting firm, was elected as president of KDI. Raising cash was the first concern. Two profitable companies were sold for $1.5 million cash, and banks loaned $550,000. That money was carefully distributed. The basic strategy was to distinguish between money producers and money bleeders. By the end of 1971, thirty-four money-eating units were sold, realizing $1.7 million in cash and the return of 206,000 KDI common shares. By the end of 1973, others that have since gone bad were sold.

In addition, corporate staff was cut from 115 to 64, and corporate expense was reduced from $10.2 million in 1970 to $3 million in 1974. A more conservative accounting policy was adopted. In 1970, KDI reported a net loss of $36.8 million. About the same time, $32.5 million of short-term debt was renegotiated into longer-term debt, and insurance companies agreed to trade $9 million of debentures and bonds for an equal face value of preferred stock. Old merger agreements with regard to support of stock prices were settled.

Problems on the Way

In November 1970, just when KDI was recovering, former owners of nine KDI units filed suit. Threatening to throw the company into involuntary receivership, they wanted rescindment of the acquisition and compensation for damages. On December 30, 1970, KDI filed under Chapter 11 of the Federal Bankruptcy Act. This allowed them to operate under their own management while trying to work out an arrangement with creditors. KDI tried to reassure former owners while letting them know they would not be let out.

Finally, one case was settled with a new employment contract and payment of certain legal fees. It looked like others would go the same way until a Minnesota court awarded a settlement of $5.1 million and $900,000 in interest to former owners. KDI agreed to sell the unit back for $1.1 million in cash and their 259,714 KDI common shares. Other cases were still pending.

1974–on

In spite of the internal conflict, in 1973, KDI became profitable. In 1974, they made a $5 million profit. The court no longer reviewed normal operations at this point. But KDI still has a long road to travel. Chapter 11 proceedings cost $500,000 in legal fees, and some suits are still pending. The company also has $38 million of debt and $9.2 million of preferred stock outstanding. However, the company has settled or refinanced practically all of its debts.

Despite the recession of 1975, the company had a healthy profit, and all twenty-four remaining operating units were expected, for the first time in KDI's history, to be in the black. Dividends were not expected to be paid in 1975, but the company indicated at that time that all other operations had returned to normal.

Rather than end up as a mere hulk of a company, with assets split among creditors, KDI evolved from court-supervised reorganization into a firm with a "reasonably promising future."

Source: "How High-Flying Firm Came Crushing Down and Survived the Fall," *Wall Street Journal,* 19 August 1976, p. 1.

The Cost of Growth

The pursuit of a company's growth—involving, as it does, taking numerous risks—is a costly endeavor. Great losses in resources are the results of ill-conceived growth. Resource losses can be traced to waste in R&D, new product failures, new venture disasters, and investments lost in acquisitions.

U.S. industry invested large sums in R&D. R&D management constitutes one of the most difficult and risky corporate endeavors. Faulty judgments, and/or a lack of effective management, can result in cost overruns and waste in resources and time. The waste in military R&D, which is widely criticized, illustrates the difficulty in managing industrial research and development activities.

LOSSES IN NEW PRODUCT DEVELOPMENT Product development has been an important approach in achieving company growth. It is a well-known fact that most of today's companies sell products that did not exist five or ten years ago. These commercially marketable products, however, represent only 20 percent of the total developed.[22] One study concluded that out of fifty-eight new ideas generated, only one results in a commercially marketable product.[23] Converting this high product failure rate into resource dollars, one can appreciate the prohibitively high cost of new product development. Large losses could result from the sudden withdrawal of a product from the market after a few years of production. The Ford Motor Company's withdrawal of the Edsel after two years' production resulted in a loss of $350 million. Du Pont's CORFAM, the synthetic leather project that was introduced in 1964, cost the company $100 million when its production was terminated in 1971. Moreover, the gross proliferation of new product development that quickens product obsolescence can be regarded as economic waste, the uneconomical use of scarce resources.

LOSSES IN VENTURES When companies diversify into new ventures, they can incur great losses. The eventual withdrawal of RCA, GE, and Xerox from the computer market cost the companies hundreds of millions of dollars. Singer's belated decision to sell its business machine operation was also a financial disaster. RCA's plunge into the computer market was a calculated risk. Its "head-on" strategy against IBM was ill-conceived and poorly executed; the company lacked comparable products and a comparable network of sales and service organizations. GE's venture into computers ran into the same difficulties as RCA's, namely, a lack of commitment once the strategy was conceived. Xerox's venture was accomplished through the acquisition of Scientific Data Systems Inc. for a high price ($900 million worth of Xerox stock). The disasters that resulted from these ventures added up initially to a loss of approximately $2.271 billion (see table 2.1).

TABLE 2.1 REPORTED LOSSES ON COMPANY VENTURES

Company	*Venture Period*	*Initial Losses (in millions)*
GE	1959–1970	$ 472
RCA	1957–1971	400
Xerox	1969–1975	1,000
Singer	1963–1975	400

Source: Business Week, *1 January 1976, p. 70, and 4 April 1976, pp. 60–68;* Wall Street Journal, *30 December 1974, p. 1, and 12 January 1976, p. 1. Xerox figures in* Financial World, *18 June 1975, pp. 8–12.*

Large losses resulting from poorly conceived and executed acquisitions was the single most injurious force behind these failures during the recent growth period. Many conglomerates approached near-bankruptcy, and a large number of growth companies were fatally injured.

THE IMPORTANCE OF BUSINESS STRATEGY

The Changing Rules

The short-lived energy crisis of 1973–1974, with its disastrous effects upon the world economy in general and the American economy in particular, dramatized once again the meaning of scarcity. Scarcity has become one of the chief economic problems of modern times. Life styles are extremely sensitive to such economic reality: changes in public and social values will affect government policies, thus reshaping priorities in resource allocation and changing the public's attitude toward business. Material shortage and inflationary pressure will alter the mode of managing business. The current sharpening of foreign competition, evidenced by the Japanese challenge in the steel, automotive, and computer industries, has deepened our concern. New competing nations—Canada, the Soviet Union, and China, to name a few—will soon join the ranks of world traders. Competition in the world market will grow ever sharper. In addition, there is the shortage of capital. The rising cost of capital for business investment and expansion will have a decisive impact on investment decision making. In a word, a set of new rules is beginning to emerge. Strategy will provide a tool with which difficulties can be overcome and competition can be subdued.[24]

Benefits

Specifically, strategy making aids management in four areas. First, strategy provides management with a perspective. Management places equal importance on the present and the future, and attacks both simultaneously. Corporate objectives are well-balanced; short-term advantages are evaluated against long-term gains. Strategic actions, thus, replace brute force and hasty actions.

Second, strategy offers a mentality, a discipline, and a technique to manage changes. Management is totally prepared to anticipate, respond, and influence its own destiny, whatever future changes may be and however the rate of change is likely to occur.

Third, strategy provides a dual approach to problem solving: (1) the exploration of the most effective means to overcome difficulties and subdue competition; and (2) the development, conservation, and deployment of limited resources to maximize returns. It provides a systematic and decisive method of problem solving; it facilitates investment decision making, thus averting large losses.

Last, strategy generates directional action. It provides a framework for guiding decision making in directing corporate operations; it supplies the organization a unified motivating force that moves a company forward in time of strength and revitalizes a company in times of distress.

SUMMARY

Given a precarious present and an uncertain future, business executives are searching for a new approach to management. Business strategy is becoming the central thrust of management because it affords four specific benefits: strategy is effective in overcoming difficulties, managing change, deploying limited resources for optimal returns, and maximizing organizational performance.

We substantiated this line of thinking by examining industrial practice of the past two decades and by citing the business setbacks of many companies. To be sure, American business grew, expanded, and proliferated phenomenally during this period, but the price was exorbitantly high. The single pursuit of growth at any cost inflicted great losses and produced side effects detrimental to society. The combined impact of the growth syndrome, the vicious cycle, and the high cost of growth cannot be allowed to repeat.

Throughout this period, the strategic concept was evolving. The early planning practiced at the functional level advanced in the 1950s to long-range planning. Long-range planning expanded to strategic planning in the late 1960s. Strategic planning is evolving into strategy-making. Significantly, business strategy has its very roots in war and politics. With today's economic reality and management challenges, these roots take on greater meaning.

NOTES

1. The more prominent of these authors are Sun Tsu, Thucydides, and Machiavelli in early times; Henri Jemini (1779–1869); Karl von Clausewitz (1780–1831); and modern writers such as Alfred Mahan (1840–1914); Guilio Douhet (1869–1930); and B. H. Lindell Hart (1895–1970).
2. For discussion, consult Marjorie Random Hershey, *The Making of Campaign Strategy* (Lexington, Mass.: Heath, 1974). For reporting on presidential campaigns, see Martin Schram, *Running for President, 1967: The Carter Campaign* (New York: Stein and Day, 1977); and Malcolm D. MacDougall, *We Almost Made It* (New York: Crown, 1977).
3. Hans J. Morgenthau, one of the most articulate spokesmen for the realistic—in contrast to the idealistic—school of morality and law in international relations, declares that "international politics like all politics is a struggle for power. Whatever the ultimate aims of international politics, power is always the immediate aim." *Politics Among Nations* (New York: Knopf, 1973), p. 27.

4. For historical development, see H. Igor Ansoff, "The State of Practice in Planning Systems," *Sloan Management Review,* Winter 1977, pp. 1–24.
5. For discussion on management thought, consult Ernest Dale, *Management: Theory and Practice* (New York: McGraw-Hill, 1973), pp. 113–54; and Henry L. Tosi and Stephen J. Carroll, *Management: Contingencies, Structure and Process* (Chicago, Illinois: St. Clair Press, 1976), pp. 14–56, 176–311. For early thought in China, see Y. N. Chang, "Early Chinese Management Thought," *California Management Review,* Winter 1976, pp. 71–76.
6. For development and practice of long-range planning, see Steward Thompson, *How Companies Plan* (New York: American Management Association, 1962); and David W. Ewing, ed., *Long-Range Planning for Management* (New York: Harper and Row, 1958). See also Y. N. Chang, "Coping with Planning Problems in Defense Industry Business," *California Management Review,* Winter 1963, pp. 49–54.
7. Reported in George A. Steiner, *Top Management Planning* (New York: Macmillan, 1969), p. 15.
8. *Top Management Planning,* p. 34.
9. Information from company-published material. For case illustration, see Melvin E. Salveson, "The Management of Strategy," *Long Range Planning,* February 1974, pp. 19–26.
10. James K. Brown and Rochelle O'Connor, *Planning and the Corporate Planning Director* (New York: Conference Board, 1974).
11. Figures, unless otherwise noted, are taken from the Bureau of Census, *Statistical Abstract of the United States* (Washington, D.C.: U.S. Government Printing Office, 1973). For GNP figures, for example, see 1973 edition, p. 319.
12. Figures quoted from Edward R. Bagley, *Beyond the Conglomerates* (New York: AMACOM, 1975), pp. 23–38, esp. pp. 24–26.
13. *Business Week,* 16 February 1976, p. 58.
14. In 1967, five industries—aircraft; electrical equipment and communication; chemical, including drugs; machine; and motor vehicles—were responsible for 80 percent of all R&D spending by industry. Edwin Mansfield et al., *Research and Innovation in the Modern Corporation* (New York: Norton, 1971), p. 4.
15. Figures reported when current in *Electronics,* March 1955, p. 66, and January 1971, pp. 35, 63, respectively.
16. *Business Week,* 22 September 1975, p. 43.
17. Among the many books against growth, see Ezra J. Mishan, *The Cost of Economic Growth* (New York: Praeger, 1967); and Mishan, *Technology and Growth* (New York: Praeger, 1970). For books favoring growth, see Wilfred Beckerman, *Two Cheers for the Affluent Society* (New York: St. Martin's Press, 1974); and Peter Passell and Leonard Ross, *The Retreat of Riches* (New York: Viking, 1973).
18. Dennis Meadows et al., *The Limits to Growth* (New York: Universe Books, 1972).
19. Also, John K. Galbraith, *The New Industrial State* (Boston: Houghton Mifflin, 1967); and John S. Gambs, *John Kenneth Galbraith* (New York: Twayne Publishers, 1975), pp. 55–81.
20. For a discussion on Wall Street crisis, see John Brooks, *The Go-Go Years* (New York: Weybright and Talley, 1973).
21. Unless cited specifically, information on companies in this section are taken from *Moody's Industrial Survey, Standard & Poor's Corporation Records,* current periodicals, and company annual reports. For Boise Cascade, for example, see *Business Week,* 1 June 1974, p. 74. Also, John McDonald, *The Game of Business* (New York: Doubleday, 1975), pp. 128–49. Company crises, in Joel E. Ross and Michael J.

Kami, *Corporate Management in Crisis: Why the Mighty Fall* (Englewood Cliffs, N.J.: Prentice-Hall, 1973).

22. One study, cited in Mansfield et al., *Research and Innovation,* p. 9, indicated a 60 percent failure rate.
23. Report from a study cited in Philip Kotler, *Marketing Management: Analysis, Planning, and Control* (Englewood Cliffs, N.J.: Prentice-Hall, 1976), p. 198.
24. Charles H. Tavel calls this the third age—the age of the strategist—distinguishing it from the first age, that of the entrepreneurs, and the second age, that of the managers, in *The Third Industrial State: Strategy for Business Survival* (Homewood, Ill.: Dow Jones-Irwin, 1975), p. 1.

Special Note: How to Analyze Policy Cases

In most policy courses, case method is used and serves a definite purpose. Our notes will delve into two aspects of case studies: case method, and case analysis. Case method can be extremely beneficial to policy teaching when it is combined with text reading and class instruction.

CASE METHOD

Purposes of Case Method

As a teaching tool, case method serves many purposes. It is a vehicle for illustrating text material and applying classroom learning to actual business situations. It serves as a basis for enlightened class discussion and a method for developing students' ability to analyze and solve complex business problems. It promotes group interaction and enriches learning. However, case method can also cause difficulties. Case analysis without guidance from a well-organized body of knowledge can lead to directionless learning. Case discussion and written analysis without the reference to a well-defined methodology can become fragmentary.

One of the major purposes of case method is the development of students' decision-making skill and analytical ability. Specifically, case study is designed to:

1. Stress methodology, not so much the merit of the solution.
2. Force students to do independent thinking in identifying major issues and attacking problems.
3. Develop oral and written communication skills to articulate and defend one's position.

Methodology, Independent Thinking, and Self-discovery

Let us clarify what we mean by *methodology* and *independent thinking*. *Methodology* refers to the scientific method of inquiry. Observing the five-step process referred to in chapter 4 and making rigorous inquiries are the qualities of a sound methodology. In this regard, solutions are hardly the central attention of a case analysis. Not only are there no "right" answers to a complex problem, but a case study is limited by available information to suggest the right answers. Indeed, to draw quick conclusions is a faulty habit. *Independent thinking* refers to thoroughness in analysis and logic in organization. It develops the student's capacity for self-discovery.

Self-discovery implies that each student depends on his or her own effort to draw conclusions rather than relying upon other people's opinions. Students are instructed to concentrate on analyzing strategic conditions, defining central issues of near- and long-term significance, and selecting courses of action. A high degree of consistency should exist between identified and proposed strategies and solutions. We also suggest the development of oral and written communication skills, which are essential to a business student's training.

CASE ANALYSIS

Case method imposes a cooperative role on instructor and students. In policy cases, the instructor serves three distinct roles. As a teacher and trainer, he/she imparts knowledge and trains students in skill development. As an organizer, he/she states course objectives, plans instruction, and organizes and assigns work. As a facilitator, he/she guides class discussions, develops resources, and promotes interaction. Students bear certain responsibilities. Each student reads and studies text and assigned materials, prepares for case discussions, participates in team activities, and writes case analysis. We will discuss preparation, class discussion and presentation, and written analysis.

Preparation, Research, and Analysis

Preparation is intended for class discussion and independent analysis. Unlike experiential exercises and short cases (generally between one and five pages), policy cases are long (twenty to fifty pages) and complex. We suggest a three-phase approach: data collection and organization; research and analysis; conclusions and recommendations.

PHASE 1: DATA COLLECTION AND ORGANIZATION

1. Read through the case rapidly to determine the general nature of the case.
2. Reread and note the background of the company—its size, product/market, organization, and brief history.
3. Study external and internal factors affecting the company's performance.
4. Jot down information concerning key executives, policies, and strategies.
5. Describe operations of important functions and personnel.
6. Single out passages to itemize the company's critical problems.
7. Study tables, exhibits, and financial statements.

PHASE 2: RESEARCH AND ANALYSIS

8. Identify missing information and facts to be researched from outside sources. (See illustration capsule A).
9. Compute ratio analysis and trend analysis to study the company's financial position. (See illustration capsule B).
10. Pinpoint internal strengths and weaknesses and external opportunities and threats.
11. Study resource expenditures concerning R&D, capital, and facilities.
12. Define the central issues (major constraints and critical problems) and comment on ongoing strategies.

PHASE 3: CONCLUSIONS AND RECOMMENDATIONS

13. Restate critical problems and propose solutions.
14. Recommend the choice of strategic alternatives.
15. State future resource needs and means for their development.
16. Refer to chapters 7, 8, or 9 to revise and reformulate strategies.
17. Consider contingency plans and methods of implementation. (Refer to chapters 10, 11, and 12 on functional strategies for implementation discussions).
18. Rethink the salient points and jot down questions for class discussion.

Class Discussion and Presentation

Class discussion can follow a variety of methods: the question/answer dialogue led by the instructor; the open discussion and critique; and team presentation. A well-conducted discussion encourages class interaction, sharing, and self-discovery. Self-discovery is an important goal that follows a spontaneous process to enable students to discover the true meaning of conceptual ideas, subtle facts and fine points, and means to obtain consensus. Sharing is an invaluable by-product. Students learn other people's viewpoints, information, and value judgments. Sharing can also lead to positive class interaction and generate the urge for "learning from peers."

On the other hand, each student is instructed to complete preparation, participate, contribute, and critique in class discussion. Students should be reminded that class discussions help develop their verbal communication. Domination of discussion, drawing quick conclusions without factual evidence, and intolerance in accepting other people's viewpoints are to be avoided at all times.

Case presentations, either through a team approach or individual reporting, is another format frequently used in policy case studies. There is a variety of team presentation methods: the consulting report; the simulated executive conference; board meetings; and staff briefings. Students are required to use charts and visual aids to sharpen skills of presentation. In such cases, group deliberation through preparation, presentation, and class critique is the essence of the team approach. Individual reporting intended for a specific aspect of strategic development or assigned research, such as the use of quantitative methods to illustrate a technical point, is often used for instructional emphasis. Needless to say, individual performance in class discussion and presentation is equitably graded.

Illustration Capsule A

SOURCES FOR CASE RESEARCH

In policy case study, outside source research is often necessary. Not only is case material limited, but outside information published at the time of case writing bears strong relevancy to the situation. Following are some of the sources:

1. Economic information:

   See illustration capsule 9.

2. Industrial sources:

   U.S. Industrial Outlook, by Department of Commerce, published annually with five-year projections.

   "Annual Report on American Industry," by *Forbes,* compilation of statistics by industry and company.

   "Fortune's Directories" on 500 largest U.S. corporations, second largest 500, and 200 foreign industrial corporations.

   Industry Survey, published quarterly by Standard and Poor's Corp.

3. Company information:

   Moody's Manual of Investments, contains a brief history of each company, its operations, and five-year financial statements.

   Standard and Poor's, *Corporation Records,* provides company statistics.

4. Trade association sources:

   A good source on individual industry's status and trends. Consult, for example, Aerospace Industries Association of America; American Petroleum Institute; Air Transport Association of America, among others.

5. Sources for ratio analysis:

   Dun's Review, by Dun and Bradstreet, Inc., published annually in September-December issues.

   Annual Statement Studies, by Robert Morris Associates, useful for small business firms.

   Almanac of Business and Industrial Financial Ratios, by Prentice-Hall.

6. General sources:

   Periodical indexes, such as *Business Periodical Index, Wall Street Journal Index, Applied Science and Technology Index, Funk and Scott's Index of Corporations and Industries,* among others.

   Journals, such as *Long-Range Planning, Harvard Business Review, Business Horizons, California Management Review,* plus popular magazines such as *Business Week, Forbes,* and *Fortune.*

Illustration Capsule B

NOTES ON BUSINESS AND FINANCIAL ANALYSIS

One of the first steps in case analysis is to quickly construct relative business and financial data. Business and financial data should be properly organized and visually presented to portray a company's position and to properly reveal its state of financial health. Like a patient's X-ray, business and financial data are essential for diagnosis.

Business Analysis
In most cases, business data of a company are supplied in the case book. Missing information can be obtained from Standard and Poor's publications. The table below shows one way of presenting business data.

Business Areas	*Principal Products*	*Sales* %	*Profits* %	*Market Share* %
A	Mainframe computer	50	60	40
B	Minicomputer	10	5	5
C	Peripheral	20	30	10
D	Miscellaneous	10	5	n.a.

Ratio Analysis
At a minimum, the following ratios should be calculated. Each ratio should be compared with industry average, and its meaning be explained. (Use Standard and Poor's and Robert Morris Associates data for industry average.)

Trend Analysis
Trend analysis is very helpful in assessing a company's performance and thus forecasting future possibilities. It should be done selectively and purposefully. It is not to be treated as a mechanical exercise. A trend analysis consists of two types: the basic, and the specific. The basic analysis should show trends in sales, profits, and return on investment (ROI). The specific type should focus on problem areas such as debt, capital spendings, R&D expenditures, and/or inventory buildups.

Ratio	Method of Calculation
I. Profitability	
1. Net profit margin	$\frac{\text{Net profit after taxes}}{\text{Sales}}$
2. Returns on total assets	$\frac{\text{Net profit after taxes}}{\text{Total assets}}$
3. Returns on net worth	$\frac{\text{Net profit after taxes}}{\text{Net worth}}$
II. Liquidity	
4. Current	$\frac{\text{Current assets}}{\text{Current liabilities}}$
5. Quick, or acid test	$\frac{\text{Current assets-inventory}}{\text{Current liabilities}}$
III. Leverage	
6. Debt to total assets	$\frac{\text{Total debt}}{\text{Total assets}}$
7. Times interest earned	$\frac{\text{Profit before taxes plus int. chgs.}}{\text{Interest charges}}$
8. Fixed charge coverage	$\frac{\text{Income available for mtg. fixed chgs.}}{\text{Fixed charges}}$
IV. Activity	
9. Inventory turnover	$\frac{\text{Sales}}{\text{Inventory}}$
10. Average collection period	$\frac{\text{Receivables}}{\text{Sales per day}}$
11. Fixed assets turnover	$\frac{\text{Sales}}{\text{Fixed assets}}$
12. Total assets turnover	$\frac{\text{Sales}}{\text{Total assets}}$

Written Analysis

Most instructors issue a format to guide written analysis. At a minimum, a format should include discussions on the central issues, the internal assessment, the environmental analysis, the business objectives, the strategy and contingency plans, and implementing programs and actions.

In preparing written analysis, a set of ground rules is developed to help actual writing. We suggest that students check with the instructor for the desired guidelines. To help effective writing, we suggest the following guide:

1. In all cases, in-depth analysis is required. For example, it is not sufficient to state the central issue without substantiation by facts, data, and clearly stated rationale.
2. Do not repeat text material; cite page number for detailed facts. Develop the ability to identify from the text the stated and implied major issues, not

trivialities, and to analytically summarize findings, not to superficially or verbatim parrot material from the text.

3. Always include a section on behavioral variations: the individuals and groups involved in the case; their personalities; motives; and their interaction.
4. Do not write in outline form but in a narrative style—concise, logical, and forceful—a position paper that justifies your position and defends its reasonableness and comprehensiveness.
5. Remember, case analysis follows a logical development. Check with your instructor for the desired format.
6. Use tables and charts to support your analysis.
7. Do not make general statements. Be precise. Use quantitative data to qualify a statement, such as "the company has grown in the last ______ years from $______ to $______ in sales, and from $______ to $______ in profits."
8. Use footnotes whenever possible to cite additional research sources and for parenthetical remarks.
9. Always cite source and data for tables and exhibits.
10. Seek additional information to supplement text material. For example, information and articles on economic climate, industry structure, competition, and financial data can be obtained from trade magazines, government publications, and investment sources.
11. Read and understand every exhibit in the text. They are there for a good reason. Sometimes, they tell more than the written text itself.

CASE SELECTION CRITERIA

In selecting policy cases for this book, we used a set of criteria. Our objective was to select a group of cases that adequately illustrated text material and that contained a wide variety of situations. This variety is expressed in size, type, time frame, length, and the difference in the main thrust of individual cases. Of special interest is the inclusion of cases concerning nonprofit organizations, which reflects the increasing interest in this area. The different types of cases in this book are summarized as follows:

Types of Cases	*Number*
Large firms	8
Medium-sized firms	8
Small firms	7
Social responsibility	3
Nonprofit organizations	4

To provide a quick review, we have constructed the case matrix (see table A), which lists each case by type and by selection criteria.

TABLE A CASE MATRIX

Company	*Annual Sales in Millions*	*Industry*	*Time Frame*	*Length of Case in Book Pages*	*Main Interest*
Sears, Roebuck	$18,011	retailer	1978–79	15	reformulation
Volkswagen Manufacturing Corp. of America	n.a.	automobile	1976–78	11	plant location
Levi Strauss & Co.	1,682	apparel	1978–79	16	growth
Gulf & Western Industries	1,670	conglomerate	1973–74	16	growth assessment
Gulf Oil Corp.	1,400	oil	1973–74	10	political contributions
Albertson's Inc.	1,270	supermarket	1975–76	29	growth
White Motor Corp.	1,229	farm machinery	1975–76	7	survival
Hewlett-Packard Co.	893	electronics	1974–75	13	strategic adjustment
Adolph Coors Co.	747	beer brewing	1978–79	9	growth
World Football League	n.a.	sports	1975–76	15	survival
Amtrak	n.a.	rail transportation	1978–79	17	quasi-public corporation
Diversified Technology Corp.	200	diversified	1974–75	20	international: general
Hesston Corp.	154	farm equipment	1974–75	23	profit slowdown
Virginia Chemicals Co.	51	industrial chemicals	1973–74	19	profit slowdown

Modern Publishing Co.	35	college textbooks	1975–76	16	growth
Paul Mueller Co.	32	stainless steel equipment	1975–76	15	international: Brazil
Rospatch Corp.	29	labels & packaging	1975–76	10	strategic planning
AMPAK International	29	sports goods	1974–75	11	international: Near East
Anaheim Memorial Hospital	24	hospital	1978–79	14	planning growth
AMMCO Tools, Inc.	16	automotive	1973–74	21	growth after initial success
Techtronics, Inc.	14	electronics	1975–76	12	penetrating strategy
American Recreation Centers	10	bowling	1975–76	19	developing strategy
Acme Steel	7	steel	1974–75	5	pollution violation
Oxygen Service Co.	2	welding supplies	1978–79	13	growth strategy
Fourwinds Marina	2	marina	1974–75	15	survival
Martinez Restaurant	1	restaurant	1977–78	14	profit slowdown
Polaroid in South Africa	n.a.	photo equipment	1977	10	foreign resentment
Consolidated Movie Theatres	——	recreation	1975–76	3	strategic analysis
Title IV-D Program	——	state government	1977–78	13	public program management
University of Arkansas	——	sports	1976–77	7	increasing attendance

CASES FOR PART I

1. CONSOLIDATED MOVIE THEATRES, INC.
2. MARTINEZ RESTAURANTS, INC.
3. HEWLETT-PACKARD COMPANY: PROBLEMS OF RAPID GROWTH

CONSOLIDATED MOVIE THEATRES, INC.

Consolidated Movie Theatres, Inc. (CMT) is composed of twenty-eight largely autonomous, previously independent theatres located throughout central Pennsylvania. Several years ago the manager-owners of privately-owned operations exchanged their theatre ownerships for CMT stock and the right to continue as theatre managers with the corporation. They believed that this freeform conglomerate arrangement would result in increased profits for all. Their corporation is run by five fulltime directors, elected by the stockholders and entrusted with the responsibility of formulating corporate strategy and directing the overall corporate activities.

Since their incorporation, CMT theatres had restricted their film offerings to those movies rated G (general audiences), PG (parental guidance suggested), and R (restricted to persons over 18), with rare exceptions when X-rated—and never pornographic-type—films were shown.

During the past year, CMT's seventh of operation, profits of the CMT theatres dropped almost 14 percent from the previous year, even though the profits of the theatre industry at-large had reached all-time high levels during the same period.

In reviewing the performance of their offerings in the past year, the CMT directors discovered that the few X-rated films that they had shown had far-and-away been the most profitable, followed by those rated R. Further, competitors of CMT who had occasionally shown pornographic-type films had outdrawn the CMT theatres on the dates when this type of film was shown.

Recently, a major film distributor approached the CMT directors with an offer to supply them with a selection of top quality X-rated and pornographic-type films for the following 12 months, the minimum contract period. These films, if ordered, would constitute approximately one-third of the films shown at any single theatre during the year, with the remaining two-thirds being supplied by the corporation's present distributor.

In discussing the possibility of contracting for films from a second distributor,

---

Prepared by Professor John A. Pearce II of the University of South Carolina.

the CMT directors foresee an opportunity for increased business by attracting a new segment of movie goers. On the other hand, they fear a twelve-month commitment to a moderately risky venture and they have expressed concern regarding the long-run impact of a rather drastic change in their film offering.

EXERCISE

INSTRUCTION This exercise is designed to gauge your skill in formulating corporate strategy.

Assume the role of a newly elected CMT director and describe the corporate strategy you would suggest for the firm. Please include in your statement an assessment of the main considerations that led to your conclusion.

To help you formulate your corporate strategy, pieces of information are available to you pertaining to the CMT situation. A listing of these pieces of information is provided below. In fifteen minutes your instructor will indicate that you can take as many as *three* of these items of information from the front desk. Subsequently, the instructor will invite you to the desk three more times at five minute intervals for additional pieces of information—a maximum of *three* each time. The largest total number of pieces of information which you can select is twelve. However, you are not required to take any.

Before approaching the desk, rank your preferences for the information by numbering the pieces you will choose on the lines provided in the page two listing. Place the number 1 beside the piece you will pick up first, should you choose any; 2 beside the second most preferred, etc., up to the number 12, if necessary.

You will be allowed forty-five minutes for this assignment and may begin to write at any time.

Pieces of information available to CMT directors:

____ 1. Labor Union Considerations

____ 2. CMT's Perceived Role in the Competitive Environment

____ 3. Concession Stand Operations

____ 4. Technological Factors

____ 5. Return-on-Investment Information on CMT and the Industry

____ 6. Inventory Control Concerns

____ 7. Manager's Commitment to a Revised Strategy

____ 8. Social Factors Affecting CMT Theatres

____ 9. Overhead Cost Changes

____ 10. CMT Ideals and Long-term Goals

____ 11. Impact on Media Advertising

____ 12. CMT Theatre Locations

____ 13. Theatre Ticketing Pricing and Film Costs

____ 14. Political and Legal Factors

____ 15. In-theatre Promotions at CMT

____ 16. CMT Corporate Performance Targets

____ 17. Theatre Hours

____ 18. Activities Valuable to the Customer

____ 19. Desired Benefits from a Revised Film Offering

____ 20. Likelihood of Success with X-rated Films

____ 21. Employee Attitudes Toward a Revised Strategy

____ 22. Economic Conditions in CMT Theatre Areas

____ 23. CMT Corporate Abilities

____ 24. Distribution Channels

____ 25. Other (Please specify at the desk)

MARTINEZ RESTAURANTS, INC.

Skip Martinez sat at his desk, leaning back in his chair and staring at the ceiling. His hands fidgeted with a paper clip that he had been turning over and over as if to give himself some sort of activity to take his mind off his troubles. He had spent the last two days in court trying to reach an agreement in a divorce settlement with his second wife. He thought, "She's really trying to take me financially and here I've lost $1,170 just this week on my newest restaurant." Going over it in his mind, Skip tried to understand how he had placed himself in such a bad position. He had been lucky with his restaurants until this last one; it was becoming a financial burden. He sat there as he recalled the days when he first entered business.

BACKGROUND OF THE MARTINEZ RESTAURANTS

He was always a hard worker and an ambitious man. He was popular among his group of friends, always willing to listen to someone else's opinion. When the problems of senior year in high school began to plague him, he took the advice of a friend and the two of them quit school to work as supervisors at the Johnson Fence Company. Soon Skip found himself wanting to own his own business. When an advertisement appeared in the paper about a service station for sale, he decided to take the opportunity; he spent the next six months working long hours to make a profitable business of the station. Soon he realized that long hours and grueling work didn't bring in the money he thought it would. He searched for another job opportunity and, on the advice of one of his suppliers, decided to go into the wholesale tire business.

For the next six years business was good for Skip. He enjoyed selling to people but found that the travel in his work interfered with his home life. He began having trouble with his wife about it, so he decided to look for work nearer home. One day as he looked through the classified ads he saw an advertisement for the

---

Prepared by Sue Graves, Russ Best, and Don Hyburn under the supervision of Professors Sexton Adams and Adelaide Griffin of North Texas State University.

sale of a restaurant in a suburb of Phoenix, Arizona that housed lower and middle-income families. He thought to himself, "A restaurant bearing the Martinez name . . . a Mexican food restaurant at that!" He knew it would be a success; the main problem would be collecting the initial money for the rent, equipment, employees, and food.

Skip sold his wholesale tire business for $35,100. He needed another $11,700 to open his new restaurant and decided to borrow it from banks. He borrowed $1,170 on his good name at the first bank. Then he used the $1,170 as collateral in the form of a Certificate of Deposit and borrowed $3,510 from a second bank. At the third bank Skip bought a $3,510 C. D., used it as collateral, and borrowed $9,360. Finally, at the fourth bank he bought a $9,360 C. D. and borrowed $12,870. Using $23,400 to buy equipment and another $23,400 to change the decor to Mexican, to lease the building, and to open, Skip started business in the first of the Martinez chain.

From 1973 to 1976 Skip turned his new business (Martinez #1) into a successful operation. The restaurant was located just a few blocks from the major highway between Phoenix and Scottsdale, as well as very near a U. S. mail facility. The restaurant seated 150 people and the bar another 50. Both of these were full seven days a week for lunch and dinner. Skip was pleased with his initial success.

Early in 1975 Skip discovered a former washateria for lease on a corner of a busy street in the same suburb; he decided to open his second restaurant, which he called Taco Villa. The equipment and opening costs amounted to $25,740. His idea was to serve Mexican food "to go." His mother was anxious to take over the management of the restaurant; since the overhead was so low and the labor requirement so small, Skip decided to give it a try. Taco Villa, however, wasn't as profitable as Skip had hoped. It only did $5,850 a month in sales; the other restaurant was doing much more. Still, since very little of Skip's time was taken, due to his mother's management of the place, Skip decided to keep the restaurant open.

Early in 1976 Skip opened another restaurant (Martinez #2) on the edge of downtown Phoenix. Again he leased the building, this time with a three-to-five-year option to renew the lease, and spent $35,100 for equipment and $29,250 for remodelling and opening costs. When he tried to pinpoint the things that had made his first restaurant a success, he decided upon a three-point rule: Good food, low prices, and close supervision. He emphasized these three things and was pleased at the promising success he was having with his second and third restaurants; the third restaurant became his corporate headquarters.

Skip thought he had his business under control until the time came to negotiate a new lease on the first restaurant; he was surprised to find that the owners were not willing to repair or remodel the building even though it was needed. Instead they offered to sell to Skip, but he decided the price was much too high. Having lost his lease, he moved his equipment and his fifteen employees to another location (Martinez #3) a few blocks away, also near a major highway. Since he already had some equipment and employees, the moving costs were $10,000 and the equipment and opening costs amounted to $40,000; the building, of course, was leased.

While all this negotiating and moving was taking place, Skip found another restaurant location that he wanted. It was in the middle of a block in a section known as Restaurant Row. This is a very cosmopolitan area of Phoenix and the streets and parking lots stay jammed with traffic from Happy Hour in the afternoon till closing time at 2 A.M.. The equipment cost him $58,500 and the opening costs another $40,950. The new restaurant, Martinez #4, shared parking facilities with two discos next door. Also situated a block away was Tony Garcia's, an expensive Mexican food restaurant located on its own block. Skip featured a Latin band in the large bar/disco area of his Mexican restaurant and tried to maintain the same good quality food and low prices that he had offered in his other restaurants. At the end of six months, however, Skip found that he was still losing $4,000 to $5,000 a month on the place.

In an attempt to change the trend of this fourth restaurant, Skip tried locating another cook. In his search, he contacted Carl Adkins, who had a reputation as an excellent cook. Even though he was talented in all areas of cooking, including Mexican, his real specialty was seafood. When Skip talked to Carl, the two of them discussed the restaurant's problems. Carl showed great interest in Skip's story. "Mr. Martinez," he said, "I know your past success has been in the Mexican food business, but have you ever thought of going into seafood? It's a higher quality food and the prices you charge can also be much higher! Besides, look around. Do you see any other seafood restaurants on this street?"

Skip realized that Carl was right—there were no other seafood places. So, he listened as Carl told him about his ideas. Within three days the Martinez Mexican food restaurant was changed into Seafood Port, a renovation that cost about $5,850. The grand opening was held in March 1977, but by mid-April Skip found that he was losing $1,170 a week on the place. He knew that, by rule of thumb, if a restaurant isn't profitable during the first six months of its existence it probably never will be; so he had thoughts of closing it down. (See Exhibit I for weekly sales figures.)

EXHIBIT I MARTINEZ CHAIN WEEKLY SALES

Taco Villa		
March	27	$1,251
April	3	1,572
	10	1,402
	17	1,427
	24	1,314
May	1	1,388
Martinez #2		
March	27	$8,355
April	3	8,420
	10	7,305
	17	8,634
	24	8,167
May	1	6,205

Martinez #3		
March	27	$8,001
April	3	8,081
	10	7,646
	17	8,127
	24	8,182
May	1	5,928

Seafood Port #4		
March	27	$4,734
April	3	5,957
	10	5,874
	17	4,824
	24	5,006
May	1	4,005

OPERATIONS

The Martinez chain now includes the four restaurants shown in Exhibit II.

EXHIBIT II

Unit	*Size*	*Lease*
Taco Villa	2000 sq. ft.	$700/month
Martinez #2	6800 sq. ft.	1,200/month
Martinez #3	3500 sq. ft.	1,250/month
Seafood Port #4	7200 sq. ft.	3,000/month

The two dinner houses specialize in Mexican food, but the managers estimate that about one-fifth of the items sold are non-Mexican—hamburgers, chicken-fried steak, spaghetti, steaks, or seafood. Taco Villa serves only Mexican food and does very little of its own food preparation. Several of its items are prepared by the dinner houses and sent to Taco Villa, where the final garnishes are added before serving. At Seafood Port the menu consists of a variety of seafood platters, many of which are served "all you can eat." A small selection of steaks is also available.

ORGANIZATION

Each restaurant is run as an autonomous unit, so the management structure varies at each location. (See Exhibit III for the organization chart of Martinez Restaurants.)

EXHIBIT III ORGANIZATION CHART

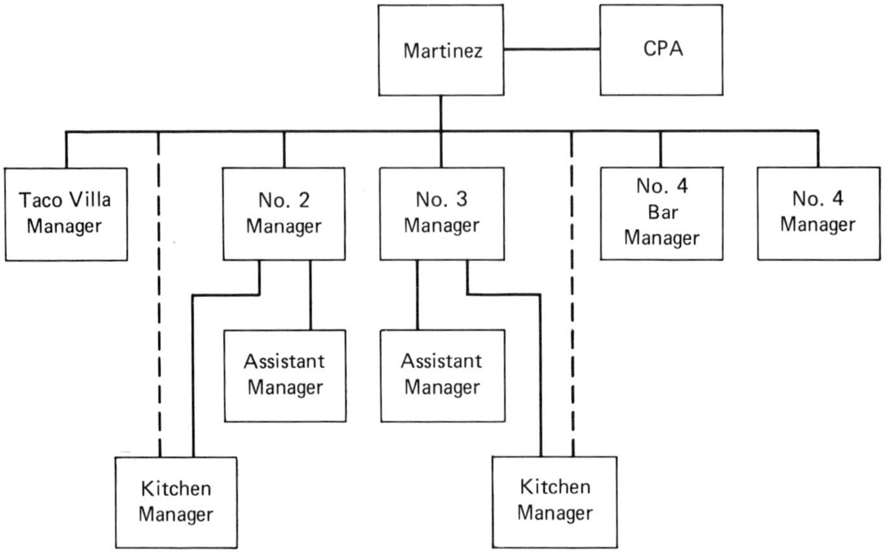

The manager at each restaurant is responsible for staffing, training, maintenance of the premises, and general operations. He also works with the kitchen manager in purchasing and food preparation.

The kitchen manager is responsible for ordering, food preparation, and general systems in the kitchen. He reports to the restaurant manager and directly to Skip. Skip feels that this system allows him to keep close control on his food costs, while holding the manager responsible for the labor costs.

All of the managers have extensive backgrounds in the food service industry and Skip has known them for lengths of time ranging from six months to four years. Within broad guidelines, each restaurant determines its own menus and operating procedures, and as long as profits and costs are in line, Skip allows the managers a free rein. When problems arise, though, he wants the managers to work closely with him. In fact, Skip feels that this was part of the problem involved in the final failure of Martinez #4 as a Mexican restaurant. He had heard that Sam Robinson, who was managing another well-known Mexican restaurant at the time, had a reputation for running a smooth operation. He hired Sam with the hope that he could make the restaurant profitable. After a few weeks of working together, though, Skip decided he had made a mistake. "Sam just took things into his own hands without talking to me first," he said. "When I found out he spent $500 on light bulbs, that was the last straw. He just wasn't used to the way I ran my restaurants." So Sam returned to Tony Garcia's and Skip finally hired Carl Adkins.

Skip admits that he has had problems with his other managers on occasion: "For one thing, I know I'm hard to work for. It's the little things that bother me; if I go into one of my restaurants and see something I don't like, I'll yell about it and just leave. When I come back a few days later I'll see if the manager's done anything about it. The other thing that bothers me is the family situation at my restaurants. Most of the employees at each store are related to the manager and if I get the manager too mad I'll lose the whole crew."

He points out the fact that the band at Seafood Port is a Latin band that came recommended by the bar manager. Skip didn't like the idea of having Latin music in his new disco but was willing to try it. When there was no increase in business, Skip suggested the band move to the #2 location, where the atmosphere was better suited to the band's style. After a few weeks at that restaurant the band complained they didn't like the set-up and moved themselves back to Seafood Port.

RECORD KEEPING

Record keeping at each restaurant is at a minimum. The total sales for liquor, food, and counter sales are sent in daily to the corporate office, where reports are prepared. These reports include daily and weekly sales, food costs, labor costs, and liquor costs for each restaurant. All invoices for purchases made by each restaurant are sent to the office to be paid and all receipts for sales are collected daily. The payroll for each restaurant is done weekly at the corporate office and all advertising is handled centrally as well.

The manager at Martinez #3 complained that this centralized system doesn't give him any feedback in that he reports his sales and expenses to the office but gets no figures back. He stated: "I have a general idea of my labor and food costs, but I have no way of knowing where I can improve because I don't know what the payroll breakdowns are or what the food costs are by item. I have some forms I used in my last job at El Chico that I think would help, but I haven't had a chance to talk to Skip about them yet."

MARKETING

Skip Martinez views his company as a success. When asked just what contributed to this success, he replied: "The low prices and the quality of the food. That kind of combination has guaranteed that once people try us, they'll come back again and again. What's more, they'll tell their friends and bring their families to my restaurants. I'm not trying to compete with the Tony Garcia type of Mexican restaurant. Instead, I try to serve the same people who would go to any casual Mexican food place, but I offer extras like not charging for coffee or tea with the dinners. It's that kind of service that brings people back."

When Skip opened each new restaurant he advertised on three of the leading radio stations and in the two major newspapers. These ads cost about $1,170 a week, but no significant difference in customer volume could be determined by Skip. Each time, after about two weeks of advertising, he would stop the advertisements and buy listings in occasional publications, such as the *Phoenix Convention Pamphlet*. This kind of advertising alone cost him $800 a month. The only exception to this policy was Seafood Port. He was so determined to increase the volume of business in this restaurant that he usually included an ad about that week's special dinner in one or the other of the major newspapers for Friday, Saturday, and Sunday editions at $140 cost per day. Again no difference in customer volume was evident, but Skip could think of nothing else to do. Now, he advertises any special items, such as price reductions or a band playing in the disco, on cloth signs hung on the building or portable metal signs placed in the parking lot; the Martinez restaurant signs are rather small and close to the buildings. At one point Skip had a catchy idea for a message on the portable metal sign in the parking lot of Seafood Port. He put on it, "Seafood is Sexfood; Get a Little . . . Here!" Shortly after he put it up, the message disappeared and was replaced with one advertising the Latin band at the restaurant. When Skip asked Carl Adkins about it, Carl replied: "Skip, this is a *family* restaurant. Parents don't want their kids asking a lot of embarrassing questions. That sign you put up made people mad. Signs are supposed to tell about days, hours, food, and bands, not be suggestive. I just decided that every day it was up, it was hurting our business; so I had it taken down."

Skip left still puzzled about what Carl had said. He liked his sign and wasn't convinced that Carl was right. He didn't want to make Carl angry since most of the employees in the restaurant were Carl's relatives, but he thought about going out there one day and putting the message back on the sign himself!

Skip designs his menus to offer something for everyone and prices his meals just at or slightly below those of his competitors. Surprisingly, some of the American foods seem to be among his best sellers, although he thinks that might be attributed to the fact that they are offered as daily specials. When asked what his very best seller is in each restaurant Skip said: "The Leon dinner is probably the most popular of the Mexican foods, but I don't really know about the seafood. I haven't been in that business long enough to get a feel for the situation. Actually, I'm planning to have new menus printed soon. I've thought of three new Mexican dishes, but I can't decide what else to keep or drop."

FINANCIAL ASPECTS

A few months after opening his first restaurant, Skip hired an accountant/bookkeeper to handle all of his accounting functions. As the business began to expand, the bookkeeper began to increase his fees accordingly. This arrangement was very acceptable until Skip began to experience substantial losses with Martinez #4 and the bookkeeper asked for another raise from $450 to $650 a month. At this point, Skip fired the bookkeeper and hired a certified public accountant to perform the accounting functions for financial statement and income tax purposes only. The new CPA, Jim Wilson, was charging only $150 a month, but he only handled the necessary tax reports and the monthly financial statements. The two office clerks were given the duties for all daily postings and other miscellaneous accounting functions. Wilson did give the clerks some basic instructions and asked that they call him if problems were encountered, since Skip has never been directly involved in any of the financial matters.

The company uses essentially the cash basis of accounting for its operations. This method is modified only to the extent of recognizing depreciation on all purchased assets. Instead of accounting for the cost of the assets when purchased, they are written-off over the life of the asset using the straight-line method of depreciation. The cash basis is also modified for large invoices. Checks are prepared and entered on the books immediately upon receipt of a vendor's invoice, even though the check is usually not mailed until five days prior to the invoice due date. All small invoices and any beer purchases are paid daily by each restaurant manager from cash receipts. The managers send the paid invoices to the corporate offices daily, where they are recorded on the books.

Wilson picks up the books monthly and prepares the tax and financial statements. He does not prepare separate monthly financial statements for each restaurant as the bookkeeper had done, except for the year-end statement. All monthly financial statements are prepared on a consolidated basis for the total corporation.

The kitchen manager in each restaurant is responsible for all purchases of food and kitchen supplies. The managers do not record any purchases and no inventory records are kept. The corporate office records the dollar amount of food purchases per month, but all other purchases are just recorded as supplies and no inventory records are kept.

No inventory records or physical counts are deemed necessary because, as Skip stated, "All my managers are good workers and very honest people, so they would probably resent any type of inventory system."

Exhibits IV and V present the income statement and balance sheet for the year ended December 31, 1976, as prepared by Wilson. The financial statement presents the operations of each restaurant separately and on a consolidated basis.

EXHIBIT IV MARTINEZ RESTAURANTS CONSOLIDATED BALANCE SHEETS (Unaudited)

Assets		
Current Assets		
Cash	$ (10,790)	
Accounts receivable	11,170	
Inventory	21,906	
Prepaid expenses	13,057	
Total Current Assets		$ 35,343
Fixed Assets		
Land	70,200	
Improvements & construction costs	16,380	
Leasehold improvements	43,012	
Equipment	190,761	
Autos & trucks	21,294	
Less: Accumulated depreciation	(41,260)	
Total Fixed Assets		300,387
Other assets-deposits		370
Total Assets		336,100
Liabilities		
Current Liabilities		
Accounts payable	28,082	
Taxes payable	14,886	
Total Current Liabilities		42,968
Notes Payable		203,547
Total liabilities		246,515
Capital stock	11,700	
Contributed stock	630	
Profit to date	77,255	89,585
		336,100

EXHIBIT V MARTINEZ RESTAURANTS STATEMENT OF INCOME AND EXPENSES (Year Ended December 31, 1976)

	Martinez #1	*Martinez #1-Club*	*Martinez #2*	*Martinez #3*	*Martinez #4*	*Taco Villa*	*Total*
Income							
Food & liquor	113,694	10,691	358,524	222,939	94,241	71,157	871,246
Counter			371	1,392			1,763
Machines	487	8	6,537	105	690	312	8,139
Cash over (under)	249	47	466	339	(706)	669	1,064
Total Income	114,430	10,746	365,898	224,775	94,225	72,138	882,212
Cost of Goods Sold							
Liquor		2,228	4,514		8,134		14,876
Food	34,302		86,576	59,926	23,942	24,795	229,541
Supplies	1,110	2,197	11,845	8,130	4,630	2,794	30,706
Salaries	38,569	2,932	119,679	69,198	39,191	16,976	286,545
Payroll taxes	2,526	192	6,357	3,192	1,528	938	14,733
Total Cost of Goods Sold	76,507	7,549	228,971	140,446	77,425	45,503	576,401
Gross Profit	37,923	3,197	136,927	84,329	16,800	26,635	305,811

Operating Expenses							
Linen	2,410		5,838	6,251			14,499
Entertainment		192	18,139		8,099		26,430
Rent-building	3,978		15,912	11,833	14,063	8,658	54,444
Maint. & repair	3,295		8,521	4,793	2,747	1,836	21,192
Advertising	2,787		6,313	5,643	1,424	328	16,495
Telephone	1,774		2,397	1,904	428	347	6,850
Utilities	2,289		17,302	7,149	8,456	5,113	40,309
Legal & accounting	234		2,259	614	293	614	4,014
Insurance	1,404	234	3,820	4,017	1,268	819	11,562
License & fees		199	2,228				2,427
Other taxes	351	117	614	702	59		1,843
Depreciation	854		10,364			1,404	12,622
Rent-equipment	560	737	5,257	1,898	1,887	1,395	11,734
Misc.	798		2,264		952	121	4,135
Total Operating Expense	20,734	1,479	101,228	44,804	39,676	20,635	228,556
Net Profit (Loss)	17,189	1,718	35,699	39,525	(22,876)	6,000	77,255

Source: Company Records

All categories of operating expenses are the same as those used for the company's daily bookkeeping operations. Separate records are maintained for expenses of each restaurant and different-colored checks are used for paying each restaurant's expenses. Since the corporate offices are located in Martinez #2, all corporate operating expenses are recorded on that restaurant's books. The corporate salaries are also charged to Martinez #2, except for Skip's salary, which is prorated equally to Martinez #2 and #3.

PRICING POLICY

Prior to the opening of his first restaurant in 1973, Skip obtained menus from three other Mexican food restaurants in the same general vicinity. After comparing the prices of his competition, Skip set all his prices below theirs. He did the same thing when he opened Seafood Port. Skip stated, "Our food is of higher quality than that of our competition, and our prices are lower. In fact, I have only raised my prices at the restaurant once. Then it was evident from our increasing meat costs that something had to be done. I had no idea how much the cost of each dinner was affected, so I increased the cost of every dinner by 8 percent. This seemed to make up for the increase in meat costs and also allowed us some hedge against future cost increases."

CONTROL

The financial operations of the corporation are controlled through the monitoring of the percentage of labor and food costs to total income. After the first year of operations at Martinez #1, Skip found that these two percentages were fairly consistent month after month. Based upon this premise, the kitchen manager is given a bonus (10 percent of his monthly salary) if food costs are kept below 28 percent of total income. Likewise, the restaurant manager receives a 10 percent bonus if labor costs are kept below 35 percent of total income. If the percentages exceed those acceptable limits no bonus is given and Skip personally investigates the cause. For instance, the bar manager at Seafood Port decided to buy a large variety of wines to complement the food menu. Naturally, this large purchase caused the percentage of food and beverage costs to total monthly income to fluctuate away from the acceptable limits. A week after the month's results were known, Skip questioned the bar manager as to the reason for the upward change in expenses. The bar manager convinced Skip with little effort that the expenditure was justified. Several weeks after this purchase, wine sales were still faltering.

The invoices for operating expenses such as repairs, utilities, food, and beverages for each restaurant are submitted directly to Skip. He then reviews each invoice in an effort to control expenditures at these individual restaurants, and he holds each restaurant manager responsible for unreasonably high expenditures on repairs, utilities, furnishings, etc.

Also submitted to the corporate office are the prenumbered daily sales receipts. The managers have been informed that the receipts are then verified as to complete sequence and mathematical accuracy. These receipts have, in fact, been verified in this manner by the office clerks only occasionally. Skip believes this process acts as a deterrent to improper control by the manager over daily sales receipts.

In July 1976 it was necessary for Martinez Restaurants, Inc. to apply for a loan with the Small Business Administration to purchase the fourth Martinez restaurant.

The SBA required a complete set of financial statements and a forecast of future operations. The financial statements presented no problem; however, a forecast of company operations had never before been prepared.

A study was conducted under the supervision of the bookkeeper in which historical sales trends were plotted graphically as shown in Exhibit VI. It was found, contrary to other published restaurant trends, that sales increased during summer months. Expenses were also examined and were found to be fairly consistent month by month when compared to sales. Sales were then forecasted monthly over a period of one year as seen in Exhibit VII. Once sales figures were established, cost of goods sold was forecast as a percent of sales. Variable expenses such as miscellaneous supplies, linen, and maintenance and repairs were forecast also as a percentage of sales. These percentages were estimated based in part upon historical data. Other expenses were estimated to remain constant with only a gradual increase over the period. Skip contends, "This budgetting deal seems like it would be helpful to me in controlling my restaurant operations. I just don't have anyone who could budget accurately and, besides, it takes too much time."

FUTURE PLANS

Skip's thoughts returned to the present as John Gomez entered the office. "Boy, you looked like you were a million miles away from here," laughed John. Skip smiled as he leaned forward in his chair. "Oh, I was just trying to think through some of the problems I've been having lately. Trying to run these four restaurants is one big headache."

"Yeah, I know you're having problems with Seafood Port," John said as he nodded, "but look at the other three . . . they're doing just great!"

"Yeah, but when I had just one restaurant," explained Skip, "I was making more money and had fewer problems than I do now. What I want to do is to sell the places I own now and move out to this land that I bought a couple of blocks from my

EXHIBIT VI MARTINEZ RESTAURANTS, INC. SALES TREND

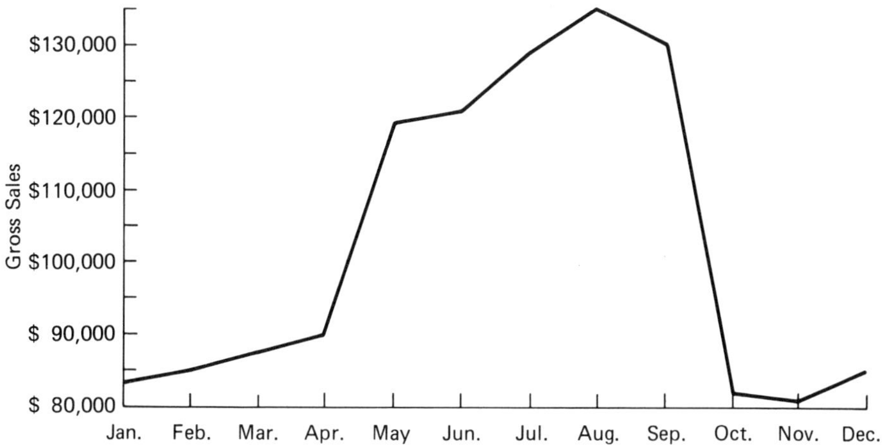

EXHIBIT VII MARTINEZ MEXICAN RESTAURANTS PROJECTED INCOME STATEMENT (Year Ending Sept. 30, 1977)

	Oct.	*Nov.*	*Dec.*	*Jan.*	*Feb.*
Total Sales	95,000	94,000	99,000	98,000	99,000
Cost of goods sold					
Food & beverage	28,900	28,200	29,700	29,400	29,700
Salaries & wages	32,715	33,075	34,980	34,290	35,180
Total Cost of Goods Sold	61,615	61,275	64,680	63,690	64,880
Gross Profit	33,385	32,725	34,320	34,310	34,120
Operating Expenses:					
Rental	6,610	6,610	6,610	6,610	6,610
Administrative salaries	3,860	3,860	3,860	4,200	4,200
Advertising	1,200	1,200	1,200	1,200	1,200
Equipment rental	860	860	860	860	860
Utilities	2,400	2,400	2,400	2,400	2,400
Supplies	1,900	1,880	1,980	1,960	1,980
Promotion & entertainment	250	250	250	250	250
Maintenance & repairs	1,900	1,880	1,980	1,960	1,980
Legal fees	300	300	300	300	300
Insurance	1,400	1,400	1,400	1,400	1,400
Licenses & fees	290	290	290	290	290
Dues & subscriptions	30	30	30	30	30
Depreciation	3,200	3,200	3,200	3,200	3,200
Interest	1,800	2,280	2,740	3,190	3,650
Misc.	120	120	120	120	120
Payroll taxes	3,125	3,100	3,400	3,300	3,400
Total Operating Expenses	29,245	29,660	30,620	31,270	31,870
Net Operating Profit	4,140	3,065	3,700	3,040	2,250
Income taxes	0	0	0	670	490
Net Profit after Taxes	4,140	3,065	3,700	2,370	1,760

first place. It's near the highway between Phoenix and Scottsdale, next to the U. S. mail building. If my old place could fill up to its 200 capacity every day it was open, then I *know* I could fill up this new restaurant I've planned."

"What's keeping you from doing it then?" asked John.

"Well, the plans I've drawn call for a building containing 10,000 square feet and seating 300 people," answered Skip. "The only real problem I have is money. The land I bought and the cost of clearing it came to about $86,580 and I've paid all but $40,950 of that off. I need a $351,000 loan to build this restaurant. If it weren't for the money I'm losing on Seafood Port . . . I have to think of a way to start it making money instead of losing it. Then I can sell all four restaurants and build the best restaurant in east Phoenix!"

EXHIBIT VII MARTINEZ MEXICAN RESTAURANTS PROJECTED INCOME STATEMENT (Year Ending Sept. 30, 1977) Continued

Mar.	*Apr.*	*May*	*June*	*July*	*Aug.*	*Sept.*	*Total*
104,000	106,000	105,000	106,000	112,000	117,000	112,000	1,247,000
31,200	31,800	31,500	31,800	33,600	35,100	33,600	374,500
35,980	36,530	33,110	32,550	35,600	37,411	33,454	414,875
67,180	68,330	64,610	64,350	69,200	72,511	67,054	789,375
36,820	37,670	40,390	41,650	42,800	44,489	44,945	457,625
6,610	6,610	6,610	6,610	6,610	6,610	6,610	79,320
4,200	4,200	4,700	4,700	4,700	4,700	4,700	51,880
1,200	1,750	1,750	1,750	1,750	1,750	1,750	17,700
860	860	860	860	860	860	860	10,320
2,400	2,400	2,400	2,400	2,400	2,400	2,400	28,800
2,080	2,120	2,800	2,820	3,000	3,200	3,080	28,800
250	350	350	450	450	450	250	3,800
2,080	2,120	2,800	2,820	3,000	3,200	3,080	28,800
300	300	300	300	300	300	300	3,600
1,400	1,400	1,400	1,400	1,400	1,400	1,400	16,800
290	290	290	290	290	290	290	3,480
30	30	30	30	30	30	30	360
3,200	3,200	3,200	3,200	3,200	3,200	3,200	33,400
4,100	4,550	5,000	5,500	6,050	6,655	7,320	52,835
120	120	120	120	120	120	120	1,440
3,500	3,650	3,500	3,600	3,800	4,000	3,700	42,075
32,620	33,950	36,110	36,850	37,960	39,165	39,090	408,410
4,200	3,720	4,280	4,800	4,840	5,324	5,856	49,215
925	820	942	1,065	1,175	1,290	1,420	8,797
3,275	2,900	3,338	3,735	3,665	4,034	4,436	40,418

HEWLETT-PACKARD COMPANY: Problems of Rapid Growth

In 1972–1973, rapid growth had created significant problems for Hewlett-Packard Company, a leading producer of electronic instruments and a major contender in minicomputers and calculators. Previous efforts to expand sales and market share had been largely successful, but had led the company to lower prices, for increased competitiveness; to reduce the percentage spent on research and development, for profitability; and to ease up on credit and payment policies, for the attraction of new customers. Sales and profits had increased substantially, but the company was faced with large increases in inventory, products put into production before they were fully developed, prices set too low to generate sufficient returns, and increased short-term borrowings. For the first time in company history, management had considered converting some of the short-term debt into long-term debt. Chairman David Packard and President William R. Hewlett, who had founded the company in 1939, decided improvements were needed in strategy, structure, and tactics.

THE INDUSTRY

Accelerating rates of technical change, increased competition, and economic uncertainty have made long-range planning and strategic decision-making increasingly complex. The world economic boom of 1972–73, followed almost immediately by depressed economic conditions, created especially difficult problems for companies in the high-technology electronics industry. Recession conditions caused large financial dislocations for many companies accustomed to rapid growth. Some of them decided to reduce expenses by cutting product development. Others increased their research spending in order to be ready for the price cuts and new products that they expected to characterize the next upturn. Since the industry is not capital intensive, a major determinant of growth is the successful development of new products, particularly those which cannot be quickly imitated. This has forced the managers of high-technology companies to make difficult decisions about the

---

Prepared by Professors Roger M. Atherton and Dennis M. Crites of the University of Oklahoma.

probable impact of price changes on sales and profits, and the probable effects of research expenditures on growth and on both short-run and long-run profitability.

As *Business Week* has reported, the management of technology—not only in electronics but also in pharmaceuticals, chemicals, and other specialties—is no longer an art but a discipline that is becoming better understood by a growing number of companies. The specialization that once separated an instrument maker from a computer company or a component supplier has largely disappeared, as semiconductor devices have taken on new complexity and instruments have been combined with calculators and computers in an extensive array of specialized systems. Semiconductor companies have integrated forward into end products, and instrument makers have started making their own data-processing equipment. As a result, a large number of potential competitors have entered almost every conceivable product-market segment and niche of high-technology electronics.

An increasingly common tactic used by companies to achieve market dominance is to price new products in relation to manufacturing costs they anticipate will be attained when the product has matured and when economies of scale have been achieved. This puts a premium on obtaining market share early in order to recover development and initial production costs, and to quickly attain sufficient volume to justify the predetermined price. As a result, many of the companies in the industry vigorously pursue strategies designed to achieve both technical and market dominance. This puts a heavy emphasis on innovation and creativity, sensitivity to market and customer needs, skills at finding useful applications of developing technology, and marketing and distribution capabilities to exploit new opportunities and to rapidly obtain dominant market share.

Although the total number of companies competing in this industry is too numerous to permit a comprehensive presentation of their performance, a representative sample is provided in Exhibit 1. Sales growth, profit margins, and earnings on net worth are shown.

HEWLETT-PACKARD: A BRIEF SKETCH

Innovative products have been the cornerstone of Hewlett-Packard's growth since 1939, when William R. Hewlett engineered a new type of audio oscillator and, with David Packard, created the company in Packard's garage. The product was cheaper and easier to use than competitive products, and it was quickly followed by a family of test instruments based on the same design principles. By the 1950s, they were turning out two dozen new products every year. By 1975, Hewlett-Packard had become one of the giants of the high-technology electronics industry. Annual sales were climbing rapidly toward $1 billion, approximately one-half of which were made to international customers. The company's 29,000 employees were involved in designing, manufacturing, and marketing more than 3,300 products. These included electronic test and measuring instruments and systems; electronic calculators, computers, and computer systems; medical electronic products; electronic instrumentation for chemical analysis; and solid-state components. According to company sources, Hewlett-Packard has remained a people-oriented company with management policies that encourage individual creativity, initiative, and contribution throughout the organization. It has also tried to retain the openness, informality, and unstructured operating procedures that marked the company in its early years. Each individual has been given the freedom and the flexibility to implement work methods and ideas to achieve both personal and company objectives and goals.

EXHIBIT 1

	Sales Growth (Percent of Change)				
	74-75*	73-74	72-73	71-72	
Beckman Instruments	7	21	10	8	
Fairchild Camera	−23	10	57	16	
General Instrument	−6	−1	34	16	
Hewlett-Packard	9	34	38	28	
National Semiconductor	11	115	65	58	
Raytheon	16	21	9	12	
Texas Instruments	−12	22	36	24	
Textronix	24	37	21	12	
Varian Associates	6	22	18	9	
	Profit Margin (Percent)				
	1975*	1974	1973	1972	1971
Beckman Instruments	4	4	4	3	3
Fairchild Camera	4	7	8	4	d
General Instrument	2	3	3	3	2
Hewlett-Packard	9	10	8	8	6
National Semiconductor	7	8	4	3	3
Raytheon	3	3	3	3	3
Texas Instruments	5	6	7	5	4
Textronix	8	8	8	7	6
Varian Associates	3	3	3	2	d
	Earnings on Net Worth (Percent)				
	1975*	1974	1973	1972	1971
Beckman Instruments	10	8	7	6	5
Fairchild Camera	8	17	20	9	d
General Instrument	5	7	9	7	4
Hewlett-Packard	16	18	15	13	10
National Semiconductor	25	35	14	16	12
Raytheon	16	14	13	12	12
Texas Instruments	11	17	18	13	10
Textronix	13	12	11	8	8
Varian Associates	5	5	6	3	d

d = deficit.
**Estimated by* Value Line.
Source: Value Line Investment Survey *and casewriters calculations.*

CORPORATE OBJECTIVES

When Hewlett-Packard was first formed, Hewlett and Packard formulated many of the management concepts that have since become the formal corporate objectives. As a result of their decision to have a decentralized organization, they believed it desirable to have a set of corporate objectives that would tie the organization more closely together and also ensure that the company as a whole was headed in a common direction. These objectives were first put into writing in 1957. They have been modified occasionally since then to reflect the changing nature of the company's business and environment. The intent and wording of the objectives in 1975 were, according to the founders, remarkably similar to the original versions.

As stated in the introduction to the Hewlett-Packard Statement of Corporate Objectives:

> The achievements of an organization are the result of the combined efforts of each individual in the organization working toward common objectives. These objectives should be realistic, should be clearly understood by everyone in the organization, and should reflect the organization's basic character and personality.

The following is a brief description of the Hewlett-Packard objectives in 1975:

1. *Profit objective:* To achieve sufficient profit to finance company growth and to provide resources needed to achieve the other corporate objectives.
2. *Customer objective:* To provide products and services of the greatest possible value to our customers, thereby gaining and holding their respect and loyalty.
3. *Fields of interest objective:* To enter new fields only when the company's ideas, together with its technical, manufacturing, and marketing skills, assure a needed and profitable contribution to the field.
4. *Growth objective:* To let growth be limited only by profits and company ability to develop and produce technical products that satisfy real customer needs.
5. *People objective:* To help Hewlett-Packard people share in the company's success, which they make possible; to provide job security based on their performance; to recognize individual achievements; and to insure the personal satisfaction that comes from a sense of accomplishment in their work.
6. *Management objective:* To foster initiative and creativity by allowing the individual great freedom of action in attaining well-defined objectives.
7. *Citizenship objective:* To honor corporate obligations to society by being an economic, intellectual, and social asset to each nation and each community in which the company operates.

Both Hewlett and Packard have indicated these objectives have served the company well in shaping the company, guiding its growth, and providing the foundation for the company's contribution to technological progress and the betterment of society.

SELECTED STRATEGIES AND RELATED POLICIES

Hewlett-Packard's product-market strategy has concentrated on developing quality products that make unique technological contributions and are so far advanced that customers are willing to pay premium prices. Products have been limited to electronic test and measurement and technologically related fields. Customer service, both before and after the sale, has been given primary emphasis. Their financial strategy has been to use profits, employee stock purchases, and other internally generated funds to finance growth. They have avoided long-term debt and have resorted to short-term debt only when sales growth exceeded the return on net worth. Their growth strategy has been to attain a position of technological strength and leadership by continually developing innovative products and by attracting high caliber and creative people. Their motivational strategy has consisted of providing employees with the opportunity to share in the success of the company through high wages, profit-sharing, and stock-purchase plans. They have also provided job security by keeping fluctuations in production schedules to a minimum, by avoiding consumer-type products, and by not making any products exclusively for the government. Their managerial strategy has been to practice "management by objective" rather than management by directive; they have used the corporate objectives to provide unity of purpose and have given employees the freedom to work toward these goals in ways they determine best for their own area of responsibility. The company has exercised its social responsibility by building plants and offices that are attractive and in harmony with the community, by helping to solve community problems, and by contributing both money and time to community projects.

STRATEGIC SITUATION

The company was fortunate to have entered the electronics industry early, before the rapid growth and expansion had started. Hewlett-Packard's leadership position in instruments was a major contributor to their success as the company diversified into computers, calculators, and components. In recent years, the original test and measurement instruments have accounted for about half of total sales. Data products, including minicomputers and calculators, brought in 40 percent. Medical electronics, a field entered largely through acquisitions, added 10 percent. Analytical instruments counted for an additional 5 percent. The trends in sales and contributions to company profit of these product groups are presented in Exhibit 2.

Sales increased 30 percent in fiscal 1972 and almost 40 percent in 1973. At first, this rapid growth was pursued vigorously because the company had been adversely affected by the computer and aerospace downturns in 1970. Earnings declined slightly in fiscal 1971, despite such austere measures as reduced work weeks for everyone, which resulted in company-wide reductions in pay. But the rapidity of the growth in 1972–73 created problems of a different kind. Inventories and accounts receivable increased substantially. There was an unaccustomed influx of new employees who needed to be trained and absorbed into the company's widely dispersed and decentralized operations. Products were put into production before they were fully developed. Prices were set too low for an adequate return on investment. These problems necessitated a higher level of short-term borrowings. By the end of 1973, these amounted to $118 million, and management considered converting some of the short-term debt to longer-term debt. The company was reluctant to do this because of the uncertain economic conditions. Since the company had policies of keeping employment steady and operating on a pay-as-you-go basis, both Hewlett and Packard believed minimal debt would be more consistent with these policies and the weakening U. S. economy.

In 1973–74, top management decided to avoid adding long-term debt and to reduce short-term debt by controlling costs, managing assets, and improving profit margins. As Packard made clear to the management at all levels, they had somehow been diverted into seeking market share as an objective. So both he and Hewlett began a year-long campaign to re-emphasize the principles they developed when they began their unique partnership. Clearly, in an industry where much of the

EXHIBIT 2 CONTRIBUTIONS TO SALES AND PRE-TAX PROFIT MARGIN BY PRODUCT GROUPS

	1975*	1974	1973	1972	1971
Sales (Millions of dollars)					
Test, measuring and related items	460.0	442.9	362.3	309.8	264.8
Electronic data products	360.0	325.7	215.2	108.0	63.1
Medical electronic equipment	95.0	76.1	56.6	40.7	30.8
Analytical instrumentation	45.0	39.4	27.2	20.6	16.4
Total	960.0	884.1	661.3	479.1	375.1
Pre-tax Profit Margin (Percent)					
Test, measuring and related items	14.5	15.1	13.3	14.5	14.3
Electronic data products	18.3	20.7	17.4	19.8	3.3
Medical electronic equipment	11.5	10.0	11.1	14.3	9.7
Analytical instrumentation	8.0	6.1	9.9	10.2	8.5
TOTAL	15.1	16.3	14.3	15.5	11.8

**Estimated by value line in* Value Line Investment Survey, *1975*
Source: Value Line Investment Survey.

competition was pushing for market share, Hewlett-Packard's decision to re-focus on profitability rather than market share presented certain risks. However, according to *Business Week*, neither Hewlett nor Packard saw themselves as risk takers and their approach was logical for a company that had consistently come up with truly innovative products. Packard toured the divisions to impose this new asset-management discipline. In addition, while other companies dropped prices to boost sales and cut research spending to improve earnings, Hewlett-Packard used quite different tactics. It raised prices by an average of 10 percent over the previous year, and it increased spending on research and development by 20 percent, to an $80 million annual rate. These two strategies were intended to improve company profitability and to slow the rate of growth that had more than doubled sales in the previous three years.

The improvements in 1974 performance compared with 1973 were quite dramatic. During fiscal 1974, inventories and receivables increased about 3 percent while sales grew 34 percent to $884 million. The effect of this better asset control, combined with improved earnings, resulted in a drop in short-term debt of approximately $77 million. Earnings were up 66 percent to $84 million and were equal to $3.08 per share compared to $1.89 per share. Only 1,000 employees were added, compared to 7,000 in the previous year. The improvement continued in fiscal 1975; sales for the first half of fiscal 1975 were up 14 percent to $460 million while profits increased 21 percent to $42 million. However, *Value Line Investment Survey* estimated that annual sales for 1975 would be up 9 percent to $960 million while profit would increase about 2 percent to $85 million.

The trends in earnings performance are shown in the Five-Year Consolidated Earnings Summary, Exhibit 3. Balance sheet effects are shown in the Comparison of 1974 and 1973 Consolidated Financial Positions, Exhibit 4. The differences in capital sources and uses are shown in the Consolidated Statement of Changes in 1974 and 1973 Financial Position, Exhibit 5.

Both Hewlett and Packard were dismayed that they had been forced to initiate and personally lead the efforts to get the company back on the track. It was particularly disconcerting to them because they believed the issues were fundamental to the basic strategy of the company. They had also had to intervene directly in day-to-day operational management, which was counter to their basic philosophy of a decentralized, product-oriented, and divisionalized organization structure.

STRUCTURAL SITUATION

Both men have been personally responsible for many of the company's new products and diversification activities. Since Packard will be 65 in 1977 and Hewlett will be 65 in 1978, both have recognized their retirements might have a substantial impact on the management structure and future success of the company. Some observers suggest that the problems in the early 1970s were the result of Packard's absence while he served in the Defense Department. As of mid-1975, the two men owned about half the company stock and could undoubtedly postpone retirement, but they felt it was very important for them to prepare the organization for an orderly succession. They also wanted to develop an organization structure that could respond more effectively to growth and diversification and would also provide more effective management of day-to-day operations. To accomplish these ends several significant changes were made, shortly before the end of the 1974 fiscal year, in the management structure of the company. The new organization is shown in Exhibit 6.

The basic product groups were realigned from four to six. The purpose was to establish a more logical grouping of products and technologies while creating group organizations of more manageable size and structure. They also established a new level of management to oversee day-to-day operations of the company. This consisted of two executive vice presidents, jointly responsible for operations, and a vice president for corporate administration. These three executives, along with Hewlett and Packard, were set up as an Executive Committee to meet weekly in order to coordinate all phases of the company's operations. This was intended to bring new people into the upper levels of management to build the long-term strength of the company. The new structure was also expected to allow both Hewlett and Packard to devote more time to matters of policy and planning the company's future.

In the new organization, the six product groups each had a general manager, who had responsibility for both domestic and foreign product divisions. The change left intact Hewlett-Packard's basic strategy of approaching established markets through relatively autonomous product-oriented division. In any high-technology operation, according to *Business Week*, a key problem is keeping new-product development focused on the needs of the market rather than on pure research and technological improvements with little market potential. Hewlett-Packard has tried to avoid this by doing most of its research and development at the division level. Of the $70.7 million spent on research and development in 1974, one-sixth was allocated to Corporate Research and Development and five-sixths was spent by the divisions. Divisions were intentionally kept small to foster open communications and quick responsiveness to their individual market segments. Each product group, in addition

EXHIBIT 3 FIVE-YEAR CONSOLIDATED EARNINGS SUMMARY (in thousands of dollars)

	1974	1973	1972	1971	1970
Net Sales	$884,053	$661,290	$479,077	$375,088	$363,593
Other Income, Net	8,732	12,108	3,570	4,202	2,802
Total Revenues	892,785	673,398	482,647	379,290	366,395
Costs and Expenses:					
Cost of goods sold	422,104	312,972	223,690	184,507	173,731
Research and development	70,685	57,798	44,163	39,426	37,212
Marketing, administrative, and general	247,232	202,999	138,716	107,822	105,587
Interest	8,502	5,057	1,764	1,239	2,212
Total Costs and Expenses	748,523	578,826	408,333	332,994	318,742
Earnings Before taxes on Income	144,262	94,572	74,314	46,296	47,653
Taxes on Income	60,240	43,823	37,064	22,415	24,146
Earnings Before Accounting Change	84,022	50,749	37,250	23,881	23,507
Accounting Change	—	—	1,211	—	—
Net Earnings	$ 84,022	$ 50,749	$ 38,461	$ 23,881	$ 23,507
Per Share					
Earnings before accounting change	$3.08	$1.89	$1.40	$0.92	$0.92
Accounting change	—	—	0.05	—	—
Net Earnings	$3.08	$1.89	$1.45	$0.92	$0.92
Common Shares Outstanding at year end	27,298	26,816	26,450	26,038	25,649

Source: 1974 Annual Report.

EXHIBIT 4 COMPARISON OF 1974 AND 1973 CONSOLIDATED FINANCIAL POSITIONS (in thousands of dollars)

	1974	1973
Assets		
Current Assets		
Cash and marketable securities	$ 13,828	$ 8,925
Notes and accounts receivable	193,735	187,472
Inventories		
Finished goods	51,627	51,652
Work in process	82,410	84,687
Raw materials	61,177	52,307
Deposits and prepaid expenses	13,791	10,147
	416,568	395,190
Property, Plant and Equipment		
Land	26,566	23,940
Buildings and improvements	128,274	87,961
Machinery and equipment	109,342	94,210
Other	26,846	21,992
Leaseholds and improvements	10,002	7,056
Construction in progress	41,541	32,493
	342,571	267,652
Accumulated depreciation	117,709	93,882
	228,862	173,770
Other Assets and Deferred Charges		
Investment in unconsolidated Japanese affiliate	4,391	3,668
Patents and other intangibles	2,243	2,798
Other	6,317	4,240
	12,951	10,706
	$654,381	$579,666
Liabilities and Stockholders' Equity		
Current Liabilities		
Notes payable	$ 43,527	$ 94,749
Commercial paper	—	25,750
Accounts payable	26,491	36,072
Accrued expenses	74,778	51,471
Income taxes	34,476	12,745
	179,272	220,787
Long-term Debt	2,899	2,182
Deferred Federal Income Taxes	14,531	7,500
Shareholders' Equity		
Common stock, par value $1	27,298	26,816
Capital in excess of par	112,157	82,763
Retained earnings	318,224	239,618
	457,679	349,197
	$654,381	$579,666

EXHIBIT 5 CONSOLIDATED STATEMENT OF CHANGES IN 1974 AND 1973 FINANCIAL POSITION (in thousands of dollars)

	1974	1973
Working Capital Provided		
Net earnings	$ 84,022	$ 50,749
Add charges not affecting working capital		
Depreciation and amortization	31,519	22,917
Deferred federal taxes on income	7,031	5,412
Stock purchase and aware plans	5,625	4,169
Other	4,549	522
Working capital provided from operations	132,746	83,769
Proceeds from sale of common stock	23,746	15,483
Proceeds of additional long-term debt	1,277	1,823
Total working capital provided	157,769	101,075
Working Capital Used		
Investment in property, plant and equipment	86,327	81,162
Dividends to shareowners	5,416	5,332
Reduction in long-term debt	560	1,558
Increase in equity in unconsolidated Japanese affiliate	723	1,054
Other, net	1,850	4,319
Total working capital used	94,876	93,425
Increase in working capital	62,893	7,650
Working Capital at Beginning of Year	174,403	166,753
Working Capital at End of Year	$237,296	$ 174,403
Increase in Working Capital Consisted of		
Increase (decrease) in current assets		
Cash and marketable securities	$ 4,903	$ (10,723)
Notes and accounts receivable	6,263	69,057
Inventories	6,568	70,083
Deposits and prepaid expenses	3,644	4,256
	21,378	132,673
Decrease (increase) in current liabilities		
Notes payable and commercial paper	76,972	(103,201)
Accounts payable and accrued expenses	(13,726)	(26,937)
Federal, foreign and state taxes on income	(21,731)	5,015
	41,515	(125,023)
Increase in working capital	$ 62,893	$ 7,650

Source: 1974 Annual Report.

to the group general manager, had a sales-service organization serving all the product divisions in the product group. Each product division had its own engineering, manufacturing, personnel, quality, accounting, and marketing functions with some of the smaller divisions in the same location sharing a functional department between them. Although H-P's divisions had considerable latitude in developing product strategies, they were not allowed to go outside their assigned markets or to borrow money. Even within the limits set by top management, new-product proposals were carefully reviewed at the preliminary investigation stage. The company considered itself conservative in funding projects and expected at least 80 percent of funded projects to be successful. Once development of a new product had been funded, the goal was to get it to the market in a hurry. The company believed that sales lost during development time could not be recovered since, if the technology were available to fill a market need, others could also conceive a product. As a result, both timing and the flexibility to exploit opportunities quickly were considered important reasons for having a multiple-product division structure.

The product-division marketing departments were responsible for order processing and shipping, sales-engineering and contract-administration, service-engineering, technical-writing, publications, and advertising and sales promotion. They also provided sales forecasts and were responsible for recommending and reviewing prices. At the initial pricing this involved a major analysis of the marketplace, competition, profitability, and overall product strategy. The actual selling and customer servicing were handled by the six group organizations. Each division competed for the time of the group's field-sales force. In order to attract the attention of the field-sales engineers, the divisions had to offer extensive marketing support and new product training to these "customers." The broad, growing, and often interacting lines of products frequently resulted in several group sales teams working with one customer. The centralized sales organization was intended to assure that cooperation and communication between sales teams were maintained; Hewlett-Packard wanted customers to feel they were dealing with one company with common policies and services. Confusion and competition were avoided by a clear assignment of sales responsibilities and by organizing the sales force in a way that put primary emphasis on functional rather than product responsibility.

As shown in Exhibit 6, both Corporate Research and Development and Corporate Development reported directly to Hewlett. Also, one or both of the founders continued to sit in on annual review sessions for each division. As the 1974 Annual Report pointed out, the restructuring represented an evolutionary step in Hewlett-Packard's continuing growth and diversification, but there had been no changes in basic operating philosophy.

OPERATING POLICY SITUATION

In addition to the tactics used in implementing the strategic and structural changes already described, there were certain operating policies that were related to the changes. The company's basic operating policy was often referred to by Hewlett-Packard people as "management by objective," and was contrasted with management by directive. Instead of leading and coordinating the organization primarily by factors such as hierarchical authority relationships, detailed rules and regulations, and a tight military-type organization, Hewlett-Packard has chosen to use clearly-stated and agreed-upon objectives. Each individual at every level in the organization has been expected to make plans to achieve the company's broader

EXHIBIT 6 HEWLETT-PACKARD CORPORATE ORGANIZATION, APRIL 1975

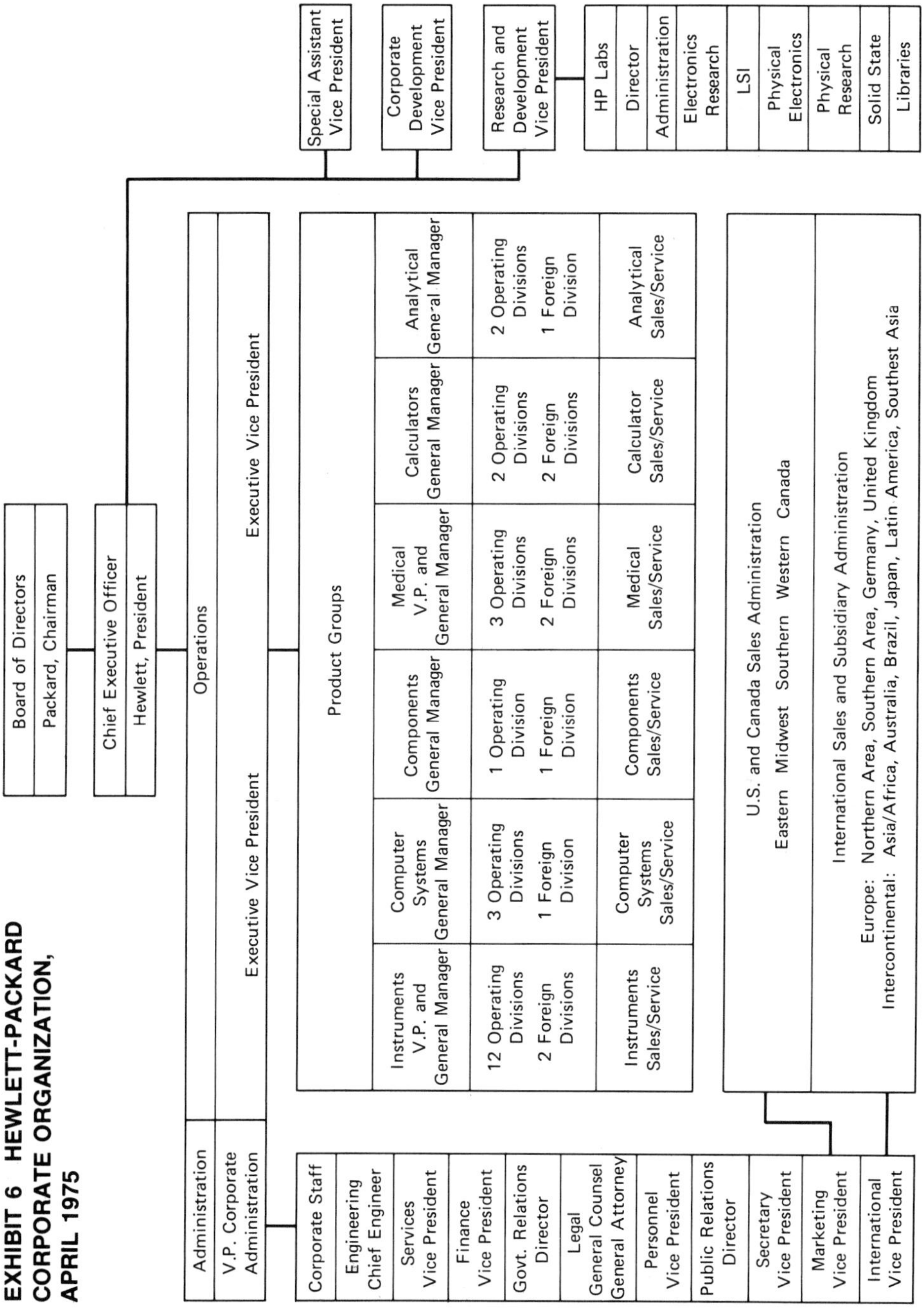

goals and objectives. After receiving supervisory approval, each individual has been given a wide degree of freedom to work within the limitations imposed by his or her own plans and by the general corporate policies. The purpose has been to offer the greatest possible freedom for individual initiative and contribution. Top management has indicated that this policy has been a major factor in Hewlett-Packard's ability to provide innovative, useful products of high quality and to develop people to accept additional responsibility as the company has grown.

As *Business Week* has suggested, the key to the success of Hewlett-Packard may well be the unusual spirit of corporate loyalty that has permeated the work force, particularly the 1,900 R & D personnel. Even though their individual stock holdings in 1975 were worth some $700 million, Hewlett and Packard still ran an egalitarian company. They drew salaries of only $156,000 each, and few top officers made more than $100,000. The company had distributed $64 million in cash profit-sharing bonuses in the previous five years, and about half the employees were participating in a stock-purchase program. Rather than run the risk of "big" layoffs, Hewlett-Packard has declined to bid on short-run government contracts. It has also avoided getting into product lines where there are wide fluctuations in sales volume, such as in many consumer products. When faced with lean times, inventories have been increased and everyone from Packard on down has worked a reduced work week. This has had the effect of dividing the available jobs among all the employees in contrast to termination or temporarily laying off somewhere between 1000 and 2000 people. As a result, Hewlett-Packard has seldom been afflicted with the migrations of people and ideas that many high-technology companies have experienced.

These general policies and the supportive attitudes of managers toward their subordinates were believed to be more important than specific details of the personnel programs. Personnel relations at Hewlett-Packard were considered good only when people demonstrated faith in the motives and integrity of their supervisors and of the company. An example was the program of flexible working hours. Under flexitime, most people at Hewlett-Packard have been allowed to work and leave within two-hour "windows." Employees could arrive within a two-hour period at the beginning of the day and leave after completing eight hours of work. In addition, individuals could vary their starting times from day to day. Hewlett-Packard has not had time clocks for many years. The company's trust in the individual was believed to be the key to the program's success. Both Hewlett and Packard have suggested that people are the essence of their organization, for people determine the character and strength of the company. As Packard has frequently said, "Motivation is the difference between a championship ball team and an ordinary ball team." The question posed by *Business Week* is whether the players will stay motivated when their two coaches are no longer with the team.

PART II

Policy Making and Strategic Planning

Effectiveness in strategy making depends upon many things: upon the company's acceptance of the concept; upon the dedication of its chief executive officers to both the theory and practice of strategy; upon a total consideration of corporate social responsibility; and above all, upon the capacity of organizing and administering the strategic function. The structure must be so designed that it ensures the assumption of proper and active roles by each entity of management and provides organizational means to coordinate their activities. A well-defined system that is systematic and streamlined will reduce excessive formality, inflexibility, and cost. In chapter 3, we discuss the development of this prerequisite.

In chapters 4 and 5, we discuss strategic planning, the policy aspect of strategy making. In chapter 4, we study environmental analysis, which is done to identify opportunities and threats, and internal assessment made to assess internal strengths and weaknesses. In chapter 5, we examine the crucial step of objective setting in matching and calculating the probability of attaining business objectives. In strategic planning, a sound methodology and a reliable mode of developing data and drawing credible conclusions are the overriding considerations.

In recent years, the relationship of business firms with government, society, and the public at large has received increasing attention. The impact of this situation upon strategies and tactics cannot be overemphasized. First, social responsibility influences the determination of a company's purpose, mission, and goal. Second, it places constraints on the selection of strategies and tactics. Third, it increases awareness of business ethics among the employees. In chapter 6, we devote our attention to such strategic issues and problems.

CHAPTER THREE

Organizing and Administering the Strategic Function

The design of the organizational structure and management system is an important aspect of management. Organizational structure provides the basic tool for accomplishing stated purposes and objectives; management systems establish the general courses of managerial action to ensure efficient coordination. The new product development system, the financial reporting system, and the performance review system are examples of company-wide management systems. Organizational structure relates functions, personnel, expertise, and activities to a logical and systematic whole. The design is based on a thorough understanding of the organization's purpose, the unique characteristics of the environment within which the organization operates, and, above all, of the management philosophy of the responsible executives. Adherence to sound management principles and behavior considerations are fundamental to the design.[1] Management systems are carefully designed to enhance the functioning of an organization and to ensure composite decision making throughout the organization. Thus, management systems that are process oriented complement the organizational structure that is function based. In this chapter, we discuss how to organize the strategic function and administer the planning system in keeping with this precept. We then discuss the structure of corporate strategies.

ORGANIZING THE STRATEGIC FUNCTION

The Organizational Setting

The management of the strategic function requires a viable organization—a structure that defines and optimizes the functioning of individual organizational units—and a system that facilitates their participation and coordination. In a large, diversified corporation, responsible individuals and units involved with the strategic function are located throughout the organization. As can be seen from figure 3.1, there are five responsible units (the board, the CEO/president and his/her general managers, the planning staff, the committee, and the line depart-

FIGURE 3.1 STRATEGIC PLANNING UNITS IN A TYPICAL LARGE CORPORATION

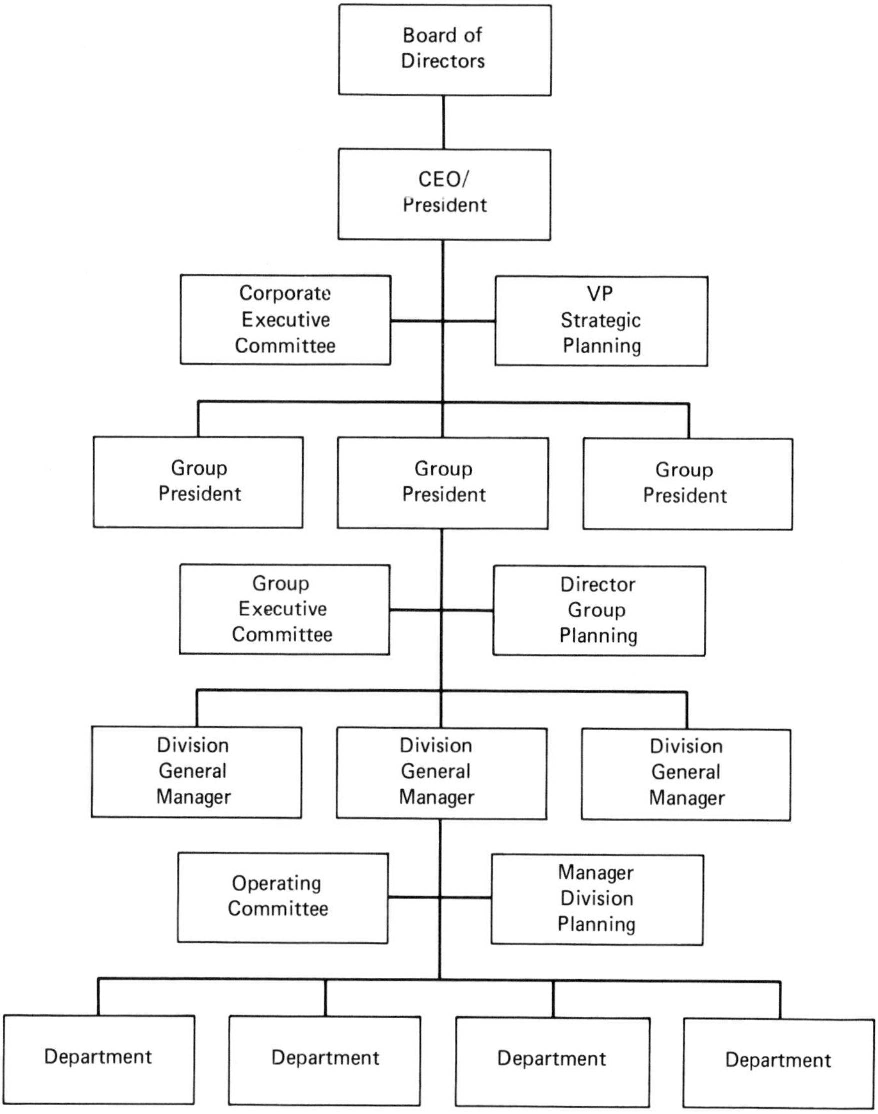

ments), and the total process has at least four tiers or levels (the board, the corporate office, the group, and the division).[2]

In a medium-sized company or a small company, the four tiers are reduced to three (the board, the corporate office, and the divisions), or to two in those companies that have not formed divisions (see figure 3.2). The individuals or units remain almost the same.

FIGURE 3.2 STRATEGIC PLANNING UNITS IN A TYPICAL MEDIUM-SIZED COMPANY

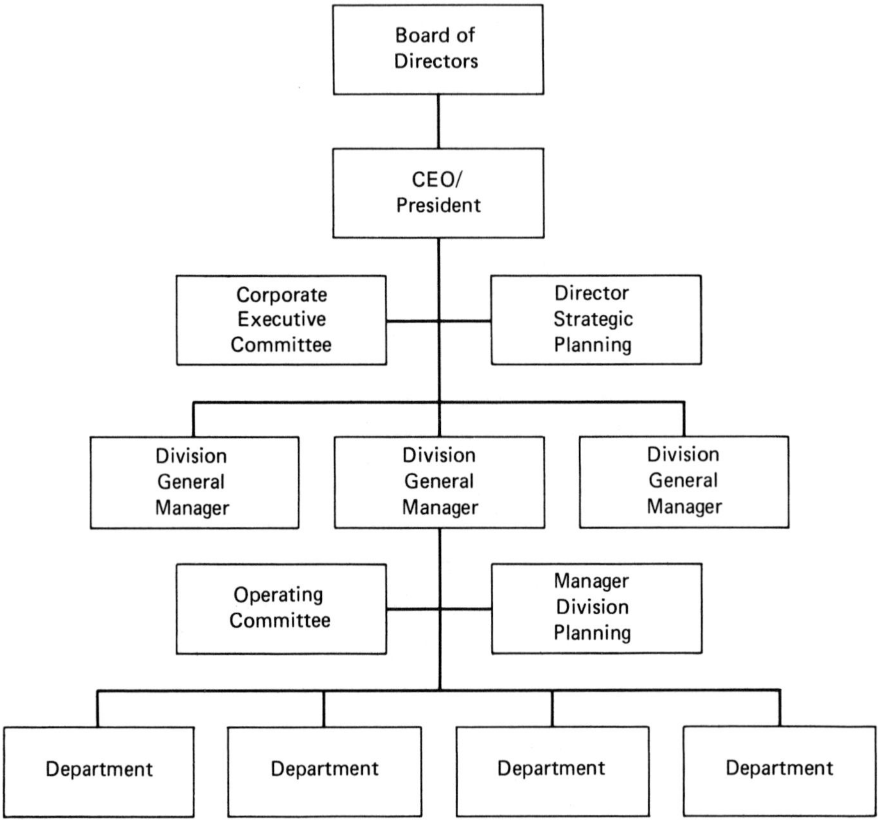

General Management and Components

In matters of policy, the board of directors deliberates basic company policies and approves the corporate strategy. The executive function rests in the hands of the CEO or president, the group executives (group presidents), and the operating division general managers (hereafter referred to as executive officers).[3] As a group, they constitute the general management. The president assumes the leading responsibility for the corporate strategy; the group executives, who command the several operating divisions, develop and direct strategies at the group level. General managers of operating divisions have the basic responsibility for developing and submitting to the group executives their respective strategic plans. Thus, it is the responsibility of these executives to ensure the optimal functioning of the five organizational units involved in the process. These five components—the board; the executive officers; the planning staff; the executive committees; and the line management—individually assuming their proper roles, and jointly operating as a team, represent the chain of command or a decision path along which strategy is developed and implemented. Let us examine each of these five components in turn.

THE BOARD The first unit is the board of directors. Myles L. Mace defines the board's functions in three major areas: (1) establishing the business objectives, corporate strategies, and broad policies of the corporation; (2) asking discerning questions; and (3) selecting the president.[4] In reality, however, the typical board member shies away from discharging legitimate responsibilities. Consequently, the responsibility for many of the recent failures and near failures of American corporations rests squarely on the shoulders of the board of directors.[5] Too often, an inactive board, dominated by inside (management) directors and staffed with unqualified members, serves merely as a "rubber stamp" to the chief executive officer.

In dealing with corporate objectives and strategies, the board assumes three functions: (1) it requests the submission by management of possible strategies; (2) it approves or disapproves them; (3) it reviews previously accepted strategies, questioning their continued validity.

THE EXECUTIVE OFFICER The next link in the chain is the executive officer. The CEO is the single most important person in strategy making, for the CEO is responsible for the company's performance and its future well-being.[6] Just as the CEO must be a generalist to properly head the organization, he/she must uniquely be a strategist. Therefore, the CEO encourages company executives to participate in strategy decision making and makes sure that the organization rewards proven performance and penalizes those who rely on short-sighted expediencies.

In discharging that responsibility, the CEO considers the following:

1. That board membership should be balanced to include both "inside" and "outside" members. A board dominated by insiders cannot judge strategies that they have developed themselves.
2. At each of the other three levels, that the planning executives are selected prudently. The selection is based on professionalism, competency, and a demonstrated skill in handling staff assignments and obtaining organizational support. Mutual trust between chief executive officers and their planning executives is an important consideration. A planning executive whose experience, disposition, and depth are not compatible to that of the chief executive officer will not function well.
3. That he/she is involved in the total management of strategies. Delegation must be exercised with prudence. It is fruitless to place blame on the planning staff or the line management for faulty strategy and failure to achieve desired objectives.
4. That the CEO's attention is properly divided between current and long-range business. Too often, the executive officer, concerned with matters of immediate urgency, ignores or slights strategic matters of future importance.[7]

THE PLANNING STAFF The planning staff, the major constituent element in the total process, gives us the third link in our chain. The planning staff provides executive officers with the needed professional assistance, conducts analyses, oversees the orderly proceedings of the process, and generates company-wide enthusiasm toward advanced planning and strategic action.[8] Organizationally, planning executives may report to the CEO/president either directly or through a senior vice president, the chairman of the board, a committee, or occasionally through a policy vice president, such as the vice president of finance. At other levels, the planning staff may report to the executive officer, to a functional vice president, or to the head of a line department, such as finance or marketing.

Being a staff function, strategic planning is a difficult task to perform. Adherence to certain guidelines will improve effectiveness.

1. The planning staff must distinguish itself through professional integrity and skillful handling of people. Professional integrity requires, at the minimum, the development of a sound methodology. Sound methodology does not mean the development of sophisticated methods for analysis, but the emphasis on a concise and rational way of developing data and addressing strategic issues. To illustrate the point, illustration capsule 5 summarizes the GE "Stoplight Strategy," which is a method of weighing decision variables involved in subjective decision making. The planner is a good communicator, capable of explaining the complexity of data, careful in justifying positions, and skillful in presentations. At times, he/she acts as a mediator between the chairman of the board and the president in reconciling differences in philosophy and approach. As a staff member, he/she advises and serves line management.

Illustration Capsule 5

STOPLIGHT STRATEGY AT GENERAL ELECTRIC

General Electric Company has developed a new framework for evaluating the qualitative factors of their businesses. With its forty-three businesses, General Electric is faced with planning in a wide diversity of industries. By the use of its Strategic Business Planning Grid, otherwise called "Stoplight Strategy," GE has found a way to refine the subjective decision-making process.

Factors, including "volatility of market share, technology needs, employee loyalty in the industry, competitive stance, and social need," are evaluated at each annual planning review. Numerical projections and qualitative factors are then combined, resulting in a high, medium, or low rating on GE's strengths in the field and industry attractiveness.

The Method

If GE's strength is high and attractiveness of the industry is medium, then a "green light" or "invest and grow" decision results, as the evaluation bars intersect in a green square. With both business strength and industry attractiveness low, the result will be a "red light" strategy. This business no longer warrants much investment by GE, but will still continue to generate earnings. A "yellow business" with high industry attractiveness and low GE strength, indicates a decision going either way.

Growth is expected from the green business, whereas the red operation may involve reduced investment, plant consolidation, limited technology, and strong cash flow. The yellow business may be composed of both green and red units.

GE planner, Reuben Gutoff says, "We don't give definite weights to the nonnumerical factors, but they do have weights. At the end of our discussion, there is a good consensus on what's green, red, or yellow. The result is semiquantitative." The final decisions and grids are made after three or four critiques at various levels by the corporate policy committee.

As one GE planner says, "Interestingly, the financial projections are often best on business that turn up worst (in the red) on the grid." The process is not just for show. Costly mistakes may be prevented.

Source: "General Electric 'Stoplight Strategy' for Planning," *Business Week*, 28 April 1975, p. 49.

2. In developing planning studies and the planning system itself, simplicity is the rule. The planning staff is responsible for the development of the planning system and acts as its agent for coordination and administration. Excessive rigidity and formality stifle innovation and participation. More than once, the planning system has acquired the reputation of being a "paper mill," an idle bystander apart from the mainstream of company operations, an obstacle rather than an asset to company progress.
3. The planning staff must be alert to company politics, able to discern the informal power structure of the company and thus to judge the possible "sensitivity" of their own findings and recommendations. Planning executives carefully clarify their functional objectives with their respective supervisors and develop strategy in achieving them. Planning depends on information and authority. Access to pertinent information from within and without the company is essential. Membership in important committees, which can be seats of power or influence, should be sought by the planning staff. Participation in reviews of the R&D budget, new product development, and acquisition proposals are legitimate planning functions.
4. The coordination and promotion of strategy making is a responsibility of the corporate staff. In addition to its assigned responsibilities, the corporate staff actively coordinates and oversees the company-wide planning process. Within the company, the respective responsibilities of the various planning units should be clearly understood. Whereas the corporate planning staff studies overall economic, industrial, and technological trends, the group and division planners focus on their specific areas of interest.

EXECUTIVE COMMITTEES The fourth link in the organizational chain we have been tracing is the executive committee on strategy. The committee provides a useful means for deliberating strategies. When properly managed, the committee can be very productive in consultation, information exchange, and group thinking.[9] The membership of a corporate executive committee usually consists of key policy vice presidents, with the president serving as committee chairman, and the planning executive as secretary. It is a standing committee from which ad hoc committees, subcommittees, or task groups can be formed to work on specific problems, such as acquisition, divestiture, or venture development. For example, Kennecott Copper Corp. established an eleven-member "strategic council" as a forum to debate strategic issues.[10] As a continual body, the committee reviews and adopts strategic plans, overseeing their implementation and recycling.

LINE MANAGEMENT Line management represents the fifth and final link in the chain. Line management plays a substantial part in both the formulation and execution of strategy. The chief executive officers and general managers of operating divisions, in particular, have the responsibility of seeing that line management's participation and support is secured. For illustration, TI's strategic planning system, an example of a company-wide commitment to strategy making, is discussed in illustration capsule 6. The company's "Objectives, Strategies, and Tactics" system is supported by a network of subsystems that involves line management and individual employees throughout the company. Illustration capsule 7 further explains the various organizational forms being practiced in several companies. The capsules help describe the part each of the five units plays in the total process.

Illustration Capsule 6

STRATEGY MAKING AT TEXAS INSTRUMENTS

One of the most successful formal planning systems is being practiced at Texas Instruments. A $2 billion company, operating in eighteen countries and expecting to grow 15 percent annually, TI feels that innovation is essential to the success of the company.

In 1963, Patrick E. Haggerty, president at that time and now honorary chairman, formalized the "objectives, strategies, and tactics" (OST) system and incorporated it into the TI structure. In the late 1960s, his successor, Mark Shepard, Jr., split the system. Strategic funds were controlled by the corporate committee who set up spending guidelines. "Under OST, a project-oriented management structure focuses entirely on tomorrow's growth, while a more conventional operating hierarchy concentrates entirely on today's profitability." This system is a check against pursuance of short-term profits. "OST is a highly decentralized bottom-up planning system, where more than 250 funded projects called tactical action programs—TAPS in TI jargon—drive more than sixty strategies that support the company's dozen business objectives."

"Management by Objectives"

TI has thirty-two divisions with sales up to $150 million each; and eighty product-customers centers, with sales up to $100 million each. Product-customer centers (PCCs) are similar to departments, except they are more independent, with some having their own engineering, marketing, and manufacturing units. Then from these, TI groups unite to support the tactics programs developed. Under the OST system, TI has a well-organized integrated company.

OST is very similar to management by objectives. However, there is a major addition. TAP managers also manage PCCs, and strategy managers are most often division heads. Therefore, TI does not have the planning group "handing off" their strategies to the operation organization.

OST has high visibility of results. Managers are constantly measured against documented goals. Monthly reviews and computerized updates on every TAP are standard procedure. Employees work in teams, with high peer pressure and recognition. There is no way to bury a mistake. Communication is thorough. Upper management has extensive knowledge of activities, and middle managers do not need day-to-day guidance. Although middle management may sometimes find OST managing them, it is a very successful system, and provides the good management and discipline needed in managing any company.

Search for Ideas

High marks are given to the TI structure by former managers. Says one: "There are a lot of middle managers running around TI talking about 'growth share matrices' and 'learning-curve pricing.' You don't get that depth of planning in other companies." TI has many systems to encourage thinking and communicating of new ideas.

In September, new tactical proposals are submitted. Using zero-based budgeting, proposals are ranked. The following March, 500 managers and the board of directors conclude the process with a week-long strategic planning conference. To overcome the problem of "slighting the more speculative development efforts," these ideas receive a separate share of the overall budget and are ranked separately. The result has been new products, and even new businesses that TI might otherwise have overlooked. The proposal ranking forces managers to plan creatively and justify the continuance of old ideas and the introduction of new ideas.

Another program to stimulate internal development and improvement of productivity is called people and asset effectiveness (P&AE). This idea, like OST, has taken a decade for full acceptance. Now, 83 percent of the employees are organized into teams to plan and organize their own work. The system is fully accepted and working well in improving both manufacturing and overhead efficiency. P&AE programs compete with other OST programs for funding and must prove their cost effectiveness.

Idea

TI recognizes that its formalized management structure may stifle innovation. Therefore, in 1973, the company funded a program called IDEA. $1 million is split annually among forty IDEA representatives, "usually senior technical staffers not managers." Grants up to $25,000 are given to employees with ideas for process or product improvement. If turned down by one representative, an employee may go to another. About half the ideas funded pay off. This system bypasses the involved presentation and documentation requirements of OST. The $19.95 digital watch, "that tore apart the market in 1976" started this way.

With all the aforementioned systems in place, TI has found a solution to managing and stimulating innovation in a large company. Through concentrated efforts on strategy, TI has developed a system that incorporates both a 15 percent growth per year program and a plan that encourages and ensures intense employee participation.

Source: "Texas Instruments Shows U.S. Business How to Survive in the 1980s," *Business Week*, 18 September 1978, pp. 66–92.

Illustration Capsule 7

STRATEGIC PLANNING AS PRACTICED IN VARIOUS FIRMS

Olin

Olin is a $1.5 billion conglomerate. In the past, profits in camping products and industrial mainstays, such as polyester film and polyvinyl chloride were "lackluster at best." Today, Olin is utilizing a planning method emphasizing total corporate goals over the potential of individual products. Olin has turned to product lines that "fit in much better with its established corporate expertise."

The planning process involves outside managers called "profilers." Profilers lend perspective and aid communication within the planning units. "Managers from each of the thirty-odd strategic planning units (components for which the company can define specific goals) meet with two or three managers from other areas of the company who generally know very little about that unit's operation." The resulting profile, a standard two-page outline format, is then passed along to top management. This system has provided a focus for Olin. According to William L. Wallace, one of the initiators of the system: "In the past, we never asked ourselves how we could win."

Mead Corp.

Another of the estimated one hundred U.S. companies using strategic planning is Mead Corp. Mead, the Dayton paper maker, attributed its 7 percent rise on returns on total capital from 1972 to 1977 to the use of strategic planning concepts. Mead has reorganized their twenty-four profit centers into as many strategic planning units. Twenty-four top executives have been moved to best utilize their expertise. Instead of "fair share" allocations, the company funds strategies. This allows the company to recognize losers and capitalize on moneymakers.

Gulf Oil Corp.

Another example of strategic planning is Gulf Oil Corp. Gulf has one of the largest systems. Gulf has thirty-five planners at the corporate level, and seventy-three planners at seven strategy centers. This system has allowed Gulf to stay clear of solar energy, "in which Gulf found it would not have competed profitably."

Daylin Inc.
Daylin is a $300 million Los Angeles retailer. In trouble two years ago, today profits are substantially better due to strategic planning. Each product manager constructs a five-year plan assessing the unit's competitive position, and sets out actions to improve it. Yet, success has come at a price. Division managers at the Diana Fashion Stores division, were resistant to a change of merchandising mix, forcing President Sanford C. Sigoloff to recruit a new management team responsive to the changes.

Fairchild Camera & Instrument Corp.
"Accelerating changes in technology and reversals in key markets" brought Fairchild Camera and Instrument Corp. into strategic planning in the fall of 1977. Fairchild has realigned top management, brought in Vice Chairman C. Lester Hogan as director of strategic planning, and set up a corporate team of six planning specialists to "map out orderly entries into new markets."

Eaton Corp.
Eaton Corp. is a $2.1 billion automotive and industrial parts maker. Four years ago, Eaton created 400 "product market segments" in its twenty-six divisions. Their form of strategic planning emphasizes recognition of and planning for "push" and "pull" factors. "Push" factors are actions the company can take to control operations. All operation divisions contribute data to monitor "pull" factors, such as inflation and exchange rates. In addition, five-year plans to accentuate "push" factors are submitted.

Source: "Strategic Planning," *Business Week*, 27 March 1978, pp. 102–5.

ADMINISTERING THE PLANNING SYSTEM

The Design

In the design of a formal strategic planning system, there are several issues that ought to be discussed at the outset. In general, a formal planning system that defines the total planning cycle, from initiation to corporate/board approval, is preferable to a looser, less-formal method of planning. A formal system ensures proper functioning and participation, facilitates systematic and streamlined progress, and thus affords time and cost economies. Above all, by instituting a clearly defined system, all crucial elements are integrated into the planning process, and a consistency is gained that makes clear-cut comparisons and evaluations possible. What the optimal system will be, of course, depends on the style of management, organizational size and complexity, and management perception of the function itself. Other issues are also basic to the design of the system; these include system simplicity; the "bottom-up" versus the "top-down" approach; "inside-out" versus "outside-in" planning; and the proper way of converting long-range planning into short-range planning. Let us deal with these issues in order.

First, simplicity in concept and implementation is essential. Simplicity applies to the design of the system and its format. The system is divided into phases. During each phase, key activities, responsibilities of the participating units, and decision points are specified. For greater flexibility, certain administrative details are left to the judgment of groups and divisions.

The time schedule is crucial. A corporate planning cycle may last for nine months to a year. At the group and division levels, a much longer preparatory phase may begin one or two quarters ahead of the official beginning of the cycle. Time is also important in determining the proper synchronization of strategic planning with annual operating plans and budgets. Simplification in the design of a given format facilitates both the preparation and the practical usefulness of the plan.

Second, the "bottom-up"/"top-down" debate refers to a choice of approach. The "bottom-up" approach engenders initiative in the operating divisions, where the most specific knowledge exists; the "top-down" approach often causes rigidity, which inhibits creativity. In practice, most companies take a combined approach. Corporate officers initiate goal setting, delineate group/division charters, define business volumes and profit targets, and seek acceptance for them in the lower echelons. Groups and divisions independently develop their positions on targets, charters, and resource requirements and search for corporate agreement. It is the responsibility of the corporate staff to enforce a certain amount of conformity in the preparation of formats and guidelines, so that quantitative data can be compared and analyzed. On the other hand, groups and divisions develop their respective strategies independently. Each conducts studies and develops criteria and rationale for their plans, which are submitted to the next management level for continual critique and review.

Third, the "inside-out"/"outside-in" debate concerns the proper sequence of goal setting and opportunity assessment—the question of which activity should happen first. The "inside-out" approach insists that goal setting take priority along with assessment of internal strength, talents, and abilities, and that only then should the company turn to external environment and ask where the opportunities lie for exploiting these abilities.[11] The "outside-in" approach considers external opportunities to the exclusion of internal capabilities. In reality, both approaches are applied simultaneously. The "inside-out"/"outside-in" dichotomy is not a choice, nor is planning a strictly "first-second" procedure. It is a methodology that ought to be practiced innovatively and flexibly.

Fourth, the transition from strategic long-range planning to annual operating planning and budgeting must be properly administered. Unless the two processes are tied together, strategic plans lack practicality and authority.[12] Annual operating plans and budgets, which focus on delineation of departmental actions and budgetary allocations, are basically a form of tactical planning and are heavily oriented toward finance. Their importance lies in the assumption of tactical actions that have great importance on long-range strategies and current operations. The formats and schedules for these related documents should be carefully thought out to ensure proper interfacing and compatibility.

The Process

The formal planning system guides the systematic development and approval of strategic plans. The design of the system, which consists of the planning cycle and planning guide, is an important responsibility of the planning staff. Illustrated in figure 3.3 is a typical planning cycle applicable to large, diversified corporations.[13] The planning cycle is divided into three phases: the initiation-guideline phase, the development-review phase, and the approval-release phase.

FIGURE 3.3 A SIMPLIFIED PLANNING SYSTEM

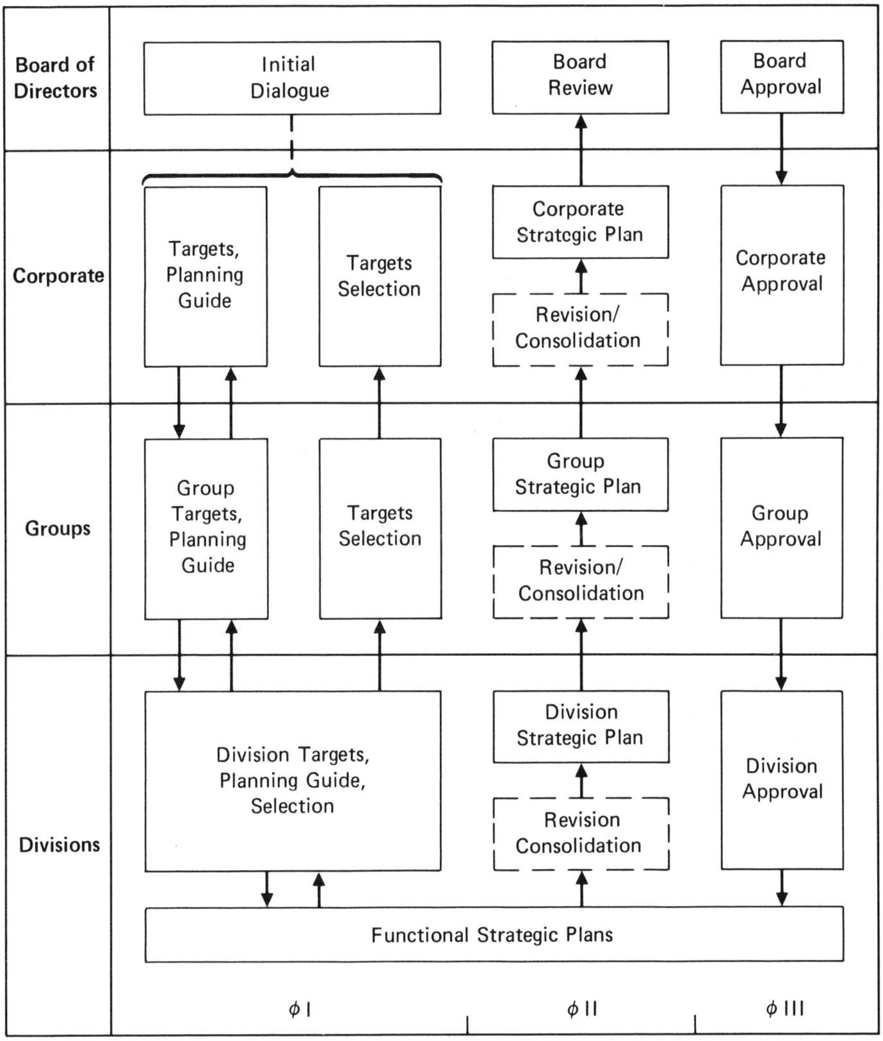

INITIATION-GUIDELINE PHASE The initiation-guideline phase begins with a dialogue between the board and the president, in which the latter is requested to formulate a corporate strategy. The board requests that the president review the corporation's purpose, mission, and objectives; evaluate its ongoing strategies; and develop a new strategic plan for submission. In initiating the company-wide planning cycle, the president directs the corporate planning staff to submit abstracts of business environmental analyses, position audits, expected broad corporate objectives, and identifiable strategic issues. Planning guides, involving format, instructions, schedules, and selected documents, will be issued to group offices. These documents, jointly developed by the corporate planning staff and the offices of policy vice presidents, serve as a basis for planning premises and constraints and as an invitation to group presidents and their staffs to confer with their counterparts at the corporate level. Group presidents, in turn, initiate the group planning cycle and issue guidelines to operating divisions. The same procedures are followed at the division level. The second part of this phase consists of a series of conferences, aimed at securing agreement on planning figures, strategic issues, and alternatives.

DEVELOPMENT-REVIEW PHASE The development-review phase consumes the most time and is obviously the most important of the three phases. It begins with the intergroup announcement of the general agreements reached in the previous phase and concludes with the official submission of strategic plans, from the divisions to groups, and from groups to the corporate level (for a sample format, see capsule 8). The group president and the president's staff hold meetings with division managers, review division plans, and integrate them into group strategic plans. Group plans are often the compilation of the approved division plans, together with an introduction defining group planning premises, goals, and strategies, and a summary critique of the separate division plans. Final review will be conducted at each management level. The president, the president's committees, and the planning staff will independently and jointly review the plans. The submission involves formal briefing of the plan by the chief executive officer to the next-higher management level at planning conferences, often held over several days at remote locations.

APPROVAL-RELEASE PHASE Phase three concerns the approval and release of strategic plans, an action that also triggers the detailed preparation of annual operating plans and budgets. In most cases, the annual operating plan undergoes a preliminary development in the strategic plan, which requires more-detailed treatment of the first year than of the remainder of the five-year period. The final submission and approval of the annual operating plan, however, is generally held up until the budget has been approved and released. Corporate, group, and division staff meetings are often held to disseminate strategic information. Henceforth, approved plans are used as controlling documents to monitor the implementation of strategies and tactical actions. Recycling to adjust and revise strategic plans is a post-strategic operation that focuses on ongoing strategic issues, contingencies, and counteractions to competitors' strategies.

Illustration Capsule 8

A FORMAT OF A CORPORATE STRATEGIC PLAN

A typical company format can be constructed on the following plan (the group format differs slightly).

Corporate purpose, mission, goals, and social responsibility

Current operations and five-year objectives

Corporate strategy: issues and programs
Group/division operations overview
  Group A
  Group B
  Group C
International operation overview
Capital expenditures and resource allocation
Contingency plans and post-strategic considerations
Appendix: financial schedules, business data, and references

THE STRUCTURE OF CORPORATE STRATEGY

In designing a formal strategic planning system, the structure of corporate strategy is a major concern. As we have seen, the planning system entails not only the design of management systems that coordinate and manage the various activities of producing a large number of business strategic plans at several general-management levels but also their substantive integration. Company strategy is constructed as a hierarchy. The levels of strategies and the complexity of integration vary depending upon the size of a company. Thus, a simple organization may have only one strategy, and large corporations may have several strategies at different levels of operations (see figure 3.4).

To coordinate and integrate the company's strategies in a large corporation poses a real challenge. We cite GE's Strategic Business Unit (SBU) as a method of integrating strategic plans. *SBU* is defined as an operating entity within a large corporation, responsible for pursuing its assigned business interests and managing its strategies. In 1971, the concept was developed by GE. Since then, the concept has been widely adopted. One author estimated that 20 percent of the Fortune 500 manufacturing firms have adopted the concept.[14] At this point, let us emphasize

FIGURE 3.4 THE HIERARCHICAL STRUCTURE OF STRATEGIC PLANS

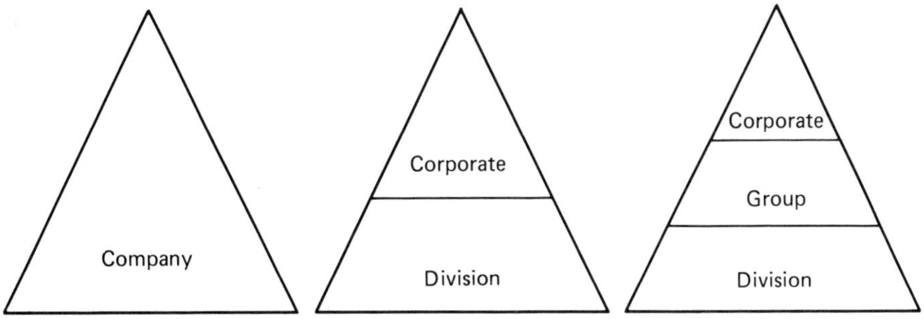

that the SBU system does not apply to product and functional organizations. It is pertinent to review the rationale of the concept, its methodology, and its relevance to our discussion. We will examine the original GE concept and its applications in large corporations.

The GE Concept

During the 1960s, while sales growth rose substantially at GE, profits increased little. Recognizing the deficiency in resource management, GE management sought a major change. At the heart of their solution is the SBU concept. Designated as the Resource Management Concept, the purpose of the new system was to facilitate resources management and to maintain a balanced business mix. Thus, by restructuring the 170 or more departments into 50 clearly identified Strategic Business Units, the corporate executive office was in a position to effectively manage resources and maintain a balanced array of businesses. In large part, the 50 SBUs somewhat parallel the organizational structure of the company, which was organized into groups and divisions at that time. Each SBU was identified to include commonality of mission, related products/market segment, similar competition, similarity in facilities and technology, and comparable size, which optimizes effective management.

In support of the SBU concept, the planning system is carefully and explicitly designed, and an elaborate organizational structure ensures the full participation of top decision makers. The SBU serves as an intermediary between corporate management and group/division management in formulating the SBU strategic plans and programs and in interfacing with corporate management in the initiation, review, submission, and approval of strategic plans. Structurally, corporate management, centering around the corporate executive office and its staff offices, assumes the policy role of determining what GE's business is and ought to be and the strategic role of centralized direction. The formulation and implementation of SBU strategies with its supportive group/division strategies is hence the responsibility of the SBU executive. Accordingly, equal if not more emphasis is placed upon strategic formulation and implementation.

The SBU Concept in Action

The institution of the SBU concept represents an important step in the development of strategic planning in the United States. It has provided a viable system to manage strategy in a greatly diversified, large corporation, and it helps focus on the substantive nature of business strategy. At GE, the SBU concept, although still evolving, is becoming the central thrust of management.[15] In other large corporations—at General Foods, Mead Corp., Gulf Oil, Union Carbide, Armco Steel, and many others—the concept has been practiced with varying degrees of success (see illustration capsule 9).

ROLE OF GENERAL MANAGEMENT Of the many innovative features derived from the concept, at least three should be singled out for emphasis. First, the concept fully recognizes the corporate management's role in strategy, particularly that of the chairman of the board, CEO/president, and his staff. Until and unless the CEO is totally committed to the concept of strategy and is competently staffed to perform that awesome responsibility, the quality of the strategy itself and its ultimate purpose of ensuring the company's present and future performance will be in doubt. Thus, the SBU concept is highly centralized in direction and at the same time fundamentally decentralized in spirit and in action.

SOUND METHODOLOGY Second, the concept has helped develop sound methodology. It provides tools to study the development of balanced business mix and resource allocation and a framework for altering business mix. In practice, three steps can be identified in SBU planning: (1) identifying SBUs; (2) strategic positioning; and (3) strategic implementation and response.[16] In identifying SBUs, the concern is with discreetly segregating and balancing the corporate business mix. This involves extensive analysis and consideration of proper mix, the practical problem of managing SBUs from the organizational perspective, and the judicious selection of criteria for identification. In strategic positioning, the industry market and competitive matrix are studied, and the trade-off decisions are made in designating those businesses for resource increases, cash generation, and withdrawal or disposition (see chapters 4 and 5). In strategic implementation and response, close attention is paid to management structure and system of implementation, control, and response.

INTEGRATED STRUCTURE The third feature worthy of discussion is the rational integration of company strategies into corporate strategy and SBU strategies, along with their supportive strategies at group/division level. The structural distinction, although not altogether clear in methodology, is significant in concept. Specifically, the corporate strategy and SBU strategies have different thrusts. Whereas corporate strategy is primarily concerned with *what* business is and ought to be, the chief concern of a SBU strategy is *how* to effectively compete in a designated single business area—in a particular industry or a product/market segment. It implies that gaining distinct competence and competitive advantages and deploying and integrating functional area strategies and activities are the underlying thrust of SBU strategies. The difference, however, ends here. What we ought to emphasize is the integrative nature of a company's strategies. Essentially, strategic direction flows downward, and strategic integration moves upward. Throughout the organization, strategic consultations occur continuously, and communication flows multidirectionally. Hence, in the pursuit of corporate business, the balance of centralized direction and decentralized initiative remains at the heart of the concept. Such is perhaps the subtle meaning of the SBU concept.

SUMMARY

In this chapter, we have examined the operational aspect of the strategic function. We recognized the general management's role in strategy making. Although the CEO assumes the prime responsibility, full support from the other four participating units is needed. No less significant than the board of directors is the executive committee on strategy, which together act as initiating and consulting bodies of senior executives in providing the CEO with collective judgment and joint consultation. The planning staff's contribution is the key to the success of a strategy. The line management links strategies and tactics into a working system. Its full participation is indispensable.

Our discussion on administering the formal planning system dramatized the complexity of developing corporate strategic plans. Our purpose in reviewing the administration of the system is to explain the formidable task of producing strategic plans and the supporting operating plans and budgets in a large organization. For the same reason, we discussed the structure of corporate strategy. We concentrated on the Strategic Business Unit concept and noted its usefulness in strategic planning.

NOTES

1. For excellent reading, see H. Eric Frank, ed., *Organizational Structure* (London: McGraw-Hill, 1971); and Lyman W. Porter, Edward E. Lawler III, and J. Richard Hackman, *Behavior In Organizations* (New York: McGraw-Hill, 1975), pt. 3, pp. 221–311.
2. This does not mean that strategy making does not apply to medium-sized and small companies. In fact, their vulnerability to faulty strategy is greater than that of large companies. Organizational structure for smaller companies is of course simpler.
3. Obviously, the number of people involved in the process, their titles, and their duties vary. For discussion, see Russell L. Ackoff, *A Concept of Corporate Planning* (New York: Wiley-Interscience, 1970), chap. 7, pp. 128–38.
4. Mace's study, based on extensive research and interview, in *Directors: Myth and Reality* (Cambridge, Mass.: Harvard University Press, 1971), esp. p. 4.
5. Joel E. Ross and Michael Kami, *Corporate Management in Crisis: Why the Mighty Fail* (Englewood Cliffs, N.J.: Prentice-Hall, 1973), p. 161.
6. C. Roland Christensen considers the president of a company as organization leader, a personal leader, and architect of organization purpose whose central concept is making of corporate strategy. C. Roland Christensen, Kenneth R. Andrew, and Joseph L. Bower, *Business Policy: Text and Cases* (Homewood, Ill.: Irwin, 1978), pp. 15–22.
7. For further discussion, see Myles L. Mace, "The President and Corporate Planning," in *Harvard Business Review on Management* (New York: Harper and Row, 1975), pp. 119–38. See also D. E. Hussey, *Introducing Corporate Planning* (Oxford: Pergamon Press, 1971), pp. 25–29.
8. Discussions on organizational forms and functions in George A. Steiner, *Top Management Planning* (New York: Macmillan, 1969), pp. 108–37; and Erwin von Allmen, "Setting Up Corporate Planning," in *A Hand Book of Strategy Planning,* ed. Bernard Taylor and Kevin Hawkins (London: Longman, 1972), pp. 34–47.
9. Antony Jay identifies six main functions of a committee: (1) identifies the team; (2) enhances group knowledge; (3) reinforces collective aim of the group; (4) facilitates individual and group commitments; (5) practices group teamwork; and (6) provides a status area, in "How to Run a Meeting," *Harvard Business Review,* March-April 1976, pp. 43–57.
10. "Why Carbborrundum Is Changing Kennecott," *Business Week,* 7 August 1978, pp. 54–60.
11. David W. Ewing, *The Human Side of Planning* (New York: Macmillan, 1969), p. 80. See also, Ewing, *The Practice of Planning* (New York: Harper and Row, 1968), pp. 32–75.
12. For a discussion of changing features and the practices of six companies, see John K. Shank, Edward G. Niblock, and William T. Sandells, Jr., "Balance in 'Creativity' and 'Practicality' in Formal Planning," in *Harvard Business Review on Management,* pp. 143–55.
13. The planning cycle is a simplified version based on review of material collected from various companies by one of the authors. See also, Richard V. Vancil and Peter

Lorenze, ''Strategic Planning in Diversified Companies,'' *Harvard Business Review,* January-February 1975, pp. 81–90.

14. William K. Hall, ''SBUs: Hot, New Topic in the Management of Diversification,'' *Business Horizons,* February 1978, pp. 17–25.
15. The institution of sector management as one more tier of management between GE's executive office and group management reflected the further evolution of the concept. ''GE's Billion-dollar Small Businesses,'' *Business Week,* 19 December 1977, pp. 78–79.
16. For detailed discussion, consult Charles W. Hofer and Dan Schendel, *Strategy Formulation: Analytical Concepts* (St. Paul, Minnesota: West Publishing, 1978), pp. 57–68.

CHAPTER FOUR

Strategic Planning I: Environmental Analysis and Internal Assessment

This chapter, in which we deal with the important area of strategic planning, is divided into three sections. In the first section, we discuss the substantive nature of the planning and formulative process, a process whereby strategic decisions are distinguished from other types of decisions. We explore the intuitive, judgmental, and rational aspects of strategic decision making and emphasize the interplay of mental processes in strategic thinking under different situations. The discussions in the next two sections treat each step of environmental analysis and internal assessment in detail and focus on the concepts, tasks, and techniques entailed. We consider environmental analysis and internal assessment as the foundation for matching the firm's capabilities with external opportunities and threats. In environmental analysis, we will review the economic, sociopolitical, industrial, and technological environment; in internal assessment, we will study position analysis and internal capability assessment.

THE PROCESS OF STRATEGIC PLANNING AND FORMULATION

The Substantive Nature of the Process

Strategic planning and formulation is a systematic and logical process following a prescribed method to facilitate rational thinking. The process entails the art of forecasting, matching, calculating, exploring, and selecting alternatives. Business strategy making is principally a mental activity, involving intuition and judgment. Neither the forecasting of future events nor the appraisal of internal capacities can be turned into an exact science. Strategic matching, calculating, and selecting, are a test of experience, depth, and risk-taking ability; at best, they are results of both an intuitive "gut feeling" and a seasoned judgment of what is possible and desirable. Thus, there is the need for a continual involvement with the concrete realities of business operation, the respect for sound methodology, and the flexibility that allows for the necessary revision of strategies.

The Three Modes

Strategic planning is a unique type of planning; it is directional, specific, and action oriented. As a mental process, however, it is rational, logical, and linear. There are two significant points that require emphasis. First, there are the different modes of strategic thinking, and second, there is a distinctive requirement for mental capacity in planning and management.

Henry Mintzberg identifies three separate modes of strategic formulation: the entrepreneurial mode; the adaptive mode; and the planning mode.[1] The entrepreneurial mode is characterized by a strong leader taking bold, risky actions on behalf of the organization; the adaptive mode applies to companies that merely respond in small, disjointed steps to a difficult environment. The planning mode that is discussed in this chapter typifies the process of systematic deliberation of strategic issues. The reality is that these three modes coexist in all organizations, and each complements, yet restrains, the others. The entrepreneurial mode is bold, intuitive, but pragmatic. The adaptive mode is flexible, seemingly disjointed, but suitable to a dynamic situation. The planning mode is obviously logical and desirable, but difficult to operate.

In another article, "Planning on the Left Side and Managing on the Right Side," Mintzberg makes a distinction between planning and managing.[2] He describes the theory that planning, which is rational, logical, and linear, differs from managing, which is holistic, relational, and intuitive. His thesis is vitally significant in that it dramatizes one of the fundamental causes of malfunction in strategic thinking. When the dichotomy persists, communication between planners and executives ceases to develop. The thoughtful planner thus recognizes that the three modes of strategic thinking are appropriate to different situations, *and* that the inherent schism between planning and managing handicaps communication. Flexibility in applying strategy in various situations reduces frustration when met with resistance.

The Five-Step Process

The five-step process described below and illustrated in figure 4.1 is designed to present a methodology that recognizes the substantive nature of the planning and formulation process.[3] For clarity, the process is divided into two parts: strategic planning (steps 1, 2, and 3) and strategic formulation (steps 4 and 5). However, although sequentially outlined, the process is not meant to be followed exactly in order, nor are the subjects under study in each step unchangeable from case to case. Indeed, the various steps interact continuously, and content varies from company to company. For instance, an internal assessment of capabilities and current strategy need not be delayed until the completion of the environmental analysis. On the other hand, it may not be possible to delay environmental analysis until an analysis is made of the firm's capabilities. Likewise, a national economic forecast may not mean as much to a local bank as to an airline. Thus, the process is flexible in content and individually oriented—a framework that is conducive to intuitive, judgmental, and independent thinking.

In the process, steps 1 and 2 represent the initial assessment of external and internal factors in the present and projected business environment. This assessment is logically followed by the determination of objectives (step 3)—the deliberation of policy issues. Steps 4 and 5 involve strategic formulation, which will be dis-

FIGURE 4.1 THE FIVE-STEP PROCESS

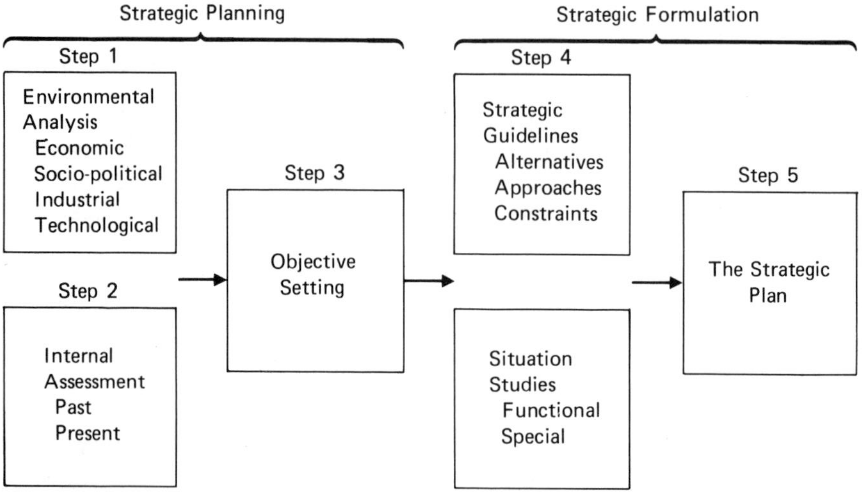

cussed in chapter 7. Altogether, the five-step process offers the business firm a sound methodology for the development of its strategy. The recycling of strategy in response to changes, however, requires the same mental processes as does the formulation of the yearly strategy.

ENVIRONMENTAL ANALYSIS

Identification of Opportunities and Threats

Business environmental analysis consists of economic, sociopolitical, industrial, and technological forecasts for the purpose of identifying long-term opportunities and threats. Opportunities fall into four areas:

1. Major profit opportunities due to anticipated economic, sociopolitical, and industrial trends.
2. New opportunities in the market/product/customer segments that the company can readily exploit, particularly in the case of technological advances.
3. Anticipated competitive advantages due to added capabilities in management, marketing, and technology.
4. Increased financial capacity due to added ability to invest without overexposure.

For similar reasons, external threats also exist in the four areas. An economic downturn, an adverse social or political condition, structural changes in an industry, market decline or product obsolescence, competitive threats, and, above all, a tight financial market can each pose considerable threats that greatly limit a company's range of choices. At this point, let us examine each of the four external environments that singularly or jointly affect a company's strategic position.

The Economic Environment

The economic environment is first and foremost in the analysis of environmental changes. At the heart of economic analysis is economic forecasting, which is a traditional means of projecting the general course of future economic development in a nation.[4] At the very minimum, economic forecasting ought to include projections of the size, changing characteristics, and trends of the economy in terms of inflation, employment, the business cycle, and the money market. Most economic forecasts are derived from the projection of the GNP. Its changes in growth rate and in the amount of each aggregate account provide important data for predicting business cycles and government economic policies. Both of these projections will have overriding importance on business decisions, thus the shaping of corporate strategies. Business cycle is a part of modern economic life. The recurring ups and downs in the economy can extend over a period of several years. Each of the four successive phases in a complete cycle—expansion, peak, recession, and trough—brings different economic conditions and problems to business firms. A firm's ability to accurately forecast the cyclical succession and adjust its strategic position is key to assessing environmental changes. To illustrate its importance, one could note the severe effects of the 1974–1975 recession, the sixth of the postwar business cycle. True, the business cycle does not affect all industries equally, nor is its impact the same in all localities. Yet, the cyclic phenomenon decisively affects government economic policies, company earnings, and investment decisions. In economic forecasting, companies consult publications and economic models. Capsule 9 presents a list of representative sources.

Illustration Capsule 9

NOTES ON SOURCES OF ECONOMIC FORECASTS

Economic forecasts serve as the framework from which industrial and business forecasts are made. There are two main sources: government; and private, which includes economic research firms, universities, and banks. Economic forecasts can be written in reports, statistics, and econometric models. Business firms generally maintain in-house economic staff; and many subscribe to national econometric forecasting services. Following is a list of representative available sources:

Public Sources

Council of Economic Advisors: Publishes the annual *Economic Report of the President.* The report reviews the economy of the past year and forecasts current trends. The Council also publishes the monthly *Economic Indicators* and special forecasts for GNP and its major components.

The Joint Economic Committee of the U.S. Congress: Publishes staff reports and hearings reports on economic policies and short- and long-term economic trends.

Department of Commerce, Office of Business Economics: Publishes the monthly *Survey of Current Business,* containing articles and statistics, plus special reports and supplements.

Department of Commerce, Bureau of Census: Offers data on population and labor, and publications, including the monthly *Business Cycle Developments,* and *Long-Term Economic Growth.*

Department of Labor, Bureau of Labor Statistics: Publishes the *Monthly Labor Review* containing articles and statistics.

Federal Reserve Board: The Board and its regional banks publish national and regional indicators and statistics on money and currency.

Private Sources

The United States Economics Corp.: A broad economic service offering monthly and quarterly forecasts on GNP and its major components.

Standard and Poor's Corp.: One of several firms engaged in security analysis. Its annual *Industry Survey* and monthly *Trends and Projections* are useful to forecasting.

Wharton Econometric Forecasting Associates: A nonprofit company owned by the University of Pennsylvania, offering research, modeling, and consulting.

Data Resources, Inc.: A publicly held company offering research, modeling, and consulting.

Chase Econometric Associates: A subsidiary of Chase Manhattan Bank offering services through computer terminals.

The UCLA Forecasting Project: A university supported research and forecasting unit offering research and regional and local forecasts.

Banks: All large banks publish regional and local forecasts.

Source: "Model Building Game," *Wall Street Journal,* 2 August 1977, p. 34.

GOVERNMENT ECONOMIC POLICIES Government economic policies on fiscal and monetary matters during the various phases of the cycle have direct effects on the business community. For instance, government attempts to tighten credit during the expansion phase may affect the availability of funds for almost all industries and increase the liabilities of those that depend on installment sales. Increases in government borrowing during recession may depress the money market, thus increasing the cost of capital. Tax policies, such as adjusting the amount of investment credit allowance, may have direct bearing on capital investment decisions. Indeed, declining earnings during a recession may induce a severe financial crunch for the company that has overextended itself through heavy borrowing. Economic forecasts of employment, productivity, and price level can have a combined effect on employment policies, labor negotiations, and the cost of production. The forecasting of capital markets is an important byproduct of the general economic forecast. Its importance in investment decisions needs no further explanation. Excessive borrowing under favorable conditions often brings on disaster as the business cycle turns downward; timely investment in an expanding industry to exploit market advantages ensures long-term gain.

ECONOMIC UNCERTAINTY AND INFLATION In recent years, economic uncertainty has been a grave concern and a practical threat to business. Economic uncertainty affects business in many ways. The uncertainty itself renders economic forecasting difficult. Vaguely pronounced government economic policies produce doubt; unsettled world economy induces fears. In addition, there is the more-pressing problem of inflation, which impacts all business decisions of strategic importance. We will briefly examine inflation to illustrate the impact on economic forecasting in general, and business decision in particular. Recent inflation is a new and highly complex phenomenon that defies the traditional method of forecasting. The traditional dependence on indexes is found to be inadequate, and alternative methodology is lacking in forecasting inflation within a business firm.[5] The severity and scope of inflation on a national and world scale challenge management in many decision areas. In large measure, a high rate of inflation affects the total operations of a firm: its profitability, cash, assets, and debt management. It also impacts on capital-spending decisions, business investment decisions, and long-term research and development choices.

On a daily basis, inflation is felt in all business areas. In marketing, pricing is obviously the most directly affected area. Flexible pricing, adopting selective pricing changes and dynamic adjustments, is becoming a viable way to guide the pricing policies and mechanism in an inflationary economy.[6] Pricing policies and strategies to cope with future prospects and problems require even more serious consideration. More pronounced, however, is the impact upon market behavior, product choices, and customer buying habits. In production, serious consideration is needed to counteract near-term and long-term inflationary effect. Purchasing, material planning and management, and cost of production must be seriously reviewed. Production plans of long-term importance require even more serious considerations: plant location (production at a cheaper labor location); capital spending; and methods of product design and production, just to cite a few. Research and development is another area in which a high inflation rate can alter project selection due to market changes, project priority (research on new material and product substitutes, and cost reduction devices, for example), and commercialization dates. These examples are intended only to illustrate the need for studying decision alternatives and strategic solutions, not to engage in technical debate.

The Sociopolitical Environment

Economic forecasting, of course, cannot be divorced from the forecasting of political and social changes. The political stability of a country and its combined political, legal, and social or ideological environment, for example, is a key consideration in investing abroad. Within the United States, political, legal, and social legislation on pollution, energy, and consumer protection, to cite just a few examples, will have an increasing impact on business operations. Local legislation and community ordinances will have an even stronger impact upon business firms that operate regionally and locally. However, the forecasting of political and social changes is such a gigantic task that very few companies are known to have attempted it with any degree of success. Nevertheless, in light of the extent of government intervention in business and the tumultuous nature of social changes, it is highly desirable to assess the sociopolitical environment and to place the more sensitive matters under constant surveillance.

PUBLIC POLICIES Any attempt to forecast sociopolitical changes should focus attention on at least two major areas: public policy, and government regulation. In studying public policy, the first concern is with economic policies, which we have discussed. In the political and legal areas, study must be made of government policies on national security, foreign trade, research and development, monopoly, and business ethics concerning the political behavior of a firm. Peace or war is the primary concern of a nation. A nation's security can be expressed in political as well as economic terms. National security policies, for example, influence foreign economic policies. Thus, trade restrictions are imposed upon sales to potentially hostile nations. National security policies, of course, determine the nation's defense spendings. Defense spending, authorized at $116 billion in fiscal 1979, representing about 25 percent of the total federal budget, is the prime source of revenue for aerospace companies. Forecasting of the nation's defense policy budgets and programs is such a necessity in aerospace companies, it is almost a ''science'' because accurate forecasts affect the industry's very survival.

In research and development, government policies hold almost the same importance as in defense. Here, federal support to research and development is enormous, averaging over 50 percent of total yearly spendings. Business firms whose survival depends on technological excellence are compelled to study policy trends for planning guidelines and sources of funding.

Legally, antitrust policy is of keen interest to business firms because it reflects the sociopolitical trend and legal/economic climate at a particular time. The accelerated rate of mergers and acquisitions in the late 1960s had once again alarmed the public to the point that government actions were direct and forceful. Early doctrinaire interpretations of stated conditions of monopoly, concentration of economic power, and mergers and acquisitions will undergo change.[7] Since the Watergate Affair, a number of firms were found to have engaged in improper activities. To what extent and in what areas a business firm can properly exercise influence upon government agencies and public officials remain key questions. A correct interpretation of public policies on business ethics is nevertheless important to the forecasting of legal environment.

GOVERNMENT REGULATION Government regulation of business activity is imposed by legislative and executive actions and is carried out at all levels of government. In recent years, government regulation has grown in scope and intensity. At the federal level, expenditures of the major regulatory agencies have risen from $2 billion in fiscal 1974 to $3.8 billion in fiscal 1978, without including the indirect costs spent by business firms to comply with regulations.[8] The proliferation of regulatory agencies and their expanded jurisdiction have led to their intervention in areas in which they have never intruded before. Of the well-publicized actions are the stiff restrictions on construction, plant operations, and energy explorations, and the harsh intervention in all business operations related to occupational safety and health. Business firms whose critical operations are subject to such regulations are well-advised to review and forecast such changes. Sudden regulation changes can result in unexpected high cost of doing business, producing delays in operations, and could even displace a product in a market altogether.

The Industrial Environment

Accurate forecasting of pertinent industry, markets, and competition is essential to survival. Industrial forecasting studies industrial trends (size and characteristics), structural changes, and competition. A growth-minded company maintains a dual forecast: a forecast of the industries it serves, and a forecast of industries it plans to enter. In a dynamic economy, industries continuously experience changes, reflecting the combined influence of the economy, technological advance, and competition. Thus, the auto industry and the appliance industry are sensitive to changing economic conditions. The electronics and pharmaceutical industries must be constantly alert to technological discoveries. In the computer industry, changes in policy or practice on the part of IBM can affect both mainframe equipment producers and peripheral equipment manufacturers.

INDUSTRIAL FORECAST A typical industrial forecast begins with a projection of the industry's future size, growth rate, and probable changes in its basic characteristics. Future size and development of an industry is naturally the primary concern. A growth industry offers a myriad of opportunities; an industry in its declining phase poses threats. Industrial characteristics of profitability, capital requirements, classification of markets and products, mode of competition, and such other characteristics as ease of entry and exit are factors of great importance. Other features unique to an industry, of course, require special attention. An industry such as trucking is highly regulated by the government. Any changes in the philosophy and methods of regulation will pose serious strategic issues. The solid-state sector of the electronics industry is volatile, due to constant technological breakthroughs and price cutting. Any changes in size, growth, potentials, and basic characteristics will constitute both short- and long-term effects that no company can ignore.

Structural changes of an industry directly affect strategic choice in several ways: in profitability, in risk, and in the mode of operations.[9] Changes in the relative strengths of rivalry, the number of competitors, and the state of competition, being stabilized or fluid, are major influences. The degree of risk of every industry is different. Labor-intensive industries, such as farming, need a large labor supply at particular times. A capital-intensive industry, such as land development, requires heavy borrowing, which increases risks when cash fails to materialize. There is still a third type of change affecting mode of operations. A company's position can be greatly affected when methods of marketing and manufacturing are basically altered either from external or internal sources. For example, Avon Products' reliance on part-time, door-to-door sales was threatened when many women sought full-time employment. Manufacturing operations can be constrained when labor supply is critical and facilities are outmoded. Such is the case of the steel industry.

COMPETITION Competition, the struggle among firms for market shares, is inherent in the business environment, and it offers opportunities as well as threats.[10] A thorough appraisal of competitive alignment and intensity is thus an important element in strategic thinking. Included in competitive analysis are: the alignment (the number and rank of competitors); the techniques (price and nonprice competition); and the philosophies and strategies of competitors. The number of competitors has direct bearing on the nature of the competition, but the identification of ranking competitors provides realism in assessing competitive strengths and weaknesses. The alignment often determines the intensity of competition. If only a few firms are competing, for instance, their rivalry tends to be quite spirited. Competition between companies such as Eastman Kodak and Polaroid, or GE and Westinghouse, is proverbially fierce. In the auto industry, the position of American Motors relative to the "Big Three" is continually precarious.

The study of types of competition offers insight into competitive behavior. Price competition, which is simple to apply, could be damaging to an industry in the long run. Nonprice competition, which is more prevalent in the United States, is varied and more difficult to counteract. Competitive philosophies may be aggressive, neutral, or defensive. They reflect a competitor's adoption of different strategies to meet different conditions. An analysis of the past behavior and strategies of ranking competitors not only reveals important insights that can be turned to account in the formulation of strategy but enables the anticipation of the competitors' counteractions. Our discussion has led us to emphasize that industry studies and forecasts are basic to strategic planning and formulation. They raise both policy and strategic issues, and they influence a firm's decisions on business mix, courses of action, and resource allocation. Their impact is both short and long term.

Technological Environment

Technology is characterized by change and uncertainty. Forecasting technological trends demands long-range strategic thinking and warrants top management's close attention. Technological forecasting serves three purposes: (1) to forecast technological trends in sciences related to the industry; (2) to serve as a basis for evaluating company-funded R&D budgets and programs, and thus the company strategy; and (3) to evaluate competitive capabilities. Technology plays a vital role in setting the pace for change and in affecting the outcome of competition. In forecasting future trends, future advances must be studied, their impact on industry or market makeup must be predicted, product implication and social effects must be assessed, and a time frame must be projected for transforming technologies from conceptual studies to commercially viable products.[11] Technologies are interrelated; the development of one often depends on advances in the others. Thus, the development of the jet engine was hastened, indeed was made possible, only by the development of high-heat-resistant material. New technologies often lead to the redefinition of an industry or market. We have seen, for instance, that the advent of digital watchmaking has placed the traditional watchmaking industry in serious jeopardy. Estimation of the feasibility of an engineering development and its time frame are crucial in predicting the commercial value of a technology. Timing is of the essence. It determines the level of investment that will be desirable and the degree of competitive advantage that can be gained.

FORECASTING R&D NEEDS U.S. industry spends an enormous sum for research and development. Large, diversified companies maintain large R&D budgets to finance laboratories and research projects whose primary purpose is to help the company gain competitive advantages. GMC, for instance, the nation's largest R&D spender, invested $1,451 million in 1977; IBM, the third-largest spender, invested $1,142 million.[12] Because R&D is a long and uncertain process, its success depends on effective planning and management. Technological forecasting provides the criteria for selecting an R&D portfolio and estimating the time scale of important events. Likewise, it supplies input for decisions on long-range investment in plant, equipment, and personnel. In particular, it clarifies and substantiates R&D objectives and sheds light on payoff possibilities. A good forecast thus supplies the needed visibility and facilitates operational decision making in R&D management.

ASSESSING COMPETITIVE TECHNOLOGIES Technological forecasting studies competitive capabilities by monitoring competitors' R&D projects and by estimating the time scale of their major research programs.[13] In performing the analysis, competitors are ranked in terms of R&D budgets, policies and strategies, research areas, personnel and publications, equipment, and facilities. By having a general knowledge of technological advances and by studying major competitors' past and present product policies and strategies, a company can readily assess their respective abilities to accomplish technical advances. It is beyond the scope of this book to discuss forecasting techniques. Econometrics, operations research, computer models, and advanced statistics are heavily used in the design of planning models (see illustration capsule 10). The choice of techniques, the information input, and the experience and insight of the people who develop and use the data are the keys to their respective application and usefulness.

Illustration Capsule 10

NOTES ON CORPORATE-PLANNING MODELS

Corporate-planning models are designed for simulating and evaluating alternatives. They have been increasingly computerized and deal primarily with overall and aggregate corporate policy and strategic matters. Frequently, however, they are composed of certain numbers of submodels of finance, production, marketing, or R&D. Today, due to economic uncertainty and rapid changes, models of various types have been in use.

Corporate Users

In September 1974, Social Systems, Inc., conducted a survey of 1,880 corporations that were thought to be either using, developing, or planning to develop a corporate-planning model. Of the 346 corporations that responded to the survey, 73 percent were either using or developing such models. Another 15 percent indicated plans to develop a model, and only 12 percent had no plans whatsoever to develop a planning model.

The overwhelming majority (95 percent) of corporate models were computer simulations that utilize case studies to determine the effect of different strategies. Most (81 percent) of the planning simulation models in use today are "what if" models, that is, models that simulate the effects of alternative managerial policies and assumptions about the firm's external environment. These models are constructed and applied in order to make inferences about future performance of the corporate system. In contrast to the system itself, a model can be manipulated easily by modifying inputs and other parameters describing the system and its planning environment to allow estimation of the impact of such modifications.

Corporate simulation models are used most often (1) to evaluate alternative policies; (2) to provide financial projections; (3) to facilitate long-term planning; (4) to make decisions; and (5) to facilitate short-term planning. Among the executives who receive and use output from the planning models, include: vice president of finance (55 percent), president (46 percent), controller (46 percent), executive vice president (30 percent), vice president of marketing (29 percent), and chairman (23 percent).

Benefits and Limitations

The major benefits that current users of corporate models have derived include: (1) ability to explore more alternatives; (2) better quality decision making; (3) more effective planning; (4) better understanding of the business; and (5) faster decision making.

Opinions about the limitations of corporate models mentioned most often are: (1) lack of flexibility; (2) poor documentation; and (3) excessive input data requirements. It should be noted that criticism of the models do not appear to be as intense or as well defined as opinions about the benefits of these models.

It is essential to recognize that many important planning functions lie beyond the scope of even the most sophisticated formal models. Most models provide increased power to explore and evaluate planning alternatives, but the identification, selection, and implementation of alternatives remain critical management responsibilities. The corporate plan can be no better than the set of alternatives considered, and the outcome of the planning process depends ultimately on successful implementation of the selected alternatives. Similarly, the development and evaluation of model inputs and assignment of appropriate values to judgmental factors are required before meaningful model studies can be conducted.

Source: G. W. Gershefski, "Corporate Models: The State of the Art," *Management Science*, February 1970, pp. 652–69; and Thomas H. Naylor and Horst Schanland, "A Survey of Users of Corporate Planning Models," *Management Science*, May 1976, pp. 671–82.

INTERNAL ASSESSMENT

Assessment of Strengths and Weaknesses

The internal assessment, a realistic and perceptive self-appraisal, is designed to evaluate a company's posture relative to its business, competition, and the overall performance and its capability in terms of strengths and weaknesses. In the total process, internal assessment together with environmental analysis is designed to prepare for the important task of matching and calculating chances of success. The environmental analysis looks outward; the position audit looks inward, defining a company position from which future objectives and positions can be reasonably projected.

An accurate assessment brings realism to strategic planning. It establishes whether or not a company is ready to risk a bold step into the future or is at a point of impending difficulties. An inexperienced management, overinspired by personal values and prejudiced by initial success, is inclined to assume a position of expansion. Without critical inquiry into the company's past performance and present capabilities, premature and overambitious growth can bring untold difficulties. A misinformed management insensitive to warning signals and internal weaknesses may find the company ill-prepared for contingencies. A critical assessment of strengths and weaknesses helps gain insight into deployment of resources and internal forces as instruments in achieving company objectives. It affords a clear view of progressive strategic planning, the step-by-step building of capabilities for future deployment. This rule applies particularly to organizations during the formative stage and to businesses confronting overwhelming competition.

The choice of methods in conducting the analysis is a point worth noting. Conducting interviews among management and operating personnel by internal consultants, though comprehensive, can be time-consuming and distorting. Evaluation by outside consultants, though valuable, can be misleading due to divergent points of view.[14] For example, an investment firm's report tends to inject investment bias and emphasize financial specifics. An internal assessment should be impartial and critical: its accuracy depends upon a well-developed data bank and the use of different methods to ensure penetrating analysis. Let us now turn to the two components of internal assessment: position analysis, and internal capability assessment.

Position Analysis

Position analysis entails three major tasks: (1) the evaluation of a company's ongoing strategy; (2) the identification of distinct competence and fundamental constraints; and (3) the determination of the company's position relative to its business, competition, and its overall performance.

First, the evaluation of the company's past and current strategies is not only directed at detecting past mistakes but at improving its capability to manage future strategies. In evaluating strategy, the focus should be on the validity of the strategy itself and the capacity to manage it. The validity of strategy is determined by the results it produces, not by the mere existence of a strategic plan, nor by the title of the office that produces the plan. A viable strategy meets the following criteria:

1. It holds up in operation and is fully involved in directing the company towards its immediate and long-range objectives.
2. It accurately meets environmental changes, as evidenced by the company's ability to exploit business opportunities and to counteract threats.
3. It is effective in resource management, as distinguished by its ability to achieve balanced business mix consistent with its purpose and mission.
4. It provides organizational coherence, unity, direction, and the flexibility to respond to changes.

Second, an accurate audit produces a genuine assessment of the company's distinct competence and certain constraints that fundamentally limit a company's probability of success. A company's distinct competence, such as a niche in the marketplace or an edge in competition, is fostered and exploited by a good strategy, and it serves as a home base from which the company's defense is organized. Every company experiences certain fundamental constraints. A large corporation cannot continue to grow. Internal strains and biological factors place limits on the size at which a large corporation can economically operate. Indeed, government policies, antitrust legislations, and competitive encroachment restrict the freedom of choice. There is, in addition, the constraint of economics. For illustration, let us cite the American Motors Corporation. Being the smallest of the four auto manufacturers (its market share has been between 2 and 6 percent of the total U.S. auto market), AMC has been struggling for stability and survival for decades. From 1957 to the present, it has experienced three major management changes. Each management change brought a change in strategy. The mid-1950s Rambler era belonged to George Romney; the quest for bigger, more luxurious cars was led by Roy Abernathy; and Roy D. Chapin, Jr., typified the "youth image" period extending from 1967 to 1978. The three periods were all marked by initial optimism, but concluded traumatically. The reality is that the company has been besieged by the fundamental constraint of economics, namely economies of size. Unless and until the company can sustain a minimum share of the market, its large capital requirements will force it to remain at the survival level.

Third, the determination of a company's present position relative to its business, competition, and its overall performance serves as the basis for projecting future capabilities and defining the posture of the company—a position of growth, a situation of profit instability, or a condition of financial insolvency. Such a posture can be determined by studying the company's financial statements and operating records. Financial analysis of profitability, debt structure, per share earnings, and other financial data can accurately reflect a company's overall position. Likewise, operating records help the study of the company's marketing position, facilities, equipment status, morale, and productivity. We will postpone our discussion of company position relative to its business and competition until the next chapter. Let us turn our attention to the procedures of conducting internal capability assessment.

The Assessment of Internal Capabilities

Internal assessment requires a deeper and more expansive investigation in addition to position analysis. The company needs to evaluate its internal capabilities, at least in five areas: marketing; finance; R&D and engineering; manufacturing; and management.

MARKETING Marketing is one of the most vital instruments in business strategy. It is the function that relates the company to the outside world and is a vital force in securing competitive advantages. An accurate appreciation of changing market mix and customer requirements leads to easier penetration into new markets and to easier enlargement of company shares in existing markets. Product development and acceptance is a key consideration. The ability to study product life cycle and product profitability to ensure constant trimming of nonprofitable products has both immediate and long-term importance. Advertising and sales promotion adds to competitive advantages. A dynamic, viable sales force is always an asset. Sales planning and controlling and the motivation of sales personnel are indispensable to the success of a sales organization. Strengths and weaknesses are evident in the channels of distribution—the simplicity (or lack of it) in their design, the efficiency of their operation, the economy of their logistics. Pricing is a traditional tool that offers financial and marketing advantages. To a great extent, marketing is a strategic game. Marketing management should search for means to strengthen its strategy- and tactics-making capabilities.

FINANCE In recent years, finance has been a focal point in management. The company's financial capacity, in terms of cash holding, debt structure, liquidity status, and inventory level, have become central issues in strategy making. Financial capacity or the lack of it is a distinct strength or weakness. The ability to explore capital markets and raise funds at a reasonable cost has become a new, demanding task for financial management. In an uncertain economy with inflation posing a constant threat, managing for profit requires active and efficient financial planning and control. The traditional, passive role played by financial management is no longer valid. The active planning and managing of profits, assets, and debts requires continual monitoring of profit improvement programs and of the divestiture projects that dispose of nonprofitable operations and unused assets. Cash management is another area that is currently receiving renewed attention. These crucial areas require critical examination.

R&D AND ENGINEERING The quest for new products, processes, and materials to achieve competitive advantage is a fact of life among many industries. Major considerations in this area include project selection, personnel and their motivation, planning and control to ensure the optimal transformation of technological advances into commercially viable items, and project management to ensure that R&D functions within the limitations imposed by cost, schedules, and technology. A company's ongoing engineering capability—its ability to meet the requirements of design, production cost, reliability goals, and customer demand—is an index registering the company's product standing in the marketplace. As in all other areas, deeper and more critical investigation is the only way to assess the company's engineering and R&D capabilities.

MANUFACTURING In many industries, such as automotive, oil refining, and certain highly automated electronics production, manufacturing is of overriding importance. The location and capacity of plants, the condition of facilities and equipment, the production process, the skills and supply of the labor force, and indeed the total manufacturing ability to meet cost, schedule, and reliability goals are the crucial areas for investigation. Purchasing, which in a time of material scarcity and high costs has become an important arm of production, plays a critical role in production management. Again, functional capabilities, which should be initially studied by functional departments and policy staffs, can be more meaningful if they are accurately related to those of ranking competitors.

MANAGEMENT Management capability encompasses all other functions that are basic to the success of the company. Management depth is an all-embracing description of a company's capacity, measured by the board of directors' success in making basic policies, by the performance of executives at the general management level, by the corresponding performance of middle management, and by the total development and management of people, resources, and technology. Once more, management abilities and deficiencies, as in other areas, must be measured and projected into the future. Strengths must be nurtured and developed; weaknesses, minimized and corrected.

SUMMARY

In this chapter, we discussed environmental analysis and internal assessment, the first two steps in the five-step process of strategic planning and formulation. We can summarize the practical implications of our discussion as follows:

1. The combined external estimation and internal appraisal leads to calculation, which is the single most important act in strategy making. Overcalculation, undercalculation, or the lack of calculation will impair the operation of a strategy.
2. In strategic planning, more time should be devoted to environmental analysis and internal assessment than to the other three steps. Once the strategic problems are well-defined and thoroughly explored, time will be saved, and better results achieved in the long run.
3. Both steps have a specific strategic meaning. The correct identification of opportunities and threats, achieved through environmental analysis, leads to realistic objective setting. The internal assessment offers direct input to the development of strategy. As in military operations, one attacks the enemy at their weakest points, not their strongest. In business strategy, the same rule applies.

NOTES

1. "Strategy Making in Three Modes," *California Management Review,* Winter 1973, pp. 44–53. In a later study, Mintzberg presents findings of a field study of twenty-five strategic decision processes and suggests that the process is "unstructured," proceeding along certain basic routines. According to the authors, they have "barely scratched the surface of organizational decision-making." Henry Mintzberg, Duru Raisinghani, and André Théorêt, "The Structure of 'Unstructured' Decision Processes," *Administrative Science Quarterly,* June 1976, pp. 246–75.
2. *Harvard Business Review,* July-August 1976, pp. 49–58.
3. Other writers conceive a process involving relatively different steps. For example, Hugo E. R. Uyterhoeven, Robert W. Ackerman, and John W. Rosenblum spoke of six steps: strategic profile, environmental dimensions, strategic forecast, company resources, strategic alternatives, test of consistency, and strategic choice, in *Strategy and Organization: Text and Cases in General Management* (Homewood, Ill.: Irwin, 1973), p. 12. Also, see Thomas J. McNichols, *Policy Making and Executive Action* (New York: McGraw-Hill, 1978), pp. 11–13.
4. For discussions on forecasting techniques, see John C. Chambers, Satinder K. Mullick, Donald D. Smith, *An Executive's Guide to Forecasting* (New York: Wiley, 1974); Ernest C. Miller, *Advanced Techniques for Strategic Planning,* (New York: American Management Association, 1971); and John Argenti, *op. cit.,* pp. 218–35.
5. D. E. Hussey, "Strategic Planning and Inflation," *Long Range Planning,* April 1976, pp. 24–27.
6. "Flexible Pricing," *Business Week,* 12 December 1977, pp. 78–88.
7. For detailed discussion, see Robert N. Corley and Robert L. Black, *The Legal Environment of Business* (New York: McGraw-Hill, 1973).
8. For a special report, see "Government Intervention," *Business Week,* 4 April 1977, pp. 42–95.

9. For a discussion, see Michael E. Porter, *Note on the Structural Analysis of Industries* (Cambridge, Mass.: Harvard Business School, 1975).
10. Competition is viewed by economists as a condition of rivalry that can be either perfect or imperfect. Viewed by business people, competition is a characteristic of behavior aiming at securing a desired share of a market.
11. Brian Twiss, *Managing Technological Innovation* (London: Longman, 1974); and P. A. White, *Effective Management of Research and Development* (New York: Wiley, 1975).
12. In 1977, the top five R&D spenders were: GMC ($1,451 million), Ford ($1,170 million), IBM ($1,142 million), AT&T ($718 million), and GE ($463 million). *Business Week,* 3 July 1978, pp. 58–77.
13. Daniel D. Roman, "Technological Forecasting in Decision Process," *Academy of Management Journal,* July 1970, pp. 127–38.
14. For a discussion on methods of conducting self-appraisal studies, see John Argenti, *Systematic Corporate Planning* (London: Wiley, 1974), pp. 96–98. Also, see David W. Ewing, *The Practice of Planning,* (New York: Harper and Row, 1968), pp. 76–97.

CHAPTER FIVE

Strategic Planning II: Objective Setting

Objective setting, a critical step in strategic planning, contains both policy and strategy meanings. In deliberating a company's objectives, company management proclaims basic policies governing its purpose, mission, and goal, while prescribing policy guidelines for business development concerning its scope, direction, and resource deployment. In establishing objectives, company management considers the reality of the situation: whether or not a set of objectives can be readily and profitably achieved within the prevailing constraints. Thus, objective setting defines the ends and at the same time sets forth conditions for strategic formulation. It should be noted that without clearly defined policies, it is impossible to set meaningful objectives. Without realistically established business objectives, strategy is impossible to formulate, and thus is totally ineffective. Accordingly, this chapter will discuss the policy nature of objective setting, policy issues, and the setting of objectives.

THE POLICY NATURE OF OBJECTIVE SETTING

Objective setting serves three distinct functions: (1) it offers a systematic method of assessing a firm's total perspective in the business world and in the community it serves; (2) it defines specific ends for future achievement and thereby a means to measure performance; and (3) it provides a common base of reference to ensure consistency of decisions and to promote joint, well-directed efforts by the total organization.[1]

In assessing their total perspectives, business firms seek multiple objectives. The traditional, single purpose of profit maximization is no longer relevant in our society. Modern business perceives a multiplicity of goals, embracing economic, social, and organizational values; it strives to satisfy the organizational as well as the economic and social goals of individuals.[2] Profit does provide incentives for business firms to perform the economic function of supplying goods and services for employment and consumption. However, business firms, as members of society and one of the three aggregates of economy, assume social responsibility toward the society as well as to their employees.

Purpose and Mission

Given a changing society and an evolving organization, modern management reviews its purpose and examines its mission for the corporation as a whole and its component charters for operating groups and divisions. We have said that corporate *purpose* gives clear recognition to what the company is and desires to be, and that *mission* declares what it plans to produce and in what businesses it plans to compete. The purpose of a corporation clarifies and defines the firm's economic, social, and management philosophies. The board of directors and the company's top management should address themselves to the question of the corporation's economic criteria for profits, for business operations, and for the quality of its goods and services. Equally, they should determine the corporation's social criteria for compliance with government and societal policies and regulations and with the image that the corporation intends to project to the public. Management philosophy normally is manifested in written statements dealing with a company's values, attitudes, and broad policies with respect to customers, suppliers, and employees. In itself, the process of writing this out serves as an important means of reconciling personal values among top management and of setting forth broad policies.

Mission and charters determine the scope of business, establishing the principal concentration of company effort in terms of customer, products, and business areas. They provide a systematic yet somewhat visionary overview of a company's position in the competitive world. For instance, when IBM regards its mission as serving the communication industry rather than as a data-processing business, and when American Can considers itself as engaged in the packaging business rather than the can business, their respective horizons are greatly broadened beyond daily realities. Group and division charters are detailed operating statements that delineate the product, market, and business areas of an operation. Because conflicts do exist among operating divisions and groups, and because authorization to pursue an expansive business scope implies power and prestige, charter definition is imperative to objective setting. An ambiguous, unclarified charter leads to the pursuit of divisive interests, the duplication of efforts, and the wasting of resources. On the other hand, a well-defined charter provides a design and a course along which the company develops and employs its resources for the pursuit of balanced business development.

In defining specific objectives for future achievement, objective setting serves the function of matching and calculating. In chapter 1, we considered matching as relating external opportunities to internal capabilities, and calculating as judging the company's probability of success in light of external threats and internal constraints. Hence, specifying short- and long-term objectives deals with business reality—whether or not a set of objectives is attainable or reasonable. It takes into consideration a myriad of variables: the company's purpose, mission, external opportunities and threats, internal strengths and weaknesses, and, above all, the feasibility of achieving them through strategic actions within the limitations of available resources.

Business Objectives

As in strategy, business objectives or goals are structured in hierarchical order.[3] A company's goals are stated at different levels: corporate; group/division; and functional. In one sense, they represent a centrally directed effort, flowing down from the corporate policy-making body throughout the organization. In another sense, however, goals are negotiated, jointly agreed targets, representing a consensus of what each organizational unit or individual is committed to accomplishing. In chapter 3, we outlined a formal planning system that stressed the participative nature of objective setting among several levels of general management.

There is one more area requiring clarification, namely the differentiation of business objectives and strategy and their close relationship. Goals or objectives define *what* is to be achieved and when it is to be accomplished; strategy concentrates on *how* it is to be accomplished. For example, a company objective of achieving an annual growth rate of 15 percent in sales is a statement of what and when a desired state will occur. A growth strategy that delineates a series of actions to be initiated and completed in a specific time frame is a statement of *how*. Thus, strategy is composed of three factors: a course of action; a commitment of organizational and material resources; and a detailed guideline for strategic actions within a time frame. The point to be made is that there is a distinct difference between objectives and strategy. Without being able to clearly distinguish them, strategy will suffer in substance. Yet, objectives and strategy mutually influence each other. Business objectives will be evaluated from the reality of strategy. They can be adjusted either upward or downward. Once strategy is placed in action, its original assumptions are continuously being tested in the realistic environment. Strategy may be altered. Revisions in strategy can very well induce changes in business objectives, or vice versa. Such a circular flow and feedback serves as a vital part of effective strategy making.

In providing a common base of reference, objective setting sets forth policy guidelines for strategic formulation. Prior to the establishment of business objectives, corporate management requests the board to deliberate on purpose, mission, and broad objectives of the corporation. Corporate management, in concert with group and division management, then discusses and negotiates a set of specific objectives, for which initial approval is obtained from the board. Policy guidelines are thus formulated. These guidelines may include planning assumptions, strategic issues, business development (the direction and the type of business mix) general performance goals, resource development and allocation, and policy statements concerning organization, personnel, and sociopolitical matters. These series of guidelines facilitate the formulation of strategies at all levels.

POLICY ISSUES

During the process of policy formulation, there are at least five policy issues requiring clear identification and critical discussion. They are: (1) the identification of present and projected posture; (2) the business mix; (3) the market share and growth or recovery rate; (4) resource allocation and risk analysis; and (5) social issues. These five issues serve as the basis for establishing goals and objectives and setting guidelines for strategic formulation. Because policies are technical in nature and judgmental in character, the assistance of staff with varied expertise is essential to policy preparation, and participative decision making at the board and CEO/president levels is crucial to policy deliberation.

Issue 1: The Business Posture

A company's business posture, which reflects its position to be assumed under a set of conditions, can be stated from two basic perspectives: (1) the current business position relative to its future development; and (2) the central issue revolving around its business and operations. Basically, almost every company can assume at one time or another any one of the three postures: a position for growth; a choice of stability; or a necessity for survival. (For detailed discussion, see chapters 8 and 9). A company can assume a growth position when external opportunities warrant aggressive actions and when internal momentum sustains such a forward movement. Thus, a company advances from one stage of growth to the next. At each stage, however, a new position can be assumed to attack the problem at hand and to cope with the anticipated situation of the future. For example, at the initial stage of growth, a position of readiness is highly advisable. At a certain point during the accelerated growth stage, a cautious and watchful position may be more prudent than the one of prolonged growth.

A company facing the difficulty of profit decline is advised to assume a position of stability, to seek for immediate reversal of the downward trend, while aiming for early recovery. A company in financial insolvency should position itself for drastic actions, aiming at quick stabilization and eventual restructuring. Such a determination can be made by studying past and present financial results and by appraising present performance vis-à-vis that of the competitors. Future position can be projected from the present, in light of projected future events and capabilities. This determination serves as the basis for objective setting.

Given accurately assessed present and future positions, company management proceeds to identify the central issue, which is the combination of the crucial element for success and any success-limiting factor, both peculiar to the particular company. For example, companies assuming a position of growth may each find a different set of issues. Technology is the crucial element in Texas Instruments' strategy for growth; portfolio management of a divergent array of businesses is the one for General Electric. A prudent long-range diversification program might be the success factor for Exxon and Mobil Oil. On the other hand, a present or pending threat that is so acute that it has become a limiting factor to the assumed position is also a strategic issue. A company's growth can be threatened by a myriad of factors: by structural changes in an industry; by a competitive challenge; by government action; or by internal constraint of resources. The chronic change in the semiconductor industry that threatens the basic survival of many companies in that industry constitutes a strategic issue. Competitive threat in the case of IBM's and Xerox's confrontation with Japanese challenge is another type. Government ban on the use of saccharin suddenly became a strategic issue for soft drink manufacturers. The succession problem at Hewlett-Packard in anticipation of its founder's retirement is a strategic issue requiring serious deliberation. Beneath the apparent ease of identifying these issues—a crucial element to success or a limiting factor to execution—lies the in-depth, more exhaustive analysis that singles out the central issue from nonstrategic issues. As in decision making, identification of the central problem is an important step in selecting decision alternatives.

Issue 2: The Business Mix[4]

At the heart of a firm's business policy is the issue of business mix. A policy on business mix states a firm's scope of business interest and proclaims policy guidelines for seeking present and future business interests through business development and occasional realignment. Here, a point of clarification is in order. Business mix is not confined to large corporations. The concept applies to small firms as well. In large firms, the portfolio can consist of businesses in several industries and markets. In a small firm, the portfolio revolves around products and markets. Their segregation, proper mix, and occasional realignment bear the same significance in policy and strategy.

Almost every company can find its business mix falling into one of the four basic forms. Each form represents a structure of a firm's business interests. The specific form of a business mix, however, decisively affects the choice of emphasis in design. These four types are summarized as follows:[5]

1. Single business: Firms that are basically committed to a single business, which can be a vertically or a nonvertically integrated company.
2. Dominant business: Firms that have diversified, but still obtain the bulk of their revenue from a single business.
3. Related business: Nonvertically integrated firms in which diversification has been primarily accomplished by relating new businesses to the old.
4. Unrelated business: Nonvertical firms that have diversified without regard to relationship between new business and current activities. For example, conglomerate companies fall into this category.

The business mix involves the structure of a firm's business in a continuous progression and is dynamic in nature. An optimal business mix enables a firm to position itself to fully exploit business opportunities available through industry, market, or product. In its design, the business mix is viable and balanced. Within its structure, the varied business interests are logically structured; they have the synergistic force to resist business downturns and sustain the overall long-term growth. In its management, the well-structured business mix demands constant vigilance on the part of management over changing characteristics and trends of industry and market needs so it can redesign and realign business interests as necessary.

A BALANCED BUSINESS MIX A viable and balanced business mix should bear two basic features: (1) the identification and strengthening of the mainline business; and (2) a common thread that ties the varied businesses together.

Overall, a firm's business strengths lie in the mainline of business from which it obtains its major share of revenue and in which it excels in competition. This simple fact dictates that a firm develop its mainline business for revenue, stability, and growth. It often serves as the central core of business, around which revolve clusters of businesses derived from newly developed products and markets. For that reason, no firm should allow its mainline business to be neglected or unprotected. Once neglected, a company will find its position vulnerable, its growth and stability threatened. This is not to say that a company's mainline business cannot be changed. However, such a change calls for the redesign of a company business mix, which is a gigantic task, requiring considerable time for planned execution.

The underlying rationale for relating varied businesses through the discovery of a common thread is the exploitation of strengths. A company's strengths may consist of its production capability, its access to a specific market, its technological excellence, its financial clout, or its management breadth and depth. Any one or combination of a few strengths can be identified as the common thread in the design of a firm's business mix. Thus, in certain electronic companies, technology is a common thread that links businesses together into a structured whole. In certain fast food companies, it is the operational/marketing identity that offers the thread for directing business acquisitions.

PORTFOLIO ANALYSIS Portfolio analysis is used to design business mix in multi-industry firms, where a large array of businesses demands advanced techniques in selection and management.[6] The central thrust of a portfolio analysis is its emphasis on achieving balanced, long-term growth in business, revenue, cash generation, and resource allocation. There are three commonly used techniques: the Boston Consulting Group's business portfolio matrix; the GE's business screen; and the product/market evolution portfolio matrix. The basic scheme of these techniques is the construction of a matrix that relates growth or its attractiveness to a firm's relative position. Illustration capsule 11 is a construct of product/market evolution matrix that shows how corporations can use a visual presentation to study business mix. When a series of such matrixes are constructed, a company's long-term business position is visualized to show the changing composition of business mix at any critical time. To conduct portfolio analysis, a series of studies must be made to assess industry attractiveness, competitive position, and the overall portfolio balance. Once the design of the portfolio is completed, portfolio management is perhaps the most challenging part of the whole scheme. On the one hand, a design of a perfectly balanced business mix is almost impossible; on the other hand, changes in portfolio must be tempered with prudence. Managing portfolio is not like managing stocks and bonds that can be bought and sold at a moment's notice. Business portfolio is a collection of organizations, people, and capital resources of significant size; its management requires as much economic consideration as the concern of people and organization.

Illustration Capsule 11

CONSTRUCTS FOR BUSINESS MIX

Business mix or portfolio composition of a corporation can be visually constructed in varied forms of charts. In addition to the Boston Consulting Group's business portfolio matrix and the GE's "business screen," Charles W. Hofer's product/market evolution performance matrix represents the third and more inclusive method.* The Hofer matrix retains most of the features of the other two

*For discussion, see Charles W. Hofer and Dan Schendel, *Strategy Formulation: Analytical Concepts* (St. Paul, Minnesota: West Publishing, 1978), pp. 30–34.

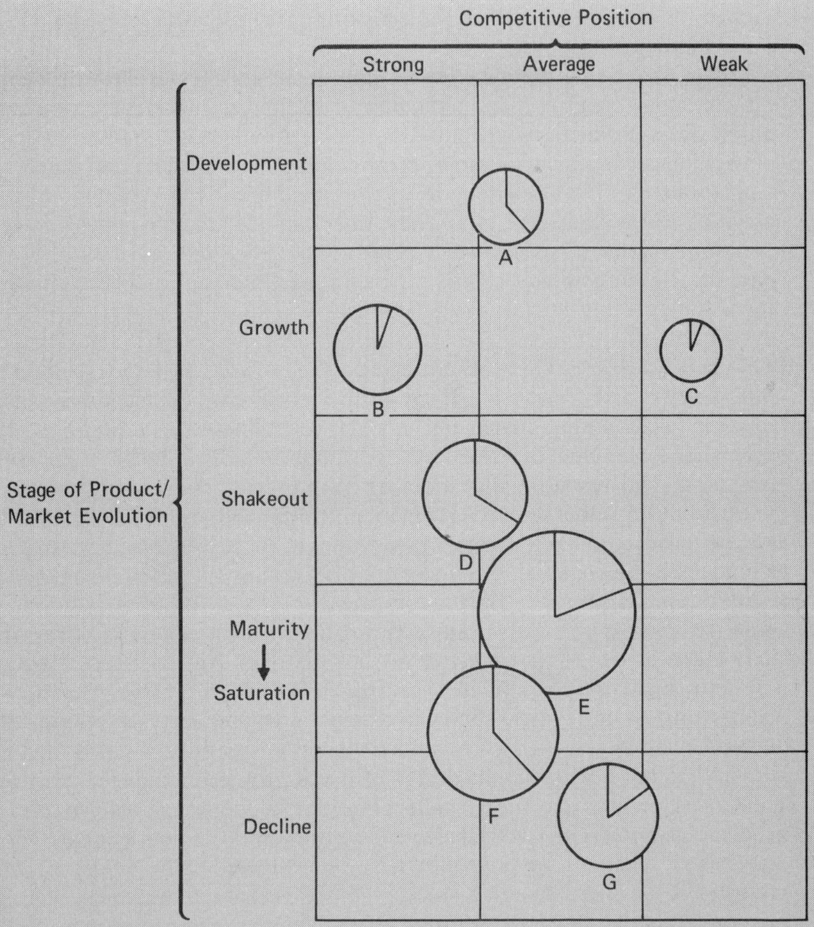

Source: Adapted from Charles W. Hofer, Conceptual Constructs for Formulating Corporate and Business Strategies *(Boston: Intercollegiate Case Clearing House, #9–378–754, 1977), p. 3.*

but includes a third dimension, depicting the stages of product/market evolution. As shown above, each circle represents the size of the industry involved; the pie slice indicates the market share of the involved business. Visual presentation is a powerful tool for initial analysis. For example, by examining the size of the slice, the stage of product/market evolution, and the competitive position, certain strategic issues can be raised. Like any quantitative measurement, the formula to assign weighted value is subject to human bias and mathematical imperfection. Indeed, visual presentation can be overly simplified to muddle up substantive deliberation.

Issue 3: Market Share and Growth/Recovery Rate

Market share and growth/recovery rate are directly related to objective setting. Market share, as it affects sales and profitability, growth rate (in case of expansion), and recovery rate (in case of profit decline) reflect management's judgment of the company's future possibilities. Market share is the percentage of industry sales made by a company over some stated time period. Strategically, a company is concerned with both the size and quality of its share. When size increases, the company's sales and earnings are expected to rise. The quality of the share is substantial when company position is not prone to large-scale invasion and when its mainline business is secured by virtue of its unique strengths. In other words, a low market share business can be as attractive as a high market share business; size and quality are not mutually exclusive. Size denotes power, which is offensive by nature, and quality implies strength, which is protective thus defensive in character. A company can assume either an offensive or defensive position. Within a corporation, it is not only prudent but natural to assign high market share for certain businesses, while acknowledging low market share for other businesses. In either case, market share significantly affects profitability.

MARKET SHARE AND PROFITABILITY Sufficient data has been produced to substantiate the assertion that there is a direct relationship between market share and profitability. Often, a high market share can outperform its rivals with low market share. It was stated in a study that "on an average, a difference of ten percentage points in market share is accomplished by a difference of about five points in pretax ROI."[7] The explanation was threefold: (1) economies of scale—the ability to capitalize on size; (2) marketing power—the capacity to apply power for competitive advantages; and (3) quality of management—the underlying strength for performance. However, there is a later study that establishes that low market share businesses can be equally attractive, although for different reasons. The study showed three low market share companies outperforming both the high market share firms as well as other lesser competitors.[8] These three companies all selected areas of competition in which they were strong, they made efficient use of limited research and development budgets, they shied away from reckless growth, and their management dared to dispute the conventional wisdom of seeking high market share as if it were the only criterion.

On the surface of these two studies, there appears to be no great difference. In reality, there is serious disagreement as to what inference should be drawn from these studies. To seek relentless increase in market share invites government intervention and defies the reality of competition; to consider high market share as the chief criterion in selecting and managing the overall business portfolio is a dangerous inference. A balanced and tempered way to deliberate such a policy issue is a flexible, contingent approach. Each posture can be assumed according to prevailing economic qualification and the difference in situations. Indeed, the real issue is not so much that of high or low market share but one of respective enhancement in size and quality. These two factors are central to the establishment of objectives.

GROWTH/RECOVERY RATE Along with the issue of market share is the question of growth rate: how fast and for how long can a company grow? The determination of a company's growth rate depends on several important variables. These may include external opportunities, internal management and financial capabilities, the firm's competitive position, and the degree of risks it is willing to assume. Most difficult, however, is the issue of control over growth. An overexpansive rate can place severe stress on a company's resources, which can lead to large losses and financial distress. Prolonged growth can generate its own momentum to an unceasing race for growth, which can lead to explosion. Thus, the issue of growth requires constant surveillance and judicious deliberation. As a general rule, the company's pursuit of genuine growth must be fully encouraged. During growth, management must remain totally aware of the precise point along the growth pattern the company has attained. (See chapter 8 for discussion on the various stages in a growth cycle.) The central issue remains to be the discovery of this pattern: the stage of its growth and its long-term progression. In the early stage, a higher rate is desirable; at the later stages, size and competition alone can force the rate to decelerate. Thus, an annual sales growth rate of over 40 percent is not at all unusual among aggressive, young companies. Needless to say, balanced growth in sales, profit, and earnings per share is the ultimate goal in determining growth objectives.

Policy consideration in determining recovery rate in times of profit decline and financial insolvency follows the same rationale as does that for growth, except that the recovery cycle operates in reverse of growth. In determining recovery rate, a series of objectives must be constructed: halting the decline, stabilization, recovery, and early resumption of growth. The rate, however, is affected more by internal effort than by external forces. (For discussion, see chapter 9.) Under the condition of stress, it is likely that management will choose a higher rate in the early stages than in the later stages. Doubtless, the task of setting objectives for recovery is more difficult than it is for growth.

Issue 4: Resource Allocation and Risk Analysis

Opportunities and constraints are the dual concepts in policy and strategy. Whereas opportunities present possibilities, constraints set limits to their realization. Of the various constraints, the lack of resources requires the most serious consideration. In a large sense, there are three types of resources: physical, human, and organization. Physical resources, in terms of money and materiel, however, are of prime importance, for their development and utilization is directly related to the firm's existence. Of the two, financial resources are by far the more important. In assessing financial resources, the concern should be for capacity, generation, and utilization. Financial capacity of a firm is determined by its total financial position, cash capacity, and the ability to raise funds. Usually, when a company is rich in cash, it is likely to pursue a more aggressive course. Substantial business opportunities can demand the enlargement of financial capacity to support expansive objectives. In addition, there is the third consideration: the initial analysis of resources utilization. Here, the analysis will show the alternative means of utilization and suggest the optimal use of limited funds. Such an early study not only will demonstrate the desired extent of a firm's financial capacity to meet its business objectives but lay the groundwork for risk analysis.

Risk analysis is a technique designed to replace subjective probability assumptions with measures of the risks associated with uncertainties. Business risk can be generated from two sources—financial risk and market risk—which are interrelated. For example, the increase of financial risk due to extended borrowing may reduce market risks, by virtue of the enhancement of the company's competitive position. Risk analysis is thus the logical extension of resource allocation. An early inquiry into a firm's risk offers a critical examination of its future possibilities. Resource allocation and risk analysis entail extensive quantitative analysis, which is beyond the scope of the book.[9]

Issue 5: Social Issues

For at least four reasons, social issues are of critical importance to corporate policy making. First, social issues are broad in scope; their impact is far-reaching, touching upon many vital activities of a corporation. Second, social responsibility is no longer an issue for public debate, but a reality of legislation and enforcement. Third, given the economic impact upon corporate decisions—for example, business cost generated to meet government regulations for social benefits—it is essential that corporate management consider the social content of every major decision.[10] Last, the process of social policy making at all levels of government is a long and evolving process. Business firms are free to participate in its generation, legislation, and reevaluation.

Emphatically stated, no corporation can safely deliberate its present and future without seriously considering certain social issues that are critical to its business. Fundamentally, social responsibility, its specific meaning and areas of concern, must be clearly defined by management. Its correct interpretation substantiates the corporation's purpose. Next, the anticipated combined impact on types and quality of products and/or services and their production and distribution, on the one hand; and on cost, profit maximization, and social benefits, on the other hand; will affect business objective setting. As guidelines to operations, corporate social policies are imperative in areas such as business ethics, environmental quality, consumerism, community needs, government regulations, and human development in hiring, health, safety, and education.

SETTING OF OBJECTIVES

Matching business opportunities with internal capabilities through environmental analysis and position audit and calculating the company's probability of success during policy deliberation logically leads to the setting of business objectives. To this end, business objectives are stated in both qualitative and quantitative terms. Qualitatively, business objectives are summarized to proclaim the company purpose and mission or charters of various operating groups and divisions and to state findings and conclusions as the result of policy deliberation. They are substantiated by analyses and studies, policy guidelines, and planning assumptions. Quantitatively, specific business objectives are reduced to performance specifications, mostly in measurable financial terms to be achieved in a specific time frame.

Planning Objectives

As we have noted previously, business objectives are hierarchically structured and arrived at through consultation. Even at the functional level, departmental objectives are well-defined to lend support to the operating division's objectives. Each set of objectives represents the expectation of the higher level of management and the commitment of management at the lower level. It is important to point out that commitment to fulfill long-term objectives must be well timed and balanced. Any drive on the part of the corporation for short-term results will cause lower-level management to disregard investment decisions of long-term significance.[11]

Of equal importance is the need to avoid pursuing an imbalanced set of goals, which can lead to the single pursuit of sales at the expense of profits and/or per share earnings. Given the importance of objective setting in policy and strategy, and that business objectives represent the articulated personal values of those in management, there must be initial agreements among general-management personnel on deployment of resources, capital spending, and available funds for venture investment. Resource allocation to research and development is essential to the attainment of business objectives; so are capital expenditures related to facilities, equipment replacement, and modernization. Venture investment is equally significant in that it represents a large expenditure and is critical to strategic formulation. Each type of resource allocation is spread over the planning period, and each is subject to the rigorous evaluation for its financial worth.

The process of objective setting is also worth noting. James B. Quinn, in a study on strategic goals, while suggesting the participative nature of the process, offers insight into the pragmatic advantages of not announcing precise, measurable goals from the top.[12] He lists undue centralization, focus on opposition, rigidity, and security as some of the reasons. The point to be noted is that establishing objectives is a delicate art. It requires a subtle balance of vision, entrepreneurship, and politics. "Broad goal setting" and "logical implementation" is the process stage calling for consultation, which then leads to precise, measurable, and integrated goals of a corporation.

Long-range objectives are stated in projections expressed in growth/recovery rates, sales, profits, and financial data, and related personnel, facility, and resource figures. They proclaim the specific targets to be achieved in the planning period. Growth/recovery rate presented in forms of sales and profits is an important criterion in "determining" objectives. Normally, sales data figured on a yearly basis contain figures for sales, orders, and backlog, and are broken down by business area, type of sales (current and new), and geographical location. Financial data, constructed in simplified income statements and balance sheets, present profit projections, return on investment, earnings per share, and cash flow projections. The projection of the number of employees is significant for personnel and facilities planning. Resource requirement figures, reflecting the level and schedule of resource allocation, are useful for evaluating capital spending and computing return on investment. Of the various projections we have discussed, sales forecasting is the most important of all because it is from the forecasted sales that many important financial and personnel projections are made. Hence, it is extremely important to achieve integrity in sales data organization and presentation.

So far as the planning period is concerned, most companies use five years as a common reference. Generally, the determination is based on two considerations: the degree of confidence in forecasting, and the investment recycling time required by the industry. In certain industries, such as airlines, forest products, and utilities, the capital recycle time makes a period of twenty years and beyond not altogether unusual.

Methods of Objective Setting

There are two basic approaches to objective setting. One method, which can be called the "scenario approach," bases its projection in qualitative terms on where a company would like to be in a distant future by tracing a path forward from the present position as a reasonable extension of the present capacity. The other method, which selects the desired projection level by superimposing the current forecast of existing business on an expansive gap and a diversification gap, thus arriving at the desired level of revised projections, can be called a "gap approach."[13] In the gap approach, a desired growth/recovery rate is used to arrive at the desired level of projection. Both approaches, particularly the former, can be used to develop a rationale for establishing objectives.

The presentation of this quantitative data reflects only management judgment and a consensus among managers. Realism and achievability are the principal considerations. Objectives that are developed without proper matching and realistic calculation are mere aspirations. Objectives that are too high or too low lack credibility. Yet, an inflexible, straitjacket prediction stifles the initiative and imagination of those who are committed to objective fulfillment. Thus, the level of achievement must be thoroughly discussed—its quantitative and qualitative value clearly understood, its constraints and contingencies properly explored, and the company's agreement to it equitably obtained.[14] Such careful deliberation and well-substantiated rationale are the substance of objective setting.

SUMMARY

We have completed discussions on strategic planning, the first phase of strategy making. Strategic planning holds special importance in policy and strategy. Strategic planning entails environmental analysis, internal assessment, and objective setting. Environmental analysis and internal assessment provide the rationale for objective setting, and objective setting facilitates the deliberation of policy issues. In turn, they establish the framework for strategic formulation.

Objective setting is judgmental in nature. It proceeds on the premise that the dynamically changing world demands occasional clarification of corporate purpose and mission. However, the clarification of what the company is and desires to be is not totally a philosophical problem, but one touching upon matters of policy importance. Equally, corporate mission and its component charters contain distinct policy meanings. What businesses to pursue and in what marketplace to compete are both policy and strategy questions. In all, we selected five issues for discussion.

Finally, we stressed again the substantive nature of objective setting. What we are emphasizing is that objective setting should not be treated as a numbers game, an expression of an individual's edict, nor a ritualistic planning totally divorced from reality.

NOTES

1. For an excellent discussion, see M. F. Cantly, "The Choice of Corporate Objective," in *A Hand Book of Strategy Planning*, ed. Bernard Taylor and Kevin Hawkins (London: Longman, 1972), pp. 9–22.
2. The multiplicity of objectives is explained by George A. Steiner as constructed on a "network of corporate aims" arranged in a hierarchical form, descending from basic

social, economic purpose to short-range goals and targets, in *Top Management Planning* (New York: Macmillan, 1969), pp. 140–95.

3. For a comprehensive discussion, see Max D. Richards, *Organizational Goal Structure* (St. Paul, Minnesota: West Publishing, 1978).
4. The authors prefer *business mix* to the more commonly used term of *portfolio management,* for the latter implies the management of business operations as if they were stocks and bonds that can be bought and sold at ease. A company's business operations are not structured for speculative purposes.
5. For details of the four types and their variations, see Richard P. Remmelt, *Strategy, Structure, and Economic Performance* (Cambridge, Mass.: Graduate School of Business Administration, Harvard University, 1974), pp. 11–32.
6. This part of the discussion is largely drawn from Charles W. Hofer and Dan Schendel, *Strategy Formulation: Analytical Concepts* (St. Paul, Minnesota: West Publishing, 1978), pp. 27–34.
7. Based on the Profit Impact of Marketing Strategy (PIMS) research in Robert D. Buzzell, Bradley T. Gale, and Ralph G. M. Sultan, "Market Share—A Key to Profitability," *Harvard Business Review,* January-February 1975, pp. 97–106.
8. A timely and excellent article in R. G. Hamermesh, M. J. Anderson, Jr., and J. E. Harris, "Strategies for Low Market Share Businesses", *Harvard Business Review,* May-June 1978, pp. 95–102.
9. For discussion on risk analysis, see Harold Bierman, Jr., Charles P. Bonini, and Warren H. Hausman, *Quantitative Analysis for Business Decisions* (Homewood, Ill.: Irwin, 1973), pp. 385–90.
10. For an excellent discussion, see Joseph W. McGuire, "Evolving Concept in Management," *Proceedings of the Academy of Management, 1964,* pp. 21–28.
11. Alfred Rappaport suggests changes in incentive systems to rectify this apparent difficulty, "Executive Incentives vs. Corporate Growth," *Harvard Business Review,* July-August 1978, pp. 81–88.
12. "Strategic Goals: Process and Politics," *Sloan Management Review,* Fall 1977, pp. 21–39.
13. Russell L. Ackoff, *A Concept of Corporate Planning* (New York: Wiley-Interscience, 1970), pp. 24–29; and H. Igor Ansoff, *Corporate Strategy* (New York: McGraw-Hill, 1965), pp. 94–151.
14. Robert L. Katz refers to *specific future achievement* as specifications that clearly specify future performance criteria in areas he calls size, market share, profitability, and life expectancy, in *Cases and Concepts in Corporate Strategy* (Englewood Cliffs, N.J.: Prentice-Hall, 1970), pp. 200–202.

CHAPTER SIX

Social Responsibility and Business Strategy

Social responsibility is a new but increasingly perplexing dimension in management.[1] The concept imposes a radically different view of business upon executives, forcing them to think beyond the confines of economics. In practice, business executives, bewildered by increasing government regulations and legal actions, usually find it difficult to respond to social changes of such magnitude. Social responsibility holds an implicit meaning in business strategy and management, both of which must be properly analyzed, assessed, and acted upon. We propose first to discuss the concept of social responsibility—those social issues of public concern and how they are perceived by business people. Social responsibilities can be met with increased effectiveness by monitoring social issues during their development and by responding, managing, and recognizing their strategic implementation in strategic planning and formulation. Hence, the study of public policy-making process, management of social responsibility, and strategic considerations involving profit, social values, and business ethics are the subjects of this chapter.

THE CONCEPT OF SOCIAL RESPONSIBILITY

Definition

Business social responsibility in its modern version stems from an era of heightened social conscience and public discontent with the American establishment—the protest against the Vietnam war, the assault on government and business, and the quest for social justice. The great debate of the 1950s and 1960s dramatically extended the traditional economic role of the business firm to matters of social concern. Such social concern, reflecting public mood at the time, embraces issues concerning human development and social justice, ecological quality, consumer protection, and most of all the basic question of the proper use of corporate power. Today, the concept of social responsibility is largely accepted by the business community. *Social responsibility* has been defined as "the obligation of decision makers to take actions which protect and improve the welfare of society as a whole along with their own interest."[2] The definition recognizes the dual nature of business functions. It broadens the meaning of business purposes, imposes social values on business decision making, and sets forth new criteria for the use of corporate power. By assuming social responsibility, modern corporations pursue their socioeconomic function and harmonize business actions with social wants.

Issues of Public Concern

Although the relationship between business and society is extremely complex, the basic issues are few and can be readily identified. Steiner divides business social accountability into two areas: those internal activities relating to employees and the use of resources; and those external activities associated with social problems, the local community, social objectives, philanthropic support, and consumerism.[3] Davis lists nine major areas: energy and environmental quality; consumerism; community needs; government regulations; business giving; minorities and disadvantaged persons; labor relations; stockholder relations; and economic activities. For our purpose, we identify three areas of social responsibility to guide our discussions.

QUALITY OF LIFE The quality of life is determined by a set of social factors that together allow people to live comfortably in their physical environment and to coexist in harmony with it. Standard of living, health, safety, and ecology are major issues of public concern.

HUMAN RESOURCE DEVELOPMENT Human dignity, civil rights, fair treatment of minority members, and equal opportunity in education and employment are the key issues in developing human resources.

CORPORATE POWER Society defines and restricts arbitrary and unreasonable use of organizational power and establishes due process for all parties concerned—government, business, and individuals. Ethics, bribery, unfair competition, and unlawful political actions are of public concern.

Nature of Social Issues

Social issues are difficult for business firms to comprehend. Not only are these issues complex, slowly evolving, and their outcome far-reaching, but their impact upon doing business is difficult to measure. Contemporary public debate is still evolving. Auto safety, pollution control, and civil rights—burning social issues of the past two decades—were first perceived by the public, identified and defined by their respective interest groups and ardent advocates, articulated and debated through democratic representation, and finally acted upon by Congress and state legislatures. Once these issues were subject to law, they proliferated, went through a process of reevaluation, and either intensified or abated in the public view. For example, the auto safety issue, once a strong and extremely agitating concern, subsided somewhat when high automobile prices turned public concern to the economics involved. Civil rights legislation widely proliferated, but eventually brought about some backlashes, as have ecological regulations.

Corporate Perception of Social Responsibility

From the perspective of a business firm, social issues cause real concerns and demand judicious handling. These concerns can be expressed in increased costs, extent of involvement, and long-term benefits. First, social legislation imposes high costs on doing business. As we will discuss in the section on government regulation, high cost of regulation is not only confined to government. Industries spend billions of dollars to comply to standards and rules. For example, at General Motors, R&D spending to meet safety and emission standards amounted to 20 percent of the firm's 1975 $1,113.9 million R&D budget; another 40 percent was allocated for meeting fuel economy standards. The estimate of private outlays for meeting pollution control were $3.8 billion, and the cost to American business in meeting occupational safety and health was estimated at about $3 billion.

Second, there is the question of the extent to which a business firm should assume social responsibility. It has been said that the social responsibility of a firm is commensurate with the size of social power it exercises:[4] the larger the company, the greater its responsibility. Large companies, such as GMC, Boeing, and Eastman Kodak, whose plants dominate the economic life of certain localities, have much greater responsibility than does a small business whose sphere of operation is limited in scope and influence. Similarly, the type of social activities a company may pursue vary from industry to industry, size notwithstanding. In a 1975 survey conducted by the Committee for Economic Development, companies were asked to rank social and economic activities to which they had made significant commitments of money and personnel. Of the fifty-eight activities reported, human development activities were ranked highest, followed by pollution and productivity.[5] Although the survey showed a large number of social activities common to all industries, such as human development, it also reflected a large degree of variations in program concentration from industry to industry.

Third, there is also the question of short-run costs versus long-run profits. The fulfillment of social duties creates short-run costs, but affords long-run profits of some kind, however nebulous and intangible. There have been numerous reports of companies that absorb short-run losses, but, by helping to solve social problems, they gain economic benefits, such as customer loyalty. One such company is Dow Chemical, whose Michigan Midland operation has recovered enough valuable chemicals and boosted its process efficiency so much that its company-funded water abatement program is more than paying its own way.

After almost a decade of debate and practice, social responsibility is now largely accepted by the business community. In a recent survey of Fortune 500 firms, it was found that the argument for and against social responsibility involvement is no longer an issue.[6] Most managers indicate strong agreement on the long-run, self-interest benefits of corporate involvement. Concerning priorities, equal opportunity in hiring and employment topped the list (82 percent), followed by pollution control (78.8 percent), employee safety (77.3 percent), resources conservation means (51.3 percent), and others. The survey also shows a large percentage of top-management involvement in establishing policy and a slightly higher participation of middle management in implementation.

PUBLIC POLICY AND SOCIAL RESPONSIBILITY

We have demonstrated that social issues constitute unique problems requiring correct interpretation and special handling. Their identification, agitation, and transformation into law is a long, laborious process of public policy making. Public issues are pluralistic, involving interrelated issues and diverse types of citizens. They are delicate, sometimes explosive, and when made into law, they are fully enforceable and legally binding. Social issues of the 1950s and 1960s burst out as public uproar. They were articulately defined, quickly and powerfully fermented, and ultimately made into law. Government agencies mushroomed, and their jurisdiction greatly extended. Under this combined assault—the heightened agitation and the proliferation of regulatory agencies—business firms found themselves engulfed in the public policy process. For business firms to be involved in the process, a discussion on public agitation and government regulation is in order.

The Public Policy-Making Process

Political scientists have long been interested in the study of public policy, its process, analysis, and administration.[7] Public policy making entails five major steps: the perception and identification of the public demand; its transformation into issues and problems; formulation of policy action and enactment of law; its administration; and evaluation and reformulation.[8] Often, social issues become public demand when large segments of the population act as a coalition of interest groups beyond the boundary of local concerns. A public demand of this magnitude will be acknowledged and studied by the government. Either Congress or the Administration will take the initiative to transform public agitation into legislation or administrative actions. Thus, the civil rights movement beginning in the mid-1950s became a monumental national issue and ultimately led to a myriad of legislation involving school integration, public housing, and equal employment opportunities, to name just a few. Once made into law, they are administered by government departments and newly established regulatory agencies. Public evaluation and renewed unrest can cause further legislation and reformulation of policies.

Interest Groups

Public agitation is an act and a movement of people. In a pluralistic society, political power is diffused among many public, semipublic, and private groups. Public agitation, however, is generally confined to interest groups and citizen volunteer organizations. Interest groups take various forms and represent virtually all kinds of citizens and goals. Predominant among them are the economic groups, which include various segments of commerce, manufacturing, labor, agriculture, and professionals. The more powerful and well-known economic interest groups are the various business lobbies, including the influential oil lobby, the AFL-CIO for the labor organizations, the Chamber of Commerce for business, and the American Medical Association. Other interest groups seeking political, ethnic, and social goals, although they do not represent "big business," are equally influential. Typical of these are the League of Women Voters, Americans for Democratic Action, the National Association for the Advancement of Colored People, and the Ralph Nader volunteer groups on consumer protection. Interest groups, of course, exert different amounts of influence, depending upon their respective membership, size, prestige, and wealth. There are various means with which they can apply power. Propaganda or persuasion, perhaps, is their chief weapon. Through publications and mass media, they direct their attention to large segments of the public. For most economic interest groups, lobbying at all levels of government is their long-standing tool. Political agitation in election campaigns is, of course, still another potent weapon. Influence of the various interest groups is most pronounced when their goals are identified with by the general public and when joint power is felt. This situation frequently occurs during turbulent times when certain explosive social issues coincide with political and economic interests.

Pollution and Consumer Protection

Such is the case involving pollution and consumer protection. We will briefly discuss them to illustrate public agitation in the making of public policy. Pollution is a social concern of physical environment degradation. During the 1950s, public resentment of air pollution in large cities aroused local protests. As soon as government and private organizations began to identify the problem through research and pollution studies, a number of interest groups and citizen antipollution groups joined forces and sprang into action. These groups soon claimed a large membership, and through public appeals local concerns became national issues. Of the many conservation groups, the National Wildlife Federation claimed 2.2 million members, and the Sierra Club, ninety-five thousand. Groups supporting the antipollution movement included the National Association of Counties and the Association of State and Interstate Water Pollution Control Administrators. Congress acknowledged the public demand and quickly enacted a series of laws culminating in the passage of the National Environmental Policy Act in 1969 and the establishment of the Environmental Protection Agency (EPA), which is given unprecedented power over pollution control and enforcement.[9]

Public demand for consumer protection is agitation on a larger scale and with more far-reaching impact. Consumer protectionism, or consumerism, is the public's protest against perceived business injustices. The movement began with the general resentment of poor quality, unsafe products, high prices, mislabelling, and misleading packaging. Until the early 1960s, as a one-man crusade, Ralph Nader led the movement. Soon, there were thousands of local groups. The movement not only attracted a great following of citizens of all ages and from all localities, but the issue proliferated to cover a broad spectrum of seller-buyer relationships. As a result, there has been a substantial increase in consumer protection legislation. To single out the more important laws, there are: the National Traffic and Motor Vehicle Safety Act and the Highway Safety Act to improve the safety of automobiles, roads, and tires; the Truth in Packaging Act, which grants power to the Federal Trade Commission and Food and Drug Administration to establish standards for packages and for the information and identification of their contents; and the Truth in Lending Act, which authorizes the Federal Reserve Board to adopt regulations to increase useful financial disclosures of credit terms.[10]

Converting public demand into legislation is the act of government that follows a political process far beyond the scope of our discussion. Suffice to say that through lobbying, interest groups exert influence at every critical point of the process. Once public demand becomes law, government agencies, including the regulatory agencies and courts, dutifully administer, enforce, and interpret the law. However, the public continues to respond and evaluate the policy and its administration. Most influential of the many public critics are the newspapers, magazines, and television. Sometimes, a new report or an article may trigger congressional investigations and/or government actions. Television journalism has a major impact. The many special news programs on social issues have emphasized the inadequacies of public policies and have aroused the public as no other medium could. The public demand is thus redefined, and the public policy-making process regenerated and recycled.

Our brief discussion on public agitation attempts to focus on the explosive nature of social issues. Business firms cannot ignore this fact. Indeed, they can take positive steps to study social issues that affect the company's business, to provide adequate information to the public, and to assume social responsibility wherever appropriate.

Government Intervention and Regulation

Government regulation of business refers to all laws and administrative process that deal with the nation's economic life.[11] In a narrower but more technical sense, government regulation refers to the public authority to prescribe rules of conduct for business behavior in a society committed to the private enterprise economy. Throughout the years, public regulation has been extensive, but largely accepted by the business community. Public regulation over interstate commerce and trade, the formation of corporations, registration and subscription of corporate stocks, employment and labor relations, unfair methods of trade and competition, plus the expansive field of business law has, in fact, contributed to the efficient operation of the American economy. Since the 1960s, however, government regulation has become a controversial issue.[12]

The power to regulate business is written in the Constitution. At the federal level, the "commerce clause" grants Congress the power to regulate business; at the state level, the "police power" grants the state the power to protect the general welfare of its people. Congress is empowered to legislate and to make law that becomes the law of the land, fully enforced through the judicial system and administrative agencies. By far, the greatest day-to-day legal impact on business is the power exercised by the local, state, and federal administrative agencies, in particular the federal regulatory agencies. This is because these regulatory agencies are empowered to make rules and to adjudicate cases. Their proliferation and expanded jurisdiction have aroused business resentment, and thus the controversy.

Proliferation of Regulatory Agencies

Referring to illustration capsule 12, a list of selected major federal regulatory agencies shows their jurisdiction has extended to five areas: banking and finance; competition and trade; employment and discrimination; energy and environment; and safety and health. The number of the more-powerful agencies totals twenty-one, excluding hundreds of lesser federal agencies and bureaus. Among them, the well-publicized ones are: Federal Reserve Board; Security and Exchange Commission; the Antitrust Division of the Justice Department; Federal Trade Commission; Equal Employment Opportunity Commission; Environmental Protection Agency; Food and Drug Administration; and Occupational Safety and Health Administration (OSHA).

The proliferation of regulatory agencies results in costs of operating these agencies and compliance with government regulations and severe impact upon business operations. Paperwork, delays, arbitrary rulings, and overextended intervention are the difficulties experienced in business firms. In light of the more turbulent social environment and the interdependency of public and private organizations, business firms are searching for a more effective way to cope with the situation. The task of interfacing with society and public agencies and managing social responsibility will induce changes in management philosophy and methods of conducting business operations.

Illustration Capsule 12

THE SCOPE OF GOVERNMENT REGULATION

Government regulation of industry and business is an established concept and a traditional institution that defines the general relationship of government to economic life. In an orderly society, all economic activity is subject to some form of regulation and control. Government regulation is purported to prescribe rules for competition by giving legal sanctions to private property rights and by providing for redress against infringement of them. Regulation is also a means to curb abuses arising from imperfections in the market and the misuse of monopoly power. In recent years, however, government regulation has gone beyond its traditional confinement of economics. Social regulation such as job safety, energy and the environment, and consumer safety and health has expanded phenomenally. Public concern of government regulation centers on the scope of intervention, impact on business operations, and the proliferation of regulatory agencies.

Scope of Intervention

Measured by federal expenditures for the forty-one agencies in fiscal year 1979, the total amounts to $4.8 billion. By percentage, social regulation constitutes 92 percent, and the traditional regulatory expenditures absorb 8 percent.

Impact on Business Operations

In a study prepared for the Joint Economic Committee, Murray L. Weidenbaum listed five major areas where government regulation deems to be overly restrictive.

Inflation: Regulation costs to business represent the "hidden tax" that is shifted from the taxpayer to the consumer.

Innovation: Excess regulation reduces the rate of initiation of new products.

Capital formation: Meeting government regulation in pollution and safety has incurred large capital expenditure, which would be otherwise spent for growth and productivity.

Employment: The minimum wage law, for example, has reduced the teenage employment.

Small Business: Paperwork alone generates $15–20 billion for 5 million small firms, not to mention high costs imposed on them to meet pollution and safety standards.

Proliferation of Agencies

There are hundreds of federal departments and bureaus having administrative power over industry and business. The more powerful independent regulatory agencies over certain areas of business activities are as follows:

Over banking and finance (5): Among them, the Comptroller of the Currency, the Federal Reserve Board, and Securities and Exchange Commission.

Over competition and trade (10): Among them, Civil Aeronautics Board, Federal Communications Commission, Federal Trade Commission, Interstate Commerce Commission, plus the Antitrust Division of the Justice Department.

Over employment and discrimination (2): Equal Employment Opportunity Commission, and National Labor Relations Board, plus the Labor Department's Pension and Benefit Welfare Programs, and Office of Federal Contract Compliance Programs.

Over energy and environment (3): Among them, Environmental Protection Agency, Federal Power Commission, and the Nuclear Regulatory Commission, plus the Federal Energy Administration being absorbed into the Department of Energy.

Over safety and health (1): Namely the Consumer Product Safety Commission. Also, other departmental agencies should include: the Transportation Department's Federal Aviation Administration and National Highway Traffic Safety Administration, the HEW department's Food & Drug Administration, the Labor Department's OSHA, and the Interior Department's Mining Enforcement and Safety Administration.

Source: Joint Economic Committee, U.S. Congress, *Hearings: The Cost of Government Regulation* (Washington, D.C.: U.S. Government Printing Office, 1978) pp. 31–59; and "Government Intervention," *Business Week*, 4 April 1977, pp. 52–56.

MANAGEMENT OF SOCIAL RESPONSIBILITY

The management of business social responsibility is a concern that is broad in scope and far-reaching in its consequences. We have suggested that a necessary conflict exists between economic and social responsibilities, and that it is difficult to say whether profit or social good should take priority in making business decisions. A short-run loss may yield long-run benefits; a costly project in one area may yield profits in other areas. The management of social responsibility thus requires a broader perspective: a realization of the need for pursuing multiple objectives, and a commitment to results of long-term significance.

The Total Involvement

The management of social responsibility requires the total commitment of the organization. It calls for conceptual acceptance of the new challenge, for a total organizational effort, and for the consideration of social issues in the formulation of policy, strategy, and tactics. Conceptually, management must consider the challenge as new and different. It must make a conscious effort and adhere to a new set of rules. Carl A. Gerstacker, chairman of the board of the Dow Chemical Company, set forth five key postulates in this area.[13]

POSTULATE 1 Social responsibility must be a firm, deep-seated belief of management. It must be a part of the ongoing strategy of the corporation. The board of directors is responsible for initiating dialogue with the company's management, which commits resources and manages specific programs. A bumper sticker campaign or a crash program is self-defeating; it cannot yield positive results.

POSTULATE 2 Management must be consistent in its support of social responsibility. Social responsibility objectives are of long-term value; their implementation requires systematic development, a consistency of attention that sustains company-wide effort toward their realization. Social programs cannot be turned on and off at will, nor should their budgets be drastically revised because of changing business conditions.

POSTULATE 3 Management commitment must be long term. Building a credible commitment requires time, as does instilling confidence and achieving results. Dow Chemical's pollution control program had its beginning in the 1930s. Throughout recent decades, the company has committed money, organization, and management to achieve pollution control goals.

POSTULATE 4 The business executives must never underestimate nonverbal communication. Actions speak louder than words in the area of social responsibility. Goals must be backed up by strategy; strategy must be substantiated by resources and administrative actions.

POSTULATE 5 The carrot is better than the stick. Management and employees should be encouraged to strive for social responsibility through open communication; neither coercion nor deception will bring lasting results.

Organizing for Social Response

To organize activities aimed at achieving social responsibility requires concerted effort. The effort starts with the board of directors, which pronounces corporate philosophy and broad policies on social matters, advises and approves plans and programs, and maintains complete surveillance over company policies and executive actions associated with business ethics.

Individually and jointly, board members provide a bridge in communicating public thinking and attitudes to the management, notifying the latter of pending legislation, crucial social issues, and government actions. In recent years, certain corporations have adopted the practice of adding to their membership individuals representing minority interest and community views.[14] Top management has the prime responsibility for organizing social responsibility activities, establishing goals, and evaluating the company's effectiveness in meeting them. Organizationally, various forms have served specifically to perform these activities: the committee; the staff department; the task group; or any combination of the three. Let us review each of these forms in turn.

POLICY COMMITTEE A policy committee for social responsibility, composed of top-management executives, is a desirable form. It fulfills the central function of selecting objectives and policies. Acting as a collective body, it provides a forum for information exchange, establishes priorities, formulates programs, monitors and assesses social consequences of company activities. Dow Chemical's eleven-member Ecology Council, composed of top-management personnel including the president and the chairman of the board, has been effective for many years. At each of the company's manufacturing locations and product departments, there is an Ecology Subcouncil that serves as a network of communication and action at all levels. However, a policy committee cannot be regarded as totally functional. It is not meant to be an operating entity; its decisions are to be carried out by the operating units. The committee runs the risk of degenerating into a "fire-fighting" operation preoccupied with handling crash problems as they arise, or into a debating society consumed with personal infighting. A policy committee needs the support of a staff department. An efficient staff will not only improve the committee's performance but will provide research work and the linkage with operating departments that is so necessary to keep policy statements operational.

PROGRAM IMPLEMENTATION A staff department is a functional organization, established at the corporate level, that has charge of social responsibility activities.[15] It advises the chief executive on corporate goals, strategy, programs, and resources allocation. It establishes policies in certain critical areas with which the company is most concerned and assists group and operating divisions in formulating their respective plans and programs. Within the company as a whole, it is the arm of management that represents the corporation's involvement in social and community affairs; it keeps management advised of legislative actions, and assimilates information internally—an educational effort that is essential to social activities. Social responsibility is necessarily an interdisciplinary function; support must be drawn from other disciplines, such as law, finance, manufacturing, and marketing. A staff department may contain a small number of specialists in the areas of urban affairs, ecology, or consumerism. The advantage of having an independent staff lies in the value of concentrated management and policy leadership.

There are also many disadvantages, one of which is the likely proliferation of activities, cost, and time. Business executives must therefore weigh requirements versus cost, determining precisely what the dimensions of the corporate social responsibility are, and in what areas the responsibility is critical. For a new organization, there is always the likelihood of excessive enthusiasm and individual crusades, but these can be contained if the proper guidelines are given and the proper individual selected. Again, a staff department of this nature depends on interdepartmental support and interdisciplinary knowledge. A small but professional organization is preferable to a large, routine-bound organization.

TASK GROUP The task group is another possible organizational form. As a component, it is temporary and operational, designed to perform certain critical tasks, not to respond to a wide range of issues. It has the single purpose of solving an operational and urgent problem. Thus, a task group might be formed in response to some aspect of consumerism or ecology, or to effect the hiring and training of the disadvantaged, as happened at Eastman Kodak in Rochester, New York, during the mid-1960s.[16] Although the task group is effective in dealing with crisis, it has many drawbacks. First, it lacks continuity. It can easily be reduced to fire fighting. From the standpoint of those making demands, the task group may show corporate shortsightedness and lack of commitment, thus generating hostility and confrontation. Second, owing to its temporary nature, the task group lacks expertise. Third, hasty action on the part of the task group and lack of communication between the group and the operating personnel who have to implement group decisions often increase difficulty in problem solving. The task group has a limited purpose and is thus ineffective in solving long-term social problems.

Formulating Strategies for Social Action

Corporate strategy for social responsibility has a different meaning from business strategy, which seeks to exploit profit opportunities and operates in a highly competitive environment. A strategy for social responsibility concentrates on developing possible, equitable solutions to designated problems and on formulating policies for the achievement of stated social goals. A corporation can choose from three different approaches: (1) unilateral actions by one company; (2) cooperative, coordinated actions by all or by the leading companies in a single industry or geographical area; and (3) actions by one company, several companies, or an industry association, for the purpose of securing or influencing some kind of governmental action.[17]

There is a sphere within which unilateral action can be quite effective: minority hiring and promotions programs, environmental containment procedures, and product design changes aimed at reducing maintenance or increasing plant safety. When the cost of a program is beyond the capacity of a given firm, and its unilateral contribution would be relatively minor, cooperative effort is desirable. Pollution control within an area where many separate firms are contributing to the pollution, along the same riverbank, for example, would be a good time for cooperative effort. Such cooperation, though difficult to arrange, offers no advantages to any given competitor and usually creates a more equitable solution for all. The third approach, which requires business firms to participate unilaterally or jointly (through trade associations) in public policy making, is a legitimate practice. But business executives must exercise extreme care in choosing the methods of such participation, cautiously anticipating the social and political consequences of the public policy they wish to influence. Tactical actions are operational in nature. Line management and responsible individuals who are required to oversee and assume tactical actions must be fully informed of the corporation's social responsibility goals, policy guidelines, and changing political and legal restrictions. In this regard, company policy guidelines and management surveillance can minimize irresponsible social actions.

STRATEGIC CONSIDERATIONS OF PROFIT, SOCIAL VALUES, AND BUSINESS ETHICS

The doctrine of social responsibility remains quite nebulous—difficult to define, continuously under debate, and awaiting crystallization. The modern concept of social responsibility originated during the turbulent 1950s and 1960s, when old values were being questioned and new ones were yet to be discovered. So long as the great debate persists, business social responsibility will remain a perplexing concept, difficult to define to the satisfaction of both the public and the business community. In reality, however, there are three concepts involved in the difficulty: profit; social values; and business ethics.

Profit Maximization

The traditional concept of profit maximization, which derives its theoretical origin from the classical economists, is sanctioned by law, has been accepted by society, and has deep roots in Western civilization. A business executive's performance is judged by his/her ability to maximize profit through the efficient use of resources and through successful competition in the marketplace. Likewise, business firms fulfill their social function, in the narrowest sense of the term, by creating employment. Profit thus provides incentive and creates jobs. Contemporary views of social responsibility not only demand that the business firm perform additional social services but even question the equitability and usefulness of profit itself. The burden imposed by ever-increasing legal constraints and government regulation, by heightened expectations by society, and by the company's own sense of an obligation to solve social problems, increases costs and thus, theoretically, must result in a loss of profits. There, apparently, lies the conflict: profit maximization versus social good at great cost. The argument that a distinction must be drawn between short-run and long-run profit goals in evaluating social programs also causes disagreement, due to the inadequacy of quantitative methods of accounting. Innovative methods, such as social accounting and cost-benefit analysis, are difficult to apply in the development of standard accounting practices and in the translation of qualitative values into quantitative terms.[18] One author has suggested that profit needs a redefinition, "one that calculates gains and losses, net worth and assets not only in terms of dollars but also in terms of people, of long-term return on social investments, and of economic benefit realized, or as yet unrealized, resulting from social action."[19] Profit is a practical problem. An enlightened executive conscientiously strives for a balance between profit maximization, the limits of which are defined by society, and socioeconomic goals, the realization of which is tempered by management.

Social Values

Policies and strategies are formulated by people. They are human decisions, reflecting the values, goals, and motives of the people participating in the process. In business strategy, personal values, professional opinions (technical, economic, social, ethical), individual motives, and group identity (formed by a blending of individual member's values) influence the selection of goals and strategy. A company's attitude toward key social issues will be influenced by the political, economic, and cultural orientations of individuals and represents a compromise between many different individual perceptions of the firm's function and responsibility.

Awareness of the role of values in decision making enhances management's feelings about value, bias, and self-interest. Social responsibility requires business executives to assess their personal values, their economic and social orientation, and their attitudes toward employees, stockholders, suppliers, and other political and social groups. The practice of corporate social responsibility demands that business executives gain knowledge of the political process and of the role that political, economic, and social organizations can play in public policy formation. We have already discussed the need for the board of directors to be thoroughly involved with social issues and have suggested various means of promoting communication within the corporation and with society. The creation of such a socially responsible environment will in the end be one key to the large problem posed by the conflict between the profit motive and social responsibility.

Business Ethics

Business ethics has become a grave issue in recent times. The much-publicized ITT affair, the oil industry's alleged conspiracy during the 1973–1974 oil crisis, the excess involvement of large corporations in election fund raising in 1972, and, most recently, widespread payoffs at home and abroad involving Lockheed and a score of other large corporations all dramatize at once the deterioration of business ethics and the public rancor incited by this deterioration.[20] Actions taken by Congress, the Securities and Exchange Commission, and corporations and their boards of directors (notably Lockheed and Gulf Oil) have exposed the nature of the problem and the difficulty of finding a solution.

Business ethics is a broad issue. It touches upon corporate behavior in the abstract and upon businesspeople as individuals in the conduct of business transactions.[21] Society places a dual ethical demand on business firms: (1) to employ knowledge and power in a fair and responsible way vis-à-vis other members of society; and (2) to discharge business activities properly and efficiently. These demands are reflected in codes written by business firms, professional societies, and business associations, and in individual conduct governed by the personal perception of moral propriety. Business ethics have religious, philosophical, and cultural roots in society; the ethics of the business community directly reflect those of society. As conventionally defined morality experiences a general decline in America, the concept of business ethics has lost its moral underpinnings and can no longer be defined as a strictly moral issue. It has expanded to include activities having political effects (such as the use of corporate power), social effects (the harm done to society), and legal effects (the disclosure of financial information). The various business wrongdoings revealed during the Watergate inquiries exemplify the misuse of corporate power. Domestic and overseas payoffs to politicians, government officials, procurement officers, and influence peddlers were clear signs of the breach of business ethics.

Bribery and Slush Funds

Companies whose survival depends on large contracts and whose operations become dependent on payoffs face a constant dilemma. To pay bribes is unethical, but there is the fear of possible elimination from competition when competitors who are more tolerant of bribery seize the opportunity to gain immediate benefits. When society condones payoffs by not punishing them, they proliferate. However, payoffs have gone far beyond society's tolerance level. Lockheed's payment of over $9 million in bribes to Japan alone has been totally disastrous to the American business image abroad, not to mention its impact on Japanese politics. The multimillion dollar "slush fund" that Gulf Oil maintained from 1960 to mid-1963 and Exxon's "special budgets" are cases that flagrantly violated the regulations of the Securities and Exchange Commission. Some remedies for the situation will no doubt be found in Congressional legislation, SEC investigations, and administrative actions.[22]

In the final analysis, corporations must bear direct responsibility for preventing or at least controlling unethical actions. Corporations must state their ethical policy in writing—the sanctioned and prohibited activities, and the various types of allowable payments, including political contributions, agents' commissions, finders' fees, gifts, favors, and entertainment allowances. Clearly established procedures for approving payments and activities are mandatory. Once a year, key executives throughout the company should be required to affirm policy and procedural compliance. The board of directors must assume an active role, requiring the complete disclosure of financial information of any confidential nature, and establishing broad policies on ethics. Whenever there is suspicion of illegal actions, a special committee of directors should be appointed to investigate, using special counsel and independent auditors.[23] Naturally, there are other management controls and surveillance mechanisms that can be used to enforce compliance.

In business strategy, personal values and business ethics are the human side of decision making. Their importance cannot be overemphasized. Corporate executives must consistently weigh the ends-means equation. Ends alone do not justify the means. Obtaining a large contract or sales order should never be used to justify any unethical action. The legitimacy of an action must be a deciding factor. Strategic thinking, with its unique potential for exploring available options, is always useful in exploring a dilemma such as this. The personal values of individual executives and the diversion of their opinions always provide checks and balances. Business ethics, society, and economics jointly constitute the composite nature of a strategic decision. Indeed, they are the basic governing factors in strategy making.

SUMMARY

Since the early 1960s, social responsibility has become a national issue, partly because of the increased public awareness of social problems and partly because of certain side effects caused by industry's preoccupation with super growth. Through the early 1970s, however, American business has learned to adapt to this new environment and has largely accepted radically imposed restrictions.

This does not mean that the industry's acceptance of the concept is without continued controversy, nor does it imply that the industry's ability to manage social responsibility needs no further improvement. Indeed, we argue for a more active role for business firms in the public policy process and in monitoring and measuring the impact of social issues and legislations upon business development and operation. In particular, we suggest that social responsibility be included in a corporation's policy and strategy deliberation. Modern state, society, and business are so interdependent that the survival of all guarantees the well-being of each.

NOTES

1. Social responsibility is not altogether a new concept. The inquiry had its beginning in the early 1930s. Its modern version is broader, more vocal, and forceful. Standard textbooks on the subject include Keith Davis and Robert L. Blomstrom, *Business Society: Environment and Responsibility* (New York: McGraw-Hill, 1975); George A. Steiner, *Business and Society* (New York: Random House, 1971); and Neil W. Chamberlain, *The Limits of Corporate Responsibility* (New York: Basic Books, 1973).
2. Davis and Blomstrom, *Business Society,* p. 39.

3. Steiner, *Business and Society,* p. 141.
4. Keith Davis calls it "the power-responsibility" equation.
5. John J. Corson and George A. Steiner, *Measuring Business' Social Performance: Corporate Social Audit* (New York: Center of Economic Development, 1974), pp. 27–29.
6. Lyman E. Ostlund, "Attitudes of Managers Toward Corporate Social Responsibility," *California Management Review,* Summer 1977, pp. 35–49.
7. For introductory work on public policy formulation, see Charles O. Jones, *An Introduction to the Study of Public Policy* (Belmont, Calif.: Wadsworth Publishing, 1970); Don Allensworth, *Public Administration: The Execution of Public Policy* (Philadelphia: Lippincott, 1973); and Francis E. Rourke, *Bureaucracy, Politics, and Public Policy* (Boston: Little, Brown, 1969).
8. Jones, *Introduction to the Study of Public Policy,* pp. 6–14.
9. Allensworth, *Public Administration,* pp. 81–102.
10. For discussion, consult Robert N. Corley and Robert L. Black, *The Legal Environment of Business* (New York: McGraw-Hill, 1973), pp. 625–44.
11. Dudley F. Pegrum, *Public Regulations of Business* (Homewood, Ill.: Irwin, 1969), p. 39.
12. James L. Houghteling, Jr., and George G. Pierce, *The Legal Environment of Business* (New York: Harcourt, Brace and World, 1963), pp. 806–78.
13. "Creating a Management Environment for Social Responsibility Performance," in *Managing the Socially Responsible Corporation,* ed. Melvin Anshen (New York: Macmillan, 1974), pp. 41–58. Joel E. Ross and Robert G. Murdick in their book, *Management Update: The Answer to Obsolescence* (New York: AMACOM, 1973), listed a ten-point guide for social actions, pp. 52–54.
14. Leon H. Sullivan, "Problems and Opportunities of Public Interest Directors," in *Managing the Socially Responsible Corporation,* ed. Anshen, pp. 168–98.
15. Anshen, *Managing the Socially Responsible Corporation,* pp. 23–40. For comments on corporate practice, see "Do Corporate Executives Plan for Social Responsibility?" *Business and Society Review,* Winter 1974–1975, pp. 80–81.
16. S. Prakash Sethi, *Up Against the Corporate Wall* (Englewood Cliffs, N.J.: Prentice-Hall, 1974), pp. 277–300, 467–82. Outstanding company practices in social responsibility are cited every year. For 1974 and 1975, for example, see *Business and Society Review,* Winter 1974–1975, and Winter 1975–1976, respectively.
17. Anshen, *Managing the Socially Responsible Corporation,* pp. 17–22.
18. For a comprehensive study, see Lee J. Seidler and Lynn L. Seidler, *Social Accounting: Theories, Issues, and Cases* (New York: Wiley-Melville, 1973). For a critical view, see Raymond A. Bauer, L. Terry Canthom, and Ranne P. Warner, "Auditing the Management Process for Social Performance," *Business and Society; Review,* Fall 1975, pp. 39–45.
19. Dan W. Lufkin, "Some Financial Implications of Corporate Social Responsibility," in *Managing the Socially Responsible Corporation,* ed. Anshen, p. 136.
20. More than 200 companies have reported to the Securities and Exchange Commission that they made questionable payments abroad, *The Wall Street Journal,* 16 September 1976, p. 8. For discussions, see Senate and House Hearings reports on *Foreign and Corporate Bribes* and *Prohibiting Bribes to Foreign Officials* (May 13, 1976, and April 5, 7, 8, 1976, respectively).
21. Davis and Blomstrom, *Business Society,* pp. 171–87; and Steiner, *Business and Society,* pp. 217–37.

22. For a fine discussion on overseas payoffs, see Peter Nehemkis, ''Business Payoffs Abroad: Rhetoric and Reality,'' *California Management Review,* Winter 1975, pp. 5–20. For comments on the Foreign Corrupt Practices Act of 1977, see Hurd Baruch, ''The Foreign Corrupt Practices Act,'' *Harvard Business Review,* January-February 1976, pp. 32–50.
23. *Business Week,* 26 July 1976, p. 19.

CASES FOR PART II

4. OXYGEN SERVICE COMPANY
5. TECHTRONICS, INCORPORATED
6. MODERN PUBLISHING COMPANY, INC.
7. ROSPATCH CORPORATION
8. GULF OIL CORPORATION: DOMESTIC AND FOREIGN POLITICAL CONTRIBUTIONS
9. CHARGE OF AIR POLLUTION AGAINST ACME STEEL CORPORATION
10. POLAROID IN SOUTH AFRICA

OXYGEN SERVICE COMPANY

For the last twenty-eight years, Charlie Miller, owner of the Oxygen Service Company (OSC) has been a distributor of welding supplies and equipment for Orange County, California. Sales over the past five years have grown at a nominal rate of 5 percent per year. However, during this same period consumer prices have averaged about 8.6 percent per year. Hence, sales have actually decreased in comparison to inflationary consumer prices. Miller attributes the flat sales to a lack of aggressiveness in the company's marketing-sales promotion effort.

In 1978, Miller, after attending seminars and doing some soul searching, realized some decisive steps should be taken. Basically, he felt these steps should include the opening of a new store to meet the growing demands of Orange County, reevaluating the management structure, implementing a new inventory control system, and redesigning his marketing-advertisement efforts.

Time was running out for Charlie Miller. With retirement only a couple of years away, any attempts to improve his company had to be implemented soon. Due to his cliental build-up of twenty-eight years and the continuing growth of Orange County, he felt the company had a strong foundation on which to build.

Company Background

Miller was raised in Phoenix, Arizona during the Great Depression of the 1930s. He finished only three years of high school. In 1941, he joined the United States Army Air Force. During his first twenty-six months in the service, he worked in altitude training units dealing with oxygen facilities. In this air force training unit, Miller met Joe Simpson (fictitious name), who later became his business partner. This training provided them with the background to start their own business.

After working three years with an Orange County firm that distributed welding supplies, they decided that they could do better on their own. In August 1950, they quit their jobs and opened a distributorship with a capital of less than $5,000. At that time in Orange County there were only a few welding supply distributors. Fortu-

---

Prepared by John E. Grob under the supervision of Dr. Y. N. Chang, California State University, Fullerton.

nately, Airco, a large manufacturer and distributor of welding supplies and equipment, did not have a distributorship in Orange County. Since Miller and Simpson had contact with Airco people on their previous job, they were able to persuade Airco to supply them with the necessities to start a business.

For the first fifteen years of the company, the hospital line was pursued almost exclusively. However, a gradual shift of emphasis took place, from supplying hospitals with gases to supplying industrial firms with welding supplies. Miller and Simpson decided to make this change because hospital technology had become so sophisticated and complex that they realized the company had to either specialize or leave the medical business entirely. Subsequently, the medical part of the business was sold to their own medical operations manager. During this period, Simpson died and left Miller as the sole proprietor.

Orange County

Orange County became incorporated on March 11, 1889. It is situated in southern California between Los Angeles County and San Diego County. Some of the physical characteristics of Orange County are sandy beaches, snow-capped mountains, and a superb mediterranean climate. The pleasant physical environment has definitely contributed to its growth.

Orange County has experienced an astronomical population growth over the last thirty years. In the 1950s, it tripled in population, thus becoming the fastest-growing county in the entire United States. Orange County had 219,390 inhabitants in 1950. Since then, the population has increased 8½ times (see Exhibit 1). However, the growth rate has now slowed.[1]

EXHIBIT 1 ORANGE COUNTY POPULATION GRAPH

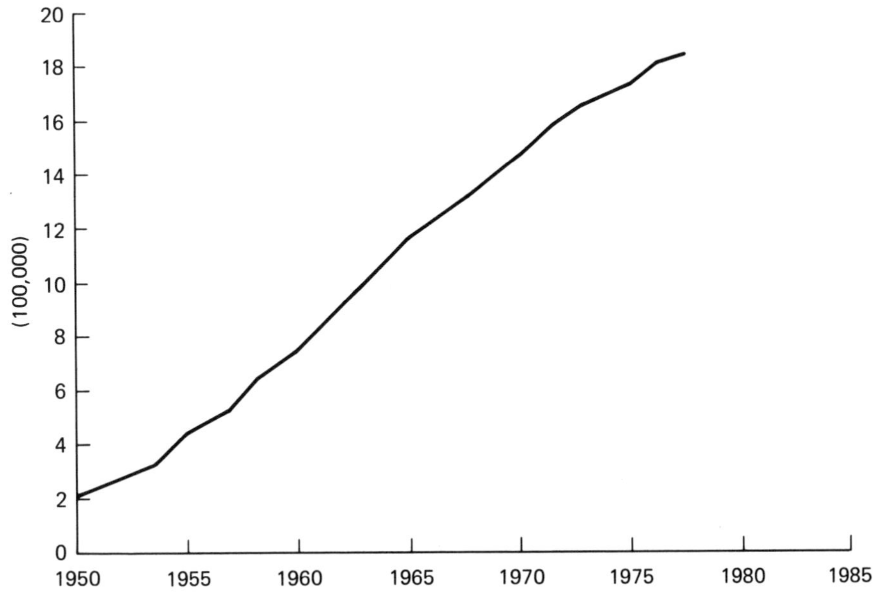

Source: Orange County Progress Report 1977–78

Internal Operations

From 1974 to 1978, company sales increased approximately 25 percent. During this same period, net profits after taxes increased 51 percent. As shown in Table 1, most of this profit growth is due to an increase of 48 percent in 1978. Net incomes of the four previous years averaged around $33,000. Miller believes that Oxygen Service's profits during 1974 to 1977 were eaten away by increasing costs and escalating gas prices. Over those years, consumer price increases in Orange County have averaged 8.6 percent per year. Simultaneously, gas prices increased exorbitantly. However, not all the rising costs could be passed on to customers. Hence, instead of profits increasing with the 8.6 percent rate of inflation, they remained stagnate, except for 1978.

TABLE 1 SALES AND EARNINGS TABLE*

Year	*Total Sales*	*Net Income***
1974	$1,243,286	$32,720
1975	1,418,891	33,018
1976	1,371,866	34,812
1977	1,479,826	33,337
1978	1,661,059	49,360

**Total sales and net income figures include income from cylinder sales and leasing.*
***Refers to net income after taxes*
Source: Company records

Product Line

Basically, 90–95 percent of the goods and services sold by OSC are to the welding and flame-cutting industry. OSC furnishes a wide variety of welding supplies. Table 2 portrays the sales and corresponding profits of the main products supplied by OSC as percents of total sales.

Gases and welding equipment represent over 60 percent of the company's total sales. However, gases are by far more profitable than equipment sales. In fact, at 0.05 percent, arc-welding machines are basically sold at cost. It is not surprising, therefore, that Miller would like to increase gas sales substantially. Other profitable items include cylinder demurrage, non-welding items, safety equipment, and filler metals and fluxes. Cylinder demurrage refers to the income made from renting and leasing cylinders. When firms keep the cylinders for more than a month, a charge on the cylinder is owed to OSC. In the future, this category will be discontinued since firms currently are required to buy their own cylinders.

Basically the three main products consist of gases, equipment, and filler metal and fluxes.

GASES The gases marketed include oxygen, acetylene, argon, helium, carbon dioxide, and mixtures of these gases. Oxygen is in heaviest demand. Oxygen prices

TABLE 2 PERCENT OF SALES TABLE

Item	*Item Sales %**	*Profits %***
Gases	31.07	17.28
Gas Equipment	9.09	2.26
Arc Equipment	22.29	0.05
Filler Metal and Fluxes	3.21	1.02
Safety Equipment	3.39	1.16
Non-Welding Items	6.83	3.37
Cylinder Demurrage	10.93	8.61
Other Misc. Sales	13.19	3.73
	100%	37.48

**Percent of item sales to total sales*
***Profits of item compared to total sales. Compared by subtracting items cost from items sales and subsequently divided by total sales.*
Source: Company records

are quoted at $152 for 244 Standard Cubic Feet, $120 for 122 S.C.F., and $100 for 80 S.C.F.

WELDING MACHINERY AND EQUIPMENT Equipment sold by OSC consists of electrical welding machines, single-stage and two-stage regulators, torches, and welding guns. Electrical welding machinery has become so specialized that a machine is needed for almost each welding function performed. In order to meet industrial demand, OSC is required to carry over ten different electrical welding machine models. Single stage regulators, contends Miller, are the best selling equipment items he carries.

FILLER METAL AND FLUXES The consumable metal sold by OSC falls into two categories of electrodes and gas rods. Both consumables vary in material composition and thickness depending upon the job required. Thus a large variety of gas rods and fluxes must be carried at all times to meet commercial demands. Spooled wire utilized by arc-welding machines is basically replacing the stick rod. Since spooled wire is faster, neater, cleaner and, more versatile, it is the consumable filler of the future.

MISCELLANEOUS ITEMS The other essential products furnished by OSC include nine styles of helmets, thirty kinds of goggles, twenty types of gloves, a line of fire extinguishing products, and a multitude of cutting and welding tips.

Operations

Most products sold by OSC are supplied by forty-five firms. All gases come from Airco. Five-year contracts guarantee OSC future supplies from Airco and simultaneously Airco is guaranteed purchases from OSC. Miller is currently negotiating with Airco over future gas prices. In the next several months negotiations should be finalized. Presently, the owner seems confident that his company will receive a 15 percent discount stemming from a larger gross purchase agreement. It should be noted that if Airco raises their price in the contract, OSC is free to change suppliers if the change in price does not correspond and meet prices of Airco's competitors.

Airco also furnishes OSC with the various consumable electrodes and rods. Welding machinery is supplied by two large firms. Accessory parts are received from forty manufacturing firms. Unlike gas, however, very little discount is given for electrodes, machinery, and accessory parts when ordered in bulk.

Lead time for orders varies from manufacturer to manufacturer. However, accessory items generally can be received within a couple of days; machinery and equipment usually arrive in about two weeks time; and welding rod orders take approximately a month. There are only five electrode manufacturers, including Airco, in the United States. Since the manufacturing process of electrodes is complex and all the firms are located in the East, there is a long delay time.

Basic operations of OSC include the filling of cylinders with gas, the delivery of the gas-filled cylinders to commercial users, and the sale of merchandise from the Orange and Costa Mesa stores. At the Orange store, there are three separate holding tanks of oxygen, nitrogen, and CO_2. The dock workers fill the cylinders from these liquid holding tanks. Since the holding tanks store the gases in liquid form, a great amount of room is saved. For example, 860 cubic feet of gas can be condensed to a single cubic foot of liquefied oxygen.

Argon and acetylene cylinders, which are received from Los Angeles in gas form, take up a lot of space on the Orange store's 200 $\times$ 300 foot lot. In the future, Miller would like to build another dock at Orange to fill argon. It would cost approximately $50,000 for the holding tank, and another $20,000 to $30,000 for pumps, manifolds, and expansion of the facilities and area. However, storage space would be saved and price discounts would be received due to larger orders.

Truck deliveries are divided into three routes. One route handles all orders north of the store. Another route delivers all orders to the south. These two routes deliver weekly, Monday through Friday. The other route is a speciality route that takes care of large customers needing several deliveries a week. There is no charge for most deliveries.

The two stores serve primarily the western and eastern parts of Orange County. The one in the city of Orange has been in operation since 1966 and is the company headquarters. The Costa Mesa store opened in 1975 and only serves as a retail outlet. In 1978, the Costa Mesa store sales represented one-fourth of the company's total sales. The owner stated that "the Costa Mesa store has done surprisingly well in its short existence."

Miller believes that store outlets are essential to satisfactorily serve commercial users and do-it-yourself welders. In the future he would like to open up a new store in either the northern or southern part of Orange County to capture a larger share of the welding market.

Marketing

Miller estimates that he supplies approximately 400 firms on open account. Presently, he would like to promote more business with major firms. However, OSC usually obtains the medium and small accounts because their competitor, V. B. Anderson, underbids them. A breakdown of regular charge customers is shown in Table 3.

Eighteen customers comprise 21 percent of total sales. (It should be noted that $701,000 or 42 percent of total sales are not listed. The bulk of these are to a multitude of industrial firms and do-it-yourself welders.)

TABLE 3 CUSTOMER ACCOUNT BREAKDOWN CHART (Fiscal Year 1978)

	Small Accounts	*Medium Accounts*		*Large Accounts*	
	$1000–2000	$3000–4000	$5000–6000	$7000–9000	$10000+
Number of Customers	199	36	10	13	18
Sales	$310,000	$135,000	$57,000	$107,000	$351,000

Source: Company records

The small accounts represent the largest customer account group. However, the bulk of these firms now receive less attention. Miller recently decided that only customer accounts that gross $200 or more a month will receive deliveries. Customers with purchases under $200 a month were asked to come to the store. Most of these customers now pick up their supplies directly from one of the two stores, but some were lost to competitors.

Since promotional efforts have been minimal, the owner believes that many potential customers have not been reached. These customers are the new industrial firms entering Orange County and the growing do-it-yourself welding market.

OSC advertising efforts have been virtually confined to five separate listings in the yellow pages. These listings are welding, rental equipment, gas equipment, and filler materials of rods and electrodes. But, in December 1978 several small ads were placed in local Pennysavers. All advertisements include the company's name, address, and phone number, and sometimes the motto, Service Is Our Middle Name. Currently, Miller is looking into newspaper and year-round Pennysaver ads as possible ways to increase sales. However, he is undecided about additional promotional efforts because of these questions: How much should be invested to obtain maximum profits? And by which channel of communication should the message be relayed?

As portrayed in Table 4, three salesmen provide the major sales promotion effort for the company. The budget for the salesmen is six times as much as the

TABLE 4 ADVERTISING AND PROMOTION EXPENDITURE CHART (1978 Fiscal Year)

Expenditure	*Amount*
Salaries & Commission—Salesmen (3)	50,856.13
Expense of Salesmen's Cars	5,010.29
Car Allowance—Salesmen's Cars	11,049.74
Advertising	8,257.54
Sales Promotion	3,874.83

Source: Company records

advertising and sales promotion expenditures. Each of the salesmen have a specific section of Orange County. One handles the southern portion, another attends to the central section, and the third serves the northern area.

OSC's good reputation for prompt service and their cliental build-up of over twenty-eight years probably constitute the company's biggest marketing tools. According to Miller, a majority of new clients stem from comments of satisfied clients.

Usually the same product price is quoted to prospective buyers. When discounts are given, it is done in an unorthodox manner. According to Miller, "we play it by ear," which means prices are determined upon the quantity of the order and the highest price they think the buyer will be willing to pay. Customers that may qualify for discounts include schools, municipalities, and large commercial firms. Discounts vary greatly.

Miller recognizes that the price of his products is a major determinant of sales growth. Thus prices are established and set to meet local competition. As a consequence, almost no profits are received from equipment sales, due to low competitive prices. However, once a customer purchases welding equipment, he usually purchases gas and consumable products, which are very profitable. Miller would like to expand his gas sales without having to sell as much "low gross" welding equipment.

Accounting and Finance

Financial statements are drawn up by a local certified public accountant firm. Exhibit 3 is the Consolidated Balance Sheet for the year ending June 30, 1978. Property and equipment in the balance sheet represent net book value. It should be noted that total accumulated depreciation for property and equipment amounted to

EXHIBIT 3 OXYGEN SERVICE COMPANY
CONSOLIDATED BALANCE SHEET, JUNE 30, 1978

Assets	
Current Assets	
Cash	$ 425.00
Accounts receivable	193,715.89
Advances receivable	42,372.83
Other receivables	2,878.00
Merchandise inventory	151,967.81
Security deposit	11,324.75
Prepaid expenses	40,403.14
Prepaid income tax	822.00
Total Current Assets	$443,909.42
Property and Equipment	
Automobiles and trucks	15,398.47
Furniture and fixtures	26,112.28
Rental equipment	12,958.17
Tools and equipment	8,492.99
Cylinders	48,897.22
Total Property & Equipment	$555,768.55

Liabilities and Stockholders Equity

Current Liabilities	
Accounts payable	156,509.07
Accrued payroll taxes	689.28
Contracts payable	48,281.40
Sales tax payable	7,093.87
Insurance loans payable	23,916.51
Income tax payable	9,683.00
Cylinder deposits	1,759.00
Total Current Liabilities	$247,932.13
Long Term Liabilities	99,136.75
Total Liabilities	$347,068.88
Stockholders Equity	
Capital stock, $10 par value, authorized and issued 2,000 shares of which 1,000 shares are held in treasury	20,000.00
Excess over par value paid in on capital stock	3,371.63
Retained earnings	185,328.04
	$208,699.67
	$555,768.55

$227,545.12, or over 67 percent of the original cost. Exhibit 4 is the Income Statement for the year ending June 30, 1978. Larger operating expenses include selling, office personnel expenditures, delivery, and administrative expenses. Office and administrative expenses comprised 11.1 percent of total sales. Another expense consists of the computer leased for $1,300 a month to help prepare financial data.

OSC does not have an established method for merchandise ordering. Miller expresses the current ordering process as "a seat of the pants operation," indicating orders are placed in an erratic manner. As a result, many slow moving items are overstocked, while shortages are frequent with popular items.

Organization and Management

As in many small businesses, the owner of OSC is the personality and backbone of the company. The company's success or failure is reflective of his attitudes, decisions, and planning. Currently, Miller is attempting to revise his organizational structure to allow himself and his vice president more time to organize, plan, and execute major programs and strategies. Exhibit 5 is the present organizational chart. The board of directors consists of the president (Miller), his wife, and his secretary. The president oversees the activities of the purchasing agent and both store managers, and heads the finance and office employees.

The sales manager, Leonard Buchanan, previously worked for Airco. He was hired by Miller partially due to his expertise in the welding field. He takes care of the activities concerned with daily operations. He supervises the three outside salesmen, the route drivers, and store employees. He is a man with great responsibility.

The office manager, Miller's son, has worked off and on with the company for ten years. Dave Miller graduated from California State University at Fullerton with a B. A. in psychology. Along with operating the computer, he is responsible for ac-

EXHIBIT 4 OXYGEN SERVICE COMPANY STATEMENT OF INCOME AND RETAINED EARNINGS FOR THE YEAR ENDED JUNE 30, 1978

Sales	$1,661,059.06
Cost of Sales	1,030,604.18
Gross Profit	630,454.88
Operating Expenses	
Warehouse and Building Expense	37,091.85
Selling Expense	182,655.29
Delivery Expense	71,378.53
Office Expense	113,762.06
Administrative Expense	70,447.02
Other Income and Expenses	61,581.20
Profit Sharing and Employee Benefits	24,934.77
Total Operating Expenses	561,850.72
Income Before Taxes	68,604.16
Federal Income Taxes	(13,070.00)
California Franchise Taxes	(6,174.00)
Net Income	$ 49,360.16
Retained Earnings—Beginning of Period	215,967.88
Retained Earnings—End of Period	$ 265,328.04

counts payable and accounts receivable. Dave works in conjunction with the bookkeeper, who does accounts payable, and two office workers who assist in receivables.

District sales, as shown in Exhibit 5, refers to the three outside salesmen. Responsibilities of these salesmen include locating new customers, establishing good communication with firms, demonstrating equipment, handling customer complaints, and thoroughly informing customers about welding equipment and supplies.

Environmental Considerations and Local Economic Trends

Orange County's population over the past few years has increased a moderate 3.2 percent. Experts predict Orange County's growth rate to stabilize at about 2–3 percent from 1978 to 1987.[2] The population is projected to increase to 2,266,400 by 1987, as shown in Table 5.

The following points are important to gain a better understanding of the growth patterns of Orange County.[3]

1. Fast growth areas from 1970 to 1976 included: Huntington Beach, Fountain Valley, Anaheim, Irvine, San Juan Capistrano, and Newport Beach.
2. Moderate growth areas from 1970 to 1976 included: Fullerton, Westminister, and Santa Ana.

EXHIBIT 5 ORGANIZATIONAL CHART

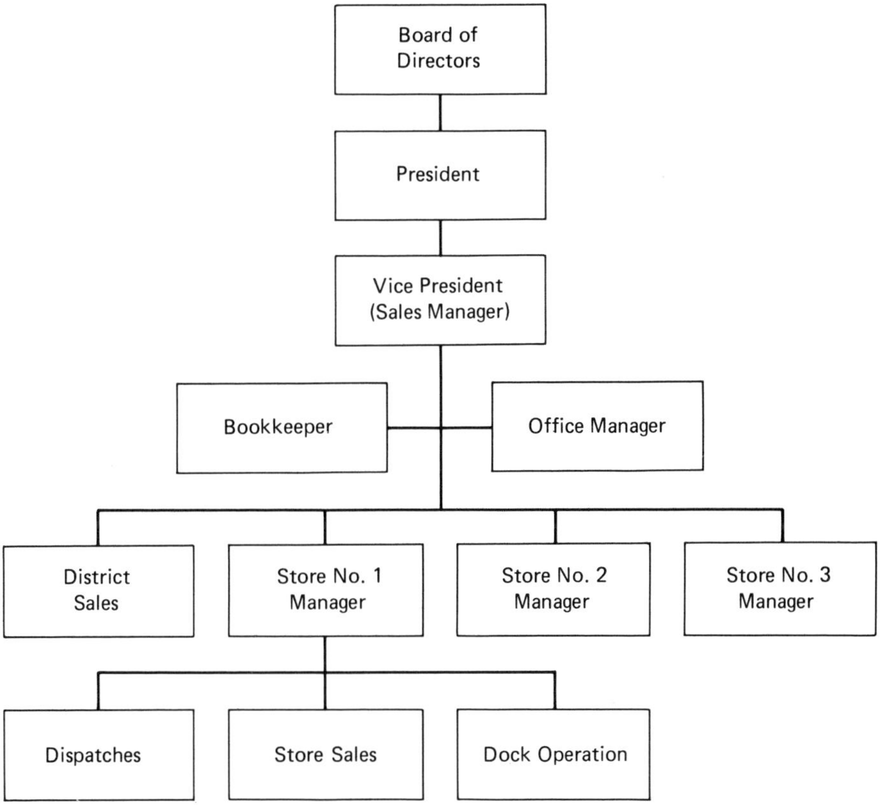

3. Stabilized or decreasing growth areas from 1970 to 1976 include: Costa Mesa, Orange, Buena Park, and Garden Grove.
4. The unincorporated areas of Orange County from 1970 to 1976 grew at a faster rate than the twenty-six incorporated cities. The vast majority of these unincorporated areas are in the southern portion of Orange County.
5. Substantial growth is projected for central, northern, and southern Irvine, East Yorba Linda, Anaheim Hills, Mission Viejo and Saddleback over the next several years.
6. The southern section of Orange County is projected to have the fastest growth rate in the years to come.[4]

Since 1950, Orange County has witnessed a substantial change in its industrial base. For years agriculture, especially oranges, constituted the primary industry. Today agriculture revenues represent only a small fragment of the economy. Presently the manufacturing sector employs 26.4 percent of the inhabitants.[5]

TABLE 5 POPULATION PROJECTIONS (1977–78 Report on the State of the County, Vol. 7)

	1976	*1978*	*1980*	*1982*	*1987*
Fullerton	98,961	101,921	105,874	109,516	120,033
Huntington Beach	158,085	164,679	169,901	174,185	185,424
Irvine	37,619	68,474	86,230	108,378	139,631
County Total	1,722,094	1,844,800	1,938,800	2,032,000	2,266,400

Fullerton, Huntington Beach, and Irvine are areas Miller is considering for store expansion.

Orange County has enjoyed substantial growth and prosperity for the past decade. In fact, it will continue to lead the state in employment and personal income growth rates.[6] Also, total employment will rise 4 percent to 5 percent annually from 1977 to 1980.[7] To accommodate this growing labor force, county administrators are attempting to draw outside firms into the county by creating an even better business atmosphere. For instance, they have approved plans for new industrial complexes to attract firms.[8]

Industrial concentration broken down by cities is shown in Table 6. This table indicates the potential market areas that OSC should be focusing upon. The cities of Irvine, Tustin, and Anaheim are heavily industry oriented. Huntington Beach has less industrial concentration.

TABLE 6 INDUSTRIAL CONCENTRATION BY SQUARE FOOTAGE OF SPACE SELECTED CITIES, ORANGE COUNTY (1976)

City	*No. of Firms*	*Sq. Ft. Occupied**
Irvine-Tustin	381	16,813,551
Anaheim	341	15,844,412
Costa Mesa	238	9,145,251
Fullerton	103	8,193,139
Buena Park	76	8,090,039
Santa Ana	233	6,374,008
Orange	87	3,716,920
Garden Grove	87	3,679,815
La Habra-Brea	23	2,893,256
Huntington Beach	99	2,752,800

**Occupied buildings of 10,000 square feet or more.*
Source: Coldwell Banker, Market Information Services

Industrial Setting

As mentioned before OSC sells 90 percent of its products to industrial firms that engage in welding and flame-cutting activities. However, the composition of the market should be broken down and closely analyzed. Table 7 dissects the welding and flame-cutting market by industry. The industry from 1975 to 1980 has approximately a 20 percent increase in demand for these jobs. Basically, durable manufactured goods represent the largest area of concentration for welders and flame cutters. The key, durable goods, consist of fabricated metal products, machinery, and transportation equipment. Fabricated metal products have enjoyed the largest rate of growth in recent years.

Competition

OSC is confronted with twelve competitors, only one of which is larger. It is three times as large as OSC and is the only competitive firm to have a retail store outlet. Likewise, OSC is twice as big as its nearest competitor.

Miller contends that the competitive situation of his company is keen. Furthermore, he believes prices for equipment and gas are kept low due to two factors: First, survival for the small firms is extremely tough; without the capital for promotion expenditures, growth for small companies is usually obtained by price cutting. Second, advertisements of Los Angeles firms, whether directed towards Los Angeles or Orange County, may lure away potential longstanding customers.

Objectives and Possible Courses of Action

In Miller's deliberation of what to do, he questions what his firm's obligations should be and what could be his firm's strategy. It is his intention to improve the company's growth in sales, profits, assets, and equity. Currently, he is attempting to strengthen the company's financial position. One of the company's intermediate goals is to increase sales by 25 percent by 1980. The regrouping of his firm's dispo-

TABLE 7 WELDERS AND FLAME CUTTERS EMPLOYMENT

Industry	*1970*	*1975*	*1980*
Construction Total	300(15.57%)	360(11.08%)	393(10.91%)
Manufacturing Total	1232(63.86%)	2107(69.26%)	2524(70.04%)
Durable goods	1175(60.90%)	2024(66.53%)	2421(67.20%)
Fabricated metal products	237(12.29%)	583(19.16%)	738(20.48%)
Machinery, except electrical	197(10.27%)	434(14.27%)	514(14.26%)
Transportation equipment	327(16.98%)	437(14.37%)	513(14.25%)
Service Total	236(12.25%)	363(11.93%)	428(11.88%)
Wholesale and Retail Trade	59(3.06%)	89(2.94%)	111(3.08%)
Government	20(1.05%)	24(0.80%)	32(0.89%)
Industry Total	1929 (100%)	3041 (100%)	3603 (100%)

Source: Orange S.M.S.A. Employment Projections for 1975 and 1980 (#61020500)

sition and increased sales may enable the company to open a new store. Miller feels the cities of Huntington Beach, Irvine, and Fullerton are the best possible areas for store expansion. Overall, he believes Orange County's growth opportunity, his company's strong position in the county, and the strength of his organization are good reasons for pursuing growth.

Notes

1. *Orange County Progress Report,* 1978–79, vol. 15, p.78.
2. *1977–78 Report on the State of the County,* vol. 7, pp.75, 76.
3. *Orange County Progress Report,* 1978–79, vol. 5, pp.79, 80.
4. *1977–78 Report on the State of the County,* vol. 7, pp.70, 71.
5. *Community Economic Profile for Orange County,* 1976, p.2.
6. *1978–79 Report on the State of the County,* vol. 8, p.61.
7. *1977–78 Report on the State of the County,* vol. 7, p.16.
8. *Orange County Manpower,* 1975–80, p. 10; *1977–78 Report on the State of the County,* vol. 7, p. 19.

TECHTRONICS, INCORPORATED

Robert J. Schmidt is putting the finishing touches on his annual report address for the shareholders in the annual meeting five weeks away. (See Exhibit 1.) He is optimistic about the future, but his concerns involve the new Scanall Corporation, which has consumed $2.5 million (if one includes cost contributed from other divisions), and the vulnerability of his products to federal spending controlled by Congress. Furthermore, a staff report on the major obstacles to wide use of scanning in the supermarkets is not encouraging. (See Appendix A.)

With the profit picture improving since 1971, he really believes he is on the right track. However, he wonders if a movement away from government-order dependence is logical, and his latest entry into the industrial field, Scanall, will use the talents of his operating companies to stimulate industrial and commercial sales.

History

Techtronics, Inc. was founded in 1947. The business began in a garage as parttime tool and die makers performed jobs that larger firms could not profitably perform or research. It remained a small proprietorship until 1956, when it was incorporated as Precision Manufacturing Company. From 1956 to 1967, it had become a reputable producer of ultra-precision components for inertial guidance, navigational and computer systems that were utilized in both government and the commercial aerospace industry.

In 1967, Precision Manufacturing Company went public, changed its name to Techtronics, Inc., and revamped its organization structure. Then a series of acquisitions took place: McGregor Corporation was acquired for $1.8 million, and United States Spectrographic Laboratories, Inc. for $.75 million, both in 1969. In 1973, Mul-Tech Electronics Corporation in Florida was purchased in exchange for shares. DuMont Ultraspec, Inc. was purchased for $115,000 in 1973. In the spring of 1974, Scanall Corporation was formed as an industrial products division that is structured to manufacture and market laser scanner label reading systems.

Prepared by Professor Charles F. Hoitash of Eastern Michigan University.

EXHIBIT 1 REPORT TO SHAREHOLDERS

Fiscal year 1975 was a year of continued growth in sales, earnings and orders for Techtronics, Inc. Net earnings were up 60% to $674,000 as compared to earnings of $428,000 for fiscal year 1974. These earnings were realized on sales of $13,671,000 and increase of 16% over last year's level of $11,784,000.

High interest rates, during the major portion of the fiscal year, had an impact on earnings. Debt, however, increased only $285,000 in spite of a significant investment in the Scanall Corp. development of $856,000. In April of 1974, a new operation, Scanall Corp., was founded for the purpose of entering the industrial and commercial product field. The product involved was a laser point-of-sale scanner for reading the Universal Product Code. This code and scanner technique will automate the checkout counters at supermarkets. Orders were received for prototype units which were delivered during the fiscal year and, as of this point in time, tentative but as yet unconfirmed production orders have been received from National Cash Register Corporation. Negotiations are underway with other suppliers of electronic cash registers and systems to whom our product is sold. The Scanall label reader has met with exceptionally fine acceptance and, through laboratory and field tests, has proven itself to be accurate and reliable. As we are now entering the production phase of this product, no further major development investment is anticipated.

Improved performance was experienced in all entities with the exception of Precision Systems Company. Price competition in this area has become very severe. Precision Manufacturing Company saw a record year in sales and earnings as did United States Spectrographic Laboratories and DuMont Ultraspec, Inc. Mul-Tech Electronic Company and McGregor Company continued to improve in accordance with expectations.

Though the first six months of the new fiscal year will show reduced earnings because of start-up costs for Scanall Production, as well as the general decline in the economy, it is anticipated that the average growth rate experienced since fiscal 1972 will continue through fiscal 1976.

ROBERT J. SCHMIDT, President

Scanall Corporation introduced its scanner and electronic processor at the May 1974 SMI (Supermarket Institute) annual convention, shortly after the division was formerly established. The following year, the Scanall laser[1] system was to be shown as part of the NCR Modular 225 Point of Sale (POS), which also includes the computer, electronic cash register (ECR), and the checkout counter. This system was designed for use with the Universal Product Code (UPC) developed by the Supermarket industry.

General

Techtronics, Inc. is engaged in four separate lines of business. (See Exhibit 2.) The first, referred to as a manufacturing business, provides ultra-precision components and assemblies to primary suppliers. This type of business is carried on by the Precision Manufacturing and Systems Division and two companies in the Technological Specialization Division (TSD), which are DuMont Ultraspec, Inc. and

*Note: 1. Laser is an acronym for Light Amplification by Stimulated Emission of Radiation. The laser is a device for amplifying light radiation, in which a beam of light is shot through a crystal causing the crystal to emit an intense direct light beam that is useful in micro-machining, surgery, and computer design.

EXHIBIT 2 CORPORATE STRUCTURE BY LINES OF BUSINESS (1975)

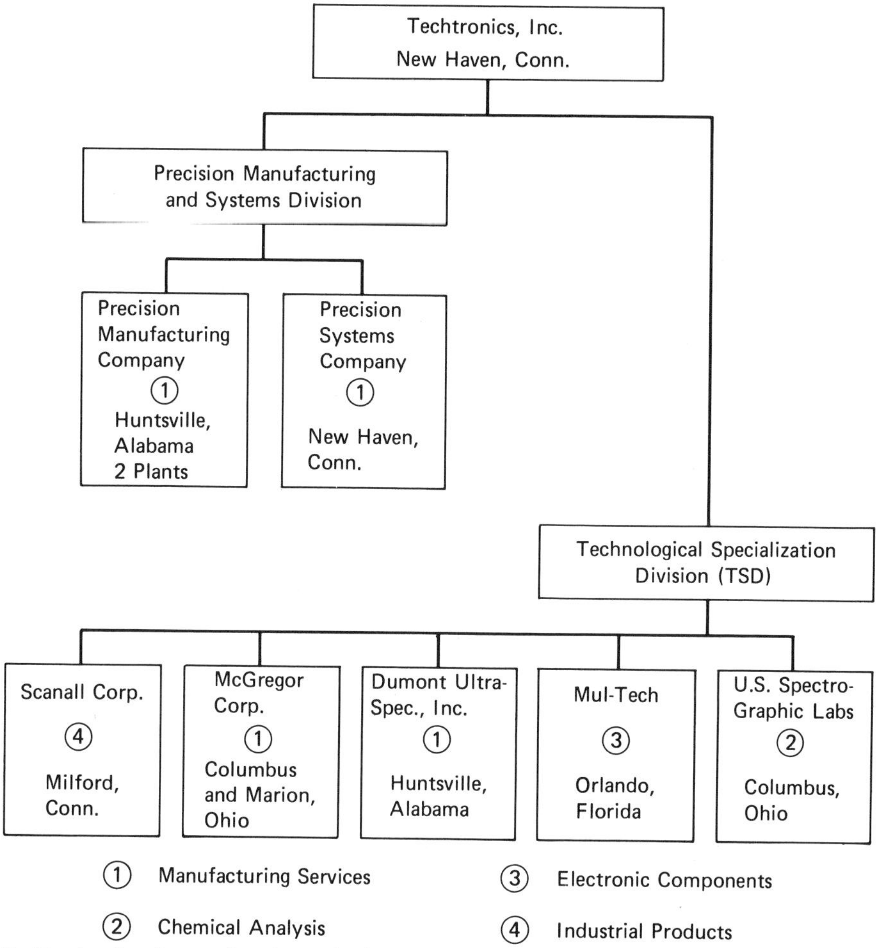

Techtronics, Inc. has no formal organization chart. Divisions have no formal status. Operating companies in the Technological Specialization Division (TSD) have functional lines of business relationships to Precision Manufacturing and Systems Division operating companies.
Source: Constructed by casewriter.

McGregor Corp. Precision Manufacturing and Systems Division and DuMont design and manufacture components and systems that require sophisticated engineering techniques and equipment. McGregor's business is principally related to the production of machined parts, primarily for the aircraft and defense industry, which require reasonably close tolerances.

Techtronics' second line of business is in the area of chemical analysis of a wide variety of materials for a broad spectrum of industry. The chemical analysis business is carried on through a company in the T. S. Division, U. S. Spectrographic Laboratories, Inc. (USSL). Techtronics' third line of business is its electronic components and assemblies operation, which commenced with the acquisition of Mul-Tech

Electronics Corporation (Mul-Tech), which was acquired in April 1973. Techtronics' fourth line of business is industrial products, involving primarily a laser scanner label reader system, using the trade name Scanall. A more detailed description of each line follows.

Exhibit 3 sets forth the contributions to net sales and earnings (loss) before income taxes and extraordinary items by line of business for the five years ended January 31, 1975. Exhibit 4 contains the percentage of total sales.

Manufacturing Services

Techtronics' manufacturing service business involved the production of products on special order to customer specifications.

The Precision Manufacturing and Systems Division has two operating companies, which are the Precision Manufacturing Company and the Precision Systems Company.

Precision Manufacturing Company primarily manufactures components on a production basis. Its products include inertial navigation components for use in missiles, space vehicles, aircraft, ships and submarines, and other items requiring extremely close tolerances. This company also manufactures gas bearings, gyro, and accelerometer components. In July 1973, Techtronics increased its manufacturing service capability with the acquisition of DuMont, which is engaged in high-precision machining of steels, aluminums, and titaniums.

Precision Systems Company produces precision optical devices presently

EXHIBIT 3 CONTRIBUTIONS TO NET SALES AND EARNINGS (LOSS) BEFORE INCOME TAXES AND EXTRAORDINARY ITEMS BY LINE OF BUSINESS FOR THE FIVE YEARS ENDED JANUARY 31

	NET SALES (In Thousands)				
	1971	1972	1973	1974	1975
Manufacturing Services	$8,349	$7,349	$9,116	$10,560	$11,622
Chemical Analysis	632	710	708	757	890
Electronic Components and Assemblies	—	—	—	467	1,009
Industrial Products	—	—	—	—	150
Total	$8,981	$8,059	$9,824	$11,784	$13,671
	Earnings (Loss) Before Income Taxes and Extraordinary Item (In Thousands)				
	1971	1972	1973	1974	1975
Manufacturing Services	$ (764)	$ (97)	$ 128	$ 708	$ 1,337
Chemical Analysis	205	186	159	170	286
Electronic Components and Assemblies	—	—	—	(73)	(23)
Industrial Products	—	—	—	—	(316)
Total	$ (559)	$ 89	$ 287	$ 803	$ 1,284

EXHIBIT 4 PERCENTAGE CONTRIBUTION TO TOTAL SALES BY LINES OF BUSINESS

	1971	1972	1973	1974	1975
Manufacturing Services High Precision Precision Mfg. and Systems and DuMont	80%	79%	78%	77%	71%
Machining Services (McGregor)	13%	12%	15%	13%	14%
Chemical Analysis (USSL)	7%	9%	7%	6%	7%
Electronic Components and Assemblies (Mul-Tech)				4%	7%
Industrial Products (Scanall)					1%
	100%	100%	100%	100%	100%

used in satellites such as the Earth Resources Technology Satellites. It also produces sensitive sensors and instruments for other outer space applications and components for nuclear applications. In addition, it designs and manufactures high-precision rotating laser and infrared scanner systems and related electronic equipment for use in communications and other applications.

In February 1969, Techtronics acquired McGregor Corporation, a firm utilizing machining processes that were numerical-controlled. McGregor's capabilities are focused upon the economical mass production of structural components requiring reasonably close tolerances. McGregor serves principally the commercial and military aircraft industries, but also does machining for torpedo housings and nuclear reactor parts. This firm suffered severe losses in the four years prior to fiscal 1975 and the first quarter of fiscal 1975. Management's efforts, which have been directed toward renegotiating existing contracts and becoming more restrictive on acceptance of new contracts without adequate profit margins, have resulted in profitable operations for the last three quarters of 1975. Management believes that the past problems causing McGregor's losses have been corrected.

Chemical Analysis

USSL is an analytical laboratory with a capability of analyzing a broad range of materials to determine chemical composition. Analysis is accomplished by an instrumental approach using spectrographs, spectrometers, atomic absorptions, x-ray analysis, and classical chemical analysis. USSL provides support supplies to other chemical analysis laboratories and its services are utilized by industries in quality control to determine, for example, whether material alloys meet required specifications or to identify causes of defects. USSL also provides analytical services in the areas of air- and water-pollution control, health, hygiene, and agriculture.

Electronic Components and Assemblies

Mul-Tech is engaged in the manufacture of electronic components and assemblies and has a particular product line of flexible multi-conductor, flat ribbon, molded electrical cable assemblies for use in computer files, business machines, guidance systems, gyro platforms, and other applications requiring high flexibility under severe operating conditions. Mul-Tech's principal customers are manufacturers of aerospace equipment, automated machinery, and business machines.

Electronic servos, (a low-power device or control mechanism used to actuate or control a more complex or more powerful mechanism), digital processors, and video processors are produced at Precision Systems Company. These units are used in control and information processing mechanisms for Techtronics products and customers products.

Industrial Products

The efforts of Scanall Corp. (in the Technological Specialization Division) are focused upon a "front-end" for the automated checkout counters for supermarkets, which will read universal product code labels on purchased goods. The Scanall system employs a laser scanner coupled with optics, video processors, and digital processors. The unit works in conjunction with electronic cash registers and computers to automate checkout and inventory control for the supermarket industry. Prototypes of this unit have been delivered to systems manufacturers who are primarily in the computer cash register or business machine fields. Orders have been received from one systems manufacturer for production units. Deliveries under these orders are expected to commence during the fiscal year ending January 31, 1976.

In the opinion of management, there is a large market potential for this device. This opinion is based on informal surveys by management; a formal market study has not been made. Other industrial products include laser measuring equipment particularly as it pertains to hardness measurement.

Marketing

The principal customers of Techtronics are federal government prime contractors and first tier subcontractors that furnish services and equipment for the use of the Department of Defense, the National Aeronautics and Space Administration, and the Atomic Energy Commission. During the fiscal year ended January 31, 1975, approximately 64 percent of the sales were for the ultimate use of the government. The remainder represented sales to customers for private use, chiefly in the commercial aircraft industry. Techtronics' business with the government is obtained primarily through competitive proposals made in response to requests for bids from prime government contractors and first tier subcontractors. Generally, the contracts are awarded on a competitive bid system.

Marketing is passive in that their business is secured through requests for bids by prime or first tier contractors. No formal sales organization exists; however, four technical sales persons representing each line of business maintain contact with potential contractors, especially the Research and Development technicians. Prints are brought back, from which quotes are developed and submitted.

Competitive Position

In view of the highly specialized fields served by Techtronics and the significance of government sponsored programs, it is difficult to make a precise evaluation of its competitive position in the manufacturing services field. However, there are a number of large and small companies engaged in supplying services and products to the aerospace industry of the type furnished by Techtronics and all of Techtronics' markets have been highly competitive for recent periods.

The electronic components and assemblies produced by Mul-Tech have one known independent competitor.

The Scanall system has several known competitors, one of which is the Sperry Univac AccuScan system, a division of Sperry Rand Corporation. Some of these competitors are independent companies who have or are attempting to develop a comparable system for sale to system manufacturers. Additional competition arises from large companies (such as IBM) that have or are attempting to develop a comparable system for their own use.

Raw Materials and Supplies

Materials purchased by Techtronics for use in the manufacture of its products consist largely of beryllium metal, stainless steel, aluminum, ceramics, refractory metals, plastics, and chemicals purchased from many national suppliers. Electronic components such as transistors, relays, lasers, and circuit boards are also purchased from various suppliers. All of these materials and supplies are presently available in ample quantities.

Backlog

On January 31, 1975, the backlog of orders for Techtronics, Inc. and its subsidiaries was $7.1 million (a new record high) compared to $6.6 million on January 31, 1974. The backlog is reasonably expected to be filled within the current fiscal year. There are no seasonal factors affecting this amount.

Research and Development

Techtronics, Inc. made expenditures associated with the development of the Scanall system of approximately $188,000 during fiscal 1974 and $856,000 during fiscal 1975. As of January 31, 1975, there were approximately twenty-five fulltime employees engaged in this activity. Customer sponsored expenditures for R and D activities amounted to approximately $62,000 during fiscal 1974 and $120,000 during fiscal 1975. Prior to 1974, there were no significant research and development activities.

Employment

As of January 31, 1975, there were 493 persons employed by Techtronics, Inc. and its subsidiaries, compared to 450 in 1969 and 297 in 1968. Of these, approximately 138 were salaried employees. None of the hourly employees belong to any union.

Management

Name	*Age*	*Position*
Robert J. Schmidt	55	Chairman of the Board of Directors and President
Robert J. Crowner	53	Executive Vice President
Willard C. Ursher	34	Vice President Finance and Treasurer
William A. Betz	46	Vice President Marketing
Richard E. Roper	43	Vice President Industrial Relations
Paul R. Trigg, Jr.	62	Secretary

There is no family relationship between any of the above persons.

Schmidt has been the chief executive officer since 1947. He holds approximately 58 percent of the outstanding stock. This includes the wholly owned companies of USSL, McGregor, Mul-Tech, DuMont, and Scanall, all of which are part of Technological Specialization Division.

Crowner joined the firm in September 1971 as executive vice president. He has a bachelor's degree from an eastern college. From 1967 until 1971 he was employed by Motorola as vice president and general manager of one of that firm's manufacturing plants.

Ursher joined the firm in December 1974 as vice president of finance and treasurer. He served as corporate controller from April 1970 to March 1972, and as vice president and treasurer of Norelco to May 1974; at that time he joined Wellesly Company as corporate controller, remaining until joining Techtronics.

Betz joined the firm in November 1971 to develop corporate planning and marketing, and was named vice president of marketing in April 1973. He graduated from an engineering college in aeronautical engineering. Like Crowner, he was employed by Motorola, as manager of engineering services, marketing manager, and director of program management.

Roper joined the firm in August 1973 as director of industrial relations, to assume the position of vice president of industrial relations in November 1974. He came to Techtronics after becoming a director of personnel in 1969 for Ken Plastics, a division of Parke-Davis Pharmaceuticals Corporation.

Trigg has been a partner of the law firm of Trigg, Goodnow, and Smith for more than five years.

Facilities

Production and service facilities have been located close to their customers, or close to the home of the firm's founder and key employees. Because of the technical nature of the manufacturing services and their specialized nature, location does not present a problem in communication or cost. Exhibit 5 lists the facilities, leased and owned, their location and approximate footage.

Finance

The balance sheet for the years 1974 through 1975 is found in Exhibit 6. The operating statement for the years 1971 through 1975 is in Exhibit 7 with key financial information in Exhibit 8. Sales and profit statistics from 1963 through 1975 are presented in Exhibit 9.

Schmidt has waived his right to any dividends since 1968, when a dividend payout ceased, and there is no intention to resume payment of them.

Net fixed assets investment is at an all-time high of $10,550 per employee.

Except for changes in the equity of the firm, net earnings have been retained entirely in the business.

Deferred income taxes are related to timing differences arising principally from the election for income tax purposes to use accelerated depreciation methods and to deduct new product development costs as incurred.

Inventories are stated at the lower of first-in, first-out cost or market.

Each year, short- and long-term debt obligations are refinanced or renewed depending on the needs and occasional restrictions on growth.

EXHIBIT 5 OWNED AND LEASED PROPERTIES

Facility	*Location*	*Approximate Square Footage*
Owned		
Precision Systems Company and Corporate Headquarters	New Haven, Conn.	55,000
McGregor Company	Columbus, Ohio	30,000
Mul-Tech Electronic Company	Orlando, Florida	15,000
DuMont Ultraspec, Inc.	Huntsville, Alabama	10,800
Precision Manufacturing Company	Huntsville, Alabama	92,000
Leased		
McGregor Company (*1987)	Marion, Ohio	34,000
United States Spectrographic Laboratories, Inc. (*1976)	Columbus, Ohio	6,500
Precision Manufacturing Company (*1977)	Huntsville, Alabama	60,000
Scanall Corp. (*Nov. 1975)	Milford, Conn.	15,000

*(*Expiration Year)*

EXHIBIT 7 PROFIT AND LOSS STATEMENT TECHTRONICS, INC. (In Thousands)

	Jan. 31 1975	*Jan. 31 1974*	*Jan. 31 1973*	*Jan. 31 1972*	*Jan. 31 1971*
Net Sales	$13,671	$11,784	$9,824	$8,060	$8,981
Cost of Products Sold	10,125	8,998	8,035	6,814	7,802
Selling & Administrative	2,108	1,811	1,352	1,040	1,561
Interest	244	217	159	169	217
Total Costs & Expenses	12,477	11,026	9,546	8,023	9,580
Operating Income	1,194	758	278	37	(599)
Other Income	90	45	9	52	40
Earnings Before Income Taxes	1,284	803	287	89	(599)
Income Taxes	95	175	100	(10)	(295)
Deferred Income Taxes	515	205	40	35	30
Write-Off of Goodwill					(614)
Net Profit	$ 674[a]	$ 423[a]	$ 147	$ 64	$ (909)

a. *See note* a *on Exhibit 9.*

EXHIBIT 6 CONSOLIDATED BALANCE SHEET TECHTRONICS, INC. (In Thousands)

Assets	*Jan. 31 1975*	*Jan. 31 1974*
Current Assets		
Cash	$ 246	$ 691
Trade Account Receivable	2,817	2,642
Inventories		
Finished and in-process products	1,241	1,141
Raw materials	272	157
	1,513	1,298
Prepaid Expenses	50	36
Total Current Assets	4,626	4,667
Properties		
Land	371	365
Buildings	2,562	1,832
Machinery and Equipment	5,809	6,478
	8,742	8,675
Less Allowances for Depreciation	3,539	4,122
	5,203	4,553
Other Assets		
Goodwill	450	463
Deferred New Product Development Costs	895	188
Miscellaneous	57	75
	1,502	726
	$11,231	$9,946

Liabilities and Net Worth	*Jan. 31 1975*	*Jan. 31 1974*
Current Liabilities		
Notes Payable		
Bank	$ 800	$ 300
Other		57
Accounts Payable	688	847
Employee Payable	462	396
Property and Other Taxes	166	208
Income Taxes	19	137
Current of Long-Term Debt	478	332
Total Current Liabilities	2,613	2,277
Long-Term Debt		
Notes Payable to Bank	1,050	1,175
Equipment Leases	285	360
Other	31	133
	1,366	1,668
Deferred Income Taxes	848	333
Net Worth		
Common Stock	1,388	1,348
Paid-In Surplus	2,480	2,457
Retained Earnings	2,536	1,863
	6,404	5,668
Total Liabilities and Net Worth	$11,231	$9,946

EXHIBIT 8 KEY FINANCIAL INFORMATION ON THE BALANCE SHEET OF TECHTRONICS, INC. (In Thousands of Dollars)

	1975	*1974*	*1973*	*1972*	*1971*
Current Assets	4,642	4,667	3,513	3,257	3,059
Current Liabilities	2,613	2,277	1,490	847	1,129
Fixed Assets Less depreciation	5,203	4,553	4,355	4,492	4,239
Long-Term Debt	1,366	1,669	1,707	2,466	2,340
Equity	6,404	5,668	4,994	4,814	4,677
Goodwill	450	463	476	488	502
Trade Account Receivable	2,817	2,642	1,851	1,739	1,274
Cash	246	691	659	638	977
Inventories	1,513	1,298	952	812	727
Accounts Payable	688	847	1,211	792	972
Deferred Income Taxes	848	333	227	193	152

EXHIBIT 9 TECHTRONICS, INC. SALES AND PROFIT STATISTICS FROM 1963 TO 1975 (In Thousands of Dollars)

Year	*Net Sales*	*Income Taxes*		*Net Profit*	
1975	13,671	610	245[a]	674	332[a]
1974	11,784	380	285[a]	423	330[a]
1973	9,824	140		147	
1972	8,060	25		64	
1971	8,981	(265)[c]		(294)[b]	
1970	11,572	640		652	
1969	8,457	595		541	
1968	7,195	420		505	
1967	6,441	270		316	
1966	5,221	220		261	
1965	4,725	n.a.		54	
1964	6,227	n.a.		129	
1963	4,641	n.a.		99	

a. As required by the FASB, the company will expense expenditures for development of new products as incurred rather than the present method of deferment and amortizing such expenditures over a period not to exceed three years. Prior to 1974, expenditures of new products or capabilities were not significant and were charged to operations as incurred. By charging the development costs as incurred, the operating income was reduced as well as the affected balance-sheet entries.

b. Before extraordinary loss item of $614,000.

c. Tax credit.

Appendix A

MAJOR OBSTACLES TO WIDE USE OF SCANNING IN THE SUPERMARKET

1. At least 60 percent of the merchandise must be symbol-marked (UPC) to receive a cost benefit with the scanner. Only recently has this been accomplished.
2. Lack of satisfactory system for in-store bar-code printing and labeling for random weight merchandise.
3. Redesigned checkstands are necessary in some cases, which have been slow in coming about.
4. Electronic Cash Registers (ECR) are very expensive and are necessary to become on-line with the computer.
5. Checkout speed (15–20 percent faster with well-trained clerks) may not happen it if means less clerks, or if the clerk has to unload as well as load.
6. Several House bills are involved with preserving pricing of items, which makes one function of the scanner unnecessary.
7. Consumer groups have applied pressure on state and federal legislatures to write item-pricing bills so the consumer knows the price, which supermarkets claim will no longer be needed when scanners are used.
8. Union groups are not only applying pressure for item-pricing legislation but also attempting to incorporate item-pricing jobs in their contracts.
9. Initial high investment cost of ECR, checkout stand, scanner, electronic processor, and computer.

MODERN PUBLISHING COMPANY, INC.

In early 1975, the management of Modern Publishing Company, Inc., a large and successful publisher of higher education materials, was considering a major reorganization of its college operations. Faced with predictions that college enrollments would stagnate and perhaps even decline over the next fifteen years, management wanted to protect the company's future profitability by formulating and evaluating its feasible strategic alternatives and then taking whatever actions were necessary to better align the organization with emerging conditions in the college market.

THE COLLEGE TEXTBOOK PUBLISHING INDUSTRY

History

Book publishing in the United States dates back to Mathew Carey, a native of Ireland, whose first significant book publication was the American edition of the Douay Bible, issued in 1790. As part of the total publishing industry, however, college textbook publishing has a much shorter history. At the turn of the twentieth century, no publisher had an organized college department, due mainly to the fact that there were less than 350,000 college students at that time. Henry Holt and Company had published several distinguished college texts, but apparently the first college department was established in 1906 by the Macmillan Company.

Shortly after the end of World War II, college textbook sales increased dramatically. Returning servicemen, taking advantage of the G. I. Bill, enrolled in colleges and universities in large numbers. This spurt in enrollments, combined with predictions of an increase in the postwar birthrate, gave rise to great optimism about the college textbook business.

THE FIFTIES During the 1950s, several college publishing companies were determined to shed the "cottage" or "country club" practices prevalent in the industry. For example, Prentice-Hall, Inc. is widely recognized as the first college publisher to truly view publishing as a *business*, and it began to aggressively secure manuscripts

---

Prepared by Professor Charles C. Snow of Pennsylvania State University.

and promote their sale in the college market. Other publishers quickly followed suit—most notably McGraw-Hill and Holt—and by continually attempting to improve the methods by which authors were located and their books produced and marketed, these and other publishing houses showed a steadily increasing annual profit.

THE SIXTIES Next came the "Golden Sixties," a period of rapid growth in which domestic sales more than tripled—from $97 million to $324 million. The compounded annual sales growth rate of 13 percent during this period was well in excess of the rates in most other areas of the economy, and to obtain the needed capital for such rapid expansion, a number of firms considered merging and/or "going public" (i.e., selling stock on the open market). In the early '60s, mergers, acquisitions, and public stock offerings reached almost feverish proportions for an industry considered to be conservative and relatively unsophisticated in its management. Also, many new firms entered the industry, and by the end of the decade there was heavy competition for the college textbook dollar.

THE SEVENTIES The flower of the '60s quickly lost its bloom in 1970 when the textbook sales growth rate fell substantially, due mainly to a decline in college FTE (fulltime equivalent) enrollments and student per capita expenditures on books. Because of the abolition of the draft and the turmoil created by the Vietnam War, students were not entering college in as large numbers as the 1960s, and those who did were simply not buying as many textbooks. Moreover, a number of other forces developed which tended to offset the previously high demand for college texts, including student sharing of books, the improved efficiency of used book dealers, and increased usage of copying machines. Finally—and perhaps most importantly in the long run—traditionally clear-cut demarcations of both markets and products were breaking down. Curricular changes in many colleges and universities made "standard" textbooks less appropriate if not obsolete for many courses (particularly in the social sciences), and many so-called "trade" books (books of general interest) began to be regularly adopted for classroom use.

Added together, these environmental conditions produced a very poor year for college textbook publishing companies in fiscal 1971 (April 1972), and due to the subsequent recession and inflation that plagued the economy, 1972 and 1973 were only marginally better. However, just when publishers' concerns were being more frequently and openly expressed, college enrollments markedly increased in the fall of 1974, particularly among parttime and female students. This enrollment increase, combined with higher per capita expenditures on texts and a general price increase reflecting the rapidly escalating cost of paper, produced excellent revenue and profit figures for most textbook publishers in fiscal 1974. However, it is still too early to tell whether or not this improvement represents a trend in the industry.

Today approximately seventy-five firms publish college textbooks, perhaps fifteen to twenty accounting for over 90 percent of total industry net sales (approximately $454 million in 1974). The majority of college publishers are located in the East (Boston, New York City, Philadelphia), with a few scattered firms in the West and Midwest. All college textbook companies can be classified as "specialty publishers" (those that publish in a limited number of academic disciplines) or "general publishers" (those that publish in most or all disciplines), and some companies, in addition to texts, publish trade books and other types of educational materials. Finally, some firms are independently owned while others are subsidiaries of larger organizations (e.g., Holt, Rinehart and Winston, Inc. is a wholly-owned subsidiary of CBS).

Key Industry Statistics

Among all the available information about the industry, statistical data concerning the following areas are of major interest to college publishers: (1) sales of all types of educational materials in the domestic market, (2) domestic and foreign sales of college textbooks, (3) sales of college materials by type of discipline, and (4) college enrollments and per capita expenditures on textbooks. This information is presented in the series of exhibits below, along with several projections concerning possible developing trends in the industry.

ALL EDUCATIONAL MATERIALS Estimated sales of all types of books and materials in the domestic educational market for 1974 are shown in Exhibit 1.

EXHIBIT 1 ESTIMATED SALES OF BOOKS AND MATERIALS IN THE DOMESTIC EDUCATIONAL MARKET, 1974

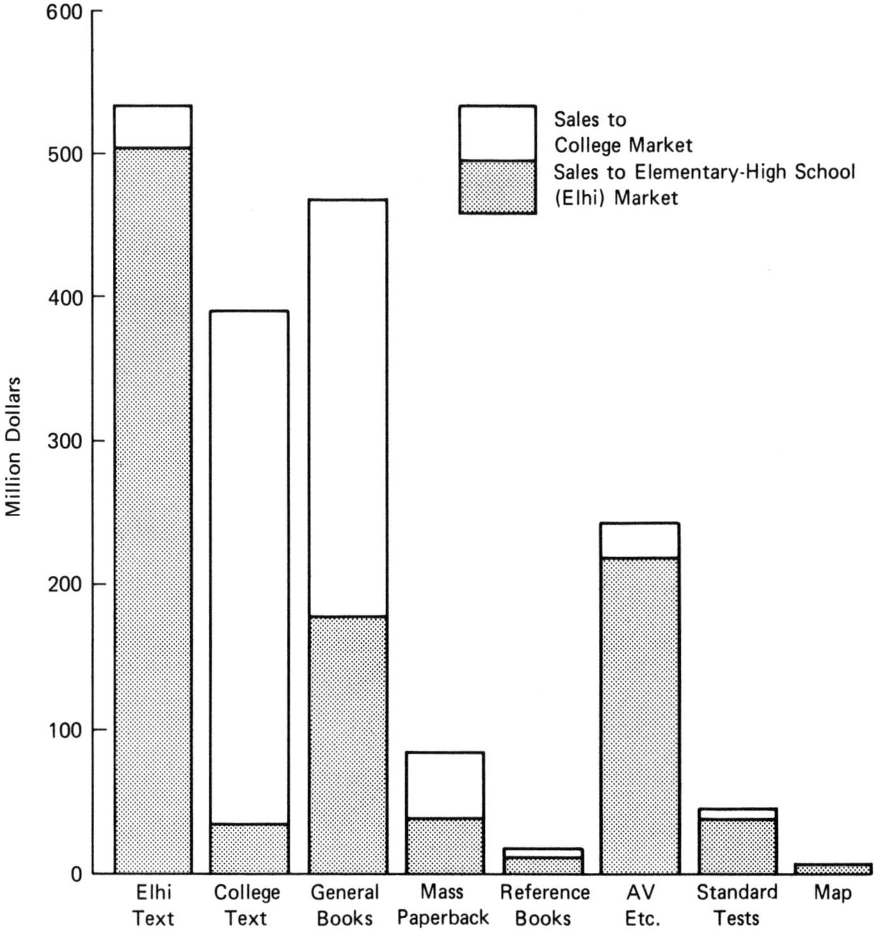

Source: Association of American Publishers, Inc., 1974 Industry Statistics

COLLEGE TEXTBOOK SALES Domestic and foreign sales of college textbooks for the years 1971–1974 are shown in Exhibit 2.

SALES BY DISCIPLINE 1973-74 sales of college textbooks and materials in major disciplines, as reported by a sample of twenty-five publishers, are shown in Exhibit 3.

ENROLLMENTS AND PER CAPITA EXPENDITURES Trend data on college enrollments, per capita expenditures, and purchases of texts are shown in Exhibit 4. For the past twenty years, opening fall degree-credit enrollments have typically grown three percentage points faster each year than the corresponding growth rate of the "college-age" 18–21-year-old population, while in recent years nondegree-credit enrollments have risen even faster. On the average, college publishers' revenues run approximately 1½ to 2 times the enrollment growth rate.

ENROLLMENT BY TYPE OF INSTITUTION In addition to projected changes in the rate of enrollment growth, the distribution of enrollments by type of educational institution is expected to change also. Over the next decade, enrollment growth in four-year colleges and universities is expected to be only slightly higher than the growth rate of the population as a whole (2–3 percent a year). By contrast, the number of students attending two-year colleges has increased by approximately 10 percent a year from 1970 to 1975 and is projected to increase by 5 percent annually from 1975 to 1980. As a result, enrollments in two-year institutions may account for one-third of total FTE (fulltime equivalent) enrollments by 1980, as opposed to about one-fourth in 1970.

EXHIBIT 2 NET SALES, RETURNS, AND FOREIGN SALES OF COLLEGE TEXTBOOKS, 1971–74

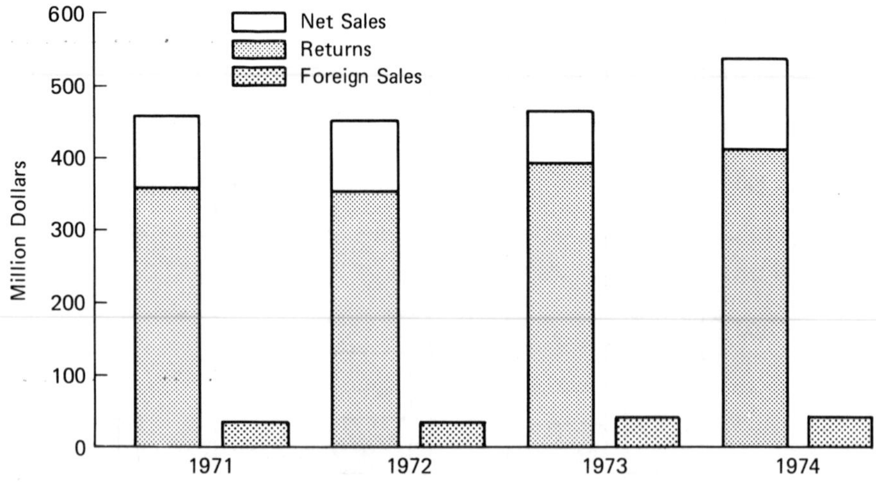

Source: Association of American Publishers, Inc., 1974 Industry Statistics

EXHIBIT 3 DOMESTIC NET SALES (AS A PERCENTAGE OF TOTAL SALES) OF COLLEGE TEXTBOOKS AND MATERIALS BY SUBJECT CATEGORIES 1973–74*

	1973 *% of Total*	*1974* *% of Total*
English Language, Literature	6.7	7.4
Speech, Drama, Mass Media	2.7	2.5
French	0.8	0.8
German	0.4	0.5
Spanish	1.1	1.0
Other Foreign Languages	0.3	0.3
Music	1.4	1.5
Art, Architecture	1.6	1.6
Religion, Philosophy	1.2	1.3
Electrical Engineering	1.3	1.1
Other Engineering	5.0	4.6
Career Education, Occupational Education	3.8	4.3
Accounting	4.8	5.2
Business Education	1.9	1.9
Business Administration	7.1	7.1
Economics	3.0	3.3
Mathematics	7.8	7.5
Chemistry (including Biochemistry)	3.5	4.2
Physics, Physical Science Survey	2.9	2.6
Astronomy	0.5	0.6
Biology	4.4	4.2
Geology, Earth Science	1.8	1.9
Home Economics	0.6	0.6
Health Education, Physical Education	1.6	1.5
Sociology	3.9	4.2
Anthropology	1.4	1.4
Political Science, Public Service, Administration	3.2	3.1
History	3.5	3.6
Psychology	7.6	7.5
Education	6.4	6.6
Nursing, Allied Health	2.8	1.4
Geography	1.2	1.1
Computers	2.2	1.9
General Reference Dictionaries	0.0	0.0
Miscellaneous	1.7	2.0
Unspecified		
TOTAL	100.0	100.0

**Twenty-five reporting publishers.*
Source: Association of American Publishers, Inc., 1974 Industry Statistics.

EXHIBIT 4 COLLEGE ENROLLMENTS, PER CAPITA EXPENDITURES, AND TEXTBOOK PURCHASES, 1945–83

	Opening Fall Degree-Credit Enrollments	*Opening Fall Nondegree-Credit Enrollments*	*Per Capita Expenditures ($)*	*Average Number of Texts Purchased per Student*	*Average Purchase Price ($)*
1945	1,457,000	NA	NA	NA	NA
1950	2,324,000	NA	NA	NA	NA
1955	2,660,000	151,000	NA	6.4	3.16
1960	3,583,000	189,000	NA	7.3	3.72
1965	5,526,000	395,000	36.00	9.6	3.84
1970	7,920,000	661,000	41.36	9.3	4.40
1975	8,665,000	1,238,000	45.65	8.9	5.63
1980	9,210,000*	1,546,000	—	—	—
1983	8,940,000*	1,637,000	—	—	—

**Projected*
Sources: National Center for Educational Statistics, Department of Health, Education and Welfare, Projections of Educational Statistics to 1983–84, *1974 edition; Association of American Publishers, 1974 Industry Statistics.*

As the composition of college students shifts more toward the two-year schools, the continuing concentration of students on a relatively small number of campuses is also likely to occur. Currently, the concentration picture is as follows:

> 270 campuses (9 percent of total) with more than 10,000 FTE students account for 52 percent of total college enrollments.
>
> 600 campuses (19 percent) with more than 5,000 FTE students account for 73 percent of enrollments.
>
> The remaining 2,600 campuses account for 27 percent of enrollments.

Geographically speaking, the Midwest and Northeast represent the two largest segments of total college enrollments.

SUBJECT MATTER GROWTH RATES As a consequence of these shifting enrollment trends, the various segments of the college textbook market may experience different growth rates in the future. For example, in 1973 one panel of industry executives forecasted the following sales trends by discipline over the next several years:

Vocational-technical	+ 19%
Business and Economics	+ 13%
Professional (engineering, law, medicine, etc.)	+ 2%
Science and Mathematics	− 6%
Social Sciences, Humanities	− 7%

Over the longer run (through 1980), sales forecasts for major types of courses according to a different breakdown are as follows:

Vocational-technical	+ 12–15%
Remedial courses	+ 6– 7%
Courses for majors	+ 6%
Introductory and basic survey courses	+ 2– 3%

DESCRIPTION OF THE COMPANY

History

Currently one of the largest college textbook publishing companies, Modern Publishing Company began as a small printing shop and bookstore in New York City. Originally a publisher of literary works, the firm, under a succession of managers who were descendants of Modern's founder, gradually moved into the publication of educational materials. By the time the firm was incorporated, approximately one hundred years later, the publication of general literature had been virtually abandoned, and the modern imprint has since become almost exclusively associated with works of a scientific and educational nature.

Definition of Business

The company, with 1974 net sales of over $52 million, currently defines its business as the publication of college textbooks and professional and reference books, including encyclopedias and scientific journals. Sales in these major product categories over the past five years are shown below.

	Years Ended April 30 (In Thousands)				
	1975	1974	1973	1972	1971
Educational materials	$27,964	$24,086	$23,312	$22,402	$21,730
Professional and reference materials and services	22,123	17,704	14,881	13,758	11,640
Journals	2,509	2,164	1,770	1,683	1,614
	$52,596	$43,954	$39,963	$37,843	$34,984

In the past, Modern largely concentrated its publishing efforts in the natural sciences, mathematics, and computers, and today these areas account for over half of the company's business. These "hard-science" sales are followed by sales in the humanities and social sciences. Modern's business and economics titles rank a distant third in total sales, while sales in the vocational-technical area represent the smallest portion of the company's overall business.

Based upon available industry statistics, Modern believes that it accounts for approximately 6 percent of the total sales of United States-developed undergraduate textbooks, approximately 4 percent of all United States-published professional and reference book sales other than medical books, and about 1 percent of United States-published medical books. The company knows of no reliable industry statistics that would enable it to determine its share of the sales of journals and encyclopedias.

Competitive Strategy

The publishing industry is highly competitive. As seen in the list below, Modern's major competitors differ according to discipline. However, the names of two competitors, McGraw-Hill and Prentice-Hall, appear in all four categories, and it may be helpful to briefly describe their publishing strategies in order to give a flavor of the competition Modern faces.

Natural Science, Math	*Humanities, Social Science*	*Business, Economics*	*Vocational, Technical*
Addison-Wesley	Harcourt Brace Jovanovich	Richard D. Irwin	ATS
McGraw-Hill	Holt, Rinehart, and Winston	McGraw-Hill	Delmar
Prentice-Hall	McGraw-Hill	Prentice-Hall	McGraw-Hill
Wiley	Macmillan	South-Western	Prentice-Hall
	Prentice-Hall		
	Scott-Foresman		
	Wiley		

As stated earlier, Prentice-Hall was the first company to conduct its publishing activities as a business operation, and this company is still recognized today as having the most aggressive (and largest) sales force. Prentice-Hall publishes in every significant field and from the "bottom" (freshman) to the "top" (Ph.D.s and practicing professionals) of the market. Its editors are expected to be aware of every professor who may have writing plans and to make certain that Prentice-Hall is an active bidder on projects in which the company is interested. Operations in this company are very tightly controlled, all employees are developed from within the organization, and management is constantly on the alert for reducing inefficiency and waste. In general, it may be said that Prentice-Hall does not "chase" new developments in the industry, but once the organization decides to pursue a new venture, it does so forcefully.

The McGraw-Hill Book Company, as only part of a larger publishing and communications organization, is listed among the *Fortune* 500. An equally strong competitor as Prentice-Hall, McGraw-Hill has tended to achieve its reputation on the editorial rather than the sales side of the business—innovative publishing techniques and programs, experiments with new and potentially profitable educational opportunities, etc. McGraw-Hill has in the past been able to draw upon a large amount of resources, allowing it to develop a number of publishing innovations, many of which were later adopted by other firms. Like Prentice-Hall, McGraw-Hill publishes widely and at all levels, but to a greater extent than its competitor; this organization is continually prospecting for new and hopefully profitable opportunities.

Against these and, it should be emphasized, other significant competitors, Modern Publishing Company has achieved a respected position in the industry without displaying the "flashiness" of some of the other publishing houses. Modern is regarded, both from within and outside the organization, as an essentially cautious but watchful analyzer of industry developments. The company is widely acknowledged as solidly managed, adaptive when it needs to be, and one of the leaders in quality publications and in sales to foreign countries.

Organization Structure

Modern's organization structure as of January 1, 1975 is shown in Exhibit 5. Prior to 1961, Modern was a unified company publishing both textbooks and professional and reference books. Beginning in that year, the first of a number of important organizational changes was made. In order to make a deeper penetration into the foreign book market, Modern acquired Euroscience, a highly regarded foreign publisher of professional and reference books primarily in the areas of chemistry, physics, the applied sciences, engineering, and technology. This firm publishes "European style"—high-level technical tracts on scientific topics for which there is a limited market. Today Modern-Euroscience operations are located in New York City, and this division's mission is to publish all Modern materials geared toward the second-year graduate student market and higher. Modern-Euroscience sales in 1974 were $13.2 million.

In 1968 the College Division was created as a separate division, and all of Modern's professional and reference books were incorporated into the Modern-Euroscience list. The College Division publishes in most fields for the freshman through first-year graduate student market. Sales in 1974 were nearly $28 million, up 16 percent over the previous year.

Eldorado Publishing Company was formed in 1971 as a small, wholly-owned subsidiary in California. Although not large, this company was intended to be a "full-service" publisher (i.e., not limited to a few disciplines) and was specifically created to give Modern West Coast "representation" along with several other major firms. Moreover, the company was to experiment with publishing briefer, better written, and more colorful books on certain "core" topics in a wide variety of disciplines. Many of Eldorado's books were to be supplemented with films and other audio-visual materials in order to form complete "learning packages." In the few years since its inception, Eldorado has published a number of successful books; in 1974, it published eleven new titles for undergraduate courses in the sciences, mathematics, computer science, business, and psychology.

The formation of Eldorado Publishing was followed in 1972 by the creation of the Fox Publishing Company, also located in California. This company was formed to publish both textbooks and professional and reference books in the fields of information science, accounting, library sciences, and computer applications. Fox was to be a "fully vertical" publisher in that it would concentrate on the freshman to professional market.

The most recent additions to the Company are the Health Care Division and Progressive Press. The objective of the Health Care Division, already partly achieved after only two years of operation, is to become an influential and well-rounded publisher of quality materials for the vast health-care market. New textbooks, reference books, and audio-visual materials are currently being developed for nursing education and in-service training and for the continuing education of physicians and allied health personnel.

EXHIBIT 5 ORGANIZATION CHART—MODERN PUBLISHING COMPANY, INC. (JANUARY 1975)

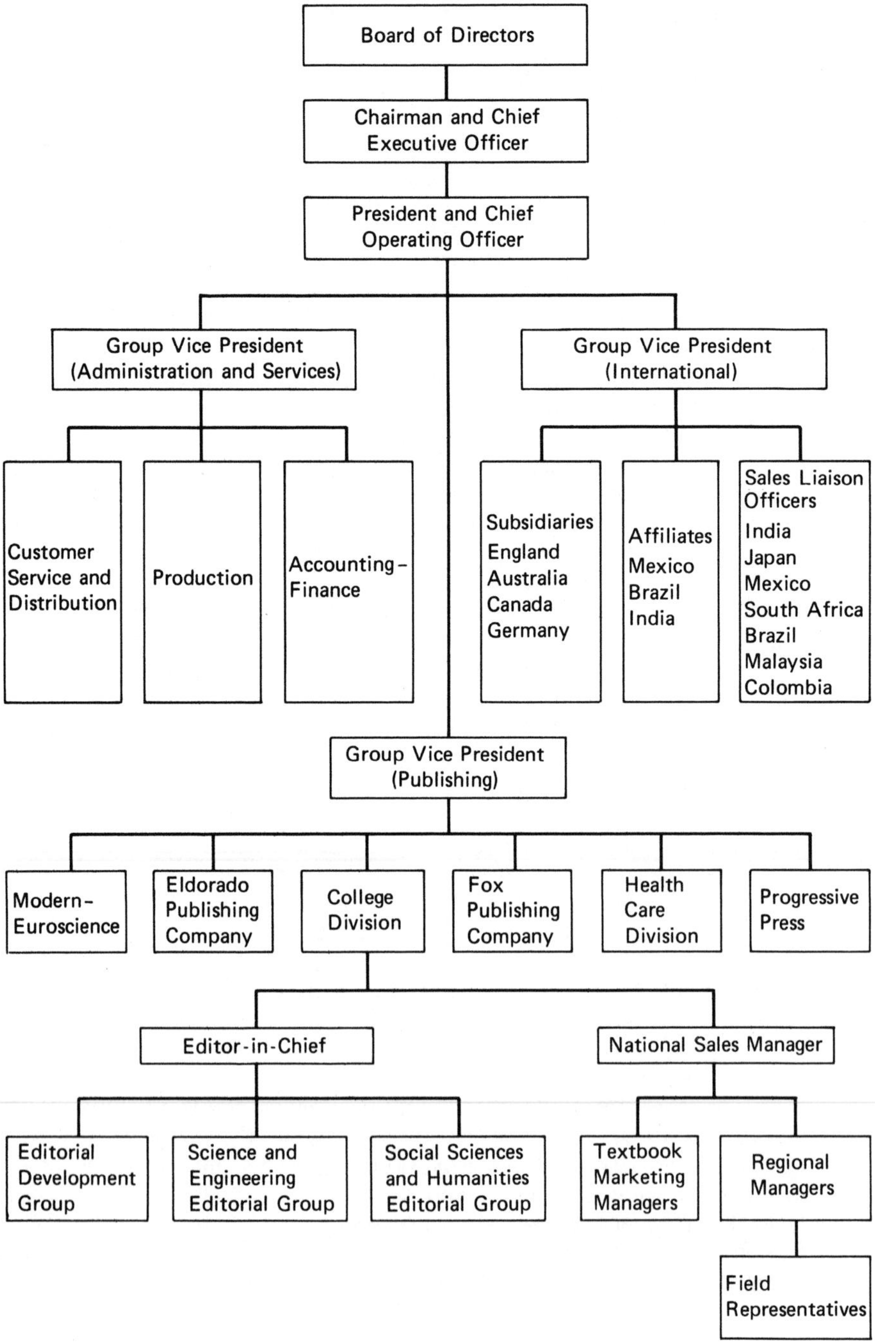

Progressive Press, an English firm, publishes books by European authors, some of which are distributed in the U.S. through Modern's facilities. Progressive Press publishes in many of the same areas as Modern, especially the life and medical sciences, earth sciences, psychology/psychiatry, and environmental, urban, and political studies. Sales of Progressive Press increased 51 percent last year, following a 106 percent increase the previous year.

Finally, the company's International Division is responsible for sales outside of the United States and has administrative responsibility for foreign subsidiaries. This division sells foreign reprint and translation rights, adapts Modern products for sale abroad, and publishes low-cost editions of textbooks for students in foreign countries.

The company's publications are sold throughout most of the world, either through the company's foreign subsidiaries or directly by the International Division to Latin America, the Middle East, the Far East, New Zealand, Southeast Asia, South Africa, Canada, the United Kingdom, Continental Europe, Central Africa, Australia, and India. Modern also maintains sales liaison offices in Japan, India, South Africa, Brazil, Malaysia, Mexico, and Colombia.

Modern's Canadian, British, and Australian subsidiaries publish titles under their own imprints. The company's Mexican affiliate, Mexico-Modern, S. A., publishes translations of Modern and other publishers' textbooks as well as original titles in the Spanish language. Its books are marketed for the most part in Mexico and in Central and South America. The company's Brazilian affiliate, Brazil-Modern, S. A., publishes translations of Modern and other publishers' books in Portuguese. Its books are marketed for the most part in Brazil. The company's Indian affiliate, Modern Eastern, Ltd., publishes reprints of U. S. editions, original Indian publications, and translations from German to English. Its books are marketed primarily in India.

Set forth below is the approximate volume of Modern's consolidated foreign sales for each of the last five fiscal years.

Fiscal Year	*Approximate Volume of Sales*
Year ended April 30, 1971	$10,300,000
Year ended April 30, 1972	11,650,000
Year ended April 30, 1973	12,400,000
Year ended April 30, 1974	14,000,000
Year ended April 30, 1975	16,950,000

Publishing, Distribution and Marketing

The "publishing" of a college textbook involves five major steps: (1) determining the type of book that is needed for a particular subject, (2) locating an author, (3) obtaining an acceptable manuscript, (4) preparing the manuscript for "production," and (5) subcontracting the manuscript to a printing and binding company to be typeset, printed, and bound. Finished books are then transferred directly to Modern's Eastern Distribution Center in New York and its Western Distribution Center in Chicago. From these distribution centers, books are distributed to college bookstores as orders are received. Modern's distribution system is frequently ranked as first or second in customer service by the National Association of College Bookstores.

Responsibility for deciding upon the type of manuscript to be obtained falls primarily on the field editors. Each editor has a list of manuscript needs in his area (e.g., biology), and he works closely with the editor-in-chief, the field sales staff, outside academic advisors, and others in order to determine the kind of text desired.

Finding potential authors, perhaps the most critical and difficult aspect of textbook publishing, can be approached in five primary ways: (1) "over-the-transom" (manuscripts that arrive unsolicited), (2) through the efforts of field editors, (3) through advisory editors (professors retained by Modern for their advice and assistance in manuscript procurement), (4) through the company's field representatives (salesmen), and (5) by commissioning authors (e.g., professors on sabbatical) to write a specific book. Modern, as do most other major publishers, obtains the majority of its authors through the efforts of the company's own editors and field representatives.

The next step is to draw up a contract with the author, setting the terms for royalties, date of completion of the manuscript, etc. Once a completed manuscript arrives—sometimes years later and usually after numerous give-and-take sessions between the author and the field editor—the manuscript is "put into production." This involves assigning the manuscript to a team of artists, designers, and copy editors in the Production Department (see Exhibit 5) who are responsible for determining the typeface, graphics, and style of paper, and for performing detailed copy editing. The Production Department serves both the College Division and Modern-Euroscience.

While the book is in production, the editor begins to develop a program for marketing the text by turning his or her needs over to a textbook marketing manager. A comprehensive marketing campaign, planned and coordinated by the textbook marketing manager, includes such things as the "packaging" of the book in terms of advertising and promotion, the timing of the book's arrival in the marketplace and at academic conventions, and the like.

When the manuscript comes out of production, it is first sent to the author for approval and then to the printer and binder. Modern, as well as all other college publishers, does not do its own printing and binding because of the high cost of the required equipment and the necessity of keeping this type of equipment running continuously. The company has contracts with many printing and binding firms in the U. S. and several foreign countries, each of which transforms manuscripts into book form and then ships them directly to Modern's warehouses.

In sum, the steps required to create a Modern textbook—from a professor's belief that "I can write the book this field needs" to the bookstore clerk's placing of the finished product on the shelf—takes on the average four to five years to complete.

Financial Resources

The company's most recent balance sheet and income statement are shown in Exhibits 6 and 7. Financial highlights for the previous five years are shown in Exhibit 8.

EXHIBIT 6 CONSOLIDATED BALANCE SHEETS
MODERN PUBLISHING COMPANY, INC.

Assets	*April 30, 1975*	*April 30, 1974*
Current Assets		
Cash	$ 928,000	$ 1,970,000
Certificates of deposit	1,200,000	2,500,000
Accounts receivable, less allowance for doubtful accounts of $347,000 and $288,000 respectively	11,871,000	9,872,000
Inventories	21,054,000	15,197,000
Prepaid expenses and income taxes	933,000	817,000
Total Current Assets	35,986,000	30,356,000
Property and Equipment, at Cost		
Land and buildings	1,579,000	1,501,000
Furniture and equipment	1,922,000	1,772,000
Leasehold improvements	774,000	563,000
	4,275,000	3,836,000
Less: Accumulated depreciation and amortization	1,403,000	1,441,000
	2,872,000	2,395,000
Cost of Titles Acquired, Less Accumulated Depreciation	488,000	—
Royalty Advances	1,991,000	1,788,000
Investments in Affiliates, at Equity	1,493,000	1,130,000
Other Assets	163,000	662,000
	$42,993,000	$36,331,000

Liabilities and Shareholders' Equity	*April 30, 1975*	*April 30, 1974*
Current Liabilities		
Notes payable	$ 2,884,000	$ 1,210,000
Accounts payable	4,720,000	3,527,000
Royalties payable	2,640,000	2,344,000
Accrued federal and foreign income taxes	2,085,000	1,752,000
Other accrued liabilities	1,500,000	1,048,000
Unearned subscription income	1,514,000	1,401,000
Total Current Liabilities	15,343,000	11,282,000
Deferred Income Taxes	104,000	—
Commitments		
Shareholders' Equity		
Capital stock $1 par value authorized, 4,000,000 shares; issued, 1,578,586 shares	1,579,000	1,579,000
Capital contributed in excess of par value of capital stock	12,465,000	12,465,000
Retained earnings	14,502,000	12,005,000
Less 36,697 Treasury Shares at Cost	1,000,000	1,000,000
	27,546,000	25,049,000
	$42,993,000	$36,331,000

Source: Annual Report, April 30, 1975

EXHIBIT 7 STATEMENTS OF CONSOLIDATED INCOME AND RETAINED EARNINGS—MODERN PUBLISHING COMPANY, INC. AND SUBSIDIARIES

	For Years Ended *April 30, 1975*	*April 30, 1974*
Net Sales	$52,596,000	$43,954,000
Cost of Sales	22,327,000	18,506,000
Gross Profit on Sales	30,269,000	25,448,000
Other Publishing Income	498,000	418,000
	30,767,000	25,866,000
Operating and Administrative Expenses	23,905,000	19,739,000
Income from operations	6,862,000	6,127,000
Other Income (Expense)		
Interest expense	(267,000)	(81,000)
Other, net	278,000	(42,000)
Income before income taxes and extraordinary item	6,873,000	6,004,000
Provision for Income Taxes		
Federal and foreign	2,996,000	2,710,000
State and local	455,000	420,000
	3,451,000	3,130,000
Income before extraordinary item	3,442,000	2,874,000
Extraordinary Item	—	(253,000)
Net Income	3,422,000	2,621,000
Retained Earnings at Beginning of Year	12,005,000	10,063,000
	15,427,000	12,684,000
Cash Dividends ($.60 per Share in 1975 and $.44 per Share in 1974)	925,000	679,000
Retained Earnings at End of Year	$14,502,000	$12,005,000
Earnings per Share of Capital Stock		
Income before extraordinary item	$2.22	$1.86
Extraordinary item	—	(.16)
Net income	$2.22	$1.70
Working Capital Provided from		
Income before extraordinary item	$ 3,422,000	$ 2,874,000
Items not affecting working capital		
Depreciation and amortization		
Property and equipment	284,000	218,000
Deferred charges and other	264,000	488,000

Write-off of deferred charges	244,000	—
Deferred income taxes	104,000	128,000
Equity in income of affiliated companies	(127,000)	(168,000)
Working capital provided from operations before extraordinary item	4,191,000	3,540,000
Working capital effect of extraordinary item	—	62,000
	4,191,000	3,602,000
Working Capital Expended for		
Cash dividends	925,000	679,000
Additions to fixed assets	761,000	834,000
Cost of titles acquired	500,000	—
Increase in investments in affiliated companies	235,000	189,000
Increase in royalty advances	204,000	191,000
Increase (decrease) in other assets	(3,000)	257,000
	2,622,000	2,150,000
Increase in Working Capital	$ 1,569,000	$ 1,452,000
Changes in Working Capital Represented by		
Current assets—increase (decrease)		
Cash	(1,042,000)	1,045,000
Certificates of deposit	(1,300,000)	1,248,000
Accounts receivable	1,999,000	1,202,000
Inventories	5,857,000	408,000
Prepaid expenses and income taxes	116,000	232,000
Net Increase	5,630,000	4,135,000
Current Liabilities—Increase (Decrease)		
Notes payable	1,674,000	1,210,000
Accounts payable	1,193,000	(89,000)
Royalties payable	296,000	233,000
Accrued Federal and foreign income taxes	333,000	591,000
Other accrued liabilities	452,000	416,000
Unearned subscription income	113,000	322,000
Net Increase	4,061,000	2,683,000
Increase in Working Capital	$ 1,569,000	$ 1,452,000

Source: Annual Report, April 30, 1975

EXHIBIT 8 CONSOLIDATED SUMMARY OF OPERATIONS

	Years Ended April 30 (In Thousands)				
	1975	*1974*	*1973*	*1972*	*1971*
Net Sales	$52,596	$43,954	$39,963	$37,843	$34,984
Cost of Sales	22,327	18,506	17,256	16,797	14,310
Gross profit on sales	30,269	25,448	22,707	21,046	20,674
Other Publishing Income	498	418	337	356	328
	30,767	25,866	23,044	21,402	21,002
Operating and Administrative Expenses	23,905	19,739	17,982	17,251	15,862
Income from Operations	6,862	6,127	5,062	4,151	5,140
Other Income (Expense)					
Interest Expense	(267)	(81)	(26)	(78)	(71)
Other, net[2]	278	(42)	(31)	142	166
	11	(123)	(57)	64	95
Income before Income Taxes and Extraordinary Items	6,873	6,004	5,005	4,125	5,235
Provision for income taxes					
Federal and foreign	2,996	2,710	2,185	1,825	2,358
State and local	455	420	339	265	278
	3,451	3,130	2,524	2,090	2,636
Income before extraordinary items	3,422	2,874	2,481	2,125	2,599
Extraordinary Items[3]	—	(253)	—	(412)	—
Net Income	$ 3,422	$ 2,621	$ 2,481	$ 1,713	$ 2,599
Earnings Per Share[1]					
Income before extraordinary items	$2.22	$1.86	$1.61	$1.37	$1.65
Net income	$2.22	$1.70	$1.61	$1.11	$1.65
Dividends Per Share	$ .60	$ .44	$ .40	$ .36	$ .30
Net Working Capital	$20,643	$19,074	$17,622	$16,423	$16,198
Shareholders' Equity	$27,546	$25,049	$23,107	$21,243	$21,044
Shareholders' Equity per Share[1]	$17.87	$16.25	$14.99	$13.78	$13.34

1. *Based on the weighted average number of shares outstanding.*
2. *Year ended April 30, 1971 restated to reflect equity method accounting for investments in non-consolidated affiliated companies.*
3. *In fiscal 1974 the company recognized a net loss of $253,000 on the sale of its subsidiary Willard Owsacker & Associates, Inc. In fiscal 1972, the excess of cost over net assets at dates of acquisition applicable to Borst and Besselink, Inc. was written off because of continued unfavorable operating results.*

Source: Annual Report, April 30, 1975

ROSPATCH CORPORATION

COMPANY BACKGROUND 1915–1968

Rospatch Corporation began in September 1915 as Rose Patch & Label Company of Grand Rapids, Michigan. The company has been publicly owned from the beginning. It was founded by Arthur Rosenthal, a one-time freelance cyclist who with his partner, Frank Lemmon, toured Europe—including a command performance for the King and Queen of England—with their "Globe of Death." Rosenthal was described by W. Jackson Chaille, former president and chairman of the board, as an "idea man but not much of a business man." The original purpose of the company was to manufacture machinery for lease—as well as final products to sell—for the cutting and folding of patches and labels.

Most of the equipment was developed from Arthur Rosenthal's ideas. This equipment was to first slit yard goods and then fold it on four sides, manufacturing the patch.

In 1924 the company began manufacturing printed cloth labels on letter presses using stationary type, intaglio engravings. These were later developed into rotary type presses using rotary intaglio engraved cylinders, which improved the production speeds of printing labels.

During the 1930s, Arthur Rosenthal sold most of his interest in the company and reduced his holdings to just below 15 percent. His stock was sold through Grand Rapids brokers.

With the '30s, a young vice president of sales, Lloyd E. Cook, conceived the objective that to succeed the company needed to develop a label that was "color-fast." In 1938, the first "vat-dye process" machines were producing printed labels that could effectively compete with color-fast woven labels. This development was said to have revolutionized the cloth label industry, resulting in printed vat-dyed labels being used in tremendous quantities by manufacturers of work garments, sheets, pillow cases, towels, wash cloths, and other articles that require frequent

---

Prepared by Dr. R. W. Allen, Visiting Professor, Grand Valley State College, F. E. Seidman Graduate College of Business.

washing. Because Rose Patch & Label Company was the first company to develop the vat-dyeing process for printed cloth labels, they became known as the source for quality fast-color printed labels throughout the industry.

In November 1939, Rosenthal died. One month later, Cook was elected president and general manager by the board. Cook inherited a company with a net worth of $161,000 and a 1939 net profit of $3,120 on $200,000 sales. He immediately appointed W. Jackson Chaille as sales manager and they consolidated and/or ceased to manufacture various novelty products in order to concentrate on labels and label machinery.

Under Cook's leadership, the company refined and improved the vat-dyed labels. The company's Machine Division was continuing to improve and modify the cloth label cutting and folding machines that were leased throughout the woven label industry.

The company's financial picture continued to improve due to the company's derived demand relationship to the textile industry, where growth relationships were approximately one for one. In 1949, $1,000,000 in sales was exceeded for the first time and by 1948 past business earnings had become sufficient to insure the first dividend.

The company's first major acquisition in 1956 was Stylecraft Packaging Service, Inc., located in Charlotte, North Carolina. The Stylecraft subsidiary was and is a film converter. Its products were flexible packaging films such as cellophane, polyethylene, polypropolene converted into attractively printed bags, and roll stock. The acquisition made possible diversification into the packaging industry.

After twenty years as president and chief executive officer, Cook was replaced as president by Chaille in 1959. Cook had increased the company's net worth 1,171 percent to $1,267,000, and net profit from $3,120 on $200,000 sales to $253,000 on $3,000,000 sales.

Under Chaille, in the early 1960s expansion planning was started for European Common Market countries. In 1964, a European screen printer was purchased and modified to enable the printing of labels using the screen printing process. This allowed for the development of metallic and opaque inks and the printing processes that were to provide sales entry into the prestige garment industry.

In 1968 the company exceeded $10,000,000 in sales. A national survey done by Rospatch, with the cooperation of one of the country's largest retail organizations, asked the public to determine which of two garments, one with a woven label and the other with a printed label, was the best. The result was that consumers rated garments with a printed label as good or better than the identical item with a woven label in terms of quality, price, and prestige associations. As a result of this survey, mass merchandisers and many of the larger textile and garment manufacturers have expedited programs to replace woven labels with Rospatch printed labels.

Prior to 1965 the company had purchased narrow fabric tape on which labels were printed from various suppliers. The company decided to expand vertically and build a plant to produce its own tape in order to assure higher quality label production. Land was purchased in Lenoir, North Carolina, and the company proceeded to build a weaving mill. It started producing tape in 1965 and is presently operating 150 high-speed modern narrow fabric looms which operate on a three-shift basis.

After ten years as president, Chaille was replaced by Richard F. Brush in 1969. Chaille had further increased the company's net worth 431 percent to $5,465,000 and net profit from $253,000 on $3,000,000 sales to $788,400 on $14,305,700 sales.

RICHARD F. BRUSH ADMINISTRATION 1969–1975

The following conversation from Lewis Carroll's *Alice's Adventures in Wonderland* might describe the preceding managements' approach to business.

> "Would you tell me please, which way I ought to go from here?" asked Alice.
>
> "That depends a good deal on where you want to get to," said the Cat.
>
> "I don't much care where—," said Alice.
>
> "Then it doesn't matter which way you go," said the Cat.
>
> "—so long as I get somewhere," Alice added as an explanation.
>
> "Oh, you're sure to do that," said the Cat, "if you only walk long enough."

The previous administrations could be defined as entrepreneurships. Administrative policies were not defined and decisions were doing what had to be done. The only unity of thought, purpose, and action was the entrepreneur himself. The only corporate staff services were finance and accounting. The need to develop an overall corporate policy and strategy, was the first priority of Brush.

Policy Formulation

Richard F. Brush was elected president of Rospatch Corporation by the board of directors on February 17, 1969. He came to Rospatch with an impressive record of successful management. He had been president of Root-Lowell Corporation in Lowell, Michigan, a prominent manufacturer of chemical application equipment for the previous eleven years. He had held divisional management positions in the East with two large firms: Orkil, Incorporated and Corn Products Company. Brush is a native of Vermont and a graduate of Duke University's School of Business.

Brush believed that the company should not have to rely on adaptation and be at the mercy of the external and internal environments. There must exist a corporate policy to be formulated and expressed in simple terms for ease of implementation. Both Brush and Chaille felt the need for a critical review of the board of directors.

To form a strong foundation for growth, it was felt that the board needed to be strengthened and higher quality outside consulting services needed to be obtained, as well as larger corporate staff. In strengthening the board, it was felt that the majority should be "outsiders" and not be their own attorney, or auditor (later made illegal, although common practice at the time), or investment banker. As Chaille once said: "If the board is made up by 'insiders' and your own consultants, how can you get them to say *no* to their boss?" Chaille began to strengthen the board composition based on the election of capable "outsiders" as early as 1964 with the addition of a college vice president and a congressman (later President Gerald R. Ford). These men then formed the foundation for the eventual addition of several competent and experienced executives and the establishment of strong board committees. The corporation also established a close relationship with William Blair and Company, investment bankers.

During Brush's first year, 1969, the Electronic Data Processing activities were removed from the Finance Department and established as a separate staff section, Manager Information Systems. The Finance Department was then subdivided into two sections, Treasury and Financial Services and Corporate Controller's Office. A corporate Industrial Relations Department was also established to organize and upgrade all aspects of personnel programming and communication.

The basic corporate objective of controlled growth through acquisitions and mergers was also established and the preliminary guidelines were developed. These guidelines were submitted to the board for approval during December 1969. The general objectives were that Rospatch should maintain its identity, the business of product identification; the company acquired should not be larger than the parent; and the corporate headquarters should remain in Grand Rapids, Michigan.

During 1970, these guidelines were supplemented by the founding of a Corporate Research and Development Department (R & D) and an outline of the long-range planning requirements and objectives of that department. These R & D efforts were to take on one or both of the two classic forms: "Innovation to order," applying presently known technology to meet specific market demands, process, and product redesign; and "Technology push," developing new products flexibly that will be added to existing lines and marketed profitably. The areas were to be new end products, new processes, machinery and methods, cost reductions in manufacturing and materials, improved patent opportunities and/or royalties, and new materials. The areas were divided into the three fields of identification products: existing narrow fabric labels and flexible packaging; special machinery, primarily cutting and folding machines with adaptive accessory hardware for processing printed and woven labels; and narrow fabric tape, for inplant imprinted labels or other than label usage.

Also during 1970, the corporate objectives were further expanded and finalized. The primary objective was to actively seek and acquire other companies which would strengthen and be compatible with present product lines and services, while maintaining a corporate identity of product identification. In a general nature the companies could be within or outside the current product line with a gross sales volume of between $2,000,000 and $10,000,000 per year with a *pre-tax* profit of between $300,000 and $1,000,000 (greater than 15 percent of sales).

There were two acceptable basic methods of acquiring defined: by either cash or stock or a combination of the two. The corporation was prepared to pay a broker's fee to agents who have been authorized by signed agreement, but would make no exclusive agreement with any agent.

On January 1, 1971, the company purchased all the outstanding stock of Textile Marking Machine Company of Syracuse, New York. This wholly owned subsidiary complements both the company's Label Division and Machine Division, inasmuch as it manufactures both machines and enjoys high repeat sales of related supplies for these machines primarily used in marking on cloth for identification purposes. A substantial portion of their products is exported to Canada, Mexico, and Europe.

Also during 1971, the Grand Rapids Rospatch Machine Division of Rospatch Corporation, which manufactures cutting and folding machines, was transferred to Syracuse to become a division of Textile Marking Machine Company, Inc., which was then renamed the Texmark Company. The company also acquired Allenson Products, Inc. of Mundelein, Illinois to complement the company's packaging operations, as it extrudes polyethylene into industrial bags and sheets in three very efficient in-line operations. Its market area is Chicago and the Midwest.

With each of these acquisitions, Rospatch has been able to retain the able and young management of these companies. During this same period, a management reorganization of the two flexible packaging companies, Stylecraft and Munson, placed them in the new Rospatch Packaging Group headquartered in Charlotte, North Carolina.

The first acquisition under the new objectives criteria was the Thermopatch Corporation of Bronx, New York in 1974. The acquisition of Thermopatch Corporation expanded the specialized machine segment of the business into the manufacturing of heat-adhesive, coated products, and heat-sealing and fusing equipment used in permanent labeling systems and the repair of textile products. Thermopatch also markets a line of thermographically produced emblems.

This acquisition satisfied the new objectives by further emphasizing the company's product identification image as well as increasing the company's net worth. Thermopatch's diversified identification product supplies and foreign market distribution capabilities have strengthened the company's machine group. The possibility existed of Texmark furnishing Thermopatch machines and Thermopatch furnishing Texmark supplies for both the European and domestic markets, while maintaining dual distributions. This would enhance market coverage as well as improve customer service capabilities. A further possibility is the restructuring of these companies.

During 1974, an overall organization and expansion plan started to take place and form a unity of purpose. The various divisions were grouped into a three-group product-centered organization. This decentralization placed the accountability and ultimate responsibility for profitable operation at the product level.

The three major groups established were the Label and Tape Group; the Packaging Group; and the Machinery, Equipment, and Specialized Supplies Group. The Label and Tape operations (production of printed fabric labels and narrow fabric tape for the textile and apparel industries) are composed of the Rospatch Label, Rospatch Fabric Tape, and Rospatch Coating Divisions. The Packaging operations (extrusion and printing of polyethylene, as well as printing of cellophane, polypropylene rolls, bags, sheets and various laminations for the textile, food, and general industries) are composed of the Stylecraft Packaging, Munson Packaging, and Allenson Products Divisions. The Machinery, Equipment, and Specialized Supplies operations manufacture a variety of cloth cutting, folding, and marking machines; mending material and heat sensitive emblems for institutions and industrial garments; expandable tapes; and coated ink ribbons used on these machines. The Machinery operation is composed largely of the Texmark Division and Thermopatch Corporation. Exhibit 1 shows a 1975 partial organization chart, and Exhibit 2 gives background information on the 1975 management group.

Results

The company has shown continued growth in sales during Brush's administration. The Five Year Summary of Operations (Table 1) reveals growth in net sales of 60 percent. Net earnings had increased 25 percent for the first four years but decreased 44 percent from 1974 to 1975.

An analysis of the percentage contributions to sales and net earnings for each of the product groups, as seen in Table 2, reveals a sales and profit decrease for the Label and Tape Group.

Financial Situation

As seen in Table 2, during the 1975 recession year sales decreased at the Label Division. Combined with a foreign sales decrease at the Texmark Division, this resulted in a consolidated sales decrease of 5 percent from 1974, excluding the acquisition of Thermopatch Corporation. The acquisition of Thermopatch was solely responsible for the 14 percent increase in sales. However, this increase in sales was offset by increased selling and administrative expenses associated with the acquisition.[1]

EXHIBIT 1 ROSPATCH CORPORATION ORGANIZATION CHART JULY 1975 (PARTIAL)

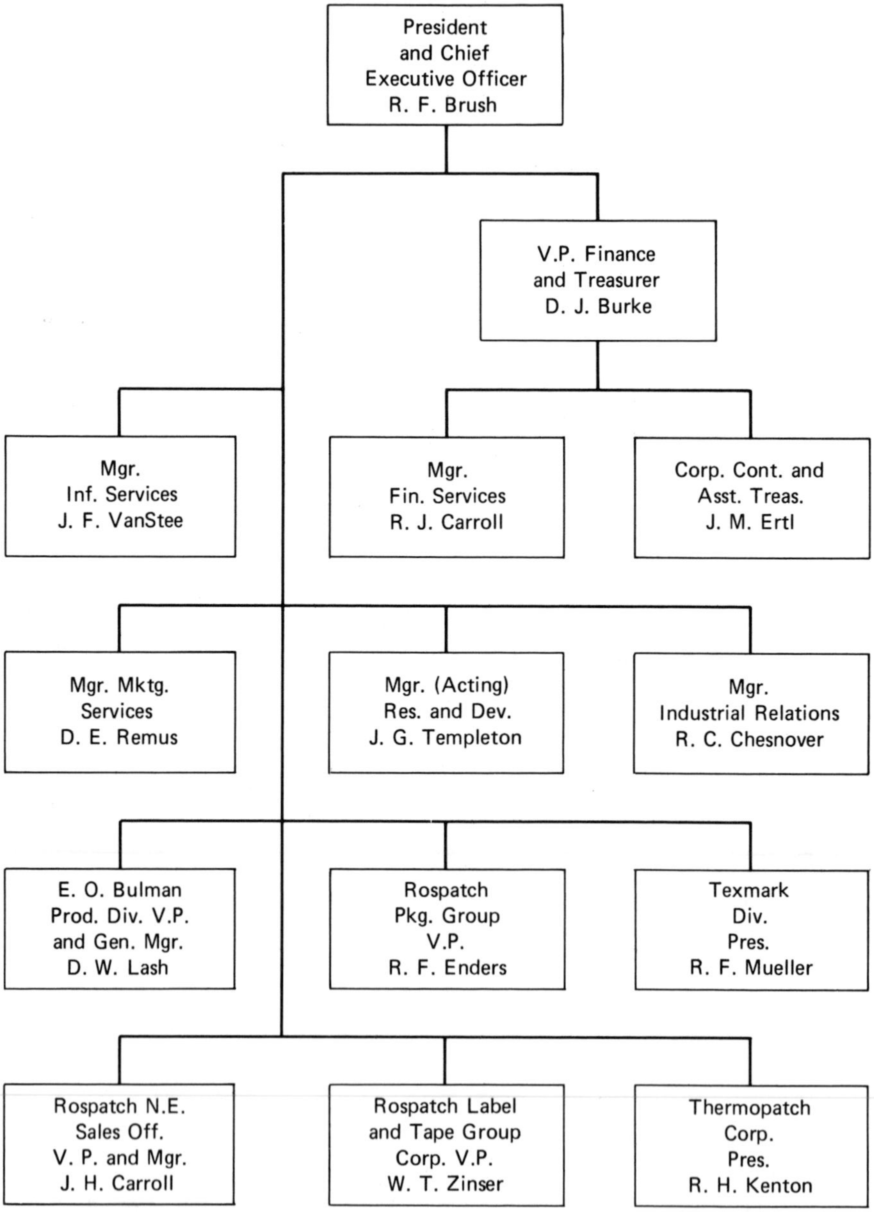

Source: Company records.

EXHIBIT 2 ROSPATCH CORPORATION MANAGEMENT PROFILE

Name	*Position*	*Years with Rospatch*	*Years in Present Position*	*Age*	*Education*	*Functional Background*
Richard F. Brush	President	7	7	57	BA	Sales
Donald J. Burke	V.P. Finance	3	1	46	BS	Control
James M. Ertl	Corp. Controller	3	1	48	BS	Control
Russell J. Carroll	Mgr. Fin. Services	7	1	30	BS	Control
Donald E. Remus	Mgr. Mktg. Services	12	1	46	AS	Control
John G. Templeton	Dir. R&D (Acting)	20	5	49	BS	Engineering
Robert C. Chesnover ...	Dir. Ind. Rels.	6	4	43	BA	Personnel
James F. VanStee	Mgr. Inf. Services	4	4	38	MBA	Engineering
Donald W. Lash	V.P.-Gen. Mgr.	26*	5	50		Mfg.
Robert F. Enders	Group V.P.	3	3	51	BA	Mfg.
Roger P. Mueller	Div. Pres.	21*	5	45	BA BS	Sales
John M. Carroll	V.P.-Sales Off. Mgr.	21	1	48	BA	Sales
William T. Zinser	Group V.P.	18	2	44	BS	Sales
Roland H. Kenton	Div. Pres.	23	1	58	BS	Sales
Robert R. Kiely	Div. V.P.-Gen. Mgr.	2	2	55	BA	Mfg.
David K. Evans	Div. Gen. Mgr.	1	1	49	MBA	Sales
Walter W. Kowalewski, Jr.	Div. Gen. Mgr.	2	1	30		Mfg.
Rudolf H. Joon	Div. Gen. Mgr.	9	1	46	BS	Mfg.

**Total years with acquired division.*
Source: Company records.

TABLE 1 ROSPATCH FIVE YEAR SUMMARY OF OPERATIONS (In Thousands of Dollars)

	1975	*1974*	*1973*	*1972*	*1971*
Net Sales	$28,745	$25,214	$24,188	$21,402	$18,001
Costs and Expenses					
Cost of sales	$21,782	$18,416	$17,699	$14,995	$12,401
Selling and administrative expenses	5,258	4,201	4,548	4,336	3,374
Interest expense	606	452	347	222	188
Other, net	(140)	(225)	(485)	(166)	(46)
	$27,506	$22,844	$22,109	$19,387	$15,917
Earnings before Income Taxes	$ 1,239	$ 2,370	$ 2,079	$ 2,015	$ 2,084
Provision for income taxes	550	1,130	923	900	1,034
Earnings before Extraordinary Charge	$ 689	$ 1,240	$ 1,156	$ 1,115	$ 1,050
Extraordinary charge					57
Net Earnings	$ 689	$ 1,240	$ 1,156	$ 1,115	$ 993
Earnings per Share*	$ .77	$ 1.39	$ 1.31	$ 1.29	$ 1.16
Cash Dividends per Share*	$ .35	$ .33	$ .30	$ .28	$ .26

**Based on weighted average number of shares outstanding during the year and adjusted for all stock splits and stock dividends.*
Source: Rospatch Corporation 1975 Annual Report.

TABLE 2 ROSPATCH GROUP STATISTICS 1971–1975

		Cloth Labels	*Flexible Packaging*	*Machinery, Equipment and Specialized Supplies*
1975	Net Sales	25.3%	46.1%	28.6%
	Earnings	0.0	37.6	62.4
1974	Net Sales	35.3	48.8	15.9
	Earnings	28.4	44.5	27.1
1973	Net Sales	39.5	45.5	15.0
	Earnings	77.2	0.0	22.8
1972	Net Sales	41.7	42.6	15.7
	Earnings	74.8	5.3	19.9
1971	Net Sales	40.1	44.7	15.2
	Earnings	63.4	20.9	15.7

Source: Rospatch Corporation Securities and Exchange Commission Form 10-k for 1975.

The decline in the other product groups' sales was due to the fact that most of the company's business is a derived demand function of the textile industry. The company will therefore follow the up and down trends of this industry with the sole note that there is a bottom for the company. This bottom is due to the fact that 30 percent of the labels go to the undergarment segment and, although the public will do without new clothes, they tend to replace their undergarments. Unfavorable economic conditions were seen as the reason for the increase in the cost of sales in 1975 as well as the net equity loss. The net equity loss of $66,000 in 1974 and $79,000 in the first half of 1975 was in the 20 percent ownership of Yokohama Tape Company, Ltd. of Japan.[2] The 1975 second half results are near break-even levels. If Japanese expansion, a $200,000 outflow, had been curtailed, the 1975 net income would have been over $900,000, which would have been favorable in light of prevailing economic conditions. It should be noted that the foreign segment of operation is divided into three sectors: partial interest in foreign companies, foreign subsidiaries, and foreign sales.[3]

FUTURE OUTLOOK

The company realizes the need for a heightened sense of corporate identity and has undertaken a higher level of verbal and written communication. Through product group reviews at management meetings and the management information newsletter, the company is trying to increase its overall level of awareness.

The company also realizes that its strength has been high technology and it must continue to emphasize research and development. The research must be blended into the long-range planning of each division in order to develop a positive synergy. Corporate management, staff, and divisional management for the first time will commence 3-year planning for fiscal year 1977.

Most importantly, the company feels that the good management of acquisitions must be retained and capitalized.

A strong consumer market orientation, as well as the basic derived demand relationship to the textile and apparel industries are now recognized by company management as significant influences. The company's objective of growth through market diversification, as well as expansion, could reduce this dependency. In addition, Rospatch has 15 percent of the available label market, representing more than any other competitor.

Brush felt justified in being optimistic about the future in 1975: "By some standards Rospatch Corporation, with 1976 sales forecasted at nearly $34,000,000, is a small company. However, it is interesting to observe that in two of our three principal business activities, we are in a *leadership position* in the United States. I am speaking of our strong innovative production and marketing capabilities in labels and tapes, and a similarly enviable position in machinery and specialized supplies for institutions, linen supply firms and industrial laundries. Furthermore, these businesses have significant market and potential.[4]

NOTES

1. Rospatch Corporation: *Securities and Exchange Commission Form 10-k for 1975*, p. 3.
2. Ibid., p. 15.
3. Ibid., pp. 7–8.

4. "Rospatch Corporation: Presentation by R. F. Brush, President, and D. J. Burke, Vice President-Finance, to the New York Society of Security Analysts, February 13, 1976," *Wall Street Transcript*, March 15, 1976, p. 43,024.

GULF OIL CORPORATION: DOMESTIC AND FOREIGN POLITICAL CONTRIBUTIONS

In 1973, following the announcement from the Watergate Special Prosecution Force that American Airlines, Inc. made a $55,000 contribution from corporate funds to President Nixon's campaign for reelection, a number of inquiries and proceedings led to a series of disclosures of political contributions by various corporations. Gulf Oil Corporation admitted having contributed about $100,000 of Gulf funds to the Finance Committee to Re-Elect the President.

This led to the formation of the Special Review Committee of the Board of Directors of Gulf Oil. The Review Committee consisted of a chairman not affiliated with Gulf and two independent members of the board. The committee was authorized to review the investigation previously made by Gulf into the use of corporate funds for contributions, gifts, entertainment, or other expenses related to political activity. In all, the Review Committee conducted interviews with more than 140 witnesses, including present and former Gulf employees, as well as third parties. Interviews were conducted in the United States, the Bahamas, Europe, and Canada.

This case is excerpted from the *Report of the Special Review Committee*, published December 1975. It describes the background events and circumstances surrounding political payments made by Gulf Oil in the United States, Korea, Italy, and Bolivia. Although Gulf made several political contributions in various other countries, the above were singled out because of the nature and magnitude of the payments.

It appears that for over a decade, from the early 1960s through the early 1970s, Gulf Oil and its subsidiaries made contributions to political parties or candidates for office and payments to government officials. The total payment over the period is in excess of $12 million. This amount, spread over more than a decade, is small compared to Gulf's total assets in 1974 of $12.5 billion, gross revenues of $18.2 billion, and net income of $1 billion. It is also small compared to Gulf's total charitable and educational contributions from 1960 to 1975 of over $56 million. However, the character of certain of the contributions and payments appeared to have greater importance than the sums involved. It was also known that for some

---

Prepared by Dr. Filemon Campo-Flores of California State University, Long Beach.

time, Gulf officials who authorized the payments for domestic political campaigns tried to suppress knowledge about them. The pattern and nature of several of these payments were in large part not recorded in the books of the company. This has raised questions as to the policy and management of the company in this matter.

A chief but not exclusive source of funds for political contributions and payments arose from surreptitious transfer of Gulf funds to and from a Gulf subsidiary known as Bahamas Exploration Company, Limited (Bahamas Ex.), located in Nassau, the Bahamas. Initially organized for exploration purposes, Bahamas Ex. became a vehicle for accumulating cash for domestic political payments and recording transfers of funds abroad for political purposes—approximately $9.6 million over a thirteen-year period. At least $4.53 million of this amount was cash funneled through a Bahamas bank account and expended in the United States. The balance was expended abroad and charged to Bahamas Ex. The principal steps in supplying cash from Bahamas Ex. to Claude Wild, former vice president of government of Gulf, as the system operated from 1966 to 1972, are outlined in Exhibit 1.

GULF'S DOMESTIC POLITICAL CONTRIBUTION

It appeared to the Review Committee that the Bahamas Ex. arrangement and related political payments may have come from Gulf's announcement in 1958 that Gulf would become more active in practical politics. Archie Gray, a senior vice president of Gulf, noted the "creeping encroachment" by the government toward industry in general and toward the oil industry in particular. Gray decried arbitrary import quotas for oil, attacks on the depletion allowance, conflicting regulatory schemes, and the lack of consideration afforded Gulf's efforts to present facts to government

EXHIBIT 1 MOVEMENT OF FUNDS UNDER THE BAHAMAS EX. ARRANGEMENT—1966–1972

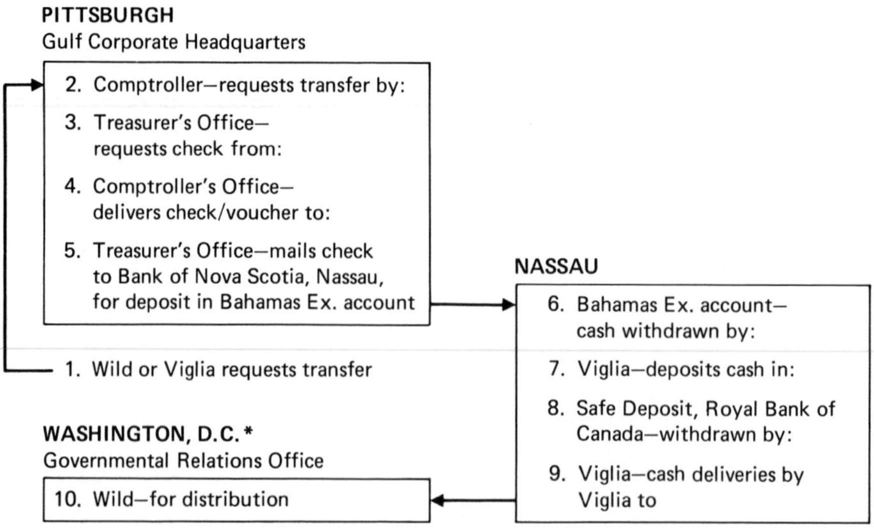

**Actual deliveries of cash by Viglia to Wild were made in various cities in the United States, not always in Washington.*

investigating committees. To combat this situation, Gulf had encouraged its employees to become involved personally in politics on the local level.

Much of the information on Gulf's domestic political activities was provided by Wild. In his testimony in December 1975, Wild said that in 1959, he was approached by Gray and Searls, Gulf's general counsel, to build an organization around the country that would give Gulf some "muscle" in politics. For this purpose, he would be provided with about $200,000 a year. It appeared that Gray and Searls realized that to be effective in the political scene contributions were "a part of life," and that was the purpose of the $200,000 yearly amount. Wild took the job and became head of Gulf's Government Relations Department in Washington, D. C. in 1963. Gray and Searls did make the money available to Wild's office.

Wild was made responsible for disbursing the cash allocated to his office. He personally took charge of national political figures. He made most of the contributions at his discretion, but on some occasions Searls and Gray specified who the recipients were. From time to time, Wild needed the assistance of others in making the payments to political figures. Some of those assisting Wild appeared to have been given discretion by Gray and Searls to make the payments, while others were also directed to make payments to specific persons. According to Wild, the only criterion ever used was that the money be spent in "the general interest of Gulf and the oil industry." Payments were initiated mostly by requests from the recipients, but on occasion, Wild did volunteer the payments.

Various national and state political figures received some contributions from Wild's office. Wild gave $25,000 for Hubert Humphrey's 1968 presidential campaign. He gave $25,000 to Maurice Stans in connection with Nixon's nomination effort in April, 1968. In the summer of 1970, Herbert Kalmbach requested $50,000 from Wild to assist in electing a Republican Senate. Wild subsequently agreed to give $25,000. Another cash contribution of $25,000 was given to John Mitchell for the Nixon campaign in October 1970.

Counsel for Gulf also testified that between 1969 and 1972, Wild made several donations to both Democratic and Republican dinners. He contributed $5,000 for each dinner to the Democrats and $10,000 for each dinner to the Republicans.

FOREIGN POLITICAL PAYMENTS

South Korea

In response to demand from certain leading political figures in South Korea, Gulf had made a $1 million contribution to the Korean Democratic Party in 1966. A contribution of $3 million was made to the same organization in 1970. There were other transactions related to the Gulf venture in Korea that had possible political implications, but these two were given closer scrutiny because of their size and character and the publicity attaching to them. Unlike the situation with domestic political contributions, there is no doubt of management responsibility involved in these payments. They were authorized by Bob R. Dorsey, then president of Gulf, being in his judgment in the best interests of the company and its shareholders.

The circumstances under which these payments were made is worthy of examination. During this period, the idea of developing industry in Korea appealed greatly to W. K. Whiteford, then chairman of Gulf. He saw it not only as an immediate outlet for a part of Gulf's Kuwait crude oil, but he also became interested in the efforts to expand Korean industry. Gulf's investment was undoubtedly the most significant private investment by any foreign country in Korea at that time. During the period from 1963 to 1964, Gulf made its original investment of $25 million in the Korean Oil Company, which was and is jointly owned with the Korean government. This was followed by plastics and fertilizer plants built by Gulf as a joint venture with the Korean government. Gulf officials estimated the company's Korean investment grew in a few years to $200 million, if not more.

While this expansion was going on, political developments were also moving forward. According to a Gulf official, operatives from United States government agencies then functioning in Korea were constantly pressing the Korean leaders for the creation and maintenance of an electoral system that could serve as a base for a stable representative government for the future. Efforts were made by United States government personnel to instruct the Koreans in election forms such as registration and election procedures. Gulf officials recognized that the Korean government was poor and had little, if any, money to carry on the usual electoral processes associated with representative government.

The driving force of the new Korean development was Korean President Park Chung Hee. Gulf officials and President Park and his representatives at times jointly participated in planning for the expansion of the country's industry. Other American companies entered the country—some according to Gulf officials, with the encouragement of Gulf—and they also became a part of the industrial development.

THE 1966 CONTRIBUTION The Review Committee's investigation showed that in 1966, with this background of national development, a substantial political contribution was requested of Gulf to help meet the expenses of a coming election campaign. Herbert Goodman, one of the key Gulf executives operating in the Far East, was approached by a high official of President Park's secretariat, who told him that the government felt a contribution should be made by Gulf to the Democratic Republican Party (DRP) in the amount of $1 million for the coming election campaign. Gulf officials did not report any nature of a threat if the contribution was not made. However, one Gulf official felt that most other companies had been or would be asked to make a contribution. Loughney, a Gulf vice president, was aware that an election in Korea could be expensive, and with most Koreans being poor the DRP would have to depend largely on industry and business for political contributions.

It was further recognized by the Review Committee that during this period there was persistent encouragement, if not pressure, from American government officials for the Korean government to establish American-style elections. The Koreans who approached Gulf for this contribution believed that to respond to this "encouragement" or policy would involve heavy expenses that they could not meet, and it was thought natural on their part to turn to foreign investors, particularly the Americans, as a source of funds. The Gulf representatives involved viewed the 1966 contribution as supportive of the developing democratic process in Korea, and they communicated this view to the Gulf corporate headquarters in Pittsburgh.

When testifying before the Senate Foreign Relations Subcommittee on Multinational Corporations, Dorsey said of the 1966 payment: "Our investigation indicates that the demand was made by high party officials and was accompanied by pressure which left little to the imagination as to what would occur if the company would choose to turn its back on the request. At that time the company had already made a huge investment in Korea. We were expanding and were faced with a myriad of problems which often confront American corporations in foreign countries. I carefully weighed the demand for a contribution in that light, and my decision to make the contribution of $1 million was based upon what I sincerely considered to be in the best interests of the company and its shareholders."

It appeared to Dorsey that the position of the Korean officials was something like this: "We are trying to adopt democratic processes after two thousand years of autocracy. Your government is encouraging us in this. We need money to do it and you have fared well here." Dorsey added that in an oblique way it was made clear that the Korean high officials well-being and the continued well-being of Gulf depended upon Gulf's acceding to the request.

Gulf made the payment using a transfer of $1,004,000 charged against Bahamas Ex.

THE 1970 CONTRIBUTION In 1970 there came another demand in the face of a heavier political challenge to the DRP. This time it was for $10 million and it was attended by a much more blunt approach. S. K. Kim, now deceased, who at that time was a sort of party head close to the administration, made the demand. Gulf officials who knew him say he was a rough customer. Kim made his demand by summoning to his office a vice president in charge of government relations for Korean Gulf Oil Company, a wholly-owned Gulf subsidiary. Kim indicated that other concerns operating in Korea were being faced with similar demands. This demand was also communicated to Pittsburgh, but no action was taken until Dorsey's visit to Korea, which had been scheduled prior to receipt of the demand. Dorsey arrived and met with Kim in what turned out to be an unpleasant encounter. Dorsey refused to meet the demand and departed from the meeting in anger. After the anger subsided, Dorsey agreed to pay $3 million. He justified this on the basis of the need for the continued goodwill and cooperation of the Korea government on which, in the newly-organized society, it was necessary for a foreign company to rely.

Dorsey stated that in their first encounter, Kim "dived right into the matter and told me that we were doing exceedingly well out there and that basically, our continued prosperity depended on our coming up with a $10 million contribution to the party." Dorsey added that when he demurred and explained why the demand was excessive, Kim became exceedingly angry and roughly said, in effect, "I'm not here to debate matters. You are either going to put up the goddamned money or suffer the consequences." The figure of $3 million was finally arrived at after some discussion and a sort of negotiation.

Dorsey summarized his reasons for making the payments as follows: "So you really are there at the mercy of the government and you are there at the sufferance of the government; if you're going to prosper and do well, you need the government on your side. You need that kind of environment, unlike any Western country."

The Review Committee found it very difficult to arrive at a satisfactory conclusion in regard to the legality under then existing Korean law of the political contributions made by Gulf to the DRP. It appeared that neither Dorsey nor the other high ranking officials of Gulf gave any thought at the time of the legality or illegality of the contributions under Korean law. They seemed to have treated it as either a request or a demand from the Korean government to be acceded to or not as the interests of the company appeared.

THE "KOREAN SYSTEM" AND THE "GRAY FUND" Various interviews by the Review Committee revealed a system of low-level tipping prevalent in South Korea. There was also the exercise of high-level influence and political influence in business affairs, the whole of which could be referred to as the "Korean system." At the lower level, the system took forms ranging from the custom of gift giving during three seasons of the year, most importantly during the Chusok season (comparable to Thanksgiving), to outright payments to key clerks in various departments in order to facilitate the routine business of government as it relates to Gulf's activities. As an example, when an application for a permit or license was received by a government agency, various clerks from the lowest level up put their name stamps on the application and pass it on to the next higher level until it reaches the section chief or the person authorized to approve it. In order to speed up the flow of the document, it was necessary to pay for the accelerated service. Most of the payments ranged from $50 to $200 depending on the level of approval needed. The system was widespread. Routine payments were required for customs approvals of all kinds, including those necessary for importation of crude oil and replacement parts. Regular payments were also made to various switchmen of the Korean national railroad to ensure that the company's railroad cars were efficiently handled.

There was also the custom of rather expensive entertainment of public officials at all levels on a recurring basis.

The Review Committee's investigations showed that a large portion of the expenditures described above were charged on the books of Gulf Korean subsidiaries as entertainment expenses and others were undoubtedly charged to various miscellaneous accounts.

The Review Committee also learned of an "off-the-books" fund maintained in Korea from which payments had been made mainly to individuals in agencies of the Korean government over a period of three years beginning 1972 and ending in 1975, when the fund was discontinued. The fund was used as a means of providing gratuities and presents of varying character to relatively low-level government personnel with which the Gulf organizations in Korea had contacts. The existence and purpose of this fund, which later came to be known as the "Gray Fund," was known to a responsible member of the executive of Gulf of Pittsburgh. According to officials familiar with the account, it was designed to ease access to government agencies that Gulf had to deal with in arranging appointments, obtaining permits, and otherwise expediting Gulf's government business through the complexities of a tightly controlled and sometimes frustrating bureaucracy. The fund and its activities were consciously kept "off-the-books" as it was believed to be less embarrassing and less compromising if its existence did not become known outside the company.

Gulf in Italy

Corporate funds of Gulf were also expended in Italy by its Italian subsidiary from time to time. The purpose was for inducing minor local functionaries to perform or expedite normal duties or to reward them for extra services. As far as the Review Committee was able to learn, the giving of gifts or "omaggi" to lubricate the sluggish machinery of petty bureaucracy was and is an accepted way of life that did not involve significant sums, considering the nature and volume of government contacts. The practice was characterized as tipping rather than bribery and was not considered unlawful.

CONTRIBUTIONS TO PUBLISHERS CONTROLLED BY POLITICAL PARTIES

During the period June 1969 through December 1972, ten separate payments totaling $627,000 were made from corporate funds. The payments were to three Italian publishing firms that were either owned or controlled by or affiliated with various political parties that were the intended beneficiaries of the payments. All of Gulf's contributions to political parties through publications were made pursuant to the initiative of Esso, ENI-AGIP (the government-owned oil company), and occasionally Shell.

The oil industry in Italy has been and is closely controlled by the national government, with all product prices set by the government. The political payments to party publications by Gulf, ENI-AGIP, and other members of Unione Petrolifera Italiana (UPI), an organization of the private sector of the oil industry in Italy, coincided with the Italian government's consideration of various matters of particular concern to the oil industry. These matters included rebates or subsidies paid by the Italian government to the oil companies upon the closing of the Suez Canal in 1967. These subsidies were in lieu of allowing the companies to increase product prices to offset freight increases.

It appears that it was the practice in Italy for political parties to solicit financial support from businesses and industry. In the case of the oil industry such solicitations were directed to Vincenzo Cazzaniga, president of both Esso Italiana and UPI. On occasion, Cazzaniga, Esso, or ENI-AGIP would make commitments to political parties without informing the other companies in advance. They would then make a determination of the total amount to be contributed to the political parties by each of the fifteen or more oil companies, including the Italian state oil company. This determination was made by a complicated formula projecting the impact upon the various companies of the governmental action. After determining the pro rata division of particular political contributions among the companies, each company would be advised of its share, and it appears that the companies had some latitude in selecting which party they would favor with contributions.

All of the payments by Gulf were made through invoices received by Gulf from the various publications for "newspaper journalistic services" or words to that effect. The payments were recorded on the books of Gulf Italiana, the Gulf marketing company in Italy. In the official company accounting records required under Italian law all payments were charged to an account designated "publicity and promotional expense." For purposes of Gulf's internal world-wide accounting system each payment was classified to an account related to that aspect of the company's activity that was thought to be affected by the particular governmental action (i.e., interest savings, increased sales revenue, or transportation savings).

The largest contribution by Gulf to political publishers was made in 1972. The allocation of contributions among the various companies was based on the impact of defiscalization. Defiscalization refers to Parliamentary decrees in 1971 and 1972 that permitted the oil companies to achieve an increase in product realizations to offset increased costs of crude oil imposed by the OPEC countries. This was achieved by decreasing excise taxes on petroleum products in lieu of granting the companies an increase in product prices. It was then alleged in the Italian press that some or all of the political payments through publications by UPI members were made for the purpose of influencing specific government action favorable to the oil industry. Gulf's Italian representative, however, has consistently insisted that in authorizing these payments there was no aspect of attempted corruption or any attempt to induce politicians or government officials to grant specific favorable treatment to Gulf or the oil industry. Rather, he regarded the political contributions as an act of good citizenship by Gulf and the other companies in supporting the existing political system in Italy and in particular the center-left democratic political parties in their efforts to retain control against radical elements of the right and left.

THE SPECIAL ACCOUNT OR "BLACK FUND" A Special account that was not recorded on the books of Gulf in Italy was opened in 1962, authorized by Whiteford, then Gulf's chairman of the board. The Special account was initially designed to serve as a confidential vehicle to receive off-the-books rebates or commissions on bank deposits in derogation of fixed interest rates agreed upon by the banks. Later it was used to provide funds, among other things, to combat a strong campaign by the press and certain political elements to nationalize Gulf's concession in the Ragusa field in Sicily. Such funds were quite common in Italy and were legal if disclosed to share-holders. The special account disbursed a total of over $400,000 over a twelve-year period. The more important categories of payments are outlined in Exhibit 2.

Gulf in Bolivia

The economy of Bolivia is based upon the production and exportation of minerals, oil, and natural gas. In 1956, a Bolivian state agency, Yacimientos Petroliferos Fiscales Bolivianos (YFPB) entered into a number of farm-out agreements with

EXHIBIT 2 SCHEDULE OF CATEGORIES OF PAYMENTS FROM SPECIAL ACCOUNT

Category	*U.S. Dollars**	*Number of Items***
(a) Political contributions or payments	235,886	22
(b) Payments for consulting services, professional fees, commissions, etc.	60,959	17
(c) Payments in connection with gasoline station marketing development	23,538	34
(d) Payments for services re Ragusa tax claims	38,462	2
(e) Payments to newspapers, editors, journalists	10,815	11
(f) Payments to Bassiano and Terranova Communes	15,385	2
(g) Payments to consulting firms for gasoline marketing studies	9,076	15
(h) Business gifts	8,545	3
(i) Payments in the nature of charitable or goodwill contributions	8,769	7
(j) Payments to professional, manufacturing or trade associations	4,333	5
(k) Payments in connection with union or dealer association problems	2,308	2
(l) Approved merit bonus paid to Gulf employee	1,538	1
(m) Bank fees	1,474	7
Total	422,526	

**These dollar amounts are based on the lire amounts converted to dollars at the rate of L.650/$1.*
***This refers to the number of transactions or withdrawals that are included in the particular category.*

United States companies. In that year Gulf, through its wholly-owned subsidiary, Bolivian Gulf Oil Company, also made its entry into Bolivia through a farm-out agreement with YFPB. This venture was not successful. But in 1957, following a new Bolivian petroleum law, Gulf was awarded the first of a number of concessions ultimately covering 3 million acres. This proved to be a successful venture yielding 34,000 barrels of crude oil a day in 1969.

In 1964, René Barrientos and another general, Alfredo Ovando, led a successful coup which resulted in the ouster of President Victor Paz Estenssors. After running the country together, it was decided that Barrientos should run as candidate for the presidency in an election in July 1966, while Ovando would direct the military. Barrientos then sought helicopters, planes, and other equipment from the United States under the Military Assistance Pact program. However, the program did not have enough funding to provide the equipment sought by Barrientos. Then Barrientos asked Gulf to supply him with a helicopter so that he could visit remote villages and provinces in Boliva for his campaign. After some consultation among Gulf officials, Gulf arranged with Fairchild Hiller Corporation to lease a helicopter and provide a qualified pilot for Barrientos's use for three months. The total cost of leasing, transportation, crew salaries, freight, and other expenses came to over $45,000.

Barrientos was elected president. At the conclusion of the rental period, Barrientos refused to return the helicopter, which was also being used by the Bolivian Air Force. The Bolivian ambassador to the U. S. told Gulf's foreign affairs representative in Washington, D. C. that some means had to be found to let Barrientos keep the helicopter, since Barrientos would not be able to understand Gulf's refusal to let him keep it. Gulf paid an additional $62,000, the net cost of purchasing the helicopter. Barrientos then donated the helicopter to the Bolivian Air Force.

The Review Committee found no evidence that the furnishing of a helicopter to Barrientos was for a specific purpose of inducing any action or omission on his part, or that Barrientos did or omitted to do any act by reason of receiving the helicopter.

PAYMENTS TO BOLIVIAN NATIONALS In 1966, Gulf discovered 4.5 trillion cubic feet of natural gas in Bolivia and decided to construct a pipeline to transport the gas to the Argentine pipeline, and thence to the existing markets. The pipeline was to be owned by Gulf. Later, opposition to the project was made by YPFB, the Bolivian state petroleum corporation. As a result, Barrientos withdrew his approval of the Gulf project and the entire agreement was renegotiated. The new arrangement involved the creation of a company owned 50 percent by Gulf and 50 percent by YPFB.

When the new agreement was in the final stage of negotiation, but before it was signed, Gulf officials were told of an obligation on the part of Gulf to make a payment to Barrientos of more than $1 million. Later, Barrientos also wanted two Bolivian nationals each to receive 10 percent of the payment. All three were to receive their payments in numbered accounts at Swiss Credit Bank in Zurich.

Just as negotiations were about to be completed, Barrientos was killed in an air crash on April 27, 1969. Despite Barrientos's death, Gulf went ahead with the payment to the other Bolivians. Gulf arranged for the transfer of a total of $140,000 to two numbered accounts at Swiss Credit Bank.

However, when Alfredo Ovando replaced the constitutional government of Bolivia with military rule, his first official act was to cancel the petroleum law under which Gulf operated its concession. Then on October 17, 1969 Ovando nationalized all of Gulf's assets in Bolivia. Extended negotiations followed, resulting in an agreement for payment of compensation approximately equal to the book value of Gulf's assets,which was at that time about $114 million. A little over half of this amount was paid.

THE FIELD HOSPITAL Gulf's Claude Wild, through a bank account of the Washington office, paid $8,000 and $10,000 towards the purchase of a field hospital that was shipped to Bolivia by the U. S. military. This amount did not cover the full cost of the hospital. It is believed that the rest of the cost was paid by the Bolivians. The Review Committee did not find any evidence that this payment was illegal under Bolivian or U. S. laws.

CHARGE OF POLLUTION AGAINST ACME STEEL

Acme Steel Corporation owns and operates several plants in the Midwest. These plants are engaged in smelting operations. Scrap metal is melted for the production of metal ingots. Acme is an Illinois corporation, and one of Acme's plants has been located in Clairmont, Illinois since 1969. The plant is located on the edge of an area zoned industrial, and there is a residential area near the Acme plant. Acme's sales in 1974 were $6.5 million.

Acme's Clairmont plant has 120 employees. Clairmont is a town with a population of 7,500 and Acme is the town's second largest employer. Clairmont suffered from an unemployment level that averaged 12 percent during 1973 and 1974, and figures for the first half of 1975 were no brighter.

The Clairmont plant utilizes sweat furnaces and reverberatory furnaces in its operation. The emissions from the furnaces are emitted through tall smokestacks. On December 2, 1975 Acme made application with the Illinois Ecology Enforcement Administration (EEA) for a pollution control operating permit for its Clairmont plant. The EEA is a state agency that enforces the Illinois Environmental Protection Act. The EEA refused the original application, and an amended permit application was filed on February 5, 1975. The EEA also refused the amended application. Both permits were refused on the EEA's contention that the pollution control precautions taken by Acme were inadequate to avoid a discharge of contaminants into the atmosphere in violation of the Act. On April 20, 1975 Acme was served as a defendant in a complaint filed with the Illinois Environmental Board by the EEA. The complaint alleged that Acme was guilty of air pollution and had also violated pollution control permit requirements, in violation of Sections 9(a) and (b) of the Illinois Ecology Enforcement Act (referred to as "the Act" hereafter). The pertinent portions of those two statutory sections are as follows:

> Section 9(a). No person shall: . . . Cause or threaten or allow the discharge or emission of any contaminant into the environment in any State so as to cause or tend to cause air

---

Prepared by Professor Kevin M. Teeven of Bradley University.

pollution in Illinois, either alone or in combination with contaminants from other sources. . . .

Section 9(b). No person shall: . . . Construct, install or operate any equipment, facility, vehicle, vessel or aircraft capable of causing or contributing to air pollution or designed to prevent air pollution . . . without a permit (being) granted (by the EEA)[1]

Acme filed an answer to the EEA's complaint, denying it was guilty.

BACKGROUND ON POLLUTION CONTROL ENFORCEMENT

In Illinois there are two administrative agencies concerned with pollution control under the Act: the EEA and the Environmental Board (the board).

The EEA investigates complaints of pollution. The investigators are trained scientists and engineers. If a complaint is of substance, the case is referred to the EEA's attorneys for prosecution before the board. The EEA also issues permits for companies who operate equipment that emits contaminants or has the potential to do so.

The board acts as the judicial body for the complaints filed by the EEA and consists of five members appointed by the governor. The board hears the arguments of the EEA and the alleged polluter and determines whether there has been a violation of the Act, and if so, what the penalty should be. The Act also provides that the board shall take into consideration all of the circumstances bearing upon the reasonableness of the discharge, including but not limited to the degree of injury, the social and economic value of the pollution source, the suitability of the pollution source to the locale, and the technical practicality and economic reasonableness of reducing or eliminating the discharge. There is a statutory presumption in favor of the EEA if the alleged polluter fails to rebut the EEA's arguments.

The hearing on a board case is held before a hearing officer appointed by the board, and the hearing is held in the county where the alleged violation occurred. The members of the board are usually not present at the hearing. The transcript of the proceedings is then forwarded to the board for decision. The board members study the arguments filed by the parties and the transcript of the proceeding, and the board then renders an opinion based on the written record before it.

The hearing of EEA vs. Acme Steel Corporation was held on September 24, 1975 in Clairmont, Illinois. Twenty members of the public were at the hearing. The EEA presented its case first, followed by Acme's defense.

EEA CASE PRESENTATION

The EEA attorney called as a witness James Schmidt, an EEA engineer and a member of the EEA's permit division. Schmidt testified that, "The EEA finds Acme's sweat furnaces #1 and #2 and its reverberatory furnaces #1 and #2 not in compliance." Schmidt also stated that Acme's two contentions contained in their permit application were inadequate. The two contentions that Acme used to justify its right to a pollution control permit were based on a modified stack test and a "settling chamber" theory.

Acme's modified stack test attempted to show that the rate of emission of contaminants from their smokestacks into the atmosphere was not in violation of the Act. Schmidt testified that Acme's permit application did not show how many sources were running at the time that the modified stack test was made. Schmidt

---

*Note: [1]Illinois Revised Statutes, Chapter 111½, Sections 9(a) and (b).

said, "The EEA's permit division never makes a stack test itself. Rather it looks at the permit application sent in and asks for more information if the application is incomplete. The Acme application contained inadequate information for the EEA to allow issuance of permit."

Schmidt further testified that there were other inadequacies in the stack test provided by Acme. Acme's modified stack test didn't tell whether all of the fans were running at the time of the test. The length of time that the test was conducted was not provided. In general, the facts presented to Schmidt by the permit application were lacking in sufficient detail for an opinion to be formed by the Permit Division. The stack test must show itself valid on the face of the application. Schmidt said that the Permit Division had pointed out to Acme the deficiencies in the application and had allowed Acme to amend their application; however, the amended permit application still failed to provide the requested data.

The EEA attorney then questioned Henry Dobbins, another EEA engineer, about the "settling chamber" theory, which Acme had used. Acme argued that their building, with a 75-foot ceiling, was a settling chamber for the particulate emissions. Acme concluded that none of the emissions escaped the building through the stacks into the atmosphere. Dobbins testified that Acme's building could not be a settling chamber because the emissions are a smaller size than what a settling chamber would collect. Dobbins also indicated that the EEA's calculations were that the uplift velocities exceeded the settling velocity of the type of particle emitted from the furnaces, and thus all of Acme's emissions were emitted into the atmosphere.

The EEA then rested its case.

ACME'S DEFENSE

The Acme attorney first called Schmidt back to the stand as an adverse witness. Schmidt was asked if any representative of the EEA made a physical inspection of Acme's Clairmont plant. Schmidt responded in the negative, though he admitted in a later answer that the surveillance section of the EEA occasionally does make physical investigations.

Carl Beyer, manager of the Clairmont plant, then testified. He said, "The opinion of the EEA regarding Acme's conformity to the law was only theoretical because the EEA made no physical inspection of the site, but Acme's tests were run on the site by experts in the field." He went on to say that the modified stack test was made under normal operating conditions. He also stated that all of the production facilities were in operation when the tests were made.

Acme's attorney then called Marvin Ledbetter to the stand. Ledbetter was an employee of an engineering consulting firm hired by Acme. Ledbetter indicated that he helped in the preparation of both permit applications made by Acme. Ledbetter testified that, "Acme's emissions were well within the requirements of the Act and an operating permit should have been granted."

The last witness called by Acme was Jacob Hodge, a vice-president of Acme. Hodge testified that, "The economic and social value of Acme's contribution to the Clairmont community far outweighs any possible violation, if there is a violation at all. Acme Steel Corporation provides jobs for 120 families. This contribution to the economic vitality of Clairmont is particularly important during this period of unemployment. The added costs of the pollution control devices which the EEA has suggested that Acme install will be detrimental to a business which has had its own share of economic difficulties during the past few years."

The Acme Steel Corporation then rested its case.

STATEMENTS OF MEMBERS OF THE PUBLIC

The board hearing officer then turned to the members of the public to ask if any of them had a statement to make. The Act requires that interested members of the public be given an opportunity to make comments.

The hearing officer recognized Donna Kruger of Clairmont. Kruger lived about two blocks from the Acme plant in a single family dwelling in the winter of 1974–75. She said that periodically in the late afternoon she would see dark gray smoke coming out of Acme's stacks. She also said that when she hung her clothes outside to dry, a dark soot collected on the clothing. She said she thought it must be coming from Acme's plant.

Richard Sonderby was then recognized by the hearing officer. Sonderby was secretary of the local chamber of commerce at the time. He said that a great deal was being made about a minor infraction. He indicated that there were much worse polluters in several neighboring towns. He thought that the EEA should begin with them. Furthermore, Sonderby stated that Acme was an extremely important force in Clairmont's economy; that if Acme was forced to cut back because of the added pollution control costs, then many people would be out of jobs. Sonderby also contended that such a layoff would have a domino effect on downtown businesses because of the weakened consumer purchasing power.

No other member of the public made a statement. The hearing officer then adjourned the hearing. The transcript of the hearing was certified by the hearing officer and forwarded to the board for decision.

APPENDIX

Penalties the Board Can Order

The Act authorizes the Board to provide for any combination of the following penalties:

1. A civil penalty of not to exceed $10,000 for a violation of the Act.
2. An additional penalty of not to exceed $1,000 for each day during which the violation continues.
3. A civil penalty of not to exceed $10,000 per day for a violation of a permit requirement.
4. An order requiring a compliance program.
5. An injunction prohibiting the conducting of business until the company comes into compliance with the Act.

EEA's Calculations Rebutting ACME's "Settling Chamber" Theory

In rebuttal, the EEA presented calculations showing that:

1. 97 percent of Acme's emissions are between 0–44 microns.
2. The settling velocity for 44 micron particles is 0.45 feet/second, and 100 micron particles is 2.5 feet/second., and
3. The calculated uplift velocity for 44 micron particles between heights of 70 feet and 74 feet due to a combination of thermal conduction and fan draft would range from 4.64 feet/second to 15.54 feet/second.

Thus the EEA concluded that since the calculated uplift velocities exceeded the settling velocity of all particles emitted from the furnaces, all of Acme's emissions were emitted to the atmosphere; i.e., a 4.64 uplift velocity will overrule 45 settling velocity for the largest of Acme's particulate (the settling velocity is weaker if you go to particles lighter than 44, of which 97 percent were).

POLAROID IN SOUTH AFRICA

On November 21, 1977, Polaroid Corporation announced its decision to terminate its distributorship in South Africa, thereby ending the "Experiment in South Africa," which it had begun six years earlier. In making this announcement, a Polaroid official stated:

> We were presented on Wednesday, November 16, with information which suggested that Frank & Hirsch Pty. Ltd., the independent distributor of Polaroid products in South Africa, has been selling film to the government of South Africa in violation of a 1971 understanding. That understanding stipulated that the distributor refrain from selling any Polaroid products to the South African government.
>
> As a consequence of this new information, we initiated that same day an investigation from which we have now learned that Frank & Hirsch has not fully conformed to the understanding with regard to sales to the government.
>
> Accordingly, Polaroid is advising Frank & Hirsch that it is terminating its business relationship with that company.
>
> In 1971, when the question arose as to whether it was appropriate for Polaroid to continue to sell to a distributor in South Africa, we examined the issue carefully. We abhor the policy of apartheid and seriously considered breaking off all business with South Africa. We felt, however, that we should consider the recommendations of black Africans before making a decision. They urged us to maintain our business relationship and try to accomplish improvements in the economic and educational opportunities for black workers. We did succeed in persuading our distributor to give to black employees responsibilities much greater than they had had in the past and substantially to improve black salary rates. We also made contributions, which aggregate about one-half million dollars, to black African scholarship funds and other programs. In much of this activity our distributor cooperated effectively. We were therefore shocked to learn that the understanding not to sell to the government was not followed.
>
> With the termination of this distributorship in South Africa, we do not plan to establish another one.

REACTION

Polaroid's 1977 sales were over $1 billion. The South African business was worth between $3 and 4 million. This amounted to about half of the revenues of Frank & Hirsch (Pty.) Ltd., the South African distributorship. Helmut Hirsch, the owner of the distributorship is a "sixty-six-year-old German-Jewish emigree who escaped to South Africa from Nazi Germany. In the South African political scene he is considered a liberal. He is a member of the Progressive Party and a friend of Helen Suzman, a well-known critic of the Vorster regime. He has been the chairman of Dorkay House," (*The Boston Globe,* November 23, 1977). The company has distributed Polaroid products for the past eighteen years and it also handled Japanese cameras, watches, and other imported equipment.

Following Polaroid's announcement, Hirsch issued a statement in Johannesburg on November 22 that said, "On hearing allegations that Frank & Hirsch have supplied Polaroid products directly to departments of the South African government, we made an immediate investigation that revealed over the past several years a very small number of isolated cases where unbeknownst to us there were deliveries to the South African government. Frank & Hirsch regrets these isolated instances because they are not in keeping with the agreement between Frank & Hirsch and Polaroid. Immediate steps have been taken to avoid any recurrences."

The Boston Globe reported that Hirsch confirmed that some sales of Polaroid products to the South African government violated the agreement with Polaroid. According to Hirsch, his investigation of the records showed three sales in 1975, two deliveries in 1976, and twelve transactions in 1977. The records do not go back further. However, he insisted that other sales to South African government agencies had not been restricted by the ban agreed upon in 1971. Hirsch claimed that "only some agencies were restricted—the Security Department, the Bantu (Black) Reference Bureaus, and the military. Muller's Pharmacy (a large Johannesburg drugstore) was officially permitted to supply anyone. They were tendering government contracts. Polaroid was well aware of it. They knew the government was putting orders through pharmacies," (*The Boston Globe,* November 23, 1977).

In the same interview, Hirsch explained that his firm supplied many government agencies, including hospitals, water supply agencies, and airports. These transactions apparently were prearranged with the government agencies through Muller's Pharmacy. Other deliveries were done as a favor. "It's possible the customers phoned, and I was not aware of it." He "begged" Polaroid management not to sever the relationship. Hirsch said he was planning a trip to the United States that weekend to try and repair his relationship. "If they give us an opportunity to talk to them, we have a good case for not abandoning Polaroid from South Africa. It's become a way of life here." Hirsch was planning to bring Sidney Kentridge, a prominent South African attorney, to represent him in discussions with Polaroid over the weekend. (Kentridge represented the Biko family at the inquest into the death of Steve Biko, a well-known black political activist.)

CIRCUMSTANCES LEADING TO THE POLAROID DECISION

Polaroid products were sold through the distributor to drugstores and photographic supply houses in South Africa. Polaroid management had known the South African government was using its film, but believed the purchases were made in the open market and not from its distributor. A 1971 agreement between Polaroid and its distributor had specified that no sales were to be made to the South African government.

Allegations of secret sales of Polaroid cameras and film to the South African military and the Bantu Reference Bureau that issues identification documents ("passbooks") to blacks (an instrument of apartheid) were made by Indrus Naidoo, a former employee of Frank & Hirsch. Naidoo made a photostat of a delivery note covering one shipment of Polaroid film going to the Bantu Reference Bureau on September 22, 1975. This photostat copy was passed on to Paul Irish, an official of the American Committee on Africa (ACOA) in New York City. Irish released the copy to the press in mid-November 1977, only after Naidoo had left South Africa as an exile.

The Boston Globe (November 21, 1977) reported that Naidoo was interviewed while in Germany, where he was on a speaking tour for the African Liberation Movement, and he detailed the transactions between Frank & Hirsch and the South African government: "Frank & Hirsch billed all the shipments to the South African government through Muller's Pharmacy, a drugstore in downtown Johnannesburg. The films and cameras were placed in unmarked cartons and then transferred to unmarked transport vans for the drive to their destination. . . . There were regular deliveries to the Voortrekker Hoogte military headquarters outside Pretoria, periodic deliveries to several local reference bureaus, and at least one large shipment of sunglasses to the Air Force. . . . Since all billing was done through Muller's Pharmacy, there would be no record of funds being received from the South African government."

Polaroid management was informed of the charges on November 16, and they dispatched Hans Jensen, the export sales manager and a British auditor, to South Africa to investigate. Polaroid officials stated, "Helmut Hirsch told us many times he was not selling to the South African government. As far as we were able to determine he had stuck to the agreement. However, we never took for granted they would follow our stipulation. That's why we have sent people there every year."

Jensen found several deliveries to the South African government in his examination of Frank & Hirsch records. In his telephone conversation with Polaroid officials, Jensen reported that Hirsch, the owner of Frank & Hirsch, was shocked: "He claimed he had no idea this was going on."

In announcing Polaroid's decision to discontinue the distributorship, Robert Palmer, director of community relations at Polaroid, described Polaroid officials as distressed: "People are upset and disappointed. . . . Over the past six years Polaroid influenced Frank & Hirsch to substantially raise its black employees' wages and we have contributed almost half a million dollars to several black groups in South Africa. Hirsch followed the program we outlined—equal pay for equal work, and black employees were moved into jobs the whites held. The distributor had only 200 black employees but I think our influence had a ripple effect on other U. S. Corporations. . . . Now this "Experiment in South Africa" has come to an end."

POLAROID'S EXPERIMENT IN SOUTH AFRICA AND CONSEQUENCES: A PERSPECTIVE

In late 1970, internal (corporate) and external (community) questions were raised regarding Polaroid Corporation's involvement in South Africa.[1] Specifically,

*Note: [1]For details describing the initial protest demonstrations and Polaroid's response, see the author's case. "Polaroid in South Africa (A)," ICH 9-372-624. The Polaroid "Experiment" along with local and worldwide reaction, are described in the sequel case "Polaroid in South Africa (B)," ICH 9-372-625. Both are distributed through the Intercollegiate Case Clearing House, Harvard University.

questions focused on the use of Polaroid's ID system by the government of South Africa in its passbook program. These passbooks had to be carried by all non-white South Africans and were seen as a means whereby the government enforced its apartheid system. In response, a Polaroid team was sent to South Africa to study the problem first hand. Based on its report, Polaroid management stated that they had reviewed their operations in South Africa and in January 1971 announced an "Experiment in South Africa." The announcement included the following statements:

> We abhor Apartheid. . . . We want to examine the question of whether or not we should continue to sell our products in South Africa. . . . We do not want to impose a course of action on black people of another country merely because we might think it was correct.

A group of Polaroid employees, both black and white, then toured South Africa and returned with a unanimous recommendation to undertake an experimental program for one year with these goals:

> To continue our business relationship there except for any direct sales to the South African government. To improve dramatically the salaries and other benefits of the non-white employees of our distributor there. To initiate through our distributor well defined programs to train non-white employees for important jobs within that company. We would commit a portion of our profits earned there to encourage black education.

At the end of 1971, Polaroid management issued their report outlining the benefits of their year-long experiment. The report concluded: "In a year's time the visible effects of the Polaroid experiment on other American companies had been limited, but the practical achievements in increased salaries, benefits, and education had shown what could be done. Therefore, the company decided to continue the program for the present."

In November 1977, following a series of reviews and audits, Polaroid issued a report specifying some of the consequences of the six years following the initial decision to undertake the "Experiment." In conclusion, the report pointed out:

> We believe it is still too soon to make a final judgement on our relationship to South Africa. We have found that the lack of knowledge concerning American business in South Africa has been as difficult to deal with as has the complexity of issues surrounding business practices in that country.
>
> We will continue to press, as constructively as possible, for change in South Africa. We will not, however, decide for black Africans what they need. The final determination will have to come from South Africans themselves. We intend to stay as long as black South Africans and moderate whites feel that progress is being made and that our presence there is helpful. We should acknowledge that our decision to continue is made easier by the fact that our South African distributor has been a willing participant in the changes affecting his work force.
>
> We agree with our thoughtful critics that the specific accomplishments of the Polaroid experiment affect relatively few black people. A growing number of people, however, are beginning to share our hope that the possibility of change in South Africa is real.

U. S. CORPORATIONS AND SOUTH AFRICA: A DIFFERENT PERSPECTIVE

The non-profit Investor Responsibility Research Center (IRRC), Washington, D. C., released a study indicating that about 320 American companies have operations in South Africa. Some of the largest (with 1976 sales in South Africa) are Mobil Corporation (over $500 million); Caltex, a joint-venture of Standard Oil of California and Texaco ($500 million); Ford ($288 million), General Motors ($250 million), Chrysler (through a 24.9 percent interest in Sigma Motors, $190 million), IBM ($163 million or less). The U. S. Commerce Department estimates book value of U. S. Investments in South Africa at $1.7 billion in 1976. For most American companies, South Africa represents 1 percent or less of their total sales. However, in the South African economy, some are significant. IRRC reported that American companies control 43 percent of the country's petroleum market, 23 percent of its auto sales and 70 percent of its computer business.

The IRRC further stated that some companies, such as General Motors, Ford, and Control Data, have indicated they will limit further expansion there. Chrysler, International Telephone, and Phelps Dodge have merged their subsidiaries into South African companies. Burlington Industries, Weyerhaeuser, Halliburton, and Interpace have completely closed down their South African operations.

The call by a number of groups for complete withdrawal of U. S. investments in South Africa has been voiced on numerous occasions. Following the Polaroid announcement, a church group introduced a shareholder's resolution calling on the Eastman Kodak Company to ban all direct and indirect sales to the South African government. This was seen as a first step in a phased withdrawal of Kodak from South Africa. The resolution called on the corporation not to "make or renew any contracts or agreements to sell photographic equipment, including cameras, film, photographic paper and processing chemicals to the South African government."

Kodak has been in South Africa since 1913. It employs 470 people, half of them black, and has sales of about $27 million in South Africa out of total sales of $5.4 billion. *The Boston Globe* (December 14, 1977) reported that a Kodak spokesman, Ian Guthrie, had confirmed sales to the South African government. However, it was pointed out that Kodak had no equipment that could be used to make passbooks or ID cards. Moreover, Kodak's policy was to stay in business in South Africa because of "strong" commitment to the 470 employees in its subsidiary, Kodak (South Africa) (Pty.) Ltd.

Kodak and fifty-three other U. S. companies to date have signed a Statement of Principles regarding their operations in South Africa. These companies point to steps they have taken to improve the lot of their black employees and express confidence that in time the existing racial barriers can be pulled down. This Statement of Principles was drawn up by Reverend Leon Sullivan, a black minister from Philadelphia and a director of General Motors Corporation. *The Los Angeles Times* (December 29, 1977) reported, "South Africa's Minister of Information, Connie Mulder, officially approved it [the Statement of Principles]. In expressing a desire to contribute to the well-being of the black workers in South Africa, these American companies are to be commended, he said."

In a press release issued September 15, 1977, Sullivan commented on the fifty-four corporate endorsements and the situation in South Africa: "We are pleased with the response to date, but we will continue to invite other companies to participate. . . . Some encouraging progress has been made during the last six months. I have been informed that racial signs are coming down; in some instances walls are being broken out to end segregation and new integrated facilities are being constructed; blacks are being selected and promoted to supervisory positions; and all companies are developing plans for aggressive future implementation of the six points. Within the next year we shall see if the effort is only a ripple or becomes a tide for change."

At a business recognition dinner on October 5, 1977, attended by many senior corporate officials, Sullivan informed the executives that the Statement of Principles was being endorsed by non-U. S. groups such as the Federation of Swedish Industries and expressed the hope that "a worldwide effort against segregation and discriminating practices will be developed by businesses on a global scale." He pointed out that the European Economic Community recently announced its South African code of ethics, which is very similar to the American Statement of Principles. (The EEC Code goes further in pushing companies to recognize black trade unions and to practice collective bargaining, as pointed out in *Business Week*, October 24, 1977.)

At the same dinner, U. S. Secretary of State Cyrus R. Vance said: "I think that all of you recognize by your presence here tonight the international business community operating in South Africa has an extremely important role to play. By adopting progressive employment practices for your South African subsidiaries, you not only enhance the lives of those who work for you, you also demonstrate the promise of a society based on racial justice. . . . We believe that your efforts will set an example which will hasten the day when all the people of South Africa will realize their full human and spiritual potential."

APPENDIX

From the 1971 Polaroid Management Report on the "Experiment in South Africa"

October 1970

Frank & Hirsch (Pty.) Ltd., South African Distributor, pay and benefits, black employees:

Range R303 to R56, average salary R75 per month (South African Rand = $1.15)

Pension plan applied to both blacks and whites

No medical plan for black Africans

Interest free loans for all employees

Christmas Bonus of one month's salary after three years

A black employees committee in existence

May 1971

Report to Congressional Sub-Committee on South Africa:

We decided whatever our course should be it should oppose the course of Apartheid.

Polaroid is a small economic force in South Africa, but we are well-known and, because of our committee's visit there, highly visible. We hope other American companies will join us in this program.

South Africa articulates a policy exactly contrary to everything we feel our company stands for. We cannot participate passively in such a political system. Nor can we ignore it.

Both our distributor and one of his suppliers have granted wage increases to all their non-white employees ranging from 13 to 33%.

An additional increase of 28% for a group of 20 non-whites Frank & Hirsch employees was announced last week (April 25, 1971).

Frank and Hirsch and one of their suppliers have agreed to guarantee the educational expenses for the children of their non-white employees through the high school level including the cost of school tuition, transportation and books.

The first installment of a financial grant to ASSECA (The Association for the Educational and Cultural Advancement of the African People of South Africa) has been completed.

A grant has been made to USSALEP (United States South African Leader Exchange Program).

We have been working to set up an educational foundation in South Africa. The foundation will be charged with selecting 500 black students and providing financial assistance to them. Administration of this program will be handled by the Institute of Race Relations.

We are not sure what the longer term decision will be regarding Polaroid's relationship with South Africa, but we are convinced that the basic approach of working for change from within deserves this kind of trial.

December 1971
End-of-the-year Report:

The average salary including bonus for black employees (at Frank and Hirsch) had now been increased by 22%.

Individual increases had ranged from 6% to 33%—the average pay was now R91 up from R75 of a few months earlier.

Eight black supervisors were appointed during the course of the year in the Computer, Administration, Services and Distribution departments. Some of these positions had been formerly held by whites and they were being paid on the same pay scale as their predecessors.

The pension plan with death benefits and the employee education plan were in full operation.

A grant of $15,000 was completed to the Association for the Educational and Cultural Advancement of the African People of South Africa (ASECA).

A second grant of $10,000 was made to the U. S.-South African Leader Exchange Program (USSALEP).

A third grant of $50,000 was used to establish a foundation to underwrite educational expenses of black students and teachers in South Africa—The American-South African Study and Educational Trust (ASSET).

A fourth grant of $1,000 was made to the American-S. A. Institute.

From Polaroid's "Experiment" Update, November 1977

Our contributions are continuing to ASSECA, though some concern has been expressed as to the slow pace of programs of this organization based mostly

EXHIBIT 1 POLAROID'S CONTRIBUTIONS IN SOUTH AFRICA (1971–77)

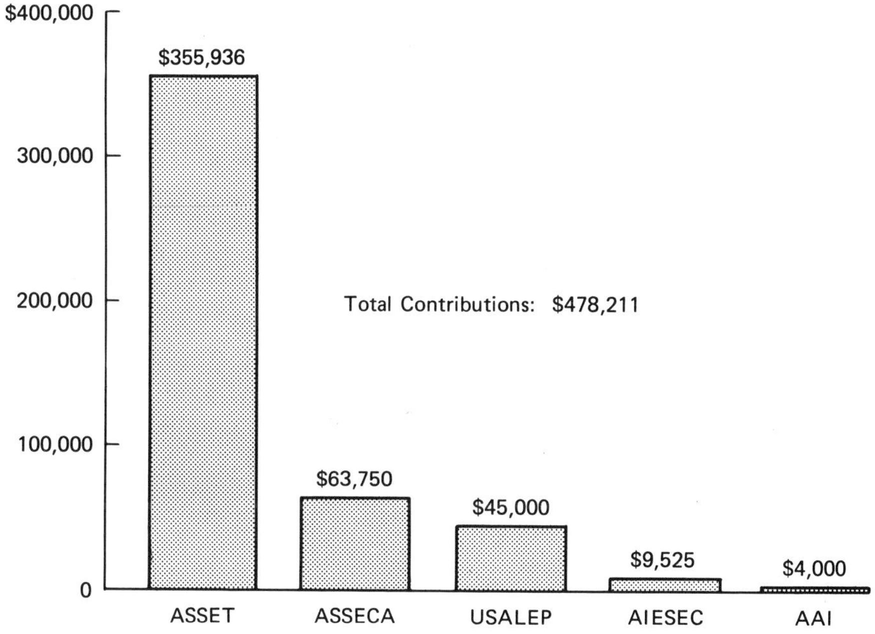

on the problem of a lack of full-time leadership. ASSECA has requested a full-time person from the United States.

Our financial contributions have also continued to ASSET. In addition we made up for the loss suffered by the recent devaluation of the dollar. Several other companies have also made substantial contributions to ASSET.

We have also made additional contributions to the United States South African Leader Exchange program, the African-American Institute, and a contribution to AIESEC in South Africa—an organization of students in economics and business administration.

With our encouragement and assistance, the Addison-Wesley Publishing Company of North Reading, Mass., donated over 22,000 new textbooks for use in black South African schools.

Training programs, medical benefits, legal aid, bursaries (scholarships) and loans have also been expanded at Frank and Hirsch.

There are some who sincerely believe that complete cessation of business with South Africa is the only solution to the existing problems. We respect that view though we continue to disagree with it. We believe that constructive engagement is the responsible course of action for an American company already there. Though Polaroid does not have plants, investments, subsidiaries or employees in South Africa, we have for a number of years sold our products through a local distributor, Frank and Hirsch (Pty.)

EXHIBIT 2 FRANK & HIRSCH PAY SCALE FOR BLACK EMPLOYEES (1970–77)

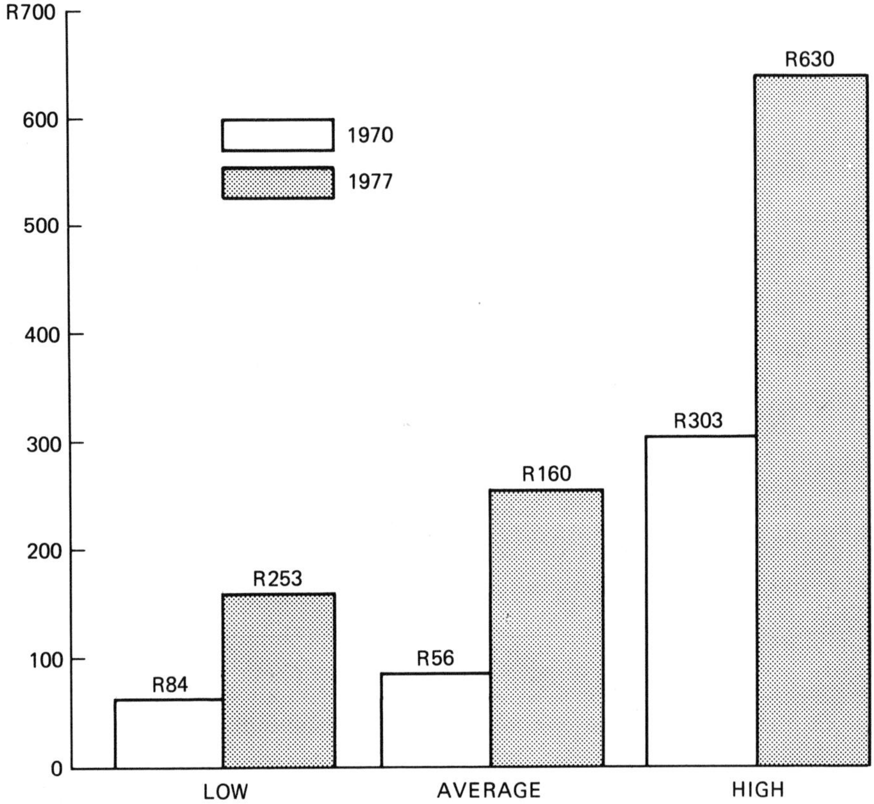

Notes: In addition to pay raises, benefits have been expanded.
Costs in this report do not include other costs of the experiment such as time, travel, audit, etc.
Total number of black employees: 1970—180; 1977—190

Ltd. We feel for that reason alone we have a responsibility not to walk away from the problem.

We are pleased that some major U. S. (and other) employers in South Africa have initiated affirmative action programs. The Company's general feeling continues to be hopeful. We are aware of a number of companies with large investments there who have started serious new programs in the country. We will continue to review our efforts with our distributor and the programs to which we are making financial contributions on an annual basis. Visitors from South Africa and many other people with whom we have corresponded have encouraged us to continue. Press reports of the effects of our experiment have reinforced our decision to proceed.

The Statement of Principles

Each of the firms endorsing the Statement of Principles have affiliates in the Republic of South Africa and support the following operating principles:

1. Non-segregation of the races in all eating, comfort, and work facilities.
2. Equal and fair employment practices for all employees.
3. Equal pay for all employees doing equal or comparable work for the same period of time.
4. Initiation of and development of training programs that will prepare, in substantial numbers, blacks and other non-whites for supervisory, administrative, clerical and technical jobs.
5. Increasing the number of blacks and other non-whites in management and supervisory positions.
6. Improving the quality of employees' lives outside the work environment in such areas as housing, transportation, schooling, recreation and health facilities.

We agree to further implement these principles. Where implementation requires a modification of existing South African working conditions, we will seek such modification through appropriate channels.

We believe that the implementation of the foregoing principles is consistent with respect for human dignity and will contribute greatly to the general economic welfare of all the people of the Republic of South Africa.

COMPANIES ENDORSING THE STATEMENT OF PRINCIPLES (AS OF SEPTEMBER 26, 1977)

Abbott Laboratories
American Cyanamid
American Hospital Supply Corporation
Avis, Inc.
The Bendix Corporation
Burroughs Corporation
Caltex Petroleum Corporation
The Carborundum Company
Carnation Company
Caterpillar Tractor Company
Citicorp
Colgate-Palmolive Company
Control Data Corporation
CPC International
Deere & Company
Del Monte Corporation
Donaldson Company, Incorporated
Eastman-Kodak Company
Envirotech Corporation
Exxon Corporation
Ford Motor Company
Franklin Electric
Gardner-Denver Company
General Motors Corporation
The Gillette Company
Goodyear Tire and Rubber Company
Heublein, Incorporated
Hewlett Packard Company
Hoover Company
Inmont Corporation
IBM Corporation
International Harvester Company
Kellogg Company
Eli Lilly & Company
Masonite Corporation
Merck & Company, Inc.
Minnesota Mining & Manufacturing Company
Mobil Corporation
Nabisco, Incorporated
Nalco Chemical Company
NCR Corporation
Otis Elevator
Pfizer, Inc.
Phelps Dodge Corporation
Phillips Petroleum
Rohm & Haas Company
Schering-Plough Corporation
The Singer Company
SmithKline Corporation
Sperry Rand Corporation
Squibb Corporation
Sterling Drug, Inc.
Union Carbide Corporation
Uniroyal, Inc.

PART III

Strategic Formulation: The Making of Company and Functional Strategies

At the midpoint of this book, let us review what we have discussed so far, and what will be covered in the remaining chapters. In Part One, The Conceptual Framework of Business Policy and Strategy, chapter 1 focused on the theoretical perspective of studying the policy course, and we introduced a conceptual model to guide our subsequent discussions. In chapter 2, we took a practical perspective in reviewing the industry practice, while stressing the importance of strategy in contemporary management. We attempt to establish that the concept is, to a certain degree, universal—is used in war, politics, and business. We introduced a few key concepts, including: the ends and means chain, the matching-calculating-selecting process, the deployment of resources, and the strategy-tactics relationship.

In Part Two, we looked into policy making and strategic planning. We covered organizing and administering the strategy function and the structure of corporate strategy from both organizational and strategic viewpoints (chapter 3). In chapters 4 and 5, we studied strategic planning. Environmental analysis and internal assessment were the topics of chapter 4, and objective setting was the subject of chapter 5. As strategic planning is largely concerned with the policy aspect of strategy making, we went into detail in discussing prerequisite analyses, from which central issues can be identified and dealt with, and policy issues can be established. Thus, strategic planning serves the function of policy formulation and defines what the company is and will be. We recognized that social responsibility impacts on the company's policy and strategic decisions. Our attempt in chapter 6 was to pinpoint its relationship with business strategy and to review public policy making and regulatory agency practices.

Developing company strategy from a group of strategic alternatives and formulating functional strategies to substantiate and implement corporate strategy are the subjects of Part Three, Strategic Formulation: The Making of Company and Functional Strategies. In chapter 7, we explore the strategic formulation process, the three strategic alternatives and behavioral aspects in strategic formulation. The strategic alternatives, not meant to be exclusive, provide a conceptual framework for assessing strategic behavior of corporations under varying conditions. Growth strategy (chapter 8) deals with one situation; in an expansive economy and market, a company chooses to pursue an offensive strategy in exploiting business and profit opportunities. Stability strategy operates in another situation, when by necessity a company chooses to fall back on a defensive-offensive strategy for temporary retrenchment and profit restoration. Survival strategy is a third alternative when for reasons of avoiding insolvency and bankruptcy, a company is compelled to form a purely defensive strategy of survival. In chapter 9, we devote our discussion to stability and survival strategies.

Strategy is a unifying concept: it unites organizational effort. Structurally, it integrates corporate strategies, functional strategies, and action plans into one mutually supportive system. Functional strategies are the links between company strategy and action plans. They serve the former and guide the latter. In chapters 10 and 11, we discuss marketing strategy and financial strategy; in chapter 12, we deal with research and development strategy and production strategy.

In the three chapters in Part Four, we will concentrate on strategy management. In chapter 13, on strategy-structure-process and human resources development, we will discuss the process of organizing strategic actions and developing human resources for organizational renewal and development. We will devote chapter 14 to tactical planning and execution, bringing strategy implementation down to working level of daily operations. In chapter 15, on strategy control and recycling, we will complete the discussion of Part Four.

In our discussion so far, we have mentioned neither strategy making in small business firms nor international business. We intentionally did so in order to keep discussions general and simple. International business strategy, like small-business strategy, has its unique features. Both small-business strategy (chapter 16) and international business strategy (chapter 17) will be discussed in Part Five. In the last chapter, chapter 18, we will summarize the essence of business strategy and suggest challenges for future executives and management.

CHAPTER SEVEN

Strategic Formulation and Choice of Alternatives

The making of strategy follows a matching-calculating-selecting process. Selecting is the concern of strategic formulation. In this chapter, we will discuss the process of assessing the company's posture, exploring and evaluating various options, selecting courses of action, and committing resources. The formulation of corporate strategy in the form of a strategic plan is, however, the practical object of the formulating process.

Strategic alternatives and their choice under certain conditions, problems likely to be encountered, anticipated outcome, and possible approaches will be the topics of the next section. We carefully developed a matrix to qualify each of the three basic alternatives: growth, profit instability, and financial insolvency. The matrix serves as a conceptual framework to assist analysis and select appropriate strategies in a given situation. Of special importance is the behavioral aspect of strategic formulation: the human element in a rational, intuitive type of decision making. We will discuss personal values, group decision making, and their interaction with one another. The impact of human element upon the choice of strategic alternatives will be emphasized.

THE FORMULATION PROCESS

Referring to the five-step process of strategic planning and strategic formulation described in chapter 4, strategic planning is the study of the policy aspect, and strategic formulation is the development of the strategic plan. The former involves conducting prerequisite studies, deliberating policy issues, and defining the ends—precisely what the company is and desires to be. The latter is the process of exploring courses of action, committing organization resources, and formulating strategies to define the means and submeans to achieve the established objectives.

The Preliminary Phase

The formulation of business strategy can be viewed as a two-phase process; the preliminary phase, and the formulation phase. Often, the preliminary phase consumes a large amount of time in developing strategic guidelines and conducting situation studies in preparing for the development of strategic plans. During the preliminary phase, there are four tasks: (1) the critical review of long-range objectives and ongoing strategies; (2) the reaffirmation of future strategic issues and the identification of critical strategic actions; (3) the preparation of strategic guidelines; and (4) the conduct of situation studies to determine the feasibility of proposed courses of actions. Let us discuss each of these briefly.

The purpose of critically reviewing long-range objectives is to ensure their realism and achievability and to check the compatibility of means and ends. When objectives are inconsistent with basic policies (for instance, a policy of retaining exclusive family control of a company would be inconsistent with the goal of rapid expansion), and when business objectives target far beyond the normal and therefore require inordinate means, strategy becomes inconsistent and thus difficult to formulate. Of course, when gross incompatibility exists between ends and means, people are inclined to use ends to justify means. Such action is detrimental to the cause of the company and is potentially disastrous.

EVALUATING ONGOING STRATEGIES Equally important is the constant evaluation of ongoing strategies. The evaluation serves two purposes: the confirmation of the viability of current strategies; and the construction of guidelines for developing new strategies. According to one author,[1] a sound strategy should meet at least the following list of criteria:

1. Is the strategy internally consistent? In a well-planned strategy, each policy fits into an integrated pattern.
2. Is the strategy consistent with the environment? A good strategy maintains consistency with the environment in both its static and its dynamic (projected) aspects.
3. Is the strategy appropriate in view of available resources? The achievement of a balance between strategic goals and available resources is an important criterion.
4. Does the strategy involve an acceptable degree of risk? Executives should be totally aware of the nature of risk—the extent of financial exposure, duration of commitment, and the size of the stakes.
5. Does the strategy have an appropriate time horizon?
6. Is the strategy workable?

Certainly, a sound strategy is judged by its ability to produce the desired short- and long-term results. A strategy that is incapable of serving as a framework for guiding critical decisions is an abstraction, totally divorced from working reality. A strategy that undergoes constant changes is one that lacks operational credibility. Indeed, a strategy that is not supported by organizational actions at the functional and project level is only partially effective, likely to suffer from inadequate implementation. Hence, in addition to the six criteria cited above, a sound strategy must meet these other criteria as well.

DEFINING STRATEGIC ISSUES The next task requires the affirmation of future strategic issues and the identification of critical strategic actions. The identification of future strategic issues requires special studies and vigilant surveillance. An impending shift in the economy, an anticipated change in government policies and regulations, or a threatening competitive action must be singled out for management attention. Likewise, critical strategic actions that are central to the success of strategy demand thorough investigation. A venture project, a divestiture program, an acquisition plan that requires long-range investment and implementation, a major advertising campaign, a large-scale borrowing program are all subjects that warrant special treatment.

The third task, the preparation of strategic guidelines, entails the discussion of a preliminary statement of business strategy. A preliminary statement discusses the company's strategic posture and possible alternatives, the level and methods of resource deployment, and guidelines for formulating functional strategies. A company's strategic posture begins with its diagnosis of its present position, from which intermediate goals are specified and future strategic development is projected, outlining decision thresholds of crucial strategic actions. The level and methods of resource deployment—the relative allocation of funds, facilities, equipment, and management among the company's key strategic functions (namely, marketing, manufacturing, R&D)—should be specified and discussed. The preliminary statement also includes guidelines to functional strategic formulation in order to avoid oversights and to ensure coordination. Strategic guidelines can be used as the basis for executive review and coordination prior to the submission of strategic plans.

Finally, situation studies are action items designed to investigate matters of utmost importance. The preparation of these studies, which is the last of the four tasks, can be assigned to whichever part of the organization possesses the competency. Thus, a close watch for shifts in the economy is a possible assignment for an economist; the monitoring of a critical technology is the function of engineering. Planning for a specific strategic action, such as an acquisition program or divestiture plan, can be assigned to task groups; an advertising campaign or fund procurement plan belongs to marketing or finance, respectively. To repeat: situation studies are not research projects of a theoretical nature, but action items that may have to be completed quickly when the needs arise in response to urgent inquiries. In other cases, they can be full-scale research requiring constant monitoring.

The Formulation Phase

The preparation of the strategic plan is the final step in the systematic and logical process of formulating strategy. Business strategy, which deals with means of achieving stated objectives is a master plan, a blueprint or a "road map." As such, it must have the virtues of clarity, brevity, dynamism. In sum, it is capable of energizing a ceaseless stream of strategic and tactical actions.

As we stated in chapter 3, a company's strategy is hierarchically constructed. Strategy, being a unified concept for organizational effort, requires the development of a series of strategic plans at the general management level and functional strategies at the functional level. Individually, each strategic plan is a part of the whole, and jointly the corporate strategy represents the total entity. Thus, the structure of the corporate strategy and the process of integrating various supporting strategic plans cannot be overlooked.

There is, of course, the central task of selecting strategic alternatives. Such a choice is of two types: the choice of a basic strategy and the choice of courses of action from among various options. The choice of a basic strategy is self-evident. Any one of the conditions—an expanding economy, a growing industry, and a strong competitive position—present growth opportunities. Sudden or prolonged profit decline, due to economic contraction, market/product obsolescence, or organizational stagnation, limits a company's choice to seek for stability. Likewise, a severe financial distress forces a company to battle for survival.

THE SELECTING PROCESS The more difficult task, however, is the selection of courses of action from among varying options. For example, growth can be obtained either from internal development through market/product development, geographic expansion, technological exploitation or from external expansion through joint venture, acquisition and merger, and/or international operations. Each course of action will be measured against many factors. These factors can include: resources expenditure; return on investment; organizational constraint; probability of success against environmental and internal assumptions; competitive counteractions; and advantages and disadvantages of the course of action itself. Above all, each course of action is viewed as a part of the central scheme and as a viable means to resolve strategic problems. Thus, an internally developed technology may serve as a spearhead for later acquisition. A new product development may be considered as an entry into a new market. Strategic selection is complex, creative, and subject to a multitude of variables. It is highly judgmental and situational, in that the final selection is largely determined by a process of trade-offs and elimination. This is accomplished by measuring each option against a set of assumptions and deploying an optimal combination of means—marketing, technological, production, and financial forces—for full impact.

In essence, a strategic plan must accurately state business objectives, define the posture, underline assumptions concerning the interplay of external and internal forces, and outline courses of action and means of deploying resources. To be sure, a good strategic plan outlines organizational and management plans for execution, showing the avenues of attack and projecting a time horizon, and specifying who does what, with whom, and how. Our discussion on formulating strategy under conditions of growth, stability, and survival will be given in chapters 8 and 9. The formulation of functional strategies will be discussed in chapters 10, 11, and 12.

CONTINGENCY PLANNING Contingency planning is a process of planning events whose occurrence is uncertain, but assumed in the original plan. The high probability of occurrences and the severe impact once they occur merit forward planning in specifying alternative action and quick regrouping to meet contingencies.

A contingency plan is a part of a company's formal strategy plan, whose basic purpose is to achieve a high state of readiness to counteract contingencies and to reduce risks.[2] Contingency planning applies to both strategic and tactical planning whenever the critical assumptions of the original plan are threatened by a high probability of uncertainty. The process itself forces management to identify and evaluate critical assumptions, to remain alert during the execution of strategy, and to respond swiftly to contingencies, thus reducing surprises and risks. One of the basic factors affecting the application of contingency planning is the environment of an organization.[3] The organization confronted with unprecedented problems and frequent changes needs flexible strategies that are highly adaptive, responsive, and amenable to risk taking.

The development of contingency plans demands special procedures. The first step is to identify critical assumptions, reflecting those assumptions of low degree of confidence, and over which the company has little control. A likely downturn of the economy, a shortage of critical material, a competitor's likely movement in the marketplace, the loss of a large contract, or a labor strike are such contingencies. The next step requires the determination of the impact of any such eventuality, its severity, and scope. A downturn in the economy may affect all business areas of a company, but with different impact for each. Once this initial analysis is complete, the planning process proceeds with reassessment of alternatives or opposite assumptions, objectives, the degree of strategic adjustment, and, if necessary, the remaking of strategy.

Finally, there is the need to establish trigger points and decision thresholds to operate contingency plans. First, the information needs must be identified, the information system selected, and its monitoring responsibilities assigned. Second, the specific measurable evidence that will cause the abandonment by management of the original assumption, if and when it occurs, must be established. Third, the amount of lead time required for a contingency response should be determined; and finally, the scenario of the response should be specified to ensure proper response to avoid overreactions or underreactions. Contingency plans can be short and/or long term. A short-term plan counteracts the contingency and accomplishes the purpose of quick regrouping with limited objectives. A long-term plan may require large redeployment of resources, if not the total remaking of strategy.

THE CHOICE OF STRATEGIC ALTERNATIVES

Almost every company faces at one time or another the crucial decisions of growth, stability, or survival. The issue is not only one of choice, but sometimes one of necessity, a compelling response to a strategic situation in time of distress. A company may view a variety of strategic situations. In the main, however, there can be three distinct situations: an opportunity for growth, a present or threatened condition of profit instability, and a clear and present danger to survival.

Growth opportunities exist in an expansive economy, in a new industry, and in a situation that is competitively advantageous due to technological advances and marketing initiative. Generally, economic prosperity benefits the auto industry with growth opportunities so auto manufacturers expand production and increase investment. The large reserves of funds among some of the oil companies, such as Exxon, Standard Oil of California, Mobil Oil, and Atlantic Richfield, have spurred a stream of acquisition activities.[4]

Profit instability occurs when a company experiences a sudden or prolonged earnings decline due to economic contraction, product obsolescence, or organizational stagnation. In 1974–1975, Sears, Roebuck experienced a sudden earnings decline during the recession;[5] several airlines suffered continuous profit deterioration for a few years. Survival problems prevailed among companies facing near-insolvency or bankruptcy. Thus, Pan American Airlines, A&P, and Chrysler went through the near-insolvency period; and Penn Central and W. T. Grant declared bankruptcy.

Conditions of Choice

The business climate, management capability, and the vicious cycle discussed in chapter 2 are the conditions giving rise to the appropriate choice of one alternative over another. The business climate reflecting the movement of the business cycle affects a company's basic position. During the 1950s, the recovery-expansion phase of the business cycle absorbed approximately seven years. The prolonged expansion in the 1960s lasted 106 months, or almost 9 years. Economic prosperity that was shared by the world economy further increased the tempo of growth.

Such economic expansion materially presents growth opportunities for most companies, particularly for those in electronics, computers, chemical, and petroleum industries. Technological explosion accompanied by favorable climate benefits almost all industries, particularly electronics, material, and pharmaceutical companies. Population growth increases personal consumption, which presents a favorable climate for companies engaging in producing consumer goods and services, including food, housing development, retailing, and service companies.

Constraint during Economic Downturn

Since the end of World War II, the United States has experienced six recessions. The moderate ones introduced periods of painful adjustments. More severe recessions, which occurred in 1957–1958 and 1973–1975, however, depressed many companies' earnings. The 1969–1970 recession, on the other hand, levied its toll mainly on the aerospace industry, and large-scale layoffs and business contraction inflicted damage to other associated industries and local economy where aerospace work was predominant. Likewise, the 1973–1975 recession hit the auto industry more severely than other industries. During periods of economic contraction, companies adopt a cautious strategy characterized by a series of actions of retrenchment, profit improvement, and, in case of continuous profit decline, even large-scale divestitures and consolidation. Thus, Sears, Roebuck's inventory reduction, price cutting, personnel layoffs, and some changes in merchandising succeeded in reverting the sudden drop of earnings. The airline companies (such as Pan American Airlines, TWA, and Eastern Airlines) made drastic cost reductions, disposed of their surplus air fleets, and readjusted route structures and schedules to reduce losses, even though the basic business climate in 1976 was primarily responsible for their recovery.

Government and Competition

Governmental regulations and competition could create a business climate that results in a drastic alteration of the strategic situations among business firms. Through positive actions—direct purchase, tax incentive allowance, and indirect promotion—government can effect favorable conditions in certain industries. The large defense and space spendings of the 1960s greatly benefited aerospace companies. Once they have become financially strong, companies such as McDonnell Douglas, Raytheon, TRW, and Texas Instruments have diversified into non-defense areas to become large, viable enterprises. The federal government's purchase of additional automobiles in 1974 and 1975 helped boost auto production. Favorable legislation is known to have benefited the oil, construction, and airline industries. The Small Business Administration has provided favorable business conditions for small business firms and minority business through loans and assistance of all types. Conversely, government and social regulations have placed restrictions on business operations.

Competition, however, is a major cause of a firm's fluctuating business situation. In the computer industry, as an illustration, IBM's dominating position has created growth opportunities for some and produced distress conditions for others. The bourgeoning computer peripheral business in the 1960s was a direct result of broadened computer applications and indirectly was a service to the mainframe computers. IBM's later expansion into certain peripheral and software work created adverse conditions for the other peripheral producers, forcing changes in their choice of strategic alternatives.

Management as a Constraint

The quality of management, which is the single most important cause of changes in a firm's fortune, requires little explanation. Successful corporations are generally blessed with outstanding business leaders; unsuccessful firms are plagued with management errors committed by their executives. Thus, GM's early success was associated with Alfred P. Sloan; Du Pont, with Pierre S. Du Pont; Sears, Roebuck, with Robert E. Woods; GE, with Ralph Cordiner; and IBM, with Thomas Watson, Sr. Two of the most important qualities that distinguish these corporate leaders from less-successful leaders are: (1) their management vision—the ability to foresee changes and the determination to challenge the future; and (2) their management depth—the capacity to successfully manage a company through a variety of strategic situations of growth, profits instability, and occasionally through periods of financial difficulties.

GE, one of the large and diversified companies, offers an illustration of good management. In the late 1940s and early 1950s, under Ralph Cordiner, GE decided to decentralize, reacting to the change of business climate and pursuing a broad strategy of diversification. By the mid-1960s, GE had grown to a company of $10 billion, a long way from a $2 billion firm of the late 1940s. Externally, GE saw the economic and social challenges. Management restructuring was centered around improving top-management decision making to achieve better balance between corporate and group-division-department and to emphasize strategic planning. GE has since weathered the dramatic business environmental changes of the 1960s, the economic hardships of the early 1970s, and is looking ahead to new challenges.

On the other hand, A&P, the largest supermarket chain until the mid-1960s, suffered prolonged stagnation, culminating in a loss of $157.1 million in 1975.[6] The underlying cause was attributed to the company's rather antiquated management structure and its insensitivity to external changes. The company management entertained no major changes for years until the installation of Jonathan L. Scott as chief executive officer in 1974, the first outsider ever presiding over the company. For years, the company maintained its old, inefficient stores in central core cities and made minimum penetration in the more affluent suburban markets. Large corporations, such as U.S. Steel, which was slow in reacting to foreign competitive threats and technological advances, and Chrysler, which was less sensitive to public desire for compact cars, also showed poor management judgment.

The Vicious Cycle as a Condition

The vicious cycle that was somewhat typical of certain companies constitutes another cause for accelerating changes in strategic situations. The dramatic impact of the cycle is not only a result of its frequency, but more important, its intensity. Most of those companies that experienced the vicious cycle (discussed in chapter 2) were largely victims of the growth syndrome. Once the growth movement begins to gather momentum, growth becomes uncontrolled. Thus, initial success often breeds the danger of errors; and moderate borrowing, for example, becomes heavy indebtedness. As the adverse business climate begins to set in, the basic assumption of success begins to crumble. Thus, the progression of the vicious cycle moves from fast growth to profit decline, and when unchecked culminates in great losses or insolvency.

STRATEGIC ALTERNATIVES

The choice of strategic alternatives is a crucial and difficult step in strategy making. It requires accurate assessment of the strategic situation and the innovative choice of approaches. An erroneous assessment of the situation leads to the choice of faulty alternatives, hence the wrong courses of action. Several reasons account for the difficulty in making accurate assessments: (1) the ever-changing environment makes forecasts uncertain. The choice represents the composite judgment about the economic, industrial, and technological trends that in turn determine the intensity of deploying forces and the timing of strategic actions. (2) A judgment of such magnitude cannot be totally rational; human emotion and economic short-sightedness often prejudice the choice. Overestimating the firm's capability and underestimating future difficulties posed by competitors' countermoves, customers' responses, and government or societal actions could result in the adoption of seemingly correct decisions. Thus, a growth strategy often appears to be an easier course than the strategy of stability, when in fact, a temporary pause is better than a quick thrust. (3) The physical inertia, brought on either by the snowballing effect of large-scale acquisition, or a persistent stagnation, often affects one's judgment. (4) The narrow margin of error in financial forecasting of return on investment and cost of capital can compound the difficulties in finding strategic solutions.

The Basic Choices

Once an accurate assessment is made on the company's present situation and its projected future, the company makes its choice among three basic alternatives: growth, stability, or survival. Within a large corporation, of course, it may pursue three strategies simultaneously. It is conceivable that one operating division may find growth as its alternative, while other divisions may be compelled to adopt stability or survival strategies. Let us briefly describe these three strategy alternatives, qualifying each with stated conditions, problems, anticipated outcome, and probable choices.[7]

GROWTH Under favorable economic, industrial, and competitive conditions, growth strategy is likely the choice. A growth cycle consists of different stages (see figure 8.1); each stage of development encounters different sets of problems.

The anticipated outcome of a growth strategy can be stated in terms of increases in sales and profits, market share, and growth rate. There are four approaches: market intensification; diversification; acquisition and merger; and international business. Each approach or course of action is selected through a tradeoff and elimination process previously discussed.

STABILITY Stability strategy is a compelling choice when a company's profit experiences decline. The decline can be a sudden or an anticipated drop, a prolonged decline, or a state of wide fluctuation (see figure 7.1). Different conditions, of course, bring different problems. However, the objective is stabilization and recovery of net income in terms of return on sales, return on assets, return on net worth, and the recovery rate. We have suggested three basic approaches: entrenchment; turnaround; and stabilization.

SURVIVAL Survival is a severe condition in which financial insolvency is visible, and bankruptcy is a possibility. The company is placed in total defense, facing drastic actions to resolve marketing, financial, and management problems. We have suggested three choices: management restructuring; marketing restructuring; and financial restructuring.

The Strategic Alternative Matrix

To facilitate analysis and to clearly identify approaches, a strategic alternative matrix is thus constructed. The matrix is designed as a framework for analyzing business policy cases, and as a basis of guiding the development of strategic actions (see table 7.1).

BEHAVIORAL ASPECT OF STRATEGIC FORMULATION

In the previous chapters, we emphasized the logical, rational process of strategic planning and formulation. We explained what "ought to be done" under a given set of external circumstances and available resources. However, we do not delude ourselves into thinking that executive decision making always follows

FIGURE 7.1 DIFFERENT CONDITIONS OF PROFIT INSTABILITY

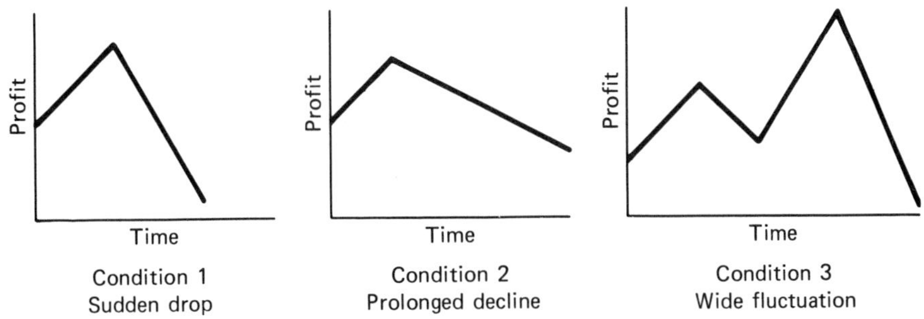

TABLE 7.1 STRATEGIC ALTERNATIVES MATRIX

Alternatives	*Criteria*	*Approaches*
Growth (offensive)	Sales Profits Market share Growth rate	Market intensification—market penetration, market development, geographical expansion Diversification—vertical, horizontal, lateral Acquisition and merger International business—exporting, foreign licensing, direct investment
Stability (defensive—offensive)	Return on sales Return on assets Return on equity Rate of recovery	Retrenchment—contraction, consolidation, recovery Turnaround—profit improvement, profit restoration, financial maturity Stabilization—selectivity, market balancing, financial retrenchment
Survival (total defense)	Critical evaluation of market and product of financial position of management	Management restructuring—structure, process, personnel Financial restructuring—capitalization restructure, divestiture, cash rebuilding Market restructuring—withdrawal, acute retrenchment, moderate expansion in selected markets

sound, objective deliberation. Scholars have long recognized the impact of other noneconomic factors. These factors make the resulting decisions less than optimum in terms of business and economic goals. We recognize them as constraints that must be understood if one is to comprehend why certain decisions are preferred over others. For the purpose of this discussion, we will examine the impact of two factors: personal values, and group process.

Personal Values and Strategic Decisions

In decision making, managers cannot separate their feelings, emotions, and personal preferences from economic considerations. True, economic factors are considered, but simultaneously personal likes and dislikes also figure in the process. At times, managers may forgo economic reasoning and proceed with what they prefer to do, paying minimal attention to other relevant factors. The overriding consideration in this case is the manager's personal values. Values refer to a conception of what an individual or group regards as desirable.[8] They are deeply rooted feelings about ideals and philosophy. Values result from the accumulation of previous experiences, perceptions, and memories; and indeed, behavior is a function of personal history.[9] Managers may not be consciously aware of their values, yet they affect their perceptions and choices, and strategic decision making is no exception. In a sense, strategy making may be a reflection of personal values.[10] One need only to look at various companies to see how their destinies have been strongly shaped by the personal preferences of key managers. To cite one example among many: Hugh Hefner, president and owner of Playboy Enterprises, imposed his life style and personality on the product/service choice, image, and character of his organization. Fortunately, his philosophy was shared by a substantial segment of the urban male population, enabling him to build a multimillion dollar publishing and entertainment empire.

Understanding values is essential to decision making in that it gives insight as to why particular decisions are selected over others. Such an awareness helps guard against biases and tendencies, operating mostly at the subconscious level. Understanding their own values also helps managers to understand other people's values, particularly those of peers and members of the organization who may be affected by managerial decisions. Such awareness can be useful in providing guidelines in discussion or negotiating with others. What may appear to be a nonrational choice may actually make sense if others' values were considered. To understand a personal value system, Guth and Tagiuri suggest that managers examine their behavior from time to time with the question of what value they hold.[11] It can also be helpful for them to compare their own behaviors with those of others facing similar situations. Another approach is for the managers to analyze the situation when they feel their values are being violated. They can also take one or more of the tests designed to identify personal values, preferably with the assistance of a competent trainer.

Group Process of Strategic Decision

Throughout our discussion, we have emphasized the value of group deliberation on strategic decisions. We recognize that the responsibility of choosing or rejecting a decision rests with the individual who alone has the final say. The deliberation, however, is not and should not be confined to one individual at all times. Deliberating strategic decisions, whether involving the adoption of a new product line or the divestiture of certain assets calls for the work of managers in group settings. Group deliberation can be carried out in committees, conferences, and task teams. There is evidence that when the problem requires few steps and where the solution can be verified either mathematically or logically and where there is need for considerable information, groups have been found to perform better than the average individual.[12] For example, group members who are more knowledgeable regarding certain areas of the problem will be able to point out any incorrect solutions. Individuals working alone do not have this advantage. There is a good chance that the sum total of knowledge, viewpoints, and skills of the group would be greater than that of any member. Thus, the group as a whole should have more resources with which to pool information, analyze situations, and think up alternatives at the same time. There may be greater interest aroused by group membership leading to greater effort at information gathering and problem solving. Of course, the group may be unable to capitalize on this wide array of resources if the members were unwilling to cooperate and share information. Finally, it is well-known that participation results in greater acceptance of the decision by the management concern. Hence, group decision may serve as a means for motivating people to implement the decision.

On the other hand, when the problem necessitates a sequence of multiple stages, when it is not easily divisible into separate parts, and when a solution is not easily demonstrable, group process may interfere with decision making. The reason is that if the problem is not divisible, the advantage of division of labor is lost. Second, if the correctness of the solution is difficult to verify, it takes much longer to reach agreement. Third, group discussion tends to interfere with the concentration necessary to put the stages of the problem into correct sequence.

Of course, there are other limitations to group process. First, social pressure can lead to conformity. Under pressure of maintaining harmony and conformity, the group may lose the ability to critically examine alternatives. Such tendencies may be harmful, particularly when the group is faced with decisions of grave consequences. This phenomenon, called "groupthink," was named and defined by Janis.[13] Drawing from information on the Bay of Pigs invasion, the escalation of the Vietnam War, and other momentous decisions, he describes a powerful social pressure that a cohesive group brings to bear upon its members whenever they demonstrate objections to the group ideas. In all, Janis identified eight main symptoms of "groupthink." Although the studies are taken from government decisions, he concludes that the phenomenon exists in industry and nonprofit organizations as well. Second, individual and/or departmental conflicts can degenerate into personality contests and harmful confrontation. Under such situations, members may expend more effort enhancing their own position, putting down others, or withholding information than they will in concentrating on the problem at hand.

All this implies that the decision maker must make some judgment in choosing the situations in which to act independently and those in which to act through group discussion. The factors to consider include the complexity of the problem, the information requirements, the structure and divisibility of the problem, and the time available.

SUMMARY

Strategic formulation centers on exploring options and selecting means to resolve central strategic issues and to achieve corporate objectives. Its practical purpose is the development of strategic plans and conversion of strategies into actions. Hence, strategic formulation follows strategic planning and precedes strategic management of implementation and recycling.

Formulation of strategies follows a two-phase process. In the preliminary phase there are four tasks. The purpose is to fully prepare management to critically review objectives and central issues and explore available options. During the formulation phase, management decides on the appropriate strategic alternatives, selects course of action, and commits resources and organization. We mention the importance of contingency planning and the necessary steps to trigger its operation.

Our strategic alternative matrix serves as a simplified conceptual framework for analyzing business situations. Its applications, however, require penetrating analysis. For example, the selection of a company's courses of action to pursue growth fundamentally depends on the state of the company's business—precisely at what stage the company is in the growth cycle. We emphasize serious studies of the prescribed conditions, the different types of problems, and the appropriate approach for each situation. Hence, familiarity with the four subgrowth strategies is a prerequisite to formulation of growth strategy. The same rigorous treatment applies to the other two alternatives of stability and survival.

To be sure, behavioral impact on strategic formulation is most elusive. We have highlighted individual and group values and suggested means to enhance individual awareness and group contribution.

NOTES

1. Seymour Tilles, "How to Evaluate Corporate Strategy," *Harvard Business Review,* July-August 1963, pp. 11–121.
2. Contingency planning is considered as one of risk-reducing strategy. John Argenti, *Systematic Corporate Planning,* pp. 238–240. Also, D. E. Hussey, *Introducing Corporate Planning* (Oxford: Pergamon Press, 1971), pp. 71–76.
3. The three environmental types are: stable; regulated flexibility; and adaptive. William H. Newman, *Strategy and Management Structure* in *Contingency Views of Organization and Management,* ed. Fremont E. Kast and James E. Rosenzweig (SRA, 1973), pp. 287–303.
4. Atlantic Richfield's attempt to acquire Anaconda, Mobil Oil's acquisition of Marco Inc., and Standard Oil of California's acquisition of AMAX (a mining company) are recent examples.
5. *Wall Street Journal,* 10 February 1975, p. 1.
6. *Business Week,* 19 May 1975, pp. 128–36.
7. The development of a series of conditional propositions about strategy selection in a given situation as suggested by Charles W. Hofer previously cited is theoretically desirable. The lack of empirical studies coupled with the reality of handling the infinite number of variables makes the approach questionable at this time. Our attempt is preliminary but quite effective in guiding strategic formulation in actual practice and in case analysis.
8. William D. Guth and Renato Tagiuri, "Personal Values and Corporate Strategies," *Harvard Business Review,* September-October 1965, p. 125.
9. James March and Herbert Simon, *Organizations* (New York: Wiley, 1958), p. 9.
10. C. Roland Christensen, Kenneth R. Andrews, and Joseph L. Bowers, *Business Policy: Text and Cases* (Homewood, Ill.: Irwin, 1978), pp. 448–49.
11. Guth and Tagiuri, "Personal Values and Corporate Strategies."
12. H. H. Kelley and J. W. Thibaut, "Group Problem Solving," in *The Handbook of Social Psychology,* 2nd ed., ed. Gardner Lindsey and Elliot Aronson (Reading, Mass.: Addison-Wesley, 1969), chap. 29.
13. Irving L. Janis, "Groupthink," *Psychology Today,* November 1971, p. 87.

CHAPTER EIGHT

Corporate Strategy I: Growth Strategy

In an expanding market and at a certain stage of a company's business development, growth is the chief concern. Growth has been a long-term goal of almost all business firms; indeed no firm would entertain a goal of consistent contraction for its own obliteration. In terms of policy, growth must be regarded as a business decision, an investment problem, and a management challenge. As a business decision, a firm can adopt either a defensive policy of expansion or an offensive policy of accelerated growth, largely depending upon the articulation of its purpose, mission, and broad business objectives. As an investment problem, growth is judged by economic and financial facts, whether or not a given investment can yield an accepted return. Increases in earnings and size lead to complexity and difficulties in management. Hence, growth poses challenges to management.

In terms of strategy, growth strategy is the single most important means to achieve a company's long-term objectives. A defensive strategy in case of normal expansion directs a company's orderly progression toward stability. An offensive strategy pursues a course through which the company takes the initiative to seize economic and marketing opportunities to aggressively expand its market share and financial gains. Inevitably, growth strengthens the internal organization. A growth-minded company attracts talent, creates a climate for achievement, and ultimately enhances its prestige and competitive position.

In this chapter, we discuss the growth pattern, the progression of a growth cycle and its control, the variations of growth strategies to direct long-term growth, and the four basic approaches to growth. We consider growth strategy basic to the three strategic alternatives. In an ordinary expansion or in a more aggressive growth, growth strategy is imperative. During a period of profit instability, growth strategy is formulated to direct the last phase of recovery. In case of financial insolvency, management depends on growth strategy to achieve early resumption of growth.

THE GROWTH PATTERN

Condition of Growth

It has been established that growth is a biological as well as a physical phenomenon. Biologically, an organ grows through a cycle, moving from one stage to the next predictable stages. Each stage contains a different set of conditions; thus varying problems are encountered. An organization, such as a business firm, if not well nurtured and sustained, can perish at any stage of its existence. Physically, growth causes changes in the physical state of things, in their size and power. Thus, a linear or accelerated growth, while increasing size and power, if unchecked, leads the organization to physical strangulation and biological degeneration.

Business growth is no exception to these biological and physical constraints. Not only does business growth follow a pattern, but it requires strategic direction, effective control, and conscientious management.

Throughout the process of growth, management is continually confronted with various strategic decisions related to products, markets, operations, and resources. To aid in analyzing these complex issues and studying alternatives, management must carefully examine the growth model of business firms. Much has been written about how business organizations grow. Structurally, business organizations can grow from a simple structure, to a functional organization, to a more complex divisionalized entity.[1] These studies are helpful in explaining the structural adaptation of the firm, but they do not lend themselves to in-depth analysis for rendering strategic decisions. What we are proposing is a five-stage model that will describe the characteristics of the changing conditions and the problems that have to be resolved during the various stages of growth. The growth model includes planning, initiation, penetration, accelerated growth, and transition, as portrayed in figure 8.1.

Decisions during a Growth Cycle

During the *planning stage,* the chief objective is to achieve a position of readiness and formulate the strategy for growth. A company's readiness exists when it has acquired the management and financial capacity to exploit external opportunities. To determine its readiness for growth, the following conditions should be taken into account:

1. Business profit opportunities have been clearly identified, and serious consideration has been given to the availability of resources in exploiting market/product/competitive advantages.
2. An aggressive commitment has been made to achieve immediate and long-range growth objectives without creating a snowballing effect that could result in a dangerous increase in indebtedness.
3. Management has acquired the capability to handle adequately the more expansive and demanding tasks of managing growth and is prepared to face changes in organizational structure and personnel to cope with a more complex business operation.

FIGURE 8.1 THE FIVE-STAGE GROWTH MODEL

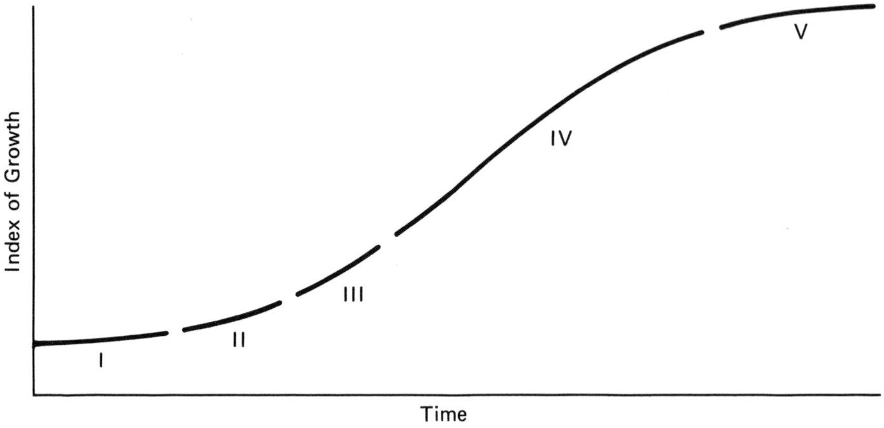

4. The company possesses the needed capacity to finance the immediate investment and is prepared to develop additional capacity to face increased obligations and anticipated requirement in case of unexpected business downturn.

In formulating growth strategy, management redefines the company's purpose, mission, and objectives, and sets forth basic policies. Growth policies state the company's growth philosophy: its views on internal development versus external growth; its guidelines on broadened business operations and management. The growth strategy prescribes the courses of action and constructs the timetable for obtaining and committing resources.

The *initiation stage* sees the company launch into growth. During this period, added constraints resulting from increased financial obligations are felt. Operational problems stemming from moving further on the learning curve, inventory buildups, and operational bottlenecks are experienced. And, administrative difficulties are expected due to newly recruited personnel and procedural confusion. Sales rise slowly, and earnings are initially depressed. Organization and personnel are taxed, but morale is high. Typically, the firm passes through this stage very quickly.

The *penetration stage* comprises a period of further penetration into the primary market, when sales and earnings are rising proportionally, and certain competitive advantages are firmly established. In case of acquisition and merger, the integration of the acquiring operations is completed, centralized planning and control is well established, and the identity of the company's integrated products and services is well defined and accepted. At this point, the company has reached a point of accelerated growth.

Accelerated growth is a period that the company attempts to prolong and fully exploit. During this period, sales and earnings rise sharply, market share expands greatly, and the organization goes into a state of euphoria. Later, the management will begin to feel strain. New facilities must be acquired, equipment and machinery await replacement. Organizational and personnel changes are made, and the financial strain can cause serious consequences.

The *transition stage* is critical to the company's long-term growth. During this stage, growth slows down, earnings increase faster than sales, but the organization shows signs of aging. Continual sales slowdown may be caused by competitors' counterattacks, industrial and market changes, and by the company's own overextended operations. Earlier success leads to complacency and stagnation. To survive this stage, the firm undertakes a planned entrenchment. This will allow for a period of digestion, consolidation, and rebuilding of management capacity and financial strength. These efforts will prepare the firm for the next cycle of long-term growth.

THE VARIATION OF GROWTH STRATEGIES

Objectives, Constraints, and Problems

In formulating growth strategy, a concise evaluation of objectives, constraints, and anticipated management difficulties associated with managing an expansive organization is important. As stated previously, growth strategy can be either defensive or offensive. It is defensive when the firm attempts to preserve its survival and to avoid stagnation. Most probably, a firm pursuing defensive growth will limit its actions to internal development, avoiding acquisition and mergers. In pursuing aggressive growth, a firm assumes an offensive position to achieve significant increases in size, market share, sales and earnings, plus other economic gains associated with size. Strategically, it employs numerous approaches (which we will discuss in the next section) through both internal and external developments.

Premature growth, overexpansion, and ill-conceived and ill-executed growth can degenerate into failures, reversing the company's forward movement In both defensive and offensive applications, growth must be treated as a long-term proposition. A company progressively advances from one stage to the next and from the first growth cycle to the next. Its overall planned growth rate is fashioned by the opportunities themselves and is controlled by internal constraints. During a growth cycle, structural changes produce changes in management style, organizational characteristics, and complexity in operations. Throughout the five-stage development, a variety of growth strategies are prescribed to anticipate and resolve difficulties during each stage and provide management with means to interact with changing realities. Let us discuss each in turn.

The Initiation Strategy

The objective of the initiation strategy is to obtain moderate growth goals, while making a concentrated effort to quickly bring the company's operations to full efficiency. Strategically, management maintains a vigilant position, contesting its early assumptions against realities and appraising the working mechanism of the expanded marketing forces. Similarly, management assumes close surveillance over internal operations, making sure that resource development actions are coordinated and all preparatory work is completed. Early production malfunctioning, operational bottlenecks, administrative difficulties, cost overruns, and cash deficiencies must be removed. An organization with heightened morale and efficient operations is ready to move to the next stage, that of penetration.

The Penetration Strategy

The penetration strategy directs the company's efforts towards making deeper penetration in the prime market areas and applying additional approaches to quicken the rate of growth. The strategy calls for management's reevaluation of company objectives, matching updated data and recalculating the probability of attainment. Limited acquisition and merger can be attempted to increase the firm's overall capacity and to test management's ability to plan and manage acquisitions and mergers. Long-range programs aimed at recruiting and developing executives; strengthening financial position; modernizing plant, equipment, and machinery; and accelerating research and development work should attract management's attention. Once the intermediate goals are achieved and initial operations are fully prepared to meet still-larger and more complex challenges, the company enters the next stage, that of accelerated growth.

Accelerated Growth Strategy

Full exploitation of external opportunities and internal capability is the objective of an accelerated growth strategy. The accelerated growth stage should be extended as long as possible; its momentum should be kept up at all times. Strategically, the company's resources are fully deployed and the four basic approaches have been attempted. Management assumes an aggressive style of management by encouraging organization members to initiate changes and by making resources available for calculated exploitation. Earning growth finally catches up and surpasses sales. Market share has been enlarged, and competitive position more deeply entrenched. In the meantime, general management at all levels must be alert to sense real and potential threats from the marketplace and to detect signs of internal complacency and fatigue. Early detection of such warnings signals the arrival of the transition stage.

The Transition Strategy

The transition strategy directs company operations during the crucial period of its long-term growth. The objective is to provide the growing organization a period of digestion, consolidation, and regrouping, launching it into the next growth cycle. After a long period of accelerated growth, the company deliberately slows down its growth rate and enters into a period of tranquility, "a breathing spell," so to speak.

A transition strategy prescribes a course of retrenchment, digesting newly acquired gains, and consolidating or trimming established business. Internally, cost reduction, cash rebuilding, profit improvement, and management audit are necessary to achieve a position of readiness. Simultaneously, management moves into the planning stage, reassessing the company's purpose, mission, and objectives, redefining policies and business interest, and formulating strategy to direct the next growth cycle. The transition strategy is the most important, yet most commonly ignored, part of the growth strategy. It slows down the snowball effect of a prolonged growth and reduces the enormous financial stress imposed upon a growth-intensive company. It corrects complacency and provides management with perspective, badly needed in times of success. The simultaneous entry into another planning stage facilitates recycling of the strategy-making process and prevents stagnation.

We have quickly provided a conceptual outline of the various strategies. Growth encompasses varied situations: the start of a new business; a young, growing company struggling for existence; a medium-sized company; and a multinational corporation striving for size and ability to survive. Hence, growth strategy offers the means to achieve these objectives.

THE BASIC APPROACHES TO GROWTH

In pursuing growth strategy, Ansoff has developed a growth vector matrix that suggests two basic approaches for growth: expansion, and diversification.[2] Expansion includes market penetration, which can increase a company's market share with its present products/markets, and product development, which assumes new product development to replace the current ones. Diversification represents a new, distinct departure seeking businesses new to the firm.

We have expanded the two basic approaches to four: market intensification; diversification; acquisition and merger; and international operation (see table 8.1). Market intensification is a basic approach in safeguarding and expanding the company's primary market. Market penetration and market development through new product development to replace the old, and geographical expansion by escalating product/market coverage to the regional or national level, are the major components of market intensification. Diversification offers a more aggressive approach. Whereas vertical and horizontal diversifications are confined to an industry, lateral, or conglomerate, diversification is a still more aggressive action across indus-

TABLE 8.1 BASIC GROWTH APPROACHES

Approaches	*Elements*	*Scope*	*Chief Means*
Market intensification	Product Product lines Market	Within industry	Market penetration Development Geographical expansion
Diversification	Business area	Within and outside industry	Internal development Vertical/Horizontal/ Lateral diversification
Acquisition and merger	Product Market Business area	All-inclusive	Purchase of a firm Merger of companies
International business	Product Market Business area	Across country lines	Exporting Foreign licensing Direct investment

try lines. Diversification is as much an investment decision as a management proposition. It poses new management challenges. Acquisitions and mergers offer quick gain in product, market, technology, financial resources, and management capabilities, not to mention profit and growth. Depending upon the purpose and scope of the venture, acquisitions and mergers call for planning and managing throughout the whole process of preacquisition, acquisition, and postacquisition. International business constitutes another option for growth. It offers countless opportunities: low-cost production; large profits; and an expanding market. International expansion can be achieved through market penetration, market development and/or acquisition and merger.

Illustration capsule 13 describes Revlon Inc. as an example. The company, through the pursuit of the four basic approaches, has maintained a continuous, steady growth in sales and profits.

Illustration Capsule 13

REVLON INC.

Revlon, worldwide leader in cosmetics, was started in 1932 by Charles Revson and his brother, Joseph. Forty years later, Michel C. Bergerac was lured from ITT to be President of Revlon, with a $1.5 million bonus for signing, and a $325,000 a year salary. When Bergerac came in, he found Revlon lacking in fundamental merchandising strengths even though they had good instincts. Bergerac came in and organized the marketing efforts and continued a controlled growth program.

Current Revlon strategy takes differences in consumer attitudes and preferences into account through a program of market segmentation that has been successful in achieving growth across a broad range of product categories. Revlon had developed a variety of product lines, targeted to correlate with the lifestyle, identity, taste, and income levels that distinguish large groups of consumers from one another. The product lines are then organized into seven houses with their own management, display areas in stores, and sometimes a separate sales force. In this way, Revlon has found an entry into each consumer group, and their marketing tactics have highly enhanced their success.

Bergerac's introduction to Revlon has brought management changes along with marketing changes. Revlon has become cash conscious. At year end 1974, cash was $108 million. At year end 1975, cash had increased to $241 million. The increase was generated by better inventory control, faster accounts receivable turnover, and the sale of $100 million of ten-year notes. Inventory control, once ignored, is being carefully monitored, as it is Bergerac's opinion that all management mistakes end up in inventory. Revlon is also beefing up their corporate staff. They have added their first financial officer, and a vice president to act as counsel to Bergerac. Once a one-man show, Revlon is now decentralizing management and making managers more informed. Bergerac has instituted marketing and management meetings with his ten or fifteen top executives for the purpose of exchanging ideas and building of company strategies.

With the entrance of Bergerac, Revlon now has a planned and highly successful approach to the market. Bergerac is also pursuing the program of planned growth put in place before his arrival. Once only a cosmetics company, Revlon now has interests in ethical drugs, proprietary drugs and toiletries, and optical products. Their plan of diversification has been to stay in related areas that can make use of many of the same distribution channels.

USV Pharmaceuticals division was purchased in 1966. It produces ethical drugs such as antibiotics and antihistamines. During the same time period, the Mitchum-Thayer division was added. Mitchum-Thayer produces proprietary drugs and toiletries such as dental adhesive and skin toning cream. In 1974, two domestic clinical labs were added along with a handful of small companies in Venezuela and Australia. Then in 1976, Meloy labs, with thirteen clinical immuno-diagnostic labs and fifteen satellite centers, was added. To Mitchum-Thayer, Norcliff labs was added. Also, in 1976 Coburn Optical, a producer of lenses and other optical equipment, was purchased. Later, in August of 1976, Barnes-Hind was purchased to fill out the optical line. By this time, entry into foreign markets had been accomplished. The West German pharmaceuticals company, ICN, gave Revlon entry into the German market. The purchase of Bozzano, the leading cosmetics house in Brazil, opened that country.

Revlon's sales have climbed from $455 million in 1972 to $959 million in 1976. Net earnings went from $40 million to $84 million in the same time frame. Revlon has achieved growth through the use of innovative marketing techniques and an orderly, well-calculated growth strategy.

Source: "Charles Revson: Marketing Genius," *Business Week*, 13 September 1976, pp. 12–14.

Approach 1: Market Intensification

Market intensification refers to the company's efforts to maintain and expand its position in its primary market area. It centers around the present product/product line/market, and its natural extension and planned expansion into related market areas. Market intensification can be either protective or expansive. Protective market intensification maintains the company's "legitimate growth rate" in the established areas; expansive market intensification penetrates into related market areas. Protective methods include market penetration by product modification, new product development to replace the old, and other pricing and nonpricing competitive means. Expansive methods include market development by means of new product development, acquisition, or joint venture, but with the basic marketing mix, such as channels of distribution and mode of selling, remaining unaltered.[3] Market intensification can be pursued along three major courses:

1. *Market penetration:* Consists of aggressive marketing activities to increase sales of present products in the company's primary markets. This effort may include three possibilities: (a) The company can try to stimulate customers to increase their present rate of consumption. Product modification to expand consumption and price incentives to increase buying are such inducements. (b) The company can introduce brand/product differentiation and increase promotion to attract new customers. (c) The company can introduce product

modification and develop new products to replace the old, thus prolonging product life cycle of current products and avoiding obsolescence.

2. *Market development:* Consists of the planned marketing of present products or the development of new products as an entry into new, related markets. This effort offers two possibilities: (a) the company can market present products, with or without modifications, appealing to those customers in the related market areas through product improvement, different channels of distribution, or use of other advertising media; and (b) the company can enter into the new market by developing new products, acquiring companies already in the market, or collaborating with other companies through joint venture.
3. *Geographical expansion:* Moves the present product into new geographical areas, escalating coverage to adjacent territorial areas for regional or national sale. It offers two possibilities: (a) the company can enlarge its internal sales force or acquire additional channels of distribution, sales agents, or manufacturing representatives; and (b) the company can franchise its operation through a chain of franchisers that, by contract, act as retailing outlets and that have made the same product/market commitment. The fast food industry, for instance, has followed this arrangement whereby the franchisee and franchiser share profit and management responsibilities.

Approach 2: Diversification

Diversification can be horizontal, vertical, or lateral, which is also classified by the Department of Justice as conglomerate.[4] Horizontal diversification takes advantage of capitalizing on a firm's strengths—its knowledge, skill, and technology in the industry it serves—to enter into major new markets of that industry. When a military electronics manufacturer diversifies into the commercial electronics market, for example, technology may be the motivator and the common thread. In such a case, the firm's marketing mix must undergo reorientation because the market characteristics of commercial electronics differs vastly from military electronics. For example, in the commercial electronics market, customer makeup, product design, channels of distribution, pricing methods, and methods of selling are very different from those of selling to the government.

TYPES OF DIVERSIFICATION *Vertical diversification* (integration) consists of company activities to absorb suppliers, intermediate manufacturers, and distribution outlets along the sequential processing of a particular product from its material origin to its ultimate consumers. Thus, a company can achieve either backward integration by absorbing material processors, suppliers, or component manufacturers, or forward integration by acquiring end product manufacturers, intermediate agents, or distributing outlets. Vertical integration is quite common among oil, rubber, basic metal, and forest products industries. The advantages of vertical diversification lie in better control of material suppliers and possible reduction in cost. There are certain disadvantages for both horizontal and vertical diversification: notably, the limited growth possibilities in one industry, and the likely risk of antitrust violations.

Horizontal diversification is commonly practiced in industry. It takes the form of internal development through product/market expansion inside an industry and/or through external acquisitions operating within the same economic/marketing environment. Vertical diversification enhances economic/marketing power of a firm; horizontal diversification adds to the firm's flexibility. Marketing and technology are the common threads underscoring the rationale for such moves. Warner-Lambert is an excellent example.[5] Based on the company's knowledge and established strengths in selling through supermarkets and drug stores, it has made thirty-one acquisitions in the past seventeen years. Among its acquired companies are American Chicklet in 1962 (sales in 1978, $578 million), Parke-Davis (sales in 1978, $528 million), and Entenmann's (1978 sales, $142 million), among others. Commonality in channels of distribution is often the rationale for acquisitions.

Lateral or conglomerate diversification is a bold attempt to diversify outside of an industry. It offers quick growth, broader stability, and greater profit potential. On the other hand, it involves higher risks and thus the potential of greater losses. A successful diversification of such magnitude requires management depth to develop sound strategy, to manage a complex unrelated business, and to conserve and develop financial resources.

REASONS FOR DIVERSIFICATION It is important to recognize that diversification is not the panacea for ending management growth problems. Should a firm consider diversification, it is of prime importance to determine the purpose or reasons for such a strategy. Precisely, why should a firm diversify? Four underlying reasons have been suggested.[6] (1) Selecting greater growth, which can no longer be realized by expansion; (2) achieving better use of financial resources when retained earnings exceed planned investment needs; (3) exploiting new potential opportunities for greater profitability wherein company resources can be better used; (4) achieving distinct competitive advantages and broader stability.

A company clearly aware of its purpose will consider diversification a long-term program, proceeding systematically step by step, and containing a common thread running through various diversification actions. When diversifying, a company capitalizes on its strengths—its production capacity, its access to a specific market, its technological capability—and avoids the pitfalls inherent in a poorly conceived diversification program.[7] Euphoric expectation, underestimation of difficulties, and lack of attention to the snowballing effect that accelerates diversification to a higher momentum are all self-destructive when not considered seriously.[8]

Another important decision is the choice between internal development through company-conducted R&D, production buildup or newly established marketing organization, and external development through acquisition and merger. Internal development offers a slower pace of growth, less initial cost, and lower risks, but it provides a company with a base of capabilities from which other diversification attempts can be developed systematically. We may safely consider internal development as a major, indispensable way of expansion. The choice between internal and external development is one of economics (the growth rate, return on investment, and payoff periods), and one of purpose (long-term versus short-term, organization character, and management philosophy).

Illustration capsules 14 and 15 explain how two such companies attained impressive growth through internal development. Digital Equipment Corp., a leading minicomputer manufacturer, managed to develop company sales in twenty-one years to $1.5 billion in 1978, mainly through internal development. Intel Corp., one of the three semiconductor leaders, achieved a strong position through well-managed R&D programs to increase sales in eight years to $226 million in 1976.

Illustration Capsule 14

DIGITAL EQUIPMENT CORP.

Digital Equipment Corporation (DEC) was founded by two Massachusetts Institute of Technology engineers in 1957, Harlan Anderson and Kenneth Olsen. It was originally a small, computer components company. Today, the company employs over 38,000 employees. DEC ranks sixth among the top fifty computer firms in the nation. The firm's revenues come from five product groups: 30 percent from minicomputer products; 11 percent from the larger mainframes; 37 percent from peripherals and terminals; 2 percent from the media and supplies; and 20 percent from software and services. Foreign sales generates about 36 percent of the volume. Net income before taxes in 1977 was $176.4 million. Revenue was about $1.4 billion in 1978.

DEC emphasizes low-cost, very fast minicomputers that can be used widely in various types of fields. DEC supplies the industry with a broad spectrum of computers priced at as low as $8,000 to as high as $1.5 million for main-frame computers.

Many employees consider DEC the "ideal" place to work. Good employee relations are emphasized as one of the keys to the company's success. During slowdowns, workers are either switched to busier departments or allowed to stay idle. There are various continuing education programs for both high school and college credits. Each year, management groups establish goals for the coming year. If successful, their budget is increased accordingly. The firm still holds a yearly outing for employees at a New Hampshire amusement park. Kenneth Olsen, one of the original founders and now company president, believes that it is DEC's attitude toward its employees that accounts for much of the company's success.

Another factor in DEC's growth is not the pursuit of "growth" as a goal, but the obligation to stick with customers once a commitment is made. Further reasons include the general growth of the computer market, part of which DEC helped create.

From the beginning, DEC "made a different product, for different customers, with different needs," and it sold and serviced its computers in different ways. When DEC's first computers hit the market, they were faster, simpler, more rugged, and less expensive than other machines on the market. They could go almost anywhere and gave immediate answers to input. Operation was simple. Connection to other apparatus was easy. Digital's first customers were scientists and engineers—not business operations. Customers wanted a different type of analysis. "On-line, interactive, general purpose, inexpensive, high performance, hands-on" were key words describing DEC's product in the marketplace.

Another tactic used to gain business was to sell to Original Equipment Manufacturers. The OEM would then incorporate DEC computers into their own products, thus broadening the applications of DEC products. Many of DEC's customers did not want or need total dependence upon DEC, so the company organized itself to give support at whatever level was cost effective for the customer. Today, DEC offers a variety of support and service packages to customers. The company encourages customer self-reliance as a matter of corporate philosophy.

DEC has, over the years, developed a family of computers known as PDP. DEC's first computer was developed in 1960. New models are constantly in development. Yet all earlier models are in use and spare parts are continuously in production. The company has 136 sales offices throughout the world and prefers to sell, not rent, its products.

It has been Digital's unique approach to both customers and employees, along with advanced technology, that have caused it to expand without the use of acquisition and with a great deal of success.

Source: David Gumpert, "Rags to Riches," *Wall Street Journal,* 18 July 1978, p. 1; "DEC's Growth Leaves Gaps for Competition to Fill," *Datamation,* January 1977, p. 141; and DEC *Annual Report,* 1977.

Illustration Capsule 15

INTEL CORP.

Intel was founded in 1968 to design, develop, and market products based on integration of complex electronic functions on a small chip of semiconductor material. These components are commonly referred to as "LSI" components. Intel has pioneered in the technology on LSI components and has set the direction of important product development.

Standard LSI circuits produced by Intel encompass random access memories, read-only memories, shift registers, and related logic arrays, and compete with magnetic core memories due to their faster performance, easier maintenance, and lower cost.

Intel sells microcomputer products as components or as complete microcomputer systems. In 1976, to handle these products and the related customers, the Microcomputer Division was established. Prior to this, in 1972, Microma Inc. was acquired. This company makes and markets digital watches using their own quality crystal.

Intel went from a relatively small company to a good sized one. In 1972, sales were $23.4 million, and profits were $2.0 million. By 1976, sales had increased to $226.0 million, and profits had jumped to $25.2 million. Factors involved in Intel's growth were multiple. By 1976, the demand for Intel's products had increased. The economy had recovered from the prolonged recession. Anticipating a product shortage by late 1976, consumers were building their inventories. Furthermore, the technology had advanced to make fuller use of this product. Intel had developed a single-board computer that combined several Intel microcomputer components and memory chips on a printed circuit board to make a complete computer. Intel had planned their progress with heavy R&D investments to have their product available when demand arose. In 1976 alone, Intel invested $20.7 million into research and development. With this investment philosophy, Intel was able to maintain an advanced product at an equal or better cost per unit than competitors.

Still another factor is that Intel has been able to internally finance their new products. Sources of investment have been profits after taxes, depreciation, deferred taxes, and stock sale to employees. Profits have been reinvested not only into R&D but in plant and production equipment.

Since Intel introduced the microcomputer, it has become central to many new and increasingly sophisticated applications. Intel started as a component business. However, they are now heavily involved in producing special purpose microcomputers. In addition, due to research expenditures, Intel was ready to market a now highly emphasized computer product and software. The value of software is cumulative in the growing library of programs and the routines developed to help customers use Intel products. Superior software has been responsible in large for the industry's standardization around Intel's 8080 as today's most widely used microprocessor.

In conclusion, Intel's remarkable growth occurred for two reasons. First, Intel developed a specialized product and got it on the market before any competition could develop. Second, Intel has had the foresight to recognize the expanding market for their products and the good sense to keep reinvesting profits into advancing their technology. Even when a slowdown threatened Intel in 1975, they recognized future opportunities and were ready with the resources and technology when the market was ripe. Through careful planning and good foresight, Intel has gone from a small components producer to a large microcomputer firm, occupying a prominent place in the industry.

Source: "New Leaders in Semiconductors," *Business Week,* 1 March 1976, pp. 40–46.

Approach 3: Acquisition and Merger

Acquisition and merger, being a part of a diversification strategy, cannot be strictly classified as a major approach in the context we are using. We choose to single it out for emphasis because of its importance in decision making and its consequence to a company's future. *Acquisition* is defined as a purchase of a company or a part of it so that the acquired company is completely absorbed by the acquiring company and thereby no longer exists as a business entity. On the other hand, *merger* is a transaction involving two or more companies in the exchange of securities, and only one company survives. The terms *acquisition* and *merger* are sometimes used interchangeably.[9]

LEGAL CONSIDERATIONS At the outset, let us emphasize the question of legality of a given acquisition and point out the legal restraints on the methods by which business may acquire assets and economic power.[10] In the first place, as we have noted, acquisition activities are classified as horizontal, vertical, and conglomerate. Each classification carries a clear definition of legal and economic terms. In the second place, the Department of Justice issued in 1968 Merger Guidelines, which in effect expanded the interpretation of the Sherman Act and the Clayton Act and strengthened the enforcement of Section 7 of the Clayton Act. The guidelines are extensive and technical. They prescribe conditions and procedures under which each of the three merger activities can be challenged. Suffice it to say that the Department of Justice will use the guidelines to question the actual legality of a case, whether or not it will oppose corporate acquisition. Indirectly, however, the guidelines stimulated the Federal Trade Commission (FTC) to intensify its enforcement. In all, the legality of every acquisition and merger must be seriously studied by management, and legal constraints must be included in the deliberation.

OBJECTIVES OF ACQUISITION From the strategic perspective, the prime concern of acquisition and merger is the clarity of the purpose. First, acquisition can entertain a limited purpose of acquiring a needed capability. Acquisition of an R&D capability, a product, or a production facility for getting competitive advantages can initially have only a limited purpose. Second, large-scale acquisition and merger for the purpose of bold and planned entry into a new industry is often the major avenue for corporate growth. Through forcing structural changes of business and management, it creates a synergistic condition—the addition of the parts is greater than the whole. Third, calculated acquisition and merger to increase assets, cash, and borrowing capacity has a special purpose. Its immediate benefits must be carefully weighed against the long-term risks. Fourth, acquisition and merger can be a defensive measure to fend off takeover maneuvers and to protect sources of raw material or distribution outlets.[11]

THE MEANING OF SYNERGY At this point, an explanation of *synergy* is in order. *Synergy,* defined as "a measure of joint efforts"[12] is a concept that considers each acquisition as a significant contribution to the total profitability of the firm. In each acquisition, the resultant effect is computed to show increase in annual rate of return on investment based on sales, costs, and investment. An acquisition can provide its synergistic effects from four areas: sales; operations; investment; and management. The possible contribution of each part logically leads to the synergy of the whole. Thus, through the use of existing channels of distribution to market newly acquired products, it brings synergistic effect. Likewise, management know-how, when applied to newly acquired operations having similar strategic, organizational, and operation problems, also produces synergy, and the whole becomes greater than the sum of its parts.

An acquisition and merger decision has both investment and management significance. As an investment decision, it is rational and seeks long-term gains. As a management decision, it takes into account the synergistic impact of acquisition—its planning and execution, the management of its integrated operation, and the planning for its consolidated future. Yet acquisition and merger contains perils and pitfalls. A study conducted by Booz, Allen, and Hamilton found that during the 1960s no more than one-third of the acquisitions made were completely successful, and the other two-thirds failed to achieve company anticipated goals.[13] Probably most failures occurred due to the lack of a planned approach. When acquisition is made on impulse without clear regard to the linkage that ties acquired activities to the dominant business activity, it fails. When an acquisition is handled in an unstructured way, lacking policy clarity and disregarding legal, financial, and operational difficulties, it cannot succeed. Finally, company management's incompetence in integrating the acquired operation into its own organization also leads to failure.

MANAGING ACQUISITION AND MERGER The central thrust of a successful acquisition and merger program is its management, which involves planning, execution, and postacquisition integration. Planning for acquisition and merger begins with the formulation of a strategic plan, which establishes policies, objectives, and the organizational responsibility for the activity. The CEO's involvement is direct and complete, and his/her early participation and subsequent involvement in certain key decision-making points are imperative.[14] A task group composed of planning, legal, and financial representatives and additional personnel from other key departments is a desired form for decision making. Although the long-range diversification plan is a central document delineating the logical linkage and paths through which acquisition and merger can be achieved, the profile containing acquisition criteria and prospect data is the operating document that guides the search, initial screening, and preliminary proposal writing.[15] The profile calls for the construction of most desired and minimum acceptable models and for the preparation of a checklist. A checklist identifies the prospective company, its history, management, product/service, finances, marketing, facilities, labor relations, geographical locations, antitrust involvement, and contains a brief evaluation of the project—whether or not it fits into the corporate schedule of management, morale, and future prospects.

Searching for prospects can be conducted through internal referrals and external sources—accountants, lawyers, brokers, and investment bankers. The chosen candidates will be subject to more-detailed financial analyses, which may include analyses of return on assets, earnings per share projection, and evaluation of tax effects on the consolidated financial position. At this point, management participation is necessary to review each candidate and to approve preliminary discussions. Subsequent inspection of plants and future evaluation of the candidate company's potentials against the criteria and checklist will lead to the next decision point, at which management either rejects or authorizes the preparation of a preliminary proposal. The meeting of chief executive officers of both companies is considered desirable at this point. Negotiations for a final offer, drafting of a consolidation plan for the transition period, and closing the deal are the major steps involved in the execution phase.

The consolidation plan, designed to guide the initial consolidation during the transition period, is a first step toward postacquisition integration. The integration of an acquired company into the parent organization is a slow process passing through three phases: initial consolidation; stabilization; and complete integration. During each phase, personnel, organization structure, policies, and communication can cause conflicts between the acquired and acquiring companies. Integration of reports, business data, and operations can be time-consuming. Administrative planning and efficient control can minimize conflicts and reduce delays while pressing ahead toward early operating integration and future development. The management of acquisition and merger is a complex task. Innovation and prudence are necessary because each transaction is different, and the ultimate outcome of each is uncertain. The final determining factor, however, lies in management's capability to plan and control the new, enlarged organization and the ability to constrain ill-defined growth.

Approach 4: International Business

International business constitutes an additional avenue for growth. It is distinguished from geographical expansion within a domestic market by several characteristics. Opportunities for international business are broad, the challenge to management is great, and the business environment can be extremely complex. Since the end of World War II, hundreds of U.S. firms have expanded their operations worldwide. The U.S. overseas activities, including the war effort and postwar foreign aid programs that greatly stimulated U.S. investment abroad, and indeed the recovery of world economy in Western Europe and Japan, provided the combined thrust to such a phenomenal growth.[16] However, to gain successful entry and growth in international business, companies are required to absorb added risk that goes beyond that normally encountered in domestic business. Thus, a company pursuing international business must first define its purpose and be prepared to face inherent hazards.

ADVANTAGES OF INTERNATIONAL BUSINESS Viewed broadly, there can be three major reasons for international expansion: (1) to increase sales and profits through expanding market outlets, exploiting growth opportunities, compensating loss in domestic sales, seeking higher profit margin abroad, and building a foothold in one nation for expanding into regional and multinational business later; (2) to gain competitive advantages by seeking low-cost production, adding channels of distribution, and accelerating technology transfer to achieve stronger marketing position in selected overseas locations; and (3) to secure raw material sources by engaging in exploration, processing, transportation, and marketing of raw materials worldwide. Industries, such as petroleum, mining and smelting, forestry and agribusiness, have long been engaged in international business for this purpose.

CONSTRAINTS International business offers countless growth opportunities, but it can also invite disaster. A company pursuing international business must be fully prepared for certain pitfalls. By its very nature, international business presents vast political, economic, legal, and cultural differences.[17] First, there are the domestic and international constraints. Foreign trade in the United States is governed by U.S. commercial policy and by international trade agreements. International business is thus subject to restrictions in the form of tariff, quota, and exchange control on movement of goods, services, personnel, investment, and capital. Currency exchange may involve several national currencies, and the exchange rates complicate transactions and increase risk when they fluctuate in time of uncertainty. Furthermore, foreign commerce is subject to international law and public and private laws of both the trading countries and the host countries. This legal complexity and its changing nature often complicates transactions and increases uncertainty.

Second, operating in a foreign environment causes great difficulties. Politically, the form of government, the legal system, and the degree of nationalism differs between regions and among nations. The stage of economic development and internal economic conditions varies between countries. This combined political and economic climate is reflected in national trading policies that determine the degree of restrictions and types of opportunities offered to an international business firm. Finally, cultural differences not only affect product market potential and mode of operations but greatly complicate management problems concerning both managerial and labor relations.[18]

COURSES OF PURSUIT International business can be pursued along three major courses: exporting; foreign licensing; and direct investment including operating wholly owned subsidiaries abroad, joint venture, acquisition, and merger. Let us briefly examine each of these courses:

1. *Exporting:* Exporting to foreign countries represents a means of entry into foreign markets without committing large assets and sizable human resources. For many firms, it signifies a determination to explore a foreign market and a learning process to gain business experience for later expansion. A long-range development plan is obviously essential. That development plan must define the objectives and outline the systematic development of international business. For example, the initial effort of marketing one product could lead to cross-product-line marketing, ultimately involving the use of direct investment for greater expansion. A successful operation in one nation could expand geographically to another, ultimately extending to regional and global scales. Once a company operates on a global basis and makes decisions with world interest and perspective, it is known as multinational business.[19]
2. *Foreign licensing:* Foreign licensing involves granting permission to a foreign firm to use the licensor's industrial property rights, know-how, patent, trademark, and/or other intangible assets for a fee (royalty). In itself, licensing income is not significant. However, to certain companies, it is the means of entry into the international market and can logically lead to technology transfer, joint venture, and other phases of international business. As a defense measure, licensing can be granted to a foreign competitor to forestall the latter's expected domination of the market. Like anything else in business ventures, it has its hazards, one of which is the fear that the licensing foreign firm may gain an unchallengeable position in that market licensed for, thus preventing the ultimate entry into that market by the licensor. Foreign licensing therefore must be viewed as a step toward the implementation of a firm's long-range goals.
3. *Direct investment:* Direct foreign investment is an expansive action, a substantial commitment involving the establishment of wholly owned foreign subsidiary, a joint venture, and the initiation of acquisitions and mergers abroad.[20] A company pursuing direct investment must consider four questions: (a) Who is to control the actual ownership of the foreign activity? The choice between a branch (the extension of parent organization operating abroad) and a subsidiary (the incorporation of a subsidiary as a legal resident of a foreign nation) must be fully analyzed. (b) Will the investment be a joint venture? If so, the percentage of ownership must be clearly established. (c) What will be the form of management structure and control of an extensive foreign operation? (d) Who will define financial policies and strategy governing investment decision, methods of overseas financing, capital structure, impact of taxes, and transfer of dividends, earnings, and assets of all types? To keep the discussion brief, suffice it to say that the determination of which of the three courses of action to pursue—foreign subsidiary, joint venture, or acquisition and merger—depends on the company's long-range goals and a host of additional considerations, such as size of commitment, policies, and investment climate of the host countries. Above all, management still constitutes the single most important challenge. Political, economic, and cultural differences in international business require an inter-

nationally oriented mentality that perceives international business in terms of varied value systems. International operations require a unique expertise and a global management capability that is sensitive to international and domestic constraints and to the needs of people having divergent cultural backgrounds and practices.[21]

SUMMARY

The strategic alternatives thus far discussed are suggested to serve as a framework for analysis. Of the three alternatives—growth, stability, and survival—the growth strategy is the most common form. It poses a persistent challenge to almost all companies, which must thrive in a competitive world and must capitalize on their strengths to exploit business opportunities and, indeed, to secure their established positions. However, growth must be controlled and well-conceived according to a long-range scheme. Our brief discussion of the growth pattern and variation of growth strategies represents an initial effort to delve into the complexity of directing a company's long-term growth, while suggesting decision options managers must face during each stage of the long process. The four approaches to growth offer a variety of options that must be selected exercising extreme care, viewing each decision as having both management and investment significance.

NOTES

1. For a detailed discussion on structural changes, see chapter 13 in this book.
2. H. Igor Ansoff, *Corporate Strategy* (New York: McGraw-Hill, 1965), pp. 109–10.
3. *Marketing mix* is defined as the set of controllable variables—product; place; promotion; price—that the firm can use to influence buyer's response. Philip Kotler, *Marketing Management: Analysis, Planning & Control* (Englewood Cliffs, N.J.: Prentice-Hall, 1976), p. 59.
4. Lateral diversification consists of what Ansoff calls concentric diversification—a common thread running either through marketing or technology that ties the diversification activities—and conglomerate diversification that has no common thread in design. Ansoff, *Corporate Strategy,* pp. 132–38. For an expansive view, see Bruno Hake, *Hazards of Growth: How to Succeed Through Company Planning* (London: Longman, 1974), pp. 53–63.
5. "Turning Warner-Lambert into a Marketing Conglomerate," *Business Week,* 5 March 1979, pp. 60–66.
6. Ansoff, *Corporate Strategy,* pp. 127–32.
7. For an example, see Paul Brown, "Diversifying Successfully," *Business Horizons,* August 1975, pp. 84–87.
8. As an example, Boise Cascade's diversification program was accelerated to a "physical" movement of feeding more needed cash to cover already dangerously extended positions.
9. Donald H. Shuckett, Harlan J. Brown, and Edward J. Mock, *Financing for Growth* (New York: American Management Association, 1971) p. 105. Discussion in John Argenti, *op. cit.,* pp. 240–41.
10. Robert N. Corley and Robert L. Black, *The Legal Environment of Business* (New York; McGraw-Hill, 1973), pp. 369–414.

11. There has been a large collection of literature on the subject. For books, see David F. Linowes, *Managing Growth Through Acquisition* (New York: American Management Association, 1968), p. 105; and Myles L. Mace and George G. Montgomery, Jr., *Management Problems of Corporate Acquisition* (Cambridge, Mass.: Harvard University, 1962).
12. Ansoff, *Corporate Strategy,* pp. 75, 75–102.
13. As noted in Shuckett, Brown, and Mock, *Financing for Growth,* p. 154.
14. Werner C. Brown, ''Development through International Diversification,'' in *The Chief Executive's Handbook,* ed. John D. Glover and Gerald A. Simon (Homewood, Ill.: Dow Jones-Irwin, 1976), pp. 348–67; and N. W. Freeman, ''The Key to Sound Acquisition Growth,'' in Glover and Simon, *Chief Executive's Handbook,* pp. 378–79.
15. Linowes, *Managing Growth,* chaps. 4–12; and Shuckett, Brown, and Mock, *Financing for Growth,* chaps. 13–16. Also, Fred W. Taylor, ''Anatomy of a Merger, Mergers and Acquisitions,'' *Journal of Corporate Venture,* November–December 1970, pp. 8–19.
16. For development of international business in the United States, see Endel J. Kolde, *International Business Enterprise,* (Englewood Cliffs, N.J.: Prentice-Hall, 1973), pp. 142–49.
17. International business is a broad and complex field of study. For standard textbooks, see Kolde, *International Business Enterprise;* Richard D. Hays, Christopher M. Korth, and Maucher Roudiani, *International Business: An Introduction to the World of Multinational Firm* (Englewood Cliffs, N.J.: Prentice-Hall, 1972); and Richard D. Robinson, *International Business Management: A Guide to Decision Making* (New York: Holt, Rinehart and Winston, 1973).
18. There has been an increasing trend to employ local nationals to fill in managerial positions for reasons of cost, efficiency, and sometimes to meet requirements of host states. Robinson, *International Business Management,* pp. 255–76.
19. In recent years, multinational business has been a controversial subject. For its economic activities, see U.S. Senate Committee on Finance's report, *Multinational Corporations* (Washington, D.C.: U.S. Government Printing Office, 1973); for strategic formulation, see William A. Dymsza, *Multinational Business Strategy* (New York: McGraw-Hill, 1972); and for management, see F. T. Haner, *Multinational Management* (Columbus, Ohio: Charles Merrill, 1973).
20. Dymsza, *Multinational Business Strategy,* chaps. 7–10; and Robinson, *International Business Management,* chaps. 4–8.
21. For the impact of these differences on strategy, see chapter 17, on international business strategy.

CHAPTER NINE

Corporate Strategy II: Stability Strategy and Survival Strategy

In situations that present companies with declining earnings and insolvency problems, the other two strategic alternatives of stability strategy and survival strategy can be developed to provide effective solutions. The development and management of these strategies is more difficult than that for growth. First, companies under economic distress are placed in a much more precarious position. Options are limited, and action is restricted. Second, in a state of organizational disarray, employee morale is low. Strong leadership, frequently with a unique management style, is required to restore confidence and arrest deterioration. Decisive actions to achieve immediate, short-term, and intermediate goals are necessary for laying a foundation for later recovery and growth. In this chapter, we will discuss these two strategic alternatives, their application, courses of action, and management.

STABILITY STRATEGY

Conditions of Profit Instability

In a distressed market and economy, companies occasionally experience a traumatic period of profit instability when declining sales and profits force the business to contract (see figure 7.1). Profit instability can be a temporary interruption manifested in a sudden decline of earnings or a prolonged condition of profit deterioration and chronic fluctuation. A prolonged growth can degenerate into profit losses; a downturn economy can cause general business contraction. Likewise, a saturated market with intense competition can produce profit instability; the television industry is a recent example of this predicament, which affects all television manufacturers.[1]

Yet, profit instability is frequently very difficult to detect. Lack of effective control mechanisms and inability to determine potential problems until they become serious can cause surprises. Likewise, management preoccupation with operational problems or complacency and overoptimism among business executives produce a series of damaging effects leading to rapid deterioration.[2] A sudden decline, if not decisively stopped, can lead to prolonged slippage after one or two years. Under such unstable situations, which occur rather frequently, a defensive-offensive strategy aimed at initial quick recovery is recommended. Resumption of gradual growth serves as an intermediate goal.

A stability strategy is directed at achieving early stabilization of profits and subsequent improvement of profitability. Early stabilization can result in the immediate arrest of earnings decline and gradual restoration of employee morale; however, in a prolonged situation, a greater and broader effort is required to attack sales, profit, assets, and debt-equity problems. In an unstable condition, major adjustment in market/product is necessary to counteract the cyclical nature of business, thus avoiding great fluctuations.

Depending upon the severity of the situation and the rate of recovery, the company can choose three distinct approaches: (1) retrenchment in a distressed economy with a clear intention of quick recovery; (2) turnaround of a continuous decline of earnings with lesser prospect for quick recovery; and (3) stabilization in a volatile market where long-range development is needed to achieve market balancing.

Approach 1: Retrenchment

Retrenchment strategy is applicable in situations in which an anticipated business slowdown is in sight, or when a sudden drop in sales and profits has occurred. It requires immediate action to effect temporary business contraction while planning for gradual recovery. Objective setting in such an urgent situation may require the establishment of a series of goals: the immediate goal of reducing sales/profit threat; the intermediate goal of making a step-by-step profit improvement; and the ultimate goal of recovery. The retrenchment strategy necessitates perceiving anticipated environmental changes, that is, the pace of the recession or the rate of economic recovery. It further delineates courses of actions, specifies methods of resource deployment, and outlines contingency plans to meet unexpected changes in external and internal situations.

A well-conceived retrenchment strategy may consist of three phases: (1) the contracting phase; (2) the consolidation phase; and (3) the recovery phase.

THE CONTRACTING PHASE During the contracting phase, most reduction represents the initial effort to reduce size. It involves a general cutback in personnel and expenditures in all administrative and functional departments. A hiring freeze, across-the-board personnel reduction, scheduled department layoffs, and cutbacks in budgetary expenditures relating to general administration, overhead, R&D, advertising, supplies, and services are all aimed at reducing size and costs. Production costs involving labor, material, purchasing, inventory, and capital equipment; marketing costs related to product development, distribution and sales; and financial costs involving interest charges, overall inventory cost, and cost generated from cash management are all areas targeted for cost savings.[3]

The actual planning and coordination is the responsibility of the finance department, which performs in-depth variance analyses and suggests cost-saving targets for the company as a whole and for each department or cost center. Cost reduction can be effected in two phases: the initial effort to stop decline, normally within two to six months; and a long-term program to direct cost savings during the consolidation phase. Even at the contracting phase for quick effect, great care and caution is necessary.[4] First, cost reduction is designed to get rid of surpluses, the fat that often exists in an organization. It must not harm the basic functioning of the organization and arouse excessive hostility among employees. Second, cost reduction during the contracting phase must be followed by a well-conceived plan to achieve long-term profit improvement during the consolidation phase when the purpose is to increase sales, improve profit, and increase productivity. In that way, a stable position for subsequent recovery and growth will be achieved.

THE CONSOLIDATION PHASE During the consolidation phase, a company must determine the rate of recovery and institute a combined profit improvement and management audit program, which is the second phase of the cost reduction program. The rate of recovery represents the company's estimation of the external environment, that is, the timing and rate of recovery of the general economy and its own ability to reach the point of internal stabilization. In turn, the rate of recovery determines the intensity and content of the combined programs. A successful profit improvement program begins with a set of realistic and attainable objectives. It takes a concerted effort; a task force, for example, is often a preferred approach.[5] Let us briefly discuss some of the more important areas targeted for the profit improvement and management audit program:[6]

1. *General management:* Improvement in general management is logically the prime target. Here, the two aspects of the program can be pursued concurrently. Cost reduction in the areas of employee salaries, fringe benefits, and administrative expenses should be examined. Management improvement in organization, management systems, and general effectiveness in areas such as decision making, policy formulation, strategic planning, and control should be attempted. The essence of a management audit is to reveal operational weaknesses and to suggest remedial actions.
2. *Marketing:* Marketing is the next area requiring close attention of management.[7] Profit improvement can be achieved through product trimming (elimination of unprofitable products), geographical contraction (reduction of sales and service offices), and personnel reduction (weeding out of less-productive sales personnel). Other saving devices derived from the more-effective use of resources in sales, advertising, distribution, and inventory can be equally effective.
3. *Production:* Productivity is a good criterion for improving manufacturing efficiency. Evaluation of the production process and reduction of labor and fixed costs can increase productivity. Disposition of unused plant and equipment, reduction in capital projects, and intensified use of value engineering can also produce positive results. The production management audit refers to a total review of management of the production department, discussion of which is beyond the scope of this book.
4. *R&D:* R&D represents a large expense. An effort should be made to review company policies on R&D expenses reporting, which can have substantial impact on its financial position. For example, the write-off of deferred R&D costs as losses rather than deferring them as assets may have significant effects on a firm's income. R&D budgets can be reduced by eliminating petty projects and nonessential services and facilities. Better cost control and

increased productivity can produce immediate cost savings. Research and development management, one of the more difficult aspects of management, can be benefited by a thorough audit.

5. *Purchasing:* It has been suggested that over two-thirds of the total expenses of an average manufacturing company are accrued through purchasing departments' orders of supplies and services. Hence, purchasing is logically an area in which large cost savings can be obtained. Here, consideration or adoption of the following practices can bring substantial savings: central purchasing; bulk purchasing; discreet buying; efficient credit financing; vendors selection; and management. To streamline the purchasing function, a management audit should review purchasing policies, procedures, costs, inspection, and warehousing.

6. *Finance:* The finance department is the central link in a profit improvement program. Management audit of a finance department has a dual purpose: to streamline financial management, and to reduce cost. Within the company's framework, the finance department studies departmental interactive costs because the reduction in one department may increase cost in another. It evaluates trade-off studies in an effort to maximize savings. Additionally, the finance department establishes guidelines and directs profit improvement activities to certain strategic areas in which 80 percent of savings results are obtained from 20 percent of the activity. Within the finance department itself, savings can be achieved from all aspects of financial management: the management of current and fixed assets, of liabilities, and of debts.

THE RECOVERY PHASE The recovery phase signifies the readiness of a company to pursue quick recovery and early resumption of growth. Following the first phase of contracting, the company has attempted to stop losses. Throughout the second phase of consolidation, company actions are streamlined, and a condition of stabilization is obtained. At this point, the retrenchment shifts emphasis from defensive to offensive strategy to be implemented through aggressive marketing and financial actions.

Market intensification, as discussed previously in connection with growth strategy, is a major approach. Product modification to prolong the product life cycle of certain high-margin and large-volume products and concentrated advertising to increase product usage can bring immediate effect. Planned entry of selected new products to coincide with recovery and offensive sales promotion concentrated upon geographical areas to increase sales are methods that can sustain the planned recovery. To be sure, marketing strategy and sales planning provide the basis for directing recovery activities. Achieving financial readiness is perhaps the next important task. Financial readiness is expressed in a company's strong financial position and evidenced by its capacity to borrow. During the recovery phase, the product improvement program should continue, although cash accumulation remains a high-priority item.

A sudden or prolonged pause in a firm's business operations is normal and sometimes desirable, as was the case for J.C. Penney. Since 1945, it experienced two such traumatic periods: a long one in the 1950s, and a brief one in 1974. In the latter situation, Penney's management skillfully adopted the retrenchment strategy. In less than one year, the company resumed its growth (see illustration capsule 16).

Illustration Capsule 16

J.C. PENNEY COMPANY, INC.

Jim Penney opened his first store in 1902 in Kemmerer, Wyoming, a small frontier town. The town was dominated by a mining company whose store offered credit or script purchases. Penney did not offer credit. Instead, he offered better deals on this same philosophy. He changed the name to J.C. Penney. By 1932, Penney had 1,500 stores. Financing was obtained through partner associates. As each store manager accumulated enough capital out of his store's earnings, he could buy a one-third partnership in a new store, if he had trained one of his employees to effectively manage the new store.

Between 1945 and 1958, Penney's growth stagnated. The causes were not selling on credit, not diversifying the line, and not moving into the urban market. In 1958, William Batten became president and started implementation of these ideas, and Penney's again progressed.

In the seventies, Penney expanded into new areas. They acquired Thrifty Drug Co., and opened discount stores under the name of Treasure Island. In addition, Penney's bought a partial interest in a Belgium retailer, Sarma. In 1971, Penney's entered the supermarket business with the purchase of Supermarkets Interstate, Inc. From 1964 to 1969, there was a 95 percent gain in earnings on a 78 percent gain in sales.

In 1974, net income decreased 33 percent from the previous year's $185 million to $125 million. In 1974, retailers were struck by the recession. J.C. Penney was caught between a sharp increase in costs and a decline in consumer spending. Because Penney bought in large quantities and in advance, markdowns hurt them severely.

Additional factors were: first, the emergence of specialized market segment that Penney's mass merchandising concept could not reach; second, the consumer was shorter on money and harder to reach, and competition became tougher; third, many primary markets were nearly saturated. Penney was financially sound and, therefore, began recovery after recognition of the above-mentioned factors.

Between 1975 and 1976, net income increased again to $228 million. In 1974, when Penney's experienced a sharp profit decline, they immediately adopted a retrenchment strategy. They reduced expenses through contraction. Penney cut back on its sales help. Many service areas in the stores were eliminated, and a personnel training center was set up. A study on productivity in turn resulted in a cost-cutting program.

By 1975, Penney's had attained a strong cash position and prepared for further growth. As a first step, Penney made better use of its space. A denser and more concentrated use of display raised overall selling floor capacity 20 percent to 40 percent, and reduced storage 50 percent or more. Merchandising speed and flexibility were concentrated upon. The sales emphasis was shifted to fast-moving items.

Furthermore, store expansion was slowed down. Marginal units were closed. Smaller markets with smaller stores were entered, and fewer giant stores were built. Higher-margin items were emphasized. Penney sought to attract new customers for its fashion items.

In 1977, there were 435 full-line Penney stores, and 1,246 soft-line stores. There were 37 Treasury stores designed for self-service, and 271 Thrifty Drug Stores. European operations consisted of 78 stores in Belgium, and Penney has discontinued its supermarket operations. Penney also now owns insurance subsidiaries, with employees numbering 183,000. Today, J.C. Penney occupies a significant position in the industry.

Source: "Can the Last Be First?" *Forbes,* 15 March 1969, p.31; "J.C. Penney: Getting More from the Same Space," *Business Week,* 18 August 1975, p. 80; and "Found: A Shining New J.C. Penney," *Sales and Marketing Management,* 17 January 1977, p. 32.

Approach 2: Turnaround

In a distressed condition of continual decline in profits and sales over an extended period, or in a prolonged state of stagnation, a company is compelled to adopt a turnaround strategy. A turnaround strategy, although a necessity, is a much-narrowed option, short of selling the operation or degenerating into insolvency. Under such a situation of large losses and widespread demoralization, a turnaround operation must be viewed as delicate because the operation demands decisive, cautious action, and sensitive because it involves changes in personnel.[8] It calls for strong management action to restore profit and rebuild morale, usually lasting up to three years or longer, depending on the degree of deterioration and the condition of the erosion.[9]

THE INITIAL GOALS At the outset, a company must face the single most important decision of who should direct the turnaround operation. Should the existing chief executive officer be retained, or should a new one be brought in from outside? This decision belongs to the board of directors, who must determine the gravity of the situation and examine each of the options with extreme care. Once a decision is made, the board of directors and the CEO jointly establish objectives of the operation. Subsequently, the strategy developed by the management is submitted to the board for approval.

A turnaround strategy delineates courses of action and outlines a series of intermediate goals to guide execution. The strategy stresses both management and functional actions that must be timed to accomplish those intermediate goals within a certain time frame. Reducing and stopping losses should be the immediate objective. Stabilization becomes an intermediate goal, and the restoration of profitability becomes a long-term objective. Once profitability is restored, a calculated growth strategy will guide the company in its long-term development.

Throughout the long and traumatic turnaround operation, decisive but cautious actions involving in-depth variances analysis and detailed evaluation of internal operation to guide decision making must be consistently pursued. Overreaction and hasty action should be avoided, lest radical surgery cripple the already weakened organization. Whereas a decisive cost reduction program reduces losses, a well-conceived and highly concentrated profit improvement program as discussed in the previous section ensures the step-by-step improved utilization of assets, facilities, and personnel. Thus, a stabilized condition, which is the intermediate goal of a turnaround operation, will have been attained. Further concentration on achieving remaining profitability goals and improved performance will prepare the organization for resumption of recovery and growth.

RESTORING PROFITABILITY Management of profitability is a serious concern of a chief executive and is the direct responsibility of the financial manager. During profitability restoration, they can assume several major actions. Two tasks, the arrest of cash drain and the generation of cash reserve, stand at the forefront. A profit improvement program ultimately results in earnings increases; however, divestiture of surplus property, nonused plants, and unprofitable operations and the disposition of excessive accounts receivables and inventory can produce positive cash flow. Hence, a comprehensive review of company's cash flow, its future cash requirements, and its financial structure defines the problem and serves as a basis on which to develop approaches and solutions. The precise analysis of cash management and detailed projection of requirements is aimed at achieving savings and determining the balance level to meet future contingencies.[10] A simplified and streamlined cash management procedure accelerates the flow of cash and thus increases its more-efficient utilization. Cash savings can be used to reduce the level of outstanding short-term debt and to reinvest in securities for increased cash reserve.

As we have noted, disposition and divestiture programs constitute a major source of cash if prudently managed.[11] The disposition of an unused facility, for example, is less complicated than the divestiture of a subsidiary or a business area. Like acquisition and merger, disposition and divestiture cause complex management problems in screening, searching, negotiating, and closing the deal. Fresh cash generated from these activities can also be used for reducing outstanding debts, increasing equity, and expanding cash reserve. When the company's financial stability is restored, a well-planned and aggressive marketing campaign and production activities can be launched to coincide with the full attainment of managing and financial readiness for recovery and growth.

The turnaround operation takes longer to complete. Cited here for illustration is RCA Corporation. The company was built in the image of David Sarnoff. After his retirement, his son Robert succeeded him but was unable to manage in his style. Illustration capsule 17 describes the continuous profit deterioration under the two managements. The new president, Ed Griffith, finally succeeded in turning the company around.

Illustration Capsule 17

RCA CORP.

RCA was founded in 1919 as a joint subsidiary of General Electric Company and Westinghouse Corporation under the leadership of David Sarnoff. It became an independent corporation in 1932 when General Electric and Westinghouse had to drop their interest in the company due to government pressures of antitrust violations.

David Sarnoff was a dynamic individual. On the evening of April 14, 1912, David Sarnoff, then a twenty-one-year-old telegraph operator, picked up the message on the historic Titanic. For the following seventy-two hours, he stayed at his post. On the basis of this dramatic beginning, he ultimately worked up to the chairmanship of Radio Corp. of America. "From then on, he and RCA would be present at the creation of every development in broadcasting and be responsible for most of them." Sarnoff promoted the first broadcast network, the first radio sets, the first TV sets, and the first color TV sets. Industry people first called Sarnoff a visionary with a premature product. However, after RCA had gone to great expense to develop a product, other companies would come in and sweep away most of the market. But Sarnoff did not care. He would have RCA involved in something newer and more advanced. This was the attitude that characterized RCA at that time. The concentration was not on profit but on bigger and more advanced technology.

Robert Sarnoff succeeded his father in 1968, in his ascending to the post of president and chief executive officer. Prior to this time, RCA was already involved in such different businesses as consumer electronics, communications, records, broadcasting, vehicle rental (Hertz), plus office and home furnishings, book publishing (Random House, Knopf, and Ballantine), carpet making, and frozen foods. Robert Sarnoff proceeded to initiate his father's bold style. He took RCA into the mainframe computer business, confronting IBM head on. What Robert could not know was that this gamble would not pay off, as had past gambles. RCA ended up taking a $490 million pretax write-off in 1971. Company losses in 1971 were $155.9 million. Robert Sarnoff made the mistake of not trimming the shaky projects soon enough, and one by one they fell apart. Two years later when the recession hit, RCA was pitifully vulnerable. NBC was the only thing that saved the company.

At the end of 1975, failing to get a raise, Robert Sarnoff surrendered his presidency to Anthony L. Conrad who had come up through the ranks. RCA was not yet stabilized. Nine months later, Conrad resigned due to unfiled income tax returns. Ed Griffith, who had been operating chief of three-fourths of the company, rose to the presidency. Griffith was blunt and straightforward in problem solving. He visited every company every month to collect reports of whether the company was meeting its target and what would be done if it was not. Every company developed a defense plan. RCA was drawn in tighter. No longer were expansion and flamboyant technology the bywords. Bywords became profitability and return.

In 1976, RCA closed a receiving tube manufacturing plant at Harrison, New Jersey, and a color-picture tube plant in Great Britain, liquidated a carpet-manufacturing plant in Belgium, and sold a furniture-making subsidiary. In 1977, much of the Canadian aerospace business was sold and recording studios in Nashville and Hollywood were closed.

In 1972, RCA had no profits. In 1977, it had more than $350 million in revenues and was profitable.

RCA went through a rapid sales growth and technology advancement, without the proper regard for future results. Robert Sarnoff extended this philosophy, and it failed. Today, RCA has slowed down and is considering the effects of today's actions on tomorrow's profits. RCA is not as glamorous as it once was, but it is far more profitable and stable.

Source: "RCA's New Vista: The Bottom Line," *Business Week,* 4 July 1977, pp. 38–44.

Approach 3: Stabilization

In a situation in which sales and profits fluctuate widely and unpredictably, or where potential threats to the company's market may cause instability, a company faces the problem of profit instability. Typical of the first situation are the aerospace companies confined to government-funded defense/space business—an industry whose survival depends on fluctuating political priorities and public sentiments. On the other hand, a growing young company whose single product is besieged by competitors' threats, or a captive manufacturing company whose prime business comes from producing private label products designated by a major buyer, represents the second situation.[12]

PRODUCT/MARKET REORIENTATION Profit instability seemingly produces few immediate consequences, but poses long-term uncertain prospects. It is a problem requiring a long-term solution, and a basic change in market/product position is designed to solve this chronic fluctuation problem and any threatened future instability. Raytheon, one of the outstanding aerospace companies, has successfully made the transition through an internal development and acquisition program guided by an effective strategic planning system. Through merger, McDonnell-Douglas has achieved market balance between the production of military and commercial aircraft. The merger of North American Aviation-Rockwell Standards since 1967 duplicated this strategy. The company today, Rockwell International, has become a well-balanced, acquisition-minded corporation, possessing a broadly based technology derived from the merger.

The reorientation of a company's market/product mix by trimming existing market/product and by acquiring new ones to offset the cyclical nature of the prime market requires a systematic, cautious development. First, a continual program of product trimming and withdrawal from an undesirable market allows a company to maximize profit and conserve cash in good times and to prepare for eventual decline of sales and profits in bad times. This softens the fluctuation effect.

A PROGRAMMED TRANSITION A gradual, systematic, long-range program to direct the transition to attain stability is a desired approach. It enables a firm to expand from internal development to planned acquisition of needed marketing, engineering, and/or production capabilities first and a more ambitious acquisition later. A single market/product company deeply rooted in its prime market or consistently dependent upon a major buyer finds it most difficult to reorient its marketing mix and to learn about the peculiarities of a new market. This process of awareness and learning requires time. Hasty action to achieve quick transition can lead to major miscalculation and repeated floundering.

Hence, a programmed transition approach requires lead time for learning and financial strengthening. A consistent attempt to develop financial capacity to finance internal development and acquisition is indispensable. In other words, a well-planned program to increase company's earnings per share and to accumulate cash must coincide with strategically planned diversification programs for greater effectiveness.

A growing young company whose position is likely to be threatened by anticipated changes in the marketplace or in its competition can also adopt a strategy of stabilization. In this case, too, hasty action is not recommended. A long-term, cautious solution that emphasizes stage-by-stage development coupled with a carefully developed financial capacity will facilitate the successful transition. A captive company manufacturing private label products for a prime buyer, such as Whirlpool's dependence on Sears, Roebuck (over 66 percent of its output) may find the adoption of stabilization strategy an intelligent action. But due to the nature of the dependency and the self-induced complacency, business executives in these companies find it difficult to adapt.

The working of a stabilization strategy thus requires a full awareness among business executives of the impending threat of profit instability. That demands their early and full attention and their willingness to adapt to new, peculiar characteristics of strange markets and industries.

SURVIVAL STRATEGY

Conditions of Financial Insolvency

In a situation of insolvency, when the firm is unable to meet its current obligations as they become due or when it is in a state of virtual organizational paralysis, a company resorts to survival strategy. Survival strategy is totally defensive, aimed primarily at battling for survival against creditors or total collapse. The multiple threats of inflation, recession, earnings decline, and overextended debt position of the early 1970s, for example, brought some companies to the brink of bankruptcy. Thus, survival strategy requires major surgery. It demands active intervention by the board of directors and unusually drastic actions on the part of the management. In almost all cases, a strategy of this nature calls for overhauling management, business/market alignment, and financial structure. Indeed, it is a severe instance of a turnaround operation. A series of urgent actions directed at quickly obtaining financial relief from creditors and replacing existing disheartened management is most desirable. Once the new CEO is installed, a long-range survival program should be instituted to complete the organizational restructuring, business realignment, and financial restructuring. Three major approaches will be discussed briefly.

Approach 1: Management Restructuring

One of the first orders of business in a survival situation is to consider the replacement of the CEO and the complete reorganization of the company. In general, because the task of survival requires a dramatic departure from previous policies, strategies, and associated failures a new CEO who can offer strong leadership and renewed determination is likely to be the desired candidate. Although the CEO's character, experience, and management style is a major concern, the method of selection, either from within the company or from outside, is equally important. During the early 1970s, several large corporations chose to replace their incumbents with new CEOs to initiate and direct the total restructuring. To name a few, John Fery was promoted to replace Robert V. Hansberger at Boise Cascade; Jonathan L. Scott, a former vice chairman and CEO of Albertson's Inc., was appointed CEO at A&P; Thomas R. Wilcox, an experienced banker, was hired from outside to head Crocker National Corp.; John J. Ricardo at Chrysler was named to replace Lynn A. Townsend; and Joseph Flavin of Xerox joined Singer to replace Donald P. Kircher.[13]

THE NEW CEO AND THE NEW THRUST The design of a revitalized organization is an immediately necessary task. A reevaluation of the company's objectives, business mission, and tasks demands in-depth appraisal. Once the initial evaluation is completed, tentative strategy and plans must be developed. At the same time, the basic structure of the organization affecting corporate staff and operating divisions must be immediately implemented. Speed rather than extreme prudence, morale restoration rather than indecisive floundering, is often preferred in a distressed situation. Team building is an urgent task. More often than not, the new CEO is likely to bring in his/her own immediate staff to plan, direct, and control the initial stage of reorganization. Ill-prepared and precipitous action on the part of the new CEO to make large-scale changes in personnel at the outset usually does more harm than good to an organization already in grave difficulty. Thus, scheduled but decisive personnel actions are preferred. Thomas R. Wilcox at Crocker National Corp., for example, fired two-thirds of the firm's senior and middle-management personnel within fifteen months—an action that was rather extreme, but apparently effective.

Once the team is installed, management, led by the new CEO, must exert all effort to restore communication. In a large-scale reorganization, changes in policy, functions, and key personnel can cause obstacles in communication. Enlarged staff meetings and management visits to distant operational units must be scheduled to inform employees at all levels of the company's short- and long-term objectives, priorities, policies, and programs. The restoration of confidence and the attainment of company-wide support for cost reduction, profit improvement programs, and personnel policies are important.

THE REDESIGN OF AN ORGANIZATION STRUCTURE The design of a viable organization should resolve the issue of centralization versus decentralization.[14] During the growth stage, a decentralized structure with multioperational divisions as autonomous units is generally preferred over a centralized form because the former provides initiative and flexibility in action. However, during the survival stage, restoring tight centralized control and direction is sometimes a necessity, especially when severe business contraction results in large-scale consolidation. For example, Westinghouse, after having suffered continuous earnings declines in the early 1970s, and after having sold some of its 256 subsidiaries and affiliated organizations, recentralized its once widely spread structure into a streamlined organization.[15] The new organization was regrouped into three companies centrally directed by the corporate office. The Kaiser Industries, Inc., after suffering poor earnings for several years, took almost the same steps in early 1975 to reduce its organization to five operating units supported by five centrally directed staff departments.

Approach 2: Financial Restructuring

The next urgent business in the survival situation is financial restructuring, centering on actions such as renegotiation of bank credits, the generation of cash, a divestiture program, and the rebuilding of a new financial structure. Financial restructuring adds a new dimension to the function of the CEO and the chief financial officer. Not only does financial restructuring require their direct involvement, but it extends decision considerations beyond normal matters to the inclusion of taxes and legal matters.

CASH REBUILDING In planning and implementing, the negotiation of expanded revolving lines of credit is often the immediate task. Funds are generally needed for working capital and for payment of urgent obligations. A tentative arrangement with major creditors requires concentrated efforts of those restructuring a company's long-term financial plans. Once the immediate danger is lessened, internal rebuilding programs must be pressed ahead vigorously. Although the company's programs to reduce cost and increase profit should continue, cash conservation and rebuilding should be given the closest attention. Streamlining cash management, adjustment of inventory level, strict control over the use of cash, and many other devices can provide surprisingly large cash savings. Rockwell International's cash crunch in 1974 was averted through company-wide financial control. A task force monitored cash flow daily. Monthly reviews at all general-management levels covered inventory and receivables in detail. The company's negative cash flow of $1 million per day was subsequently eliminated.[16]

DIVESTITURE Disposition and divestiture offer a major potential source of cash. Although the write-off of losses and the discontinuance of operations combine to have a positive impact on future earnings and cash, the disposition of unused facilities, plants and equipment, and divestiture of a subsidiary or a business operation to reduce debt have been frequently used in the sobering early 1970s. For example, Boise Cascade's successful sale of its subsidiaries and business operations helped to improve its financial position ahead of schedule. Since the initiation of the divestiture program in July 1972, Boise Cascade sold about $370 million of its assets including almost all of its domestic businesses unrelated to forest products. It also sold $120 million of its Northern California timberlands and $50 million of South American bonds. The cash from these divestitures helped Boise Cascade reduce short-term borrowing to a minimum and greatly reduced overall, long-term debt from $979 million at the end of 1971 to $622 million in April 1973.[17]

Another company, Whittaker Corporation, which instituted its divestiture program in 1971, encountered greater difficulties than Boise Cascade did. The company was reorganized to concentrate in five specific business areas. Some twenty or so units that did not fit into the company's business plan were initially scheduled for divestiture. Two years after the program, of the units identified for divestiture, approximately 80 percent had been sold, yielding $35 million in cash and over $10 million in notes and securities. At the close of 1975, Whittaker claimed the successful conclusion of the restructuring program. At that date, the company managed to reduce its debt to equity ratio from 1.9 to 1 to almost 1 to 1.2. But continuous adjustments in the company's business structure extended the program beyond that date.[18] Of course, divestiture programs must be governed by the company's long-range objectives and strategy. The common thread that provides the basic rationale for the company's very existence and integration is one of the overriding determinants.[19] Future environmental changes and growth opportunities are the other governing factors. Essentially, the restructuring of a company's business/market interest serves as a basic framework for financial decision.

The ultimate restructuring of the company's capital structure, the permanent long-term financing of a firm, is a slow process necessitating intelligent and judicious thinking. An optimal capital structure reflects the character and needs of a firm. A conservative structure emphasizes safety; and an aggressive model stresses leverage—a lower level of debts to assets ratio. This will be discussed in more detail in chapter 11 concerning financial strategy. Suffice it to say that the optimal structural mix of common stock, preferred stock, long-term debts, and net worth depends not solely on the company's design but primarily on the cost of capital and the much-restricted capital source under a condition of financial strain.

Approach 3: Marketing Restructuring

Marketing restructuring, the reverse of diversification, is the effort to redefine the basic line of business and to discover a common thread for the firm's very existence and consolidation. In marketing restructuring, as in management regrouping and financial restructuring, management presses for an immediate consolidation while pursuing long-range planning for restructuring of a firm's business interests.

An initial decision to consolidate begins with a quick reevaluation of the company's basic line of operation.[20] First, it should thoroughly reexamine its purpose, mission, and objectives. What type of company does the management desire it to be, and what are the things the company can do best? Second, it restudies its industry and the potentials, competition, and trends of its prime market. Third, it appraises its internal strengths—its capabilities in technology, marketing, and production—and the required financial capacity in light of the firm's cash needs and future requirements.

The next task shifts focus from the redefinition to the search for a common thread that ties its basic lines of business into related business and market interests. Thus, the combined thrust of technology, marketing, and production strengths forms the basic design, from which consolidation can be logically planned and implemented. Those business/market areas that do not fit into the basic business structure, especially those offering little potential, constitute the first group of candidates for elimination. Others that have unsatisfactory earnings, a weakened competitive position, or management incompatibility, form the second group for discontinuation. A third group, which can attract a good price but cannot justify further company investment, may be considered for divestiture.[21] We have seen that Boise Cascade consolidated its regrouped business structure around forest products; A&P regrouped by closing one-third of its 3,500 stores at a total write-off of some $200 million. And, Westinghouse restructured its mainline business around manufacturing equipment that "generates, distributes, controls, and uses electrical energy." By the end of 1974, the company had sold its major appliance business, the French and Belgian elevator subsidiary, and had discontinued the record club and direct mailing operation, water quality control equipment manufacturing, and the low income housing project, a portion of Urban Systems Development Corp.

In a persistent effort to press toward complete long-range marketing restructuring and the readiness of resumption of growth, a company conducts intensive analysis of its mainline business, reevaluating potentials of each operation and establishing short- and long-term objectives. Within the restructured business groups, continuous consolidation at the functional level is desirable. This may include restructuring R&D projects and streamlining marketing, manufacturing, and purchasing activities that are necessary for the eventual return of the company to a vigorous fighting status, ready for resumption of growth. A sound strategy will guide this development.

Again, an illustration capsule can illustrate the scenario of a survival strategy in action. The case of Rohr Industries, Inc. is one of many such companies that has survived a period of severe financial distress. Rohr's problem can be blamed on miscalculating environmental factors and its early acquisition actions. However, its amazing recovery can be attributed to the management's sound strategy to incite decisive actions (see illustration capsule 18).

Illustration Capsule 18

ROHR INDUSTRIES, INC.

Rohr was founded in 1940 by Fred Rohr. The first product of the company was the complex metal plumbing for aircraft engines. Next, the company began building complete power packages for mounting on commercial and military airplanes. With such a specialized product, Rohr's marketing amounted to finding out how many units aircraft manufacturers needed for the year.

In 1965, Burt Raynes became president and chief executive officer of Rohr. Raynes joined the company shortly after it was founded and served as chief inspector and right-hand man to Rohr, until Rohr's death in 1965. By 1967, sales had climbed to $249 million. In 1968, sales were $262 million and profits were $10 million.

Raynes was a progressive man, deemed so even by his critics. He felt a company "should exist to fill valid, rational human needs." As president, Raynes put his visions into play. Rohr was a major supplier for practically every important aircraft program ranging from the Lockheed C5A to the SST transport. However, successful as the aircraft business was, by 1970, Raynes had his sights set on five other areas: rapid transit; space; marine; antenna; and materials handling.

Rohr made its first move into the transportation industry. With the purchase of Flexible Co. in 1970, Rohr entered into both bus and rail transportation and was awarded the contracts to build cars for the Bay Area Rapid Transit system (BART), and the Washington Metropolitan Area Transit Authority (WMATA). Raynes felt that the fuel shortage would push the public to rapid transit systems.

What Raynes did not foresee was that the venture would prove too costly in several ways. R&D expenditures were very high causing Rohr to commit too much of its resources to one project. The second problem was in the government contracts. First thought to be a bonanza, the government contract turned out to be a technical nightmare. The contract requirements were beyond the state of technology at that time. Rohr had accepted the contracts at a fixed rate, and the lack of room for error caused Rohr in 1975 to have huge write-offs. In late 1975, the transportation write-offs had risen to the point that the company was in technical default on its long-term debt of $164 million, or 60 percent of its total invested capital.

Rohr was in a bad position. In late 1975, Raynes was replaced as CEO by Fred Garry. Garry was conservative on the company position and predicted that 1975 performance would not improve over 1974. Dividends were suspended.

Garry then began restructuring the company. Financial was first. Then came marketing. Rohr was brought back to the things it could do well and reentered the aircraft industry. Rohr went out of the land transportation business. The railcar venture was written off and Flexible Co. was sold. The only area of expansion retained was the marine activity, with a $160 million cost-plus contract for the Navy to build an 80 knot surface-effect ship. The technology for the marine venture was close to the aircraft technology.

In 1977, Rohr earned a profit of $1.1 million. The income from discontinuing operations jumped to $6.4 million in 1977 from a dismal $79,000 in 1976. One of the greatest improvements is morale. Managers felt they were really managing, something they could not do with the autocratic Raynes.

Rohr started as a highly successful aircraft industry supplier. But when they moved to transportation, they got in over their heads. Their technology was not advanced enough, and the public was not as ready for rapid transit as Rohr had envisioned. Rohr forgot their original market. Today, they are more prudent and are back in their original field. Rohr is once again in a good position both financially and successfully in their marketplace.

Source: "Rohr: New Peas in the Old Pods?" *Financial World,* 8 June 1970, p. 14; *Wall Street Journal,* 10 November 1975, p. 15; and "How Rohr's Move into Transportation Backfired," *Business Week,* 19 January 1976, p. 46.

SUMMARY

The formulation of stability strategy and survival strategy to counter profit instability and company survival problems is as difficult as it is urgent. In attacking profit instability problems, we examined three distinct approaches: the retrenchment strategy; the turnaround strategy; and the stabilization strategy. In attacking company survival problems, we posed the combined application of three approaches, which require the undertaking of strategic actions concurrently but separately in management, financial, and marketing areas. Stability and survival strategies both demand varied degrees of regrouping a company's basic business structure and call for the definition of company purpose, mission, and objectives. We consider pressing for immediate actions and striving for long-range development to be of equal importance. In addition, we emphasize the necessity of gradually attaining complete readiness for early resumption of growth. Finally, we strongly suggest that a successful business executive is the one who possesses the total ability to effectively manage the three strategies of growth, stability, and survival, though always hoping to avert a survival crisis.

NOTES

1. Zenith Radio Corp., the number one producer, experienced sharp decline. *Business Week,* 10 October 1977, pp. 128–32; *Wall Street Journal,* 25 October 1977, p. 1.
2. Research on management in instability and insolvency situations is sketchy. For studies on causes and symptoms of corporate failures, consult John Argenti, *Corporate Collapse* (New York: Wiley, 1976); and Joel E. Ross and Michael J. Kami, *Corporate Management in Crisis: Why the Mighty Fall* (Englewood Cliffs, N.J.:

Prentice-Hall, 1973). For an initial attempt, consult Allan Easton, *Managing for Negative Growth: A Handbook for Practitioners* (Reston, Virginia: Reston Publishing, 1977).

3. During recession, many companies reported large savings from well-managed cost-saving programs. For an example, consult report on Emerson Electric Co.'s program, *Wall Street Journal,* 4 June 1975, p. 1.
4. Herbert Roth, Jr., "Turning a Company Around from Regression to Growth," in *The Chief Executive's Handbook,* ed. John D. Glover and Gerald A. Simon (Homewood, Ill.: Dow Jones-Irwin, 1976), pp. 390–400.
5. For discussion, see Joseph Eisenberg, *Turnaround Management: A Manual for Profit Improvement and Growth* (New York: McGraw-Hill, 1972), chap. 5, pp. 103–25.
6. For discussion on profit improvement in functional areas, see John Winkler, *Company Survival During Inflation: A Systematic Approach to Profit Improvement* (New York: Wiley, 1975). Also, Charles R. Ferguson, *Measuring Corporate Strategy* (Homewood, Ill.: Dow Jones-Irwin, 1974).
7. For detailed discussion on marketing audit, see Philip Kotler, *Marketing Management: Analysis, Planning & Control* (Englewood Cliffs, N.J.: Prentice-Hall, 1976), pp. 447–50.
8. Roth, "Turning a Company Around," p. 390.
9. In a series of studies, Dan Schendel, G. Richard Pallon, and James Riggs describe the characteristics of fifty-four companies in turnaround situations. Their data show a downturn phase of four years. They single out seven causes for downturn and seven cures for upturn. Their studies suggest that decisive actions and viable strategies make the difference between success and failure in turnaround. For an early study, see "Corporate Turnaround Strategies," in William E. Glueck, *Business Policy: Strategy Formulation and Management Action* (New York: McGraw-Hill, 1976), pp. 171–82; for the later study, see illustration capsule 2.
10. For techniques of streamlining cash management, see Eisenberg, *Turnaround Management,* pp. 127–65.
11. For an excellent discussion, see Albert H. Gordon, "Getting Out of a Business—When and How," in *Chief Executive's Handbook,* ed. Glover and Simon, pp. 401–11.
12. Sears, Roebuck buys from 20,000 private label suppliers, of which 13,000 probably could be considered as captive. Glueck, *Business Policy,* p. 187.
13. Most of these companies have been discussed in previous chapters. For information on Crocker National Corp., Singer, and Chrysler, see *Business Week,* 11 August 1975, pp. 38–44; *Fortune,* December 1975, p. 100; and *Wall Street Journal,* 7 July 1976, p. 1.
14. For review, see Harold Koontz and Cyril O'Connell, *Management: A Systems and Contingency Analysis of Managerial Functions* (New York: McGraw-Hill, 1976), pp. 343–70.
15. *Business Week,* 20 July 1974.
16. *Business Week,* 29 May 1978, p. 63.
17. *Wall Street Journal,* 1 May 1975, p. 40.
18. *Whittaker Annual Report,* 1970 through 1975.
19. The term "common thread" is used here in a more specific way than the original version introduced by H. Igor Ansoff.
20. See, for a review, chapter 5 of this book.
21. Gordon listed six reasons for divestiture, "Getting Out of a Business," p. 403.

CHAPTER TEN

Functional Strategies I: Marketing Strategy

Making functional strategies falls within the sphere of functional departments, those key areas of marketing, finance, R&D, and production that provide the instruments of corporate strategy. Functional strategies support the overall corporate objectives and provide substance to corporate strategy by specifying methods of organizing and applying resources to achieve functional objectives and by setting forth strategic guidelines to incite well-planned and organized actions for implementation. Indeed, they are the driving forces of corporate strategy. In binding together the corporate strategy, functional strategies, and action plans, management creates an integrated system of strategy making. Within the framework of the corporate strategy, each functional strategy deals with the decision area of a function, defining its goals and objectives, and detailing the deployment of component forces to accomplish given tasks. A functional strategy is thus technical by its nature, innovative in its character, and heavily action oriented in its implementation.

Functional strategies will be discussed in three parts: in this chapter, we will be confined to marketing strategy; in chapter 11, we discuss financial strategy; and in chapter 12, we discuss research and development (R&D) strategy and production strategy. In each chapter, the discussion will begin with an overview of the function concerning its technical aspect of decision elements, will be followed by strategic issues peculiar to the function, and then component strategies that convert plans to actions.

Our discussions are not intended as a review of core courses. Rather, we present the strategic aspect of each functional specialty and point out their interrelationship and required integration from the viewpoint of corporate strategy.

The making of marketing strategy requires the study of marketing as a function within a corporate structure, the various strategic issues involved, and the formulation of component strategies.

AN OVERVIEW OF THE MARKETING FUNCTION

Marketing is one of the most important functions; its effective management is essential to a company's success. As an operation, it is dynamic and challenging, driving constantly toward the attainment of a complex set of goals. Furthermore, the marketing environment exhibits rapid changes in buying habits, government regulations, new technological advances, and ever-intensified competition. The combined thrust of management pressure for sales and the rapidly changing environment demand intelligent thinking and action. In essence, marketing is a strategic game in which the application of strategic concepts and approaches is basic to its management.[1] As an instrument of corporate strategy, it is the most indispensable of the functional strategies. At its disposal, there is a variety of vital means to interact with customers, competitors, and society at large and to influence the outcome of a business operation, thereby assuring the success of the overall corporate strategy.

Modern marketing concepts, centering on studying, developing, and meeting customer satisfaction, are predicated on three basic assumptions: (1) marketing is customer oriented, being seen as the means rather than the end; (2) it is profit oriented, emphasizing profitability, not sales volume; and (3) it is an integrated function, stressing a variety of decision variables whose combined use assures customer satisfaction. These assumptions, in turn, dramatically affect marketing management.

Marketing Management

First, marketing management has become analytical, strategic, and at the same time action oriented, seeking better knowledge of the marketplace and a more effective approach to marketing. Second, the chief marketing executive has become an indispensable member of the management team, signifying the pressing need for his/her active participation in corporate strategy making and for advice concerning the changing dynamics of industry, market, and competition. Third, there is a great emphasis on marketing information, marketing research, planning and control, and resource allocation in marketing management.

The quest for better knowledge of the marketplace leads to the study of customer structure: their wants, total requirements for complete and lasting satisfaction, buying habits, and decision-making process. In studying market structure and behavior, one focuses on market segmentation. A consumer market, for example, can be segmented by age, income, and geographic differences. An institutional market can be classified by type of users (industrial or government), customer size (large versus small), product type, and geographical segmentation. Structural differences can lead to further study of behavioral variations, matters dealing with buying habits, total requirements, and decision-making process. For example, an institutional market such as the aerospace market, which generates up to $100 billion R&D and production business, entirely managed within the defense establishment of bureaus and laboratories, has a setting totally different from a consumer market.[2] Here, a thorough understanding of the institutional customers' varying requirements of functional, technical, and logistic significance, and their decision-making processes for selecting suppliers based on proposal submission is crucial to successful marketing. Thus, market segmentation and customer behavior studies provide the basic information for marketing strategy making. These, in turn, help direct marketing activities and resources to concentrated areas, and develop marketing mix as a means to secure marketing objectives.

The Marketing Executives

Marketing executives' participation in corporate strategy making is not only a necessity but is also a means to ensure a close working relationship between the chief executive officer and the marketing executive, thereby ensuring the compatibility of corporate strategy and marketing strategy.[3] A marketing executive is responsible for providing marketing information and expertise to top management. In strategy making and in directing business operation relating to the company's external affairs, he/she initiates discussions on strategic issues and sounds out advanced warnings on changing market conditions, on aggressive competitive actions, and on major government regulations. He/she provides information and alerts management to future industrial trends, new sources of competition, technological implications, and structural changes concerning suppliers, distributors, and customers. Externally, he/she assumes an active role in interfacing with the outside world, keeping himself/herself and the organization informed of changing marketing dynamics, trends, and regulations. He/she maintains cordial business relationships with key customer organizations, suppliers, competitors, and distributors, seeking out information about changing requirements and marketing information. And above all, he/she must consider himself/herself and the organization as an important reservoir of information and expertise on marketing matters and as active participants in external activities.

Marketing Performance

Modern marketing management demands a high level of performance. On the one hand, there is the demanding management of an ongoing operation of great complexity and high intensity. On the other hand, there is a strong need for advanced planning to counter changing dynamics and persistent uncertainty. This combined requirement calls for emphasis on marketing information, marketing research, resource allocation, planning, and control.[4] Whereas marketing information and marketing research provide information and analysis, planning and control ensures the systematic development of marketing activities, focuses on judicious allocation of resources, and measures performance in achieving short-term and long-term objectives. In our view, an effective marketing executive is a strategist, a tactician, and a manager of vision, decisiveness, and action.

MARKETING STRATEGIC ISSUES

The art of strategy making calls for the identification of crucial issues: those concepts that are fundamentally important to strategy making, and those central strategic issues that require constant attention. We have identified five such issues, which form the basis for formulating marketing strategies.

Marketing Strategy Making

Marketing strategy making is governed by the same concepts and methodology as the making of corporate strategy. The ends and means equation, the logical and substantive nature of the process, and the strategy-tactics connection are fully applicable. In formulating marketing strategies, marketing objectives that are subordinate to corporate strategy must be clearly established and structured in product, market, and geographical areas. The process follows a sequential development.[5]

The Three Strategic Alternatives

The three alternatives, which we discussed under corporate strategy, provide the framework for developing marketing approaches. A growth strategy calls for a combination of various marketing activities to pursue aggressively such goals as market intensification, diversification, acquisition and merger, and international business. A stability strategy requires a different set of activities to achieve retrenchment, turnaround, and stabilization goals. So does the survival strategy, under which marketing restructuring reorients marketing goals and efforts.

Market Positioning[6]

Market positioning refers to the selection of specific areas for marketing concentration, which can be expressed in terms of market, product, and geographical locations. Market positioning is of crucial importance. It is an economical way to deploy resources and assign priorities. It determines the products the company will produce, the customer the company will serve, the level of resources the company will allocate, and the competitors the company will face. Market positioning can be established by examining the size of the market segment, the potential of future growth, the ease of penetration, and the competitive advantages a firm achieves and maintains.

Marketing Mix

Marketing mix refers to the set of marketing means a firm can employ to influence the buyers' responses and to gain competitive advantages. The basic means are: product; channel of distribution; promotion; and price. These individual means are referred to in this book as "marketing component strategies." Each of the component strategies is an integral part of the total marketing strategy, and each must be compatible with the others. These component strategies are interrelated, closely coordinated, and their actions sequentially or jointly delivered in the marketplace for desired impact. The introduction of a new product, for example, requires the total coordination of marketing activities, especially sales promotion, to coincide with final phases of market testing and commercialization.

Public Policy and Marketing Strategy

Marketing, having the widest interaction with the public, must be extremely sensitive to legal and regulatory constraints. Product decisions concerning the maintenance of quality standards, packaging and brand design, or patents are subject to government regulation. Similarly, channel decisions affecting monopolistic practices, franchising agreements, and territorial allocation to distributors are areas requiring close scrutiny for possible violation. To also avoid misleading advertising, deception, and coercion in sales, additional constraints are placed upon sales promotion. Discriminatory pricing, price fixing, and unfair pricing represent other illegal practices prohibited by law. Business ethics concerning bribery and gift giving is a new area requiring supervision by management.[7] Any potential violations of the law or practices intended to deceive are means that cannot be used to justify the ends of producing sales.

MARKETING COMPONENT STRATEGIES

At the outset, let us single out a few essential points for clarification and emphasis:

1. Component strategies specify methods of employing marketing means to achieve marketing objectives and incite marketing activities.
2. There are four decision areas requiring strategic thinking and action: product; channel of distribution; sales promotion; and pricing. We prefer to name them in this sequence to emphasize the thought process as it should occur.
3. For each decision area, component strategy can have a number of substrategies. The selection of any combination of substrategies can be multiplied to an infinite number of options. Simplicity is a cardinal rule in strategy making. We choose only a few strategic variations for that reason. Yet, the differences in situations, capabilities, and constraints will ultimately determine the combination.
4. Component strategy is governed by marketing strategy that optimizes the trade-offs and accomplishes the integration process. In turn, marketing strategy must be consistent with the overriding corporate strategy and be structured to achieve business goals specified under the three strategic situations.
5. The total management of strategy is a responsibility of the marketing executive, who integrates the component strategies into a whole and who oversees the total process of formulation, implementation, control, and recycling.

The selection of component strategies and their attendant substrategies represents a limitless number of approaches. At the heart is the firm's perception of its relative competitive position, individuals involved in each encounter, and the peculiar problems at hand. For quick reference, table 10.1 provides a summary.

Product Strategy

In formulating product strategy, management starts by selecting certain policy decisions whose definition and clarity affect the soundness of product strategy. First, the term *product* refers not only to the physical design of a product, its function, and cost but also expands to include all the peripheral factors that contribute to customer satisfaction. For example, a consumer purchasing a television conceives of the set as a physical product to create personal viewing pleasure, but that set also represents the manufacturer's engineering reputation, the prestige associated with the brand name, its warranty, and the credit and delivery terms as well as the services available from the marketing outlet. Knowing how expansive this concept is, management can develop product objectives consistent with overall corporate objectives.[8]

Second, packaging and branding policies deserve consideration. Packaging

TABLE 10.1 MARKETING COMPONENT STRATEGIES

Component Strategies	*Substrategies*	*Typical Approaches*
Product strategy	Product modification	Market/product modification
	New product development	Penetration, growth, harvesting
	Product elimination	Trimming, run-out
Channel of distribution strategies	Multiple channel	Channel expansion
	Channel change	Partial adjustment
Sales promotion strategy	Sales strategy	Personal selling, negotiation, closing
	Communication	Theme selection
	Media	Selection, scheduling
Pricing strategy	Price setting	Penetration
	Price change	Initiation, responding
	Promotional pricing	Skimming, promotional

gives products both functional and aesthetic advantages. Containers of varied types and packages of different designs offer choices of sizes, convenience, and indeed the identification and sensory appeal that help to move merchandise. Using a brand name and trademark establishes product identity and provides legal protection.

Product Mix and Product Life Cycle

Two more variables must also be studied: product mix, and product life cycle. Product mix refers to the decision to achieve the proper mix of a manufacturer's product items, product lines, and the composite of products offered for sale by a firm or a business unit. A company's product mix can be described as having a certain width (the number of product lines), depth (the average number of items within each product line), and consistency (its relationships to customers, distributors, and other variables). Marketing advantages, simplicity, and cost are the factors coloring all decisions made to create an optimal mix.

Product life cycle is such a fundamental concept of product strategy that it warrants thorough understanding. A product normally lives through a life cycle of introduction, growth, maturity, and decline (see figure 10.1). At each stage of the cycle, there is a certain relationship between sales and profit. This relationship can be developed and modified through varied marketing means. (For a discussion, see New Product Development Strategy.) The definition of product life cycle and the formulation of decisions dealing with product objectives, packaging and branding, and product mix are necessary to product strategy, as they decisively affect its outcome.

Product strategy can be divided into three substrategies: product modification strategy; new product development strategy; and product elimination strategy. Each type deals with a specific situation, and each complements the others.

FIGURE 10.1 PRODUCT LIFE CYCLE

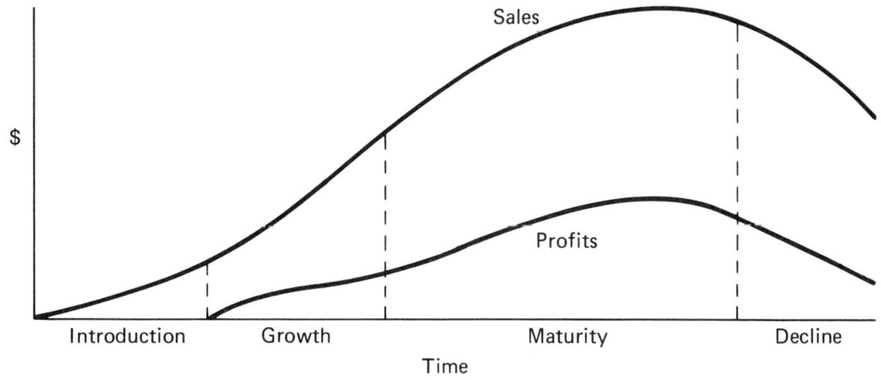

PRODUCT MODIFICATION STRATEGY A large portion of a company's business consists of current business—sales derived from products living through the stages of introduction, growth, and maturity. These products should receive primary attention. Product modification strategy, in its broad sense, can dictate two courses of action: market modification and product modification.

Market modification is directed at market expansion through product improvement, market stretching to prolong a product life cycle, and recycling to repeat its new life cycle.[9] Through product design changes, functional expansion, and a combination of packaging and branding techniques, new users and new markets can be created. A good illustration is the success of nylon, which was expanded from its original use for military purposes to novel applications for women's hosiery, clothing, and tires. Careful use of market segmentation can direct market modification to increase number of users and to penetrate related market areas.

Product modification can be manifested in many ways. Design modification can be achieved by alteration of material, by redesigning the original product to meet varied customer wants, and by expanding product range, thereby expanding usage. Feature modification to provide ease in usage, safety, or other product benefits can increase product options and enhance product appeal. Styling modification, notably in automobile and women's clothing, has now been adopted by other industries to increase product appeal and create a firm's image as a stylish designer and pace setter. Product modification is an important instrument with which to sustain a firm's operation and expand its business base. Too often, however, product modification is neglected in favor of new product development, thereby quickening the pace of product obsolescence and sales deterioration.

NEW PRODUCT DEVELOPMENT STRATEGY New product development is vital for firms seeking long-term stability and growth. During the 1950s and 1960s, when growth was the byword, new product development was widely practiced in the United States, although the cost was exorbitantly high. (See chapter 2.) New product development poses management as well as marketing challenges.

A successful new product development program requires an efficient organization to manage the total process. Although a well-prescribed procedure includes idea generation, screening, business analysis, product development, manufacturing planning, marketing planning, test marketing, and commercialization to guide the development, an effective decision-making and control apparatus in the form of a task-oriented organization controls expenditures, time span, and technical progress.[10] Marketing's role is crucial. In particular, it assumes the prime responsibility for managing the product life, and its related strategies.

Penetration Strategy Penetration strategy guides the initial introduction of a new product. Four possible approaches arise from the varying combinations of pricing and promotional activities: (1) a high-profile approach characterized by launching a new product with high price and high promotion effort; (2) a selective penetration approach with a high price and low promotion combination; (3) a preemptive penetration approach with low price and heavy promotion mix; and (4) a low-profile approach with low price and low-level promotion.

Product Growth Strategy During the product growth stage, the firm tries to sustain a rapid growth as long as possible, but at the same time remains fully guarded against customer's shifting behavior and competitors' actions. A cautious but aggressive strategy is thus desirable. Usually, a company can use the combination of product, promotion, and distribution to achieve a dominant position for a new product, while aggressively moving it into related areas. Product improvement in quality, features, and model, enlargement of distribution channels, and heavy promotion, and perhaps even price reductions are considered as alternate means.

Harvest Strategy When a product reaches the final phase of maturity and begins to show signs of decline, product harvest strategy is formulated to direct the remaining life of the product.[11] A harvest strategy is aimed at reducing investment and achieving short-term cash flow. Cutbacks in plant investment and R&D expenditures are the investment options; reduction in sales costs, sporadically intensifying advertising, and increasing prices are the marketing choices. The trade-off lies in the balance of reducing costs to the point where sales are not depressed. Yet, the calculated action will not alarm the customers and give away one's intention to the competitors. When applied skillfully, harvest strategy can extend product life and aggressively plan for replacement or slow down decline.

PRODUCT ELIMINATION STRATEGY Product elimination strategy not only applies to situations during business contraction but is a standard practice in marketing management. It follows a procedure of selecting candidates for product elimination (those products exhibiting downward sales, price, and profit trends), determining products for ultimate elimination, and subsequently launching the elimination program. There can be four substrategies:

Product Trimming Strategy Also called product pruning or simplification, product trimming strategy refers to the periodical reduction of nonprofitable products. A "20–80 rule" is generally used to facilitate the process by trimming products that constitute only 20 percent of sales but absorb 80 percent of costs of sales.

Run-out Strategy Under a run-out strategy, all supporting effort to a product is reduced to the minimum level to increase product profitability over its remaining life. Reduction in sales expenditure, advertising, and distribution costs are the options.

Contract Marketing Strategy A declining product that does not call for immediate abandonment can be allowed to continue production but is contracted to other firms who market it. Through licensing, a product can also be produced by other firms.

Product Abandonment Strategy Product abandonment strategy facilitates the redeployment of released personnel, facilities, capital, and inventory and allows orderly withdrawal from the marketplace without undue damage to the firm's commitment to customers and distributors. Timing, speed, and orderly execution are important considerations.

Channel of Distribution Strategy

Channel of distribution decision is concerned with the selection of marketing institutions to form channels through which goods and services are distributed from the producer to the final user.[12] An efficient distribution system from the manufacturer, to channel institutions or the middleman, to the final users is designed to achieve efficient physical distribution.

The first task is to determine channel objectives in terms of sales, profitability, and indexes of channel members' allegiance and customer product preference. Its objective is simply to increase volume and profit. The second policy issue is channel structure, which is concerned with the number of channel members—the wholesalers, jobbers, and retailers—and the number of channel levels. The selection, though different in every case, is guided by two basic considerations: (1) a company must decide which markets are to be covered and through what means they can be reached; and (2) the selection is based on certain criteria, such as customer characteristics (number of customers, geographical distance, and purchasing patterns, for example), product characteristics, middleman characteristics, competitor characteristics, company characteristics, and environmental characteristics (economic and legal).

Management and marketing considerations constitute the third area of policy deliberation. Channel institutions are members of the marketing team. Each member performs certain tasks. Wholesalers perform marketing, warehousing, pricing, promotion, and financing; retailers discharge responsibilities in marketing, inventory management, promotion, and selling. At the outset, a manufacturer must work out with channel members the terms and conditions, pricing policy, territorial arrangements, and specific services to be performed by each party. Performance standards and quota assignments need mutual agreement. Motivation of channel members constitutes a challenge to the manufacturer, who applies incentives and supervision to encourage member participation and cooperation in developing joint marketing strategies to attain channel objectives. Management control in evaluating channel members' performance, in determining causes of and remedies for below-standard performance, and in planning for joint strategies are essential to good channel management.

MULTIPLE CHANNEL STRATEGY When a company decides to develop multiple channels of distribution, it intends to use added channels to supplement direct distribution. The design of the channel structure is thus necessarily an immediate task. Simplicity, economics, and profits are the criteria governing the selection of members, their individual responsibilities, and trade relationships. Trade relationships can be established according to the different modes of distribution. Whereas intense distribution creates a large number of outlets to maximize product exposure, selective distribution limits the number of wholesalers and/or retailers to achieve better concentration and control.

Another mode, exclusive distribution, grants distributors the exclusive rights to distribute the company's products to a given geographical market. The producers must define trade relationships and clarify their position concerning their retailers' support program—those price concessions, financial assistance, and protective provisions that the manufacturers must develop to properly motivate the members and negotiate the channel to achieve channel objectives.

CHANNEL CHANGE STRATEGY Channel of distribution is dynamic in nature, reflecting changes in competition, market, law, and the producers' consistent effort to improve. Modifying the channel strategy therefore is a necessary part of channel management but a slow process in effecting changes. There can be three approaches: (1) partial modification—the effort to replace channel members due to normal turnover and to add new members to extend coverage to new customers/market segments; (2) channel revitalization—an action to replace older, inefficient members with new distributors of vitality and potential and to revitalize the channel system, improving its performance through efficient supervision, incentives, training, and sales planning; and (3) second channel addition—the attempt to open up a second channel to serve an entirely new market. In introducing modification, consideration must be given to the design, construction, and management of the channel system. However, channel modification must be regarded as a periodic requirement and an important means of implementing marketing strategy, seeking solutions to growth, profit instability, and survival problems.

Sales Promotion Strategy

Modern marketing relies heavily on personal selling and sales promotion. Sales promotion in its totality is considered a means of selling and communication, the ability to manage a viable sales force and employ a variety of media to persuade, educate, condition, and remind a specific segment of customer audience.[13] Depending on persuasive communication to achieve sales goals, a marketing organization mixes advertising, personal selling, specialized promotion, and publicity. It is a cost area in which large expenditures can be expected and for which economic allocation and close scrutiny is an absolute necessity. Additionally, sales promotion poses management challenges especially in the recruiting, selecting, training, motivating, and managing of a sales force. A well-directed and well-motivated sales force is the vital organ of a marketing organization. A good salesperson is a tactician, an achiever, and an executor who can operate independently without undue supervision, and who plans strategy and tactics before plunging into a sales encounter.

Sales promotion strategy must be guided by a clear statement of objectives. They can be general, dealing with increased sales, maintenance or improvement of market share, creation or improvement of climate for future sales, and improved promotional efficiency. Alternatively, they can be specific, dealing with a part of the promotion mix, an element in marketing strategy in launching a new product, or reducing marketing cost. As such, sales promotion strategy involves many decision choices and covers a broad range of activities. We single out three promotion strategies for illustration:[14]

SALES STRATEGY Sales strategy deals with the deployment of the sales force—the total process of sales planning[15]—and the choice of sales techniques. Sales techniques differ from situation to situation. There can be four types of selling: trade; missionary; technical; and new business selling. They can be programmed to meet the needs of traditional vendor-customer relationships, system selling (requiring the salesperson's comprehension of the technical limitations and requirements of the customers' systems), and programmed selling (the maintenance of an ongoing sales operation once the product has been sold).

COMMUNICATION STRATEGY Communication strategy refers to the selection of the theme of an advertisement, determining precisely what will make the advertising different from that of the competitor and most meaningful to the customers. A creative strategy depends on a thorough analysis of the motivating factor of the customers' buying decision and the competitors' advertising program. It also depends on execution—the adherence to certain guidelines of good advertising, which may include orchestrating a television commercial and the presentation of an advertising message.

MEDIA STRATEGY Media strategy refers to the selection of the best commercial channels to carry the message to the target audience. Communication channel may include radio, television, newspapers, magazines, or outdoor signs. The choice singles out the medium (the specific television station or a specific magazine), the media scheduling (its reach and frequency), and the development of the media plan, including techniques to measure advertising effectiveness.

Pricing Strategy

Pricing is the single most important consideration in marketing decisions. This is because pricing has a direct relationship with demand and supply, constitutes a source of revenue for the company (sales), and is the prime determinant of profit.[16] In economics, pricing is considered a crucial variable in break-even analysis, and through marginal analysis of varied demand and supply conditions, profit maximization models can be readily developed to guide business decisions. Pricing is thus an economic function. Similarly, it is a powerful marketing tool. Its impact upon sales, profit, and competition is direct and dramatic. In fact, pricing can produce immediate and far-reaching results in the marketplace not equaled by any other means in the marketing mix. For this reason, it is also a dangerous and explosive instrument; improper pricing can result in destroying a product, and persistent price cutting can create chaos in a marketplace. Violation of pricing laws can bring expensive lawsuits and indirectly damage a firm's standing in the marketplace.

Because of these seemingly conflicting roles, pricing is a complex subject and thus poses policy and strategy problems. In the first place, a firm must establish its pricing objectives. The increase of sales and maintenance or improvement of market shares are objectives of a general nature; specific pricing goals for profit and return on investment help define policies and strategies. Pricing policies guide everyday pricing and sales activities. Pricing policies can include a broad range of guidelines: in general, however, a firm establishes policies on price level (price leader or follower), geographical pricing, discount policies, product life cycle pricing, and policies relating to the management of a pricing function including procedures, analysis, determination, and maintenance. For simplicity, pricing strategy can be grouped into three areas.

PRICE-SETTING STRATEGY In setting prices, there can be three approaches: cost-oriented pricing; demand-oriented pricing; and competition-oriented pricing. Cost-oriented pricing is generally based on the total cost of a product including the allocation earmarked for overhead and general administration cost. Markup pricing by resellers and target pricing by manufacturers based on a desired rate of return on their cost at an established standard volume are the variations. Demand-oriented pricing is based on market conditions; a particular product is priced depending on the intensity of demand, exemplified by auto prices, which fluctuate with seasonal demand. Competition-oriented pricing refers to a firm's pricing its products chiefly based on what its competitors are charging. It can take the form of ongoing, competitive rates of pricing or, in the case of industrial sales and governmental contractual selection, the form of competitive bidding.

PRICE CHANGE STRATEGY Price change strategy concerns two aspects: the initiation of a change, and meeting pricing changes. Whereas initiating price changes takes into account price elasticity of demand and the perceptual factors in buyers' response, meeting price changes considers a firm's competitive and profit position, which can be strong or passive.

PROMOTIONAL PRICING STRATEGY Promotional pricing strategy refers to a number of means a firm can select to secure temporary, promotional price advantages. "Skimming" pricing is aimed at getting the "cream" of the market at a high price, usually during the early phase of a new product's introduction. Penetration pricing is the opposite; a lower price is used to capture a large share of market at the time of penetration or saturation. Other means, such as prestige pricing to connote high quality or status, leader pricing to attract customers to stores, bait pricing to attract bargain hunters, and odd-even pricing to end the price tag with an odd or even number for psychological effects, are the various means to achieve such temporary price advantages.

SUMMARY

Marketing is a powerful instrument in achieving corporate objectives and is a vital part of corporate strategy. Modern marketing is a strategic function; it interacts with the external world and directly encounters competition. As such, it assumes a triple role of advisor, manager, and strategist.

We have reviewed marketing strategic issues and emphasized equal application of corporate strategic concepts to marketing. The discussion on the four component strategies with over ten substrategies is only an overview. Indeed, it is the unlimited number of situations, the infinite patterns of human behavior, and the dynamic nature of marketing that complicate the attempt to describe the varying approaches.

NOTES

1. Strategic marketing is viewed by many authors as a basic approach to marketing. It can be a process, an integrated plan, or a method of planning and problem solving. Philip Kotler, *Marketing Management: Analysis, Planning & Control* (Englewood Cliffs, N.J.: Prentice-Hall, 1976), pp. 45–46; David T. Kollat, Roger D. Blackwell, and James F. Robeson, *Strategic Marketing* (New York: Holt, Rinehart and Winston, 1972), pp. 28–45; Martin L. Bell, *Marketing: Concepts and Strategy* (Boston: Houghton Mifflin, 1972), pp. 546–72; and David W. Cravens, Gerald E. Hills, and Robert B. Woodruff, *Marketing Decision Making: Concepts and Strategy* (Homewood, Ill.: Irwin, 1976), pp. 321–47.
2. Kotler, *Marketing Management,* chap. 5, pp. 98–116.
3. Gerald A. Simon, "The Top Marketing Executive," in *The Chief Executive's Handbook,* ed. John D. Glover and Gerald A. Simon (Homewood, Ill.: Dow Jones-Irwin, 1976), pp. 571–85.
4. Standard marketing textbooks give full treatment to the subject material. David J. Luck, Hugh G. Wales, and Donald A. Taylor, *Marketing Research* (Englewood Cliffs, N.J.: Prentice-Hall, 1974); William J. Stanton, *Fundamentals of Marketing* (New York: McGraw-Hill, 1971); and E. Jerome McCarthy, *Basic Marketing: A Managerial Approach* (Homewood, Ill.: Irwin, 1975).
5. For example, David T. Kollat lists marketing objectives, target market selection, general marketing strategy, marketing programming, the market plan, and controlling and evaluating marketing ends as the six steps. Kollat, Blackwell, and Robeson, *Strategic Marketing,* pp. 35–45.
6. Philip Kotler listed five strategic concepts: market segmentation, market positioning, market entry strategy, marketing mix strategy, and time strategy. *Marketing Management,* pp. 57–61.
7. For discussions on social responsibility and marketing, see David J. Schwartz, *Marketing Today: A Basic Approach* (New York: Harcourt Brace Jovanovich, 1973), pp. 599–621.
8. For detailed discussions, refer to Kotler, *Marketing Management,* pp. 183–98; and Bell, *Marketing,* pp. 617–32.
9. Bell listed three approaches to the management of mature products: a trade-off approach; a dynamic approach; and a recycle approach. *Marketing,* pp. 674–82.
10. For detailed discussion, see appropriate chapters in Bell, *Marketing;* Kollat, Blackwell, and Robeson, *Strategic Marketing;* and Kotler, *Marketing Management.*
11. Philip Kotler, "Harvesting Strategies for Weak Products," *Business Horizons,* August 1978, pp. 15–22.
12. Bell, *Marketing,* pp. 694–726.
13. Kotler, *Marketing Management,* pp. 322–46.
14. Kollat, Blackwell, and Robeson, *Strategic Marketing,* pp. 347–65, 372–78.
15. Sales planning consists of organizing sales force, establishing quota, programming sales activities, and execution and control. Cravens, Hills, and Woodruff, *Marketing Decision Making,* chaps. 21, 22.
16. Kotler, *Marketing Management,* pp. 249–73. Also, Alfred R. Oxenfeldt, *Pricing Strategies* (New York: AMACOM, 1975), esp. pp. 1–34.

CHAPTER ELEVEN

Functional Strategy II: Financial Strategy

Financial strategy, the second functional strategy, defines the use of financial resources to implement corporate strategy and outlines courses of action. It enables the finance department to develop, conserve, and alter financial resources and to specify the optimal deployment of such resources towards the achievement of financial and corporate objectives under varied strategic situations. In this chapter, we discuss the financial function in its modern setting and the additional dimension of its external and internal responsibility, the financial strategic issues that require early identification and discussion, the component strategies dealing with capitalization, debts, dividends, and assets, and, finally, some special applications.

THE FINANCIAL FUNCTION

The Changing Image

Since the 1950s and 1960s, increasing importance has been placed on financial management. Financial management was seen as vital to the development of sources of capital for growth and expansion. Later, in the early 1970s, financial management focused on strategies to improve profits and to solve business contraction and survival problems. These two tasks brought about a reorientation of financial management. Contemporary financial management acknowledges its responsibilities towards external financial markets and institutions, its full participation in internal decision making, and in managing corporate financial resources to assure a profitable business.

The Chief Financial Officer

In a new role as an active member of the management team, the chief financial officer (CFO) maintains a close relationship with the chief executive officer.[1] The CFO and his/her organization supply management with financial data, analyses, and expertise. As the corporation's representative in external financial affairs, he/she maintains a good relationship with selected banks and investment institutions fully aware of the changing financial market whose condition affects cost, timing, and the selection of sources of capital to meet corporate needs whenever required. He/she is also regarded as a close adviser to the CEO on internal financial matters dealing with taxes, depreciation, interests, insurance, and matters relating to government reporting practices. He/she formulates short- and long-range profit plans and controls to oversee corporate profit performance, analyzing and measuring profitability in its total perspective and in all crucial decision areas of investment, debt, and assets management.[2]

Additionally, he/she raises advanced warning signals to alert management when a hidden profit crisis is forthcoming and when a shift of business direction is warranted. He/she actively participates in decision making by reviewing proposals on capital investment, acquisition, and merger. He/she reviews and advises on large expenditures, such as make-or-buy decisions, major purchases, inventories, and R&D expenditures. In his/her relationships with operating division heads, the CFO advises and assesses their business decisions with credibility that invites mutual respect and cooperation. In his/her role as a senior financial officer of the corporation, he/she maintains a highly competent staff that applies advanced quantitative methods and sound financial reasoning to substantiate its findings and recommendations, formulates corporate financial policies, and assumes a leadership role among financial organizations throughout the corporation, especially in directing company-wide programs, including profit improvement, cash generation, and financial planning and control.

FINANCIAL STRATEGY ISSUES

In financial strategy making, we have identified four strategic issues: (1) the proper use of ratio analysis; (2) the determination of financial capacity; (3) the dynamic process of financial management; and (4) the importance of strategy upon finance.

The Proper Use of Ratio Analysis

The proper use of ratio analysis is an issue simply because ratio analysis serves a definite purpose in strategic analysis. It provides a quick diagnostic look at a company's financial health and it triggers subsequent financial and operational analyses. Its proper use must be stressed in order to avoid the "number game" syndrome that is prevalent among financial analysts.

Ratio analysis is traditionally used by external institutions, banks, and stockholders to assess the advisability of making funds available to a firm; it is extensively used by business firms for internal analysis and control. Its shortcomings, however, must be thoroughly understood; without judicious interpretation and comparative analysis, ratio analysis could be misleading. Without further-developed techniques, it is limited in predicting future trends.[3] Ratio analysis can be grouped into four types:[4]

1. Liquidity ratios, consisting of (a) current ratio, and (b) quick ratio to measure a firm's ability to meet its maturing short-term obligations.

2. Leverage ratios, consisting of (a) debt to total assets; (b) times-interest-earned; and (c) fixed charge coverage ratio to measure the extent to which the firm has been financed by debt.
3. Activity ratios, consisting of (a) inventory turnover; (b) average collection period; (c) fixed assets turnover; and (d) total assets turnover to measure how effectively the firm is using its resources.
4. Profitability ratios, consisting of (a) profit margin on sales; (b) return on total assets; and (c) return on net worth to measure management's overall effectiveness.

During the formulation of business strategy, financial ratios are constructed selectively. The complete calculation of the twelve ratios as a routine financial exercise is not warranted because management needs to know only those crucial ratios related to the problem at hand. For instance, a simple problem requires few ratios; a large problem calls for extensive analysis. Thus, although ratio analysis serves to identify problems, other comparative analysis must be introduced to explore likely solutions. Comparing a firm's ratios to an industrial average and/or major competitors, relating past year's ratios to present ratios for trend analysis, and converting dollar amounts into percentages for common-size analysis[5] are all efficient techniques for focusing on problem identification and thereby facilitate decisions on strategic issues.

Financial Capacity

Financial capacity of a firm refers to its present and future capacity for funding, its size, and sources. Not only do studies of financial capacity determine the degree of the company's readiness to pursue intended strategic action, but they place constraints on selecting courses of action. A company pursuing growth, for example, must first ascertain the amount of funds required to finance the varied new product development, diversification, or international business activities. An analysis of financial capacity establishes the size and availability of its internal source of funding—cash on hand, depreciation, and convertible cash.

External sources of financing, which accounted for one-third of the total corporate financing in the United States in 1973, offers a wide range of selection. The CFO is expected to determine the immediate and future needs of funds and to assess the advisability and feasibility of obtaining them. He/she must consider whether the basic financial philosophy of the company is either aggressive or conservative and what will be the combined effects on the changed financial structure and the enlarged business operation. Furthermore, he/she must establish the limit of financial exposure (what degree of borrowing the company can assume) and the extent of risk (what margins of safety the company must have for unanticipated crises). A company under business contraction needs to know how long and to what degree it can sustain earnings decline and losses. In a survival situation, the company's financial capacity to achieve solvency is positively the prime concern in deciding courses of action.

The Dynamic Process of Financial Management

Modern financial management is a dynamic process, which requires active participation and the capacity to manage change. It must be sensitive to the business cycle, inflation, and industrial changes. Government policies and regulations deeply affect financial operations, levying financial impact directly or indirectly, and thus requiring judicious interpretation. A company's financial structure undergoes constant changes and adjustment demanding almost continual assessment of a firm's financial position.

Financial decision making involving capitalization (long-term debt and equity financing), debt, dividend, and assets management is in essence a strategic game. It requires the use of advanced quantitative methods to simulate and compare alternatives and facilitate intuitive and judgmental thinking to select courses of action.

Additionally, financial decisions bear long-range significance. They focus on long-term economic gains, and their implementation requires lead time and well-planned actions to succeed. A cash generation program, for example, needs time to implement; a large loan request needs time to be developed, negotiated, and concluded. Financial management is thus a function capable of managing changes, strategy, and programs of long-term importance.

The Importance of Strategy to Finance

Financial decisions are essentially investment decisions, aimed at maximizing the present value of future benefits. At the core of the activity is the ability to develop and utilize capital resources. Recent scarcity of capital has dramatically demonstrated the competitive nature of the capital market and the associated high cost of capital. Indeed, a company competes for capital resources in the financial market in much the same way it competes in the marketplace for products and services. Strategy-minded management thus attaches prime importance to capitalization structure and debt management. The excessive use of heavy borrowing to finance growth in the 1960s is now under severe examination. Management of current and fixed assets to conserve and produce resources requires advanced planning and strategic action, as does the management of dividends. We choose four areas of decision to illustrate the importance of strategy making in financial management and to emphasize its importance in implementing corporate strategy.

FINANCIAL COMPONENT STRATEGIES

We consider four financial decisions of overriding importance in financial strategy making: (1) capitalization structure strategy, which seeks to develop long-term sources of financing; (2) debt strategy, which examines the use of debt as a means of developing long-term financing; (3) dividend strategy, which specifies a firm's posture toward internal financing; and (4) assets management strategy, which determines the optimal development of current and fixed assets. Our discussion will be brief, viewing the decisions purely from a strategic perspective because the technical and quantitative aspects of the decisions are beyond the scope of the book.[6]

Capitalization Structure Strategy

Capitalization structure strategy spells out the composition of a firm's long-term financing of debt, preferred stocks, and common stockholders' equity. The decision itself is affected by a score of variables, among them: the company's basic philosophy on borrowing, income tax savings, the cost of capital, and the leverage ratio. A company such as du Pont entertains little thought about debt financing, preferring to use internal financing as a major source. U.S. Steel and Sears, Roebuck pursue a cautious policy of borrowing; yet expansion-minded companies, such as Dow Chemical and the Aluminum Company of America, maintain debt as a means of financing growth. Income tax savings from payment of interest on indebtedness expensed for tax purposes is a decisive consideration, making debt cheaper than other forms of financing. Another important variable is the weighted average of cost of capital, which widens the gap between cost of borrowed funds and the equity fund. The use of leverage by enlarging debt to equity ratio was a popular alternative in the 1960s.

In developing capitalization structure, three basic rules govern its formulation: simplicity; safety; and flexibility. A simple structure involving the minimum number of sources and instruments facilitates selection and efficient management. Care in applying proper leverage, avoiding dilution of earnings per share and assets per share, retaining ownership control, and basically maintaining a conservative structure provides earnings stability and prevents disastrous effects from adverse business situations. Flexibility refers to the contractual relationship between a corporation and its security holders. Unfavorable terms and conditions restrict a firm's freedom of operation. Together with the firm's financial position, timing, and condition of the financial market, these variables influence the formulation of the strategies.

Adjusting capital sources is also a part of the capitalization structure strategy. It can be accomplished, for example, by initially using short-term loans to finance rapid growth or the beginning of long-term projects. The short-term loan can be completely repaid at a later date, such as within a few months when long-term financing is consummated. Other adjustments can be made in preferred stocks, in the hope of increasing the market price of common stock and thus eliminate any potential burden on the firm's working capital. Adjustments in common stock through stock dividends, stock splits, and planned purchases of a corporation's own stock also affect the company's market price or capitalization. Restructuring of capitalization occurs in insolvency and survival situations. However, once the firm is placed under severe distress it has a much limited option and essentially is at the mercy of the creditors.

Debt Strategy

In times of capital scarcity or economic uncertainty, debt strategy has become one of the most crucial decisions in financial management. Yet, the decision is most difficult because it is closely interrelated with the other three decisions (capitalization structure, dividend, and assets), and its outcome decisively affects a firm's future solvency, growth, and profitability. Major considerations in debt strategy center around the determination of a firm's debt capacity and the use of leverage, the debt ratio itself. Debt capacity can be initially determined by two basic ratios: the current ratio, which measures the short-term solvency; and the times-interest-earned ratio (or interest coverage ratio), which measures the degree of a firm's ability to meet annual interest payments. Although the size of the two ratios differ from company to company and from industry to industry, lending institutions generally consider current ratio as two or more times, and times-interest-earned ratio at four or more times as minimum.

Financial leverage indicates a firm's indebtedness in relation to equity, and is, in reality, a decision calculated on a firm's projected ability to meet debt obligations. A debt to equity ratio of 0.9 to 1 is considered desirable. However, high income tax savings, lack of internal financing, and the increasing demands of funds for growth provided the impetus for corporations to use high-debt ratio.[7] Highly leveraged companies reason according to the premise that the anticipated future cash stream is large enough to meet annual interest and principal payments. However, when earnings decline and cash begins to dwindle, the partial solvency problem can escalate into a real threat. Leverage is thus a double-edged weapon: it provides funds, but it also invites disasters. A prudent management must seriously consider the downside risk of the economy and at the same time accurately ascertain its cash flow projection and future requirements. Briefly stated, the choice between growth and solvency is largely a strategic decision, one requiring the clear determination of policies to guide the quantitative simulation of a wide range of alternatives and the development of the debt strategy.

One of the basic policies a company must determine is its policy on borrowing. A policy of no long-term debt is clear and easy to communicate. A policy of borrowing to guide decision making, however, may offer several acceptable options: (1) borrowing the maximum amount available at the lowest market rate of interest, but limiting bond rating either to Aaa or Aa; (2) borrowing the maximum amount available while keeping the bond rate at A; (3) borrowing up to some fixed leverage ratio; (4) borrowing until the interest coverage reaches some minimum acceptable level; and (5) borrowing the maximum amount available but limited by what the market is willing to accept.[8]

Dividend Strategy

The dividend decision is an integral part of a firm's approach to internal financing. Dividend is a type of payment to stockholders that is deductible from a firm's earnings with a residual amount as retained earnings. The decision is influenced by profitability, growth rate, stability of earnings and dividends, market price of the stock, and the desired retained earnings. The size and methods of payments, either cash or stock dividends, affect the level of income and thus the profitability. A company's growth rate is influenced by the decision. Lower dividend payments increase the level of earnings, thus the company's growth rate. We have seen many growth-minded companies consistently maintain a policy of no dividend for that purpose. Stability of earnings and dividend is a sign of consistency, which encourages stockholders' support and produces positive effects on the market price of the stock. Stockholders expect a well-managed company to produce fixed dividend payments on a continuous basis. The market price of the stock can be affected by the size and methods of payment. A moderate growth company is expected to pay higher dividends, and when it fails to pay, the market price drops. Most important, the company's debt strategy, which is greatly influenced by the amount of internal financing, is a controlling factor in deliberating dividend strategy. Internal financing is more desirable than external financing, due to its cost, flexibility, and the advantages to stockholders. These major considerations, plus minor ones including directors' attitude and legal requirements, form the basis for formulating the strategy.

In developing dividend strategy, a company can choose among five options: (1) regular cash dividends only, a practice among the majority of U.S. companies; (2) regular and extra cash dividends; (3) cash and stock dividends; (4) consistent use of stock dividends to conserve cash and adjust capitalization structure; and (5) no dividends at all, widely practiced among aggressively growing and emerging young companies.[9]

Assets Management Strategy

In view of the broad scope of the subject and the gravity of its effects, assets management is indeed a critical area for financial management. Long-term assets management refers to managing assets whose cash contribution exceeds a period of one year. This includes all types of fixed assets and capital investment decisions of new product development, acquisition and merger, modification, replacement, and disposition of existing fixed assets. Current assets management deals with two crucial problems: the appropriate mix of each of the component items, and the effects of short-term financing. Recently, much concentrated attention, however, has been placed on cash management, which affects the firm's solvency and requires strategic solutions.[10]

CASH MANAGEMENT Cash management is affected by four major factors: flow of receipts and disbursements; cash balance (the synchronization of cash inflows and outflows to achieve a balanced position); short-term interest rate; and efficient handling of receipts and disbursements. A cash strategy reflects the interplay of several important variables, such as size, seasonal and cyclical fluctuations, and the predictability of receipts and disbursements patterns. Further, it depends on an accurate projection of cash flow and the ability to conserve and rebuild cash when required. Cash strategy is dynamic in nature, reflecting the constantly changing conditions, and is guided by policies and decisions for continual adjustments. A good cash strategy clearly defines cash management objectives and delineates courses of action in cash projection and planning, cash conservation (for example, handling excess cash and cash rebuilding), cash balance (its upper and lower limits), and efficient management of accounts receivable and inventory.

LONG-TERM ASSETS MANAGEMENT Long-term assets management is the area generally referred to as capital budgeting. It entails a process of evaluation, selection, and execution and is an investment decision. As a process, it is related to the annual long-range planning activity, the planning, submission, and approval of capital expenditures. As an investment decision, it employs economic and financial analyses and advanced quantitative methods of allocating resources; the prime concern of these methods is maximizing the market value of the firm.

Capital investment can be classified into three categories:[11] (1) social investments involving government-required projects for health, safety, and pollution protections; (2) cost improvement investments for improving equipment and facilities; and (3) capacity investments consisting of equipment for new products, new plants, and new facilities. Investment for new products, purchase of a firm, or R&D expenditures are dealt with separately on functional and ad hoc bases. Their evaluation and selection require consistently good management.

Investment decisions on capital spending has captured the attention of financial management.[12] In capital budgeting, the initial decision centers around evaluating and selecting techniques. The net present value (NPV), internal rate of return (IRR), and payback method are well-known techniques.[13] Each technique has its unique application and limitations. Their combined uses have pragmatic value for comparing computation and for ranking projects. Selection of capital projects rests on capital rationing and classification of projects based on purposes and usages. Capital rationing is an important policy issue whereby a company sets limits to its planned investment for a specific year based on the amount of cash available. The classification of projects by purpose and usage establishes another selection criterion. Projects classified by purpose as described above specify dollar limits to these categories. Investments classified by usage can be divided by independent, competing, and complementary or dependent projects whereby each project is evaluated vis-à-vis other competing projects. Advanced techniques including risk analysis, probabilistic analysis, sensitivity analysis, and portfolio selection techniques can be introduced at the later stage of selection to analyze more complicated, conflicting projects.

Leasing is another choice in capital acquisition. Leasing offers the advantage of minimizing initial capital outlay, thus preserving the lessee's borrowing capacity. However, it may positively affect future financial costs because leasing prevents the lessee from claiming depreciation and investment tax credit, among other disadvantages. The choice lies in the depreciable life of the property, the borrowing ability, and the total use of assets.

SPECIAL APPLICATION OF FINANCIAL STRATEGIES

Financial strategy, like marketing strategy, requires the optimal use of component strategies. Functional strategies are called upon to implement corporate strategy to meet a specific situational need. In recent years, financial strategies have been applied to finance growth and direct divestiture. As an illustration, we will discuss growth-financing strategy and divestiture strategy.

Growth-Financing Strategy

In the process of strategy making, finance is an important participant. During corporate policy deliberation and objective setting, the CFO and the finance staff prepare financial assumptions and participate in discussions. They raise critical questions on present posture, future business mix, risk, growth rate, and general courses of action. Once the policy issues are defined, the finance staff proceeds to study and interpret these issues in quantitative terms, conduct analysis and trade-off studies, and formulate financial strategy.

Financial strategy deals basically with capital acquisition and value maintenance. In pursuing growth, financial strategy centers on financing growth. It specifies criteria in locating source of financing (internal, public, and private), establishing cost of capital, and evaluating return and risk.[14] The financial strategic plan also specifies guidelines for each component strategy. For example, the company's borrowing capacity (influenced by the maximum amount of debt outstanding), sources of financing, and cost of capital are guidelines for capitalization structure decision. Financing through debt and thus its relationship with internal financing is a consideration of debt decision. Cost of capital and financial risk, which represents the company's projected ability to meet debt obligations, are problems to be considered in dividend and assets management strategies. To be sure, these considerations are interrelated, and each decision impacts the other. In the final analysis, it is the financial evaluation of return on investment that determines the economics of financing and thus courses of action.

In executing corporate strategy, the financing plan provides action guidelines. Here, consideration of certain tactical actions are important. First, the CFO must make sure that growth financing will be available on reasonable terms. Decisions on amount and timing are action items. Second, he/she must determine the minimum return that must be met by growth investments. Actions in determining type (equity versus debt financing), cost, and risk are specific assignments. And, third, he/she must determine the maintenance of the highest intrinsic value for the stock. Risk and ownership control are important studies to be accomplished. Of course, these actions interact. Together, they constitute the complex interaction requiring quantitative analysis and simulation modeling.[15]

Additionally, the CFO and the staff actively participate in all phases of execution. For example, in acquisition/merger and international operations, finance representatives prepare financial evaluations of acquisition and financial projection of the combined operations. The establishment of financial criteria for acquisition, prospects selection, preliminary evaluation of purchases, pro forma projection of tax impact on cash flow, and additional commitment of resources, among others, are decision inputs required of the finance department. In case of international operations, international financing constitutes an even more complex problem. Financial input is hence indispensable to the formulation and execution of corporate strategies.

Divestiture Strategy

Divestiture strategy operates in two environments: the normal disposition of "losing" business in part or in whole; and the forced divestiture of a large number of businesses in times of financial stress.[16] Corporations decide on divestiture for different reasons. Those businesses that have separated from the main business of the company form one group of candidates for divestiture. This occurs mostly during marketing restructuring, when ill-conceived acquisitions have overextended the company's financial capacity. The widespread "dumping" of businesses in the mid-1970s was a result of such a phenomenon. The objective of divestiture of this type is reduction of debt level, thus the generation of cash. Those businesses showing the lowest earnings and cash due to product aging, market degeneration, and plant obsolescence have reasons for the second type of divestiture.

A third reason can be positive responses. In such a case, a company may find that an operation can command a high price, and yet its retention is not indispensable in the corporate revised business operations. The cash from its divestiture can be reallocated to meet the needs of the corporation, either for reinvestment or achieving intended financial objectives.

In formulating divestiture strategy, guidelines are specified to direct the operation. Divestiture follows a three-phase procedure: planning; divestiture; and postdivestiture. Planning divestiture entails the establishment of objectives and criteria for divestiture. For example, the estimation of proceeds and cost, the urgency, and methods of divestiture (selling the parts or the whole) are important preliminary actions. The divestiture phase begins with the identification of prospects and selecting a preferred purchaser. Negotiation follows when the buyer is identified. It centers on valuation, submission of the divestiture package, and resolution of differences on common tax problems and accounting financial reporting. Final negotiation, which requires the meeting of management of the two companies, does not take place until the general agreement is reached and financial differences are resolved. When the purchase contract is drawn and the financial audit is completed by independent accountants, a long period of anxiety and wrangling takes place between middle-management personnel of the two parties. Financial personnel are deeply involved in interpreting, clarifying, and analyzing agreement on figures and accounting details. The final signature on the contract signifies the official change of ownership.

The postdivestiture phase is equally important. Financial considerations call for reporting divestiture to government agencies, settling accounts with suppliers and distributors, and scheduling the use of proceeds. These are the strategic and tactical guidelines to be included in a divestiture strategy. A good divestiture strategy is a management as much as a financial decision. Management involvement and functional participation, including marketing, legal, personnel, and other involved departments are doubtlessly imperative.

SUMMARY

So far, we have discussed two of the four functional strategies—marketing and financial. We should remember that functional strategies are heavily action oriented and need constant attention and adjustments in response to dynamic changes at the functional level. We have shown that there is a great variety of component strategies. In marketing strategy, we discussed the four component strategies with over ten substrategies. In financial strategy, we singled out four representing the major decision areas demanding strategic thinking and action. In particular, we briefly discussed growth-financing strategy and divestiture strategy to illustrate this interplay of component strategies. For reasons also stated, our discussions are confined to strategic issues more than to technical specialties. The essence of functional strategies, let us repeat, is to substantiate corporate strategy on the one hand, and incite tactical actions at the functional level on the other hand.

NOTES

1. Robert Anderson, "The Chief Financial Officer: What to Look for, How to Get Top Performance," in *The Chief Executive's Handbook,* ed. John D. Glover and Gerald A. Simon (Homewood, Ill.: Dow Jones-Irwin, 1976), pp. 657–63.
2. For an expansive view, see Ezra Solomon, "Recent Trends and Developments in Academic and Professional Thinking on Financial Management," in *Frontiers of Financial Management: Selected Readings,* ed. William J. Serraino, Surendra S. Singhvi, and Robert M. Soldofsky (Cincinnati, Ohio: South Western Publishing, 1971), pp. 11–20.
3. Robert M. Soldofsky and Garnet D. Olive, *Financial Management* (Cincinnati, Ohio: South-Western Pub. Co. 1974), pp. 344–350, and Baruch Lev, *Financial Statement Analysis: A New Approach* (Englewood Cliffs, N.J.: Prentice-Hall, 1974), pp. 109–51.
4. J. Fred Weston and Eugene F. Brigham, *Managerial Finance* (Hinsdale, Illinois: The Dryden Press, 1975), pp. 19–45.
5. Common-size analysis is useful in showing the relative importance of each individual

account in the total and their percentage changes in identifying trends. Carl L. Moore and Robert K. Jaedicke, *Managerial Accounting* (Cincinnati, Ohio: South-Western Publishing, 1972), pp. 164–67.

6. This section draws heavily on material from financial management textbooks. Soldofsky and Olive, *Financial Management;* Stephen H. Archer and Charles A. D'Ambrosio, *Business Finance: Theory and Management* (New York: Macmillan, 1972); and Weston and Brigham, *Managerial Finance*.
7. The year 1966 is a landmark signifying the end of an era of relatively stable and low-cost financial market. Eli Shapiro and Barbara Negri Opper, ''Changing Structure of the Financial Markets,'' in *Chief Executive's Handbook,* ed. Glover and Simon, pp. 715–30.
8. Soldofsky and Olive, *Financial Management,* pp. 189–91.
9. Ibid., pp. 225–28.
10. For example, see S. D. Slater, *The Strategy of Cash: A Liquidity Approach to Maximizing the Company Profits,* (New York: Wiley, 1974). An excellent book centering on the thesis that cash is the core principle of all business activity.
11. For an excellent discussion on industry practice, see Hershner Cross, ''Capital Project Approval'' in *Chief Executive's Handbook,* ed. Glover and Simon, pp. 731–43.
12. Solomon, ''Recent Trends and Developments,'' pp. 11–18.
13. Textbook on capital budgeting in Robert W. Johnson, *Capital Budgeting* (Belmont, Calif.: Wadsworth Publishing, 1970); and Harold Bierman, Jr., and Seymour Smidt, *The Capital Budgeting Decision* (London: Collier-Macmillan, 1971).
14. For detailed discussion, see Leslie F. Murphy, ''Corporate Financial Strategy,'' in *Corporate Growth Strategies,* ed. Isay Stemp (New York: American Management Association, 1970), pp. 291–356.
15. Henry I. Meyer, *Corporate Financial Planning Models,* (New York: Wiley, 1977).
16. For discussion see, Arthur Bettauer, ''Strategy For Divestments,'' *Harvard Business Review,* March-April 1967, pp. 116–24, and Leonard Vignola, *Strategic Divestment* (New York: AMACOM, 1974).

CHAPTER TWELVE

Functional Strategies III: Research and Development Strategy and Production Strategy

Almost all modern business firms perform four essential functions: marketing to distribute goods and services; finance to supply resources; R&D to provide a means for future growth and stability; and production to produce. R&D is a relatively new function, difficult to perform, and often requiring sizable investment for somewhat uncertain returns.[1] Yet, it is a critical instrument of corporate strategy, decisively influencing the firm's long-range strategic posture, and greatly affecting the respective competitive position in marketing and production.

Production is crucial to a business operation by virtue of the size of its required investment (a major portion of the fixed and current assets), and the large number of employees it is required to manage. Effective management in a manufacturing operation reduces the cost of production, enhances return on assets, and improves human relations. In both functional areas, there are certain critical aspects requiring strategic thinking and action. We shall discuss the uniqueness of the two functions, identifying strategic issues peculiar to each, and examining component strategies whose formulation creates the substance of a corporate strategy.

RESEARCH AND DEVELOPMENT STRATEGY

Research and development is a big business. U.S. annual expenditures on R&D amounted to over $35 billion in 1975. The expenditures of individual companies ranged from more than $1 million by companies on sales of $50 million, to GM's $1,114 million, making GM the number one spender among the 730 companies surveyed by *Business Week*.[2] In times of capital scarcity and in search of better return on such large expenditures, business firms reexamine the value of R&D and look for more effective management of the operation.[3] R&D strategy is one of the vital means of forcing management to clarify objectives, develop courses of action, and respond to environmental changes in business and technology. Let us first review the nature of the R&D function.

The Unique Nature of R&D Function

Few large R&D organizations existed in the United States before the mid-1950s. Today, R&D organizations are sizable and fully interrelated with other organizations within the corporation. In a large corporation, R&D laboratories are numerous, consisting of central laboratories and division research centers for varied sciences, often located distantly. We have seen in the aerospace industry, for example, that operation of large R&D organizations amounts to tens of millions of dollars and involves thousands of engineers and technicians. Management of R&D organization is complex and calls for special consideration. There are two observations worth making: first, due to its youth compared to the traditional arts of selling and production, R&D management can draw upon few theories and minimal experience from the past. Second, perhaps the most fundamental explanation is the inherent contradictions of the function itself.

R&D is an activity of innovation and to some extent of individual achievement. A relatively free and nonregimented working environment is, therefore, a prerequisite to creativity and ingenuity. On the other hand, a business firm is a highly regimented organization, continuously seeking results and placing strict restrictions on time, cost, and scheduled accomplishments. An R&D organization within a business firm is thus subject to perpetual contradiction, struggling to perform its assigned responsibilities and to communicate with those who must authorize the expenditures and those who use its output.

R&D management assumes a dual responsibility, externally keeping abreast of the technological world and internally serving as an active member of the management team. It is keenly interested in the activities of the external technological community—universities, its competitors, and privately funded laboratories. It develops technological forecasts about the broad spectrum of related technological development as an input to corporate strategic planning and identifies outstanding discoveries and technically strong firms whose potential acquisition or joint venture may become desirable. Above all, an organization sensitive to the external world finds technological exchange and contact not only beneficial to its own planning and project selection but also to the recruitment of highly sought specialists known only to a small circle of the technological community.

Internally, the chief R&D officer of a corporation is a member of the management team. He/she advises and consults with the CEO on technological developments and on decisions whose technical content requires an expert's input.[4] He/she and his/her designees participate actively in the making of corporate strategy and in serving on committees and task forces planning and directing new product development, diversification, and other activities where technology is a constituent part. Indeed, communications between the technically minded and innovative-oriented R&D organization and the rest of the corporation, both at the top-management and operating-management levels, is a real challenge.[5]

In the development of corporate R&D programs, this officer formulates long-range technological objectives, R&D strategy, and proposes the budget. In its management, he/she selects projects, oversees project management, approves capital equipment and facilities, and recruits competent staff. As a chief R&D officer, he/she establishes policies, stimulates technical information exchange, and coordinates corporate-wide R&D activities, making certain that the central laboratories and division R&D activities are fully efficient and mutually complementary.

Strategy Issues

We identify three strategy issues for discussion: (1) technological forecasting and planning, which provides a useful input to corporate strategic planning; (2) the R&D mix that determines the size and composition of the program (that is, research versus development, or one technology versus another); and (3) R&D management concerning issues of centralization versus decentralization, project selection, and project planning and controlling.

TECHNOLOGICAL FORECASTING AND PLANNING As we discussed in chapter 4, technological forecasting is a constituent part of business environmental analysis involving forecasting of economic, sociopolitical, industrial, and technological trends. In technological forecasting, company management and R&D executives must accept the fact that the accuracy of predicting technical trends, new discoveries, and time horizons of future events remains inadequate. Ultimately, however, forecasting guides operating decision making on R&D planning and budgeting and provides a framework for adjusting and recycling R&D strategy making.

R&D planning focuses on two fundamental issues: the role of an R&D operation in the total corporate scheme of business development, and the allocation of resources within its sphere of operations. A company that depends upon technology as the spearhead for its business development would assign an important role to its R&D operations. Conversely, a company that employs methods other than technology for achieving competitive advantages would dictate a lesser role to its R&D work. Measuring in terms of expenditures, it is noted that industries such as computer and pharmaceutical spent an average of 4.9 percent to 5.9 percent of their sales dollars for R&D work as compared to less than 1 percent for many others. Equally, a company's R&D strategy, being aggressive or defensive, determines the role and thus the size of its R&D operations. As far as budgetary needs are concerned, they can be determined by considering economic criteria (percentage of sales, for example), technological advantages (the preservation of a company's technological leadership), and financial qualifications (return on investments). Final budget decisions, however, will be colored by how management perceives the task performance and the achievements of the R&D organization.

R&D MIX R&D mix refers to the operational structure of an R&D program, which provides both near-term and long-term benefits. In structuring an R&D program, there are two basic concerns: the optimal blend of research and development activities to achieve balanced benefits; and the methods of organizing R&D projects to implement R&D strategy.

Balancing Research and Development The differences between research and development can be established by their time horizons, their rates of development, and their technical contents. Research deals with a long-term horizon, such as three to five years; the rate of development is of a factoring magnitude above a significant number of one. Its management generally resides in centralized laboratories. In contrast, development is short term, about one to three years; its technical thrust is to improve the product life cycle. Its rate of development is fractional; its technical content is hardware oriented beyond the stage of material, process, or devices. Its management is scattered among the operating divisions.[6] An optimal blend of the two activities reflects the company's business objectives and the nature of the technology. Thus, a company pursuing an aggressive objective and confronting severe competition maintains an R&D blend slightly favoring research in contrast to development, relatively speaking.

Classifying R&D Work R&D work can be classified by business areas: those related to existing products and services; and those serving as a basis for diversification. Projects intended for products and services can be structured into business areas, markets, and product and are identified as primary and supporting projects. Projects in search of new technology for diversification adhere to the corporate classification "diversification activities" for easy identification and evaluation.

Classifying R&D by technology is another method to construct the desired R&D mix. Such a classification dramatizes the lateral relationship of varied technologies involved in a large corporation. It facilitates the projection of critical paths through which future technological development can be structured. Whereas classification by business area shows the impact of an R&D program, classification by technologies focuses on the logical linkage of the driving forces of the technology. Technologies are portrayed as a common link between business activities—the importance and relationship of each technology are logically established, and the transition from research to development of commercial products is visibly identified.

R&D MANAGEMENT Management of an R&D operation, because of its unique requirements and characteristics, is most challenging. There are three basic issues: (1) centralization versus decentralization; (2) project selection; and (3) project planning and controlling.

Centralization versus Decentralization Centralization versus decentralization is a pressing issue among large corporations with multiple products and technologies to serve. The decision affects the basic structure of the corporate R&D organization and its effectiveness in operation. Centralized R&D operations that limit activities to the centrally established laboratories, such as the Bell Telephone Laboratories and similar operations in oil and pharmaceutical industries, is one type that offers economy and efficient control. Decentralized R&D operations having many geographical scattered centers, such as du Pont's Experimentation Station in support of division operations, is another type. In between is the mixed mode; centralized and decentralized laboratories coexist—thus, a clear separation of research by centrally organized corporate-group laboratories, and development by product-oriented operating division centers. A company deciding on this structural issue gives full consideration to the pros and cons of each mode and adopts one that is compatible with its technological requirements and its internal operation.[7]

Selecting R&D Projects Project management refers to the actual selection of projects under the predetermined R&D mix and stated budget restrictions. A project is basically selected on its own merit—the relevancy and impact criteria that focus on a project's relationship with others and its impact upon business development. Other selection consideration can be given to: (1) the best use of skills and facilities available in the laboratories; (2) a good balance of prime and supporting projects to achieve a degree of self-sufficiency; (3) a desired mix of project completion dates to temper the speed of R&D, thereby minimizing sudden, intense use of resources and the uncalled for "fire-fighting" practices; (4) a conservative portfolio structure to achieve stability and continuity, thus avoiding continual and drastic changes of portfolio and direction; and (5) the judicious use of quantitative methods of project selection.[8] Closely associated with portfolio selection is project transferring and activity dealing with timely transferring of mature technologies from research to development, for example. Project transferring is an important activity in which lateral and vertical coordination is essential.

Planning and Controlling R&D Work Planning and controlling in R&D management deserves special treatment. First, R&D management is surrounded at all times by uncertainty. Technical difficulties, physical limitations (lack of facilities), and economic constraints and competitive actions can force project abandonment or structural reorientation of the program. Too often, technological forecasts are overly optimistic: rapid scientific progress is forecasted but frequently postponed; early commercialization may have been projected but is slow in developing. Second, R&D is a long-term investment whose payback period is usually long; moreover, total capitalization of a commercialized product is high, considering the cost of test and evaluation, pilot production, and marketing expenses. Good project planning and controlling can alleviate some of these difficulties and contribute to minimizing work slippage, cost overruns, and poor performance.

Such planning must: (1) define projects by specifying performance goals, cost limitation, and project time span; (2) detail work/cost breakdowns and milestone events; and (3) control and evaluate by establishing information flow, periodical reviews, and evaluation criteria.

R&D Component Strategies

In developing R&D strategy, we consider three component strategies to meet the needs of three different situations: (1) the basic strategy wherein a company can choose between a defensive or an offensive strategy, or both; (2) the penetration strategy employing new technology as a prime means to enter a new market; and (3) the response strategy to counteract a technological threat either from competitors or from the technology itself.

THE BASIC R&D STRATEGY A company's basic R&D strategy can have three different emphases—defensive, offensive, or both. Defensive strategy is directed at maintaining and bolstering its established technical position in its prime market areas; offensive strategy is designed to assume aggressive R&D activities to achieve marketing expansion and diversification.

The Defensive R&D Strategy The central thrust of a defensive strategy lies in the selection of projects and actions needed to maintain a company's position, which is dictated by its own established position vis-à-vis that of the competitors (a leading position or a follower's position, for example), and the anticipated trends of the technology. The overriding task, however, boils down to the two distinct but related decisions: (1) undertaking technical development to bolster the product life cycle of a company's prime products; and (2) calculated selection of technologies to achieve short- and long-term competitive advantages. On the one hand, a certain amount of R&D work is required to engage in product modification, improvements, and new production techniques to extend product life cycle and reduce cost of production. Much technical development is concentrated on new product development to replace old products that have reached saturation and decline (see chapter 10 on marketing strategy). On the other hand, technologies must be so selected that a calculated blend of research and development is achieved. Indeed, this is an important decision requiring high-level intuitive and judgmental thinking by an experienced R&D executive.

The Offensive R&D Strategy An offensive R&D strategy is designed to pursue advanced technology in a concentrated and aggressive manner in order to implement marketing expansion and diversification. A growing young company, by virtue of its strong technical staff and uniquely equipped capability, customarily espouses an offensive strategy. The fact that such a company is generally weak in marketing and production capacities confines its choice of strategies.[9]

In large corporations, an offensive strategy can be construed as an extension of a defensive strategy—the dictum that the best defense is a good offense. As growth is often a firm's long-term objective, an offensive strategy is not only a protective means but is a vital instrument when technology is an influential determinant in a firm's growth strategy. On the other hand, this high-risk and potentially high-payoff strategy demands considerable skill in technological innovation, the ability to identify emerging opportunities, and the competence to quickly translate them into commercial products either through the company's own discoveries or through acquisition. For this purpose, the R&D organization must remain alert and keep abreast of the technological community to detect and exploit such opportunities. We have learned that the Japanese business firms have frequently purchased needed technologies from other industrial nations, such as the United States and West Germany. In this manner, Japanese firms made extensive use of integrated circuit modules developed and manufactured in the United States for their large-scale entry into the electronic calculators market.

A combined defensive/offensive strategy usually applies to companies holding technological leadership. Such companies pursue both strategies equally aggressively. Thus, IBM in the computer industry, Texas Instruments in the semiconductor industry, GM in the auto industry, GE in the electrical industry, and Dow Chemical in the chemical industry, all maintain large R&D capabilities to pursue such a dual strategy. The allocation of resources to these two areas is a judgment dictated by corporate objectives and the nature of the technology with which the company is concerned.

THE R&D PENETRATION STRATEGY When a new technology is discovered, or when technology is considered a key to implementing corporate strategy in penetrating a new market, penetration R&D strategy is formulated to meet varying needs. Let us cite a few specific cases to illustrate the variations. Hewlett-Packard, a well-diversified $1 billion electronics company, relies heavily on high technology. The guiding principle of its penetration strategy is the development of innovative, advanced products that command a premium price.[10] It does not compete on the basis of low pricing. The company's R&D budget has been large ($125.4 million in 1977), and the management and process of R&D work is effective and rigid. Timing is key. During the 1973–1974 recession, the company increased R&D spending to time its new product introduction to coincide with the economic recovery in early 1975. Once development of a new product is funded for introduction, management pushes hard to get it rapidly to the market. Efficient coordination with marketing and production activities underscores the total strategy.

Texas Instruments (TI), a leader in the semiconductor industry, skillfully exploits its new technology through pricing on low-cost, quantity production to achieve competitive advantages. The process of accelerating technology to effect price cutting thereby forces weaker competitors out of the market. The company's attempt to enlarge its leading position in the digital watch market and to gain entry into the minicomputer and microcomputer markets were characterized by its low-price approach.[11] TI calculatedly delayed its entry into the digital watch market until it had accomplished substantial reduction in production cost. By using the same hardware and software for both computers to achieve low-cost production, TI priced their computers below market price. The central thrust of TI's penetration strategy lies basically in its R&D competence, greatly supplemented by advanced production technology and aggressive marketing activities (for example, the wide-range distribution).

There can be two other variations on penetration strategy: the interstitial strategy and maverick strategy. The interstitial strategy is an approach whereby a challenger selects the leader's technological weak spot as a wedge for penetration. Thus, Control Data Corp. succeeded in maintaining a dominant position in the scientific computer area of the computer market where IBM is weak. The maverick strategy is another version that can be used when the market leaders are reluctant to apply the new technology once discovered because the impact may do harm to its already established market. This reluctance on the part of the leaders offers an opportunity for the challenger to invade the market. Thus, Gillette's reluctance allowed Wilkinson Sword Ltd.'s entry into the razor blade market with the introduction of stainless steel blades. This initial advantage, however, can only be maintained if it is backed by subsequent aggressive actions in marketing and technology.

THE R&D RESPONSE STRATEGY Technological threats occur occasionally in all industries. More acute threats, however, must be taken seriously in certain industries. It is a recurring event confronting technological leaders as well as followers. IBM, the dominant computer manufacturer, is constantly threatened by new technologies, often pioneered by young, growing companies. The newly developed central processing unit designed by Amdahl Corp. and Intel Corp. for their powerful new computers is typical of these kinds of technological threats.[12] Similarly, Digital Equipment Corp.'s advanced minicomputer is luring users away from the massive, central mainframe computers to the more sophisticated and economic minicomputer network; this is a serious threat IBM cannot ignore.[13] A response strategy demands that a company's strategic actions effectively counteract the threat.

Depending upon the nature and urgency of the threat, and the type of industry, a firm may choose a basic policy somewhere between a passive and aggressive response: a "do-nothing" approach or a token investment in improving old technology is a passive response. A dual strategy of improving old technology and committing major investments to new technology is an aggressive response. A combination of varying actions is noted in a study of seven industries' responses to technological threat.[14] When a firm chooses a passive approach, it can assume any of the following actions: (1) do nothing; (2) monitor new development in the competing technology through vigorous study and forecasting activity; (3) remain flexible to respond at a later date; (4) hold back the new threat by fighting it through public relations and legal action; (5) avoid the threat through decreasing dependency on the most threatened submarkets; (6) expand work to improve existing technology; and (7) attempt to maintain sales through actions not related to technology, such as promotion or price cutting. However, if a company chooses to respond aggressively, it must make major commitments to the new technology, accelerate development, consider timing and means of entry through internal development, acquisition, or joint venture. Response strategy requires thorough assessment of the threat and its surrounding situation, establishment of well-defined objectives, and formulation of counterstrategies, considering factors such as resource, risks, and legal limitations, and the use of other alternatives not directly related to technology.

Summary

Technology, as a motivating force behind innovation, generates changes. Through technological change, business firms grow. Through social and economic changes, society forges ahead. From this perspective, technology is not only a business problem but a public issue about which spirited debate is far from over (see chapter 2). However, within the realm of business, technology and its advancements depend upon the effective management of R&D work; we cannot overemphasize this.

For many companies, R&D is a vital function, a potent instrument of corporate strategy; for some, however, it plays a much lesser role than do marketing and production. As a vital function, R&D must be dealt with squarely. We have established that R&D is a perplexing function. It requires special understanding and skill. Its cost and productivity, in light of large investment and the uncertainty of its return, demand vision and risk-taking capacity. The three strategic issues we have discussed in this chapter reflect the nature of the problem. As a potent instrument of corporate strategy, R&D seeks long-term advantages. The very nature of long lead time and large investment required of R&D work restricts its development for immediate, short-term effects. That is the function of marketing strategies. Our identification of the three component strategies—the basic defensive-offensive strategy, the penetration strategy, and the response strategy to technological threats—is an attempt to establish a framework for R&D strategy making and organized analysis.

PRODUCTION STRATEGY

Frequently, production strategy receives only insignificant discussion in corporate strategy making because more conspicuous and close attention has been given to the other more direct and pressing functional strategies, such as marketing, finance, and R&D.[15] Yet, production contributes greatly to a firm's profitability and significantly affects its basic competitive position. We will discuss three topics: (1) the modern meaning of production, emphasizing its positive role in corporate strategy making; (2) strategic issues of a production operation concerning planning, productivity, human factors, and government impact; and (3) production component strategies centering on the basic production strategy, product engineering strategy, and plant location strategy.

The Modern Production Function

Production is considered an economic activity revolving around the input-output equation, the process of converting input (raw material, supplies, people, and machine) into production output. Its purpose is the maximization of the created value. Production thus demands total efficiency of management and the full application of economics—the use of microeconomics, managerial economics, and quantitative models. Although methods of production have evolved slowly, production management has occasionally experienced dramatic changes. Often, they reflect changes in the contemporary business environment or in the workers' attitudes. Modern production calls for intelligent and timely response to these changes. They may include high cost of capital, technology, sporadic material shortage, rising labor cost, government regulations, and, above all, human demand for job satisfaction.

Today, a production manager must view himself/herself and his/her organization as a key element in shaping the ultimate success of the firm. He/she plays a significant role in corporate strategy making by participating in decision making on growth, stability, and survival strategies and develops production strategy to assume organized actions and achieve corporate objectives. He/she keeps management informed of union activities, material shortage, level of productivity, governmental and societal regulations on health, safety, pollution, and the ramifications of short-term and long-term energy problems. As a chief production officer of the corporation, he/she establishes policies, recommends research and development to achieve technological innovation, and oversees corporate-wide production to improve standards and practices.

Within the corporate structure, he/she and his/her organization maintain full coordination with marketing and engineering to formulate plans to improve products and services. At the same time, he/she keeps in constant communication with finance and personnel to achieve the optimal use of assets (purchases and disposition), cost control, recruitment of production personnel, management of labor disputes and negotiations, and methods of human resource management.

Within the production organization, the production manager constantly reviews the proper balance of capital investment (plant, equipment, and inventory); personnel commitment (direct labor and support labor); the efficient operation of the production system (its flexibility and versatility in response to schedule fluctuation, product mix, and variations in raw material and quality control); the planning and control of inventory, material handling, and facilities planning; and the institution of innovative methods for managing people.[16]

Strategy Issues

Among many operational problems in production management, we choose to identify four strategic issues: (1) planning and control whose integration with corporate strategic planning is deemed essential; (2) productivity improvement, a central determinant of economic decisions and a perennial goal of production operations; (3) human factors related to management of people to increase job satisfaction and performance; and (4) government impact on industry practices regarding health, safety, pollution, and human resource development.

PRODUCTION PLANNING AND CONTROL Internal production planning and control, involving production control and scheduling, facilities planning, material handling, and inventory control, has always been a integral part of production management. Long-range production strategic planning, however, is not widely practiced. The production department's participation in corporate strategic planning has generally been passive; operational planning is not coordinated with its own strategic planning.[17] To be sure, the production department submits annual capital budgets, personnel plans, and facilities plans and participates in new product development and divestiture planning. But the department's participation is carried out in such a routine fashion that it lacks initiative, central direction, and strategic thinking. In emphasizing production strategic planning, it is highly desirable that the production department vigorously pursue the following activities:

1. Submit for management consideration production trends and requirements, including production technology, assets replacement and modernization, competitive assessment, union negotiations, and government policies and regulations.
2. Analyze the company's present operations, its effectiveness in employing assets to meet changes in production rate, product mix, production technology and process, level of productivity, and, above all, to determine the precise status of the company's production capacity.
3. Study overall corporate objectives and strategy and define specific objectives for the production function.
4. Coordinate with marketing, R&D, and finance in new product development, diversification studies, and divestiture planning to determine if they are feasible from the viewpoint of production.

PRODUCTIVITY IMPROVEMENT Productivity can be defined as output per person, per hour, per dollar of investment, or as a measurement of production efficiency according to the input-output equation. An efficient production operation constantly strives for productivity improvement—the increase in production output is greater than the increase in investment input. The detailed analysis of individual aggregates on both sides of the equation and the study of past trends of this relation are the initial steps in defining productivity improvement objectives and programs. Productivity improvement can be pursued along two lines: the management approach, and the program approach. The management approach is aimed at improving the total effectiveness of the production department. Such fundamental methods as improving organizational structure to consolidate all related productivity functions, or making economic use of computer services and automation, can produce positive results.[18] The program approach is directed at instituting productivity improvement programs, which can include plant productivity improvement, job enrichment, cost reduction, and inventory reduction programs, among others.[19]

HUMAN FACTORS IN PRODUCTION Human resource is often the most important element in a production system. Not only do men and women have an effect in the conversion process of transforming investment input to production output, but their attitudes and performances determine productivity. To stimulate human performance and maximize satisfaction and productivity, the company can draw from many significant contributions made by behavioral scientists and from personnel management competent in the areas of recruitment and training, wage and salary administration, and industrial relations. However, we will concentrate on job satisfaction—an issue that we believe is of contemporary importance and relevancy.

Job Satisfaction Job satisfaction is the state of workers' attitude toward their work. A high level of satisfaction could result in high performance; a low level of job satisfaction can result in high turnover rate, absenteeism, and vandalism, which cause further harm to workers' morale and are very expensive for the company. In a factory, job satisfaction can be approached from two perspectives: physical, and behavioral.

Physical environment includes the design and ambience of the factory and the person-machine relationship. For example, if employees perform physical tasks requiring a great deal of energy, and the interior temperature increases beyond 80 degrees Fahrenheit, they tend to become less productive. Noise is another design consideration because when the noise level gets too high, it becomes annoying, physically painful, and can cause permanent disability in the long run. Illumination and interior decor also affect concentration and fatigue, which leads to accidents and errors. Health and safety are the other two considerations. Their minimum standards are specified and regulated by government inspectors. Conformity to these standards reduces industrial accidents and indirectly heightens productivity. The person-machine relationship, often regarded as human engineering, is an area of modern concern. In the broad sense, a machine should always be used whenever excess strength is required and when simple, routine, and repetitive jobs would cause extreme boredom. In a technical sense, human engineering is rather a new science that methodically analyzes the person-machine relationship. The design of machines should lead to increasing productivity and safety of machine operations. Machines are now designed not only to perform their tasks but also to fit the needs of the operators. Such improvements as running lubrication tubing from bearings to a central position where all of the fittings are located for quick and easy lubrication, or designing control gauges, dials, and lights to be located within easy reach of operators, are good examples. Production engineering and value engineering are related engineering disciplines that significantly contribute to cost reduction as well as to worker productivity.

Job Enlargement The behavioral approach centers on the complex subject of job design. Job design can be approached in two ways:[20] the traditional scientific management, and the modern practice of job enlargement or job enrichment. The scientific management approach stresses analysis of the work by breaking it into simple subtasks, selecting and training the right person for the job, preparing detailed procedures and instructions for the work, and instituting monetary bonuses to reward more efficient workers.

The job enlargement approach, widely practiced in the mid-1960s, is the response to generally observed assembly line boredom resulting from workers having to perform identical operations over and over again during a single day. Job enlargement can be viewed simply as increasing the variety of tasks. This can be done vertically or horizontally. Vertical enlargement assigns a person some tasks from a higher level, in addition to regular tasks, and horizontal enlargement assigns additional tasks at the same level. The purpose is to increase a worker's job satisfaction by reinforcing his/her sense of growth, achievement, and responsibility. To be sure, job satisfaction is extremely difficult to achieve because it is dependent on the individual's personal needs, goals, and work attitudes. The combined physical design of the factory environment and the behavioral development of job satisfaction and management, however, offers a promising approach towards the increase of productivity in factory operations.

GOVERNMENT IMPACT Production actions are regulated by the government in three areas: pollution control; safety and health; and personnel practices. Pollution control is perhaps the most pressing, affecting each industry differently. The Environmental Pollution Agency (EPA), created in December 1970, and its comparable departments and boards at state and local levels, rigidly enforce air and water pollution standards, and violations are severely penalized.[21] Production managers must take concrete steps to correct deficiencies in air and water purity, comply with company policies and procedures, and recommend new equipment and processes for pollutant treatment and disposal.

The Occupational Safety and Health Administration (OSHA), created in April 1971, and other regulatory agencies, such as Food and Drug Administration, Federal Aviation Agency, and analogous state and local boards, specify and enforce a myriad of standards. Legislation of this nature greatly affects facilities layout, work environment design, production process, machine and material handling, quality control, and inspection. In fiscal 1975, industry violations cited by OSHA, for example, included violations of national electrical codes, safety of abrasive wheel machinery, construction and placement of compressed gas containers, marking of exits, safety of drives in mechanical power-transmission gears, and other offenses relating to fire hazards, safety, and health.[22]

Under the Equal Employment Opportunity Commission (EEOC) since 1972, and the Office of Federal Contract Compliance (OFCC) of the Department of Labor since 1971, industry personnel policies and procedures are given close scrutiny. Legislation such as the Civil Rights Act, Title VII of 1964, and the Equal Rights Act for Women (ERA) of 1972 make it illegal to discriminate against any individuals in hiring, discharging, or compensating because of the individual's race, color, religion, sex, or national origin.[23] Production managers and supervisors not only must acquire a thorough knowledge of company-prescribed policies and procedures, union restrictions, and government regulations but must also work closely with the personnel department on all activities dealing with employees. Violations can bring suits and jeopardize the firm doing business with government departments.

Production Component Strategies

The three production component strategies we have selected for discussion are: (1) the basic production strategy outlining the nature of the system, and its optimal balance between investment input and production output; (2) product-engineering strategy in developing and manufacturing competitive and economically viable products and services; and (3) plant location strategy, an investment decision affecting future courses of the firm.

THE BASIC PRODUCTION STRATEGY The planning of the basic production strategy naturally begins with the thorough appreciation of the corporate business mix. Specific questions, such as the nature of the production system (job shop versus continuous flow, labor intensive versus capital intensive) and the mode of operation (the flexibility to meet schedule fluctuation, degree of automation, and quality control) must be studied by production management. The substance of the strategy, however, is the optimal balance between plant investment and production output. The former is decided by the degree of modernization (technology), the production process, and the inventory level; the latter is based on trade-offs between direct labor and support labor, and between long-run production versus short-run variations to meet customer requirements.

Investment Input Decisions Investment input decisions mandate the planning of production process, machinery requirements, and the quality of operation. Production process refers to the design of a series of operations to transform inputs to desired outputs. It gives detailed consideration to product design, process design, selection of machinery, and the basic mode of operation (for example, process-oriented processing by manufacturing activity versus product-oriented assembly line processing).[24] Production output decisions determine production capacity and its management to meet fluctuating rates and product mix. A factory can only operate at the lowest unit cost if its capacity is employed full time to gain continuous flow. Thus, the desired level of capacity utilization depends on good planning and control. Accurate forecasting of production needs—the rate of production, delivery schedules, personnel needs, material needs, and inventory levels—serves as the basis for planning production. Planning for desired operating levels and the balanced use of facilities among working units and departments to secure continuous, smooth production is the next decision variable.

Production decisions depend on quantitative analyses. Capsule 19 presents two commonly used planning techniques, decision tree and Program Evaluation and Review Technique (PERT), for review and reminder.

Production Planning Strategies Richard Tellier introduced three basic strategies to organize production resources for matching long-range, overall demand.[25] These strategies are: demand matching, operations smoothing, and subcontracting. Often, demand appears somewhat seasonal—it is at minimum in one month and peaks in another. A demand-matching strategy will plan an operation to exactly meet the demand. In this case, a minimum inventory is maintained, but the operational cost is high. An operations-smoothing strategy will produce continuously at the average value of demand, thereby keeping a high inventory when demand slackens and drawing from these inventories when demand peaks. There is still a third alternative, the subcontracting strategy, where production is kept at a minimum level, leaving the high production to subcontractors. The choice depends on the changes in resource costs in each of these strategic approaches. There may include costs of equipment, hiring/termination, overtime, inventory, and subcontracting.

Illustration Capsule 19

NOTES ON PLANNING TECHNIQUES

Solutions to production problems require the use of quantitative methods. Two commonly used planning techniques are cited here.

Decision Tree

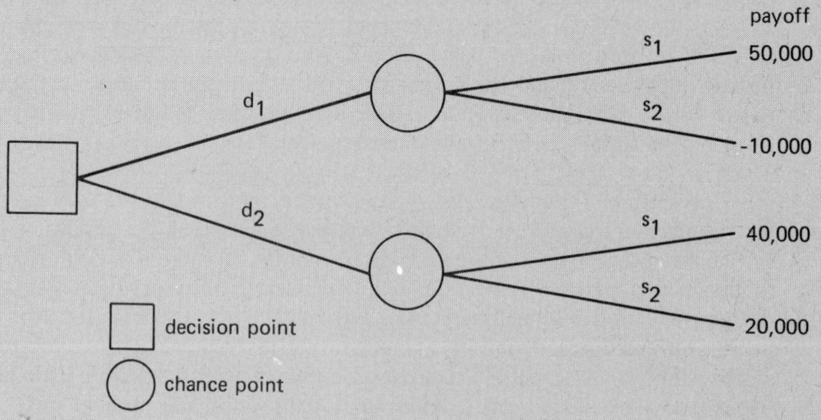

A decision tree is a graphical representation of the decision-making process. It shows directions that actions might take from various decision points. A decision tree is most useful for complex multistage decision problems that are sequenced over time. To clarify the interpretation of the tree, decision points are represented by squares, and chance points, points over which the decision maker has no control, are represented by circles. From each alternative, the decision tree constructs the chronological path, leading through chance points and other decision points, to each assumed possible terminal outcome. Payoffs associated with each path and probabilities of occurrence associated with chance events are shown on the tree.

As cited in the example, the firm must make a decision (d_1 or d_2), and as the firm starts operation, the state of nature (s_1 or s_2) will occur. The biggest payoff of 50,000 occurs when management makes the decision to purchase the system represented by d_1, and the market acceptance turns out to be s_1. The next point of $-10{,}000$ occurs when management chooses d_1 and s_2 occurs.

PERT

PERT (Program Evaluation and Review Technique) is used to assist management in planning, scheduling, and controlling a variety of large-scale projects, such as research and development, construction of plants, and so forth. It uses time-event network analysis. Each circle represents an event-plan whose completion can be measured at a given time. Each activity is represented by an arrow-time-consuming element of a program that occurs between events.

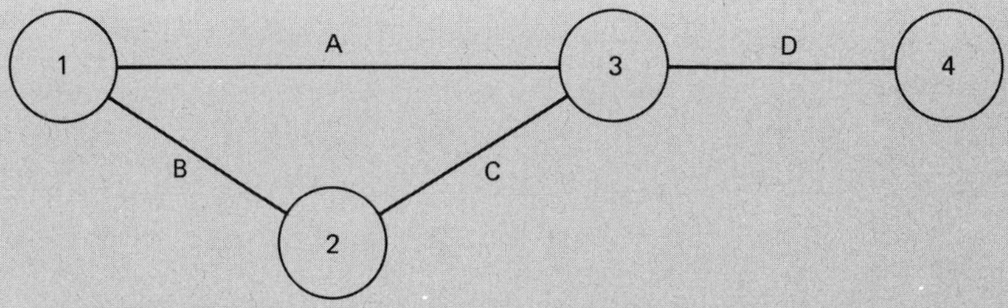

The activity time is the time required to accomplish an event. Three time estimates are made: optimistic time; most probable time; and pessimistic time. These estimates enable management to make their best estimate of the likely activity time and range within which it may fall. The critical path is the sequence of events that takes the longest time. Identifying the critical path at all times enables close supervision of this sequence of events to assure total program will be completed on time.

The example above can illustrate the process of purchasing a piece of equipment. The activities are represented by (A, B, C, D). The circles represent events that follow activities. For example, circle 3 follows the completion of A and C. Activities cannot be completed without the completion of the prior activity.

Refer to Richard Tellier, *Operations Management: Fundamental Concepts and Methods* (New York: Harper and Row, 1978), pp. 59–61, 169–70.

PRODUCT-ENGINEERING STRATEGY Product engineering provides designs, specifications, and manufacturing drawings for a company's current and newly developed products.[26] Administratively, a product-engineering department can be a part of the production department or a separate department with which production maintains a close working relationship. A product-engineering strategy is designed to ensure the production department's total participation in shaping product design decisions. A well-engineered product is one meeting the changing needs of the customer, complying with various laws pertaining to safety and consumer protection, and basically satisfying manufacturing requirements of low-cost and efficient operation. Production requirements on engineering design include choice of materials, ease of production, standardization and interchangeability, and human engineering. Overengineering in design and reliability, and poor engineering practices without full consideration given to cost and ability to produce are frequent deficiencies in engineering design. Production must exert strong influence in shaping basic product designs and in transforming them from engineering designs into production specifications.

In initiating product modification, the production department consults with marketing and engineering to study product deficiencies and investigate effects of changes on tooling, production process, safety, and warranty provisions. In new product development, production actively participates in the total process especially in product design, tooling design, and pilot run installation. Further, the production department analyzes alternative manufacturing facilities and studies plant modifications. Of special importance is the pilot run installation, which can be very expensive and yet crucial to estimating the cost of new production facilities. In addition, the production department on a regular basis solicits full cooperation of marketing and field services organizations to monitor product deficiency reports and competitive production techniques. These activities, then, help formulate product-engineering strategy and specify the production objectives and policies.

PLANT LOCATION STRATEGY Plant location is essentially an investment decision, one that has long-term significance and implied economic effects. A good decision pays off; a bad decision can cause severe financial difficulties. Once a plant is acquired, it is a permanent site that cannot readily be sold. Plant location decisions can arise when operational environment has been significantly altered due to anticipated long-term changes in level of demand, availability of raw materials, or in distribution and operating costs. Plant relocation becomes necessary when business expansion and advanced technology require additional facilities to serve new market areas, to produce new products, or simply to replace the old, obsolete plants to increase a company's production capacity.[27]

Plant location decisions require intensive study of economic and sociopolitical facts. Long-range forecasting concerning trends in market demand, geographical distribution, material and labor supply, and social climate of the community in which the plant will be located are the basic strategic considerations. The accuracy of forecasting is essential in regard to rising demand and anticipated sales increases. Companies that have miscalculated in such situations find themselves incapable of occupying the new facilities once constructed, and unable to expand the new facility at a later date due to land and environmental restrictions.

Conventional capital budgeting techniques and simulation models are available for evaluating economic feasibility of plant investment and decision alternatives. A sequential analysis has also been developed to include selection decisions on a specific geographical area, a site, and a community. Factors such as access to market, distribution and logistic costs, labor costs, tax advantages, and the projected economic and social stability of the community are important considerations. Decision guidelines are always desirable in formulating strategies. In this regard, company management in conjunction with production management should consider several fundamental questions.[28] First, how accurate are the planning assumptions, how accurate are the demand forecasts, and how reliable is production technology when the use of new equipment and automation is involved? Second, what is the inflation factor used to determine the timing of investment and costs of operation and maintenance of a new plant? Third, what is the company's ability to finance a new plant, or what use can it make of alternate means such as the lease or build/lease of a plant? In essence, plant location is essentially a corporate decision in which production management is fully involved; however, its implementation, once the decision is made, is the sole responsibility of the production department.

SUMMARY

We have completed the discussion of the four functional strategies: marketing, financial, R&D, and production. It is desirable once again to summarize several points for special emphasis: (1) functional strategies are the second tier of our strategy model, which links corporate strategy on the one hand, and action plans and tactical actions on the other hand; (2) the art of strategy making calls for creative and optimal use of instruments to achieve specific objectives, although we have repeatedly warned that means do not justify the ends; (3) functional strategies involve technical aspects of a function, which means that discussions of them cannot be totally divorced from technical content. We choose the middle-of-the-road approach and do not involve ourselves too deeply with quantitative methods and the technical content of each of these four functions. We discuss issues from the viewpoint of general management and present materials from the perspective of strategy; and (4) an additional reminder—developing functional strategies is of substantive nature and is systematic in process. It follows the same methodology as does developing corporate strategy. Yet, functional strategies are action oriented, eliciting constant reappraisal and recycling.

The relative importance of R&D strategy and production strategy to a company depends on the characteristics of the company and the industry it serves. We have demonstrated the new challenges of these two functions, the strategic issues each confronts, and the component strategies involving each function. Our attempt to describe these component strategies is tentative because of the lack of attention given to functional strategies in general. They are presented in such a way that provides an organized framework for analyzing strategic decisions in those functional areas.

NOTES

1. In our context, R&D is largely confined to technology for product and methods of production; however, it also applies to technology for services.
2. *Business Week,* 28 June 1976, pp. 26–84.
3. The rethinking centers on reducing R&D investment and improving R&D management. Brian C. Twiss, *Managing Technological Innovation* (London: Longman, 1974), pp. xv–xix.
4. Simon Ramo, "The Director of Research and Development," in *The Chief Executive's Handbook,* ed. John D. Glover and Gerald A. Simon (Homewood, Ill.: Dow Jones-Irwin, 1976), pp. 447–60.
5. Lowell W. Steele, in his book, *Innovation in Big Business* (New York: American Elsevier Publishing, 1975), considers the "we and they" attitude among R&D organizations undesirable, and recommends means to correct the problem. See Introduction and chaps. 12 and 13.
6. Charles H. Tavel categorizes R&D work into five types: exploratory research, new product or process research, improvement research, cost reduction research, and raw material adaptation research. *The Third Industrial State: Strategy for Business Survival* (Homewood, Ill.: Dow Jones-Irwin, 1975), pp. 265–66. Also, Twiss, *Managing Technological Innovation,* pp. 30–33.
7. Twiss, *Managing Technological Innovation,* chap. 2; and Steele, *Innovation in Big Business,* pp. 80–85.
8. Methods such as PABLA (Problem Analysis by Logical Approach), critical path planning and branched networks, and cost benefit analysis are discussed in P. A. White, *Effective Management of Research and Development* (New York: Wiley, 1975), pp. 118–50.
9. In the electronics industry, where technology plays an important role, new companies had adopted an offensive R&D strategy. But due to large investment, technological difficulties and poor management, many had failed to achieve their business goals.

10. *Business Week,* 7 June 1975, pp. 50–58. For the company's entry into the computer market, see same issue, pp. 91–92.
11. *Business Week,* 27 October 1975, pp. 102–5; for discussion on digital watch market, see same issue, pp. 78–92.
12. *Business Week,* 25 October 1976, pp. 74–76.
13. *Business Week,* 26 April 1976, pp. 58–63.
14. Arnold C. Cooper and Dan Schendel, ''Strategic Responses to Technological Threats,'' *Business Horizons,* February 1976, pp. 61–69.
15. For standard books on production management, see Richard I. Levin, Curtis P. McLaughlin, and others, *Production/Operation Management: Contemporary/Policy for Managing Operating Systems* (New York: McGraw-Hill, 1972), and Thomas E. Vollmann, *Operation Management: A Systems Model-Building Approach* (Reading, Mass.: Addison-Wesley, 1973).
16. Richard F. Cole, ''The Director of Manufacturing: A Careful Look at Leadership,'' in *Chief Executive's Handbook,* ed. Glover and Simon, pp. 511–19.
17. Wickham Skinner, ''Manufacturing: Missing Link in Corporate Strategy,'' *Harvard Business Review,* May-June 1969, p. 136; also Robert J. Mockler, *Business Planning and Policy Formulation* (New York: Appleton-Century-Crofts, 1972), pp. 152–71.
18. For discussion, see Gerald B. Mitchell, ''Manufacturing Productivity'' in *Chief Executive's Handbook,* ed. Glover and Simon, pp. 520–35.
19. Levin et al., *Production/Operation Management,* pp. 209–29.
20. For discussions, see Henry L. Tosi and Stephen J. Carrol, *Management: Contingencies, Structure, and Process* (Chicago, Illinois: St. Clair Press, 1976), pp. 355–57; and Lyman W. Porter, Edward E. Lawler III, and J. Richard Hackman, *Behavior in Organizations* (New York: McGraw-Hill, 1975), pp. 274–311.
21. For example, Kaiser Steel's Fontana plant in California was fined for alleged violation in September 1976 for excess visible emissions, which could result in more than $15 million in fines. *Los Angeles Times,* 19 November 1976, pt. 2, p. 1.
22. *Business Week,* 14 June 1976, pp. 64–72.
23. For details, see Paul Pigors and Charles A. Myers, *Personnel Administration: A Point of View and a Method* (New York: McGraw-Hill, 1977), pp. 59–78.
24. Levin et al. *Production/Operation Management,* chaps. 7–9, 12.
25. Richard Tellier, *Operations Management: Fundamental Concepts and Methods* (New York: Harper and Row, 1978), pp. 150–77.
26. For discussion, see James W. Wilcock, ''Product Engineering'' in *Chief Executive's Handbook,* ed. Glover and Simon, pp. 494–508.
27. Levin et al., *Production/Operation Management,* pp. 273–89.
28. Goldon R. Corey, ''Planning for Plant; How Big, When, and How to Finance'' in *Chief Executive's Handbook,* ed. Glover and Simon, pp. 554–67.

CASES FOR PART III

ANAHEIM MEMORIAL HOSPITAL

Judy Thams, director of planning and research, pointed to the stack of blueprints near the door. "See that?" she said. "It represents Phase IV of our construction program." I was dutifully impressed; the stack must have been five inches thick.

"I think our building program represents our biggest administrative problem," Bill Platt, the planning analyst, added. "Our Phase IV plan will basically update the older facilities. We're going to tear down the original brick building and replace it with a new two-story building."

"How old is the original building?"

"It was built in 1956, so it's around twenty-three years old."

"Twenty-three years old and you're going to tear it down?"

"Yes, we're going to make a parking-lot out of it."

Anaheim Memorial Hospital (AMH) is located in Anaheim, Orange County, California. The hospital grew in twenty years from 72 to 240 beds. The current construction (1979), referred to as Phase IV, will update seventy-six original beds by constructing new facilities and tearing down the old building; the old building does not meet AMH's present requirements.

Current growth for AMH follows the Master Plan for Development drawn up in 1965. This plan was approved by the Orange County Area Hospital Planning Committee, a voluntary county committee. The plan called for a multiphase building program to increase the hospital's bed capacity from 76 to 680 beds. Phase IV plans, affecting the original building, stem from this Master Plan.

The original building, located on the southeast corner of the property, is still in use. Several supportive departments are located there. Patient rooms contain two to four beds and bath facilities are shared. The beds in the original two wings show low utilization; doctors prefer the newer facilities located in Cromer Tower and schedule their patients there. Hospital administrators feel bed occupancy will increase upon completion of Phase IV.

Prepared by Jerome L. Youderian and Jack Van Haaster under the supervision of Dr. Y. N. Chang of California State University, Fullerton.

Continued growth according to the Master Plan for Development presents a problem. The legal environment changed during the 1970s. Strict government regulations alter the ability of hospitals to continue construction as they planned. Phase IV growth was exempted from Certificate of Need regulation because it consisted of remodeling efforts.

HISTORY OF AMH

AMH was scheduled to open in 1956 as a proprietary institution. The private enterprise failed, and the building remained empty until February 24, 1958. At that time, a group of citizens reopened the hospital as a nonprofit institution. During 1964, the hospital's capacity was increased to 76 beds with the addition of a 5-bed Intensive Care Unit (ICU).

In 1965, studies were undertaken by the hospital and the Economics Research Associates to determine a proper development program that would meet the increased demand for services. AMH experienced high utilization because of a rapidly expanding population base. In 1967, the year before the first expansion, the occupancy rate was 103.59 percent. Patients were sometimes held in the halls till space was available in licensed rooms. High utilization led to studies formulating the Master Plan for Development.

The Master Plan for Development was a multiphase plan designed to increase the hospital's bed capacity from 76 to 680. Along with the increase in beds, plans were laid for opening a 24 hour-a-day, 7 days-a-week emergency service; business in the area requested this feature. The Orange County Area Hospital Planning Committee approved the Master Plan and Phase I of this plan for construction in 1965.

In February 1968, the hospital began constructing Clyde Cromer Tower, Phase I (the first three floors), which was completed on schedule and opened for service in August 1969. The new tower provided all new ancillary services for the hospital, plus eighty-eight additional single (private) care beds. Following this, Phase II was the completion of the two shelled floors of Cromer Tower. The fourth floor became a 44-bed general medical/surgical floor. The fifth floor became a 32-bed intensive care unit called the Acute Care Center.

The Acute Care Center was an unique and progressive concept, developing a four-wing unit to include a coronary care unit, two medical/surgical wings, and a progressive care unit. This particular phase of the hospital's development specialized the hospital's services, especially in the area of cardiology. An open-heart-surgery program derived great success because of the Acute Care Center. Clyde Cromer Tower increased the hospital's capacity to 240 beds.

Subsequent to the completion of Phase II construction, the hospital began development and construction of an office and administrative building. The building is designed to house a 24-hour-a-day, 7-days-a-week pharmacy, outpatient laboratory facility, education complex, hospital administration, and sixty private-practice physician offices. These offices continue to remain full since they opened.

In 1975, the hospital began construction of Phase III, which represented an addition to the emergency room, surgery, and radiology. Upon its completion in 1976, Phase III added two more surgical suites, a three-bed trauma room to the emergency room, exam rooms to radiology including a CAT scanner, two heart catheterization labs, a special procedure room, and a bulk storage room.

A nurse paramedic team was established in 1976 to provide needed paramedic services until Anaheim could train its fire personnel. AMH was designated as a paramedic base station and has become an accepted trauma center for its hospital service area.

The development of critical care medicine at AMH made possible the establishment of an open-heart-surgery program that performs the largest volume of surgeries and heart catheterizations in north Orange County, with one of the lowest mortality rates in the nation.

A community health-need assessment identified deaths attributable to cancer in Orange County as increasing by 51 percent between 1971 and 1975. The Oncology-Hematology Program was established and it accounts for 31 percent of the total patients admitted by internal medicine. The program received a three-year approval from the Commission on Cancer of the American College of Surgeons. This is the first designation in north Orange County.

The hospital is currently implementing Phase IV of its facility development plan. The project involves the replacement of the original 1956 hospital building in order to remodel seventy-six nonconforming beds and modernize the intensive care unit. AMH received a Certificate of Exemption for this project and has consistently complied with the intent and letter of all planning laws in effect since the trustees of the hospital authorized planning of the project.

AMH dropped its Obstetrics Program in 1977. The program accounted for nearly 4 percent of patient day use up to that time. It was terminated because Martin Luther Hospital, located a mile away, opened a new obstetrics ward. AMH was unable to update their facilities because of government regulation, so the obstetrics doctors on staff left for the new facilities.

ENVIRONMENTAL FACTORS

Environmental factors confronting the hospital industry include governmental regulations, the Health Systems Agency, competition, and industrial changes. Though other factors exist, these elements constitute the major factors. A short summary of each of these areas follows.

Government Regulations

Legislation regulating the hospital industry proliferated in the 1970s. Rationale for increased regulation springs from spiralling health-care costs. Hospital costs rose 89 percent in California between 1971 and 1976. Federal and state legislatures passed bills in an attempt to control costs. The Orange County Health Planning Council (OCHPC) represents the end product of government regulations for Orange County. The relationship between AMH and OCHPC is seen in Exhibit 1. Descriptions of several important bills affecting AMH follow.

In 1971, the California Health Facilities Commission (CHFC) was created by the California Health Facilities Act. The CHFC, an independent state agency, reports directly to the governor and legislature on matters affecting health facilities' cost. It maintains broad authority to set standards for hospital accounting and reporting. It requires a Hospital Disclosure Report at the end of each fiscal year.

In 1973, California passed the Duffy Act. This required state approval for expansion and new construction. A grandfather clause incorporated in the bill allowed current construction to proceed without approval. Fourteen new hospitals were

EXHIBIT 1 THE RELATIONSHIP BETWEEN AMH AND GOVERNMENT AGENCIES

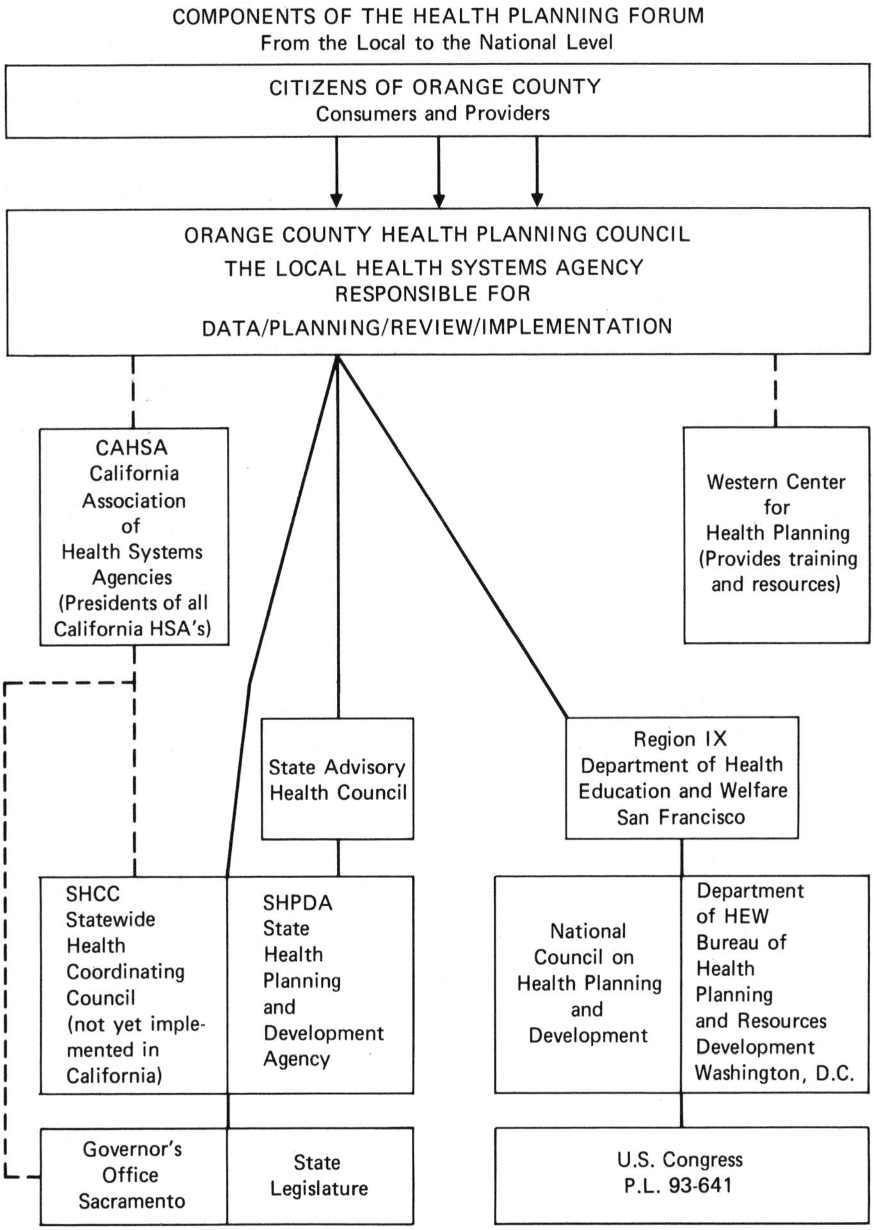
COMPONENTS OF THE HEALTH PLANNING FORUM
From the Local to the National Level
CITIZENS OF ORANGE COUNTY
Consumers and Providers
ORANGE COUNTY HEALTH PLANNING COUNCIL
THE LOCAL HEALTH SYSTEMS AGENCY
RESPONSIBLE FOR
DATA/PLANNING/REVIEW/IMPLEMENTATION
CAHSA
California Association of Health Systems Agencies
(Presidents of all California HSA's)
Western Center for Health Planning
(Provides training and resources)
State Advisory Health Council
Region IX
Department of Health Education and Welfare
San Francisco
SHCC
Statewide Health Coordinating Council
(not yet implemented in California)
SHPDA
State Health Planning and Development Agency
National Council on Health Planning and Development
Department of HEW
Bureau of Health Planning and Resources Development
Washington, D.C.
Governor's Office Sacramento
State Legislature
U.S. Congress
P.L. 93-641

Source: OCHPC

started in Orange County before the bill became effective; these were primarily proprietary hospitals.

The National Health Planning and Resource Development Act, Public Law 93-641, became effective in 1974. This federal law works through HEW, as seen in Exhibit 2. Chapter 854 of the California Statutes of 1976 is similar to the federal bill. The statute is known as the Certificate of Need. Both the state and federal laws require a Health Systems Agency (HSA) to develop a Health Systems Plan.

The Health Systems Plan determines the need for the number, type, and location of health care resources in each HSA area. The plan in Orange County is developed by the OCHPC. To ensure compliance with the plan, hospitals must file a Certificate of Need request for any capital expenditure of $150,000 or more. The OCHPC must approve the request before the expenditure can be made.

The Certificate of Need request restricts administrative decisions on the part of hospital staff. The CAT scanner gives a prime example of this. Most doctors desire this piece of equipment because it aids diagnosis without the use of exploratory surgery. It currently costs between $350,000 and $1 million. HSA policy restricts the number of CAT scanners available in any given area, forcing hospitals to share facilities.

The Orange County Health Planning Council

OCHPC adopted several policies in 1976. These policies have not changed appreciably since that time and include

1. There will be no increase in the Acute Care Hospital bed inventory.
2. In reviewing Certificate of Need applications, the Council will give consideration to: consolidation of services and facilities between two or more hospitals, regionalization of specialized services, and conversion of beds from one type or level of service to another to increase utilization.
3. The Council will not entertain proposals for the replacement of existing facilities at the same site if the facility is located in an overbedded area.

These policies are in accordance with federal guidelines that call for 4.0 beds per 1,000, operating at 80 percent of occupancy; Orange County has 4.1 beds per 1,000, with a 60.5 percent occupancy rate.

Competition

The county is divided into seven planning areas. The vast majority of the population lives within 5 miles of at least one hospital. Half of the licensed beds are located in Anaheim-Garden Grove, Orange-Santa Ana areas. These areas contain one-third of the total county population. Hospitals range in size from 24 to 708 beds. The number of beds in Orange County increased 72 percent between 1970 and 1976. This increase may be attributed to a reaction to the Duffy Act. The occupancy rate fell by 5 percent during this period, while the average length of stay (ALOS) increased (Exhibit 2).

Orange County hospitals are operated under three types of ownership: proprietary (29), nonprofit (8), and government (1). Of the twenty-nine proprietary hospitals, ten are owned by national corporate chains, one is owned by a health maintenance organization and the rest are owned by private investors. (Health

EXHIBIT 2 PROFILE OF LICENSED GENERAL ACUTE CARE BEDS, PERCENT OCCUPANCY AND AVERAGE LENGTH OF STAY, ORANGE COUNTY, 1970–76.

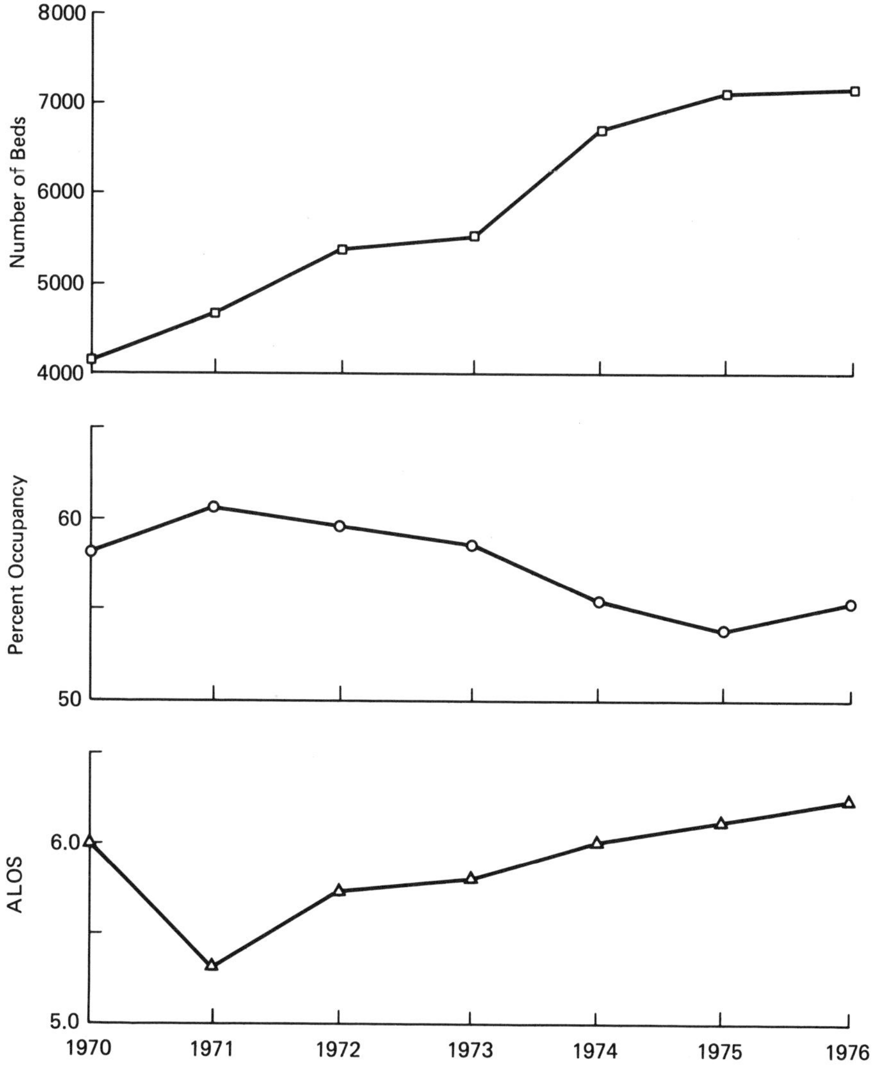

Source: OCHPC

maintenance organizations primarily service individuals who subscribe to their medical plans.) The ownership mix in Orange County differs from the rest of California (Exhibit 3). Orange County maintains a larger number of small proprietary hospitals.

Competition appears as a distinct problem in the health-care industry. The economic supply and demand curves that hold true for most business concerns

EXHIBIT 3 COMPARISON OF NUMBER OF ACUTE HOSPITALS AND ACUTE HOSPITAL BEDS BY TYPE OF OWNERSHIP, ORANGE COUNTY AND CALIFORNIA, 1975–76.

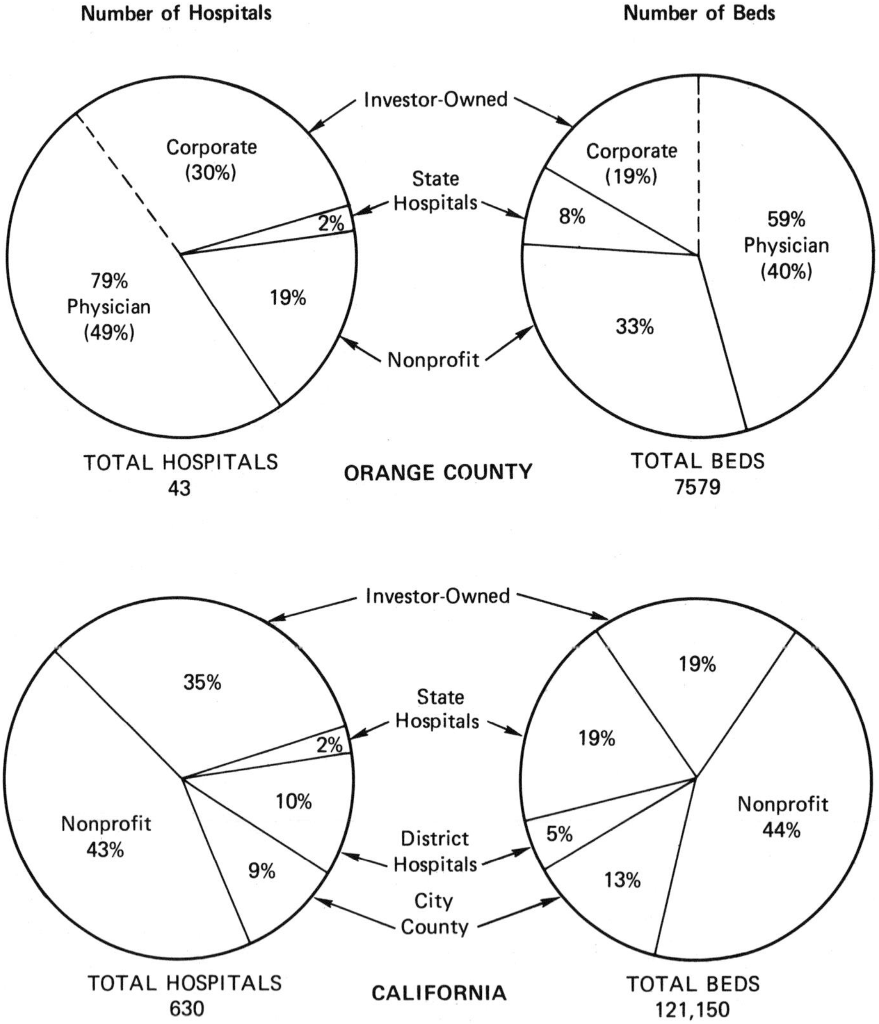

Source: OCHPC

assume that the consumer can refuse services if the price is too high. Within the medical world this is not so. An emergency patient is not likely to refuse the nearest qualified help.

Hospital competition centers around attracting the services of qualified physicians. Physicians are an important element in the health-care delivery system. While an individual usually decides when to consult a physician, thereafter most of his or her medical care is chosen by the physician. This includes whether the individual should be admitted to a hospital and which one. Therefore, hospitals keep their facilities up-to-date to attract physicians.

Industrial Trends

Of the services offered most frequently in general acute-care hospitals, medical/surgical services had the highest overall occupancy rate for Orange County (63.4 percent). The medical/surgical beds represent the main concentration in AMH's mix; 199 out of 240 beds are medical/surgical.

As noted previously, costs rose dramatically in Orange County from 1971 to 1976. The HSA and hospital administrators have looked into ways to reduce these costs. To analyze these costs, a breakdown of service areas was made. Costs were attributed to categories: *daily hospital service* (the various levels and intensities of nursing care services and supportive services—housekeeping, dietary, and administration); *ancillary services* (organized units of a hospital that assist physicians in diagnosis or treatment of patients—for example, special surgical services, laboratory, and x-ray); *education* (LVN and nursing programs); *fiscal and administrative expenses* (all costs of the administration and unassigned costs, such as depreciation, leases and interest); and *general service* (all categories assigned to support cost centers—for example, kitchen, security, and maintenance). Ancillary services represent the largest single contribution to expenditures in the acute-care facilities.

MANAGEMENT AND OPERATIONS OF AMH

The managerial and operational aspects of AMH break down into the areas of management, operations, marketing, and finance. The hospital industry contains distinctive administrative problems peculiar to the industry. The eleemosynary nature of AMH represents one of these peculiarities. This factor will be evident in the following discussion.

Management

The nonprofit nature of AMH affects the management structure. Exhibit 4 portrays the chart of organization for the AMH Association. Membership to the AMH Association is controlled by its charter. The members of AMH Association elect the board of directors for AMH. The members on the board serve on a voluntary basis.

Two members of the board are Herbert B. Leo and David Proctor, M. D. Leo has served for one year as the chairman of the board; he is also president of Mutual Citrus Products in Anaheim. Proctor serves as chief of the medical staff in conjunction with his duties on the board. He ties the administration closer to the medical staff.

A symbiotic relationship exists between medical staff and administrative staff. Physicians require a place for their patients; hospitals need physicians to fill their beds. Physicians may staff more than one hospital in Orange County; thus, they choose the hospital that they will admit their patients to.

Physicians interrelate with the management structure. They are organized under standing committees and set standards for quality. They function in various line positions such as ancillary and nursing services, making innumerable decisions that affect daily management.

James McAlvin holds the chief executive officer position. His entire career centers in the acute-care-facility industry. His early years were spent in several Ore-

EXHIBIT 4 THE AMH ASSOCIATION CHART OF ORGANIZATION

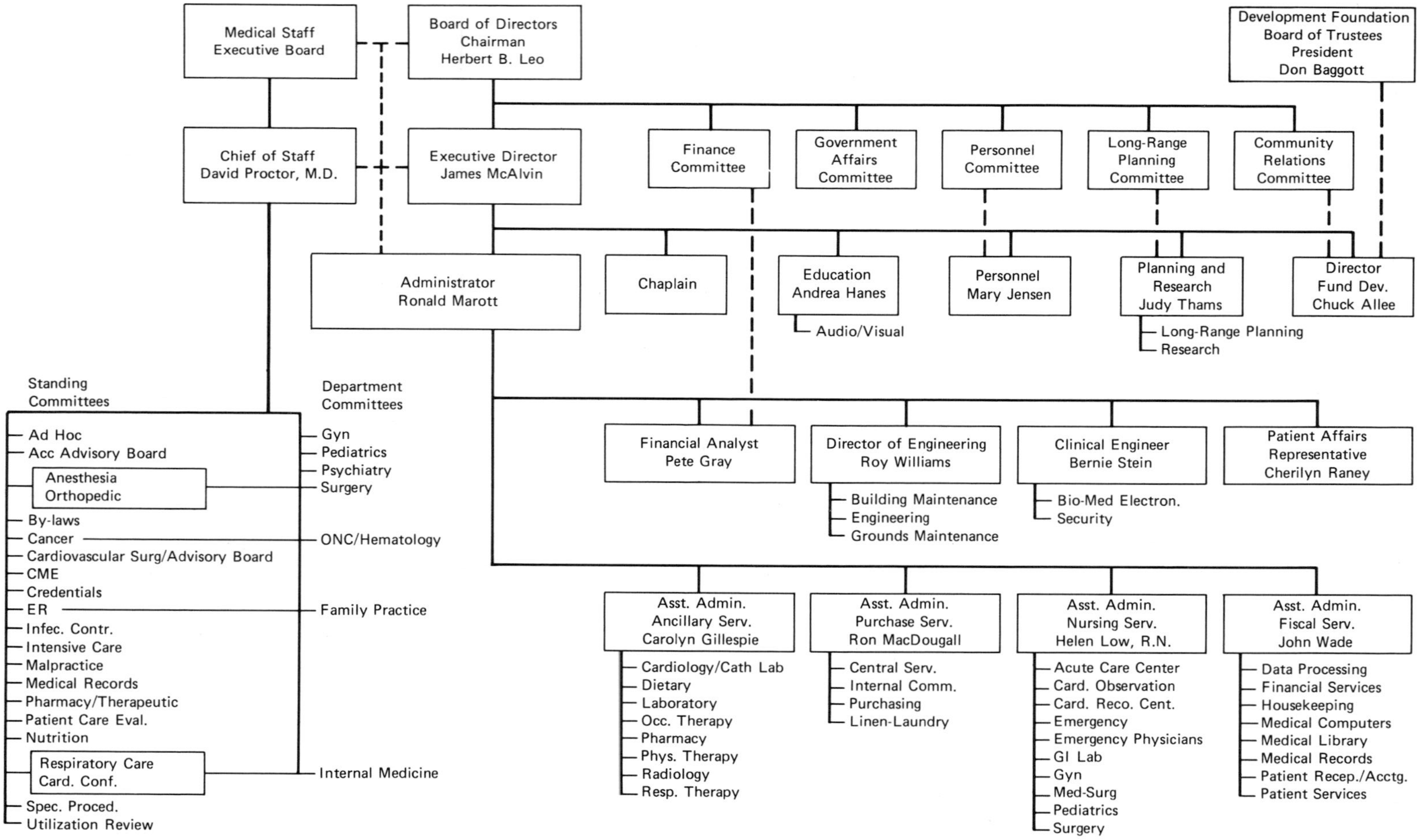

gon hospitals. Prior to moving to AMH he worked in several hospitals in Los Angeles. He has served as the CEO of the AMH since it opened, except for several years as the CEO in a hospital in San Jose.

The various staff positions appear on the organization chart. An interesting point to notice is the relationship between the director of fund development and the AMH Development Foundation. The AMH Development Foundation is a separate nonprofit organization created to solicit funds for AMH. The organization actively solicits funds and services with the aid of three suborganizations: the Double Eleven, a men's club; the Guild, a voluntary hospital service group; and the Guardian Angels, who solicit funds. The director of fund development coordinates the activities between AMH and the AMH Development Foundation.

Operations

The operations of AMH are broadly divided into ancillary, purchasing, nursing, and fiscal services as indicated on the organization chart. Operations are designed for inpatient and outpatient care. Inpatient care involves a patient occupying a hospital bed; outpatient service does not require admittance to a bed (emergency and certain ancillary services). Operations basically revolve around providing support services for the medical/surgical beds and the intensive care unit (ICU). Selected volume statistics involving these services are provided in Exhibit 5.

Patient days are broken down into ICU and general/medical-pediatric categories. The thirty-two-bed ICU facility shows high utilization; this ties in with the

EXHIBIT 5 SELECTED VOLUME STATISTICS FOR AMH

	1974	*1975*	*1976*	*1977*	*1978*
Patient Days					
ICU	5,165	6,202	8,655	8,387	7,179
Other	42,125	46,830	42,953	48,903	49,688
Total	47,290	53,032	51,608	57,290	56,867
% increase (decrease)	8%	12%	(3%)	11%	(1%)
Percent Occupancy	54%	61%	59%	65%	65%
Other Volume Statistics					
Surgeries	3,847	3,897	3,785	4,433	4,209
% increase (decrease)	1%	1%	(3%)	17%	(5%)
Open heart surgeries	162	260	417	351	295
% increase (decrease)	103%	60%	60%	(15%)	(15%)
Heart catheterizations	440	718	925	918	803
% increase (decrease)	273%	63%	29%	(1%)	(12%)
Radiological exams	28,639	34,814	36,955	47,850	47,893
% increase (decrease)		22%	6%	29%	
Emergency room visits	15,743	17,505	29,860	24,918	23,582
% increase (decrease)	5%	11%	71%	(16%)	(5%)
Per patient day revenue	$228	$270	$341	$413	$445
% increase (decrease)	14%	18%	27%	21%	7%

increase in open heart surgeries. An emphasis on the medical staff centers in internal medicine; 59 of the 161 active physicians on staff specialize in internal medicine. Nineteen of the fifty-nine physicians specializing in internal medicine are cardiologists. Twenty percent of the active physicians on staff fill 50 percent of the hospital beds.

AMH underwent two declines in the number of surgeries performed in the last few years. In 1976, fear over malpractice suits caused elective surgeries to decrease by 3 percent. In 1977, a shortage occurred among critical care nurses. At that time nursing registers became popular in Orange County, and nurses left AMH to work for these registers. This shortage was eased by a change in benefits and recruitment; however, maintaining an adequate nursing staff presents problems for growth.

Marketing

AMH incorporated marketing principles into their organization, but as with most hospitals, they did not develop a separate marketing department. In 1978, administrators proposed a separate marketing department. Howard J. Broad, with a background in mass marketing, joined the staff to develop the marketing department.

Marketing will focus on two areas: professionals and communities. The marketing directed towards professionals emphasizes the benefits of working with AMH. The marketing aimed towards the community stresses the services AMH provides the community.

Financial Trends

AMH's patient revenue increased over the last few years (Exhibit 6). Costs rose at a higher rate and net operating income failed to increase proportionately with revenues. The failure to increase net operating income did not hurt the relationship with creditors.

AMH's sources of finance include bank notes payable and long-term debt. AMH may borrow up to $400,000 in bank notes payable, with interest at one-fourth percent above 120 percent of the bank's prime interest rate. Long-term debt has increased with the sale of bonds to five insurance companies. The increase in debt is shown in Exhibit 7. The first mortgage bonds were issued under a security agreement that provides, among other things, certain restrictions as to additional AMH financing, requiring monthly deposits, including all unrestricted donations not to exceed $125,000 annually, to a trust account. Deposits held by the trustee are available for payment of bond principal and interest and for purchase of hospital equipment.

All property, plant, and equipment has been pledged as collateral for payment of the bonds and the trust deed note payable. The hospital has also entered into a security agreement with the bank wherein AMH assigned its accounts receivable as collateral for all its indebtedness to the bank. The agreement contains a current ratio of 1.25 along with other restrictions.

AMH receives approximately 45 percent of its revenues under terms of third-party reimbursement contracts (for example, Medical and Medicaid). Payments are made at interim rates by the agencies administering the programs and are subject to audit of the allocation of costs by various payment formulas. Third-party reimbursement contracts present a problem in the financial statements. Third-party contracts are listed as a liability when the amount billed exceeds the payment formulas. This difference, the excess of billings to government payment formulas, is known as the

EXHIBIT 6 STATEMENT OF REVENUES, EXPENSES, AND FUND BALANCE, 1974–78 (In Thousands of Dollars)

	1974	*1975*	*1976*	*1977*	*1978*
Revenue					
Patient service	$11,364	$15,192	$18,411	$23,218	$25,865
Allowance for uncollectibles	710	1,195	1,408	2,153	2,440
	10,654	13,997	17,003	21,065	23,425
Other operating revenue	160	323	642	795	796
	10,814	14,320	17,645	21,860	24,221
Operating Expenses					
Salaries and wages	4,466	5,451	6,624	8,126	9,500
Supplies, services	4,815	6,986	9,106	11,355	12,206
Interest and write-off of mortgage expense	470	620	882	1,041	1,100
Depreciation	340	457	576	750	938
	10,091	13,514	17,188	21,272	23,745
Income from Operations	723	806	457	588	476
Unrestricted Donations	31	23	21	—	—
Excess of Revenue over Expenses	754	829	478	588	476
Fund Balance at Beginning of Year	2,174	2,928	3,757	4,255	4,928
Restricted Donations	—	—	20	85	99
Fund Balance at End of Year	2,928	3,757	4,255	4,928	5,503

contractual-difference. The collectivity of these sums is uncertain, leading to negotiation.

The hospital uses accelerated depreciation methods in determining reimbursable costs under certain reimbursement programs. Depreciation is recorded on a straight-line basis for financial statement purposes. Revenue resulting from such differences appears as deferred revenue on the balance sheet.

FUTURE PROJECTIONS

Discussions with AMH planners and executives concerning the future of AMH pointed to AMH's image of a progressive medical center as being crucial. Although occupancy rates are now around 68 percent, projections for 1985 show a 90 percent occupancy rate (Exhibit 8). The higher projected occupancy rates stem from the completion of Phase IV construction.

Two problems involved in expansion center around the medical staff. The medical executive board would like to broaden the emphasis of the physicians on staff. This may cause problems in providing equipment for their specialties.

Nursing personnel also present a problem. When the hospital begins to function at the 90 percent occupancy level, it will require more nurses. The administration is looking into the possibility of affiliating with a nursing school to ensure an increased supply of competent personnel.

EXHIBIT 7 AMH BALANCE SHEET, 1974–78 (In Thousands of Dollars)

	1974	1975	1976	1977	1978
Assets					
Current Assets					
Cash	$136	$96	$159	$171	$226
Accounts receivable	2,314	2,773	3,369	4,365	4,578
(Uncollected accounts)	(233)	(333)	(380)	(400)	(450)
Supplies	290	305	375	463	652
Prepaid expenses	53	129	139	164	115
Total Current	2,560	2,970	3,662	4,763	5,121
Long-term Assets					
Land	840	873	1,058	1,139	1,178
Buildings	6,503	10,962	12,893	12,898	12,950
Equipment	1,887	2,358	2,917	4,348	5,049
Construction	3,525	—	—	35	925
Allowance for dep.	(1,792)	(2,232)	(2,784)	(3,490)	(4,476)
Other assets	243	286	892	737	3,184
Total Assets	13,766	15,217	18,638	20,430	23,931
Liabilities and Fund Balance					
Current Liabilities					
Notes to bank	150	250	400	400	400
Accounts payable	1,095	957	1,940	2,740	3,327
Third-party reimbursements	—	363	132	130	101
Employee compensation	285	357	261	381	471
Advances for Current fin.	85	88	110	123	157
Current L-T D	254	310	403	521	654
Total Current	1,868	2,325	3,246	4,295	5,110
Long-term debt (Less current portion)	8,770	8,924	10,922	10,996	13,136
Deferred revenue	200	211	215	211	182
Fund balance	2,928	3,757	4,255	4,928	5,503
Total Liability Fund Balance	13,766	15,217	18,638	20,430	23,931

McAlvin states that the objectives of AMH are to complete current Phase IV construction and increase the size of AMH. The current legal environment does not permit further expansion, but McAlvin sees acquisition as the strategy to acquire more beds. Several offers are being made to small proprietary hospitals. Reasonable offers based on book value of the assets to be acquired are extended. Negotiations failed to materialize at this time due to the exorbitant amount of goodwill demanded. Acquisition represents the only alternative for expansion at the current time.

EXHIBIT 8 PROJECTED OCCUPANCY RATES FOR AMH, 1980–85

Occupancy	*1980*	*1981*	*1982*	*1983*	*1984*	*1985*
ICU	9,300	9,300	10,200	11,200	12,300	13,500
Other	52,000	52,000	55,500	58,900	62,200	65,300
Total	61,300	61,300	65,700	70,100	74,500	78,800
% Occupancy	70%	70%	75%	80%	85%	90%

THE WORLD FOOTBALL LEAGUE—WHAT PRICE RISK, REWARD, AND RECOGNITION?

Of all professional sports, football is the one with the most excess demand for its product.—(*Government and the Sports Business,* The Brookings Institution)

In October 1973, Gary Davidson announced the formation of the World Football League. Davidson, 40, a California attorney, had experience in organizing professional sports leagues, being founder of the American Basketball Association and co-founder of the World Hockey Association.

In his announcement, Davidson said "The NFL has grown arrogant and complacent. The doors are open to a rival." Play was scheduled to begin in 1974 for United States teams. However, the U. S. teams were to constitute only the American Division of the WFL, as the league planned within five years to have teams in most of the major cities of the world—Tokyo, Madrid, London, Paris, Rome, etc. In addition, the WFL planned a number of innovations to enliven the spectator appeal of football and announced the intention of signing name players. According to Davidson, as quoted by Wells Twombly in the *New York Times Magazine* ("Superflop I," January 12, 1975), "The mania for pro football is not any different from the hunger for good rock music. It's all entertainment, and people are willing to pay big money to be entertained."

ORGANIZERS

Gary Davidson, as the central figure in the formation of the WFL, stood to profit by more than a million dollars. To him there was nothing "sinister in this; you enter business to make money," he told Twombly. Davidson, like the other organizers, received a franchise. Although initially thinking of the Southern California area, he finally decided on Philadelphia. It is reported he invested $100,000 of his own money in the team but immediately sold the franchise for $690,000 to a group headed by Jack Kelly, Jr., a former AAU president and Olympic rowing champion and at the time a Philadelphia city councilman.

Prepared by Zoe-Vonna Milligan, graduate student, under the supervision of Professor D. J. Piehl, University of Washington, Seattle.

Davidson received other compensation from the league. He had a no-cut contract as league commissioner for $100,000 annually. The contract, among other provisions, required the WFL headquarters to be located in Newport Beach, California, close to Davidson's home. As WFL commissioner, Davidson had the final say in all league matters, unlike the NFL, where three-fourths of the twenty-six owners must approve every major decision. In addition, Davidson was to receive 10 percent of all WFL television revenues for the first ten years.

Besides his law partner, Donald Reagan, who had aided in past ventures, Davidson was supported in his organizational efforts by four other key people. Reports vary but these four either paid nothing or a token $100,000 each for the franchises they received in return for their efforts.

John Bassett, Jr., 35, a former Davis Cupper and heir to a Canadian fortune, was one of the few very wealthy investors in the league. Bassett's father owned a successful Toronto television station and had owned an interest in the Toronto Argonauts of the Canadian Football League (CFL) and the Toronto Maple Leafs of the National Hockey League. Bassett received the Toronto franchise but was forced to abandon Toronto because of opposition among Canadians, who feared the WFL would undermine the stability of the CFL. Bassett moved his team to Memphis while the Canadian House of Commons approved in principle a bill prohibiting U. S. football leagues from entering Canada.

Robert Schmertz, past owner of the Boston Celtics, and R. Steven Arnold, president of Pro Sports, Inc., a business management firm for professional athletes, received franchises, as noted in Exhibit I. Nick Mileti, formerly involved with the Cleveland Indians, Cavaliers, and Crusaders, also aided in the WFL organizational efforts but sold his right to the Chicago area franchise for a reported $400,000, all profit.

INVESTORS

According to Davidson, he carefully explained not only the potentials for profit from WFL franchise ownership to each interested investor but also the risks involved. It was expected that each franchise would lose between $500,000 and $1 million during the first year of play, and that most would be operating at a loss during the second and possibly the third year as well.

At the time of the WFL organization, the tax laws provided advantages to owners of professional sports teams that made the true rate of return on investment substantially improved than would initially appear from just financial records.[1] This may partly explain why even in the face of book losses, the values of established professional sports teams, including football (as measured by sales price), have generally risen. For example, the WFL in the summer of 1974 placed a $4.2 million price on any new franchises issued in 1975.

Unique to professional sports is the treatment of player (employee) contracts as capital assets subject to depreciation. The greatest benefit from this treatment accrues on the purchase of an existing team when the incentive is to allocate as large a portion of the purchase price as possible to the depreciable player contracts. However, even to the initial franchise investors, as is the case in the WFL, the depreciation on player contracts can make a significant difference between antici-

*Note: [1]The 1976 Tax Reform Act significantly changed the regulations applying to sports franchises. For example, the act provides that purchaser and seller must allocate the same amount of the sales price to player contracts. In addition, the act contains the presumption that not more than 50 percent of the sales price can be allocated to player contracts.

EXHIBIT I PROFILE OF THE WFL

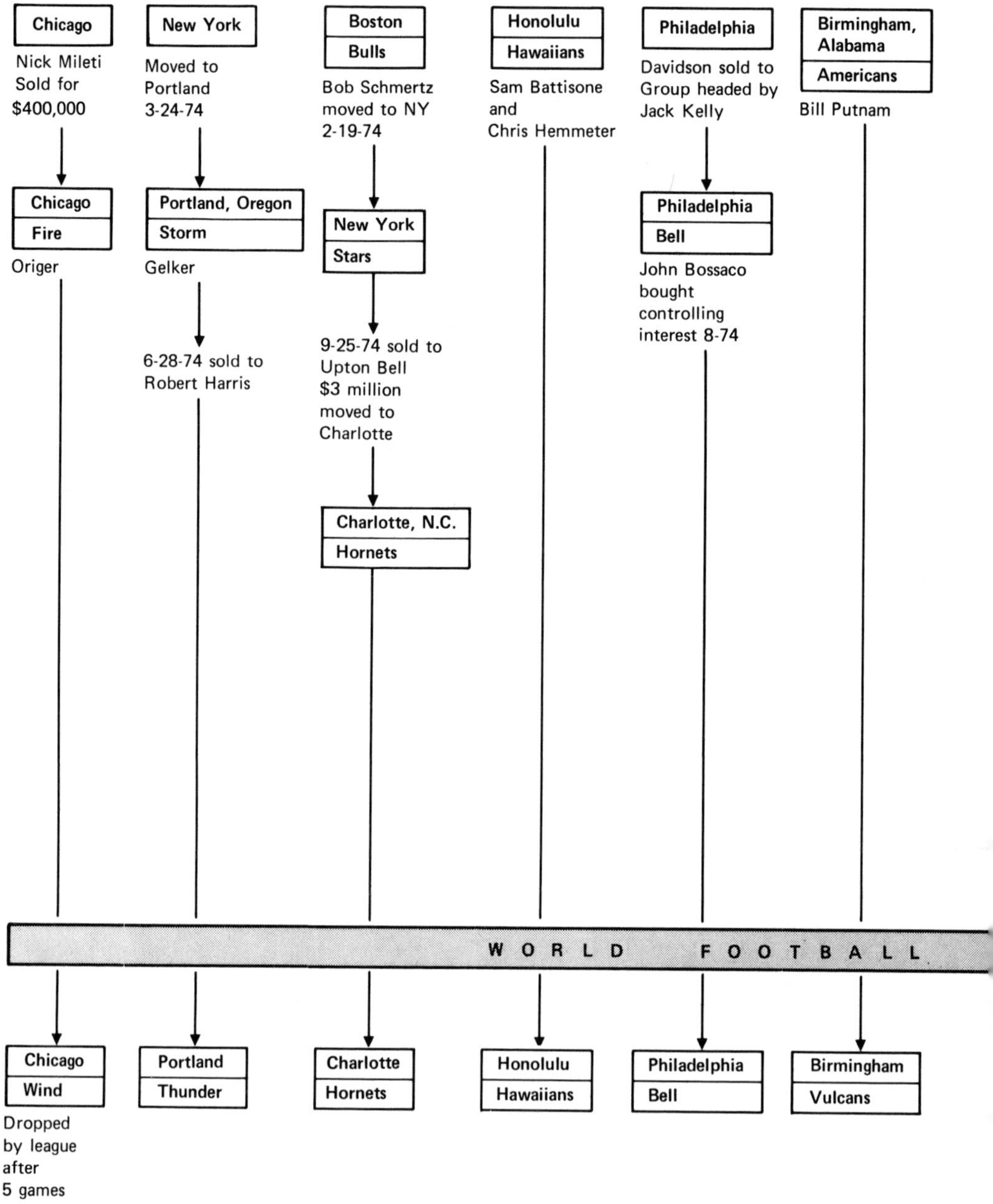

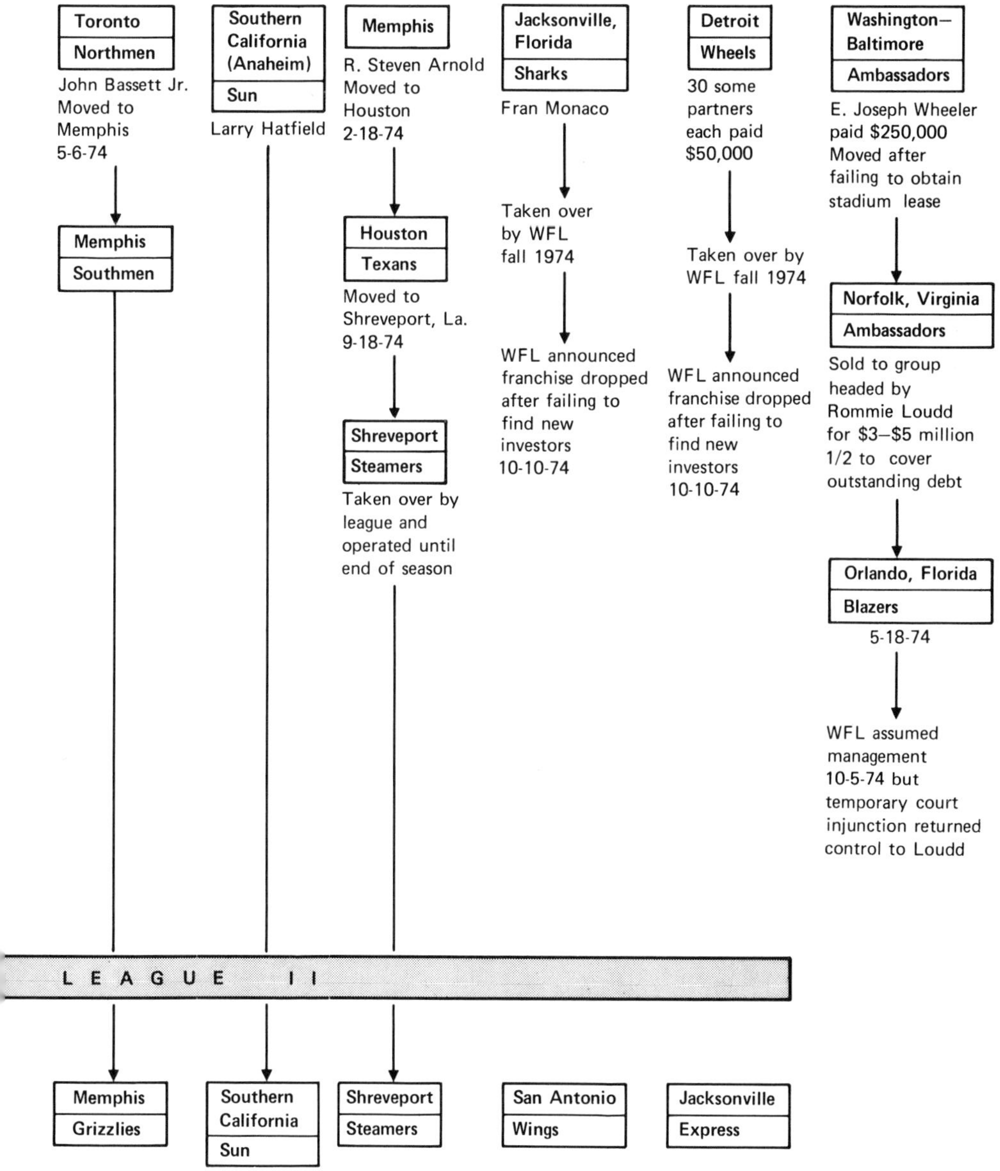
Toronto
Northmen
John Bassett Jr.
Moved to
Memphis
5-6-74
Memphis
Southmen
Southern
California
(Anaheim)
Sun
Larry Hatfield
Memphis
R. Steven Arnold
Moved to
Houston
2-18-74
Houston
Texans
Moved to
Shreveport, La.
9-18-74
Shreveport
Steamers
Taken over by
league and
operated until
end of season
Jacksonville,
Florida
Sharks
Fran Monaco
Taken over
by WFL
fall 1974
WFL announced
franchise dropped
after failing to
find new
investors
10-10-74
Detroit
Wheels
30 some
partners
each paid
$50,000
Taken over by
WFL fall 1974
WFL announced
franchise dropped
after failing to
find new
investors
10-10-74
Washington—
Baltimore
Ambassadors
E. Joseph Wheeler
paid $250,000
Moved after
failing to obtain
stadium lease
Norfolk, Virginia
Ambassadors
Sold to group
headed by
Rommie Loudd
for $3—$5 million
1/2 to cover
outstanding debt
Orlando, Florida
Blazers
5-18-74
WFL assumed
management
10-5-74 but
temporary court
injunction returned
control to Loudd
LEAGUE II
Memphis
Grizzlies
Southern
California
Sun
Shreveport
Steamers
San Antonio
Wings
Jacksonville
Express

pated first-year book losses and actual cash outflow. To take advantage of these and other tax losses and improve cash flow, the Subchapter-S election can be made for tax purposes. This election allows franchise operating losses to be offset against personal income from other sources, thus reducing the overall income tax paid by the individual investor. The Subchapter-S election does not affect the legal corporate status.

On the sale of a franchise, the depreciation on player contracts is subject to recapture provisions under ordinary income rates. However, the Subchapter-S election need not be made in the year of sale, and thus the lower maximum tax rates for corporations would apply. There is also an incentive on the part of the selling team to assign as large a portion of the sales price as possible to the franchise which avoids the recapture provisions and allows capital gains treatment on the difference between the book value of the franchise and the sales price.

According to Davidson, prospective owners were motivated to invest in the WFL not just because of profit potential via tax shelters and capital appreciation, but also for the new challenge and ego gratification. Davidson felt that wealthy men needed a means of nourishing their vanity. He told *Fortune* writer C. G. Burck ("Why Those WFL Owners Expect to Score Profits," September 1974), "The position of owner carries the aura of power over events that touch the emotions of tens of thousands of fans and boosters. The team owner acquires a particularly gratifying form of public stature as a unique blend of entertainment celebrity and civic leader."

Whatever the reasons, Davidson was able to sell the potential of the WFL to other individual investors or investment groups, people largely unknown in sports circles, to make a total of twelve franchises for the 1974 starting season (see Exhibit I). Long-term financing was up to each franchise, but it was expected that success in organizing the league would attract backing from the very wealthy such as Lamar Hunt and Barron Hilton in the AFL.

Franchises sold for between \$100,000 and \$750,000. Fran Monaco is quoted as saying that he was the only franchise owner who paid the full price. However, Monaco apparently purchased the franchises for three Florida cities—Tampa, Orlando, and Jacksonville—for \$750,000. He settled on Jacksonville after abandoning Tampa because of the NFL expansion and reselling the Orlando franchise for \$1 million with half the selling price going to the league.

Monaco became interested in the WFL after trying for years to obtain an NFL franchise in Florida and being disappointed with the \$16 million price and the NFL stipulation that the new Tampa franchise owner would not be able to share in the NFL national television revenues for five years. Besides, as the Brookings Institution study noted, one major consequence of the formation of a new league in any professional sport has *always* been that some owners in the new league will obtain major-league franchises when peace is restored between the leagues. And, with the formation of a new league, all teams supposedly start equal so that everyone has a chance to win the championship.

PLAYERS AND COACHES

The WFL held its first college draft January 22 and 23, 1974, and on March 18, 1974 held a draft to assign negotiating rights for NFL and CFL players. At the time of the college draft, several teams were without coaches, general managers, playing fields, and even cities. Actually, the January draft only went through six rounds, because the WFL had to wait until the NFL had carried out its draft in February in order to use the NFL draft list as a guide. The draft information that was available to the WFL prior to that time was supplied by the former director of player personnel, recently fired by New Orleans, who came to the WFL along with his sheets of player ratings.

Although the early college draft was aimed more at establishing credibility than obtaining players, the draft did have several effects on the NFL. One player agent estimated that the WFL helped move the average player salary from $27,000 to $42,000. In addition, the NFL hurried in its attempts to tie down draft choices. By April, the WFL had failed to place one NFL first or second-round draft choice under contract. But, as one WFL spokesman was quoted in *Sports Illustrated*, "The NFL can have all its first-round draft choices if we can have the established players."

To attract the NFL players, the WFL not only offered potential salary increases but also additional player freedom. The freedom issue was one of the controversial aspects of negotiations between the striking NFL Players Association and the NFL owners in the summer of 1974. The WFL did not adopt the NFL option system and the so-called Rozelle Rule. The option system, professional football's variation of the reserve clause, gives a team exclusive right to retain a player's services without the player's consent for one year after the term of his contract has expired. The purpose of such a reserve clause is to restrict competition for players, thus ensuring that strong teams do not "rob" weaker teams of key players.

If a player does not sign a new contract after his old one expires, his salary is a lesser percentage (supposedly 90 percent) of what it was the previous year. At the end of the year of playing without a contract, the player is free to negotiate with other teams. However, the Rozelle Rule provides that a team signing a player who has played out his option must still indemnify the player's former team. The NFL commissioner has the authority from which there is no appeal to determine the amount of compensation which can be in any form of rights to future draft choices or veteran players or cash payments.

NFL players generally looked favorably on the WFL organizational efforts, although Ed Garvey of the NFL Players Association, in his concern for player bargaining position, expressed fears that the WFL would destroy the CFL and then merge with the NFL. Merlin Olson told *Sports Illustrated*, "If the NFL established a franchise in Honolulu overnight to put the WFL out of business, I think the Players Association would sue." And, as Calvin Hill expressed to *Sports Illustrated* in signing for $500,000 for three years with the Hawaiians, "I just want to get paid $100 for every $100 worth of effort. There is nothing that salves my ego about playing in the NFL."

The WFL also attracted a number of free agents trying for the chance to participate in the mystique of professional football. Detroit had 665 men appear for team tryouts.

Owners in the WFL were of two opinions regarding player acquisitions. Some felt it was necessary to have at least a few big name professional players on a team. Others such as Origer of Chicago felt that no player was indispensable. Finances, of course, limited the number of name NFL acquisitions possible. The general manager of the Detroit team, a team that did not sign any NFL players for future play, told *Sports Illustrated* that, "My own ethics aren't going to allow me to promise something I can't deliver."

John Bassett, who was willing to sign in April 1974 a $3 to $4 million contract for the combined services of the Miami Dolphin trio of Csonka, Warfield, and Kiick for play beginning in 1974, was of the opposite frame of mind. Bassett felt the signing of the three could make his team and the league. According to him, a struggling franchise can afford such contracts because the name players attract attendance, which increases revenue, while an established team already has near capacity attendance.

On the player's side, Ed Keating, business manager for Csonka, Warfield, and Kiick, put together the contract in which the three were immune from trades and dismissals and which was guaranteed by a letter of credit from a Canadian bank. In addition to the basic contract, each player expected to benefit from endorsements and commercials. NFL player reaction to the deal was more one of envy than animosity. John Brockington told *Sports Illustrated*, "that bona fides the WFL for me." The contract signing triggered a number of NFL players to move to the WFL. Ken Stabler, a local Alabama product and hero, signed with Bill Putnam, owner of the Birmingham franchise, for play two years in the future. After the signing, Putnam reported ticket sales jumped 1,000 ahead of the expected rate.

As would be expected, NFL owners were not pleased with the WFL player raids. Some kept silent fearing anti-trust action or aiding the striking NFL players' cause. Some, like Carroll Rosenbloom of the Los Angeles Rams, spoke against Davidson. Twombly, in his *New York Times Magazine* article, quoted Rosenbloom: "If you'll notice, most of the ventures break down financially after he has put them in gear. He comes out of these deals with more money than he puts in, mostly because he hardly ever puts anything other than imagination and hustle into them." However, some sought court action in attempts to void WFL player contracts. In April 1974, Cincinnati and Dallas were granted a temporary restraining order blocking the WFL from signing their players. The NFL teams had argued that players with WFL contracts would not perform up to their abilities and that organization morale would be disrupted by strained relations between WFL contract players and their NFL teammates and coaches. However, in May 1974, the court reversed itself and refused to grant an injunction since "such an injunction would harm the goal of fostering free competition in the market place for the sports dollar."

Many of the coaches, like the players, came to the WFL from the NFL. As Jack Pardee said to *Sports Illustrated* when jumping to Orlando after fifteen years in the NFL with the Rams and Redskins, "I looked around the NFL and I saw plenty of good assistant coaches who never got a chance to be a head coach. I couldn't see waiting five years, or who knows how long, for an opportunity that might never come."

ODDS FOR SUCCESS

In the spring of 1974, while the WFL was organizing itself for its first season, observers were largely negative on its chances for success. Lamar Hunt, founder of the AFL, said there was little similarity between the AFL and the WFL. The AFL had chosen franchise locations where the NFL did not have teams, while the WFL had seven of twelve teams in NFL cities. When the AFL was organized, only one of the three major networks televised professional football. In addition, the AFL competed with the NFL almost exclusively for rookies, not established players as the WFL was doing.

TELEVISION COVERAGE

From 1964 to 1974, sports programming on each of the three major networks doubled to about 1,000 hours per year. A Brookings Institution study estimated that only a handful of the most successful professional football teams might be profitable without broadcasting. Although both local and national broadcasts result in revenue to teams, revenue from national broadcasts is the most significant. It was estimated in 1974 that each NFL franchise received about $2 million from the NFL contracts with the three major networks.

Since the three major networks were committed to the NFL through 1977, it was not expected that the WFL would obtain television coverage. However, in February 1974 the WFL signed a contract with TVS Television Network. The contract called for thirteen WFL games to be shown nationally by the up to 130 stations affiliated with TVS. Ten other games were to be shown by TVS affiliates considered to be in the top audience drawing markets. Since the TVS contract was expected to bring in only about $1 million in revenues to the WFL in 1974, or approximately $80,000 per team, the real importance of the contract was not in covering operating expenses but in providing exposure for the WFL.

TVS, a small, independent operation, bought rights to sports events and then contracted out with both independent and network affiliated stations to carry the events. TVS also sold the commercial time to advertisers and on a free-lance basis hired the manpower to broadcast the events. The TVS network had to convince stations to air the WFL games during the entire season, not just the summer when there were no NFL games or program ratings. Some felt the major networks were not going to look favorably on an affiliate station that substituted WFL games for the network's prime time programming in the autumn months.

WFL INNOVATIONS—SCHEDULING AND RULES

The WFL planned to have a playing season from July to November with twenty regular games (ten home, ten road) and no exhibitions. In 1974, the opening game was set for July 17. Play was scheduled for mid-week so as not to compete with high school, college, and NFL play. Regular games were planned for Wednesday night, with a single Thursday evening nationally televised game.

A spokesman for Davidson stated the WFL projections for break-even attendance as 25,000 to 30,000 per game. Ticket prices were set at around $7.50, with 75 percent of the gate to be retained by the home team and 25 percent going to the visiting team. However, the gate-sharing arrangement was dropped partway through the season.

In setting the playing season from July to November, the WFL lessened the effect of NFL competition but increased the competition for fans between different sports. *Fortune Magazine* presented a typical sports programming schedule for the week of October 14–20, 1974 in New York City (major networks only and excluding the multi-theme sports shows):

Monday	Football
Tuesday	Baseball
Wednesday	Baseball, hockey
Thursday	Football, baseball, basketball
Friday	Open (federal law prohibits conflict between professional games and high school and college from Labor Day to December)
Saturday	Football (2), baseball, basketball, horse racing
Sunday	Football (4), baseball

To help make play more appealing to fans, the WFL made a number of rule changes designed to open up the offensive game and promote touchdown scoring. Most of the WFL rule changes were subsequently adopted by the NFL in April 1974 when Pete Rozelle announced the most radical changes in NFL rules since 1933. Rozelle said the NFL had been considering the rule changes for several years.

OPENING SEASON SURPRISES

Since the announcement of the formation of the WFL, the typical news article had dealt with WFL problems: confusion of ownership, shifting sites, raiding of NFL personnel, and legal hassles. But with the start of the season, the press coverage shifted towards characterizing the WFL as a "competent operation," a phrase used in a *Sports Illustrated* article just prior to the opening game.

The first week of the season the *New York Times* carried an article on the caliber of play that noted WFL mistakes were at a minimum even though the WFL did not have exhibition games and many teams had inexperienced players (see Exhibit III). Attendance at the opening games received very favorable coverage (see Exhibit II). The only negative note was that the high-scoring games expected because of the rule changes did not materialize. Only two teams scored more than 17 points.

A Dave Anderson editorial in the *New York Times* on July 13, 1974 noted that not everyone was pleased with the positive opening game showing by the WFL. Anderson accused the NFL of seeking to sabotage the WFL's impact by "leaking alleged inside information to newsmen regarding WFL attendance and policy." According to Anderson, "Pete Rozelle's agents were whispering such rumors as, 'did you know that the Chicago Fire announced attendance of 42,000 but only had about 27,000 paid?'"

PAPERGATE

The papergate, as it came to be called, involved several WFL teams. John B. Kelly, Jr. resigned as president when he learned that the Bell's vice president had announced 120,153 people in attendance at the two Philadelphia home games, when 100,000 or so attended free.

EXHIBIT II OPENING GAME STATISTICS

	Attendance
Portland (8) at Philadelphia (33)	55,534 (20,000 paid)
Southern California (7) at Birmingham (11)	53,231 (all but 1,000 paid)
Detroit (15) at Memphis (34)	30,122
Houston (0) at Chicago (17)	42,000 (approximately 30,000 paid)
Hawaii (7) at Florida (Orlando) (8)	18,625
New York (7) at Florida (Jacksonville) (14)	59,112 (approximately 15,000 tickets given away)

Total opening games attendance: 258,624.
Total attendance was 70 percent of total capacity of stadiums.
New York at Florida was the first WFL nationally televised game.

EXHIBIT III COMPARISON STATISTICS BY LEAGUE

	WFL Opening Night Average	*NFL 1973 Season Per-Game Average*
Paid attendance	35,000	58,961
Points scored	28	39
Net yardage	517	571
Passes attempted	50	49
Passes completed	26	25
Interceptions	2.2	2.6
Fumbles	4.4	4.5
Fumbles lost	2.4	2.3
Penalties	11	10
Yards penalized	105	95

To counter the unfavorable publicity, Gary Davidson requested that all teams break down attendance figures by paid and unpaid.

FINANCIAL TROUBLES

As the season progressed, attendance began to drop off, which caused revenues to decline, creating cash flow problems. Detroit and Jacksonville were the first to experience major troubles. Detroit actually had problems from the beginning. The Wheels had to settle for play in Ypsilanti at the East Michigan State University Stadium, 35 miles from downtown Detroit, because the Lions had exclusive football rights to Tiger Stadium until 1975.

The thirty-two or so individuals who owned the Detroit franchise had hoped to raise an additional $4 million in capital through a public stock offering. But, the offering failed to take place when the franchise was declared too risky to go public. The owners did not exactly get rave reviews from the players for management. According to Detroit punter Chuck Collins, as reported by Twombly, "The owners of the Wheels were a bunch of jerks. They just wanted to run around saying they had a part of a professional football team. All they had to do was put in $50,000 each and they thought they'd be millionaires overnight. They must have told us a million lies. They wanted us to stay in tents during training camp. We won that battle but that was the only one."

Things went from bad to worse financially, and other league members were assessed a total of $265,000 to help Detroit meet back payrolls. The money went instead to creditors. The WFL took the franchise over but announced in October 1974 that Detroit was being dropped because new investors could not be found.

Jacksonville met a fate similar to Detroit under somewhat different circumstances. Although the Sharks were second in the league in attendance, Jacksonville players were not being paid. Monaco borrowed $27,000 from his coach, Bud Asher, to make a payroll, and then turned around and fired him. The team was finally taken over by the league, then dropped. But as Monaco said, according to Twombly, "I never told them I was Lamar Hunt. This thing happened too fast. If we had waited until 1975 to get going, the Jacksonville Sharks would have lasted. My cash loss will be around $800,000." League owners met in Los Angeles at the end of October to hold a special draft for players from Detroit and Jacksonville. At the meeting they promised to honor all contracts signed by the defunct teams.

Other teams missed paydays, including Portland and Orlando. Orlando stopped paying its players September 6. Portland players were not paid the last two months of the regular season and the standing joke became, reports Twombly, "On the road the Storm would receive food stamps instead of team meals." The league also had to take over the Houston franchise and move it to Shreveport. The Sun's owner, Larry Hatfield, was indicted by a federal grand jury on three counts of making false statements to obtain bank loans. Davidson announced that each of these problems were team specific and that the league was facing and dealing with them.

LOSS OF THE NEW YORK FRANCHISE

Traditionally, because the wire services, the major television networks, and most advertising agencies who purchase television air time are located in New York, it has been thought necessary for a league to have a franchise in that city. In addition, it has been assumed that the networks and network advertisers buy the population figures of large metropolitan areas. Professional sports leagues have in the past been caught in the dilemma of needing the large city franchises for the reasons elaborated but having the smaller cities, anxious for major league sports, have more successful franchises; as a result, large city audiences usually find it insulting to lose to the smaller city teams and thus do not support their franchises.

The WFL's New York franchise was forced to move to Charlotte, North Carolina, ostensibly because of stadium facility problems. Downing Stadium, the only one available, was dimly lit and inaccessible by mass transit and had turf in poor condition. Upton Bell, son of the former NFL commissioner and himself once general manager of the New England Patriots, was head of the syndicate that bought and moved the New York franchise to Charlotte. The syndicate reportedly paid between $3 and $5 million to Schmertz, who was said to be over $2 million in debt at the time of sale. As the Stars were leaving, the WFL awarded an expansion franchise to New York to play in 1976 when the Yankee Stadium renovation was to be completed.

DAVIDSON RESIGNS

On October 29, Gary Davidson resigned under pressure as league commissioner. The situation was forced by Tom Origer, owner of the Chicago team, when he threatened to take his team out of the league if a new commissioner was not installed and the league headquarters shifted to New York. Press reaction was that Davidson had lost his credibility.

Donald Reagan served as temporary commissioner until November 22, when Chris Hemmeter, co-president of the Hawaiian franchise, was elected as Davidson's replacement. Hemmeter claimed to have originally become involved with the WFL as a civic gesture when Honolulu built a 50,000 seat stadium but had no one to back the Hawaiian team. Hemmeter, 36, a real-estate developer, and Sam Battistone, owner of Sambo's restaurant chain, finally stepped forward and persuaded friends and associates to do likewise. Hemmeter consented to head up the WFL primarily to protect his reputation and because "the bigger the challenge, the happier I am." He told *Sports Illustrated*, "I'm doing all this to show people that it can be done. I don't mind losing money, but when you lose it looking like a fool, well, that's not my idea of a good time. I want a reputation that says, if you invest with me I'll do everything possible to protect that investment."

WORLD BOWL

Hemmeter waited until after the December 5 championship game to deal with the problems facing the WFL. In the World Bowl, 32,376 fans watched Birmingham defeat Orlando 22-21. For a time it was unclear if the game would be played. Three days before the game, the Birmingham players announced they would not play unless they received five weeks of unpaid wages. They eventually relented; so did the IRS on $237,000 in back taxes with the promise of a share of the Birmingham Legion Field gate. The players settled for the promise of championship rings.

HEMMETER'S ATTEMPTS TO SAVE THE WFL

After the World Bowl, Hemmeter announced that the WFL would collapse if new owner-investors were not found by March 1975. According to him, there were three strong franchises—Hawaii, Philadelphia, and Memphis. The league had taken over the Chicago, Orlando, Portland, and Charlotte franchises during December. Hemmeter, in attempting to save the WFL, said it had three powerful assets: "Quality performances by the teams, public recognition achieved by weekly telecasts of games in over 100 cities, and the structure of the league."

An article in the *New York Times* also noted the above positive factors of the WFL and characterized the WFL problems as "terrifying only when compared to the prosperity of the established leagues." The article went on to add that the WFL was better off in attendance than the AFL in 1960, the ABA in 1968, the NBA in 1947, or the WHA in 1973 (making appropriate adjustments for the difference in attendance between sports).

In mid-December, the WFL owners voted that all present owners would have to post a $750,000 bond by December 31 to protect their current franchises. The bond would be used to meet 1975 operating expenses and pay back salaries from 1974.

WFL 1974 LOSSES

As Hemmeter was attempting to save the league, reports were circulating about the team losses for 1974. Estimates of the total WFL losses for the year varied between $5 and $20 million. The Associated Press published a survey towards the end of November that reported the league lost more than $20 million, including the following:

Memphis—$700,000 loss, the lowest in the league. Believed to be the strongest franchise.

Birmingham—as high as $1 million. Putnam attempted to raise $1.5 million but only received $175,000.

Portland—at least $1 million loss.

Charlotte—assets of $95,000 and liabilities of $2.5 million.

Southern California—estimated $1 million loss.

Hawaii—$3 million loss.

Chicago—$800,000 loss; Origer had received $150,000 loan in mid-season from other WFL owners.

Shreveport—estimated $1.5 million loss.

Detroit and Jacksonville—$4 million loss.

Orlando and Philadelphia—no details reported.

Up to this time the largest annual operating loss for a professional football team was thought to be less than $2 million—Barron Hilton's loss before moving the Chargers from Los Angeles to San Diego.

HEMMETER PLAN FOR WFL II

Hemmeter designed a unique reorganization and revenue sharing plan for operating the WFL in its second season. The plan emphasized frugality in operations and was based on the concept of relating a team's expenses to its revenues. Maximum revenue percentages were allocated to the various categories of expenses. The capital requirements were also revised under Hemmeter's plan and included the stipulation that each owner deposit between $600,000 and $1.2 million in cash, depending on team liabilities.

Hemmeter's plan was obviously complex, but it depended on two key factors—attendance of at least 17,000 per game and players willing to work for a percentage of team gross income. The player's percentage salary formulas averaged about 1 percent of gross income or $500 per game, whichever was higher. The actual percentage varied with the player's negotiating ability. The plan did not preclude lucrative contract negotiations for name players; it did, however, guarantee every player at least something.

A simple example of a player's salary for a week based on game attendance of 12,000 and an average ticket price of $7.50 would be

Home team player: 60% of $90,000 = $54,000 × 1% = $540

Visiting team player: 40% of $90,000 = $36,000 × 1% = $360

Hemmeter's plan reinstituted sharing of gate receipts between home and visiting teams. It was reported that one-half of the league players signed percentage contracts.

Hemmeter found backers for eleven franchises in WFL II. Only a few of the first season investors returned—Bassett of Memphis, Bossaco of Philadelphia, and several Hawaiian investors; Battistone purchased a substantial portion of the Southern California franchise.

TELEVISION CONTRACT CANCELLED

During April and May of 1975, while Hemmeter's reorganization plan was taking shape, the WFL announced its intentions of trying to attract Joe Namath to sign a $4 million contract with the Chicago franchise. At the end of May, Namath officially rejected the offer. Eddie Einhorn of TVS claimed that advertisers would not buy time for the WFL broadcasts after the WFL failed to sign Namath. Einhorn felt that by

EXHIBIT IV WFL FINAL STANDINGS 1974

	Won	Lost	Tied	Pct.	Points Scored	Points Allowed
Eastern Division						
Orlando, Florida	14	6	0	.700	419	280
Charlotte, N.C.	10	10	0	.500	467	350
Philadelphia	9	11	0	.450	491	413
Jacksonville	4	10	0	.286	258	359
Central Division						
Memphis	17	3	0	.850	629	365
Birmingham	15	5	0	.750	500	394
Chicago	7	13	0	.350	446	600
Detroit	1	13	0	.071	209	358
Western Division						
Southern California	13	7	0	.650	486	440
Hawaii	9	11	0	.450	413	422
Portland	7	12	1	.375	264	426
Shreveport	7	12	1	.375	240	415

Philadelphia won one game against Chicago by forfeit.
Jacksonville and Detroit were suspended from the league.
Birmingham defeated Orlando for the league championship.

announcing their intentions of signing Namath, the WFL II tied their credibility to Namath's contract. TVS did not renew their contract for coverage of the 1975 games. Hemmeter hoped that after 1975 the WFL would have proved itself and the networks and sponsors would be willing to deal in 1976.

1975 SEASON

Shortly after the second season was under way, the Chicago franchise was dropped for failing to meet Hemmeter's financial requirements. Troubles also plagued San Antonio, Shreveport, and Jacksonville, who each had to renegotiate contracts to keep from folding. In October, the league had to assess the other teams a total of $300,000 to keep Portland and Philadelphia operational.

By October, average attendance figures for the first six games ranged from the Memphis high of 19,776 to a low for Philadelphia of 3,705 for four home games (see Exhibit V). The sagging attendance was enough to undermine Hemmeter's carefully calculated revenue sharing plan, and was critical enough to move the league to attempt a national marketing campaign.

But it was too late. October 22, twelve weeks into the season, Hemmeter announced that WFL II was ceasing operations. The WFL II deficit was said to have reached $10 million; another two years and an expenditure of $25 to $40 million was estimated to be necessary to make it successful. In his announcement, Hemmeter said that WFL II could not withstand the combined ill effects of bad weather, NFL and media skepticism, and the reputation from WFL I. Hemmeter also cited an un-

EXHIBIT V WFL II AVERAGE ATTENDANCE

Thru Six Home Games:	
Memphis	19,776
Birmingham	19,278
Shreveport	16,081
Hawaii	15,881
Southern California	13,518
Jacksonville	12,984
Charlotte	12,007
San Antonio	11,058
Portland	8,861
Thru Four Home Games	
Philadelphia	3,705

stable economy, continuing inflation, the failure to secure a national television contract, and a softening in the market for new professional sports teams.

Hemmeter ended his parting announcement on a personal note, reported in *Sports Illustrated*: "I thought that righting a wrong would certainly be rewarded and we would attract strong public support due to our insistence on a businesslike atmosphere. This was not the case. The 1974 problems haunted us, the lack of credibility stayed with us. We found that paying bills was not enough to save the WFL. We failed in marketing. Possibly I was the wrong person to head up the league. Maybe pro sports are a little too swinging for me. I'm conservative and I don't have public appeal and flamboyance. We had excitement on the field but the league lacked excitement. Most of us are bankers, and we lacked charisma, mystique."

Birmingham and Memphis, the two strongest WFL teams, planned to petition the NFL for membership.

HESSTON CORPORATION

Following a dramatic growth in 1974 in net sales of 58 percent, a growth in net income of 34 percent, and a growth in employment of 33 percent, along with a strong first half performance in 1975, the Hesston Corporation, in late August 1975, announced a reduction of employment amounting to 12 percent of the work force at its main plant in Hesston, Kansas. This comprised 6 percent of the company's worldwide payroll. This layoff may indicate a reversal of its recent rapid growth in income and employment. Hesston's lifelong performance in the specialized farm equipment industry had been spectacular. The layoff hit the home plant, which was previously its most profitable and rapidly growing plant and which specialized in production and distribution of hay and forage handling equipment.

INDUSTRY RELATIONSHIPS AND DERIVED DEMAND

The agricultural machinery and equipment industry encompasses the primary products of Hesston Corporation. As is the case for all intermediate industries that produce for other industries, the demand for the product is derived from the demand for the final product. This relationship causes a time lag in the impact of changes in demand for the final product upon the demand in the intermediate industry, often referred to as the ripple effect. Business cycle swings are similarly affected in their timing among industries.

The final product in Hesston's industrial market is food. Distributors and processors buy raw food products from agricultural producers who, in turn, are induced by many economic forces to use the most efficient means of production. Due to the strong forces of competition in agriculture, coupled with the rapid rate of technological change, the forces inducing the producers of food to update their methods and machinery are strong indeed.

To complete the requirements for the decision to buy, the necessary desire needs to be complemented by sufficient purchasing power. Slightly less than 20

Prepared by Dr. Forrest W. Price of West Virginia University and Dr. Albert L. Winkler of Kansas State University.

percent (only 16 percent in 1971) of the total income of the U. S. economy has been spent for food recently. Of this amount, about 40 percent is spent for meat and meat products. Part of this revenue filters down through the distribution and processing system to animal producers.

Beef comprises the largest item of meat expenditures, and dairy products are also major items in the food budget. Beef and dairy producers are major users of hay and other forage feeds since these animals are ruminants. Grains are also included in the rations, depending upon the level and quality of production desired as well as upon the costs and availability of alternative feeds. Pork, or swine, are fed grain almost exclusively, corn being the principal feed. When grain is relatively low in cost, a large percentage of beef cattle are fed to a high-quality finish on grain, a process known as "cattle feeding," as opposed to cattle production of the more common cow-calf producer on the range.

The production of pork and grain finishing of beef cattle has historically been confined to the corn belt. Increased use of irrigation and production of grain sorghum, a more heat and drought-tolerant crop than corn, has caused grain feeding to spread across the central plains and into Texas and the Southwest.

It is in this industrial, geographical, and technological setting that Hesston Corporation was born and grew in the heart of the plains at Hesston, Kansas. The types of farm equipment that were the initial sources of Hesston's success were those originated and adapted to the geography, crops, and climate of the plains. The hay windrower and a special grain-saving attachment for combine harvesters of grain sorghum are two examples. Emphasis upon innovation in hay and forage equipment and technological advance in designing specialized equipment and attachments for other farm machines have been the key to Hesston's continued growth.

The sales of Hesston are directly linked to the incomes of the livestock and grain producers through the relationships described. Due to the geographic factors and the relative importance of hay and forage equipment in their total product line, Hesston has been more dependent upon the incomes of cow-calf producers for their total sales than other producers of farm equipment.

International Harvester (IH) is the largest producer of farm equipment in the United States and was listed twenty-second in Fortune's 500 largest manufacturing firms in 1974. John Deere, second largest, was ranked seventy-eighth. IH is also a large producer of heavy industrial equipment, trucks, sport vehicles, and appliances. Deere produces tractors and other farm equipment not included in the Hesston line. New Holland is considered to be the major and most direct competitor of Hesston in specialty farm equipment manufacture and sales.

THE HESSTON APPROACH

"There has to be a better way," thought Lyle Yost, a custom harvester in 1947, as he waited for hours for a crew to unload the bins of his self-propelled combines. He had an idea which he took to the owner of the Hesston Machine Shop, and together they worked out an unloading auger attachment to the combine. Additional models were made for sale, other equipment ideas were developed, and in 1949 the Hesston Corporation was formed. In 1955 a self-propelled windrower, which made Hesston's name known throughout the world, was added. The company's first major acquisition occurred in 1969 with the purchase of Wood Brothers,

Inc., of Oregon, Illinois, another innovator of specialized farm equipment, especially corn pickers and heavy-duty rotary mowers. Hesston rapidly became the leader in rotary-mower production at the agricultural and industrial level.

Into the 1970s Hesston continued to grow very rapidly through expansion in production and distribution of its initial product line and through diversification. In 1971 the design and manufacture of advanced office furniture was undertaken. In 1972 two firms who were producers of industrial incinerators were purchased, forming the Waste Disposal Division. Also in 1972, a manufacturer of farm equipment in France was acquired. Acquisitions continued in 1973 with additions of a producer of self-propelled forage harvesting equipment, a producer of waste compacting and handling machines, and a producer of specialized farm and light industrial equipment. These extensions and added divisions are discussed in more detail in subsequent sections of the case study.

Throughout this history of rapid expansion and diversification, Hesston had successfully grown in managerial talent, from both within and without. Growth through acquisition and diversification led to a divisional management system with eight operating divisions in North America and two in Europe, each with virtually autonomous profit centers but under general administration of corporate headquarters.

After completion of divisional organizations in Europe, Hesston advanced its international operations to Australia and South America. The new manufacturing division and sales branch in Australia almost immediately reported severely depressed sales of hay and forage equipment in late August of 1975.

MANAGEMENT PHILOSOPHY AND PRODUCT DEVELOPMENT

At the annual meeting on January 20, 1975, Howard L. Brenneman, 34, was elected president and chief operating officer. He expressed a philosophy of successful business management, which included five major factors, the first of which was the product. The other four factors, which are included as topics of business analysis following the organization section of this case, are market penetration, plant facilities, people, and profits.

Said Brenneman: "Hesston has achieved a unique place in world agriculture business because of product innovation and by selecting specific needs that exist in the marketplace in which we believe a contribution can be made. Our objective has always been to deliver a product to the customer that will save labor and increase output, thereby increasing his return on investment. Our thrust must be to increase product innovation as we reach around the globe to help all nations provide a balanced diet to their populace."

References have been made to this philosophy throughout the entire history of the company. This was emphasized in the search for complementary products back in 1966 when Hesston purchased the assets and product lines of a firm in Logan, Utah, which manufactured hay-handling equipment and again when it purchased its first overseas plant at Udine, Italy, for the manufacture of windrowers for the European market.

In 1965 plans were laid for four major product developments. In 1966 ten were achieved, several of them industry firsts. The engineering staff reported: "Specific attention to preplanning by manufacturing and product engineers on products in the final states of development adds substantial promise to the objective of compressing the transition time from development to production. The initial results of this emphasis are already being realized in the form of lower new-model introduction costs, improved quality control, and more effective communication."

A more formal product-proving program was introduced in 1966 involving intensified field testing. The company indicated the prospects for improved product performance and reliability would result, and during 1967 fourteen significant product developments were completed, including a new high-capacity windrower, a hay harvester, a sugar-beet harvester, and a trash-removal unit for the cotton harvester.

In addition to the products acquired through the purchase of Wood Brothers, an important new development in 1969 was the introduction of the Hesston StakHand, a new hay-handling machine with which one man picks up cut hay from windrows and stacks it in stacks as large as six tons. These stacks are compressed for field storage and the operator does not leave his tractor. As time progressed, Hesston developed a product line with which one man could harvest, store, and feed hay and forage without manual operations and farm labor. The decision to concentrate in hay and forage products was made after intensive research by Hesston and after independent research indicated growth potential.

In line with this decision, many modifications, variations in size, and new products were developed in the hay-handling system in the early 1970s, including a StackHandler that loads or unloads a six-ton haystack in less than one minute, and a machine that will slice it and deliver it into feeding windrows, bunks, or grinder hoppers, all without the man leaving his tractor.

ORGANIZATION

During 1973, Hesston adopted a divisional management system in order to more effectively manage the anticipated growth. An organization chart of central management was made. Under this concept, each division operated relatively autonomously, relying on corporate headquarters for general guidelines and for funds as required. Hesston was then operating ten divisions, eight of which were located in the U. S. and two in Europe. A brief description of the divisions and their major functions follows.

Farm Equipment Division. Sixty percent of Hesston's net consolidated sales have been generated by this division, located in Hesston, Kansas. Many of the wide range of harvesting and handling equipment units described elsewhere are manufactured in this plant.

Field Queen Division. This unit, acquired in 1973, manufactures commercial self-propelled forage harvesters designed primarily for use by alfalfa dehydrator operators and a large self-propelled forage harvester for farmers and ranchers.

Woods Division. This division, located in Oregon, Illinois, is the largest manufacturer of tractor-mounted rotary mowers in the world. The line of mowers manufactured in the Woods Division has been continuously expanded since it was acquired in 1969 and development continues.

Logan Division. This division manufactures equipment for harvesting sugar beets, potatoes, and other root crops. Others are under study and existing methods such as windrowing are being applied. An onion harvester has most recently been added.

Lawn Equipment Division. This division manufactures several models of lawn and garden tractors and accessories. It was organized in 1973 and new production facilities were leased in Indianapolis, Indiana.

Waste Equipment Division. With the addition of the Val-Jac Company in 1973, this division provides a full line of waste-disposal equipment such as compactors, containers, truck-mounted compactors, incinerators, and related items. This division was recently moved to a new plant in Bartlesville, Oklahoma, and the original plants were sold.

Hesco Division. This division, located in Hesston, designs and manufactures a complete line of high-quality wood office furniture.

Danuser Division. This 1973 addition manufactures several models of tractor-mounted rotary mowers, backhoes, and snow blowers sold primarily to original equipment manufacturers.

International Operations. This operation, consisting of two divisions, has increased from 11 percent of company revenues in 1973 to 13 percent in 1974 and has a current goal of 20 percent of sales, exclusive of sales in Canada. Rochland S. A., of Coex, France, manufactures Hesston's windrower and a low-density hay baler. Production has also begun on the Field Queen forage harvester for the European market. Hesston S. p. A., located in Udine, Italy, manufactures a self-propelled windrower for the same market. Hesston products are sold in other parts of the world through licensees such as those in Brazil, Argentina, and Australia and through trading companies in Japan, Russia, and others.

A number of changes in management assignments were made in 1974; Exhibit 1 lists the directors and officers for the past ten years. On January 20, 1975, L. E. Yost, president and chairman of the board of directors, announced the election of a new president, Howard Brenneman: "After serving as president and chief executive officer for over twenty-five years, I feel this is a most appropriate time to move over for the next generation of management. In 1957, a young farm boy who grew up in the Hesston community began his employment at Hesston as a bookkeeper. An honor graduate with a bachelor's degree in business economics, he quickly moved through several departments in accounting. In 1969, he was appointed assistant to the president, and in 1972 was elected vice president of operations, and he became a member of the executive committee in 1974. This last June he was elected vice president and chief operating officer. As a young executive, 34 years old, he has shown his professional ability in the community and industry. . . .He is a graduate of the American Management Association Management Course and other management courses."

MARKETING

Distribution of Hesston equipment was made through distributors during the early years, with distributors being replaced by company operated sales facilities at the rate of about one each year throughout the 1960s and into the early 1970s. In 1966, 48 percent of Hesston sales were made through company-owned units serving thirty-six states. In 1967, the review of operations stated: "In recent years Hesston's marketing and product strategy has been to match specialized products to specialized market opportunities. This marketing policy has led to the addition of such product lines as cotton harvesters, sugar beet harvesters, and hay-handling wagons—all of which are specialized and limited to regional markets. With the company's development of a more effective nation-wide distribution system, its capabilities allow for consideration of products for broader markets and greater potential dollar volume. However, Hesston will, as it has in the past, continue to give careful consideration to expansion possibilities in new models and options for the existing product lines."

EXHIBIT I DIRECTORS AND OFFICERS, HESSTON CORPORATION

DIRECTORS	1966	'67	'68	'69	'70	'71	'72	'73	'74	'75
L. E. Yost	—	—	—	—	—	—	—	—	—	—
H. P. Dyck	—	—	—	—	—	—	—	—	—	—
R. C. Schlichting	—	—	—	—	—	—	—	—	—	—
C. G. Stutzman	—	—	—	—	—	—	—	—	—	—
W. C. Claassen	—	—	—	—	—	—	—	—	—	—
J. Siemens, Jr.		—	—	—	—	—	—	—	—	—
R. A. Adee		—	—	—	—	—	—	—	—	—
E. L. Melcher		—	—	—	—	—	—	—	—	—
L. T. Smith		—	—	—	—					
George Reuland			—	—	—	—	—	—	—	—
Keith Wood					—					
O. C. Jensen							—	—	—	—
H. L. Brenneman									—	—
R. F. Hardlicka									—	—

EXECUTIVES	1966	'67	'68	'69	'70	'71	'72	'73	'74	'75
L. E. Yost, President	—	—	—	—	—	—	—	—	—	—
H. P. Dyck, Vice Pres. & Director of Sales	—	—								
Vice Pres.			—	—						
R. C. Schlichting, Secretary-Treas. & Director of Finance	—	—	—	—						
Treasurer & Vice Pres. Finance					—	—	—	—		
Vice Pres. Finance									—	
Senior Vice Pres.										—
J. Siemens, Director of Industrial Relations	—	—	—	—						
Vice Pres. Industrial Relations					—	—	—	—		
Vice Pres. Administration									—	
Senior Vice Pres.										—
L. T. Smith, Director of Marketing Development	—	—	—	—						
Vice Pres. Marketing					—					
E. L. Melcher, Director of Manufacturing	—	—	—	—						
Vice Pres. Manufacturing					—	—	—			
Vice Pres. Diversified Products								—	—	—
R. A. Adee, Director of Engineering	—	—	—	—						
Vice Pres. Engineering					—	—	—			
Vice Pres. Corporate Engineering								—	—	—
R. F. Hardlicka, Secretary					—	—				
Vice Pres. Legal & Secretary							—			
Vice Pres. General Counsel & Secretary								—	—	
Senior Vice Pres.										—
M. H. Voth, Assistant Treasurer					—	—	—			
Assistant Treasurer & Assistant Secretary								—		

Corporate Treasurer		—	
Vice Pres.			—
F. S. Depew, Vice Pres. Marketing	—		
Vice Pres. & General Manager Farm Equipment		————	
H. L. Brenneman, Vice Pres. Divisional Operations	—		
Group Vice Pres. North American Operations		———	
President & Chief Officer			—
H. Hershberger, Corporate Controller		———	

In 1966, after having dominated the straw-chopper market, negotiations were completed to manufacture adaptations of this attachment for each major manufacturer of appropriate equipment, so that Hesston straw choppers might be sold as original equipment or as additions to the equipment of other manufacturers under other trade names. By the end of 1967 it was reported that accounts to original equipment manufacturers had grown to 30 percent of sales. It was then decided to discontinue most of the straw-chopper sales through Hesston outlets in favor of direct sales of major combine manufacturers.

However, the year 1967 was a disappointing year with extended drought in the farm areas resulting in limited purchases of farm equipment. This change in market conditions was not apparent until late in the year and adjustment of production was difficult in the industry. Excess inventory and start-up costs at the Logan plant resulted in a loss there, and production was then limited until new products could be developed for that facility. At that time, domestic sales were made through five Hesston branches and ten independent farm implement distributors who also carried other brands of farm equipment. International sales by Hesston were increased 61 percent from the previous year, including both products manufactured abroad and those shipped abroad.

Growth in sales brought the total to $25 million in 1967, almost ten times sales of ten years earlier. Distribution planning continued to emphasize the importance of retail implement dealers, providing them with product knowledge and supporting their sales efforts with advertising and direct mail to customers. Insistence on quality of manufacture was rewarded by customer endorsement as reflected in used-equipment sales at prices above the prices listed in the dealer association's price guide.

Annual sales growth at Hesston had fluctuated from increases of 15 percent to 69 percent during a period of ten years and during the most recent five years averaged a 21 percent increase. In 1968, sales increased only 8.4 percent and consolidated net income fell from $1.1 million in 1967 to 0.7 million. The president issued the following statement at the end of that year: "The major factors contributing to the decrease in earnings were higher capacity costs and the modifications required on the model 600 and PT10 windrowers. These expenditures were made in keeping with the company's policy to make complete and thorough modifications in situations such as this in order to enhance the company's image and its customer relations even though the costs adversely affect current earnings."

Continued expansion was anticipated however, along with some new personnel, new products, new distribution facilities, and new capital. On July 2, 1968, 300,000 shares of common stock were sold to the public, opening the company to public ownership for the first time.

In 1969, sales returned to a more normal increase of 16.8 percent and this resulted in a net earnings per share increase of about 50 percent. Approximately half of the sales increase resulted from the purchase of Wood Brothers Manufacturing Co., whose sales totaled about $5.5 million in 1969. Its product line included rotary mowers, flail choppers, and minimum tillage tools. The industrial and residential sales of mowers was a first step in the program of diversification for Hesston. This move into the light-industrial and consumer-good market was seen as a significant new market potential for the firm. Other acquisitions and new products were being studied at the end of that year.

Overseas sales in 1969 increased by 22 percent, making possible a fair profit in the Italian subsidiary, in contrast to the three previous years of operating losses. Prospects were good for recovery of the balance of the previous losses during 1970, and that year did result in another increase in sales of 17 percent overseas, $880,610 of which came from Hesston, S. p. A., the Udine, Italy, subsidiary.

Also in keeping with the policy of diversification and the acquisition of profitable growth companies, Hesco, a local designer and manufacturer of office furniture, was acquired for cash in November 1971. Hesco was a new company (four years old) producing one-half million dollars in volume at that time. It was said to have good management as well as good growth and profit potential.

Hesston had a good year in 1972, with corporate sales up 36 percent from 1971 and net income up 64 percent. The basic reasons for this success were given as enthusiastic customer acceptance of new products and a strong agricultural market during the year. Production had reached the limits of plant capacity and construction was begun on a new 86,000-square-foot assembly building at the Hesston plant. This added capacity was designed to double production capacity of hay-handling equipment. Plans were also made to expand office and manufacturing facilities in 1973 to meet the needs of several years to come. Capital expenditures were increased from $850,000 in 1971 to $2,750,000 in 1972 and planned to total $5,750,000 at the various facilities in 1973.

Two new companies were purchased for cash in 1972 when the Waste Disposal Division was created. The Goder Company of Chicago and McNaulin of Milwaukee were seen as complementing firms in production and marketing of solid-waste-disposal equipment. Then, in November 1972, 62 percent of the stock of Rochland S. A., a farm equipment manufacturing company based in western France, was also acquired for cash. Rochland had been producing Hesston farm equipment under license for several years, and plans were set to manufacture much of Hesston's forage harvester equipment for Europe and Africa at the Rochland plant.

The marketing organization was strengthened in 1972 by the formation of the Marketing Research Department and by the addition of several key people with extensive experience in the farm-equipment industry. The marketing planning and product management functions were strengthened in an effort to make the entire company more responsive to the needs of farmers and ranchers.

Through the company-owned distribution system, the number of franchised dealers was increasing steadily and acceptance by customers of the one-man hay-handling system increased the volume for each dealer. A dealer development program was undertaken in 1972 in which Hesston dealers were brought by company aircraft to the home office for an exchange of information and ideas between dealers and Hesston personnel. Also in this year, a retail sales and service center was formed in the highly productive farming area of the Magic Valley of the Snake River in Idaho. This retail center was an experiment in marketing to determine the feasibility of this type of distribution for Hesston farm products.

The year 1972 was the twenty-fifth year of operation and sales exceeded $50 million for the first time. This was an increase of 36 percent from 1971 sales and almost all products were included in the sales increase. Hay-handling equipment led the way, and all sales increases were made at 1971 prices.

At the end of 1972, management issued the following evaluation: "A glance at Hesston's performance during fiscal 1972 shows that record levels were achieved. Sales were ahead of forecast—field inventories were at all-time low levels—new horizons in growth and expansion through diversification were achieved and the year ended on a high note of satisfaction. This enthusiasm will carry into 1973 with equal momentum. The agricultural economy in North America is well balanced and in excellent condition. There are new indications that the worldwide agricultural market is continuing to expand. Hesston is responding to the international market with an expanded sales thrust while increasing our manufacturing capability in Europe. We expect that our international market will grow at a rate equal to our domestic market."

In May 1973, Hesston offered another 350,000 shares of common stock to the public and received $6,912,328 net for the offering. These funds were used primarily for construction and for equipping of new facilities at a cost of $8,976,850 for the year, about 50 percent more than was announced a year earlier for 1973. The sale of these shares to the public qualified Hesston for listing on the New York Stock Exchange and the company was listed in August. Plans were then announced for additional plant expansions in 1974 amounting to $11 million. Dividends were also increased for the second consecutive year.

During the fiscal year 1973, Hesston acquired or completed negotiations for the purchase of four new companies. In December 1972, Field Queen, Inc., of Maize, Kansas, one of the largest manufacturers of self-propelled forage harvesters, was acquired. In July 1973, Val-Jac, a manufacturer of waste-handling equipment, also located in Maize, was acquired. Its products strengthened the Waste Equipment Division product line. In October 1973, the Danuser Machine Works of Claremore, Oklahoma, was purchased. Several product lines from the Farm Equipment Division at Hesston were scheduled for transfer to the Danuser Division to complement the farm and industrial equipment being manufactured and sold there. The final acquisition for the year was the planning of the purchase of the remaining 38 percent of the stock of Rochland S. A., the French subsidiary.

At the close of 1973, the following statement was made by the president: "We are carefully tracking the agricultural economy and the business environment worldwide. Never during the twenty-six-year history of our company has the outlook been more positive. Inventories are at a lower percentage of sales than at any time in the last several years, and worldwide demand increases faster than our capability to increase the supply."

In 1974, sales increased 58 percent to another new record of over $154 million and net income increased by 34 percent to a record $8,250,435. Cash dividends were again raised to 10-cent per quarter. International sales exceeded $2 million and represented 13 percent of total revenues, an increase of 86 percent over 1973 international sales. Capital expenditures for plant and equipment reached $16.5 million, again 50 percent above the amount announced at the beginning of the year. Substantial new production capacity was put into use, particularly in the Farm Equipment Division, where demand for agricultural equipment had exceeded production capacity for many years.

At the annual meeting on January 20, 1975, Yost, now chairman of the board, made the following assessment: "We're optimistic about the balance of 1975. Orders from dealers have been received for about 90 percent of the farm equipment production planned for fiscal 1975. The 1975 first quarter retail sales were very close to being on target even though some softening appeared during December—please note these are retail sales. Since the first of January retail has again picked up and it's our consensus that farmers will be buying new machinery to harvest the increased acreage of crops which most of them have planted or are planning to plant in 1975.

"We entered the year with dealer inventories of our products at a very low level. Should any softness in retail appear, it would help only to correct the low dealer inventories, which we consider too low for proper distribution and market penetration of our products."

The second factor of successful business management referred to by Brenneman in January 1975 was market penetration. This, it appears, was achieved at that time, and he made the observation that, "A strong position in the North American markets has been achieved. We are on the threshold of duplicating this around the world. Our marketing network must be strengthened by providing better customer services, training, and product distribution. We must continually make better products in terms of quality and useful lines. Expansion of Hesston's distribution in Europe, Australia, South America, and the Middle and Far East is a must."

MANUFACTURING CAPACITY

Brenneman's third key-essential to the meeting of corporate objectives was plant facilities "that will allow us the flexibility to produce the products efficiently." He concluded that the company was in an "excellent competitive position to do just that. . . . Continual plant expansion and modifications are occurring worldwide to achieve this goal. Extra emphasis is being placed on procurement of materials in plant and industrial engineering to lower the cost of the end product."

Hesston production over the years was irregular in quantity and frequently inconvenienced by inadequate capacity. In 1966, multiple shifts were being used and duties transferred between plants in an attempt to regularize work flows. In 1967, manufacturing space of 75,600 square feet was added at the Hesston plant while the newly constructed plant at Logan, Utah, operated only until July and was closed for an undetermined period. New products for manufacture at the Logan plant were actively sought.

Efforts to improve efficiency were continuous and some savings were claimed in 1967. Scrap losses and rejected parts were reduced and warranty costs on the products sold were reduced more than 50 percent compared to net sales. It was in that year that the machine-shop workload scheduling was computerized in an effort to improve manpower and machine scheduling. Other applications were planned for the computer in manufacturing. The computer itself was replaced in 1968 and programming then included a complete shop workload and scheduling system.

In 1969, another 60,000 square feet of floor space was added to the Hesston plant. This steel fabrication facility was designed to include material handling by conveyors with capacity of 20 tons to move all types of steel and components from the point of delivery to the various points of preparation, storage and fabrication. Mechanization of this kind was considered necessary due to the increasing size and sophistication of the products being manufactured. However, in 1970 the production of the StakMover 60 and the StakFeeder 60 were moved to the Logan plant to help relieve the heavy production schedule at the Hesston, Kansas, facility. All beet and potato-harvesting equipment remained at the Logan plant.

While not all capital expenditures were made for production space and facilities, the financial statements include a summary of additions to property, plant, and equipment, which grew from over $1 million in 1965 to over $16.5 million in 1974, most of which was for production purposes.

PERSONNEL AND INDUSTRIAL RELATIONS

The fourth factor cited by Brenneman as a key to success was "the people side of our business. Today we have excellent employees in every phase of our business around the world." There were times, however, when the availability of skilled labor posed a difficult problem and it still remains a major consideration in location decisions. The following table shows the progression in number of employees in recent years.

1959	390	1967	1080
1960	400	1968	1260
1961	430	1969	1330
1962	450	1970	1403
1963	520	1971	1271
1964	560	1972	1484
1965	700	1973	2490
1966	1050	1974	4359

The policy of the company to locate plants in rural communities has caused various comments over the years. In 1966 the president said: "An unusual effort was necessary to achieve this additional build-up of personnel because of a local manpower shortage. An adverse effect of the present manpower shortage is inefficiency and an increased rate of turnover. This, unfortunately, adversely affects both plant capacity and production costs." The next year he again pointed to the problem but said, "A labor supply of good-quality personnel continues to be available, even though it is difficult to accomplish any rapid build-up in the work force since there is only a limited reserve supply from which to draw." However, in 1969 the company reported that good-quality applicants were available at the rate of employee turnover. Management continued to report its satisfaction with the qualities of a stable rural community in each of its locations, high standards of workmanship, and excellent safety records.

The company has maintained an active and well-developed personnel and industrial relations program since its early years. In 1966, when the number of employees first reached 1,000, management development and supervisory training programs were being expanded and coordinated to facilitate in-company training for personnel from the pre-supervisory level through executive levels. Efforts were begun to improve communications and employee relations throughout the company. The employees' deferred-compensation profit-sharing program was modified to include payments based on the entire results for parent and subsidiary firms combined. Efforts were also being made to include subordinate management people in the decision-making process for the purposes of improved decision making, training, and morale.

Employee relations at the Hesston plants have been peaceful over the years and employee organizations at the major plants have not been affiliated with national labor organizations. The community of Hesston, 35 miles north of Wichita, Kansas, is a quiet farming community with clean, up-to-date facilities. Many of the people are Mennonite and Yost has been a director of the Mennonite Economic Development Associates, along with many other important offices. M. H. Voth, vice president, made the following comments about the nature of the workers at the home plant: "We are most fortunate in this area of the country. Many of our first employees were farmers, used to doing a day's work for a day's pay. That philosophy has carried through to our present capable work force. A visitor summed it up by saying, 'People in this shop seem to know what they are doing and are about doing it.'"

Richard Huxman, a farmer who joined Hesston twenty years earlier, was, in 1975, manager of manufacturing at the Hesston plant. He made the following comments to illustrate the relationship with employees.

> We realize that a company is only as good as its people. We pay wages that are comparable to wages in this area. Our top management people meet with officers of our independent union every other week and discuss possible problem areas.
>
> We have a five-day orientation program for new employees. A training manager and two training secretaries handle the course. It starts with classroom sessions where we cover everything from safety, policy, procedures, insurance programs, and the products we manufacture. They see the product and promotional films so they know what is being sold and how it's used. They have films on the areas where they will work and get a look at their supervisors before they even meet them.
>
> Three-and-a-half days are spent in the classroom and three afternoons are used for touring the plant, looking at parts they will be handling and seeing how the machines are assembled. At the end of their first week on the job, they fill out a critique sheet which is evaluated at the end of the month.

Huxman also said that the shortage of labor (unemployment in Harvey County was 1.3 percent at that time) had caused them to start hiring women for factory work some time ago. "We now have about 70 women in the plant and we are most pleased with their performance. Many of them are doing welding and similar work."

Employees are represented by the Hesston Corporation Workers Association. Three-year contracts have been the custom for a number of years and they usually provided for a wage increase during each of the years covered by a contract period. The 1967 Annual Statement included a comment that "all of this was done in keeping with the policy of paying wages and salaries above the average of those paid by related industries in the area." New contracts were negotiated in 1967, 1970, and 1973, each time with harmonious relationships. The scheduled wage increases agreed upon for October 1, 1971, could not be implemented due to the national wage-price freeze and assurances were given and accepted that the pay increases would be implemented when the controls permitted.

When labor contracts expired in 1973, it was not practical to include all employees under a single contract. Differences were recognized when the Farm Equipment Division headquartered at Hesston negotiated another three-year contract with increases in wages and benefits which were consistent with guidelines established by the Cost of Living Council, and employees of the Waste Equipment Division headquartered in the Chicago area signed a different two-year contract.

FINANCE AND PROFITS

The final key to good business management, according to Brenneman, was profits—a level adequate to satisfy stockholders and to finance corporate growth objectives. These are not always compatible objectives, for stockholders frequently seek safety and dividends when rapid growth involves some risks and retention of earnings to finance growth. The management of Hesston demonstrated early their understanding of these needs and their willingness to assume risks by paying no dividends until 1966 and by the use of leverage to improve the return on equity at that time. The rate of return on total capital employed was good but was becoming increasingly difficult to maintain with rising capital investment requirements dictated by technological advances throughout the industry.

Sales and profits in 1967 were below expectations due to lower farm income and adverse weather conditions in many states. Dividends were kept low to allow 80 percent of net earnings to be retained and re-employed in the business. Earnings were not sufficient, however, to provide adequate working capital to finance the higher level of receivables and inventories and the accelerated tax payment schedule due to suspension of the investment credit by Congress. Seasonal bank loans were therefore used in larger amounts and for a greater portion of the year to supplement working capital. This resulted in increased interest expense. Other costs were added due to the use of term loan funds for the full year and to finance longer terms to dealers through Commercial Credit Equipment Corporation.

During 1968, the firm was recapitalized by changing 3 million shares of $1 par value common stock (Class A and Class B) to 3 million shares of $2 par value common stock. Outstanding shares were traded on a 1 for 2 basis so the dollar amounts of equity accounts were unchanged. The company then sold 300,000 shares to the public, resulting in net proceeds of $2,565,000 in new equity capital to Hesston. In the same year, long-term debt arrangements were renegotiated to increase borrowing from $2,600,000 to $5,600,000, one million to be received on June 30, 1968, and the remainder the following fiscal year. Repayment at $400,000 annually was scheduled to begin in 1970.

Consolidated sales for the year 1970 increased for the twelfth consecutive year but net earnings fell from $1,510,356 ($1.50 per share) in 1969 to $920,815 (92 cents per share) in 1970. A significant sales increase for 1970 did not materialize, and when this was determined extensive cost reduction efforts were undertaken. Inventories were also abnormally high at the beginning of the fiscal year, and efforts were instituted to reduce inventories for the remainder of the year and the subsequent period.

The amount of accounts receivable that customers had accumulated at the end of 1970 was considerably greater than a year earlier. During this year, the tight money situation resulted in a curtailment of the amount of sales being financed through independent finance companies and consequently it became necessary to finance a greater portion of the sales through open accounts. By the close of the 1970 fiscal year, Hesston had arranged for sales financing through several independent finance companies to avoid the problem of insufficient sales financing being available at peak sales periods.

HESSTON CORPORATION CONSOLIDATED INCOME STATEMENTS

	1965	1966	1967	1968	1969
Net Sales	16,516,645	21,863,045	25,093,575	26,926,951	36,661,247
Cost of Goods Sold	11,063,006	14,340,315	16,489,205	17,590,098	23,755,250
Gross Profit	5,453,639	7,522,730	8,604,370	9,336,853	12,905,997
Operating Expenses:					
Selling and marketing	1,784,959	2,455,456	2,659,225	3,528,248	3,696,926
General and administrative	1,330,523	1,787,499	2,165,470	2,271,622	3,567,159
Engineering, research & development	661,964	826,361	935,477	1,034,011	1,209,317
	3,777,446	5,069,316	5,760,172	6,833,881	8,473,402
Operating Profit	1,676,193	2,453,414	2,844,198	2,502,972	4,432,595
Other Deductions:					
Interest expense	169,598	341,267	660,373	842,602	1,313,131
Other expense	19,792	6,590	(23,405)	59,399	(21,001)
	189,390	347,857	639,968	902,001	1,292,130
Income Before Income Taxes	1,486,803	2,105,557	2,207,230	1,600,971	3,140,465
Provision for Income Taxes	717,445	1,073,000	1,036,000	822,000	1,667,982
Net Income	769,358	1,032,557	1,171,230	722,651	1,510,356
Net Income Per Dollar of Sales	4.7 %	4.7 %	4.7 %	4.5 %	4.1 %
Net Income Per Share (1965 Base)	1.11	1.49	1.67	.96	1.50
Dividends	—	136,610	140,060	262,800	326,388
Additions to Property, Plant & Equipment	1,145,435	1,499,996	1,781,561	1,402,265	1,770,451
Working Capital—Ending	1,819,316	4,080,196	3,763,206	7,320,271	9,551,579
Ratio CA/CL	1.6	2.0	1.5	3.0	2.9
Common Stock Equity	3,665,707	4,694,854	5,780,024	8,731,588	10,965,579
Book Value per Share	2.64	3.35	4.11	* 10.00	10.91
Depreciation	289,478	395,994	556,980	665,420	861,472

*Note recapitalization in 1968 and 50 percent stock dividend in 1972.

HESSTON CORPORATION CONSOLIDATED INCOME STATEMENTS (cont.)

	1970	*1971*	*1972*	*1973*	*1974*
Net Sales	39,078,763	41,807,859	56,846,077	98,215,327	154,881,383
Cost of Goods Sold	25,633,274	25,389,213	35,089,076	61,374,557	100,150,139
Gross Profit	13,445,489	16,418,646	21,757,001	36,840,770	54,731,244
Operating Expenses:					
Selling and marketing	4,706,285	5,187,714	6,604,548	9,807,578	13,453,903
General and administrative	3,643,292	3,956,193	5,336,160	9,508,551	16,064,444
Engineering, research & development	1,278,339	1,303,417	1,729,039	2,453,434	3,715,826
	9,627,916	10,447,324	13,669,747	21,769,563	33,234,173
Operating Profit	3,817,573	5,971,322	8,087,254	15,071,207	21,497,071
Other Deductions:					
Interest expense	1,924,121	2,672,543	2,714,014	3,405,437	6,292,874
Other expense	(88,389)	(58,644)	(22,563)	(161,862)	(224,471)
	1,835,732	2,613,899	2,691,451	3,243,575	6,068,403
Income Before Income Taxes	1,981,841	3,357,423	5,395,803	11,827,632	15,428,668
Provision for Income Taxes	1,061,026	1,678,074	2,636,384	5,650,708	7,178,233
Net Income	920,815	1,679,349	2,759,419	6,176,924	8,250,435
Net Income Per Dollar of Sales	2.4 %	4.0 %	4.9 %	6.3 %	5.3 %
Net Income Per Share (1965 Base)	.92	1.67	1.83	3.48	4.15
Dividends	402,127	402,127	402,127	479,057	636,079
Additions to Property, Plant & Equipment	1,668,542	554,817	3,320,921	9,634,877	16,582,685
Working Capital—Ending	10,401,110	12,859,388	13,495,386	18,788,729	41,866,479
Ratio CA/CL	2.1	3.1	2.3	1.9	2.0
Common Stock Equity	11,484,267	12,761,489	15,118,781	28,628,909	36,243,265
Book Value per Share	11.42	12.69	* 10.03	14.40	18.23
Depreciation	989,895	1,015,772	996,853	1,606,704	2,244,145

*Note recapitalization in 1968 and 50 percent stock dividend in 1972.

The long-term financial requirements of the company were reviewed in 1971. The need for additional financial arrangements was evident and with a generally favorable long-term market prevailing, a new long-term loan was negotiated with the insurance company. The new agreement provided for $3 million of additional funds, half of which would be received in 1971 and half in 1972. The total loan amount was $8 million at the rate of 7¾ percent and the old loan was to be paid with a portion of the proceeds.

A profitable year and the twenty-fifth anniversary of the company was the occasion for a 50 percent stock dividend in 1972, in addition to the regular distributions in cash. The stock dividend resulted in an additional 502,438 shares being distributed.

A new program of wholesale floor-planning by Hesston Industries, Ltd., was begun in 1972. Under this program, the Hesston sales subsidiary in Canada carried all its own receivables with the use of a credit line supplied by a Canadian bank. All machines sold to Hesston dealers in Canada were included in this financing. The change was made to reduce the high cost of sales financing in Canada. Floor-plan financing of sales to Hesston dealers in the U. S. continued through agreements with several independent sales finance companies at reasonable cost.

Several acquisitions were consummated in 1973. All new firms were purchased for cash with the exception of Field Queen, which was obtained on a pooling of interests basis for 129,987 shares of Hesston common stock. The 62 percent interest in Rochland S. A. was acquired for $600,000; Val-Jac for $200,000; and Danuser for $3,600,000.

Although profit margins narrowed somewhat in 1974, the trend of Hesston profitability was favorable when viewed over a longer period. During the ten years ended in 1974, sales grew at a compounded annual rate of 25 percent and profits increased by an annual average of 27 percent. Late in 1974 the company negotiated a 10¾ percent, fifteen-year loan of $35 million from Prudential Insurance Company. Of that amount, $20 million was used to refund the existing loan and the balance was to be used to finance capital expansion programs, reduce short-term debt, and provide a higher level of working capital in support of expanding operations.

At the annual stockholders' meeting on January 20, 1975, the stockholders approved a proposal that authorized the board of directors to issue a class of preferred stock consisting of two million shares of $2 par value, with other terms to be fixed by the Board.

1975 AND CHANGE

At a presentation before the New York Society of Security Analysts on May 21, 1975, Yost included these comments:

> Net farm income dropped from the all-time high of $32.2 billion in 1973 to $26.5 billion last year. There is some pretty persuasive talk around that net farm income will be down again in 1975—perhaps to about $23 billion. This will occur, in our opinion, while cash farm receipts are rising to an all-time high of close to $100 billion. Two weeks ago, when Congress was attempting to override the President's veto of the farm bill, there was talk of even lower net farm income.
>
> The Department of Commerce, however, is optimistic about farm machinery shipments. They are forecasting that the industry at factory level will ship about $6.2 billion versus $5.9 billion in 1974—about a 9 percent increase. Of course, a good part of the dollar

gain may be attributable to inflationary price increases, but perhaps not as severe as in the past two years.

Our strategy is to anticipate market opportunities instead of responding to them. This product strategy is relayed to all our divisions and is an integral part of our forward planning.

Ray Schlichting, senior vice president—finance made the following report.

It's no secret that corporations, in the past few years, have been facing extreme difficulties related to reliance upon the capital markets for funds to support corporate growth. Indeed, I'm certain there have been many lost expansion opportunities because companies deemed it imprudent to grasp those opportunities without proper financing—no matter how profitable the promise of such expanded operations appeared.

Fortunately, throughout the good times and the pressure times, Hesston Corporation has been able to assemble the financial resources required of a company growing from the $30 million sales level in 1967–68 to the $155 million sales peak of last year. Believe me, there have been days in the past few years when we weren't too certain about our ability to obtain the needed funds. However, we did succeed when we needed to, but most notably last year, our capital funds acquisitions did leave us quite heavily leveraged with term debt. . . .

As a result of the 1974 financing, our debt-to-equity ratio rose to about 1 to 1, a higher level than was considered desirable and twice as high as existed during the prior five-year period when the ratio was generally around .5 to 1. . . . In March 1975 we successfully completed an equity financing involving the sale of 500,000 shares of convertible preferred stock, which netted the company about $11.7 million. Five million was utilized immediately to reduce intermediate-term debt and the balance was added to working capital. This has not only provided us with additional resources to finance profitable growth through 1976, but has substantially improved our liquidity and financial strength. As a result, our debt to equity ratio now stands at a more acceptable .7 to 1.

We also feel that we have adequate seasonal borrowing capabilities with the unsecured lines arranged with our banks. Moreover, while current arrangements for sales financing are adequate for fiscal 1975, plans are currently being implemented to gradually develop a captive finance company beginning in fiscal 1976 to provide for an increasing portion of sales financing in the future.

At the same meeting, Brenneman added these comments:

Our profitability is up for a number of reasons. First, the labor supply, the shortage of which plagued us in 1974, has become adequate in all operating divisions. Second, raw materials, which were in short supply in 1974, are freeing up, and we are monitoring quotations and pushing for better buys. In addition, we are actively engaged in inventory monitoring and making reductions to meet our turn objectives. Third, our 1975 price lists reflect all known cost increases, and, with few exceptions, margins are expected to be satisfactory. Fourth, we are working hard on production efficiency with an objective of a minimum of 10 percent improvement—and we are on target. Production efficiency has top priority in all of our operations. We believe that if the inflation spiral is to be stopped, it must begin with us. We are striving to keep prices in line through production efficiencies, rather than merely passing along costs imposed on us by our suppliers.

We should mention to you that the current year is one in which dealer inventories in our industry are being filled to normal levels. Unlike many industries, our dealer inventories going into 1975 were at a near, all-time low . . . completely unsatisfactory for Hesston to

> obtain the share of market we strive to achieve. It may be of more than passing interest to some of you that one of the methods we have used for years to achieve out-of-season retail sales during the winter months and to obtain greater market penetration is a "check from the factory" or "cashback," which has been so widely used by the automotive industry lately. The big difference in our plan is that we send the farmer a check for buying pre-season in the amount it would normally cost in interest to floor plan the equipment until the use season . . . rather than as a "distress sale" gimmick. Our plan has made us money and put the equipment in the hands of customers months earlier at a saving.
>
> With inventories getting back to a more normal level and equipment shortages on dealer lots being a thing of the past, we can anticipate a return by farmers to the traditional seasonal pattern of purchasing equipment immediately prior to and during the use season. We at Hesston are geared to slug it out at retail worldwide because we can specialize in our product lines. Our main competitors diffuse their efforts among tractors, combines, and huge volume of conventional equipment and have to give secondary emphasis to specialized products of our field.

The drought in 1974 and the resulting inflation of grain prices occurred when livestock numbers and meat supplies were at record highs. The meat supplies were augmented by large numbers of livestock being finished to relatively heavy weights on high grain rations. As grain prices shot upwards in 1974 and feeding margins plummeted at the heavy weights, marketings increased substantially to drive prices of livestock downward. Due to shorter feeding periods and/or reproduction cycles, supply adjustments occur more rapidly in certain classes of livestock.

In January 1975, at Hesston's annual meeting, Pioneer Seed Company, the world's largest hybrid seed company, reported that compared to a year ago there were only 90 percent as many chickens, 90 percent as many hogs, 70 percent as many cattle on feed of grain-finishing rations, but 105 percent as many cattle available as compared to the previous year. As a result, incomes to the cow-calf and subsequent feeder cattle producers were reduced more in amount and durations than that of other livestock producers. Losses per calf were running at one-half the production costs.

Ken Monfort, president of Monfort of Colorado, reportedly operating the largest feedlots in the world, spoke at the meeting also. He stated that losses in the feedlot business in the previous seventeen months had been astronomical—in the neighborhood of four to five billion dollars. And now these losses were being passed on to the range cattle producer as indicated by feeder cattle costs being only half of what they were the previous year. The result to the rancher was a reduction in revenue per cow of 50 percent. Monfort predicted that within four years, the rancher and the feeder would have a profitable industry again.

By early September 1975 the cattle industry was showing signs of a more rapid adjustment than normal and perhaps an earlier recovery. While slaughter numbers of cattle were breaking all-time weekly highs, a drastic reduction in slaughter weights and yields of meat per animal was resulting in shortages of fresh dressed meat at the current prices. During the last week of August, record amounts of frozen beef were reported to be moving out of storage. Confidence was returning to the beef industry, resulting in higher prices both for grain-fed animals and for feeder cattle and calves, the primary products of the producers who use hay and forage equipment.

The third-quarter report for Hesston was issued September 2, 1975. Selected statements from that and previous quarterly reports are attached. In it, Hesston con-

EXHIBIT 3 SELECTED STATEMENTS FROM QUARTERLY REPORTS, HESSTON CORPORATION

	Quarter Ending		*Quarter Ending*		*Quarter Ending*	
	Dec 1974	*Dec 1973*	*Mar 1975*	*Mar 1974*	*June 1975*	*June 1974*
Sales	47,640,079	32,723,168	52,475,776	36,415,470	65,485,000	44,985,000
Net Income	2,387,725	1,546,789	3,104,342	2,046,833	3,612,000	2,689,000
Net Income per Share	1.20	.78	1.54	1.03	1.72	1.35
Shares Outstanding	1,987,747	1,987,747	1,987,747	1,987,747	1,987,747	1,987,747
	Accumulated:		*6 Months*		*9 Months*	
			1975	*1974*	*1975*	*1974*
Sales			100,115,855	69,138,638	165,601,000	114,124,000
Net Income			5,492,067	3,593,622	9,104,000	6,282,000
Net Income per Share			2.74	1.81	4.46	3.16
Shares Outstanding			1,987,747	1,987,747	1,987,747	1,987,747

EXHIBIT 4 HESSTON CORPORATION CONSOLIDATED BALANCE SHEET, SEPT 30

	1965	*1966*	*1967*	*1968*
Current Assets:				
Cash	30,481	145,306	552,958	309,839
Marketable securities	—	—	—	—
Accounts receivable	1,227,742	2,210,338	3,100,563	4,411,046
Inventories	3,252,664	5,695,332	7,068,008	6,174,508
Prepaid expenses	120,449	105,137	99,661	158,789
Total Current Assets	4,631,336	8,156,113	10,791,190	11,054,182
Other Assets	106,062	149,999	307,749	348,022
Property, plant and equipment (cost)				
Land	114,575	112,896	163,611	219,235
Buildings	1,433,239	2,234,075	3,011,862	3,373,912
Machinery and equipment	1,307,526	1,795,816	2,462,604	2,949,439
Office furniture and fixtures	296,117	372,461	493,895	518,305
Automobiles and trucks	159,731	205,302	203,628	292,820
	3,311,188	4,720,550	6,362,600	7,353,711
Less accumulated depreciation	1,045,697	1,414,283	1,917,079	2,482,916
Net Plant and Equipment	2,265,491	3,306,267	4,445,512	4,870,795
Total Assets	7,002,889	11,612,379	15,544,460	16,272,999
Current Liabilities:				
Notes payable to banks	597,500	218,668	4,204,854	1,050,000
Accounts payable	859,044	1,644,390	975,017	1,501,397
Accrued sales discounts & allowances	—	—	—	—
Federal and state income taxes	510,411	805,500	478,189	27,927
Accrued payroll and profit sharing	438,497	670,443	618,724	525,853
Other accrued liabilities	378,014	509,362	639,044	601,180
Long-term debt payable in one year	28,554	227,554	228,054	27,554
Total Current Liabilities	2,812,020	4,075,917	7,143,882	3,733,911
Long-Term Debt Payable after One Year				
Notes payable to bank	—	—	—	1,000,000
Notes payable to insurance co.	260,000	2,600,000	2,400,000	2,600,000
Other notes and mortgages	28,662	19,108	9,554	—
Subordinated debenture bonds	236,500	222,500	211,000	207,500
	525,162	2,841,608	2,620,554	3,807,500
Deferred Tax	—	—	—	—
Minority Interest	—	—	—	—
Stockholders Equity				
Common stock	1,373,600	1,391,200	1,397,200	1,745,700
Capital in excess of par value	—	165,000	213,600	2,416,813
Retained earnings	2,292,107	3,138,054	4,169,224	4,569,075
Total Stockholders Equity	3,665,707	4,694,854	5,780,024	8,731,588
Total Liabilities and Equity	7,002,889	11,612,379	15,544,460	16,272,999

1969	*1970*	*1971*	*1972*	*1973*	*1974*
567,622	585,734	824,528	1,714,143	1,734,004	6,429,950
—	—	—	750,000	—	—
5,806,449	8,267,892	5,836,035	7,874,879	11,078,765	19,740,809
7,889,869	10,518,877	12,223,330	13,245,827	25,894,717	56,337,941
226,044	278,335	215,888	194,422	223,899	483,692
14,489,984	19,650,838	19,099,781	23,779,271	38,931,385	82,992,392
492,648	381,695	452,257	862,496	1,398,829	1,337,685
242,039	242,039	241,139	368,693	653,644	854,017
4,291,042	5,411,873	5,452,186	7,287,680	12,125,720	19,051,469
4,165,534	4,699,748	5,093,324	6,174,349	10,630,063	18,119,950
660,615	752,051	810,731	1,013,524	1,263,333	1,941,942
425,041	487,423	550,571	634,626	1,093,359	1,552,089
9,784,291	11,593,134	12,147,951	15,478,872	25,766,119	41,519,467
3,985,226	4,915,326	5,735,886	6,629,697	8,717,083	10,648,997
5,799,045	6,677,808	6,412,065	8,849,175	17,049,036	30,870,470
20,781,677	26,710,341	25,964,103	33,490,942	57,379,250	115,200,547
—	3,568,427	—	941,132	3,270,699	16,374,388
1,524,724	1,569,116	1,706,771	2,310,347	5,859,258	11,636,058
—	2,050,232	1,306,589	1,908,333	1,181,032	1,937,906
854,190	194,124	691,273	960,714	2,565,341	2,820,318
1,096,366	920,567	1,432,017	2,448,276	4,704,603	5,399,534
1,311,625	495,762	676,243	883,411	1,917,215	2,795,528
151,500	451,500	427,500	831,672	644,508	162,181
4,938,405	9,249,728	6,240,393	10,283,885	20,142,656	41,125,913
—	500,000	—	—	—	—
3,616,000	4,600,000	6,500,000	7,430,000	6,860,000	23,000,000
900,000	488,000	100,000	285,408	702,454	13,856,787
214,500	241,000	221,500	220,000	218,500	203,000
4,757,500	5,829,000	6,821,500	7,935,408	7,780,954	37,059,787
120,193	147,346	140,721	152,868	464,909	771,582
—	—	—	—	361,822	—
2,010,644	2,010,644	2,010,644	2,010,644	3,975,494	3,975,494
2,386,443	2,386,443	2,386,443	2,386,443	7,636,414	7,636,414
6,568,492	7,087,180	8,364,402	10,721,694	17,017,001	24,631,357
10,965,579	11,484,267	12,761,489	15,118,781	28,628,909	36,243,265
20,781,677	26,710,341	25,964,103	33,490,942	57,379,250	115,200,547

tinued to report increased sales and earnings and the board declared an increase of 100 percent in the quarterly dividend, bringing it to 20 cents per common share. The regular cash dividend of 40 cents was also declared on preferred. Sales for the first nine months of 1975 fiscal year rose 45 percent and net income increased from $3.16 to $4.46 per share and the following statement was issued: "The exceptionally strong third quarter assures us that our objective of over $200 million sales for the entire fiscal year will be met. Most operating divisions are expected to be on target by the end of the year. However, we have lowered production schedules of farm machinery in the fourth quarter to eliminate further buildup of field inventories going into the new fiscal year. Consequently, we are anticipating net income for the fourth quarter to be moderately lower than initially planned. We are continuing to move at full speed on new-product development and are viewing fiscal 1976 with considerable optimism, fully anticipating a more favorable market for beef and milk producers, as well as a respectable net farm income that will create a continued receptive climate."

In the August 21, 1975 issue of *The Wall Street Journal*, John Deere Co. reported a relatively modest rise in earnings for its third quarter ended July 31, 1975, and reported expectations for the fourth-quarter profit to decline from year earlier levels. Sales for the third quarter were up 14 percent and profits increased 6.2 percent. These third-quarter results were much lower than earnings increases in the first and second quarters of the current fiscal year of 29 percent and 36 percent respectively.

Deere indicated that expected lower demand for industrial equipment, cotton harvesting equipment, hay machinery, and consumer products will contribute to the lower earnings in the fourth quarter. They also cited higher interest, material and labor costs, and "costs associated with capital expenditure programs" as causes. For the nine months, retail demand for large tractors and combines continued to be strong and field inventories in these two products were still considered below desirable levels.

At the time of this announcement by Deere, the common stock of Hesston was selling at $26 on the New York Exchange. Hesston shares immediately lost 3 points and leveled out at about 23. Six days later, under the date August 27, 1975, Hesston issued the following announcement.

> Hesston Corporation President Howard L. Brenneman today announced a reduction in the Hesston Division labor force which would affect up to 250 employees at the main plant at Hesston. Effective Sept. 2, 1975, 125 employees will be put on layoff with a similar size reduction scheduled in mid September. After the layoff Hesston Division employment will be 1850 employees, compared with approximately 2000 a year ago. Worldwide employment of the Hesston Corporation is nearly 4300.
>
> "We regret that the cyclical nature of the farm-equipment industry has forced us to this decision to reduce the Hesston Division work force," Brenneman stated. "Reduced industry retail sales have resulted in a buildup of dealer inventories. Consequently, production schedules are being lowered during the fourth quarter of this fiscal year."
>
> "We are optimistic, however, that fiscal 1976 (the year beginning Oct. 1) will be a year of economic recovery for the farm equipment industry and we are hopeful that an improved market for Hesston products will allow us to recall those employees affected by this reduction."

This news release was quoted in an article in *The Wall Street Journal* on September 3, 1975. The next day *The Wall Street Journal* carried a report from

EXHIBIT 5 INVENTORIES LOWER OF COST OR MARKET (FIFO)

	Total	*Finished Goods*	*Parts*	*Work in Process*	*Raw Materials*
1966	5,695,332	2,306,876	715,221	1,223,864	1,449,371
1967	7,068,008	3,286,559	742,878	1,207,119	1,831,452
1968	6,174,508	1,932,509	884,939	1,872,488	1,524,572
1969	7,889,869	2,917,488	1,225,775	1,569,861	2,176,745
1970	10,518,877	3,487,364	2,030,459	1,794,666	3,206,388
1971	12,223,330	4,190,331	2,207,184	2,486,803	3,339,012
1972	13,245,827	4,602,946	2,509,360	2,609,630	3,523,891
1973	25,894,717	7,298,811	4,697,411	6,454,068	7,444,427
1974	56,337,941	10,657,876	8,229,401	12,983,622	24,467,042

Massey-Ferguson that third-quarter results dated July 31 were at record highs with net income 34 percent ahead of one year earlier on sales of 41 percent higher. The president of Massey-Ferguson said, "For the remainder of 1975 the worldwide outlook for farm machinery and diesel engines remains strong and will require the company to produce at full capacity. . . . Our sales and income for the fiscal fourth quarter are expected to improve from a year before."

Hesston common stock closed at 22½ for the week ending September 5, 1975.

DIVERSIFIED TECHNOLOGY CORPORATION

During a period of about six years, Diversified Technology Corporation (DTC) has evolved from a tightly family owned and managed concern to a non-owner, professionally managed company with gross sales increasing from around $75 million a year to about $200 million. Corporate profitability has also increased significantly, but not as significantly as sales, and profitability performance has been quite erratic at times, even in recent years.

The stock of the corporation has been faced with a relatively low price-earnings ratio for some time, in spite of markedly improved financial performance. The founding family continues to own a clear majority of the outstanding shares of common stock and is represented on the board of directors, which is still chaired by a family member.

The founding family built a diversified corporation that has had and continues to have a very good reputation for its integrity and for several of its relatively high-technology product lines and types of software knowhow that it has developed internally or acquired. A very substantial amount of the firm's growth over the years has come through acquisitions. DTC continues to be overdiversified in terms of its total volume of business, professional manpower, internal systems, and infrastructure and organization structure. One consultant working closely with DTC recently said that DTC's degree of product and service diversification suggests that it is a multi-billion-dollar corporation, while its distribution system and infrastructure suggests a $10 million or $20 million firm. Top management is now interested in getting out of some of the corporation's weaker businesses, but at the same time exploring and pursuing acquisitions and mergers that are synergistic and could significantly improve the firm's profitability.

DTC is in the following types of businesses, among others:

1. Various kinds of industrial gears, with high-speed gears being one of their strongest product lines. Such gears are used in turbines, petrochemical plants, and various kinds of industrial technology and operations.

Prepared by Professor Barry Richman of University of California, Los Angeles.

2. Various petroleum exploration and production products, some of a proprietary nature. They have both onshore and offshore products.
3. Various kinds of ship machinery, shipyard equipment, and technology relating to the shipbuilding industry, as well as marine architecture and a capability to do major turnkey projects in this sector.
4. Various kinds of products for the aviation and aerospace sector.
5. Various kinds of materials handling equipment.
6. Software services and turnkey management capability for the steel industry (especially relating to the design and construction of blast furnaces, soaking pits, and a new proprietary energy-saving steel-manufacturing process).
7. Business forms and commercial printing presses.
8. Powered work platforms used primarily in construction, shipbuilding, utilities, and the petrochemical sectors.

The company is organized on a product (or service) division basis, but there is considerable overlap, and interfacing is required with regard to some of the products produced in various divisions. On the other hand, management feels that not nearly as much synergy or economies are being derived from a number of different products as could be. It has recently been redivisionalizing and reorganizing divisions and other parts of the company to some extent, with the aim of improving efficiency and overall financial performance.

At the corporate headquarters in the Los Angeles area there is the president, several group vice presidents (each responsible for certain divisions), and functional vice presidents or managers in charge of such things as finance, marketing, production, engineering, procurement, and personnel. Most of these corporate functional managers do not exert much direct line authority over the product divisions, but rather act in an advisory staff and/or service capacity and exert some functional authority over certain policies and procedures.

The most notable exception is the marketing vice president, who is responsible for the corporation's field sales force, with regional and some other sales managers reporting to him. This sales force handles the sale of a majority of the company's products, with the others being handled by those divisions that have their own sales forces. Most of the divisions have their own marketing managers, and under them are product line managers who serve in staff positions as product coordinators and information centers, though in some cases they also exert power of their own. These marketing and product managers have reporting relationships both to divisional management and the marketing vice president.

The corporate vice president for marketing also has had primary responsibility for DTC's international marketing and sales, as well as many other aspects of the company's international business activities. A limited number of foreign sales and other personnel working abroad also report to this vice president. The corporation does not have an international division. This vice president is the newest member of the top management group, having joined the company less than two years ago.

In the last several years, about one-third of DTC's total sales have been derived from exports, and a somewhat higher percent of its total profits have been derived from foreign sales.

The corporation has had only two plants outside of the United States. One manufactures powered work platforms in the European Common Market, and the other is a low-cost production facility in Mexicali, Mexico that supplies various parts and other items to some of the firm's U. S. plants. DTC has been seriously exploring the possibility of a new plant in Ireland, as well as an acquisition or joint venture involving a relatively small western European turbine manufacturer that is involved in the aerospace-aviation industry. DTC has very recently acquired a West German printing-press firm and feels that this puts the company in a stronger competitive position with regard to its printing press (graphic arts) business. It is also felt that this acquisition will give DTC better access to markets in eastern Europe and possibly South America and elsewhere.

Most of the top managers of DTC have become convinced that the most profitable opportunities and/or greatest growth potential for a number of the firm's products and services are now and will increasingly continue to be outside the United States. At the same time, they feel that company exports of various products will be increasingly threatened by competitors who set up plants and offices or expand their existing operations in foreign countries where DTC has actual or potential markets for its products and services. As a result, it is felt that DTC must establish an on-going presence in countries in which potentially lucrative opportunities are identified.

Depending on the particular country, products and services, and other opportunities that are identified and analyzed, this could possibly involve wholly owned subsidiaries; majority or minority-owned joint ventures with private partners, local stockholders, or the host government; various kinds of production, marketing and/or supply arrangements not involving equity joint ventures per se; licensing agreements; technical and/or managerial service or assistance contracts; relatively long-term turnkey projects; new sales offices or offices handling negotiations of various types in different countries; etc. Even for various DTC products that form only a relatively small part of a much bigger and more expensive finished product or where DTC cannot be the prime contractor, it is felt that a DTC office or facility of some type is likely to be warranted in various countries. (For example, this might be the case for some kinds of industrial gears or ship machinery manufactured by DTC.)

To date, DTC has tended to be reactive or opportunistic rather than deterministic or systematic in its consideration and exploration of potential or new international business ventures and activities. Divisional and sales personnel have often presented ideas to top management that have happened to come their way— typically with little or no real research and analysis undertaken by them. People from different divisions have made trips to explore opportunities in various countries without knowing or finding out whether other divisions were also sending people or exploring opportunities in similar countries. Much time and money has been spent and wasted on such trips, exploration, and negotiations in an uncoordinated way, usually without anything being finalized or implemented.

There have been very few clearly stated or operational corporate objectives, plans, strategies, policies, programs, controls, research, methodologies, or information systems relating to international business prospects and new opportunities. And, as indicated earlier, there has not been nearly enough interdivisional coordination or communication with regard to international business. In addition, most of the divisions have not dealt systematically or deterministically with international opportunities, apart from effectively pursuing export orders in some notable cases.

The limited data that the company already has combined with the experience, reasoned judgment, and intuition of some key managers do indicate that there are likely to be new and potentially lucrative opportunities for DTC in various countries.

However, for the most part the company and its management do not have enough information and have not undertaken adequate planning, research, or analysis to know confidently what specific opportunities are worth pursuing in terms of corporate capabilities or priority countries beyond the U. S.

Top management now realizes that the longer the company and they delay in identifying, investigating, analyzing, and pursuing international opportunities in a much more systematic, rational, and deterministic way, the more potentially lucrative opportunities will be lost to DTC.

It is clear that not only a rapidly growing number of competing U. S. firms, but also European, Japanese and other companies, have already made and will continue to make major inroads—and often very sizeable profits and returns—in the Mid-East, Latin American, Asia, and even in the communist and in African countries, as well as in other parts of the world. DTC and its managers and other key personnel generally know considerably less about developing and communist countries as compared to developed countries such as Canada, western Europe, and Japan. However, some of the most potentially lucrative opportunities for DTC are likely to involve various developing and/or communist countries.

QUESTIONS FOR DTC CASE

1. What steps should the top management of Diversified Technology Corporation take at this time to effectively and efficiently identify, investigate, screen, analyze, decide on, capitalize on, and implement new international business ventures and opportunities? Outline the major steps or phases that the corporation should follow in this regard in conjunction with (a) the major questions that should be asked; (b) the kinds of information that should be sought and from where; (c) the types of methodologies and techniques that might be used; and (d) the kinds of analyses and feasibility studies that should be undertaken; at each step or phase. In essence, design and outline an overall comprehensive approach for effective and adequately comprehensive international business planning, decision making, program design, and implementation. If your overall approach is sound it should be basically or largely applicable to numerous other companies and not just to DTC. You are encouraged to think about, consider, discuss, and analyze what your own organization is or should be doing in this regard.
2. What suggestions do you have for DTC regarding its (a) degree of business diversification; (b) organization structure; and (c) managerial and other professional manpower situation and requirements, especially as these issues relate to its international business activities and opportunities?
3. In your opinion, which countries might offer the best relatively long-term potential opportunities warranting a DTC physical presence for each of the eight businesses that the company is in? What are the major reasons for your choices? What kinds of ventures might DTC consider in each case and why? Make any reasonable assumptions that you wish.

LEVI STRAUSS & COMPANY

Going between here and Big Basin, we found a man who had run his car off the highway and was stuck. We had no chains or rope but found a pair of old Levi's in the back of the car and tied one leg to our car and one to the front of his. We really had to pull, but the pants held, and out he came—Customer Letter[1]

People have been praising Levi's jeans for over a hundred years, whether it be for durability or for styling. In fact, one third of the branded jeans worn by Americans carry the Levi's name and over one billion pairs have been sold since the early days of the company. Consequently, Levi Strauss & Company is one of the fastest growing companies in the United States. In 1978, sales reached over $1.5 billion, more than six times 1969 sales (an approximately 20 percent annually compounded growth rate). More than 35 percent of sales is contributed by the jeanswear line, variations on the basic pants first made in the 1870s. This growth was attained through internal growth rather than acquisition or merger.

Levi Strauss achieved a large part of these successes as a privately held, family run company. The chairman of the board, Walter Haas, Jr., and the president, Peter Haas, are great-grandnephews of the founder, Levi Strauss. Furthermore, the fifth generation, Robert and Peter, Jr. (sons of Walter, Jr.), are working their way up the corporate ladder. Robert Haas is senior vice-president of corporate planning and policy and his brother Peter is a middle-manager in the international division. Family members were never forced into the company, neither did they join out of a sense of duty. All came to work with Levi Strauss by choice. The family feeling carries over to non-family employees as well as to the community. A non-profit foundation and teams of employees provide assistance to service programs in communities where the company has production and distribution facilities. (See Exhibit 1 for organization chart.)

Up to 1971, Levi Strauss was privately owned by descendants of the founders and by a few employees. To 1966 it had been feasible to finance growth through

---

Prepared by Susanne Franklin and Margaret Krasnick, under the supervision of Dr. Y. N. Chang of California State University, Fullerton. This case is prepared from published information. The company in no way participated in its preparation.

EXHIBIT 1 LEVI STRAUSS & CO. OFFICE OF THE PRESIDENT

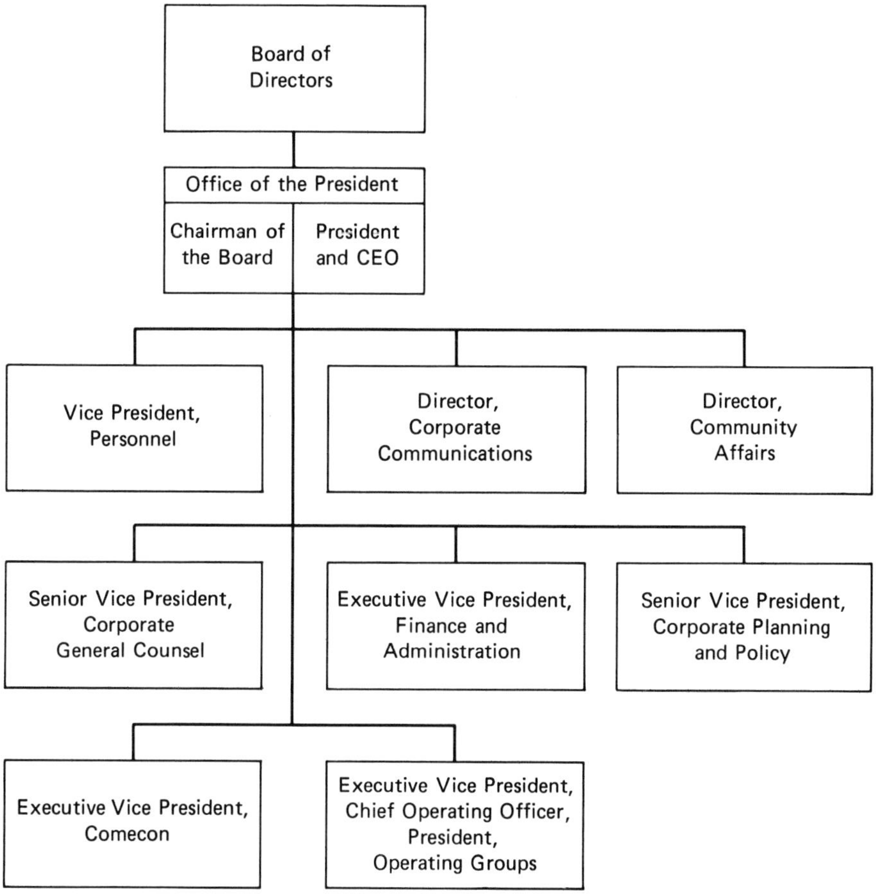

retained earning and short-term borrowings. However, in that year it was necessary to obtain long-term funds through a loan from an insurance company. Then, in late 1970 after much speculation by employees and the investment community, Walter Haas, Jr. announced that they would go public after being privately held for more than 120 years. Wall Street analysts categorized the stock offering as a hot new issue and the initial offering was sold out at premium prices, $17 over the asking price of $47.50 per share.

The glamorous corporation developed unexpected problems in 1973. Throughout the '60s and early '70s demand for denim pants (especially Levi's) grew tremendously. Nowhere could this explosive demand be better evidenced than in Europe, where a worn and torn pair of Levi's could be sold for $25 or $30 in a Paris boutique. When news of an arriving shipment of Levi's leaked out, distributors would line up outside the company's warehouses to get merchandise. Suddenly demand shifted and Levi Strauss' European division was stuck with large inventories of unwanted styles as well as uncollectible receivables. Reducing the inventory and writing off receivables in the last quarter of 1973 caused a large drop in profits for the entire company. Amazed analysts and investors lost faith in the high-flying apparel maker when the loss was disclosed. The price of their common stock dropped from $29 to $21.50 per share in one day on the New York Stock Exchange. Management made some immediate and longer-range changes and the following year the company bounced back with profit increased by 194 percent.

Moving into the last half of the 1970s and on into the 1980s, the managers of this singular company have strived to continue the successes of their past and meet greater challenges in the future.

HISTORY

When young Levi Strauss arrived in San Francisco in 1850 he found a city filled with opportunity. As a result of the gold rush, dry goods of all kinds were in short supply, with available merchandise selling at premium prices. Strauss found he could sell his goods (shipped from New York by his brothers Jonas and Louis) almost as soon as the ship carrying them docked.

Eventually, Strauss and his brother-in-law David Stern opened a shop, with Strauss wholeselling some goods to retail merchants in the gold towns of northern California. The mix of merchandise changed with every shipload, but the only thing that mattered to the partners was quick-selling stock that turned a small profit.

By the 1860s there were five partners in the business: Levi, Jonas, and Louis Strauss and their brothers-in-law David Stern and William Sahlein. The prosperous dry-goods business no longer sold only supplies for gold prospectors but also Irish linen, Italian shawls, and Belgian lace as well as French and German-made clothing.

Despite the fine European goods, it was a riveted pair of pants that would bring fame to the partnership. In 1873 Levi Strauss and Company and Jacob W. Davis, a Nevada tailor, were granted a patent on pants reinforced at pockets and seams by copper rivets. Made in duck or denim, these "waist overalls" were so successful that riveted hunting coats and blanket-lined pants were added to the line.

By 1877, all patented riveted pants were made in one design: slim legged, fitting low on the hips. All the denim used was from one mill to ensure a uniform blue color. Orange thread was used for the seams and for stitching the curving Vs on the rear pockets. Metal suspender buttons were embossed with the company name and a leather label with the "Two Horse Brand" was permanently sewn to the rear waistband. This garment, nicknamed the 501 after its lot number, has been sold essentially unchanged for more than 100 years.

The company continued to sell the riveted clothing, adding a line of shirts. The line was popular with laborers of all kinds and demand was always greater than the supply. Children's playclothes and nightwear was also manufactured and sold. The company, now run by the four nephews of the Strauss brothers and the son of Jacob Davis, survived the San Francisco earthquake of 1906 and the Bankers' Panic of 1907, relying more and more on the Two Horse Brand riveted clothes, Koveralls, the children's line, and men's dresswear manufactured in the East and sold on the Pacific Coast as "Sunset Clothes." Koveralls was the only item sold nationally. Eventually, sales of imported fabrics and sundry items such as ladies corsets and umbrellas were discontinued.

THE HAAS MANAGEMENT

Because there were no sons old enough to come into the family business when the second generation retired, one of the nephews brought in his son-in-law, Walter Haas, in 1919 as heir-apparent to the family firm. Haas met resistance from the older clerks and bookkeepers when he revised their accounting systems (bringing in adding machines also), implementing financial controls, shifting personnel, and putting more supervision on the sales force. Realizing the company's great potential, he felt this restructuring was justified. Daniel Koshland, Walter Haas's cousin, came to work two years later when profits declined sharply as a consequence of inefficiency in the Koveralls production process and the falling price of cotton. When cotton prices dropped, inventories of raw materials and finished goods were adjusted downward in price. California manufacturers were already at a competitive disadvantage with clothing manufacturers in other parts of the country, who were not restricted by minimum wage laws as in California. When these competitors lowered their retail price, Levi Strauss had to follow, reducing profit margins. Both men worked to return to more profitable times, with the situation evolving in which Haas was accountable for finance and merchandising and Koshland for personnel and production.

Despite declining sales and losses during the Depression, Levi Strauss built up large inventories of denim pants. Rather than fire factory workers and clerks, production was continued three days a week so that everyone would have work. When the Depression ended and orders began coming in, the vast inventories were depleted. The 501 was a staple good like sugar and flour. As consumers went back to work, they wore Levi pants and the workclothes.

The 501 acquired an image as the cowboy's pants and early marketing managers capitalized on the linkage, pushing a western theme in advertising. The pants were promoted at rodeos and dude ranches. Even today westernwear, designed for ranchers, is still considered a strong product line. Customer loyalty, durability, and brand identification were also stressed. The distinguished arcuate design (the curved stitching on the rear pockets), the Two Horse Brand label and a ribbon Levi's tag sewn into the pocket seam heightened brand awareness. Eventually the tag was added to other garments, the first time an apparel manufacturer had put brand on the outside of an article of clothing. In time this trademark would become a status symbol copied by others (over 200 patent infringement lawsuits were brought by Levi Strauss from 1975 to 1977).

THE TRANSITION

Following World War II, several important changes were made. First, at a time when wholeselling made up three-fourths of the business, a decision was made to shift from jobbing to manufacturing branded items. Changing demographics during the post-war baby-boom era necessitated a switch in sales and advertising emphasis from cowboys to the youth market and the growing urban population. Levi's were to be marketed as playclothes as well as workclothes.

As Walter Haas's sons took over management in the mid-1950s, a phenomenon was developing. James Dean and Marlon Brando, wearing a uniform of Levi's, T-shirts, and boots, became heroes to the nation's youth. Identifying with their actor-heroes, young people adopted the same uniform. The 501, garment of workman and cowboy, began to signify the anti-establishment and became a means of proclaiming dissatisfaction with a society that measured success by affluence. Although this association did not please all the company's executives, it was helping to push sales to record levels. Levi Strauss continued to aim the bulk of its products throughout the '50s, '60s and on into the '70s at the youth market.

In the meantime, the possibility of international markets was surfacing. Levi Strauss always had scattered sales overseas, but its primary market was the western United States. There were indications that foreign demand existed: American mining engineers working in South African diamond mines sent in mail orders for Levi's; Sea Bees during World War II wore the 501s across the Pacific Ocean, creating a new sales territory; and in the post-war German black market, Levi's were fast sellers along with nylon stockings and American cigarettes. In 1960, Levi Strauss acquired its first European distributor, in France, who contracted to buy 5,000 pairs of 501s to sell to French dealers. A few months later, Haas and his brother Peter chose a chain of local distributors in Great Britain and the European continent to market Levi's. In 1960 they acquired 75 percent of a Canadian work-garment manufacturer, Great Western Garment, for $2.85 million.

International sales, principally in Europe, was a major means of growth for the company. As the craze for corduroy and denim pants exploded in the U. S. during the '60s, it was also swept overseas, particularly into Europe. Battling with small European manufacturers as well as H. D. Lee and Blue Bell (Wrangler jeans), the company fought for market share. A subsidiary, Levi Strauss Europe (LSE) had been formed to coordinate activities there. This subsidiary, based in Brussels, sold pants and jackets made in Levi Strauss factories in the U. S. and Hong Kong to independent distributors. Levi Strauss' small-scale exports to Europe suddenly grew to a very large scale in 1969.

PROBLEMS IN EUROPE

Edward Combs, a corporate vice president in charge of international operations, conferred with Peter Haas and made a strategic decision to expand rapidly to gain as large a market share as possible and impose managerial and financial controls later. There seemed to be no real need for inventory control at that time because demand was so far ahead of supply. While the demand for pants seemed to be insatiable, LSE acquired its ten Levi Strauss distributors in Europe and turned them into subsidiaries, each with a national manager. Integration proved difficult: each firm's president resisted changing individual operation methods. Those who persisted in blocking changes were shifted to other jobs.

Problems were beginning to develop as a result of the lax controls and the organization of LSE. As each manager followed a company tradition of operating autonomously with profit responsibility, the new subsidiaries had their own inventory control and accounting systems. Only one was computerized (Switzerland) and even that did not fit in with the existing system of LSE. Consequently, financial information received at LSE headquarters in Brussels was outdated and inventory levels were inaccurately reported. Also, the inventory mix was not tracked correctly; managers did not know which styles and sizes were moving. The chaos, multiplied twelve-fold by the number of subsidiaries, was overwhelming.

Concurrently, Europeans began demanding jeans in a wide range of styles, colors, and fabrics beyond the standard straight-legged denim and corduroy. European retailers suddenly wanted bell-bottomed pants, and because of long lead times the company found it difficult to switch production. They shifted to bell-bottoms as fast as they could, but the straight-legged pants ordered months before continued to arrive in Europe. Then, when Levi's plants were reaching full production of corduroy pants, consumer tastes suddenly moved to denim, but it was too late to respond to the market. For six months LSE was importing and manufacturing hard-to-sell pants.

In January 1973, Carroll Robinson, who had replaced Combs as international manager, and Peter Thigpen, general manager of LSE, realized that they had serious problems. Year-end figures had shown an inventory level that would support six months of sales and was still increasing. Independent-minded national managers resisted efforts to unload inventories, insisting that the situation was temporary. By cutting prices and offering large discounts, Thigpen unloaded as much inventory as was possible. Competitors were also trying to reduce their inventories and it was difficult to close out all the inventory, since LSE was left with odd sizes and unusual styles. Also, a large amount of uncollectible receivables was building up.

When year-end financial statements for LSE arrived in corporate headquarters in San Francisco, the true magnitude of the markdowns and inventory losses was revealed and analyzed. The $12 million loss in Europe would cause a loss in the international division and the whole corporation as well in the fourth quarter. Wall Street analysts questioned the ability of Levi Strauss management as its common stock price fell dramatically.

THE QUICK RECOVERY

In 1974, as a result of the setback that was so damaging to the corporate profit and reputation, tighter controls were instituted. In the words of Robert Groman, the newly appointed international vice president, "The company booked its losses and took its lumps in 1973. It hadn't necessarily identified all the problems, nor assured itself that they wouldn't recur. But it had wiped the slate clean."[2]

The European operating divisions were divided into three self-sufficient areas, since reduced to two: Continental Europe and the United Kingdom/Scandinavia. Unprofitable countries were eliminated (e.g., Portugal). Each area had its own manager and a staff for operations, marketing, and finance. Collections were tightened on overdue receivables; accounts that were not creditworthy and unsuitable outlets were eliminated. Most importantly, production and sales concentrated more on basic jeans rather than trying (usually unsuccessfully) to produce pants to satisfy every European consumer's taste. Manufacturing operations were made safer and more efficient.

The objective in Europe was not to grab a large market share; rather, it was redefined as selective and controlled growth utilizing assets fully. The 1974 operating results were dramatic: 1974 showed a 194 percent increase in earnings and a resumption of their normal growth pattern (20 percent per year). Recently, sales in the European division were up 33 percent from the prior year and the division's contribution to total sales dollars was increased 3.5 percent to 18.7 percent.[3] (See Exhibit 2 for International Group organization.)

Expansion is also occurring elsewhere: Latin America has the group's second highest growth rate, with sales increasing 31 percent in one year. Australia and Japan have the largest market share potential for growth. In the early 1970s, Levi Strauss defied the Japanese tradition of a complex system of middlemen and set up its own distribution system, letting its importers act as distributors also. After some setbacks, the American way won out and is successful.[4]

EXHIBIT 2 INTERNATIONAL GROUP

Division	*Important Characteristics*
Europe:	
Northern Europe Continental Europe	Production Facilities: United Kingdom Market Areas: U.K., France, Belgium, Italy, The Netherlands, Spain, Switzerland, Scandinavia
Canada:	
Levi Strauss of Canada, Inc. Great Western Garment, Ltd. (GWG)	Two separate, non-competing companies producing jeans, womenswear, youthwear, sportswear, and workclothes
Latin America:	
Brazil, Mexico, Puerto Rico, Argentina	All self-sufficient for raw materials and production except Puerto Rico
Asia/Pacific:	
Australia, New Zealand, Japan, Malaysia, Singapore, Indonesia, Thailand	Production facilities in Hong Kong and the Philippines

THE APPAREL INDUSTRY

The apparel industry includes firms that manufacture sportswear, men's tailored clothing, dress shirts, jeans, dresses, career apparel, headwear, hosiery, and footwear.

Competition within the industry is keen due to the large number of firms in the industry and the relative ease of entry. Although the domestic industry is dispersed throughout the U. S., 71 percent is concentrated in the eight states of New Jersey, Pennsylvania, California, North Carolina, New York, Georgia, Texas, and Tennessee. Sectors that produce garments with more required manufacturing operations or frequent style changes tend to be concentrated in the middle-Atlantic states and California, while those segments of the industry that produce garments requiring fewer manufacturing operations tend to be concentrated in the southern and southwestern states.

IMPACT OF CHANGES IN THE MINIMUM WAGE More than two-thirds of the 15,000 apparel manufacturers in the U.S. are family owned and run. Only forty companies have sales greater than $100 million. Apparel is a labor intensive industry, employing 72 percent of all U. S. production workers in 1978. Eighty-six percent of the labor force works in production, compared with 72 percent for all manufacturers. Eighty percent are women and 17 percent are minorities. Total employment in 1978 was 1,256,600, down 2,500 from 1977 and 10 percent lower than the peak employment year, 1973. Unemployment in the first half of 1978 was 9.8 percent, versus 5.8 percent for all manufacturing. Payroll costs account for 52 percent of value added, and average wages are $3.90 per hour versus $6.00 in all manufacturing.

The degree of unionization varies with the type of apparel produced and the area of the country. Union membership tends to be higher in metropolitan areas and for segments of the industry with higher skills requirements. The two major unions are the International Ladies' Garment Workers Union and the Amalgamated Clothing and Textile Workers Union, both AFL-CIO.

Skills required of the labor force are relatively low, and technology relatively simple. Capital requirements are low, with gross plant and equipment equal to $332 per worker, as compared with $2,169 in all manufacturing.

IMPACT OF TECHNOLOGY Technological advancement involves modifications to traditional cutting and sewing machinery. Lasers and computerized pattern grading and cutting have only been applied to a limited extent and have not had much impact on the employment level of cutters and stitchers, who account for 50 percent of the total work force and more than two-thirds of the production force. According to a recent trade association survey of 200 companies, 62 percent were undermechanized and were not taking full advantage of technological developments.

There has been a long-term trend toward larger factories and fewer plants. Today there are 15,000 companies; ten years ago there were 18,000. Diversified firms have consistently out-performed the industry in return on sales and return on equity. The larger, diversified firms are also susceptible to cyclical fashion swings, but to a lesser extent than those firms concentrating in women's and children's wear.

IMPACT OF CHANGING DEMOGRAPHICS Sales in the apparel industry reflect fashion trends and disposable income. Total expenditures for apparel increased over the period 1968–78, although they show a falling trend when expressed as a percentage of disposable income.

Fashion trends are cyclical. Retailers now tend to order close (two to four months) to the time of sale to avoid markdowns, and this means that manufacturers must move rapidly to capitalize on trends. In late 1978, these trends were toward dressing up more for both men and women, resulting in a higher outlay per item. Sportswear is projected to continue to make gains as Americans continue to stress casual lifestyles. Active sportswear, related separates, and the disco look are areas of opportunity for manufacturers.

Changing demographics—the 19 percent increase in the 25–40 year age group projected by 1980 and the increase in the over-40 age group—and the increase in the number of working women present other opportunities for growth.

THREATS OF FOREIGN COMPETITION Threats are posed by competition from lower-priced imports. Scheduled increases in the minimum wage point to the increased likelihood of more foreign competition because foreign labor is paid less. Relative currency values also affect foreign competition.

Imports are projected to account for 22 percent of the U. S. apparel market in 1979, versus 13.7 percent in 1975 and 6 percent in 1967. Originally, imports were thought to be shoddy merchandise. This is no longer the case. The less industrialized countries, with abundant cheap labor, entered the market in the early 1950s and since then have reinvested profits to modernize equipment, eliminating the technological advantages held by U. S. domestic producers and opening the way for higher quality, more expensive imports. Foreign producers have a cost advantage in cheap labor, but also face longer lead times of six months. To some extent, industrialization of the less developed countries tends to eliminate the labor savings that originally attracted apparel manufacturers.

Imports have the greatest market share for items that are less fashion-sensitive but still involve high labor content, such as sweaters, men's shirts and trousers, and tailored clothing. Imports may well account for half of the market in the 1980s. Since 1972, agreements have been negotiated with eighteen nations to hold the annual growth rate of imports to 6 percent; real growth in the market is estimated to be 2 percent.

LEGAL ENVIRONMENT To protect the ribbon tab trademark, Levi Strauss uses a variety of ribbon colors, varies the location of the tab, and puts blank tabs on approximately 10 percent of the items. In 1977, Levi Strauss won a patent infringement suit against Blue Bell, producers of Wrangler. There were approximately 200 such cases handled by the corporate legal department during 1975–77.

Counterfeit Levi's jeans are a growing phenomenon. Levi Strauss maintains a corporate security force of eight, which includes former agents of the Secret Service, FBI, and British Intelligence. This group's investigations led to five major lawsuits filed in 1977 in San Francisco, London, Hong Kong, Switzerland, and the Netherlands charging international conspiracy to manufacture and market counterfeit Levi's. This sophisticated worldwide operation involved approximately 110,000 pairs of jeans, but most counterfeiting operations are much smaller, producing about 3,000 or 4,000 units before being shut down.

In September, 1978, Levi Strauss announced that an injunction had been granted and the company would receive $500,000 in settlement of this lawsuit. The company is attempting to form a consortium with other firms also affected by counterfeiting to lobby for stricter sanctions worldwide against counterfeiters.

During 1974–78, Levi Strauss was the subject of several lawsuits alleging illegal price maintenance and antitrust claims. A suit initiated by the Federal Trade Commission in 1974 was settled in August 1978 and affirmed Levi Strauss's right to select and control distribution channels. Later in 1978, suits were filed by the attorneys general of California, Massachusetts, New York, and Connecticut on similar charges. The New York and Massachusetts suits have been settled with payments of $20,000 to each, while the others are still in litigation.

LEVI STRAUSS & CO.: ITS POSITION

ORGANIZATIONS AND MANAGEMENT In 1972, Levi Strauss was divisionalized into functional areas: Jeans, Panetela Sportswear, Boyswear, Levi's for Gals, and International operations, providing more managing units for meeting the needs of the marketplace. In 1977 the fundamental structure was revamped to include two operational groups, U.S. and International. Divisions in the U.S. group were jeanswear, youthwear, sportswear, womenswear, and diversified products. International was divided along geographic lines into Europe, Canada, Latin America, and Asia/Pacific. In mid-1978, U. S. divisions were "fine-tuned" into Jeanswear (including Youthwear and Jeanswear) and Sportswear (four product areas: sportswear, Womenswear, Activewear, and accessories). Diversified products were incorporated into these operating units. Each operating unit has a president who is overseen by an executive vice president (corporate) of their division (Jeanswear, Sportswear, or International). The president of each operating unit runs his area autonomously, with help from the corporate staff for financial and administrative support. Each division maintains its own sales force and production facilities.

MARKETING Domestic operations account for two-thirds of total sales, with the remaining third from International. The Jeanswear division experienced a decline in sales dollar volume due to a return in demand for straight-legged jeans in heavy denim. This styling trend is reinforced by designer label jeans, a basic in high fashion. The Youthwear division experienced a similar styling change in silhouette and increased demand for fashion jeans in lighter fabrics. Girlswear, for ages 7 to 14, and toddler sizes are recent product developments, meeting the goal of supplying leisure wear in all sizes for both sexes.

Leisure attire is the central unifying factor of the sportswear group. The sportswear unit markets separates under different brands aimed at the older male and the younger male customer. Womenswear is the company's fastest growing unit as a result of a strong retail environment for women's clothing and recently implemented strategies:

1. Recognition of the distinctly different junior and misses market, responding with independent merchandising and sales support
2. Reestablishing department stores as key retail outlets
3. Improved customer service and redirecting product offerings to key products rather than a random orientation.

Womenswear has also introduced a line of larger sizes for women, further diversifying the product line. Both the Accessories and Activewear units are being developed after having been transferred from the former Diversified products and the Sportswear division, respectively. The three broad categories of Accessories—belts and billfolds, dress items such as briefcases and hats, and casual luggage—all showed substantial sales growth. New product categories for sportswear are being studied and it is felt sporting goods stores will widen the company's channels of distribution.

An expanded line of Activewear will be marketed in conjunction with the 1980 Olympics, in hopes of expanding sales and moving into the potentially lucrative USSR market. Levi Strauss will be a key sponsor of the U. S. Olympic team in 1980. They are providing warm-up suits developed specifically for the team, tote bags, and other clothing and have also contributed $300,000. A gift of this size means that the company may use the Olympic logo in its advertising campaign. Levi Strauss's campaign will include an expenditure of $8 million for 123 half-minute commercials during the games. Total promotional expenditures for the Olympics are planned to be $12 million.

To expand product lines and move into new market areas, Levi Strauss is constantly on the lookout for products that might successfully carry the Levi's brand under licensing agreements. Following a successful association with the Brown Shoe Company, which was licensed to manufacture casual shoes for men with the Levi's label, Levi Strauss entered into an agreement with Burlington Industries in 1978 for Burlington to produce men's socks with the Levi's label on the cuff. Their ad campaign is a good example of the company's innovative promotional tactics.

To get a toehold on the socks market, Levi Strauss launched a half-million-dollar ad campaign in five western states, three times the average spent on campaigns for a single item of apparel. The campaign was aimed at a narrow market, attempting to establish market dominance, and stressed quality, durability, and the

Levi's brand. At its introduction, the line consisted of seven styles of sport and casual socks, with premium prices ranging from $2.75 to $5.50 per pair. To provide the customer with the quality expected from Levi's products, the socks are unconditionally guaranteed and come in colors dyed to match the blue, brown, and tan jeans and cords. The socks were test marketed in the winter in San Diego, Sacramento, and Denver to determine if there was indeed a market for premium socks, and if so, whether it would be possible to generate sufficient volume at a premium price. The socks bore the Levi's label in an attempt to transfer brand loyalty to the sock market. The line, test marketed at Christmas, was a success and has been expanded to eleven styles, including boot socks. (See Exhibit 3 for product lines and Exhibit 4 for divisional contributions to sales.)

RESEARCH AND DEVELOPMENT In 1971, Levi Strauss created a research and development lab in Stamford, Connecticut, and spent $2.25 million in 1972, 19 percent of total research and development in the industry for that year. An equipment research and development center is now maintained in Texas.

In 1973, Levi Strauss made its first steps toward automated assembly lines to increase productivity and increase sales. In the pants-making lines, 25 percent automation was targeted for 1978, with an additional 25 percent in the prototype stages. The goal of this extensive research and development is to put Levi Strauss into a more profitable industry position. Automated fabric inspection equipment (a series of electronic optical sensors), shade markers to eliminate hand numbering to match pieces cut from the same bolt, and a marker/grader for pattern-making and waste-reduction are the major innovation areas.

EXHIBIT 3 PRODUCT LINES

Jeanswear	
Jeanswear	**Youthwear**
Jeans and Fashion Jeans Jackets, shirts and knit tops, vests, shorts and westernwear	Boys and girls jeans and pants, jackets, shirts, coveralls, T-shirts and vests
Sportswear	
Sportswear	**Womenswear**
Dress and casual slacks, sports jackets, vests, shirts, sweaters and outerwear	Junior and misses jeans and pants, shirts, skirts, dresses, shorts, and sweaters
Activewear	**Accessories**
Men's and women's ski overalls, down parkas and vests, windshirts and outerwear	Belts, wallets, briefcases, knapsacks, hats, luggage totebags and leather goods

Source: 1978 Annual Report

EXHIBIT 4 DIVISIONAL CONTRIBUTIONS TO SALES (millions)

	1978	*1977*
Jeanswear		
Jeanswear	$ 649.6	$ 695.3
Youthwear	184.2	171.6
Sportswear		
Sportswear	118.5	108.8
Womenswear	99.2	62.8
Activewear and accessories	36.3	33.6
International		
Europe	314.9	237.4
Canada	114.8	122.7
Latin America	103.5	79.3
Asia/Pacific	61.0	47.6
Totals	$1,682.0	$1,559.3

Source: 1978 Annual Report

The Corporate Marketing Research department utilizes an on-line computerized data bank to get immediate information and results of surveys about major fashion trends, retailing sales trends, and apparel pricing. Also, separate marketing research functions were developed for each division to focus on different consumer sectors. Additional information on the company image and consumer attitudes towards the company's products are also monitored. To aid advertising and product managers, the department pre-tests proposed advertising and new products.

Since 1930, one agency has handled Levi Strauss's domestic advertising. In 1967, they moved from 100 percent newspaper advertising to television commercials aimed at the youth market. The advertisements emphasized the quality and style with contemporary animation techniques. Since then other media such as radio, magazines, trade journals, poster art, and in-store displays have been used to reach youth and other market segments.

SOCIAL RESPONSIBILITY When Levi Strauss and Company was born over 100 years ago, the founders realized the importance of business to the community. Consequently, the corporate managers measure the company's success not only by dollars of profit, but in the overall well-being of the communities where their divisions are located. The long standing feeling of social responsibility is strong; "It's in the genes," as Walter Haas, Jr. once remarked.

An important part of their annual reports is the Equal Opportunity Statistics section. In 1978, minorities comprised almost 46 percent of total employees in the

EXHIBIT 5 CONSOLIDATED BALANCE SHEET
LEVI STRAUSS & COMPANY AND SUBSIDIARIES (Dollar amounts in thousands)

Assets	1978	1977	1976	1975	1974	1973	1972	1971
Current Assets								
Cash & Short Term Investments	$254,821	$160,941	$137,934	$ 76,939	$ 23,737	$ 15,940	$ 14,972	$ 15,399
Accounts Receivable (net)	241,125	203,239	172,980	139,375	116,909	101,764	73,804	64,487
Inventory	298,494	296,103	236,010	173,487	220,098	177,038	154,485	117,994
Other	29,787	35,975	24,186	17,798	22,709	10,801	9,124	4,871
Total Current Assets	$824,227	$694,258	$570,110	$407,599	$383,453	$305,543	$252,385	$202,751
Property, Plant & Equipment (net)	141,319	119,255	88,774	82,081	82,272	68,010	47,998	39,579
Other Assets	8,328	10,640	5,538	6,596	4,637	9,106	6,678	5,577
Total Assets	$973,874	$824,153	$664,422	$496,276	$470,362	$382,659	$307,061	$247,907
Liabilities & Stockholders' Equity								
Current Liabilities								
Short Term Liabilities & Current Maturities of Long Term Debt	$ 21,364	$ 41,654	$ 47,264	$ 28,696	$ 58,693	$ 57,146	$ 35,849	$ 13,096
Accounts Payable & Accrued Liabilities	155,064	103,081	78,193	46,864	83,159	75,833	39,617	41,014
Other Current Liabilities	125,977	118,791	99,373	79,874	46,284	22,684	22,780	13,779
Total Current Liabilities	$302,405	$263,526	$224,830	$155,434	$188,136	$155,663	$ 98,246	$ 67,889

Long Term Debt less Current Maturities	83,292	80,647	66,627	68,728	72,236	48,110	37,604	28,385
Deferred Liabilities	12,859	16,125	10,448	6,923	3,985	2,528	1,366	502
Minority Interest in Consolidated Subsidiary	—	—	—	—	—	—	121	2,301
Total Liabilities	$398,556	$360,298	$301,905	$231,085	$264,357	$206,301	$137,337	$ 99,077
Stockholders' Equity								
Common Stock, $1 Par	21,999	21,999	21,957*	49,067	48,960	48,960	48,960	48,960
Additional Paid in Capital	71,895	73,178	73,480	43,999	43,563	43,563	43,563	43,563
Retained Earnings	484,947	374,950	267,080	172,125	113,482	83,835	77,201	56,307
Less: Treasury Stock at Cost	(3,523)	(6,272)	—	—	—	—	—	—
Total Stockholders' Equity	$575,318	$463,855	$362,517	$265,191	$206,005	$176,358	$169,724	$148,830
Total Liabilities & Stockholders' Equity	$973,874	$824,153	$664,422	$496,276	$470,362	$382,659	$307,061	$247,907

**In mid-1976, the company transferred $3.50 per share from common stock to additional paid in capital to equate its per share stated value of $4.50 per share and the par value ($1.00). Also in mid-1976, the company split its stock 2 for 1; as a result, transfer was made from additional paid in capital to common stock in accordance with generally accepted accounting principles.*

EXHIBIT 6 CONSOLIDATED INCOME STATEMENT
LEVI STRAUSS & COMPANY AND SUBSIDIARIES
(Dollar amounts in thousands except per share data)

	1978	*1977*	*1976*
Net Sales	$1,682,019	$1,559,341	$1,219,741
Cost of Goods Sold	1,058,439	996,767	780,061
Gross Profit	$ 623,580	$ 562,574	$ 439,680
Marketing, General & Administrative Expenses	344,536	286,473	232,114
Operating Income	$ 279,044	$ 276,101	$ 207,566
Interest Expense	11,178	20,048	10,890
Other Expenses & Income (net)	(12,503)	(13,913)	(10,740)
Income Before Taxes	$ 280,369	$ 269,966	$ 207,416
Provision for Taxes on Income	135,400	140,174	102,596
Minority Interest in NI of Consolidated Subsidiaries*	—	—	—
Net Income	$ 144,969	$ 129,793	$ 104,820
Earnings per Share**	$ 6.56	$ 5.87	$ 4.71
Cash Dividends Declared	$ 1.60	$ 1.00	$ .45
Book Value of Shares Outstanding at Year-end	$26.28	$21.32	$16.50
Average Common & Common Equivalent Shares Outstanding	22,114,936	22,128,673	22,238,734

**In 1972, the company extended its basis of consolidation to include a previously unconsolidated Canadian subsidiary.*
***Per share data adjusted for a 2 for 1 stock split in 1976.*

U. S. facilities, with women making up 80.5 percent. Twenty-four percent of officials and managers are women and about 15.5 percent are minorities. In 1972, these figures were 13.8 percent and 10.1 percent respectively.

Employee stock ownership is jokingly referred to as "golden-handcuffs." Whatever the plan is called, it has helped maintain employee loyalty and a family feeling while facilitating wider ownership of the common stock. Family members and related trusts still own about 49 percent of the common stock outstanding.

FINANCIAL POSITION Exhibits 5 and 6 present consolidated balance sheet and income statement figures as shown in Levi Strauss & Company's Annual Reports for the years 1971 to 1978. Because the company was privately held prior to 1971, no detailed financial statements are available for the period. In fact, even stockholders were not permitted to take financial statements out of the room where annual meetings were held.

In 1972, the company extended its basis of consolidation to include the previously unconsolidated Canadian subsidiary, Great Western Garment, Ltd. Also, per share data was adjusted for a two-for-one stock split in 1976.

EXHIBIT 6 CONSOLIDATED INCOME STATEMENT (Cont.)

1975	1974	1973	1972	1971
$1,015,215	$897,696	$653,042	$504,104	$432,042
667,809	662,214	468,650	343,829	302,436
$ 347,406	$275,482	$184,392	$160,275	$129,606
207,641	186,175	139,179	107,068	89,056
$ 139,765	$ 89,307	$ 45,213	$ 53,207	$ 40,550
13,134	13,675	10,133	4,328	4,358
(10,048)	2,901	1,272	810	482
$ 136,679	$ 72,731	$ 33,808	$ 48,311	$ 35,985
71,937	37,862	21,952	23,046	15,980
—	—	—	242	275
$ 64,742	$ 34,869	$ 11,856	$ 25,023	$ 19,730
$ 2.95	$1.60	$ .54	$1.15	$ .93
$ .28	$ .24	$ .24	$ .19	$ .16
$12.16	$9.47	$8.10	$7.80	$6.84
21,949,514	21,760,160	21,760,160	21,760,160	21,172,000

CONCLUSION

As Levi Strauss & Company moves toward a new decade, the challenges of the past grow more complex. A new generation of managers from within the company family and those recruited from other companies and universities will face the task of steering their company to take advantage of new opportunities and successfully overcome problems that develop. Present managers have confidence in their products, financial position, strategy, and most of all, their people. In the 1973 Annual Report, the following issues are identified:

1. Markets: Eastern U. S., specialized marketing units, and Eastern Europe
2. Products: Activewear line and new product categories
3. Operations: Controlling discretionary expenses, and wage and price guidelines.

NOTES

1. Ed Cray, *Levi's* (Houghton Mifflin Company, 1978), p. 91.
2. *Forbes*, "Back to Basic Bottoms" (March 15, 1975).
3. *Levi Strauss & Company 1978 Annual Report.*
4. *Forbes*, "Beating the System: Levi Strauss in Japan" (August 15, 1973).

VIRGINIA CHEMICALS, INC.

1973 was another growth year for Virginia Chemicals, Inc. For the thirteenth consecutive year sales increased, exceeding $50 million for the first time. Net sales billed in 1973 amounted to $51,216,000, an increase of $7,083,000 or 16 percent over the previous all-time high of $44,133,000 in 1972. (For financial statements and an analysis of sales, see Exhibits 1, 2 and 3.) Sales of industrial chemical products, about 75 percent of the company's total sales, increased by 18 percent over the previous year. The air conditioning and refrigeration products activity recorded a sales increase of 12 percent over the previous year. Aerosol insecticide sales increased 7 percent. The 1973 profit increase came primarily from improved sales in the industrial chemical division.

The company experienced an earnings decline in 1970, but since then has demonstrated steady growth in sales and earnings to the record levels achieved in 1973. The decline in earnings in 1970 was attributable to generally poor economic conditions, the pressures of competitive prices in the chemical industry, and higher overall costs of doing business. In addition, multi-plant startup and other development costs related to plants, new products, and expansion projects in their early stages were charged against income. This practice was in line with the company's long established financial policies and a result of the rapidly changing technology within the industry. The manufacturing and selling of the industrial and commercial lines of products has been a highly competitive business. The company competes with a number of well-established companies, some of which are the largest chemical corporations in the U. S.

As of December 1973, the air conditioning-refrigeration and the aerosol-insecticide activities were still in accelerated programs for market development, research, and new products. These programs have resulted in the company's manufacturing a greater percent of the products it sells. In the past, these established activities have contributed to the company's growth and earnings, and despite the charges now being absorbed by them for developmental cost, they are showing progress in returning to their former profitability.

Prepared by Thomas L. Wheelen, J. David Hunger, and C. Allan Foster. Copyright © 1975 by Thomas L. Wheelen, J. David Hunger, and C. Allan Foster.

EXHIBIT 1 VIRGINIA CHEMICALS, INC., SUMMARY OF EARNINGS (in Thousands of Dollars)

	DECEMBER 31									
	1969		1970		1971		1972		1973	
	$	%	$	%	$	%	$	%	$	%
Net Sales	31,369	100.0	31,613	100.0	36,395	100.0	44,133	100.0	51,216	100.0
Cost of Sales	22,342	71.2	24,210	76.6	27,602	75.8	35,560	80.6	40,329	78.7
Gross Profit	9,027	28.8	7,403	23.4	8,793	24.2	8,573	19.4	10,887	21.3
Operating Expenses										
Selling, G&A	3,477	11.1	4,028	12.7	4,271	11.7	5,091	11.5	5,992	11.7
Research & development	928	3.0	954	3.0	950	2.6	1,168	2.6	1,197	2.3
Interest expense (income)	(44)	(.1)	136	.4	117	.3	96	.2	121	.2
Depreciation	1,023	3.3	1,159	3.7	1,472	4.1	—[1]	—	—	—
Total Operating Expenses	5,384	17.2	6,277	19.8	6,810	18.7	6,355	14.4	7,310	14.2
Net Income before Tax	3,643	11.6	1,126	3.6	1,983	5.4	2,218	5.0	3,577	7.0
Federal Income Taxes	1,944	6.2	561	1.8	991	2.7	1,033	2.3	1,707	3.3
Net Income	1,699	5.4	565	1.8	992	2.7	1,185	2.7	1,870	3.7
Per Share of Common Stock										
Net income	$ 1.72		$ .58		$ 1.01		$ 1.18		$ 1.84	
Dividends declared	.53		.56		.56		.56		.61	
Book value	13.24		13.26		13.69		14.42		15.73	

1. In 1972–73 reports, the company did not list depreciation in Income Statements but included it in other categories as appropriate. Depreciation in 1972 was $1,454 and depreciation for 1973 was $1,739.

EXHIBIT 2 VIRGINIA CHEMICALS, INC., CONSOLIDATED BALANCE SHEETS (in Thousands of Dollars)

	DECEMBER 31				
Assets	1969	1970	1971	1972	1973
Current Assets					
Cash	422	524	561	693	677
Certificates of deposit	329	354	913	—	—
Marketable securities	289	389	302	604	—
Receivables	3,808	4,028	4,804	6,755	7,005
Inventories	5,075	5,381	5,488	5,916	5,752
Prepayments	274	154	106	198	123
Total Current	10,197	10,830	12,174	14,166	13,557
Plant and Equipment (Net)	9,201	9,235	8,704	8,322	12,720
Deferred Charges	370	273	420	516	280
Total Assets	19,768	20,338	21,298	23,004	26,557
Liabilities & Equity					
Current Liabilities					
Notes payable—bank	700	—	—	—	—
Current maturities—long-term debt	—	—	—	784	184
Accounts payable & accruals	3,785	2,962	3,299	3,298	3,982
Dividends payable	143	136	—	141	163
Accrued federal taxes	185	305	220	84	273
Customer deposits	549	421	507	459	623
Total Current Liabilities	5,362	3,824	4,026	4,766	5,225
Deferred Income Tax	1,212	1,325	1,252	1,756	2,006
Deferred Tax Credit	331	280	235	588	951
Commitment Long-Term Debt		2,000	2,121	1,338	2,321
Stockholders Equity					
Preferred stock	—	—	—	—	—
Common stock	1,943	1,948	1,996	2,019	2,041
Paid-in surplus	144	165	432	678	903
Retained	10,776	10,796	11,236	11,859	13,110
Total Equity	12,863	12,909	13,664	14,556	16,054
Total Liabilities & Equity	19,768	20,338	21,298	23,004	26,557

Orders for Virginia Chemicals' products during 1973 continued to grow, and at year-end the company was still not able to meet shipment requests for many of its major chemical products. Harry W. Buchanan, chairman of the board and president of Virginia Chemicals, stated in a message to the company's shareholders in the 1973 annual report that "the combination of this strong sales demand and increased chemical production capacity resulted in an improvement in profit margins." He went on to say that improved cost control procedures also played a role. Furthermore,

EXHIBIT 3 VIRGINIA CHEMICALS INC., SUMMARY OF SOURCES AND APPLICATIONS OF FUNDS (in Thousands of Dollars)

	DECEMBER 31			
Sources	1970	1971	1972	1973
Net Income	565	992	1,185	1,870
Depreciation	1,159	1,472	1,454	1,739
Deferred Income Taxes	113	(73)	504	250
Deferred Inventory Tax Credit (net)	(51)	(45)	353	363
Amortization and Write-off of Deferred Charges	97	198	102	236
Loss on Retirement of Plant and Equipment	—	23	77	4
Proceeds from New Long-Term Debt	2,000	121	—	500
Proceeds from Refinanced Short-Term Debt	—	—	—	667
Proceeds from Stock Issuances	26	315	269	247
Total Sources	3,909	3,003	3,944	5,876
Applications				
Plant and Equipment Additions	1,193	964	1,149	6,141
Deferred Charges Additions	—	345	198	—
Long Term Debt Becoming Current	—	—	783	184
Common Stock Dividends	545	552	562	619
Total Applications	1,738	1,861	2,692	6,944
Additions to Working Capital	2,171	1,142	1,252	(1,068)

Buchanan reported that "the improvement in this margin was accomplished in another year of federal price control programs and in spite of sharply rising manufacturing costs due principally to higher costs of key raw materials and energy. Our profit margin, like that of many other manufacturing companies, is still below appropriate levels."

HISTORY

Virginia Chemicals, Inc., a manufacturer of industrial chemicals and chemical products, is a Maine corporation originally organized in 1909 as a copper smelter under the name Virginia Smelting Company. The business had been founded by E. C. Eustis in 1899.

In 1916 the company began to deemphasize copper-smelting operations in favor of production of liquid sulfur dioxide. This was originally made from a by-product of the smelting process. Eventually the company ceased copper smelting and concentrated upon the production of industrial chemicals, particularly liquid sulfur dioxide and sulfur-dioxide-based chemicals. The company has expanded its product lines into air conditioning-refrigeration chemicals and components, and aerosol-insecticide products.

The company has grown not only internally, but also through acquisition. In 1967 the company acquired the Refrigeration-Air Conditioning Division of Ansul

Company. In May 1970, Monsanto Company's liquid sulfur dioxide business including equipment, storage tanks, and tank cars was acquired. Later in 1970, the sulfur dioxide facility of Dow Chemical Company in Selby, California was acquired. Furthermore, in December 1971, the company acquired the assets and inventories of Components Manufacturing Company, Oklahoma City, Oklahoma, producer of mechanical components for automotive air conditioning systems. These operations were consolidated with the company's refrigeration mechanical components plant at Staatsburg, New York. As a result of these acquisitions plus facilities expansion, Virginia Chemicals has plants in numerous locations. (See Exhibit 8.)

ORGANIZATION

Virginia Chemicals employs 535 people. In December 1973, top management was organized as shown in Exhibit 4.

The company has two subsidiaries. Each is wholly owned. Financial statements were not available for these firms. The first of these subsidiaries, Virchem of Canada, Ltd., was incorporated under federal laws July 12, 1963, and originally manufactured hydrous zinc. It has since been converted to hydrosulfite blending and the making of defoamers. The subsidiary is headquartered in Cornwall, Ontario.

Virchem Export, Inc., was chartered in April 1972, under the provisions of the Revenue Act of 1971, for Domestic International Sales Corporations (DISC). It was organized to act as an export sales or leasing corporation and to perform other export-related activities either for Virginia Chemicals, its own manufacturing parent, or for other unrelated manufacturers of export products.

RESEARCH AND DEVELOPMENT

In its research and development efforts the company has developed proprietary products and alternate sources of raw materials. Prominent among the recent accomplishments has been the refinement of a new process for producing sodium hydrosulfite, patented in the U. S. and five other countries.

The R & D department has twenty-one professionals including eight PhD's and eleven technicians. It is organized into six groups, each with a group leader. Each group concentrates in a major research area. Over the years the company has obtained title to 103 patents and has developed proprietary formulae and new products.

In addition to the R & D group there is a department of commercial development, which develops new areas of activity for the company, negotiates with groups outside of the company, and works closely with the management of personnel in the development of new works.

Except for patents and patent applications relating to the process used by the company at Bucks, Alabama and Leeds, South Carolina for the production of formate-based sodium hydrosulfite, none of the patents owned by or licensed to the company were considered to be of major significance to its total business. The plants at Bucks and Leeds employ a process on which the company and Mitsubishi Gas Company have patents granted and pending. These two companies have entered into a cross-licensing agreement for the use of this process. The estimated amount spent during each of the last five years on research activities relating to the development of new products, improvement of existing products, and technical service to customers was approximately $1 million. As of December 1973, approximately fifty-five professional employees were engaged full time in research activities.

EXHIBIT 4 VIRGINIA CHEMICALS, INC. ORGANIZATION CHART

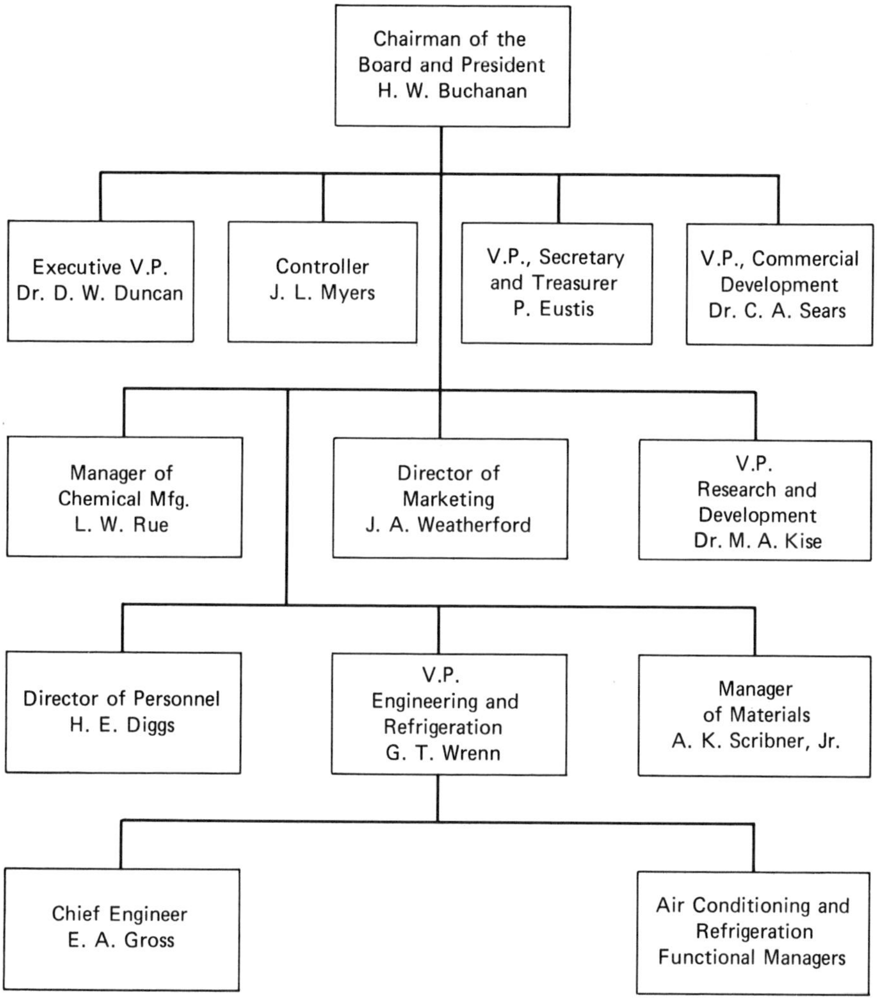

SALES AND MARKETING

Virginia Chemicals employs sixty-six people in sales and marketing for the three product lines. Products of all three are sold directly to end users and to wholesalers through the company's field sales force. Coordinated selling by the field sales personnel and the product managers is used to ensure total coverage of the purchasers' needs.

The company maintains sales offices in nine states and markets its products both inside and outside the U. S. Sales outside the U. S., other than those by the company's Canadian subsidiary, are made through VirChem Export Inc., a DISC.

Sales outside the U. S., including those of the company's Canadian subsidiary, accounted for less than 10 percent of the company's total sales in 1973.

Sales of the air conditioning-refrigeration and aerosol-insecticide products are seasonal and generally are highest during the second and third quarters of the fiscal year.

PRODUCTS

The company is organized into three major product lines: industrial chemical products, air conditioning-refrigeration products, and other products, primarily aerosol-insecticide products. Shown in Exhibit 5 are the net sales billed and income before taxes attributable to each of these lines, including export sales and income.

The company buys and manufactures sulfur dioxide and sells the product to more than forty industries. The company's more important customers for sulfur dioxide include other chemical manufacturers, pulp and paper manufacturers, food processing and agricultural industries, and textile dyers and finishers (see Exhibit 7). The company uses substantial amounts of this chemical in the manufacture of its other industrial chemicals. The company's product offerings are as follows.

Sodium bisulfite (anhydrous) is used as a mild acid and reducing agent in finishing and in the production of photographic developers and synthetic fibers; as a reducing agent in finishing and in the production of photographic developers and synthetic fibers; as a reducing agent in textile and wood pulp processing; and as a preservative of fruits, vegetables, and other food products.

Sodium hydrosulfite is principally used as a powerful reducing agent in the application of vat dyes to cotton textiles and as a bleaching and brightening agent for groundwood pulp from which newsprint is made; is also a basic ingredient in the manufacture of chemicals, plastics, and rubber. The company manufactures formate-based sodium hydrosulfite at its plants in Bucks and Leeds, utilizing a process covered by patents granted to, applied for and licensed to the company. The company also manufactures sodium hydrosulfite by a zinc process at its Portsmouth, Virginia plant.

Zinc hydrosulfite is also used for bleaching groundwood pulp. The sharply increased world price for zinc, coupled with environmental considerations associated with zinc, has substantially reduced the use of zinc hydrosulfite in some areas of North America. This was reflected in lower volume of production, particularly at the company's Cornwall plant, and a change from zinc hydrosulfite to other chemicals, including proprietary sodium hydrosulfite products produced by the company.

Hydroxylamine sulfate is used in the manufacture of oxime anti-skinning agents for paint and printing inks, in production of synthetic rubber, photographic developers, dyes, pharmaceuticals, dyeing of textiles, and in the syntheses of many organic compounds.

Sulfur dioxide is used extensively throughout the processing industries—chemicals, foods, paper pulps, glass, glue, gelatin, metallurgy, paint and varnish, oil refining, tanning, textiles, water treatment, plastics, and cosmetics. More specifically, sulfur dioxide is sold for such varied processes as a bleaching agent in foods, as a major ingredient in controlling the effluent of chrome and other plating processes, to make glass stronger, to improve the odor and taste of water, and in the production of soft drinks and wines.

Amines are derivatives of ammonia and alcohol and are sold to the agricultural chemicals, pharmaceutical, photographic, textile, rubber, and plastics industries.

EXHIBIT 5 SALES AND OPERATING INCOME BY ACTIVITY (in Thousands of Dollars)

	For the Years Ended December 31,				
Net Sales Billed	1969	1970	1971	1972	1973
Industrial chemicals	$23,047	$22,958	$26,982	$33,251	$39,099
Air-conditioning/ refrigeration	6,992	7,294	7,791	9,131	10,249
Other	1,330	1,361	1,622	1,751	1,868
Total	$31,369	$31,613	$36,395	$44,133	$51,216
Income before Taxes					
Industrial chemicals	$ 3,327	$ 1,791	$ 2,337	$ 2,783	$ 3,977
Air-conditioning/ refrigeration	334	(570)	(227)	(442)	(332)
Other	(18)	(95)	(127)	(123)	(68)
Total	$ 3,643	$ 1,126	$ 1,983	$ 2,218	$ 3,577

Zinc sulfate is used in chemical manufacturing, rayon processing, electroplating, glue and adhesives, fungicides, insecticides, micronutrient, and fertilizer mixtures.

Virchem[R] is a group of nontoxic chemical products for the control of corrosion in municipal drinking water systems, industrial fresh or brackish cooling water systems, and desalination operations.

Virtex[R] specialty products which are used as wetting agents, detergents, and defoamers in the preparation, dyeing, and finishing of textiles.

Virtex[R]*500* is used as a defoamer in beck dyeing of tufted carpets without contributing to the flammability of the finished carpet.

Virtex[R]*-FRJ-1* is used as a fire retardant for jute matting in compliance with new fire protection regulations in the automotive industry.

Hydrogen peroxide is used in the bleaching of paper pulp.

Industrial Chemical Products

The principal products of the company's industrial line of products are sulfur dioxide and sulfur dioxide-based chemicals, such as hydrosulfide and sodium metabisulfite. The company also manufactures organic chemicals, a group of amine products, and other industrial chemicals not derived from sulfur dioxide. Approximate sales billed (including international sales) of these classes of products for each of the past five years is shown in Exhibit 6.

Air Conditioning-Refrigeration Products

The company also manufactures and buys for resale a broad range of refrigeration and air-conditioning installation and maintenance products sold primarily to

EXHIBIT 6 INDUSTRIAL CHEMICAL PRODUCTS SALES BILLED (in Thousands of Dollars)

	1969	*1970*	*1971*	*1972*	*1973*
Sulfur dioxide and derivative products	$15,699	$15,874	$18,632	$23,104	$27,651
Organic Chemicals	3,446	3,432	3,784	4,908	6,108
Other	3,902	3,652	4,566	5,239	5,340

EXHIBIT 7 VIRGINIA CHEMICALS INC., INDUSTRIAL CHEMICALS PRODUCTS & MARKETS

	Sulfur Dioxide	*Sodium Hydro-Sulfite*	*Zinc Hydro-Sulfite*	*Zinc Sulfate*	*Sodium Bi-Sulfite*	*Hydroxyl Amine Sulfate*	*Amine*
Chemical Manufacturing	x	x		x	x	x	x
Pharmaceutical	x	x		x	x	x	x
Photographic	x			x	x	x	x
Pulp & Paper	x	x	x	x	x		
Textile	x	x		x	x	x	x
Food	x	x			x		
Rubber		x		x		x	x
Textile Specialties				x	x		x
Water Treatment	x	x		x	x		x
Chrome Waste	x	x		x	x		
Clay	x	x	x				
Dyestuff		x			x	x	x
Glue	x			x	x		
Synthetic Fibers	x			x	x		
Agriculture				x			x
Leather	x				x		
Sugar	x	x					
Glass	x						
Herbicides							x
Insecticides							x
Organic Intermediates							x
Protein	x						
Plastic							x
Resins							x

wholesalers and to some major original equipment manufacturers. These products are also sold to the automotive field—both original equipment manufacturer and aftermarket—by the company's field sales force. The company entered this business when sulfur dioxide was the principal chemical used in refrigeration. After freon refrigerants came into this market, the company entered into a sales agreement with E. I. DuPont Nemours Company to help market DuPont's freon to air conditioning and refrigeration wholesalers. This sales agreement has been continued for many years. The company also has sales contracts with other major manufacturers to market their insulation products, sealants, mastics, and refrigeration oils. The product lines manufactured by the company include mechanical components (e.g., filter driers for air conditioning and refrigeration systems), canned refrigerants, water treatment chemicals, and cleaners. The mechanical components business was purchased from the Ansul Company of Marinette, Wisconsin in 1967 and these products are manufactured in Staatsburg, New York.

Aerosol-Insecticides Products

A third group of products are specialty high-pressure aerosol insecticides and related equipment designed specifically for professional pest control application. This business grew from the company's interest in freon, which is the principal propellant for the aerosol insecticides, together with the company's research and development work on insecticides.

The insect control products offered include automatic (pre-timed) dispensers of insecticides to eliminate flying insects. Similar dispensers are marketed for the dispersing of odor control products under the Virmist label. These independently operated dispensers can be programmed to fire on demand with each unit treating from 1,000 to 12,000 cubic feet. The company also offers custom-designed systems for insect control in large areas—i.e., factories and warehouses.

Also marketed are products registered with the Environmental Protection Agency for flying insect control in places where food is processed, prepared, or served. Pressurized sprays with special applicators for the control of such insects as wasps, hornets, and roaches are offered, as well as specialized products for insect control in greenhouses, nurseries, and mushroom houses. Miscellaneous products marketed in this department include Turf-Green, for ornamentals or grass coloring, and a product for cleaning synthetic turf.

PRODUCTION-OPERATION FACILITIES

Orders during 1973 were strong and at year end the company was not able to meet shipment requests for many of its major chemical products. This was due in part to a shortage of raw materials used in production.

The major raw materials used by the company are sulfur dioxide, sodium formate, caustic soda, sulfur, zinc dust, sulfuric acid, alcohol, hydrogen, ammonia, and soda ash. The company manufactures some of its own sulfur dioxide and has entered into an arrangement to use and to market sulfur dioxide recovered by a major West Coast smelting and refining company from its stack gases. During 1973 the company experienced sporadic plant shutdowns due to a temporary lack of raw materials. While management anticipates possible recurrences during 1974, its evaluation of raw material sources and markets was that the frequency and duration of such shutdowns would not have a material impact on 1974 earnings.

In addition to shortages, there have been major increases in the prices of some raw materials. These increases in company costs have generally been reflected in increased selling prices for the company products that were affected.

With respect to the general shortage of energy, the major areas of possible concern in considering the present situation were considered to be: (1) ability to fuel plants to continue production; (2) ability to deliver products to customers; and (3) availability of raw materials (especially petrochemical products) to the company.

All of Virginia Chemicals' major plants were equipped to be heated and operated by at least two of the following alternate forms of energy: fuel oil, natural gas, and coal. The company estimates that, provided the alternate fuel sources are available, conversion in any plant could be completed within two weeks should any curtailment occur, and there is little or no chance that production would be slowed significantly during the changeover. During 1973, the cost of electric power and fuels for energy was approximately 2 percent of dollar sales.

The company delivers most of its products to customers through common carriers or company-owned or leased trucks and railcars. Management estimates that the company would experience the same difficulties as any of its competitors in the use of common carriers for deliveries should service be disrupted, and that no competitive advantage would be gained or lost in the event of a disruption. The extensive use of railcars for delivery and the company's own fleet of these cars give relative assurance of delivery.

Properties

The locations and activities of the production are listed in Exhibit 8.

Alcohols used in the production of amines are the only petrochemical feedstocks used by the company. These products are supplied primarily from three major suppliers. Management is currently investigating new sources and additional quantities of alcohol. There are indications of industry shortages of alcohols, but management believes their suppliers will continue deliveries at the required levels.

ACCOUNTING PROCEDURES—FINANCIAL CONTROL

The accounting policy was to expense cost when incurred for research and development, computer programming, plant start-up inefficiencies, and similar items. Investment tax credits were amortized over the lives of related facilities rather than taken into current earnings. Useful lives of plants were shortened for depreciation purposes when, in the opinion of management, this was appropriate to recognize technological developments that could necessitate early replacement or retirement of equipment.

The consolidated financial statements include the accounts of the company and its totally held subsidiary, Virchem of Canada, Ltd. All material inter-company transactions have been eliminated. Canadian operations have been translated using (1) prevailing exchange rates at year end for current assets and liabilities, (2) historical exchange rates for long-term assets and liabilities, and (3) average prevailing rates during each year for revenues and expenses.

In 1967 the company engaged the management systems division of Arthur Andersen and Co., its public accountants, to work with management in order to effect a more formal growth plan through the establishment of strong financial planning, including cost control and management information systems. This financial program provided the basis for long-range plans, budgets, and control systems and,

EXHIBIT 8 PLANT LOCATIONS

LOCATION	*LEASED OR OWNED*	*PRODUCTS*
Portsmouth, Virginia	Owned	Amines Sodium hydrosulfite Zinc hydrosulfite Zinc sulfate Sodium bisulfite Aerosol filling and freon packaging Sulfur dioxide (Research & Development) (Corporate Headquarters)
Bucks, Alabama	Leased[1]	Sodium hydrosulfite-based products, sodium bisulfite
Leeds, South Carolina (Initial operations)	Owned[2]	Sodium hydrosulfite-based products
Kalama, Washington	Owned	Zinc hydrosulfite
Cornwall, Ontario	Owned	Hydrosulfite blending and defoamers[3]
Selby, California	Leased[4] and Owned	Sulfur dioxide
Staatsburg, New York	Leased[5] and Owned	Mechanical components for air-conditioning and refrigeration equipment

1. The company leases the Bucks plant from the Industrial Development Board of Mobile, Alabama, which financed the plant with a $4,500,000 industrial revenue bond issue. The company has not capitalized the cost of the land and plant or recorded its commitment with respect to the remaining $4,275,000 indebtedness.
2. In connection with the planned issuance of $1 million of Industrial Revenue bonds, the company expects to sell a portion of the Leeds plant to Chester County, South Carolina and lease it back.
3. Previously manufactured zinc hydrosulfite.
4. Lease related to land and building only.
5. Lease related to land and building expires September, 1974.

when integrated with an appropriate computer system, provided management information for planning.

The company prepares a five-year plan to identify market movements or improvements and permit the company to react quickly to market changes. The five-year plan also includes estimates of cost, capital requirements, and financing alternatives. The five-year plan is augmented by a one-year plan or budget that is created from input and projections from the product managers, division heads, cost center supervisors, and the budget committee. The system produces a monthly report as well as a variance analysis of actual versus budgeted sales and costs. The budget committee is made up of the vice president, secretary and treasurer, controller, executive vice president, and marketing vice president. The budget committee reviews the previously mentioned reports monthly, and a monthly report is sent to the chairman and to each person directly responsible for the variances. A bimonthly report of progress against these guidelines is then forwarded to the board of directors. In addition, the budget committee meets each month with division heads and product managers to discuss monthly reports and any plans to correct deficiencies.

Non-capitalized financing leases include leases on the plant at Bucks and a company airplane. The present values of minimum rental commitments for both non-capitalized financing leases aggregate $4,406,000 at December 31, 1973, of which $4,275,000 is applicable to the Bucks plant and $131,000 to the airplane. The average interest rate applicable to the Bucks plant is 7 percent and the average interest rate applicable to the airplane is 11 percent. Exhibit 9 reflects the impact on net income if both non-capitalized financing leases had been capitalized.

The company also has non-cancellable operating leases for railroad cars and trucks. The majority of these leases are for tank cars commonly used in the chemical industry. Minimum rental commitments under non-cancellable leases for railroad cars, trucks, the airplane, and the Bucks plant as of December 31, 1973 are given in Exhibit 10.

Inventories

Inventories are valued at the lower of standard cost, which approximates average cost, or market. Inventories used in the computation of cost of goods sold are given in Exhibit 11.

EXHIBIT 9 EFFECT ON NET INCOME OF CAPITALIZED LEASES (in Thousands)

	1973	*1972*
Decrease in rent expense	$ 786	$ 356
Increase in depreciation	(455)	(213)
Increase in interest expense	(319)	(153)
Decrease (increase) in income taxes	(6)	5
Increase (decrease) in net income	$ 6	$(5)

EXHIBIT 10 RENTAL COMMITMENTS

1974	$ 1,158,000
1975	1,118,000
1976	1,061,000
1977	998,000
1978	958,000
1979 through 1983	4,619,000
1984 through 1988	2,549,000
1989 through 1991	1,239,000
Total Rental Commitment	$13,700,000

EXHIBIT 11 INVENTORIES (in Thousands)

	Dec. 31, 1973	*Dec. 31, 1972*	*Dec. 31, 1971*
Finished Goods	$2,723	$3,275	$2,753
Raw Materials	2,346	2,183	2,274
Manufacturing Supplies	683	458	461
Total	$5,752	$5,916	$5,488

Depreciation Method

The company provides depreciation using the straight-line method over various estimated useful lives ranging from five to thirty-five years. Maintenance and repairs are charged to expense as incurred. Renewals and betterments are capitalized in the property accounts. When property or equipment is replaced, retired, or otherwise disposed of, the cost and related accumulated depreciation are removed from the accounts. Any gain or loss is credited or charged to income or expense. Additions to and retirements of property, plant, and equipment during 1972 and 1973 are shown in Exhibit 12.

Additions in 1973 included $4,600,000 for a new sodium hydrosulfite facility in Leeds, for which there was an additional commitment of approximately $800,000 to the contractor.

Additions to and retirements from accumulated depreciation accounts for 1972 and 1973 are shown in Exhibit 13.

CAPITAL PROGRAM—FUTURE DIRECTIONS

Common Stock

The company has authorized capital consisting of 2,500,000 shares of common stock at the par value of $2 each and 300,000 shares of preference stock

EXHIBIT 12 DEPRECIATION (in Thousands)

	Total	*Land*	*Buildings and Equipment*	*Returnable Containers*
Balance Jan. 1, 1972	$18,220	$526	$16,981	$713
Additions	1,149	24	1,016	109
Retirements	(262)	(2)	(256)	(4)
Balance Dec. 31, 1972	$19,107	$548	$17,741	$818
Additions	6,141	164	5,976	1
Retirements	(135)		(135)	
Balance Dec. 31, 1973	$25,113	$712	$23,582	$819

EXHIBIT 13 ACCUMULATED DEPRECIATION ACCOUNTS (in Thousands)

	Total	*Buildings and Equipment*	*Returnable Containers*
Balance Jan. 1, 1972	$ 9,516	$ 8,993	$523
Additions	1,454	1,403	51
Retirements	(185)	(181)	(4)
Balance Dec. 31, 1972	$10,785	$10,215	$570
Additions	1,739	1,709	30
Retirements	(131)	(131)	
Balance Dec. 31, 1973	$12,393	$11,793	$600

without par value. As of December 31, 1973, there were 1,020,333 shares of common stock outstanding. No preferred stock has yet been issued, and the company has no plans or commitments involving the issue of such stock. Holders of common stock are entitled to dividends out of all funds legally available therefore, payable when, as, and if declared by the board of directors. Cash dividends on the common stock have been declared and paid regularly since 1956, and on a quarterly basis since 1961. A dividend of fifty-nine cents per share was paid in 1973.

The holders of the common stock have the sole voting power and each share is entitled to one vote in the election of directors and other matters. There is no cumulative voting.

As of December 31, 1973 the only equity security of the company outstanding was its common stock. The only persons known to the company to own of record, or to own beneficially, more than 10 percent of the stock outstanding are listed in Exhibit 14.

Exhibit 15 shows the range of the market prices for the common stock of the company, adjusted to allow for the 3-for-2 split of this stock in April 1969. The stock is traded over the counter and the quotations are from *The Wall Street Journal* based on the average of the bid and asked prices without adjustments for retail mark-up, mark-down, or commissions.

Debt and Lines of Credit

Long-term debt includes a $2,500,000 unsecured note payable to a bank, less current maturities of $179,000 under a long-term loan agreement. The loan agreement permits the company to borrow up to $7,000,000, including the $2,500,000 that was outstanding at December 31, 1973. When borrowing under this agreement, the interest is payable quarterly at 1/2 percent above the prime rate. The loan is to be paid in fourteen equal semi-annual installments beginning July 1974. Under the agreement the company must maintain net worth in excess of $12 million, net working capital in excess of $5 million and unencumbered gross fixed assets of $12 million.

EXHIBIT 14 PRINCIPAL STOCKHOLDERS

	Type of Ownership	*Common Shares Owned*	*Percentage of Class Owned*
William E. C. Eustis and Peter Eustis as trustees of Voting Trust dated November 30, 1951, as amended.	Record	215,325	21.4
Bowen, David & Co.	Record	143,550	14.2
Elizabeth E. Williamson	Record	None	None
	Beneficial direct and indirect	123,514	12.2
Margaret E. Richardson	Record	None	None
	Beneficial direct and indirect	123,859	12.2
Frederic A. Eustis, II	Record	None	None
	Beneficial direct and indirect	125,508	12.4

EXHIBIT 15 STOCK MARKET PRICES

Year	*High*	*Low*
1969	36	25
1970	25	14½
1971	21⅝	14⅞
1972	30½	18⅛
1973	29¾	15½

The company also has a line of credit with the same bank permitting seasonal borrowings for up to $3 million at the prime rate, subject to review in April of each year.

Also included in long-term debt is $121,000 payable in two installments of $116,000 and $5,000 due in 1973 and 1974 respectively, with interest at 6 percent per annum in connection with the acquisition of certain assets of a components manufacturing company on December 15, 1971.

The company has entered into an agreement with the Industrial Development Board of Mobile, Alabama, whereby the board will construct and the company will lease the plant in Bucks. The agreement calls for rental payments of approximately

$430,000 a year for twenty years beginning February 1, 1971. The payments made to the board will be used to retire the $4,500,000 industrial bond issue, plus interest, issued by the board. The company has not capitalized the cost of the land and plant or recorded its commitment with respect to the remaining $4,275,000 indebtedness. The company intends to expense the majority of the rental cost over eleven years, commencing with the start of operations of the plant. The company has an option to purchase the plant at any time for an amount equal to the unretired principal portion of the bonds plus accrued interest to the date of redemption and a prepayment penalty of no more than one year's interest. Should the bond issue, on which interest to the bond holders is tax exempt, lose such tax status, the board may immediately require the company to exercise its option to purchase the plant.

Recent Developments

In the late 1960s the company reviewed its markets, products, and production processes in light of forecasted national and industry growth and initiated a more formal growth plan. One of the first accomplishments was the establishment of strong financial planning, including cost control and management information systems.

At the same time that the company was reviewing its financial planning programs, other phases of the company's operations were revaluated. Revaluation was concerned with (1) developing new and modified products for the company's markets and (2) determining the most desirable manufacturing process and raw materials usage for production of existing and new products. Buchanan reported that "in these efforts we emphasized research and development and a consciousness of the needs of our customers, both from the standpoint of longer term economics and the important environmental considerations." He further stated that these efforts "were and are to strengthen the company's competitive position in each of our markets. Our goals were and are to provide our customers with innovative quality products and proprietaries, and to produce these with the technology and raw materials mix that will enable us to be a low cost producer."

The revaluation of all phases of the company's operations has resulted in development of new products, construction of new plants, modernization of some existing plants, and the gradual phase-down of other plants that did not utilize the more economical processes. Having carefully evaluated the opportunities, management decided to concentrate recent and projected capital expenditures in industrial chemicals. This has resulted in larger capital expenditure programs, which management feels are essential to growth. The plants and related pollution control facilities that will be constructed through these capital expenditure programs are designed to (1) increase the productive capacity and market penetration in the three major industrial chemical areas in which the company is presently active (sodium hydrosulfite, sodium bisulfite, and organic chemicals) and to (2) complete the major required pollution control expenditures. With regard to environmental expenditures, the company completed during 1973 a major phase of a long-term pollution control program. This program was initiated some years ago, at a cost of $1 million at the original headquarters plant in Portsmouth. Remaining pollution control expenditures are estimated at $700,000 for the Leeds plant and $500,000 for Portsmouth. Operating expenses for pollution control facilities in Portsmouth were $100,000 in 1973.

Opportunities in air conditioning-refrigeration, aerosol insecticide products, and other areas are under continuous review. Management feels that planned projects would not require substantial amounts of capital before 1976. It is believed that the projects can be financed from cash generated internally through 1978.

Capital Programs

The company in 1970 began to plan for construction of a plant to manufacture sodium hydrosulfite and proprietaries. This resulted in the new plant in Bucks. It uses a process covered by patents granted to, applied for, and licensed to the company. The reception of the products produced at Bucks led to the construction during 1973 of a similar plant at Leeds. As the new Leeds plant begins commercial operations, it is anticipated that the output of these plants will be used principally by customers currently served by the company.

It is obvious that the continuance of the desired rate of growth is dependent upon the funds available to finance these capital expenditure programs. In 1973 capital expenditures were $6,141,000 and included $4,600,000 for the new plant in Leeds. The company was able to finance 1973 capital expenditures largely from internal cash sources. Sixty-five percent of cash required for 1973 came from operations. Sources of cash are listed below for 1973:

From operations, including depreciation and amortization, deferred income taxes, and investment tax credits	$4,462,000
Increase in current liabilities net of a small increase in current assets (other than cash items and current maturities of long-term debt)	1,025,000
Sale of marketable securities on hand at December 31, 1972	604,000
Proceeds from new long-term bank debt	500,000
Sale of stock under employee plans	247,000
Decrease in cash in banks	16,000
Total cash available for needs	$6,854,000

Of cash used, nearly 90 percent was invested in new plant and equipment. The principal uses of cash during 1973 were:

New capital investment including principally the Leeds, South Carolina, plant	$6,141,000
Cash dividends ($.59 per share) paid to shareholders	597,000
Retirement of a long-term obligation with cash	116,000
Total uses of cash	$6,854,000

The company projects capital expenditures for 1974 of up to $8 million and for 1975 of up to $8 million. The projected expenditures for 1974 and 1975 include approximately $7 million for a proposed new organic chemical facility including related pollution control equipment. A final decision on this facility will be made after feasibility studies are completed.

Projected 1974 and 1975 capital expenditures for which capital expenditures have been completed include (1) approximately $800,000 for completion of the Leeds sodium hydrosulfite facility, which began test operations in December 1973, and $1,300,000 for related facilities, including pollution control equipment; and (2) approximately $2,200,000 at Portsmouth for completion of a new solid sodium bisulfite facility ($1,700,000) and related pollution control equipment ($500,000). The balance of the capital expenditures is for other corporate programs.

Buchanan stated that "as is customary throughout the chemical industry, a large amount of output of current and projected plants is covered by short and long-term arrangements." Based on the manner in which the company conducts its business and on current information about the company's long-established markets, management believes that the capital expenditures will be recovered from earnings attributable to the program within an acceptable number of years.

The financing necessary for these capital expenditures and related working capital and for retirement of $2,500,000 of long-term bank debt outstanding on December 31, 1973, has been studied. Present plans contemplate the issuance in 1974 of $2 million of tax-exempt industrial development bonds, $1,200,000 of tax-exempt pollution control bonds, and $5 million of long-term senior notes. Depending on the results of the feasibility studies for the proposed organic chemical facility and the company's capital needs, an additional $5 million of long-term debt securities, that may include $1 million of pollution control bonds, may be issued in 1975. Management feels that the funds to be derived from this financing, the sale of stock under existing employee benefit programs, and operations will be sufficient to pay for the capital expenditures, retire the $2,500,000 long-term bank debt, and provide necessary additional working capital.

AMMCO TOOLS, INC.

"I have always believed in people. I love to work with creative people regardless of the field they are in. People are an important part of business, and I would like to draw from the best part of these people. Our best man does not have a degree; he has only a seventh-grade education; he is long on common sense; he's an inventor," said Mr. Fred G. Wacker, Jr., president of AMMCO Tools, Inc., which was a North-Chicago-based, family-owned manufacturer and marketer of engine rebuilding, brake service, and wheel alignment tools and equipment. Under the leadership of Wacker, AMMCO had enjoyed continued growth, especially since 1960. Sales and profit grew from $4.5 million and $143,000, respectively, to $15.9 million and $1.6 million in 1973. (See Exhibit 1 for selected financial data for the company.)

THE AUTOMOTIVE AFTERMARKET INDUSTRY

The automotive aftermarket industry was, according to Merritt Hursh, vice president of research for *Jobber Topics* (an aftermarket industry trade journal), a very nebulous industry that was "hard to get your arms around." In a general sense it incorporated the entire spectrum of repair and service of cars: engine repair and rebuilding, brake relining, wheel balancing and alignment, exhaust system repairs and replacement, painting, replacement parts, tires, batteries, etc. AMMCO was part of the diverse and individualized tool sector, composed of many small firms and divisions of larger companies. Competition within the tool sector was hard to pinpoint because numerous firms specialized in only one specific aspect of the industry while others participated in two or three different aspects. For example, one company manufactured one tool to tighten one bolt on a certain type of car, while AMMCO produced various tools for engine rebuilding, brake service and repair, and wheel alignment and balancing. Thus, no two firms were in direct competition throughout their entire product lines.

Prepared by Lawrence D. Chrzanowski and Charles S. Wilson, under the supervision of Professor Ram Charan of Northwestern University.

EXHIBIT 1 AMMCO TOOLS, INC., CONSOLIDATED BALANCE SHEETS (Thousands of Dollars)

	1960	*1963*	*1966*	*1967*	*1968*	*1971*	*1972*	*1973*
Assets								
Cash and Liquid Securities	312.2	65.3	117.4	225.6	1,564.6	2,439.3	1,215.5	528.7
Receivables	389.2	554.6	957.7	694.3	786.9	1,037.6	1,691.9*	1,365.3
Due from LCC	258.2	267.0	229.0	641.8	122.1	40.9	5.6	76.6
Inventories (Auto)	755.3	1,102.5	1,407.7	1,101.5	1,292.9	1,526.9	1,554.7	2,202.9
Inventories (Meters)	479.8	798.0	193.8	56.4	—	—	—	—
Prepaid Expenses	13.3	31.1	86.1	89.4	71.0	99.6	62.1	33.1
Current Assets	2,208.0	2,818.5	2,991.7	2,809.0	3,837.5	5,144.3	4,529.8	4,206.6
Investment—LCC	—	—	800.0	800.0	800.0	800.0	800.0	850.0
Other Investments	152.2	167.9	146.7	147.3	153.0	166.2	211.3	531.1
Patents & Trademarks	10.6	10.0	13.1	12.9	12.3	10.8	11.2	13.1
Property, Plant & Equipment	1,525.9	2,007.1	2,496.7	2,618.6	2,684.0	4,120.8	6,072.7	7,408.0
(Accumulated Depreciation)	(698.8)	(996.3)	(1,516.0)	(1,686.8)	(1,836.5)	(2,077.0)	(2,429.2)	(2,724.7)
Net Plant & Equipment	827.1	1,010.8	980.7	931.8	847.5	2,043.8	3,643.5	4,683.3
Deferred Fed. Income Tax	—	—	—	—	—	73.0	147.0	193.0
Total Assets	3,197.9	4,007.2	4,932.2	4,701.0	5,650.3	8,238.1	9,342.8	10,477.1
Liabilities								
Payables	690.6	378.3	331.8	70.9	257.1	314.1	366.2	448.8
Accrued Expenses	334.1	175.0	337.1	378.6	840.4	1,290.9	1,060.4	879.6
Current Liabilities	1,024.7	553.3	668.9	449.5	1,097.5	1,605.0	1,426.6	1,328.4
Long-Term Debt								
Stockholders & Others	138.0	69.0	—	—	—	63.6	125.3	190.0
Prudential	—	805.0	1,450.0	1,350.0	1,250.0	950.0	850.0	750.0
Total Liabilities	1,162.7	1,427.3	2,118.9	1,799.5	2,347.5	2,618.6	2,401.9	2,268.4

Equity	1,891.8	2,471.6	2,726.6	2,813.3	2,901.5	4,478.5	6,519.4	6,940.9
Current Year Earnings	143.4	108.4	86.7	88.2	401.3	1,310.8	1,661.1	1,607.4
(Less Dividends)	(-)	(-)	(-)	(-)	(-)	(169.8)	(339.6)	(339.6)
(Other)	(-)	(-)	(-)	(-)	(-)	(-)	(900.0)	(-)
Total Equity	2,035.2	2,579.9	2,713.3	2,901.5	3,302.8	5,619.5	6,941.0	8,208.7
Total Liability & Equity	3,197.9	4,007.2	4,932.2	4,701.0	5,650.3	8,238.1	9,342.8	10,477.1

Consolidated Income Statement

Gross Shipments	4,592.9	5,279.5	6,369.0	6,359.4	7,780.7	12,545.9	14,965.5	16,206.9
Less: Returns/Allowances	111.8	110.1	138.4	189.9	192.1	274.0	189.3	236.9
Net Shipments	4,481.1	5,169.4	6,230.6	6,169.5	7,588.6	12,271.9	14,776.2	15,970.0
Cost of Sales	2,206.2	2,790.2	3,442.4	3,447.5	3,740.3	5,198.7	6,301.1	7,192.0
Gross Profit on Sales	2,274.9	2,379.2	2,788.2	2,722.0	3,848.3	7,073.2	8,475.1	8,778.0
Meter Income**	41.2	44.8	145.3	81.6	29.8	3.8	2.9	4.1
Other Costs & Expenses								
Commissions	810.6	536.2	763.0	749.5	931.4	1,621.4	1,963.9	2,141.0
Engineering	206.8	214.2	289.9	193.2	244.4	188.3	215.2	332.3
Selling, Admin., General	952.5	1,355.5	1,599.3	1,569.8	1,768.7	2,578.2	2,962.0	3,111.7
Operating Income	346.2	318.1	281.3	291.1	933.6	2,689.1	3,336.9	3,197.1
Interest expense	40.8	71.8	92.6	112.9	77.3	61.3	56.8	56.8
Net Income	305.4	246.3	188.7	178.2	856.3	2,627.8	3,280.1	3,140.3
Tax Provision	162.0	138.0	102.0	90.0	455.0	1,317.0	1,619.0	1,533.0
Net Profit	143.4	108.3	86.7	88.2	401.3	1,310.8	1,661.1	1,607.3

**A small tools promotion that encouraged orders by the end of 1972 is the primary cause for the increase in year-end accounts receivable.*
***Minimal subcontracted machining for LCC.*

One measure of the aftermarket industry is given in Exhibit 2, which is based on sales by wholesalers. Also shown are the two major categories in which AMMCO competed.

AMMCO's product groups of heavy equipment (brake lathes and brake-shoe grinders), accessories (shop benches, facing sets, silencers, adapters, etc.), parts (replacement parts for the heavy equipment), and wheel service (auto ramp and rack alignment systems) were included in the equipment (all types) category. AMMCO's product groups of small tools (cylinder and brake hones, ridge reamers, torque wrenches, decelerometers, etc.) and stones and cutters (tool bits, stone sets, and abrasive belts) were included in the small hand-tools category. A sales summary of AMMCO's products by groups is provided in Exhibit 3.

While not requiring tremendous capital to enter, the industry's tool sector was characterized by a high degree of technology and a need for creative engineering talents. Design was based on ease of operation with maximum performance. Since the basic structure of the automobile was not subject to frequent, radically new inventions, the automotive aftermarket tool industry had potential for growth, but not to the degree associated with the glamour industries of recent years. Thus, it was basically concerned with refining and increasing the efficiency of tools for repairing cars.

Although car sales and servicing were seasonal, the tool sector of the industry was not. The actual market for automotive aftermarket tools was the car, truck, and bus repair industry, which consisted of small operations such as auto repair shops and service stations; the auto centers of large chainstores such as Sears and K-Mart; tire stores such as Firestone and Goodyear; the franchised service stations of large oil companies; the federal government; some exports; and auto enthusiasts such as hobbyists and do-it-yourselvers. The structure of the aftermarket and its changing nature are shown in Exhibits 4, and 5.

AMMCO TOOLS, INC.

Fred G. Wacker, Sr. started AMMCO Tools, Inc. (then known as Automotive Maintenance Machine Co.) in 1922 by purchasing the patent rights for an engine-cylinder grinder (a tool used to smooth out the walls of a worn cylinder that had lost its shape, leaving the piston without a complete seal inside the cylinder.) AMMCO started manufacturing hand and machine tools in Chicago with six employees, and by 1929 had a sales volume of $350,000. In 1935 the senior Wacker moved AMMCO to a purchased building in North Chicago. By developing and expanding its line of engine rebuilding tools, the company was able to rebound from the Depression and rëach a $500,000 sales level by 1940. During the war AMMCO produced a small toolroom shaper, used for shaping metal, which the government bought in quantity. The company later sold the machine to Delta, a division of Rockwell Man-

EXHIBIT 2 SALES BY WHOLESALERS (Millions)

	1967	*1968*	*1969*	*1970*	*1971*	*1972*
Total	$4,960	$5,200	$5,442	$5,460	$5,650	$5,933
Equipment (all types)	274	252	146	127	106	147
Small hand tools	82	69	80	101	93	106

ufacturing Company, because AMMCO had decided not to produce any of the complementary machinery to make a complete line (i.e., lathes and milling machines). Rockwell had sold only a few thousand shapers since the war.

In 1947, when Wacker, Jr. entered the company, there was a stabilization in the demand for engine rebuilding tools because better materials, lubricants, and paved roads increased the time engines could last between repairs; auto owners began taking increasingly complicated engines to centralized engine rebuilders rather than to individual garages or doing their own repairs. This centralization of engine rebuilding reduced the individual garages' demand for tools. Frequently, a tool was used on many jobs continuously in a centralized rebuilding shop rather than on a few jobs in many individual garages. Hence, AMMCO decided to move into brake-service tools because with larger and more powerful cars coming into the market, the brakes were wearing out faster than the engines.

AMMCO pursued brake-service tools by purchasing the rights for a brake-shoe gauge in 1950 from a West Coast inventor, who, later that year, also sold AMMCO a new design for a brake-shoe grinder, something AMMCO had worked on for a year without success. Wacker, Jr. modified the traditional pricing formula to get market acceptance for the new grinder, and the difference between profit and loss in 1950 was due to AMMCO's brake related business.

In 1952 AMMCO produced its own brake-drum lathe. Wacker, Jr. made attempts to buy out two companies already producing lathes, but he was not able to get together with the owners on price. Therefore, AMMCO developed its own lathe, which turned out to be better than the others and became the industry standard. "I was very disappointed when we couldn't buy either of those companies," Wacker, Jr. said, "but the Man upstairs must have been looking out for us."

In 1954, Wacker, Jr. looked to diversify from the company's great dependence on the automobile industry. AMMCO's patent attorney was asked to look for a product that would fit in with AMMCO's production methods and facilities. In the meantime, AMMCO experimented with bicycle engines and food machinery such as orange juicers, but with poor results. The attorney told Wacker that a neighbor, George Richards, had invented a positive displacement meter for measuring heavy fluids such as oil. Wacker purchased the Richards patents and formed the Liquid Controls Corporation (LCC). During the 1950s and early 1960s, Wacker spent half his time setting up LCC, which took a long while to produce a profit. LCC initially operated from the AMMCO plant, but it was soon moved to a separate facility. Richards, disliking the design of the new plant, refused to carry out Wacker's instructions. There was more trouble when Richards, who was paid a guaranteed minimum and a percentage of yearly sales, wanted a larger percentage, and although Wacker talked him out of resigning twice, Richards eventually left in 1967. LCC did not produce attractive profits until 1974 (about 7 percent of sales, after taxes).

Starting in the mid 1950s a number of problems developed in AMMCO. The company became very new-product-oriented, using a scatter-shot approach, under which products were introduced before they were properly tested. Five or six products had to be recalled and redesigned at great expense. The emphasis on new products resulted in less concentration on AMMCO's old-line products, which subsequently declined in quality. At the same time, AMMCO's plant and equipment were becoming outdated compared to the rest of the industry, and AMMCO experienced bottlenecks and tie-ups in production. Communications were beginning to break down, and the engineering department began to develop a philosophy different from Wacker's.

EXHIBIT 3 AMMCO TOOLS, INC., SALES SUMMARY (in Dollars)

	1960	*1963*	*1966*	*1967*
Sales by Product Group				
Heavy Equipment	1,948,683	2,333,970	2,849,866	2,568,244
Accessories	391,062	464,508	654,474	745,332
Small Tools	1,049,083	1,123,974	1,201,324	1,294,544
Stones & Cutters	721,407	879,418	934,906	966,241
Wheel Service	—	44,888	306,453	275,253
Parts	360,067	275,595	278,717	317,827
Miscellaneous	10,768	47,059	4,876	2,059
Total	4,481,070	5,169,412	6,230,616	6,169,500
Cost of Sales by Group				
Heavy Equipment	1,009,145	1,323,779	1,648,859	1,518,784
Accessories	202,515	223,795	344,624	399,597
Small Tools	423,861	469,495	590,935	659,098
Stones & Cutters	302,442	307,192	377,246	369,611
Wheel Service	—	24,922	212,573	188,111
Parts	142,309	122,417	98,285	112,779
Miscellaneous	7,981	25,360	4,060	442
Total	2,088,253	2,496,960	3,276,582	3,248,422
Gross Profit by Group				
Heavy Equipment	939,538	1,010,191	1,201,007	1,049,460
Accessories	188,547	240,713	309,850	345,735
Small Tools	625,222	654,479	610,389	635,446
Stones & Cutters	418,965	572,226	557,660	596,630
Wheel Service	—	19,966	93,880	87,142
Parts	217,758	153,178	180,432	205,048
Miscellaneous	2,787	21,699	816	1,617
Total	2,392,817	2,672,452	2,954,034	2,921,078
Sales—Domestic & Export				
Territories	3,877,414	4,333,292	5,392,349	5,343,597
House	104,703	131,477	352,284	384,275
Canada	154,718	125,071	153,943	127,923
Subtotal	4,136,835	4,589,840	5,989,576	5,855,795
Export	344,235	579,572	332,040	313,705
Total	4,481,070	5,169,412	6,230,616	6,169,500
Unshipped Orders	43,713	63,432	207,849	527,089

EXHIBIT 3 AMMCO TOOLS, INC. (Cont.)

	1968	*1971*	*1972*	*1973*
Sales by Product Group				
Heavy Equipment	3,281,601	6,575,378	8,274,743	9,139,876
Accessories	823,069	1,926,006	2,183,295	2,279,829
Small Tools	1,716,908	1,751,667	1,903,761	1,931,794
Stones & Cutters	1,032,249	1,470,178	1,697,580	1,839,385
Wheel Service	368,290	219,181	303,662	272,166
Parts	361,581	305,888	397,933	505,234
Miscellaneous	4,893	23,582	15,206	1,750
Total	7,588,591	12,271,880	14,776,180	15,970,034
Cost of Sales by Group				
Heavy Equipment	1,609,716	2,556,467	3,143,546	3,906,451
Accessories	359,476	702,407	817,150	918,694
Small Tools	811,252	773,748	835,624	968,781
Stones & Cutters	405,406	555,174	697,467	771,804
Wheel Service	208,389	105,919	158,916	156,535
Parts	123,758	81,385	107,858	157,528
Miscellaneous	988	12,164	13,527	3,454
Total	3,518,985	4,787,264	5,774,088	6,883,247
Gross Profit by Group				
Heavy Equipment	1,671,885	4,018,911	5,131,197	5,233,425
Accessories	463,593	1,223,599	1,366,145	1,361,135
Small Tools	905,656	977,919	1,068,119	963,013
Stones & Cutters	626,843	915,004	1,000,113	1,067,581
Wheel Service	159,901	113,262	144,746	115,631
Parts	237,823	224,503	290,075	347,706
Miscellaneous	3,905	11,418	1,679	1,704
Total	4,069,606	7,484,616	9,002,074	9,090,195
Sales—Domestic & Export				
Territories	6,650,566	11,449,851	13,774,515	15,064,398
House	398,539	180,828	125,198	56,114
Canada	171,445	286,554	319,334	326,432
Subtotal	7,220,550	11,917,233	14,219,047	15,446,944
Export	368,041	354,647	557,133	523,090
Total	7,588,591	12,271,880	14,776,180	15,970,034
Unshipped Orders	880,319	441,563	1,125,999	5,806,606

EXHIBIT 4 THE AUTOMOTIVE AFTERMARKET IN THE 1970S

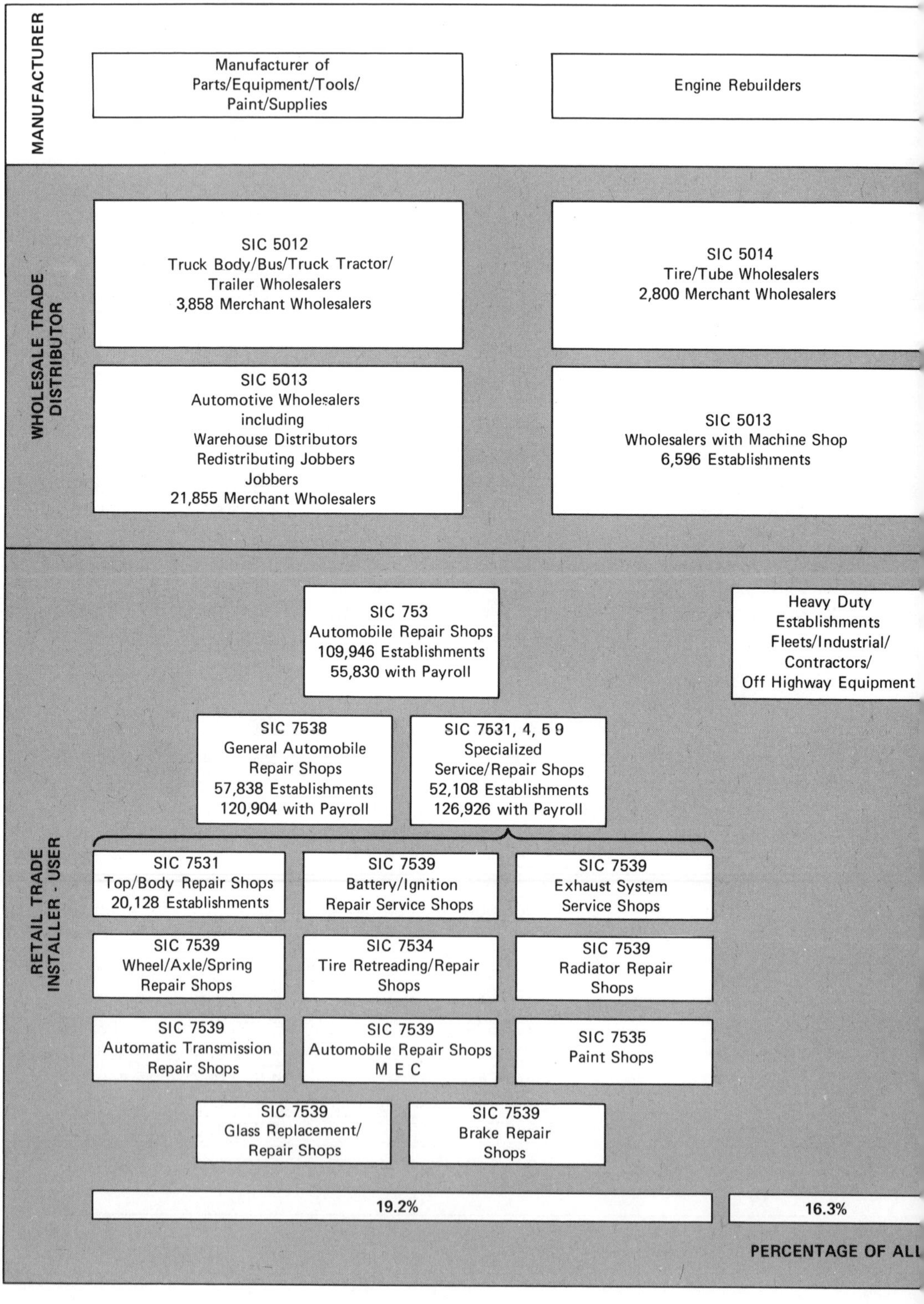
MANUFACTURER
Manufacturer of Parts/Equipment/Tools/ Paint/Supplies
Engine Rebuilders
WHOLESALE TRADE DISTRIBUTOR
SIC 5012 Truck Body/Bus/Truck Tractor/ Trailer Wholesalers 3,858 Merchant Wholesalers
SIC 5014 Tire/Tube Wholesalers 2,800 Merchant Wholesalers
SIC 5013 Automotive Wholesalers including Warehouse Distributors Redistributing Jobbers Jobbers 21,855 Merchant Wholesalers
SIC 5013 Wholesalers with Machine Shop 6,596 Establishments
RETAIL TRADE INSTALLER - USER
SIC 753 Automobile Repair Shops 109,946 Establishments 55,830 with Payroll
Heavy Duty Establishments Fleets/Industrial/ Contractors/ Off Highway Equipment
SIC 7538 General Automobile Repair Shops 57,838 Establishments 120,904 with Payroll
SIC 7531, 4, 5 9 Specialized Service/Repair Shops 52,108 Establishments 126,926 with Payroll
SIC 7531 Top/Body Repair Shops 20,128 Establishments
SIC 7539 Battery/Ignition Repair Service Shops
SIC 7539 Exhaust System Service Shops
SIC 7539 Wheel/Axle/Spring Repair Shops
SIC 7534 Tire Retreading/Repair Shops
SIC 7539 Radiator Repair Shops
SIC 7539 Automatic Transmission Repair Shops
SIC 7539 Automobile Repair Shops M E C
SIC 7535 Paint Shops
SIC 7539 Glass Replacement/ Repair Shops
SIC 7539 Brake Repair Shops
19.2%
16.3%
PERCENTAGE OF ALL

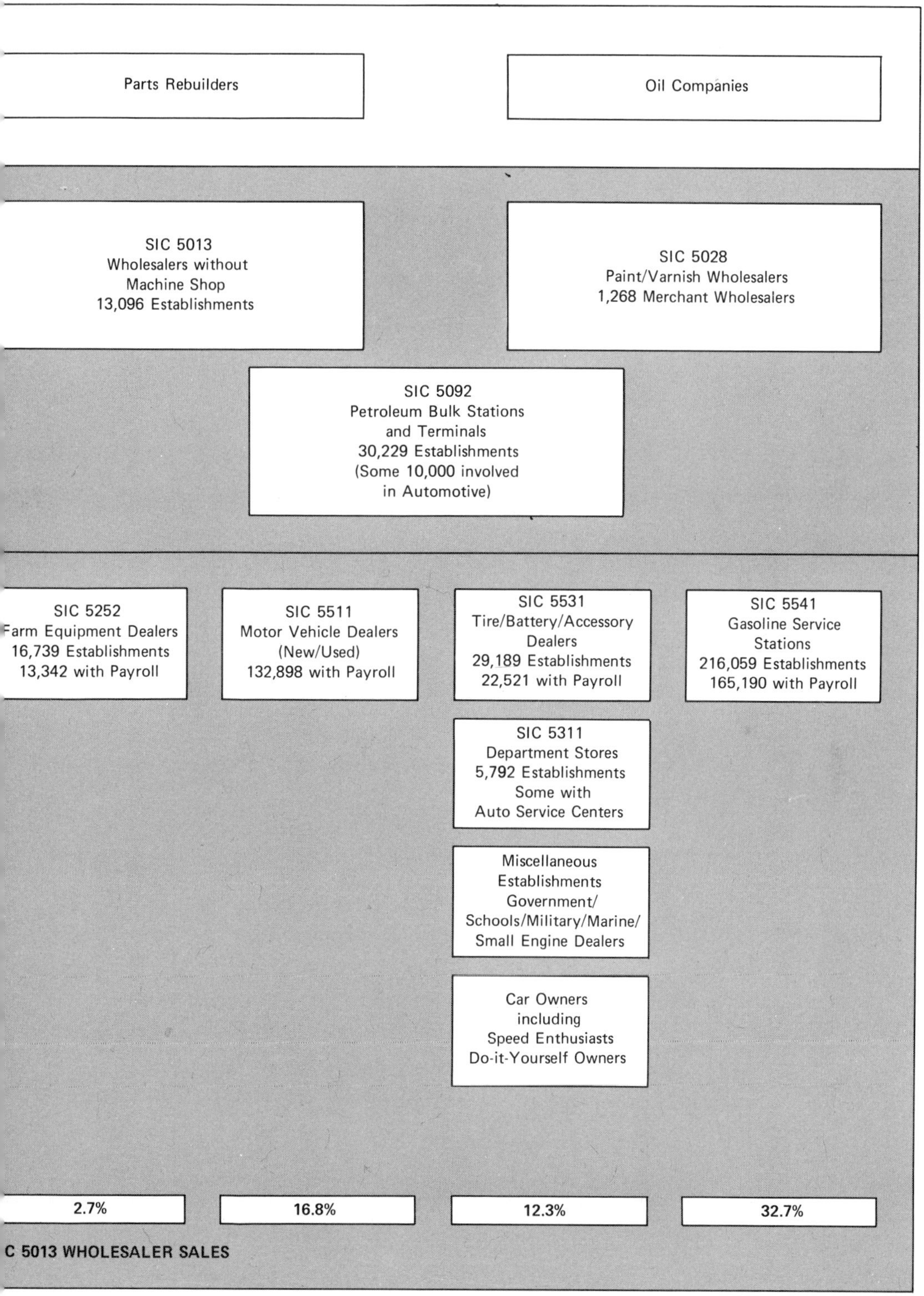

Parts Rebuilders
Oil Companies
SIC 5013
Wholesalers without
Machine Shop
13,096 Establishments
SIC 5028
Paint/Varnish Wholesalers
1,268 Merchant Wholesalers
SIC 5092
Petroleum Bulk Stations
and Terminals
30,229 Establishments
(Some 10,000 involved
in Automotive)
SIC 5252
Farm Equipment Dealers
16,739 Establishments
13,342 with Payroll
SIC 5511
Motor Vehicle Dealers
(New/Used)
132,898 with Payroll
SIC 5531
Tire/Battery/Accessory
Dealers
29,189 Establishments
22,521 with Payroll
SIC 5541
Gasoline Service
Stations
216,059 Establishments
165,190 with Payroll
SIC 5311
Department Stores
5,792 Establishments
Some with
Auto Service Centers
Miscellaneous
Establishments
Government/
Schools/Military/Marine/
Small Engine Dealers
Car Owners
including
Speed Enthusiasts
Do-it-Yourself Owners
2.7%
16.8%
12.3%
32.7%
C 5013 WHOLESALER SALES

EXHIBIT 5 AUTOMOTIVE WHOLESALERS (MERCHANT WHOLESALERS)

	Number of Establishments by Sales Size						
Sales Volume	1971*	1967	1963	1958	1954	1948	1939
$10,000,000 or more	—	88	16	11	—	—	—
$ 5,000,000–$9,999,999	—		38	29	25	11	—
$ 2,000,000–$4,999,999	—	329	192	112	82	68	6
$ 1,000,000–$1,999,999	—	2,650	633	372	240	190	33
$ 500,000–$ 999,999	—		1,646	1,092	675	573	81
Over $500,000	4,200	3,067	2,525	1,616	1,022	842	120
$ 300,000–$ 499,999	—	5,807	2,307	1,480	1,126	941	132
$ 200,000–$ 299,999	—		2,869	1,854	1,481	1,134	223
$ 100,000–$ 199,999	—	6,075	5,949	4,080	3,418	2,778	769
$ 50,000–$ 99,999	—	6,381	6,517	2,788	2,984	2,598	1,401
Under $50,000	—			1,901	2,182	2,666	3,492
Under $500,000	17,800	18,263	17,642	12,103	11,191	10,117	6,017
Not Operated Entire Year	500	525	885	389	350	—	—
Total Establishments	22,500	21,855	21,052[1]	14,108[1]	12,563	10,959	6,137

**Market PROBE estimate*
1. Totals based on U.S. Business Census figures published as of given year. Details not available based on adjusted figures reported in later U.S. Business Census Reports.
Source: U.S. Department of Commerce/Bureau of the Census

Problems were pyramiding in 1967 when cost-of-goods-sold reached 56 percent of sales, profit dropped to 1.4 percent of sales, and Wacker felt he might not be able to meet AMMCO's payroll in a few weeks. Appendix A presents quarterly accounting statements for 1967. Also during this time, the lead time for supplies dropped sharply so that AMMCO developed huge inventories of both finished goods and raw materials, and inventories became greater than unfilled orders. The sales prediction for 1967 was a 10 percent increase in sales, but demand actually dropped. AMMCO's debt-to-equity ratio reached a high of 70 percent.

Meanwhile, a new computerized inventory system was received with antagonism. Wacker asked for changes but none came—no one seemed to care. Thus in August 1967, Wacker, with the aid of Wally Mitchell, vice president and director of manufacturing and engineering, and Robert Pranke, treasurer and controller, acted to bail out the company. They devised five steps to generate cash and improve employee morale:

1. 117 people were fired or left including the chief engineer. Internal bugs in the basic operation were eliminated, and all new research and development was stopped so that more time could be spent improving the old standard lines.
2. Bottlenecks were reduced by using new machinery and by redesigning the products so that they were easier to manufacture; overtime, second, and third shifts were eliminated.

   (The two steps allowed AMMCO to generate enough cash to pay off $800,000 in debt in six months and to improve the plant. Wacker was no longer "paying bodies." During this time, Wacker moved his office into the plant so that he would have a more direct control over the operation.)
3. Control was enhanced through the use of a computer to monitor the flow of goods through the plant, so that all parts would be ready when needed.
4. Research and development was reinstituted.
5. The total operation was refined and expanded.

During this time Wacker also began using control charts, produced by the W. C. Heath Company, which graphically showed trends in the company's inventories, accounts receivables, assets, etc. Wacker felt that these charts gave the viewer an immediate picture of AMMCO's performance and the direction in which the company was moving. By 1973 AMMCO had $16 million in sales with 319 people compared to $6 million in sales with 475 people in 1967. This was accomplished with no overtime and using only one shift. By 1973 AMMCO had its cost of goods sold down to 44 percent of sales and its after-tax profit up to 10.6 percent of sales.

PRODUCT POLICY

"I do not believe in planned obsolescence; I like to produce value for the money the customer pays. We build things by which other people make a living," Wacker said. "The company makes and sells the same tool (cylinder grinder) today as my father sold when he started the business in 1922. Nothing that AMMCO Tools manufactures is designed to ever wear out, given reasonable care."

AMMCO has striven continually for increased product quality while minimizing the operating complexity for the user. For example, a vibration dampener for the lathes was produced to improve the machine finish on the disc brakes. Two nylon pads used to accomplish the dampening eventually wore out, thereby creating a replacement market. Two years later, a friction material was tried experimentally. This new material extended the life of the dampener pads to such an extent that the replacement market would be eliminated altogether were the design change to be made. Wacker made the change regardless of some internal opposition. Also, a very successful double-boring bar was introduced as an accessory, making it possible to machine both faces of a disc brake simultaneously.

This concern for quality often manifested itself in a product's delayed market introduction due to thorough testing by AMMCO. Also, after a product was released, the company would follow up to see that it still operated correctly.

MANUFACTURING

Production at AMMCO basically consisted of machining and assembly operations using bar stock, castings, forgings, and electric motors as basic inventories. Although increasing its dependence on machines, the operation required highly skilled labor. From 1968 to 1973, the number of direct and indirect employees involved in actual production had decreased from 191 to 182.

AMMCO's product line was composed of over 150 items, which consisted of 5 to 6,000 different parts for each item. Some individual parts required as many as ten separate operations.

The plant had been expanded piecemeal. As Wacker said, "We did what we had to do at the time. In retrospect it shows poor planning, but it worked." The current additions or purchases of new machinery were on a pay-as-you-go basis, which was best summed up by Wally Mitchell. "I am a believer in the Bohemian plan," he said. "We must earn and have the money before we spend." At Mitchell's recommendation, investments in plant and equipment were made to eliminate production bottlenecks and enhance finished goods turnover.

Considerable emphasis was placed on rationalizing the manufacturing processes to facilitate the flow of materials and reduce scrap losses. Scrap losses were reduced from 6.5 percent of direct material input in 1968 to 1.2 percent in 1973. Mitchell was responsible for product design and manufacturing processing. A recent employee, Lenny Morrison, introduced sophisticated technology in the form of lasers and optical processes to AMMCO's wheel-alignment products. Morrison had formerly been associated with the Technological Institute of Northwestern University.

MARKETING AND SALES

In sales, AMMCO covered the U. S. with six regions staffed by eighty-six district managers under six regional managers. The regional managers were salaried and given bonuses on volume while district managers were paid a straight commission from which they paid their own expenses. Commissions were a percentage of the net invoice amount; the percentage was 10 percent, 15 percent, or 20 percent, depending on the particular item. The district manager in the area where a product was set up and used received the commission regardless of whether he took the initial order. Returns necessitated that the district manager in that area forfeit his portion of the commission for those items returned. Sales were highly dependent upon service after the sale. Therefore, the commission system was an incentive not strictly for sales but for high levels of customer service. The district managers' duties included filling orders, installing and teaching people to use machines, servicing for both dealers and jobbers, and soliciting new orders, which the district managers then sent either to a jobber or to AMMCO directly. House accounts were handled by the home office. Car registrations, counties, and sales volume were used to determine sales areas. As sales volume increased the areas were trimmed to handle the concentration, allowing AMMCO to take advantage of greater sales at less cost. Initially the salesmen did not like this method, but experience showed that it increased their sales.

By 1973, 20 percent of AMMCO's sales were national accounts such as Sears & Roebuck and Goodyear. This figure was expected to continue to grow.

The company had a strict pricing policy: it marked up each item in the product line 100 percent above manufacturing cost and rigidly controlled costs. Price changes were made once a year at most. When an unprofitable item was identified from the computer outputs as making significantly less than 100 percent return on cost, the price of this item was raised, and if the sales volume and higher price did not enhance the item's profitability, it was dropped from the product line by designating the item as discontinued and eventually deleting it from the price list.

The district managers were free to work autonomously in their dealings with customers in implementing programs to increase sales as long as they followed the discount and pricing policies set by the company. The district managers were also free to share commissions when a distributor's area overlapped sales areas. Advertising and marketing vice president Richard Stevenson said the AMMCO sales force was more conscientious than some of its competitors; AMMCO men worked only for AMMCO, whereas in some cases salesmen in the industry represented many companies at the same time. Also, many of AMMCO's salespeople began working in AMMCO's plant so that they knew their product much better. Adding his personal touch at a gathering of the regional managers, Wacker was very proud to show the improvements in the work processes at locations where many of the regional managers had begun their careers at AMMCO.

AMMCO did some subcontracting for companies under their brand name (such as Craftsman for Sears & Roebuck), but this was a small part of total sales, as were exports. Twenty direct mailings a year and ads at car races were also used. But AMMCO's biggest publicity was through word of mouth among people using the products in their own businesses, which Stevenson said tended to cause the company to minimize field problems.

In 1973, AMMCO spent $300,000 on promotion such as advertising, catalogs, and trade shows. The total selling expense for 1973 was $1 million, and AMMCO paid almost $150,000 for sales bonuses, while commissions were about $2.1 million.

For 1973, the top selling item (brake-drum lathe) accounted for 38 percent of total sales. The top five and ten selling items accounted for 54 percent and 64 percent of total sales, respectively.

Dick Manning, vice president and general sales manager, felt the best way to view AMMCO and its competition was to divide AMMCO into three groups: brake equipment, small tools, and wheel alignment equipment. Although few figures were available, Manning referred to a study performed by a competitor in 1970 that showed AMMCO was responsible for about 65 percent of the brake business; the rest of the brake business was divided among five competitors. Manning felt the percentage was presently down to about 55 percent because AMMCO was unable to fill all orders due to the castings shortage. In small tools, Manning felt that although AMMCO did not produce the diverse selection of tools as its four competitors, AMMCO was the sales leader (or second highest) in the products it produced. In wheel alignment AMMCO was about ninth in a field of ten competitors. This was due to AMMCO's recent entry into the field.

Another AMMCO executive felt that AMMCO was the Rolls-Royce of the industry, and that because of this superior quality, AMMCO's prices were higher than the prices of its competitors.

Stevenson suggested the company diversify from brake equipment by placing more emphasis on hand tools, which would reduce the selling costs of instruction, set-up, and service. He also said he thought the company should improve its engineering staff and strengthen its product development.

FINANCE

AMMCO made much use of historical data in planning current finances. Monthly estimates were generated from a base of actual performance in previous years. A sales forecast was established and the historical percentages of sales for the various items were used to determine the budgeted amounts, which were used as standards and not as specific authorizations. Expenses continually were compared to sales in order to see if historical percentages were maintained or could be improved. A very modest seasonality was involved, with sales from April 1 to October 1 approximately 53 percent of yearly volume.

Profitability had been hampered during 1973 because of governmental price controls. These controls applied more stringently to AMMCO's products than to some of AMMCO's material and labor inputs. After the price controls were lifted, AMMCO made plans to raise prices where needed.

PERSONNEL

"We look for two things in a potential employee: attitude and the ability to do the job. With the right attitude you can move mountains," said John Lauten, industrial relations manager. "We're a shirt-sleeve organization where communication is on a one-to-one basis," he continued. "We don't waste time with memos and notes. We just pick up the phone or go see the guy."

Lauten came from Chicago Hardware Foundry in North Chicago, which had been taken over by a larger company in 1967. Lauten had been assistant to the personnel manager at the foundry, where he also had much experience in the industry.

AMMCO employed few college graduates. Most of the people in high positions had advanced from within the company, and many of the district managers had started out working in the factory. The company used a registration method for advancement. Everyone could sign up to be considered for any new opening, and 80 percent to 90 percent of those who registered were advanced. When a man was put ahead, he stayed on a trial basis for a few months, and if he and his supervisor felt he disliked the new position or did poorly, he was given his old job back. The most senior personnel were given the first chance to advance; the decision was made by Lauten, the plant manager, and all the foremen and supervisors involved with the individual.

"People working as a team is what makes AMMCO," Lauten said proudly. "We have few rules because everyone knows what's expected of him." As of December 1973 all the foremen were in their late thirties or early forties, except the general foreman, who was in his early fifties. The two exceptions: Pranke, 50, and Mitchell, 69. Half the factory workers had been with the company more than five years. One of the two turnovers in the managerial staff in the past four years was due to age.

AMMCO's relationship with the union was generally good, although there had been two strikes within the past five years; the most recent strike lasted four months.

Lauten indicated that the company faced the problem of getting good workers for the factory and for the engineering department because the North Chicago area had virtually no unemployment.

ORGANIZATION

AMMCO was a privately owned corporation whose board of directors was composed of Fred G. Wacker, Jr., his mother, sister, brother, and two bank trustees for Fred G. Wacker, Sr.'s estate. Wacker, Jr. was president and chairman of the board; he had held both of these positions since his father's death in 1948.

Wally Mitchell. Though Mitchell, vice president and director of manufacturing and engineering, had a seventh-grade education, he had patented more than 150 inventions. He had previously worked with several companies including Victor Comptometer and Dacor—a manufacturer of scuba-diving equipment. For a while, he and two partners had operated their company, Dukes Manufacturing Company.

Mitchell had worked at AMMCO in the 1930s until a difference of opinion with Wacker, Sr. led to his resignation. When Wacker, Jr. entered the company, his father told him to contact Mitchell if he needed help with certain products he had invented. Wacker, Jr. later did hire Mitchell as a consultant.

The friendship between Mitchell and Wacker, Jr. was built on common interests. When Wacker was racing with the French auto racing team, he brought Mitchell with him as his chief mechanic. In 1967, Wacker had Mitchell survey metal-working firms in Europe and make suggestions for streamlining AMMCO's manufacturing operation. Mitchell had designed some of the company's product line and revamped the production process and also was responsible for some of AMMCO's literary contributions. He established a research group to develop new AMMCO products to solve problems experienced by the large auto and brake companies in which Wacker had contacts. It was Mitchell's feeling that "in U.S. business, most problems are solved by small to medium-sized firms. The big companies don't solve problems, they overwhelm them."

Mitchell, in his spare time, developed a meter that surpassed all existing meters in accuracy of measurement for LCC. Besides his creative ability, Mitchell always kept in mind that his inventions had to be put together by people. In this vein, he designed AMMCO's products in such a way as to allow them to be assembled as easily and as efficiently as possible. One of AMMCO's executives fondly referred to Mitchell as "the maestro who got the production and engineer people to play the same tune."

Mitchell's business philosophy centered on manufacturing. "To increase sales, you first have to increase capacity before the salesmen push sales," he said. He extensively tested products before he would permit market introduction; there was some criticism of Mitchell by those who felt this testing delayed a product's market entry for too long a time. "We need good people to take an idea and pursue it," Mitchell said. "An idea is only as good as what you make it. We must build a better mousetrap; then we'll get the customers."

EXHIBIT 6 AMMCO TOOLS, INC., ORGANIZATION CHART

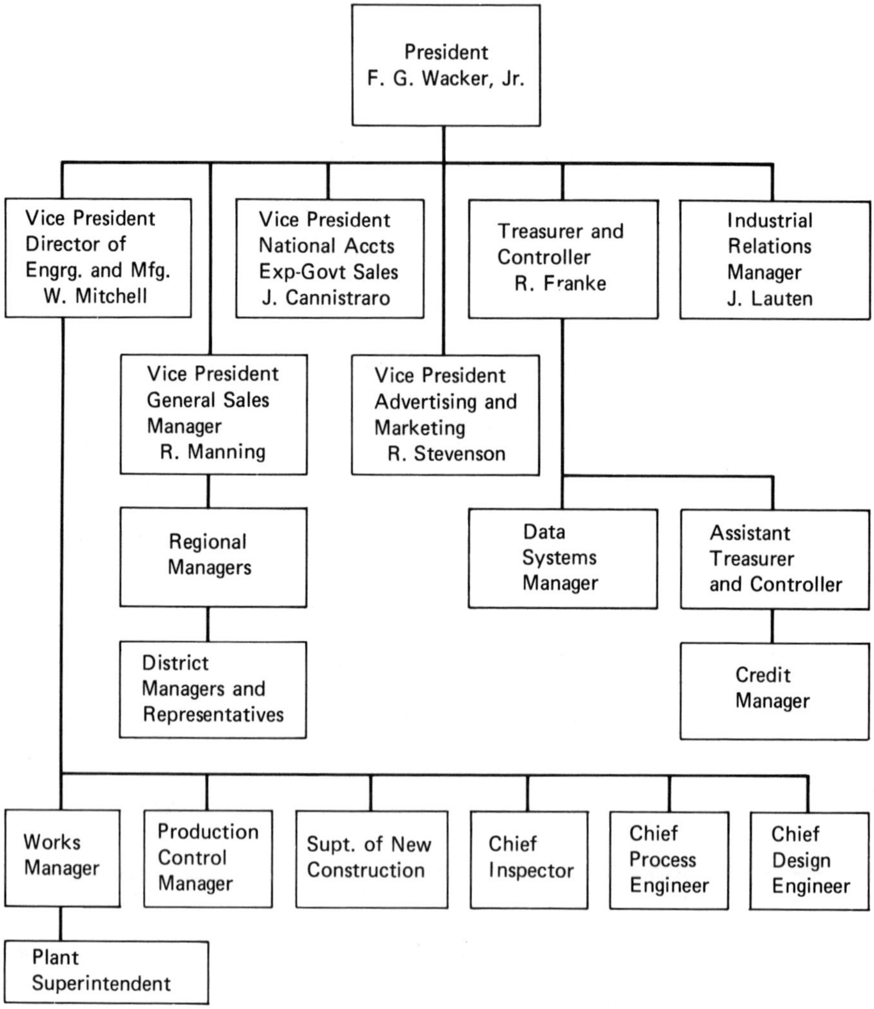

One thing that was beginning to bother Mitchell was the requirement that every manager affected by a proposed investment sign the request. For example, to spend $31,000 for a machine to handle a new supplier's proposed aluminum castings (to alleviate the shortage of iron castings) required eight signatures.

Mitchell was not only vice president and director of manufacturing and engineering at AMMCO, but he filled the same position at LCC. His compensation was in the form of a consultant's fee rather than a fixed salary; generally, Mitchell left work at 3 P.M.

Robert Pranke. Pranke, treasurer and controller, was responsible for pricing policy, forecasts, and budgets. He had developed an early interest in electronic data

EXHIBIT 7 AMMCO TOOLS, INC., PERSONNEL SUMMARY

POSITION	*AGE*	*YEARS AT AMMCO*
President	56	27
Vice-President and Director Engineering & Manufacturing	69	35
Vice-President General Sales Manager	53	11
Vice-President National Accounts, Export, Govt. Sales	56	20
Vice-President Advertising and Marketing	52	28
Treasurer and Controller	50	13
Industrial Relations Manager	41	7
Works Manager	56	15
Prod. Control Manager	58	16
Supt. of New Construction	68	15
Chief Inspector	61	40
Chief Process Engineer	55	10
Chief Design Engineer	39	20
Plant Superintendent	46	4
Regional Manager	65	20
Regional Manager	49	18
Regional Manager	64	29
Regional Manager	61	36
Regional Manager	57	37
Regional Manager	38	12
Credit Manager	42	14
Asst. Treasurer & Controller	37	15
Data Systems Manager	37	10

processing through his past experiences: first with a small company that printed business forms, then later with the Toni Company, a division of Gillette. He came to AMMCO as a controller in 1961, when the company's modest computer system was used for order processing and payroll applications. Two and one-half years later the treasurer resigned with a nervous condition, and Pranke was promoted to treasurer and controller.

Describing how he came to AMMCO, Pranke said, "I was in Chicago working for Toni, and I wanted to leave; one day, while passing an employment agency, I took a chance and went in. The agency had just received AMMCO's job listing. I came to visit AMMCO, and I decided to work here. It shows that if you don't take a chance nothing will ever happen.

"The computer does not necessarily reduce the office staff, but it halts the growth of the office employees with much more information at the user's disposal." Without an increase in the office staff, AMMCO was able to handle a doubling in sales and the proportional increase in the paperwork volume. Pranke considered the computer "the office man's tool."

Pranke, realizing the threatening feeling that the computer gave many of

AMMCO's employees, felt that the only way to get people to accept the computer was to have it supply foremen and department heads with the information they had collected before on their own. This information should be presented in a format identical to the one used by those receiving the information. After this was accomplished, then the computer could provide other information that could be helpful to the foremen and department heads. "You don't have the information user change for the sake of the computer," said Pranke, "but have the computer change for the information user."

Pranke described the interaction between the computer and the manufacturing process at AMMCO: "AMMCO is an industrial engineering textbook case of a metal working company. For example, the machining operations are all done on an incentive pay plan. The flow of any item is monitored with the computer at each work station to provide payroll information. You have an exact recording of what went on, an accountant's dream. You can't find a better source of information than the measure of activity of 180 people trying to make a buck, and operating our incentive payroll system. Thus, the system automatically provides information on our finished and in process inventory."

Pranke was also treasurer and controller for LCC.

Richard Stevenson. Stevenson, vice president of advertising and marketing, was responsible for all promotional advertising and marketing information. He came to AMMCO in 1946 for a summer job before enrolling at Yale University, but for personal reasons he could not attend Yale, and he has been with AMMCO ever since.

Stevenson felt that because of the great amount of "word-of-mouth" publicity that AMMCO enjoyed, the marketing department was continually "dragging its feet" before introducing a product, to be sure the product was perfect and did not tarnish AMMCO's reputation.

Besides feeling that AMMCO had "too many eggs in one basket" and that it should diversify more into hand tools, Stevenson expressed, "I think we are under-engineered; our engineers should be younger, travel with the salesmen, and listen more to the salesmen. I don't think our product development is as aggressive as it should be."

John Lauten. Lauten, industrial relations manager, was responsible for personnel and all labor related matters. "When I came to AMMCO in May 1967, I thought I was joining a sinking ship," Lauten said. "My secretary told me not to bother her because it was her last day, the chief engineer was fired, and over 100 people left or were fired by December. This place was a mess."

Lauten, having already worked with the union representing AMMCO's employees and having brought many of the better workers over from Chicago Hardware Foundry (including the present union president), was on good terms with the employees and trusted by the union. Lauten felt his job basically consisted of eliminating the barriers that existed between management and labor. "People are the strength of AMMCO; people working as a team is what makes AMMCO," said Lauten.

Lauten felt that he would like to see AMMCO grow to about 500 people but no larger. "After about 500 people," said Lauten, "personal contact begins to die and walls begin to be erected between management and labor."

Although admitting that he enjoyed working at AMMCO and that he had no desire to leave, Lauten did have some reservations concerning the future. "Mr. Wacker, through his trust and open-door policy, has created the atmosphere here; if he were to die, I don't know what would happen to the company. I don't think his brother or sister would want to run the company, and his mother is too old (84), even though she came to the plant and signed the checks every week until a few years ago. I think Bob Pranke could do a good job of running the company and keeping the same atmosphere. I worry about them selling AMMCO to a larger company. If AMMCO was left alone, it would be fine; but if the new owners brought in their own management, not only would I be out of a job, but AMMCO wouldn't be the same. Those are the risks of working for a privately held company."

Fred Wacker, Jr. Wacker attended Yale University, where his classmates were Roy Chapin, current president of American Motors Company, and Henry Ford II, chairman of the board of Ford Motor Company. After graduating from college in 1940 with a B.A. in English, he worked in the machine shop at the AC sparkplug division of General Motors, while also studying at the General Motors Institute. Wacker said that "the experience as low man on the totem pole in the machine shop gave me an understanding of the employees' point of view; I learned what it was like to have a six-foot, six-inch foreman stand over you all day." Subsequently, he was moved to the time-study department of AC. He left General Motors to serve in the Navy from 1943 to 1945, and on his return he formed and conducted the Fred Wacker Swing Band, earning $165 a week.

Greatly involved in auto racing, Wacker drove in the European Grand Prix Circuit as a member of the French racing team after World War II; and in addition, he and Phil Hill (the only American to win the championship on the Grand Prix Circuit) raced as a team in the Le Mans 24-hour race. Wacker also won the first Sebring endurance race (1951). He attempted to break a motorcycle world speed record at the Bonneville Salt Flats in 1972. The impression that "business wasn't very exciting" kept Wacker from entering AMMCO, until his father's health was failing in 1947. Drawing on his experience at GM, Wacker improved company efficiency; and after his father's death in 1948, he became president and chairman of the board of directors.

Wacker said his formula for a successful business was a fortuitous combination of men, product, money, and machines; he quoted this equation: (Raw Material + Human Energy) × Tools = Man's Material Welfare. "The multiplying factor is tools, because man has a limited amount of human energy," he said. "And remember always, too, that none of it will be productive unless the entire enterprise is carried out with Christian principles and spiritual guidance throughout."

Wacker felt that too many company presidents spent most of their time doing the wrong things—such as going to seminars, arranging financing, having their companies go public, and devoting their attention to advertising, mergers, and acquisitions. "But if their manufacturing costs are 65 percent," said Wacker, "shouldn't they be spending their time on the floor in order to reduce those costs? Furthermore, without the reduction in costs, how can they improve the earnings for the company?" These reductions in costs could only be accomplished by hard work on the president's part, and even then the reductions could only be achieved gradually, according to Wacker.

Wacker, in talking of his beliefs in fair play and people, pointed out that even before President Johnson's executive order regarding equal employment, he employed blacks against the advice of his management team. Admitting that he made mistakes concerning certain blacks in his initial recruitment, Wacker was very proud of the fact that a black the company hired in 1967 was the union president by 1973. The union was 80 percent white.

Wacker felt it was unfortunate that labor often did not work together with management as in other countries. Wacker kept a card catalog with a photograph of each employee in it on each card. He would memorize the face and name of every employee and attempt to talk to each one when he was in the plant.

AMMCO had considered going public but resisted. "If the outstanding stock is worth more on the marketplace than the true value of the company, then in a sense we have gulled the stockholders," Wacker said. "If it is less, we have gulled the original investors. The Bible says in effect, 'Neither a lender or borrower be, or the borrower is the servant of the lender.' It is for this reason, among others, that AMMCO has generated its growth from its own earnings rather than by borrowing. The growth may take longer, but it is slow, solid, and sure."

With a view to the future, Wacker said he would like to see AMMCO grow at an annual rate of 10 percent. In the last few years, growth had been around 25 percent per year; over the company's lifetime growth had been about 13 percent per year. Wacker felt the growth in the past few years had been too fast and was putting pressure on his limited management team since he, Pranke, and Mitchell held the same positions in AMMCO and LCC. AMMCO had not as yet been able to find good management people to alleviate some of the pressure. Because of the castings shortage in 1973, AMMCO was considering purchasing a casting foundry; the company was "feeling out" a few possibilities. AMMCO was experimenting with aluminum castings in their products; however, aluminum was also in tight supply. The fuel crisis caused some concern for AMMCO. However, Wacker felt AMMCO would not be too seriously affected. His feeling was that man would find alternative power sources for cars and that wheel alignment and brake repairs would still be needed. Concerning his replacement, Wacker felt there was no need for worry; Pranke and Mitchell, he said, would be able to fill his place with no problem.

"When I came to AMMCO in 1947, things were not up to snuff, and I had no management experience," Wacker said. "I've made some mistakes along the way and the company is growing faster than I would like, but we have gone from a day-to-day existence to now being able to plan on a year-to-year basis."

APPENDIX A AMMCO TOOLS, INC. CONSOLIDATED BALANCE SHEETS (in Thousands of Dollars)

Assets	*1Q-67*	*2Q-67*	*3Q-67*	*4Q-67*
Cash & Liquid Securities	(240,000)*	(124.1)*	140.8	225.6
Receivables	796.0	890.7	908.5	694.3
Due from LCC	415.7	664.0	847.4	641.8
Inventories (Auto)	1,866.0	1,821.4	1,485.7	1,101.5
Inventories (Meters)	278.8	234.0	160.6	56.4
Prepaid Expenses	67.6	75.7	57.2	89.4
Current Assets	3,184.1	3,561.7	3,600.2	2,808.9
Investment—LCC	800.0	800.0	800.0	800.0
Other Investments	146.8	141.6	141.6	147.3
Patents and Trademarks	12.8	12.5	12.2	12.9

Property, Plant & Equipment	2,540.3	2,615.4	2,620.6	2,618.6
(Accumulated Depreciation)	(1,570.0)	(1,618.0)	(1,666.0)	(1,686.8)
New Plant & Equipment	970.3	997.4	954.6	931.8
Total Assets	5,114.0	5,513.2	5,508.6	4,700.9
Liabilities				
Note Payable	400.0	700.0	700.0	—
Payables	200.1	181.2	148.3	70.9
Accrued Expenses	296.1	373.7	382.6	378.5
Current Liabilities	896.2	1,254.9	1,230.9	449.4
Long-Term Debt				
Stockholders & Others	—	—	—	—
Prudential	1,400.0	1,400.0	1,350.0	1,350.0
Total Liabilities	2,296.2	2,654.9	2,580.9	1,799.4
Equity	2,813.2	2,813.2	2,813.2	2,813.2
Year to Date Profit	4.6	45.1	114.5	88.2
Total Equity	2,817.8	2,858.3	2,927.7	2,901.4
Total Liability & Equity	5,114.0	5,513.2	5,508.6	4,700.8
Consolidated Income Statement				
Gross Shipments	N.A.	N.A.	1,760.6	1,586.5
Less: Returns/Allowances	N.A.	N.A.	47.9	63.3
Net Shipments	1,304.8	1,628.7	1,712.7	1,523.2
Cost of Sales	631.3	878.8	954.2	983.1
Gross Profit on Sales	673.5	749.9	758.5	540.1
Meter Income	23.4	30.5	19.4	8.3
Other Costs and Expenses				
Commissions	150.2	206.9	200.8	191.6
Engineering	74.1	66.0	30.8	22.3
Selling, Admin., General	439.8	398.9	379.4	351.6
Operating Income	32.8	108.6	166.9	(17.1)
Interest Expense	23.6	30.8	31.4	27.2
Net Income	9.2	77.8	135.5	(44.3)
Tax Provision	4.6	37.3	66.1	(18.0)
Net Profit	4.6	40.5	69.4	(26.3)

**The balances are negative in these accounts due to the practice of predating a check for a bill prior to the date on which the check is mailed (a date when the cash reserves covered the amount of the check). N.A. means Not Available*

WHITE MOTOR CORPORATION: FIGHT FOR SURVIVAL

When Semon E. Knudsen became chief executive at White Motor Corporation in 1971, all but five top executives had left, and the corporation needed $290 million in bank loans to stay in business. After three consecutive years of declining earnings, White Motor was then $21 million in the red. While expanding into the farm-equipment area, the market had drastically declined and left White Motor dealers with over $130 million in unsold farm machinery. Also, White Motor trucks had been steadily losing market share.

Knudsen, former executive vice president of General Motors Corporation and former president of Ford Motor Company, became the chief executive of White Motor with no money, no organization, and no staff. By the end of 1971, however, White Motor was in the black with earnings of $2.4 million on sales of $837 million. In 1974, with earnings of $38.6 million on sales of $1.3 billion, White Motor paid dividends on its common stock for the first time in four years.

Then, in 1975, because of a recession, customers stopped buying trucks and farm machinery. Added to recessionary problems was a government regulation that required all trucks manufactured after March 1, 1975 to have anti-skid devices—adding $2,000 to the cost of each truck. White Motor reported a net loss of $69.4 million on sales of $1.228 billion for 1975. At the end of that year, White Motor had $131 million in long-term debt. A subsidiary, White Motor Credit Corporation, had a long-term debt of $112.5 million. White Motor also was short on working capital. Only one segment of White Motor—its industrial and construction group (off-highway haulers, large engines, compressors, and heavy diesel engines)—showed profitable operation for the year. The group had a 1975 pre-tax profit of $47.4 million compared with its 1974 profit of $26.5 million.

With the incurrence of additional debt, White Motor was ill-prepared to cope with a business downturn. White Motor was unable to handle its short-term liability position with either its banks or its suppliers.

Prepared by Ephraim Smith and Eleanor Schwartz of Cleveland State University.

HOW WHITE MOTOR GREW

White Motor Corporation began in 1900 as a producer of "horseless carriages." By 1906 auto sales were twice those of its nearest competitor. Cars were discontinued in 1918 to manufacture heavy-duty trucks. An economy downturn in 1949 adversely affected the trucking industry, and White Motor stock slipped to the \$13–\$14 level, compared with a book value of \$56 per share. White Motor became what *Forbes* called a "loaded laggard"—a company whose stock price has lagged behind the value of its assets, making it a prime target for bargain-hunting conglomerates. White Motor management decided the best way to avoid becoming merged into a larger company was to become big on its own. The logical area for expansion was the truck industry. White Motor management, foreseeing that the heavy-duty truck market (then only 2 percent of total 1950 unit sales) would quadruple in the fifties and sixties, acquired several small truck-manufacturing firms (e.g., Sterling Motor Truck Company, Reo Motor, Inc., Diamond T. Motor Car Company, Montepelier Manufacturing Company).

Management also began to look at an unfamiliar industry for expansion and purchased the farm-machinery assets of several marginal companies (e.g., Oliver Corporation; Cockshutt Farm Equipment, Limited of Canada; and Minneapolis-Moline). Although the farm-equipment industry was then depressed, White management saw the farm market as cyclical and ready for an upturn. Research indicated that the farm-machinery market had a favorable near-term and long-range future, based on an accelerated shortage of farm labor, worldwide population explosion, and the huge replacement market. Not only were distribution, engineering, and manufacturing techniques of the farm-machinery industry similar to the heavy-duty truck business, but also it was undergoing a competitive shakedown that made established manufacturers susceptible to acquisition on advantageous terms.

The industrial power equipment industry was seen as another logical area of company diversification. As a result, White's industrial group included four divisions in 1976: Hercules (producer of engines up to 200 H.P.), Euclid (a world leader in off-highway haulers for forty years), Alco (American Locomotive Company, producer of diesel engines 800–4500 H.P.), and White Superior (maker of engines and compressors in the 400–2400 H.P. range–in diesel and in natural-gas fuels).

PROBLEMS

The truck acquisitions in the fifties increased White Motor's heavy-duty truck-market share. To maximize efficiency, White Motor moved its Diamond T plant from Chicago to its Reo plant in Lansing, Michigan. Because the two trucks began to compete with each other rather than other manufacturers, both divisions showed poor sales during the booming truck market from 1959 to 1966. To correct this, the two divisions were combined into one operation with one nameplate—Diamond-Reo.

Part of an internal growth plan was to increase the truck-market share by cutting into competition's market share. The company made its start and drew its best profits from the owner-operator who was willing to pay a higher price for a truck customized to his needs. He might require, for instance, a heavier axle or a wider wheelbase for his particular truck. He was unable to acquire this type of service from the mass producers, such as Ford and General Motors. Long the producer of heavy-duty trucks aimed at this owner-operator market, White Motor began to concentrate also on two segments of the mass-produced market: The light-heavy market (trucks used for short-haul and in-city cartage) and the heavy-duty truck-fleet market (companies with several trucks as opposed to the single owner-operator).

In the light-heavy market White Motor sold only 1500 of its 5000 entries, which it aimed at the farm delivery market and dubbed "The Trend." Dealers responded cooly because they were moved into the hotly competitive light-truck class where mass producers had a distinct advantage.

The fleet market was dominated by mass producers, particularly Ford. To cater to this market and to meet the stiffer competition, White Motor had to economize and standardize production. Custom work became secondary, and the gap between customized trucks and mass-produced trucks narrowed. The close relationship between the truck manufacturing market and the truck buyer dissolved. Many loyal owner-operator buyers took their business elsewhere.

As a whole, truck sales boomed in the sixties. Though hampered with marketing problems, cumulative White Motor truck sales increased each year except for 1964 and 1967, which were relatively poor years for trucks in general. White remained the number-two independent heavy-duty truck producer, behind only International.

White Motor's main marketing strategy for the sixties, however, revolved around the farm equipment assets of Oliver Corporation, Minneapolis-Moline, and Cockshutt, which continued to operate as separate units. White Motor management was convinced that the farm-equipment industry cycle was about to change. Substantial gains did occur until the severe 1968 nosedive. Marginal producers were in trouble, and White Motor owned only marginal producers. Management dismissed the downturn as temporary and kept building up inventories, tying up large amounts of capital. When the market failed to rebound, the company was forced to cut prices and sustain heavy losses. White Motor lost $20 million in 1970, due almost exclusively to the $43 million loss for the farm group.

Meanwhile, an engine plant had been built in Canton, Ohio, at an estimated cost of $45 million. The plant's profit potential was centered around volume. For instance, according to one analysis in *Forbes,* "to make the plant break-even, 25,000 farm tractor engines must be built in a year." In the 1969 economy, only about 18,000 farm-tractor engines could be sold. Since White Motor would operate at a loss at that level, the plant, equipped and nearly ready to operate, remained idle.

Hard-pressed for cash after the farm-market downturn, White Motor sought to merge with White Consolidated, a diversified producer of major household appliances and industrial equipment. The Justice Department opposed the merger. At this point, White Motor had neither the financial nor managerial resources. At the edge of liquidation, the outside directors in an emergency meeting selected Knudsen chairman and chief executive.

In a program to put White Motor back into a profitable direction, Knudsen attacked the financial, inventory, and marketing problems. He obtained a $290 million line of credit from forty-two banks, recruited a new top management team, liquidated some operations, sold a major division, reduced inventories, and developed new lines in the truck- and farm-equipment fields. R & D was increased for development of new products and improvement of existing ones. The farm group was restructured and consolidated (e.g., the two farm lines, Minneapolis-Moline and Oliver were combined). The new management admitted money could be made in the farm-equipment business, but did not want it to dominate the total operation. A program was launched to increase White's international operations, also.

RESULTS

During 1972, sales rose 13 percent and profits from operations also rose significantly. Total profit in 1972 was $6.9 million. These earnings were achieved despite the loss of truck production caused by a supplier strike, truck-component shortages, the costs of the idle Canton plant, and a strike at the Hercules Engine Division.

In 1973 White Motor sales increased by over 26 percent, net income increased from $7 million to $19.4 million, and earnings per share went from 76 cents per share in 1972 to $2.22 per share. Sales continued to climb in 1974, reaching $1.389 billion, a 17.8 percent increase over 1973. Income from operations increased by 16.5 percent.

However, in 1975 sales fell 12 percent to $1.23 billion from $1.39 billion in 1974. Only the industrial and construction group showed profitable operations. The group had a 1975 pre-tax profit of $47.4 million compared with a 1974 profit of $26.5 million. White Motor was most hurt by the more than 37 percent decrease in sales in its truck division. A net loss of $69.4 million was incurred. White Motor officials noted that this loss, however, included more than $42.7 million that resulted from decisions in the second and third quarters to sell or liquidate several loss operations and related product lines.

Merger with White Consolidated again was sought as a solution to financial difficulties. Although the Justice Department had prohibited the merger previously, the 1976 proposal was approved under the failing company doctrine.

Under the merger agreement, White Motor was to be a subsidiary of White Consolidated, separately financed. White Consolidated was not to guarantee any of the White Motor financing. The merger agreement provided also that White Consolidated could cancel the transaction if White Motor did not get additional loans of at least $60 million under terms satisfactory to White Consolidated. In addition, the lending bank had to agree to extend all White Motor's existing losses for at least five years.

Lender banks and insurance companies cooperated extensively with White Motor to meet the financing demands of the merger agreement. They agreed to give White Motor three additional months. Nevertheless, a majority of White Consolidated's directors determined that the proposed financing did not meet the conditions of the agreement and denied the merger. The transaction would have been a substantial gamble for White Consolidated, who though prospering, already had a heavy debt load as a result of a series of acquisitions.

The breakoff of the merger appeared to leave White Motor three possibilities: an early filing for protection from creditors under Chapter 11 of the Federal Bankruptcy Statutes, under which it would attempt to seek a long-term arrangement with creditors that would allow it to continue operating; another merger agreement, either with White Consolidated or with some other company; or possibly selling off some assets to raise cash so the company could continue until the resurgent economy would help the company resolve its problems. White Motor management chose to accept the resignation of its president; slash the corporate staff by 17 percent; close the advance-products division in Farmington Hills, Michigan; move corporate head-

TEN-YEAR SUMMARY, WHITE MOTOR CORPORATION AND CONSOLIDATED SUBSIDIARIES (In Millions except per Share Amounts)

Results for the Year	*1975*	*1974*	*1973*
Net Sales			
Truck	$ 527.9	$ 840.5	$ 773.2
Industrial & Construction	349.0	261.1	202.9
North American Farm	341.7	276.8	194.4
European Farm	10.1	11.4	8.9
	$1228.7	$1389.8	$1179.4
Income (Loss) before extraordinary Items	$ (69.4)	$ 22.6	$ 19.4
% of Sales	(5.6)%	1.6%	1.6%
% of Total Shareholders' Equity[1]	(28.2)%	9.3%	8.8%
Net Income (Loss)	$ (69.4)	$ 22.6	$ 21.7
% of Sales	(5.6)%	1.6%	1.8%
% of Total Shareholders' Equity[1]	(28.2)%	9.3%	9.9%
Cash Dividends			
Preferred Stock	$ 1.1	$ 1.1	$ 1.1
Common Stock	—	3.3	—
Property; Plant and Equipment Additions—Gross			
Current Operations	$ 40.6	$ 53.3	$ 22.9
Corporate Acquisitions	—	—	—
Depreciation and Amortization	12.3	10.1	9.2
Interest Charges	a	25.8	15.5
Balance Sheet (December 31)			
Working Capital	$ 98.9	$ 208.3	$ 220.3
Current Ratio	1.2 to 1	1.5 to 1	2 to 1
Long-Term Debt	131.1	169.9	148.3
Preferred Shareholders' Equity	9.5	12.6	15.8
Common Shareholders' Equity	162.8	233.4	226.2
Total Capital[2]	303.3	415.9	390.3
% of Long-Term Debt to Total Capital	43.2%	40. %	38.0%
Shares Outstanding			
Preferred	.13	.16	.16
Common	8.3	8.3	8.2
Number of Common Shareholders	a	.025	.025
Per Common Share[3]			
Shareholders' Equity	$ 19.72	$ 29.80	$ 27.42
Income (Loss) before Extraordinary Items			
Primary	(8.52)	2.61	2.22
Fully diluted	(8.52)	2.54	2.17
Net Income (Loss)			
Primary	(8.52)	2.61	2.50
Fully diluted	(8.52)	2.54	2.43
Cash Dividends	—	.40	—

**Figures may not add due to rounding*

1. Percentage is based on the balance at the beginning of the year.

2. Total Capital is the sum of Long-Term Debt and Shareholders' Equity.

3. Adjusted to give retroactive effect to a 10% Common Stock dividend in 1967.

4. Adjusted to reflect retroactive adjustment of the extraordinary charge for additional retirement benefits at the discontinued farm equipment operations.

TEN-YEAR SUMMARY, WHITE MOTOR CORPORATION AND CONSOLIDATED SUBSIDIARIES (Cont.)

1972	*1971*	*1970*	*1969*	*1968*	*1967*	*1966*
$611.4	$522.3	$507.7	$613.2	$518.6	$431.8	$508.9
182.0	189.3	202.0	191.6	135.3	106.5	48.2
142.3	117.9	93.5	137.5	190.3	225.2	221.6
7.6	8.3	6.9	8.1	6.9	6.2	—
$943.3	$837.9	$810.1	$950.5	$851.0	$769.8	$778.7
$ 6.9	$ .9	$ (21.0)	$ 17.5	$ 23.0	$ 28.9	$ 32.1
.7%	.1%	(2.6)%	1.8%	2.7%	3.7%	4.1%
3.6%	.4%	(9.1)%	8.1%	11.2%	15.3%	19.5%
$ 8.4	$ (17.3)	$ (21.0)	$ 12.4	$ 23.0	$ 28.9	$ 32.1
.9%	(2.1)%	(2.6)%	1.3%	2.7%	3.7%	4.1%
4.5%	(8.4)%	(9.1)%	5.7%	11.2%	15.3%	19.5%
$ 1.1	$ 1.1	$ 1.1	$ .5	$ —	$ —	$ —
—	—	3.3	13.0	13.0	11.8	9.7
$ 8.3	$ 10.0	$ 59.7	$ 19.8	$ 13.8	$ 12.6	$ 13.9
—	—	—	6.3	11.2	1.2	3.7
9.0	9.3	8.6	9.2	8.2	8.4	6.5
15.1	15.5	16.5	11.2	7.7	5.8	3.9
$214.0	$132.2	$122.4	$171.9	$178.3	$145.6	$143.4
2.3 to 1	1.5 to 1	1.4 to 1	1.7 to 1	2.0 to 1	1.9 to 1	1.9 to 1
155.7	105.1	114.4	84.0	82.2	39.5	36.4
15.8	15.8	15.8	15.8	—	—	—
203.3	172.9	189.7	214.1	216.6	206.2	188.4
374.8	293.8	319.9	313.8	298.8	245.7	224.7
41.5%	35.8%	35.8%	26.8%	27.5%	16.1%	16.2%
.16	.16	.16	.16	—	—	—
8.2	7.0	6.9	6.5	6.5	6.5	5.9
.023	.024	.028	.025	.025	.026	.025
$ 24.70	$ 24.83	$ 27.37	$ 32.88	$ 33.13	$ 31.63	$ 29.09
.76	(.03)	(3.27)	2.60	3.52	4.44	4.96
.76	(.03)	(3.27)	2.52	3.40	4.42	4.92
.96	(2.64)	(3.27)	1.83	3.52	4.44	4.96
.96	(2.64)	(3.27)	1.79	3.40	4.42	4.92
—	—	.50	2.00	2.00	1.82	1.50

5. *Figures for 1970 have been restated to include Rectrans, Inc.*
a. *Unable to determine*
Sources: *White Motor Corporation Annual Report, 1974; White Motor Corporation Financial Statements for 1975; White Motor Corporation Prospectus, March 25, 1976.*

quarters from Erieview Plaza in downtown Cleveland to Eastlake, where its truck group was headquartered; work the company's debt to suppliers from $50 million to $25 million; sell the White Superior Division for $36.5 million.

Sale of the White Superior Division to Cooper Industries for $36.5 million eased the liquidity problem. Sale proceeds were used to reduce the backlog of bills from suppliers. Knudsen commented that it was a major step in improving the financial strength of the company. Several weeks after the sale of the White Superior Division, the firm reported profits for the first half and second quarter of 1976. Knudsen, commenting on the profit upturn, credited the slash in salaried workers (1,181 persons or 17 percent) and the reduction of corporate staff (from 175 to 75 people during the second quarter of 1976). Knudsen felt that with satisfactory financial arrangements and the support of lenders as well as normal flow of material from suppliers, White Motor could become profitable again. In August 1976, he announced that 364-day revolving credit agreements totalling $347.4 million with a consortium of banks had been reached. The credit agreements were divided between the parent firm, the White Motor Credit Corporation (a subsidiary), and White's Canadian subsidiary. The credit agreements involved $303.5 million associated with U. S. obligations and $43.9 million with Canadian, and replaced notes outstanding on a demand basis. Knudsen, in a public statement, said that the sale of the White Superior Division and the credit agreements were "two major steps towards establishing the company's financial stability and providing increased funds to respond to the growing demand for its products, primarily trucks. We now have the liquidity to meet and maintain obligations of the company on a timely basis."

ALBERTSON'S, INC.

Joseph A. Albertson opened the first Albertson's store in Boise, Idaho in 1939. The store was a supermarket, one of the largest and most modern in the West. Formerly a district manager with Safeway Stores, Albertson was considered to be one of the original pioneers of the complete one-stop, self-service concept of supermarketing. Thirty-seven years after the opening of that first store, the company was operating 252 Albertson's supermarkets in eleven western states in addition to being an equal partner in 61 Skaggs-Albertson's drug and grocery supermarkets in five southern states.

Consolidated sales in fiscal 1975 reached $1.27 billion, with net profit after taxes of $15.8 million (see ten-year summary, Exhibit 1). Total assets on January 31, 1976 were nearly $222 million, with stockholder's equity of more than $91 million (see balance sheets, Exhibit 2). *Fortune* ranked Albertson's in July 1976 as the twenty-ninth largest retailer in the U. S. (in terms of sales), but the eighth highest in returns on equity capital of all U. S. retailers. *Forbes* ranked Albertson's on January 1, 1976 as eighty-third in American industry in terms of five-year average return on equity. In that same issue of *Forbes,* Albertson's was number four out of twenty-five regional chain stores in five-year average return on equity, number four in five-year average return on total capital and number four in five-year average earnings per share growth. In the summer of 1976, Albertson's management was looking forward to further growth and profitability for the company.

CORPORATE PHILOSOPHY

Albertson's operating philosophy placed strong emphasis on responsiveness to the consumer, a centralized management information system with decentralized merchandising responsibility, and a fully integrated property development operation. In the low-margin supermarket industry, Albertson's executives believed that careful management of inventory turnover and debt leveraging of real estate and store equipment were the keys to a good return on stockholders' equity. They sought to

---

Prepared by Professor Melvin J. Stanford of Brigham Young University.

EXHIBIT 1 TEN-YEAR SUMMARY

Operating Results	*52 Weeks 1/31/76*	*52 Weeks 2/1/75*	*52 Weeks 2/2/74*	*53 Weeks 2/3/73*
Consolidated:				
Sales	$1,271,124,076	$1,046,104,683	$852,491,046	$681,623,075
Gross margin	268,269,799	216,637,108	175,511,334	145,151,751
Real estate rent expense	16,591,847	13,529,937	11,168,028	9,429,955
Interest expense	3,534,464	2,373,402	1,616,360	927,792
Earnings before taxes	30,794,099	23,103,686	17,573,612	14,231,827
Taxes on income	15,001,632	11,402,146	8,435,319	6,761,937
Net earnings	15,792,467	11,701,540	9,138,293	7,469,890
Net earnings as a percent of sales	1.24%	1.12%	1.07%	1.10%
Skaggs-Albertson's:[3]				
Sales	$ 424,443,391	$ 281,954,708	$184,574,005	$119,646,314
Earnings before taxes	13,094,462	7,760,930	5,386,591	3,779,722
Net earnings	6,879,017	4,078,454	2,829,728	1,977,725
Common Stock Data:				
Net earnings per share[1,2]	$ 2.38	$ 1.85	$ 1.45	$ 1.19
Dividends	4,195,005	3,331,629	2,660,076	2,178,367
Dividends per share[1]	.63	.525	.42	.35
Book value per share[1]	12.51	9.54	8.19	7.17
Financial Position:				
Total assets	$ 221,908,501	$ 172,797,127	$134,604,709	$105,032,505
Working capital	50,556,897	23,556,671	25,908,937	20,336,525
Long-term debt	34,404,703	27,608,062	23,520,935	16,819,640
Stockholders' equity	91,241,497	60,727,942	51,655,625	45,225,188
Other Statistics				
Number of stores at end of year:				
Albertson's	252	246	229	218
Skaggs-Albertson's	61	49	40	33
Total	313	295	269	251
Number of employees:				
Albertson's	12,400	12,110	11,391	10,501
Skaggs-Albertson's	6,250	4,350	3,456	2,110

1. *Adjusted for 10 percent stock dividend paid June 1, 1973.*
2. *Based on average number of shares and equivalents outstanding.*
3. *Total, 50 percent included in Albertson's, Inc. financial statements.*

protect margins by concentrating on store productivity, diversification, implementation of selected private label lines, tight management control through a highly sophisticated management information system, and "most important. . .the training of its key assets. . .people."

Responsiveness to the consumer was the basis of a strategy of integrating consumerism programs. Albertson's executives believed that "it is the heart of our business to initiate consumer services." The company sought to emphasize to its customers that it was the "buying agent" for the customer and not the "selling agent" for the manufacturer.

The company sought to maintain a traditionally conservative financial structure. It had for some years been using its capital primarily to build stores rather than a distribution system. New store buildings were financed to a large extent by sale

EXHIBIT 1 TEN-YEAR SUMMARY (Cont.)

52 Weeks 4/1/72	*53 Weeks 4/3/71*	*52 Weeks 3/28/70*	*52 Weeks 3/29/69*	*52 Weeks 3/30/68*	*53 Weeks 4/1/67*
$550,175,100	$487,932,657	$449,313,324	$420,126,478	$390,902,189	$324,166,383
118,188,907	103,562,549	94,926,140	92,387,854	84,244,639	71,190,756
8,259,118	7,232,338	6,528,833	6,250,527	5,594,652	4,423,935
575,367	402,318	373,985	379,694	441,302	320,602
11,924,661	10,088,498	9,544,541	9,897,468	9,554,293	8,072,109
5,667,543	4,814,696	4,912,071	5,216,600	4,789,696	3,728,059
6,257,118	5,273,802	4,632,470[4]	4,680,868	4,764,597	4,344,050
1.14%	1.08%	1.03%	1.11%	1.22%	1.34%
$ 69,944,231	$ 31,124,003				
1,438,860	998,971				
763,129	513,390				
$ .98	$ .83	$ .73	$ .74	$ .76	$ .69
2,072,645	2,084,593	2,080,533	2,064,089	2,057,581	2,052,429
.33	.33	.33	.33	.33	.33
6.41	5.83	5.42	4.85	4.42	3.99
$ 87,149,962	$ 73,948,906	$ 64,389,304	$ 58,959,262	$ 55,677,401	$ 49,786,250
19,503,355	14,786,136	14,374,481	10,380,914	10,185,317	7,126,182
11,456,754	7,190,284	5,070,152	5,701,576	6,856,984	6,882,148
40,354,485	37,158,207	34,539,684	30,704,474	27,821,196	25,093,761
219	214	212	213	202	184
28	17	9			
247	231	221	213	202	184
8,926	8,847	8,478	8,494	8,443	8,036
1,654	1,424				

4. Excludes extraordinary gain of $568,034 net of taxes or the equivalent of $.09 per share of common stock.

and leaseback, with Albertson's internal capital being applied to equipment, inventory, and remodeling. In the long run, management felt that once enough stores were established in a sector of its geographically-diversified trading area, investments could then be made in warehouses and distribution facilities with a greater profitability than if such "backstage" support was developed concurrently with the stores. New stores were supplied primarily by wholesalers in their area of operation. Locations for new stores were generally selected in growth areas where price competition would not be intense from existing firms.

Geographically, Albertson's believed that well-run conventional supermarkets still had an important place in the western market. However, the company's management also saw a trend toward one-stop stores with greater emphasis on nonfood, household, recreational, and automotive needs. Accordingly, considerable priority was being given to expansion of the Skaggs-Albertson's partnership stores.

EXHIBIT 2 CONSOLIDATED BALANCE SHEETS

	January 31, 1976	February 1, 1975
Current Assets:		
Cash and short-term securities	$ 34,958,943	$ 9,793,128
Accounts and notes receivable	17,952,603	11,881,877
Inventories	76,205,747	63,853,240
Prepaid expenses	3,746,589	2,860,973
Property held for resale	4,794,493	12,364,876
Total Current Assets	137,658,375	100,754,094
Other Assets:		
Notes receivable	529,864	826,137
Securities, licenses and other investments, at cost which approximates market	5,170,617	4,127,138
	5,700,481	4,953,275
Land, Buildings, and Equipment:		
Land	8,784,461	7,290,384
Buildings	9,095,814	10,473,099
Fixtures and equipment	90,926,109	76,530,644
Leasehold improvements	14,089,024	9,547,123
	122,895,408	103,841,250
Less acc. depreciation and amortization	47,830,223	41,347,409
	75,065,185	62,493,841
Deferred Costs, less amortization	3,484,460	4,595,917
	$221,908,501	$172,797,127
Current Liabilities:		
Note payable to bank		2,000,000
Accounts payable	65,409,799	58,568,329
Salaries and amounts withheld employ.	7,880,167	6,409,048
Taxes other than income taxes	5,683,244	4,697,428
Interest payable	1,185,398	190,617
Taxes on income	4,235,931	1,998,928
Dividends payable	1,312,852	967,768
Current maturities of long-term debt	1,394,087	2,365,305
Total Current Liabilities	87,101,478	77,197,423
Long-Term Debt, due after one year	34,404,703	27,608,062
Deferred Compensation	714,979	
Deferred Income Taxes	4,633,000	4,933,000
Deferred Investment Credit	3,812,844	2,330,700
Stockholders' Equity:		
Common stock	7,293,621	6,385,275
Capital in excess of par value	32,726,167	14,894,117
Retained earnings	51,221,709	39,681,097
	91,241,497	60,960,489
Less treasury stock		232,547
	91,241,497	60,727,942
	$221,908,501	$172,797,127

In addition, Albertson's hoped to develop its own nonfood operation through acquisition or internal growth so that combination units would be available in all of the company's operating areas.

A theme of "Grow with the West" had been expressed by Albertson's a decade earlier, but by 1976, in addition to developing its partnership stores in the South, management thought that there were many opportunities for new stores in other states where the company was not operating, as well as throughout its current operating area. Albertson's referred to itself as the "walking" regional chain. Management believed that the decentralized operation first learned in Idaho would permit the company to go to any attractive store location in its chosen operating area, no matter how remote, rather than slowly expand outward from a central base to neighboring areas. The company expansion which was taking place in the mid-1970s, however, led to Albertson's being called by some observers a multi-regional and even a national company. There were Albertson's stores within 20 miles of the Canadian border. In 1974, plans were made to enter western Canada the following year with three or more stores and to have at least ten stores in the Calgary-Edmonton area by mid-1977. However, the company dropped the Canada expansion because it decided to increase efforts on the partnership in Florida and avoid expansion so far afield at the same time.

ECONOMIC TRENDS AND CONDITIONS

The years 1973 and 1974 had brought an unfamiliar and unwelcome condition to the American economy: simultaneous high price inflation and high unemployment. Then the economy began to slip in 1974 and by early 1975 the worst recession since World War Two was in progress. During the recession, however, price deflation did not occur, but inflation actually continued, though at a moderate rate. Recovery started in the second quarter of 1975, and by mid-1976 the situation had improved to the extent that the general level of U. S. economic activity had returned to the level where it had been when it started to fall in 1974. Price inflation had been moderate in early 1976, but consumers, businessmen, and politicians were all concerned that the strength of the recovery would accelerate inflation.

Food expenditures by the American people had amounted to about 26 percent of income in 1947, declining to about 21 percent a decade later and to about 18 percent by 1966. The downward trend continued until 1972, when the percentage began to rise again to just above 16 percent in 1974 and 1975.

Standard and Poor's expected that food expenditures as a percentage of disposable income would at least remain above the 1972 low point and could increase in the late 1970s to levels closer to 22 percent or 23 percent.

Food price increases during 1973–74 were attributed by Standard and Poor's to the following reasons:

1. Economic activity increased. Employment, hourly earnings and consumer spending all rose, increasing the demand for food.
2. Foreign countries bought more U. S. farm products, decreasing the domestic supply levels.
3. U. S. livestock production was down slightly.
4. People bid up the price of meat in 1973, causing a rapid price rise with the small cutback in meat production.

5. Food marketing margins had increased more sharply in recent years. (The Department of Agriculture estimated in 1973 that the farmer received 38 percent of the retail food dollar, with labor receiving 31 percent, packaging 8 percent, transportation 5 percent, and taxes, rent, interest, advertising and profit, etc. accounting for the other 18 percent.
6. U. S. food stamp and food distribution programs were helping 15 million lower income people (over twice as many as in 1969); they were spending more on food, adding to the demand.

The food retailing industry had been subjected to customer boycotts and other negative consumer reactions during the times of the highest inflation in 1973 and 1974. These reactions were particularly intense during times of shortages and high prices of specific items, such as beef and sugar. Food processors and retailers were accused of raising prices more than the increase in their costs, and farmers especially complained that they were being hurt by inflation and that middlemen were taking the profits. This kind of activity had subsided by 1976, but the general mood of the food shopper still seemed to be cautious, thrifty, and worried about prices.

In mid-1975, Albertson's Economic Research Department noted a slowing down in inflationary trends for food-at-home purchases. It was estimated by that department that while overall cost of living might increase at a somewhat higher rate, the allotted weekly expenditure by families for food in supermarkets would increase by only 5 percent between mid-1975 and mid-1977. However, the economic staff monitored the consumer price index and other indicators and was prepared to adjust its estimates if conditions changed enough to warrant it.

THE SUPERMARKET INDUSTRY

Total food store sales in the U. S. were reported by industry and government sources as $143 billion in 1975, up from $131 billion in 1974 and $113 billion in 1973. The total number of stores, however, had declined from 199,600 in 1973 to 198,000 in 1974 and 192,000 in 1975. This pattern was a continuation of the general trend in the U.S. between 1963 and 1972, during which time the average sales per grocery store increased faster than that of both retail trade and of drug stores.*

Total sales by U. S. supermarkets were nearly $104 billion in 1975, up 10 percent over 1974. The largest increase (45 percent) in sales between those two years was for chain supermarkets (a "chain" was a company with more than ten stores) with annual sales levels of more than $4 million per store; in 1974, there were 3,680 of these large chain stores, and their sales accounted for 15.4 percent of all grocery store sales. In 1975, the number of these large (over $4 million annual sales) chain stores increased to 5,400, and their combined sales totaled 20.4 percent of all U. S. grocery sales.

Independent supermarkets (ten or fewer stores in the company) increased from 1,560 stores in 1974 to 1,650 stores in 1975, while their aggregate sales rose from $10.9 billion to $12.4 billion in the same one-year period. Independent grocery stores with annual volumes between $0.5 million and $4 million increased in the range of 8 percent to 16 percent in both number of stores and aggregate sales volume between 1974 and 1975, but independent stores below $0.5 million volume

---

*Note: These government totals were between 3 percent and 4 percent lower than industry figures because the latter included some specialty stores that the former did not.

decreased 8 percent in number while maintaining about the same aggregate volume in that period.

All chain stores with less than $4 million annual sales decreased in number of stores between 1974 and 1975 and also decreased in aggregate sales volume, except for the stores under $1 million, which maintained about the same aggregate sales volume (but with fewer stores).

Convenience stores, such as Seven-Eleven, which tend to stay open longer hours and offer a limited variety of food and related items at higher prices than grocery stores, are not included in the foregoing data on chains and independents (but are included in the industry totals). The number of convenience stores increased from 22,700 in 1974 to 25,000 in 1975, and their aggregate sales volume rose from $5.3 billion to $6.2 billion in that time. A summary of the market share in number of stores and sales volume for all three categories of store (in 1973, 1974, and 1975) is as follows:

	1973	*1974*	*1975*
Number of stores:			
Independents	77.3%	76.3%	74.9%
Chains	12.5%	12.3%	12.0%
Convenience	10.2%	11.4%	13.0%
	100.0%	100.0%	99.9%
Dollar sales volume:			
Independents	49.3%	49.1%	49.1%
Chains	46.8%	46.8%	46.6%
Convenience	3.9%	4.1%	4.3%
	100.0%	100.0%	100.0%

Supermarkets were defined in the food store industry as any store, chain, or independent doing $1 million or more in sales per year. Gross profits of supermarkets (without profits of warehouses by those stores that had them) had remained near a median of 19 percent of sales during the period 1969 to 1974, according to one industry survey (see Exhibit 3), with net profit before taxes ranging between 1.3 percent of sales and 1.8 percent of sales during that same period. Geographically the number of grocery stores, between 1967 and 1972, was decreasing faster in the northeast than in other parts of the U. S. During that same period, total grocery store sales increased proportionally more in the south and the west than in other regions. The same pattern was generally visible in the case of drug stores. Between 1973 and 1974, the dollar sales volume gain for grocery stores in the U. S. was nearly double that of drugstores.

Food retailing in the U. S. was generally regarded by investment analysts as a mature industry with little overall growth potential. Traditionally a highly competitive, low-margin business, food retailing also faced risks of labor contract negotiation (for larger chains) and pressures from consumer groups and Washington bureaucrats, some of whom advocated government control of food production and distribution. Despite these conditions, investment observers suggested a consolidation trend in

EXHIBIT 3 SUPERMARKET INDUSTRY DATA

	Medians of Stores with Sales above $1 Million per Year†					
	1969	1970	1971	1972	1973	1974
Gross profit with warehouse	21.2%	20.8%	21.3%	21.3%	21.1%	20.9%
Gross profit without warehouse	19.3%	19.4%	19.3%	19.4%	18.8%	19.0%
Sales per man hour	$34.39	$36.37	$38.66	$40.24	$42.63	$47.70
Sales per square foot (per week)	$ 4.15	$ 4.16	$ 4.55	$ 4.34	$ 4.71	$ 5.09
Sales per customer transaction	$ 6.02	$ 6.29	$ 6.50	$ 6.58	$ 7.47	$ 8.23
Average hourly labor cost*	$ 2.77	$ 2.87	$ 3.15	$ 3.29	$ 3.43	$ 3.69
Store labor expense	8.0%	8.1%	8.1%	8.4%	8.3%	8.1%
Fringe benefit expense	1.1%	1.1%	1.0%	1.2%	1.3%	1.4%
Grocery department shrink	0.4%	0.6%	0.6%	0.7%	0.8%	0.6%
Net profit before taxes	1.5%	1.7%	1.6%	1.3%	1.3%	1.8%

†Based on reports by about half of Super Market Institute member companies in U.S. and Canada.
**Excludes fringe benefits.*
Percentages are of sales.
Source: The Supermarket Industry Speaks: 1975

the industry, expecting that better-managed food retailing companies would achieve relative growth by increasing their market shares and also improve their profitability. Factors for industry growth more important than market share were thought by analysts to be the prospects for a more favorable industry pricing structure and bigger stores capable of carrying a much larger mix of higher-margined merchandise, such as convenience foods (including wines, party cheeses, bakery goods, delicatessen items, frozen foods, and private label items) and general merchandise. Because tight cost control and high sales volume were required in order to make a satisfactory return on investment in the low-margin business, food retailers had traditionally sought special merchandising concepts to stimulate sales and had also developed various promotional techniques to improve productivity and reduce costs. Self-service in grocery stores was an innovation in the 1930s, and the constantly increasing store size of supermarkets over the years was the result of efforts to generate higher volume and to increase employee productivity. Other food retailing techniques included intensive advertising, loss leaders, private brands, central meat processing, and captive food processing plants for dairy, bakery, and other high-volume staple items.

During the 1950s, food retailing was in a strong expansion phase. Substantial conversion of the industry to large supermarkets was taking place. That period was characterized by growth and high profits. However, it came to an end when industry capacity became excessive and competition grew more intense. The use of stamps and games became widespread and then subsided. In the 1960s there was a gradual adoption by more food retailers of the discount concept, reaching a climax in 1972 with A & P's WEO (Where Economy Originates) program; in 1972, the industry's average profits (after tax) dropped to 0.49 percent of sales, compared to 1 percent in the 1960s.

Discount merchandising was essentially the selling of food in high-volume stores, with all games, gimmicks, stamps, and special services eliminated to achieve lowest prices. With lower overhead and higher volume, earnings could be achieved in spite of lower gross margins.

Greater emphasis on general merchandise appeared to be a major trend for the food industry in the 1970s. Previously, some food retailers had gone into non-food blindly, on the theory that there was no need to start with expertise in the field. Such firms learned to their regret that general merchandise was a specialty and that a good grocery buyer was not necessarily a good housewares or apparel buyer. More recently, companies achieving better results in such diversification reasoned that, with proper training on the store level and the hiring of experienced buying and merchandising personnel, supermarkets could compete with general merchandise stores.

Some companies, such as Lucky (automotive, department stores, fabrics, drugs) and Supermarkets General (drugs, department stores, home improvement centers, catalog showrooms), believed that the supermarket industry needed to diversify into a variety of retailing fields in order to improve profitability. Other food retailers, such as Winn-Dixie and Colonial stores, were sticking close to more traditional supermarket operations, on the theory that the supermarket industry was courting trouble if it got beyond its known sphere of operations and competed with professionals in other fields. Investment analysts generally believed that the strength of an operation, not its form (supermarket, discount center, drug store, etc.), determined profitability.

Supermarkets were considered to be in a strong position to capitalize on the one-stop shopping concept, because their stores were generally more conveniently located for the average customer than were other retail stores. Moreover, the average customer visited a supermarket about four times per month, compared to only about twice a month for general merchandise stores.

A major investment cycle for the supermarket industry was said to be in its early stages in 1974 by Standard and Poor's, which also observed that the industry expansion was in the hands of a few strong companies (such as Albertson's, American Stores, Colonial Stores, Dillon Companies, Fisher Foods, Jewel Cos., Kroger, Lucky Stores, Safeway, and Winn-Dixie Stores). That same source also observed that rapid growth of drugstores may be ending. The drugstore field was becoming more competitive, as chains began to battle with one another in some markets, as supermarkets and discount stores began to rely more on sundry merchandise to improve their own profitability, and as independents began to fight to regain business lost to chains in recent years. Overstoring was not considered to be a problem in the retail drug industry, but trade sources indicated that expenses were a problem and had risen faster than sales for several years and that profit margins on prescription medicines had peaked.

COMPETITION

In the food retailing industry, competition was perhaps most visible among the large supermarket chains, but the independent operator was also a formidable competitor for several reasons. The independent proprietor was a part of the community in which he lived and operated. He knew the people and their needs, responded quickly to market changes and trends, worked closely with his employees, and had a positive local image. Albertson's management saw this as the challenge to its own growth: to try to maintain these characteristics of local operation in its present and new market areas.

Safeway Stores, Inc. was the largest food retailing firm in sales, number of stores, and total earnings (see Exhibit 4). In return on equity capital, Safeway was strong but was behind several other firms in the industry (see Exhibit 5). Although it did not rank especially high in balance sheet analysis compared to ten other firms in a recent investment study (see Exhibit 6), Safeway had a reputation of being the best-managed firm in the industry. Albertson's executives regarded Safeway as an "excellent operation, well-managed, good competitors and predictable" (predictable in the sense that Safeway's size, maturity, and stability of operation would enable others to anticipate what its activities, sales, and profits would likely be in the future).

Safeway was a highly integrated company with its own distribution system. It neither bought nor sold, to any extent, from or to other wholesalers or retailers in the industry. Safeway operated a cost center type of organization that was believed to be typical among large food chains. In 1972 it had overtaken A & P as the number-one food retailer in the U. S. Both Safeway and A & P owned large food processing facilities for their own respective private label merchandise; A & P was one of the largest food product manufacturers in the U. S.

A & P had fallen on hard times during the late 1960s. After being for many years America's largest food retailer, A & P had allowed some of its stores to become obsolete. Customer relations had also suffered, with a resulting decline in sales and profits. The WEO program of A & P was believed by the industry to have been overdone to the point that not only did A & P lose money by cutting margins so deeply, but many competitors in its predominantly eastern U. S. trading area suffered also from the resulting price competition. In an effort to turn the company around, A & P directors in December 1974 brought in J. L. Scott as the new chairman and chief executive officer. Prior to being hired by A & P, Scott had been the vice chairman and chief executive officer of Albertson's.

GOVERNMENT CONTROLS

Government regulation had not directly impinged upon the retail food industry since retail price controls, which had been temporarily established in 1972, had expired. The high cost of living, with food prices as a key element of that total cost, was receiving close and continuous government attention, especially in the presidential election year 1976. The Joint Economic Committee of Congress had, in 1975, subpoenaed the records and documents of the seventeen largest U. S. food chains, including Albertson's. That committee was interested in the structure of the food retailing industry and the resulting impact on prices. Albertson's management believed that the committee would find that the food retailing industry was very competitive and that the consumer benefitted from the efficiencies and economies of scale of the larger chains. As of mid-1976, no information had been released by the committee on the progress of its study.

UNIVERSAL PRODUCT CODE

A possible target for legislative restriction was the Universal Product Code (UPC) system. The code itself was essentially a ten-digit number. The first five digits identified the manufacturer or the company that controlled the label. The last five

EXHIBIT 4 SALES AND EARNINGS OF 22 PUBLICLY HELD FOOD CHAINS

	SALES (000$)			EARNINGS (000$)			1975 Number of Food Stores
Company	1975	1974	1973	1975	1974	1973	
Safeway	9,716,889	8,185,190	6,773,687	148,700	79,205	86,180	2,451
A & P	6,379,800	6,874,611	6,747,689	(177,400)	(157,071)	12,227	2,151
Kroger	5,339,225	4,803,032	4,204,677	34,441	45,239	29,916	1,228
Lucky	3,109,000	2,702,000	2,340,000	47,900	41,400	33,700	222
American Stores	3,011,300	2,734,710	2,320,322	26,200	19,321	18,063	742
Winn-Dixie	2,962,165	2,528,014	2,109,738	55,552	51,500	42,720	1,009
Jewel	2,772,100	2,598,913	2,219,601	28,100	30,230	36,336	393
Food Fair	2,482,539	2,369,761	2,092,127	(3,434)	8,926	6,200	459
Grand Union	1,634,622	1,562,736	1,493,969		9,504	2,309	508
Super Market Gen.	1,556,700	1,498,475	1,333,798	2,300	2,673	7,739	103
National Tea	1,472,340	1,403,815	934,511	(5,950)	(2,635)	(15,357)	525
Fisher Foods	1,379,994	1,124,404	868,758	12,426	12,581	9,435	181
Stop & Shop	1,318,200	1,223,791	1,082,957	12,600	11,992	8,860	158
Albertson's	1,271,124	1,046,105	852,491	15,792	11,722	9,138	313
Allied Supermkt.	1,049,859	1,027,598	1,035,856	(3,426)	762	4,281	254
Colonial	982,002	934,171	827,214	13,367	9,672	11,114	385
First National	962,600	934,803	859,598	800	5,708	(14,858)	265
Dillon	969,231	790,914	602,647	17,652	13,708	10,691	364
Giant Food	792,700	741,043	669,060	10,900	6,979	7,438	107
Waldbaum	688,947	570,320	459,637		3,425	3,543	118
Fred Meyer	612,443	536,760	425,620		8,251	8,191	42
Pueblo International	600,309	589,432	560,029	(4,700)	1,937	4,394	93

EXHIBIT 5 NET PROFITS AFTER INCOME TAXES AS PERCENT OF STOCKHOLDERS' EQUITY FOR LEADING FOOD CHAINS, 1965 to 1974

Company and 1973 Sales Size	*1965*	*1966*	*1967*	*1968*	*1969*	*1970*	*1971*	*1972*	*1973*	*1974*
$1 billion and over										
Allied Supermarkets	10.5	9.5	7.0	3.4	−10.8	−36.9	3.7	9.9	1.7	n.a.
American Stores	6.6	5.8	5.1	6.4	7.1	8.1	6.5	0.5	9.0	n.a.
Food Fair	11.6	10.7	9.2	9.7	n.a.	8.1	8.1	−1.0	1.6	6.4
Grand Union	11.2	10.4	10.0	10.2	11.2	10.8	8.5	5.4	1.5	n.a.
A & P	8.8	9.2	8.9	7.1	8.0	7.4	2.2	−8.6	2.0	−35.4
Jewel	12.8	12.2	12.3	13.1	13.0	11.9	12.2	12.5	13.8	10.6
Kroger	12.8	11.3	9.6	12.1	12.5	12.0	9.2	5.2	7.6	10.8
Lucky	22.6	22.6	26.4	26.7	26.8	23.0	22.6	19.7	18.9	20.5
Safeway	13.9	15.7	12.6	12.8	11.9	13.9	14.7	15.0	13.1	11.4
Southland	18.0	18.3	20.4	12.1	13.1	13.2	13.0	10.5	10.9	12.2
Stop & Shop	9.5	12.6	16.2	12.7	12.6	9.1	5.6	9.6	12.2	14.7
Supermarkets Gen.	24.5	17.6	22.4	19.9	13.4	14.4	16.1	6.4	10.9	3.7
Winn-Dixie	23.5	20.2	20.2	20.0	18.7	20.3	19.7	19.1	18.8	n.a.
Weighted average	11.9	11.9	11.1	11.0	11.2	11.0	10.1	6.8	9.5	n.a.

$500 to $999 million

Albertson's	22.2	17.9	17.5	15.2	15.5	14.2	15.5	16.5	17.7	19.3
Arden-Mayfair	13.5	10.2	1.0	6.6	5.2	−7.4	5.0	−2.6	−82.6	9.9
Colonial Stores	12.1	13.2	11.8	13.0	11.0	11.9	12.7	10.8	13.7	11.2
Dillon	17.9	16.7	17.8	15.5	16.0	17.6	19.2	19.3	21.0	n.a.
First National	2.5	−0.8	−7.8	1.4	5.6	4.2	−0.9	0.04	−22.7	n.a.
Fisher Foods	−0.5	10.8	19.9	22.0	17.6	17.5	19.0	16.8	16.8	19.0
Giant Food	14.0	11.5	13.8	14.3	15.6	9.8	16.9	12.4	12.3	n.a.
National Tea	8.9	9.2	8.8	6.0	8.0	6.1	7.0	−38.7	−19.8	−3.5
Pueblo International	21.5	21.4	18.2	23.6	19.9	11.1	14.3	−1.6	9.5	4.1
Weighted average	9.8	9.0	7.2	9.7	10.8	8.4	10.3	0.8	1.3	n.a.

EXHIBIT 6 FINANCIAL DATA ON ELEVEN SUPERMARKET CHAINS BALANCE SHEET ANALYSIS

	Albertsons	*Bi Lo*	*Colonial*	*Dillon*
Sales and Earnings				
Annual increase Sales 1970–74	21.0%	34.0%	9.0%	32.0%
Annual increase E.P.S. 1970–74	22.0	38.0	6.4	18.2
Number of down years E.P.S. 1970–74	-0-	1	1	-0-
1974 Pretax margins	2.2%	3.6%	1.8%	3.2%
Balance Sheet				
Current Ratio				
1970	1.59	2.41	2.36	1.60
1974	1.31	1.76	2.38	1.32
Debt/Worth				
1970	0.99	0.71	0.65	1.11
1974	1.84	0.87	0.87	1.26
Debt and Leases to Capitalization				
1970	70.8%	35.3%	60.3%	56.5%
1974	78.3	62.0	63.8	69.1
Cash Flows/Total Liabilities				
1970	32.8%	34.2%	33.0%	24.0%
1974	20.0	41.0	25.9	24.8
Accounts Payable Turn				
1970	17 days	12 days	13 days	N/A
1974	26 days	12 days	13 days	N/A
Balance Sheet Overall Rank				
1970	8	3	5	7
1974	10	5	4	7

Source: Investment Firm Study

digits identified the item of merchandise. The code had been talked about in American industry for more than 40 years, but in order to be widely useful a standard symbol had to be selected which could be read by optical scanners. The coding scheme was adopted in May 1971, and two years later a bar code symbol was chosen:

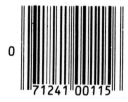

0 71241 00115

EXHIBIT 6 FINANCIAL DATA ON ELEVEN SUPERMARKET CHAINS (Cont.)

Fisher	*Foodtown*	*Jewel*	*Lucky*	*Safeway*	*Weis*	*Winn-Dixie*
29.5%	43.0%	12.3%	14.4%	13.9%	12.1%	16.5%
22.4	42.0	4.4	9.5	3.3	11.2	13.5
-0-	-0-	-0-	1	2	-0-	-0-
2.0%	4.4%	1.9%	3.0%	1.7%	8.5%	3.6%
1.66	1.85	1.64	1.36	1.52	3.26	2.82
1.30	1.58	1.49	1.40	1.26	3.77	2.13
2.59	0.56	1.41	1.69	0.76	0.20	0.39
2.97	0.58	1.63	1.53	1.15	0.18	0.54
73.4%	42.6%	35.5%	56.4%	72.6%	22.9%	58.1%
78.4	39.4	56.9	75.0	72.8	21.6	61.6
13.5%	47.9%	16.2%	21.5%	32.1%	84.8%	77.7%
13.0	48.7	145.1	21.2	20.7	126.1	59.7
28 days	16 days	31 days	29 days	25 days	16 days	10 days
29 days	15 days	17 days	23 days	29 days	15 days	13 days
11	4	6	10	9	1	2
11	3	6	8	9	1	2

There were three levels of electronic systems that could utilize UPC. The first was a "stand alone" electronic cash register (ECR) which would perform all of the functions of mechanical cash registers plus other functions. Some ECRs were upgradable to terminals for a scanning system.

A processor-driven terminal system was the second level, with a mini-computer located in the store and connected to terminals with cables. The processor would contain the memory and logic to drive the terminals. Its computer power would enable it to perform many additional functions, such as:

perform price look-up using item codes

accumulate sales for individual items

perform check authorization

accumulate information for store scheduling

consolidate sales from all checkstands

control the accumulation of excess cash in the store

It appeared that the processor-driven system could be expanded to handle numerous other store functions, such as monitoring of refrigerated cases, direct delivery accounting, and payroll timekeeping.

The highest level of electronic system was the full-scan system, which consisted of attaching optical scanners to the processor driven system. At its full capability, prices of all items would be stored in the computer, and as the symbol was scanned at the checkout stand, the price would be obtained from computer memory, displayed, and printed on the customer's receipt.

The full-scan system opened up numerous other possibilities. Manual price marking of each item, and marking and checkout errors, could be virtually eliminated. Perpetual inventory information could be maintained in the system to reduce both ordering time and stockouts. Such a system could also greatly minimize shrink by pinpointing items that are not rung up at the checkstand. Valuable marketing information on customers and their shopping patterns could also be compiled by a full-scan system.

In order for the full-scan system to be economically feasible, a minimum of about 75 percent of the merchandise had to be UPC-marked. Industry experts also estimated that potential savings from a full-scan system could be as much as 1 to $1\frac{1}{2}$ percent of sales (as much or more than the industry net profit margins). However, it appeared that POS (point-of-sale) scanner devices would be delayed. There was consumer resistance to the idea of not having prices marked on each item they took from the shelf to put into their shopping baskets. This concern gave rise to various legislative proposals that would require that marking of prices on each item be continued throughout the retailing industry. As of mid-1976, no legislation to this effect had been passed.

ALBERTSON'S OPERATIONS

Every Albertson's store was a full-line supermarket, with meat department, produce, groceries, and non-food items. Many stores had hot bakeries, and some offered a delicatessen and prepared hot foods for take-out. All stores carried a broad range of national brands and also offered private labels in most merchandising categories. About 20 percent of Albertson's merchandise was private label, up from 5 percent in 1971. On most items, private labels had wider margins.

Consumer programs were focused on a theme of, "We Care About What You Care About," and each store manager wore a gold-colored blazer jacket so that customers could readily identify and visit with him. He was identified in consumer advertising as the "Man in Gold," with the role of the consumer advisor as a part of his store management duties. Management believed that customers were responding positively to this approach to personal service. A customer who complained was personally visited by the store manager and sometimes a division officer as soon as possible.

Consumer programs of the company included:

"Tru-value" unit pricing. Albertson's had been one of the industry leaders in showing on each shelf label the cost per ounce or other unit of measure for each packaged product.

Uniform beef labeling, using meat industry terminology.

Freshness code dating.

Buyer's choice ground-beef program (which shows fat content in percentage).

"See-thru" meat trays.

Fresh bakery products without preservatives.

Longer hours for customer convenience (in 1976 over half of all Albertson's stores were open 24 hours a day, seven days a week).

Another theme, "Something's always on sale at Albertson's," was not meant to offer loss-leader weekend specials but to pass on to the consumer cost reductions arising from special purchases, promotional discounted items, seasonal merchandise, and perishables.

The management information system of the company included both detailed cost controls and budgets and a sophisticated inventory control system. Store managers prepared operating budgets for a year ahead, and these were reviewed by district and regional management and then consolidated into a corporate budget. Corporate headquarters prepared weekly operating statements for each store, showing both budgeted and actual figures, and these statements were distributed to regional, district, and store managers, as well as to corporate staff divisions, along with labor analysis, product movement, and other data.

The inventory control system was operated by computer. Normally, computerized inventory control was not considered feasible unless a supermarket company had its own distribution system. Since Albertson's supplied its stores primarily from outside wholesalers, it had arranged for its major suppliers to provide direct entry data on purchases for its inventory control system. The system was considered by management to be a major factor in achieving an annual inventory turnover of about fifteen compared to the industry 1975 average of about thirteen and in reducing shrinkage to 0.75 percent of sales compared to the industry 1975 average of 1 percent.

Electronic cash registers that were upgradable to scanning units had been installed in all new and remodeled Albertson's stores from 1974 onward. More than 20 percent of all the company's stores had ECRs in place by mid-1975. The newest store, Five Mile Road in Boise, which opened in May of 1976, also had fixed optical scanners (not wands) installed and operating full-scan at the checkstands; however, price labels were still being placed on each packaged item on the shelves in order for the customer to be able to see the unit prices in the usual manner. The system appeared to be working well, and Albertson's management looked forward to the time when the company could proceed to install the full-scan system in all of its stores. They had not gone rapidly into using the system but were watching to see what pioneering in the UPC was being done by other large retailers so that Albertson's could move ahead with the full-scan system when it became both technically feasible and acceptable to consumers. The technical feasibility seemed to be near at hand. As to consumer attitude, it was believed by Albertson's that after customers got used to the idea they would accept merchandise marked only on shelf labels and not on individual packages. The new store operation in Boise was being watched to see what kind of a transition pattern it would reveal.

UPC markings were becoming more prevalent in American packaging. By 1976, Albertson's estimated that more than 75 percent of the tonnage of all merchandise going over its checkstands was UPC marked at the source of packaging.

SKAGGS-ALBERTSON'S

The partnership of Skaggs-Albertson's was started as a joint venture in 1970, with the opening of seventeen stores in Texas. A summary of the subsequent expansion follows:

Fiscal Year	*Beginning Stores*	*Added*	*Closed*	*Ending Stores*	*Ending Total* Square Feet (000)*
1971	17	11		28	950
1972	28	16	1	33	1,215
1973	33	7		40	1,631
1974	40	9		49	2,120
1975	49	12		61	2,732

Skaggs was the second largest drug retailer in the U. S., with headquarters in Salt Lake City. Sales and net income for Skaggs from 1965 to 1974 are shown in Exhibit 7.

The partnership had built forty-seven new superdrug-supermarket combination stores between 1970 and 1976. In addition, it had acquired and was operating fifteen superdrug units in the same market area (refer to Exhibit 1). Albertson's and Skaggs had equal investment in the partnership and shared equally in the profit. Half of the sales, expense, net income, assets, liabilities, and capital for the partnership were consolidated into each partner's financial statements (refer to Exhibit 2).

A separate management organization operated the partnership from its headquarters in Dallas, Texas. In the stores, a single set of checkstands was used for all customer checkout. The combination drug and food stores included a full line of pharmaceutical, variety, cosmetic, recreational, and photographic merchandise in addition to the usual lines of food and limited general merchandise carried by an Albertson's store.

Albertson's management believed that the partnership had some important advantages for both partners. For Skaggs, the food store would draw more customer traffic than a drugstore alone would, and for Albertson's the higher margins in non-foods would offer increased earnings. Both partner companies believed that the combination store offered each of them a stable form of diversification, with experienced management in both drugs and food coming primarily to the partnership from the partner companies. Moreover, it was believed that Skaggs-Albertson's had a local image in its operating area, for both customers and employees, separate from either partner company and that such local identification would strengthen the position of combined stores beyond that which separate stores of each partner in these areas might attain.

Sales of non-food items in the combination stores had lagged behind that of food to the extent that some investment analysts questioned the balance of contribution to overall store gross margin. It had also been observed that the rapid expansion of the partnership had led to inefficiencies which had resulted in a decline in operating performance. However, both partner companies were satisfied with the 50-50 arrangement and believed it equitable. Moreover, they were generally pleased with the operating results of the partnership and expected further improvements as its management gained experience.

---

*Note: About 70 percent of total square footage is considered to be selling space.

EXHIBIT 7 SALES AND NET INCOME FOR SKAGGS (IN MILLIONS OF DOLLARS) (about 38 percent owned or controlled by directors)

	Net Sales	*Oper. Income*	*Net Before Taxes*	*Net Income*
1974	498.7	24.39	19.28	10.01
1973	412.3	17.69	13.42	7.20
1972	357.4	12.07	8.41	4.58
1971	320.0	13.02	10.21	5.12
1970	183.4	11.78	10.41	5.16
1969	172.2	11.25	9.85	4.68
1968	160.9	9.54	7.90	4.04
1967	138.7	7.00	5.44	2.94
1966	112.0	4.94	3.75	2.12
1965	88.9	3.64	2.94	1.58

GROWTH AND MARKET SHARE

Expansion of Albertson's operations was categorized as three major thrusts:

1. Building new stores
2. Updating new stores through remodeling and renovation
3. Increasing "backstage" distribution facilities

Older stores that were declining in profitability were sold if they were not considered feasible to remodel or replace. Although in the past some new market areas such as Denver and Los Angeles had been entered by acquiring existing independent local food chain stores, all of the new stores and remodels were currently being constructed by the company (or its Skaggs-Albertson's partnership for those stores) by its fully integrated property development function consisting of real estate negotiations, lawyers, economic analysts, architects, and construction supervisors. Within the preceding ten-year period, a total of 198 new stores (operating in 1976) were newly constructed and an additional 67 stores were completely remodeled. About one-fourth of floor space was allocated to non-food items in new stores. A five-year summary of the recent expansion program for Albertson's stores (not including the partnership) follows:

Fiscal Year	*Beginning Stores*	*Added*	*Closed*	*Ending Stores*	*Ending Total Square Feet (in thousands)*
1971	214	8	3	219	4,440
1972	219	7	8	218	4,461
1973	218	19	8	229	4,816
1974	229	25	8	246	5,456
1975	246	15	9	252	5,776

About 88 percent of all company stores were less than ten years old in 1975, and 80 percent were profitable at a satisfactory level (compared to 60 percent at the end of the 1960s).

The net growth of Albertson's stores was taking place primarily in the California and Denver areas (see sales analysis, Exhibit 8). As the concentration of stores began to increase, the company proceeded to build or buy its own "backstage" distribution facilities. A wholesale distribution center in Boise served company stores in Idaho, eastern Oregon, and other parts of the Northwest. Produce warehouses were operated in Seattle and San Francisco (and in Dallas and Orlando by Skaggs-Albertson's). A 200,000 square foot distribution center in Brea, California served stores in southern California, southern Nevada, and Arizona with groceries and produce. The company's wholesale grocery facilities sold also to outside retailers. During 1976, the company was opening two new distribution facilities. A 340,000-square-foot full-line distribution center in Salt Lake City costing $10 million would serve stores in Utah, eastern Idaho, and portions of Colorado, Wyoming, and Nevada. Also in Brea, California was the company's new 135,000-square-foot meat-service center. This $10 million facility was designed to improve productivity through central processing and provide greater meat quality control and merchandising capabilities at the store level in its service areas of California, Utah, Nevada, and Arizona. These new facilities would increase the merchandise supplied by Albertson's to its own stores to 38 percent of volume sold at retail in 1976, up from 25 percent in 1975. However, management intended to continue to rely on its traditional method of using outside wholesale warehouses and seek maximum investment re-

EXHIBIT 8 SALES ANALYSIS

	Idaho	*Inland Empire*	*Utah*	*Western Washington*
March 29, 1969:				
Sales	$41,544,309	$46,653,930	$56,999,681	$ 61,912,226
No. of stores*	22	23	27	36
Sq. footage	359,332	458,092	528,258	645,408
February 1, 1975:				
Sales	75,558,270	78,666,388	82,508,937	94,063,776
No. of stores*	21	24	28	31
Sq. footage	425,294	533,700	587,016	606,605
January 31, 1976:				
Sales	85,400,000	86,883,000	99,840,000	105,696,000
No. of stores*	20	24	28	32
Sq. footage	435,207	546,444	596,412	630,405
Stores closed or replaced from				
3/29/69 to 2/01/75	8	2	9	9
2/01/75 to 1/31/76	2	1	1	0

The above does not include Skaggs-Albertson's partnership
**Number of stores at end of period.*

EXHIBIT 8 SALES ANALYSIS (Cont.)

	Oregon	*Southern California*	*Northern California*	*Rocky Mountains*
March 29, 1969:				
Sales	$ 61,811,954	$ 62,351,121	$ 51,966,654	$ 35,024,609
No. of stores*	33	28	25	19
Sq. footage	609,002	561,807	568,077	343,317
February 1, 1975:				
Sales	99,629,023	179,645,362	156,789,210	93,105,110
No. of stores*	31	39	43	29
Sq. footage	603,841	857,228	931,136	647,593
January 31, 1976:				
Sales	108,030,000	202,600,000	212,310,000	107,734,000
No. of stores*	31	43	45	29
Sq. footage	632,725	993,535	1,197,848	671,826
Stores closed or replaced from				
3/29/69 to 2/01/75	4	5	3	5
2/01/75 to 1/31/76	2	1	0	2

turn in retailing. At the same time, each operating area was continually being evaluated for other worthwhile distribution investments in the future.

The market position of Albertson's stores varied considerably in various parts of its operating area. In Boise, Albertson's was first in food retailing volume. The company was third in Portland, Oregon and also in Salt Lake City, fourth in Seattle, and fifth in Denver. Despite intense competition in southern California, a substantial portion of the company's total sales volume came from that area (see Exhibit 9).

A study of Albertson's market activity in eighteen major metropolitan areas was made by an investment firm in 1974. The study concluded that Albertson's was in a strong position to grow market-wise, but that the company's financial position and sales in low-share markets would significantly hinder growth prospects.

ORGANIZATION AND MANAGEMENT

Albertson's was organized into eight geographical divisions in addition to the Skaggs-Albertson's partnership. Each division included several districts, and each district in turn supervised a group of stores. Merchandising policy was a large part of each division's responsibility, recognizing the different nature of the various market areas. A profit-center accountability was followed at all levels down to the store. A division staff as well as district managers were supervised by the vice president in charge of a division, and all vice presidents reported to the executive vice president for operations. The latter, together with the corporate headquarters staff reported to the president, who reported to the vice-chairman and chief executive officer. The corporate secretary and the president of the Skaggs-Albertson's division (representing Albertson's interest in the partnership) also reported to the vice-chairman, who in turn was responsible to the chairman of the board.

EXHIBIT 9 ALBERTSON'S MARKET POSITIONS ($1,046,105 TOTAL SALES 1974)

Market	Supermarket Sales Growth 1970–1974	1974 Supermarket Saturation	Total Food Sales (000's)	1972 Market Share	1974 Market Share	1974 Albertson's Sales (000's)	% Total Albertson's Sales
California							
Bakersfield	19.0%	94.1%	$ 208,985	0 %	4.9%	$ 10,240	1.0%
Los Angeles	7.4	90.4	5,423,007	2.1	2.4	130,152	12.4
Riverside-San Bernardino	8.9	91.6	675,306	1.8	2.0	13,506	1.3
Sacramento	15.0	94.2	595,752	3.6	4.3	25,617	2.4
Salinas-Seaside-Monterey	19.9	92.0	156,135	2.6	3.3	5,152	0.5
San Diego	14.4	93.4	875,494	0	0.6	5,253	0.5
San Francisco	10.0	90.9	1,935,933	1.2	1.8	34,847	3.3
San Jose	17.3	93.7	826,862	3.7	4.9	40,516	3.9
Stockton	10.2	92.4	161,544	4.1	5.9	9,531	0.9
Vallejo-Napa	15.2	89.7	154,713	4.0	6.0	9,283	0.9
Colorado							
Denver	12.4	94.9	761,990	5.0	5.1	38,861	3.7

Nevada							
Las Vegas	10.6	96.6	202,949	6.0	6.2	12,580	1.2
Oklahoma							
Oklahoma City	16.1	96.4	456,094	0	1.3	5,929	0.6
Oregon							
Eugene	18.1	93.7	138,025	10.5	12.3	16,977	1.6
Portland	21.5	95.1	845,343	16.2	10.5	88,761	8.5
Utah							
Salt Lake City	21.0	93.7	421,096	20.5	18.2	76,639	7.3
Washington							
Seattle-Everett	17.6	94.6	1,051,556	8.0	10.2	107,259	10.3
Spokane	12.1	94.5	185,642	13.0	10.9	20,235	1.9
			$15,076,426	N/A	4.3%	$646,086	61.8%

Overall growth 16.0%
Source: Investment Firm Survey

The organizational philosophy of Albertson's placed considerable emphasis on the role of the store manager. The organization chart which was displayed in the 1970 Annual Report (see Exhibit 10) was still representative of management's viewpoint on organization in 1976. Training received considerable emphasis in the company, and each division had its own training function in addition to the corporate training staff. Store management personnel were well paid and could earn bonuses totaling up to 16 percent of store profits if the profit goals were met or exceeded.

Employees of Albertson's were largely unionized; more than 89 percent of the employees were covered by a total of over 350 separate union contracts. Management believed that one of the advantages of its labor relations program was its widespread geographical operation in that a problem with any one contract would not materially affect the entire company. Albertson's negotiated union contracts through employers' associations in most areas.

Top management's average age in Albertson's was among the youngest in the food retailing industry. Six of nine senior operating executives were not over 45 years of age in 1976. Mr. Albertson, who owned about 25 percent of the issued common stock, gave his senior executives a relatively free hand in running the company. About 10 percent of common stock was held by other officers and directors of the company.

Management policy was largely established by three executives: Albertson, as chairman and major stockholder; Robert D. Bolinder, vice chairman and chief executive officer; and Warren E. McCain, president. Bolinder had been with the company since 1965. Prior to joining Albertson's as a vice president and treasurer, he had graduated from college in accounting and had received an M.B.A. degree and also attended a senior executive course. In 1972, Bolinder became president when J. L. Scott, the former president, became vice chairman. When Scott left in 1974 to become chairman of A & P, Bolinder became vice chairman and chief executive officer of Albertson's; Bolinder was succeeded as president by Warren E. McCain. McCain had joined Albertson's in 1959. Prior to becoming president he had served as executive vice president, vice president of operations, a regional director of retail operations, division manager, and a non-food and grocery merchandising supervisor.

According to Bolinder, he and McCain generally agreed on principal corporate objectives and strategies although their management styles were considerably different. "We provide a good balance for the company," stated Bolinder, "as he is much more intent on concentrating on current profit opportunities and the short-run problems, whereas I have a tendency to take a longer-range broader approach. McCain is a strong, aggressive-type individual and whether my input is having a proper effect upon the company will only be determined by time. Mr. Albertson feels we should concentrate on improving current operations and save diversification until after adequate improvement has been obtained."

Bolinder saw the company primarily in the "food-retailing" business in 1976 but expected that it would be more in the "retailing" business in the future. He looked toward the possibility of small acquisitions in perhaps home-improvement hardware stores or in sporting goods. With respect to Albertson's "backstage" development, he expressed concern that the company would lose its customer orientation, indicating that this was a danger for a company with a significant portion of its total operations in non-retail-store activities.

McCain visualized the development of more backstage distribution and even light manufacturing, such as candy packaging, ice cream production, central

EXHIBIT 10 ALBERTSON'S, INC. ORGANIZATION CHART

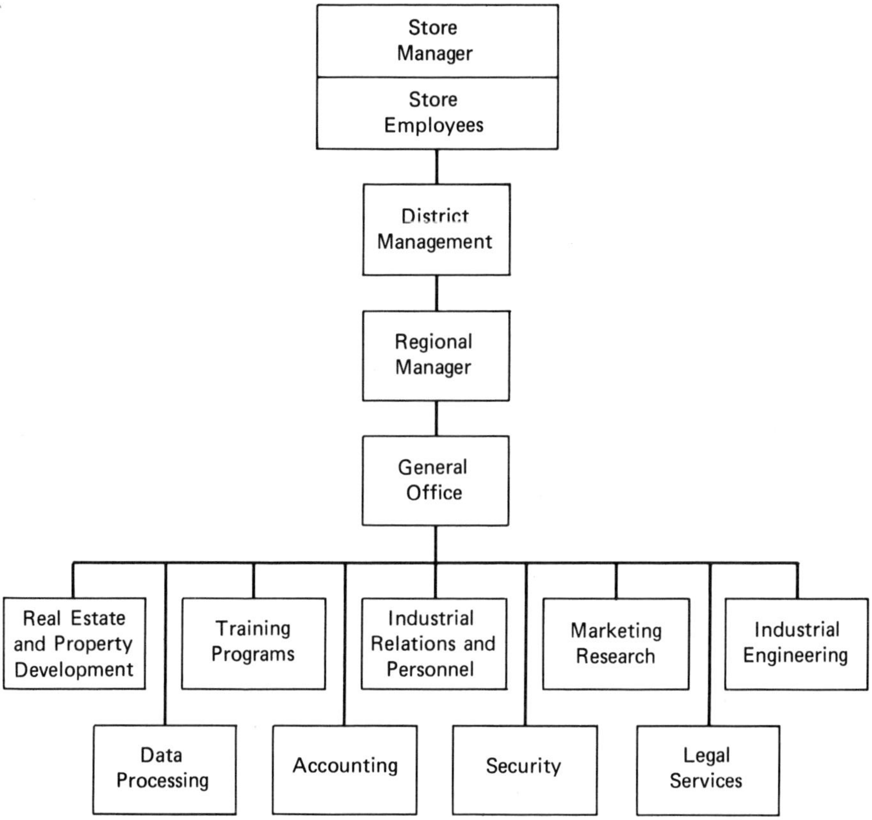

Are We A Backward Company?

"Well, in one respect. Our organization chart starts in reverse when compared with other corporations. At the very top is the store manager and his people who serve our customers. . .

"A typical Albertson's supermarket with its grocery, meat, produce, variety and complex in-store production bakery is a complex business unit. . .and its manager must be a man of many talents. . .

"Would you believe he is chief buyer, price setter, goal setter, advertising manager, personnel director, community relations expert, teacher, money manager, accountant, building supervisor, safety engineer, security agent, and merchandise promoter? Enough? No wonder Albertson's puts him at the top of the organization chart. . .

"The Company is not interested in building empires for headquarters executives. . . our primary concern is developing the store manager and his people. In the end this is the only place it really counts. Motivated by one of the most forward-looking bonus systems, our Albertson's manager is taught to run his store as though he owns it. . ."

bakeries, etc. "We have quite a ways to go to support the stores we already have," he said. "Every facility needs to stand on its own. If we sell meat too cheap in one area, then it is being supported by other operations. We have to have tough cost control. We watch every part of the company on cost-spread sheets. Every cost has to fit into our formula, or if we find that the formula is not right then we change it. A good financial system is a big part of our success. But we need more sophisticated information in the divisions to control the pricing mix, to see what changes in price will have what effect."

According to McCain, "Safeway goes on cost center for distribution—charges groceries to stores at cost. They are completely integrated. Albertson's buys and sells outside and has a profit center operation. Scott is changing A & P to the Albertson's pattern, not Safeway's; this is not an industry trend but is unique."

Training was another area mentioned by McCain. "Our store and division-level people need to become better businessmen. They are presently good operators but not necessarily good businessmen. They need to know more about ROI. In some cases we have spent too much on remodeling, and we didn't look close enough at the ROI. Construction has not had complete accountability, but it will have six months from now."

Members of the Board of Directors of the company, in addition to the three principal executives already mentioned, were as follows:

Kathryn Albertson, Housewife

John B. Fery, President and Chief Executive Officer, Boise Cascade Corporation

R. V. Hansberger, Chairman, President and Chief Executive Officer, Futura Industries

W. H. Langroise, Chairman and Chief Executive Officer, Continental Life and Accident Co.

Charles D. Lein, Professor and Dean of the School of Business, Boise State University

David Little, Cattleman and Idaho State Legislator

Barbara Rasmussen, Housewife

T. E. Roach, Retired; formerly Chairman and Chief Executive Officer, Idaho Power Co.

L. S. Skaggs, Chairman and Chief Executive Officer of Skaggs Companies, Inc.

Directors were elected or reelected each year by the stockholders at the annual stockholders' meeting. In turn, the directors elected or reelected each year the chairman, vice chairman and president; these three executives made the appointments to all other executive positions in the company.

The Board of Directors met quarterly. A director's role, according to Bolinder, was to evaluate the management of the company. "A good board member doesn't interfere with management but gives the input asked for . . . constructive evaluation." Three outside members of the Board served on an audit committee, and there was also a compensation committee. Otherwise, there was not much board involvement beyond the quarterly meetings except for occasional informal calls by management to discuss interim matters.

FINANCIAL MATTERS

Common stock of Albertson's was first sold to the public in 1959 and was traded over the counter. In 1970, the company was first listed on the New York Stock Exchange, which at that time traded the stock of 1,300 of America's 1.5 million business firms. By 1976 there were nearly 7.3 million shares of common stock outstanding, including 825,000 shares that had been issued in a public offering during January 1976 at a net yield of just under $18 million.

The balance sheet of the company had been strengthened by the sale of stock and by a private placement of $20 million in debentures during 1975. "Off-balance-sheet financing" was the description given by investment analysts of Albertson's use of sale and leaseback of new buildings, because the lease obligations did not show directly in balance sheet accounts. Footnotes to the balance sheets in January 1976 revealed that net minimum rental (lease) payment commitments outstanding were about $303 million, which had a present value of about $135 million when discounted at an average interest rate of 7.8 percent. The company's rate of return on equity was attributed, in part, to the financing leverage of such non-capitalized leases.

Total lease payments in 1975 were $16.2 million, up from $13.9 million in 1974. For 1976, payments on leases existing at the beginning of the fiscal year were projected at $15.9 million.

Interest payments in 1975 were $3.5 million and in 1974 $2.4 million. Short-term financing was obtained primarily through borrowings on unsecured lines of credit from banks. In January 1976, Albertson's had short-term lines of credit, at the prime interest rate, of $18.5 million, and it was required to maintain compensating balances of 10 percent of the total lines of credit plus 10 percent of the credit utilized. The company's average short-term borrowings during 1975 were $4 million, with a maximum of $10.5 million.

FUTURE PLANS

The outlook of the food distribution industry in 1976 was described by industry publications as more confident and optimistic than in recent years, although profitability of retailing had some negative indications. Four critical questions regarding the future of the industry were posed by *Progressive Grocer:*

1. Margins. The traditional gross-margin structure was described as inadequate to support either operations or growth. The validity of the idea of price competition resulting in selling groceries at breakeven needed to be reexamined.
2. Distribution had been called a wasteland. Appreciable savings were thought to be possible by eliminating overlap, improving coordination and scheduling, and updating regulations.
3. Merchandising was said to need some fresh thinking.
4. Information becoming available from electronic front-end equipment and consumer research could materially increase turnover, reduce stockouts, and optimize shelf and display space use. However, these kinds of data were not yet being used productively in the grocery distribution system.

Gross National Product forecasts by different U.S. publications to 1985 varied in the range of about 2 percent to 10 percent annual growth in current dollars. A composite forecast by *Predicasts* was 8 percent in current dollars and 3.1 percent in real dollars. A quoted forecast for aggregate U. S. grocery store sales growth to 1985 was 7.3 percent annually, with all drugstore sales growth at 7.1 percent annually.

Bolinder recognized several changes in the business environment that could affect Albertson's way of doing business:

1. Concern over food prices and food expenditures as a percent of disposable income would put pressure on improving productivity, store design, and merchandising concepts.
2. The need to reduce time and distance necessary to shop would require more "one-stop" stores.
3. Eating out would have an effect on grocery sales.
4. More convenience foods.
5. Larger quantity sales, such as case lots.

"We have led out in such areas as consumer programs," he said. "We are definitely large enough in the industry to lead out when we have the foresight and courage."

Albertson's was still committed to the strategies of "aggressively meeting or challenging all price competition" and an "aggressive expansion program." The major portion of Skaggs-Albertson's business was coming from competitors, who "reacted in the usual manner—hotter ads, promotions, etc." Bolinder stated, "We are sold on the Skaggs-Albertson's stores and we will move as fast as Skaggs is willing and capable."

Plans for the expansion of Albertson's stores were concentrated in the company's current area of operations, with emphasis on California and Denver, where additional market depth was wanted. Funds for expansion over the next five years were projected to be obtained primarily from earnings and sale and leaseback of stores, with a gradual reduction in long-term debt. It was expected that additional capital of about $3.6 million in fiscal 1978 and about $3.7 million in fiscal 1979 would be needed to maintain the desired current ratio. However no outside capital, other than funds anticipated from exercise of stock options for the next two years, was projected to be added to working capital.

A Portland investment firm in 1975 suggested that in the next five years Albertson's earnings per share could double, despite the dilution considered necessary to finance the expansion. It projected Albertson's position in 1980 as follows:

	Albertson's	*Skaggs-Albertson's*	*Combined*
Number of stores	346	106	450
Sales per store (millions)	$4.0	$9–10	
Total sales (billions)	$1.4–1.5	$1.0	$1.9–2.0
Net profit margin %	1.2–1.3	1.7–1.8	
Net income (millions)	$17–19	$17–18	$25–28

(Only half of Skaggs-Albertson's sales were included in the combined figure, and number of stores excluded drug units).

Albertson's was projecting, in early 1976, a doubling of sales by 1980, with substantial increases in sales per square foot.

The biggest challenge faced by Albertson's, according to a Lehman Brothers report in 1976, was the result of "a fundamental shift in its location strategy." In the past, the company's supermarkets had been broadly dispersed geographically, "and the principal strategy was to place new stores in areas with limited competition according to the desirability of location, potential sales volume, rent costs, and profit potentials. But the number of such sites has diminished over time, and Albertson's is now moving toward a policy of building strength in promising growth markets."

THE ADOLPH COORS COMPANY: A COMMITMENT TO MANAGEMENT CHANGE

The Adolph Coors Company was founded more than a century ago on the principle that the public would accept and purchase a quality product offered at a fair price. This has proven to be the driving force behind the success of Coors. Even today, when prices seemingly rise overnight and the quality of products is always in question, Coors keeps its founding principle of being responsible to its customers. The success of Coors was aided by hard work, investment after investment in operations to keep things up-to-date, and a strong commitment to some basic business principles. But even companies that are successful are not immune from problems and so it is with Coors. Of late, Coors has been plagued by many problems, some of which have only recently been recognized by management. Fortunately for Coors, management realizes that they are in a critical period and that a commitment to management change is in order. It will be a slow, arduous transition for a company that is so devoutly dedicated to tradition, but that must change to survive.

HISTORY

Coors was founded more than a century ago by a German immigrant who found the American Dream. Born in Germany in 1847, Adolph Herman Joseph Coors was orphaned at age fifteen. After serving an indentureship in brewing, he ventured to America at twenty-one by stowing away on a ship. Slowly but surely, Coors worked his way west. In 1872, he opened a beer and wine bottling business outside of Denver, Colorado. But this still was not what he wanted to do, so in 1873 he and a partner converted an old tannery into a brewing plant. The site was in the Rocky Mountain foothills west of Denver. After working at the brewery for seven years, Coors' partner sold out to Coors, who became the sole owner. In the years that followed, Coors put in much hard work and witnessed both success and setbacks, but the company always continued to grow. Even when Colorado proclaimed prohibition in 1916, the company kept its operation going and profitable by switching

Prepared by Patrick Manterer, under the supervision of Dr. Y. N. Chang of California State University, Fullerton. This case is prepared from published information. The company in no way participated in its preparation.

its production to near-beer, malted milk, sweet cream butter, and skim milk crystals. During this time, Coors also sold the alcohol distilled off of the near-beer to drug companies and hospitals. When prohibition was repealed, Coors started to grow once again as a viable new force in the brewing industry.

INDUSTRY

The brewing industry in the U.S. is the world leading producer of beer, producing 156,948,000 tax-paid barrels in 1977. Since the industry is large and because the market for beer does not increase by any appreciable amount, it is a highly competitive business.

The intensive nature of competition among the beer brewing companies directly reflects the changing characteristics of the industry. Notably, there has been a decline in numbers of brewing companies. In 1971 there were no more than eighty brewers in the United States, compared to the hundreds of family-owned brewers in the 1930s. Economy in production and national distribution typify large operations. Second, beer is hard to market profitably because the product is bulky, distribution is costly, and labor costs are high. Third, the large brewers can command premium prices over locally marketed beers. Last, changing consumer characteristics increase marketing expenses. Although about half of the adult population drink beer, 60 percent of these adults are men. Heavy beer drinkers, however, consume 80 to 90 percent of the beer sold in the U. S.

To saturate this broad spectrum of market and to cope with the stiff competition, large breweries rely on product innovation and aggressive advertising. For example, since Miller introduced its light beer in 1975, brewers have been falling over themselves to introduce light beer. In fact, Anheuser-Busch brought out two lights: one under the Anheuser-Busch name and one under its Michelob name. Coors was one of the last companies to produce a light beer; theirs came out in the spring of 1978. Another product, the super-premium beer, is under development.

Advertising is the second competitive weapon. It has been acknowledged that beers are becoming bland in taste and the difference between beers is minimal. Thus the only way to gain customer attention is to make the beer distinctive through advertising. Companies that have the catchiest, most inventive advertising are bound to be spending the most money and holding the largest market share. For example, Schlitz Malt Liquor advertises with a bull and sells quite well. Table 1 and Table 2 show the advertising expenditures for the top five brewers and indicate the market shares of the same five brewers.

ENVIRONMENTAL IMPACT

Coors is trying to minimize the pollution caused by its packaging materials. Coors uses recyclable, non-biodegradable materials. The glass in Coors bottles is easily crushed but does not chemically decompose and hence does not cause water or air pollution. Also, all Coors bottles are redeemable for 1 cent to encourage consumers to recycle the bottles. As for the aluminum cans, aluminum is indefinitely recyclable. To encourage recycling of aluminum, Coors instituted the "Cash for Cans" program, in which all Coors distributors pay 17 cents a pound for aluminum cans of any beverage. Because of this program, 17,236,000 pounds of aluminum cans were recycled by Coors in 1977; in 1978, out of every hundred cans Coors put into the marketplace, they got 85 cans back for recycling.

In an effort to stop pollution by pull tabs, Coors came up with a can opening

TABLE 1 BEER SALES/MARKET SHARE

	31-Gallon Barrels Sold 1977	*Market Share* 1978
Anheuser-Busch	36,640,000	25.3%
Miller Brewing Co.	24,218,000	19.0%
Joseph Schlitz Brewing Co.	22,130,000	11.9%
Pabst Brewing Co.	16,300,000	9.4%
Adolph Coors Co.	12,824,000	7.7%

Sources: Standard and Poor's Industry Survey, *Vol. I, A-L, April 1979.* Los Angeles Times, *Part VII, p. 1, May 27, 1979.*

system that stays on the can. To prevent pollution of water, Coors built a waste treatment plant to process more than 4 million gallons of industrial waste a day.

Coors is also committed to energy conservation. It presently uses natural gas from its own gas wells, though this is only a short-term plan. Coors also owns a coal field and is converting its plant over to coal-fired boilers. Through its recycling aluminum cans program, Coors is saving 95 percent of the energy necessary to make new metal. In addition to these saving measures, Coors uses a process that benefits fuel conservation and helps give Coors its special taste. The company eliminates heat pasteurization in the making of its beer and saves 50 percent of the total thermal energy needed to run the brewery, which amounts to enough energy to heat 13,000 Colorado homes for a year.

MANAGEMENT

Coors has an unusual management style. The company is run by third generation family members who are brothers. Bill Coors is the older of the two and holds the position of chairman and chief executive officer, while Joe Coors, the younger brother, is president. There is no apparent rivalry between the brothers and no formal lines of responsibility. Bill generally handles the technical side and is known for his near-genius in the brewing industry. The financial and administrative affairs fall under the jurisdiction of Joe. A fourth generation of the Coors family is at work, too. Joe's three sons, Peter, Jeffrey, and Joseph Jr., are all in on the family business. Peter is the senior vice-president for sales and marketing, Jeffrey is the senior vice-president in charge of technical operations, and Joe, Jr. runs one of the company's industrial porcelain operations. Also employed in the company is Adolph IV, son of the late brother of Joe and Bill. Adolph is a chemist. All members of the board are presently working or had at one time worked for Coors. Four of the eight directors are Bill, Joe, Jeffrey, and Peter. Presently, only one seat is filled by a non-Coors employee, but he just recently retired from their operations.

MARKETING

Product and Distribution

The company, deliberately limiting its distribution to sixteen states, presently serves only 29 percent of the nation. Coors' only brewery is in Golden, Colorado,

TABLE 2 ADVERTISING EXPENDITURE

	1977
Anheuser-Busch	
Advertising investment	$58,687,200
Advertising cost per barrel	$1.60
Advertising cost per case	11¢
Miller Brewing Company	
Advertising investment	$43,283,400
Advertising cost per barrel	$1.78
Advertising cost per case	12¢
Joseph Schlitz Brewing Co.	
Advertising investment	$43,928,800
Advertising cost per barrel	$1.98
Advertising cost per case	14¢
Pabst Brewing Co.	
Advertising investment	$10,969,789
Advertising cost per barrel	68¢
Advertising cost per case	4¢
Adolph Coors Co.	
Advertising investment	$ 4,355,333
Advertising cost per barrel	33¢
Advertising cost per case	2¢

Source: Advertising Age, *October 9, 1978, p. 122.*

and it markets its product through company-owned distributors. Until 1978, Coors only brewed one beer, Coors Banquet Beer, which is the original Coors beer. It has been marketed under the slogan "America's Fine Light Beer." It was given this title even though it had 145 calories per 12-ounce can. The birth of Coors Light in the spring of 1978 was marked by great disagreement in the Coors organization, but the decision proved to be a wise one. Coors Light has a caloric content of 105 calories per 12-ounce can. It is being marketed through a spirited advertising campaign and a slogan that says "Something no other light beer has—the real taste of Coors."

Packaging

Coors has remained a self-sufficient company. It has contractual agreements with independent farmers to grow barley, with Coors supplying the seed to the farmers. Coors malts almost all of its own barley in company facilities. The water used in the beer is from springs located on company grounds. Coors also maintains its own source of energy in that it owns a natural gas field containing some 90 gas wells and also owns a coal field.

In addition, Coors owns its own facilities to produce containers to package the beer. In 1971, Coors completely converted to all-aluminum cans. It decided that aluminum was versatile and light. Coors built its own aluminum plant and has the largest single-metal container manufacturing plant in the U.S. It produces mainly lightweight, seamless aluminum can bodies and easy-open lids.

Coors also produces its own glass bottles. In 1976, it acquired a glass plant. The Coors Container Glass Division manufactures all the bottles for the brewery. The company uses glass because of its impermeability and lack of odor and taste. Coors also has its own transportation and distribution companies to provide flexibility, ease, and direct contact with retailers.

Diversified Activities

Coors has dabbled in companies not directly related to its beer operation, but they complement the primary product. Through three subsidiaries Coors produces a number of ceramic and porcelain products. Coors Porcelain Company, Wilbanks International, Inc., and R. I. Ceramic Company operate in four states. The companies convert raw materials such as aluminum oxide and clay into various types of mechanical and electronic ceramic and porcelain products. Coors also maintains a food company. Coors Food Products Company was created in 1977 and operates out of a rice processing facility in Arkansas. Coors experimentation with food introduced a cocoa powder replacement that contains no chocolate. Coors eventually wants to develop the food products company into a diversified food company.

Marketing Mix and Advertising

The Coors Company has recently had to change its marketing strategy. Coors was faced with a problem that most firms only dream about; namely, that the demand for its beer outstripped its production capacity. Since its product sold so well, Coors' only marketing strategy was to let the "superior" quality of the beer sell the beer and the company's attitude took on tones of arrogance. In fact, from 1941 to 1975, company sales grew steadily and doubled between 1968 and 1973. Until 1977, Coors remained in the single brewery in Golden, brewed only one type of beer, and held on to fourth place in beer sales.

Coors started a whole new marketing strategy aimed at reconquering its market position. The company brought out a new beer, Coors Light, to cover the then rapidly growing light market. Coors also decided to go public and hired a new public relations staff. Finally, Coors went back to market research, after a 35-year absence, to put the public's desires over those of the company. Coors also adopted a program of sponsoring sporting events. The company has a long way to go to catch up with the industry, but it has made a big start.

PRODUCTION OPERATIONS

The operations take place in the single brewery in Golden, Colorado. The making of the product is a long and meticulous process. The brewing process takes about seventy days, longer than any of Coors' major competitors. The process combines basic engineering practices and biochemical technology into an exact sequence that is maintained around-the-clock. Coors malts its own barley. The barley is wet down and aerated, then allowed to sprout in germinating bins. This allows all the starches in the grains to convert into usable forms. Finally, the barley is heated in large kilns to retard any further growth and is moved to silos to be aged. When brewing time comes, the barley is ground up and mixed with rice and water and this mixture is heated to convert starches and carbohydrates into sugar. Coors' trademark is the use of only "Pure Rocky Mountain Spring Water" and this is one of the factors in its special clean taste. After the mixing is accomplished, the husks and hulls are removed and the extract is brewed for two hours, during which time a blend of hops is added. At the end of two hours, the hops are strained and unfermented beer is cooled and combined with yeast and left to ferment. After a carefully controlled period of time and temperature, the yeast is separated from the beer and the beer is pumped to storage tanks, where it is allowed to age for seven to eight weeks.

Coors approaches the problem of germ control in an unusual manner. Most companies employ heat pasteurization to kill any germs in the beer. Coors uses a process in which the beer is placed in containers under conditions as sterile as that found in an operating room of a hospital. Coors does this because it was discovered that heat has the effect of taking away some of the body and taste from the beer.

PERSONNEL

At present, Coors employs 3,800 people, which includes its own engineering force. The company believes that the only way to get its employees interested in the business is to promote from within. To this end, Coors also provides educational and training programs to help upgrade employee skills. Coors is an equal opportunity employer and everyone is given an equal chance in employment, training, and advancement. The company enlists the help of minority employment agencies to recruit minorities. Coors also has a program, the Employment Opportunity Training Program, through which it hires and trains ex-convicts and the disadvantaged. The company sponsors many recreational activities to boost employee morale. Coors has always been a staunch advocate of the open-shop theory of running a business and therefore has long been plagued by union problems. The union problems have not been about salary because the average brewery worker makes over $20,000 a year. The problems have always been over civil rights issues such as mandatory polygraph tests. But in 1978, management gained a foothold when a twenty-month strike ended. Seventy-one percent of the workers in one union voted to oust that union and have a one-to-one relationship with management.

RESEARCH AND DEVELOPMENT

Research and development at Coors takes the form of developing improved brewing and packaging techniques and new products. In 1978, Coors spent $9,444,000 in research and development, 1.5 percent of its net sales. This is a drop of 29 percent over 1977 R&D expenditure of $13,280,000, which was 2.2 percent of net sales. This decreased expenditure can be partially attributed to the introduction of Coors Light in the spring of 1978. With this beer on the market, there was no longer any need for the expensive pre-market research and testing. The company is always looking for new ways to update and improve its operation. In fact, in 1977, Coors spent $6 million for the right and license to use certain technology to improve aluminum can recycling abilities and reduce cost. Although Coors has not spent a great deal on R&D, it has recognized its importance in the company's strategic development.

FINANCE

The gross sales figure for the year ending December 31, 1978 was $746,756,000, while the net sales figure was $624,804,000. The net sales increased 5.3 percent in 1978 over a 1977 net sales figure of $593,120,000. The increase in sales was primarily due to price increases that were instituted in March and

TABLE 1 BALANCE SHEET (In Thousands)

Assets	Dec. 31, 1978	Dec. 31, 1977
Current Assets		
Cash	$ 88,550	$ 72,001
Accounts and notes receivable	40,292	34,293
Inventory	115,083	119,560
Prepaid expenses and other assets	19,547	15,226
Accumulated income tax prepayments	7,214	7,135
Total Current Assets	$270,686	$248,215
Properties, at cost, less accumulated depreciation	$475,780	$435,673
Excess of cost over net assets of businesses acquired, less amortization	2,808	2,893
Other assets	2,336	4,787
Total Assets	$751,610	$691,568
Liabilities and Stockholders' Equity		
Current Liabilities		
Accounts payable	$ 37,413	$ 34,439
Accrued salaries and vacations	18,236	14,675
Taxes, other than income taxes	15,256	16,840
Federal and state income taxes	16,853	17,008
Accrued interest	5,988	4,989
Accrued expenses and other liabilities	13,874	11,087
Total Current Liabilities	$107,620	$ 99,038
Accumulated Deferred Income Taxes	$ 41,237	$ 33,251
Other Long-Term Liabilities	5,237	5,256
Stockholders' Equity		
Capital Stock		
Class A common stock, voting, $1 par value	1,260	1,260
Class B common stock, non-voting, no par value	11,000	11,000
	$ 12,260	$ 12,260
Paid-in capital	2,011	2,011
Retained earnings	609,250	563,278
	$623,521	$577,549
Less—treasury stock, at cost	26,005	23,526
Total Stockholders' Equity	$597,516	$554,023
Total Liabilities and Equity	$751,610	$691,568

November 1978 and were in compliance with the President's anti-inflation guidelines. The net profit for Coors in 1978 was $54,774,000, which is an 8.7 percent net profit after taxes on sales, while in 1977 Coors had an 11.4 percent profit on sales. This decline from 1977–78 was due to increased packaging costs, higher fixed costs, and a decline of 2 percent in the volume of beer sold in barrels. The company also incurred increased operating costs for maintenance and repairs, due to the substantial additions to the property. In determining the value of its inventories, Coors uses the lower of cost or market value. Of the stock that is issued, the Coors family owns all of the Class A common, which has full voting rights and a par value of $1. The Coors family also owns 41 percent of the Class B common stock, which has no voting rights and no par value, but which had a value of $4.20 per share on December 31, 1978. The balance sheet and income statement for Coors are in Tables 1 and 2.

FUTURE OUTLOOK

According to management, commitment of change marked the company's operations in 1978. The company has switched to offense: the commitment to break a twenty-year tradition of brewing just one product by introducing Coors Light. The company continues to develop a super-premium beer and intends to begin test marketing during 1979. To implement the segmented marketing strategy, the marketing

TABLE 2 INCOME STATEMENT (In Thousands)

	December 31, 1978	*December 31, 1977*
Sales	$746,756	$716,609
Less—Federal and state beer excise taxes	121,952	123,489
Net Sales	$624,804	$593,120
Costs and expenses		
Cost of goods sold	450,439	413,884
Marketing, general and administrative	79,369	49,842
Research and development	9,444	13,280
	$539,252	$477,006
Operating Income	$ 85,552	$116,114
Other expense (income)	$ (7,975)	$ (3,448)
Income before income taxes	$ 93,527	$119,562
Income taxes		
Current	$ 30,846	$ 44,887
Deferred	7,907	6,975
Net Income	$ 54,774	$ 67,700

organization has been enlarged, strengthened, and reorganized to facilitate distribution and decentralized decision-making at distribution and retail levels. Management regards the ability to market as equal to the ability to produce.

Expansion in brewery capacity is a commitment to change. Two potential sites are under study: one in Rockingham County, Virginia, and the other in Anson County, North Carolina. Capital expenditures for 1978 amount to $86 million.

There are also management changes. The tight hold by the Coors family, however, remains strong. Corporate policy towards unions remains unchanged.

A commitment of management change has begun; management is confident of the growth the future will bring.

REFERENCES

Adolph Coors Company Annual Report 1978.

Adolph Coors Company Profile (company publication).

A Handful of Questions About Coors (company publication).

"A Test for the Coors Dynasty," *Business Week,* May 8, 1978.

"Coors Beer: What Hit Us?" *Forbes,* October 16, 1978.

"Coors Undercuts Its Last Big Union," *Business Week,* July 24, 1978.

Dun & Bradstreet Industry Ratios 1974–1977.

O-T-C Regional Exchange Stock Reports. Standard & Poor's Corp., New York, 1976–1979.

Standard & Poor's Industry Surveys 1979. Standard & Poor's Corp., New York.

"The Men at Coors Beer Find Old Ways Don't Work Anymore," *Wall Street Journal,* January 19, 1979.

VOLKSWAGEN MANUFACTURING CORPORATION OF AMERICA: A CASE IN POINT

At one time, in the late 1960s, Volkswagen could call 50 percent of the U.S. foreign car market its own. This market share contributed one third of its corporate profit. The primary reason for this success was a car model called the "Beetle," or "Bug." In the early 1970s, however, Volkswagen's market share in the U.S. started slipping due to the Beetle nearing the end of its product life cycle.

This dilemma, coupled with the OPEC oil embargo of 1974, the dollar's devaluation, and the increasing Japanese competition, produced a record loss of $807 million for Volkswagen in 1974.

This situation put Volkswagen in front of a problem that could hardly be mastered by many businesses: How can you reduce your loss, simultaneously establish yourself a base from which you can increase your U.S. foreign car market share, and within four years present increasing profits to your stockholders again?

In the short run, three to five years, Volkswagen planned to maintain its share in the U. S. market in spite of increasing competition from Detroit and Japan with the falling dollar posing and ever-enlarging problem. A production facility in the U. S. seemed to be the best strategy to counter these threats.

In the long run, ten to twenty years, this production facility would give Volkswagen a means for expansion in the mature but gigantic American market, with its annual projected growth rate of 2 percent over the next decade.

VOLKSWAGEN—A BRIEF COMPANY HISTORY

Volkswagen as a company evolved around the Beetle. The idea for the small, economical car was developed by Ferdinand Porsche, the famous automobile engineer, in the early 1930s. His attempts to sell the concept to manufacturers failed, however, until he caught the attention of Hitler, who liked the idea and in 1937 had the Volkswagen Development Company established. A year later, he laid the cor-

---

Prepared by Robert Jechart, Francis J. MacBride, and Steven M. Elliott, under the supervision of Dr. Y. N. Chang of California State University, Fullerton. Case prepared from published information; the company described in no way participated in its preparation.

nerstone for a huge factory to produce Volkswagens in a new town later to be known as Wolfsburg. However, when the war came, the new plant was rapidly converted to produce military adaptations of the Volkswagen. The plant was virtually destroyed by Allied bombing raids in 1945.

Volkswagen's post-war growth was largely due to the efforts of Heinz Nordhoff, its president from 1948 to 1968. His autocratic manner and his production background provided the small VW company with the leadership necessary to revive it.

The adherence to one automobile model—the Beetle—and its gradual perfection was the philosophy of Nordhoff. His goal: to develop a car of the highest technical excellence and quality at the lowest price.

In 1949, VW's annual production was up to over 46,000 cars, all Beetles. By 1954 it was turning out an annual total of 202,000 Beetles and 40,000 Type IIs (Transporters). Fortunately for Volkswagen, demand for the Beetle continued to grow. In fact, by 1960 sales had reached 860,000 vehicles. A small plant at Brunswick and a new large facility at Hanover were added to handle the increased demand. Towards the end of the 1960s—the decade of fantastic growth for the company—VW was turning out 1,775,500 vehicles yearly (1968).

Volkswagen's greatest marketing success remarkably enough was in the U. S.—home of the big car. The first VW car entered the U. S. in 1950. In 1958, Volkswagen of America (VWOA), a wholly-owned subsidiary of the Volkswagen in Germany, was established and appointed sole VW importer for the U. S. By 1968, the U. S. absorbed 569,300 Beetles, Microbuses, and other models—57 percent of the total U. S. imported car market. By this time, VW's dealer network, consisting of 1,070 dealers in exclusive territories across the country, had become one of the biggest in the U. S.

Nordhoff died in April 1968 and was succeeded by Kurt Lotz, whose first priority was to pursue the model diversification. He was determined to break out of the Beetle image before the car lost ground in the marketplace.

In 1969, Lotz acquired and subsequently merged with Audi. In the same year he led VW into a joint venture with Porsche.

Lotz's diversification plans were largely unsuccessful. Dependence on the Beetle remained.

By 1971, difficulties started to plague the company. In 1971 profits were reduced to DM (Deutschmark) 147 million, due to soaring costs and the mark's revaluation, down from DM 540 million earned in 1968.

At the end of 1971, Lotz resigned and Rudolf Leiding took over his post. His first task was to devote his entire effort to building a handful of water-cooled, front wheel-drive, front-engined cars to be introduced in 1973/74.

In the meantime Leiding attempted to reduce VW's dependence on the U. S. market. The continuing revaluation of the Deutschmark, the U. S. import surtax imposed on foreign cars, and the U. S. customers' gradual disenchantment with the aging Beetle let VW unit sales plunge 18 percent between 1971 and 1972 and another 14 percent between 1972 and 1973. Also, production costs in Germany were too high to permit construction of a successful export car. The solution to Leiding was to transfer increasingly production abroad, especially to developing countries.

Already by 1972, production companies had been set up in Brazil, Mexico, and South Africa and assembly companies created in Australia, Belgium, Indonesia,

Yugoslavia, and Spain. It was this insistence on transferring production abroad that contributed to Leiding's resignation in 1974.

This was VW's worst year—it recorded a record loss of $807 million. Car sales continued to plunge, especially in the U. S., where VW sales were decreasing rapidly. The OPEC oil embargo, the dollar's devaluation, and the increased Japanese competition were the main factors for this high loss.

VW's third president in seven years was Toni Schmuecker, who was faced with a grim and almost hopeless situation.

However, by 1975 Schmuecker reduced VW's loss considerably and considered a U. S. plant the only way to regain the VW's market share in the U. S. foreign car market.

In June 1975, a U. S. "project team" was assembled to study the feasibility of an American VW production facility. By April 1976, the Supervisory Board of Directors, consisting of six government officials (due to the government's 40 percent share in the company), two union officials, three factory council members, and nine industry officials, gave the final go-ahead for a U. S. production plant.

PLANNING STAGE

On September 1, 1973, Volkswagen A. G. of Germany established a "U. S. Team" to study the possibility of establishing manufacturing or assembly operations in the United States to help overcome the effect of the dollar's weakness versus the mark's strength. This study team travelled to major U. S. cities in late 1973 to evaluate the situation.

However, on August 1, 1974, the first comprehensive feasibility study indicated that the time was not yet right for the start of an American production or assembly operation.

Then, in June 1975, another project team was assembled in Wolfsburg with members drawn from all pertinent departments to again study the feasibility of a U. S. plant. Simultaneously, various consulting firms were retained to assist in comprehensive studies relating to strategic concept, alternative plant locations, labor market conditions, and other essential considerations regarding a U. S. plant.

In November 1975, the results of the preliminary studies were presented to Volkswagen's Supervisory Board of Directors, who authorized the continuation of the U. S. study project.

In April 1976, the final go-ahead for assembly of Volkswagen vehicles in the U. S. was given by the Supervisory Board of Directors based on continued project feasibility studies.

During the end of 1975 and the beginning of 1976, every state in the United States except Alaska and Hawaii submitted proposals for establishing a Volkswagen plant in their states.

In June 1976, following comprehensive review of all proposed plant sites, three locations were named finalists in the "logistically optimal" U. S. Northeast. Each had an existing plant adaptable to Volkswagen requirements: Columbus, Ohio; Cleveland, Ohio; and New Stanton, Pennsylvania.

Simultaneously, VODECO (Volkswagen Development Company) was incorporated in Detroit to begin seeking component sources for an "Americanized" Rabbit.

Finally, in July 1976, New Stanton was selected to be the location for Volkswagen's first American assembly plant. (See Exhibit 1 for sequence of events.)

EXHIBIT 1 VWMOA SEQUENCE OF EVENTS

Sept. 1, 1973	Volkswagenwerk AG establishes a "U.S. Team" to study possibility of establishing manufacturing operations in the U.S. to help overcome the dollar's devaluation.
May 1974	Volkswagen Rabbit introduced in Germany.
Aug. 1, 1974	First feasibility study indicates that the time is not yet right for start of an American production operation.
Feb. 1975	VW Rabbit introduced to the U.S. market.
June 1, 1975	New U.S. "project team" is assembled and various consulting firms retained to assist in comprehensive studies relating to a possible U.S. plant.
April 23, 1976	VWAG's Supervisory Board of Directors votes unanimously for ultimate assembly of VW vehicles in the U.S.
June 1976	Three locations are named finalists for possible VW U.S. plant: Columbus, Ohio; Cleveland, Ohio; and New Stanton, Pennsylvania.
July 1976	New Stanton is selected to be the location for Volkswagen's first American assembly plant.
Sept. 15, 1976	"Final Master Agreement" for VW's U.S. Project signed between Volkswagen and the Commonwealth of Pennsylvania.
Feb. 1, 1977	VWMOA acquires metal stamping plant in South Charleston, West Virginia from AMC.
Feb. 14, 1977	Construction starts in the Westmoreland plant.
Aug. 3, 1977	First plant production personnel placed on VW Westmoreland payroll.
April 10, 1978	First American made Rabbit comes off the line.
Jan. 15, 1979	Production of 400 Rabbits daily on first shift; employment now about 3,500 persons.
March 1979	Production geared up to 800 Rabbits daily by utilizing second shift.

LOGISTICS AND OPERATIONS SET-UP

Plant and Site

The plant chosen was an unfinished shell, modern in design and laid out expressly for automobile production, owned by Chrysler Corporation, who had stopped construction in 1972 before it was completed. This plant is located 35 miles southeast of Pittsburgh near New Stanton in Westmoreland County.

The site included 1,300 acres of land and a 2.5 million square feet of main factory building.

Richard S. Cummins, former plant manager at Chrysler Corp., was hired as plant manager for VWMOA and put in charge of supervising the final construction of the building and surrounding grounds.

Access and Transportation

With 4,000 to 5,000 employees and a production schedule of about 800 cars per day, and each car made up of over 10,000 parts, transportation in and out of the plant was a large factor to be considered.

Access roads into the plant area involved some fairly complicated on and off-ramps from Interstate Highway 70 and Route 119 and were constructed by the state of Pennsylvania. In addition, Pennsylvania constructed railroad facilities, which included a rail spur from Mt. Pleasant to the plant area and a railyard. Two railroads, the Baltimore & Ohio and the Norfolk & Western, are users of these facilities.

Other transportation considerations concerning choosing this plant were:

1. *Airline system:* Pennsylvania has five international airports; ninety-six full-service airports served by fourteen commercial airlines and seventy charter services. There are ninety-two other licensed commercial landing fields, and 547 personal use landing fields.
2. *Water system:* It includes 402 river terminals and three major ports; Philadelphia, the largest freshwater port in the world; Pittsburgh, the largest inland port in the U.S.; and Erie, which reaches the Atlantic Ocean via the St. Lawrence Seaway and all of the five Great Lakes, with their numerous Canadian and U.S. ports.
3. *Highway system:* Pennsylvania's turnpike and limited interstate highway system contains 45,000 miles of modern highways that put every motor carrier's shipment within two hours of a major cargo terminal.
4. *Rail system:* Pennsylvania's rail system carries one-sixth of the nation's total rail tonnage. Forty-three rail lines, including nine major trunk lines, operate on over 18,000 miles of track within the state.

VWMOA also purchased a 31.6 acre pier located at the Port of Wilmington in Delaware. This new port facility will enable the company to expedite the delivery of cars in the South and Midwest. This port also provided an easy access between West Germany and the U. S. for the shipments of component parts. The port will also be used to import and distribute Porsches and Audis into the South and Midwest. It was estimated that about 70,000 cars will pass through this port yearly.

Energy Resources

Energy availability and proximity were also very important considerations in deciding for the New Stanton plant. Available energy resources in Pennsylvania are:

1. *Coal:* Recoverable coal reserves are estimated at 35 billion tons, enough to last several centuries.
2. *Nuclear:* Six operating nuclear power stations have a combined capacity of 3,902 megawatts, with five more units under construction, representing another 5,946 megawatts of capacity.
3. *Petroleum:* Pennsylvania is the fifth largest oil refining state and exports substantial quantities of refined petroleum products. The crude extracted from Pennsylvania wells has excellent lubricating qualities.

EXHIBIT 2 VWMOA BASIC DATA

Location:	About 2½ miles south of New Stanton, Pa., at the intersection of VW Drive and "old" U.S. Route 119.
Plant Site:	1,180 acres.
Total Floor Area of All Buildings:	2,566,786 sq. feet.
Building Size:	
Assembly Plant:	Overall dimensions approximately 1,700 by 1,000 feet.
East Annex:	Total area approximately 39,840 sq. feet.
West Annex:	Total area approximately 95,250 sq. feet.
Administration Building:	Total area approximately 102,200 sq. feet.
Rail Facilities:	VW Westmoreland is served by both the Baltimore & Ohio and the Norfolk & Western Railroads over a state-owned rail system linking the plant with Mt. Pleasant, Pa. Rail facilities at the plant include a 15-track-wide railroad support yard south of the assembly building and a five-spur auto loading facility east of the plant in the finished vehicle storage lot.
Truck Marshalling Area:	Room for approximately 75 car-transports in the finished vehicle storage area.
Utility Services:	Include electric, water, stand-by-fire protection, gas, sewage, and compressed air.

4. *Electricity:* Pennsylvania is an exporter of electricity and the electric utility sector is the nation's third largest. Coal generates 80 percent of their electrical production.
5. *Natural gas:* Pennsylvania produces only 12 percent of its total natural gas needs, but it has the largest gas storage facilities in the U. S. and expects to tap natural gas under Lake Erie in the near future.

Parts Supply

A great deal of importance, of course, was given the problem of supplies. Approximately 10,000 parts were needed for the manufacture of the Rabbit. To tackle this task, VODECO (Volkswagen Development Company) was founded, its headquarters located in Detroit, Michigan. This location was chosen because the majority of part suppliers are set up in this area, the traditional home of the American automobile industry. A staff of 160 persons was hired by VODECO to manage and plan the purchasing of all the parts needed. In 1977, it was estimated that VWMOA would purchase over $60 million in component parts. VWMOA estimated that by 1985, 80–85 percent of the components will be U. S. built. Among the start-up components in 1977 were: glass, wheels, steering wheels, interior plastic parts, door panels, carpets, exhaust components, rear suspensions, shock absorbers, fuel tanks, weatherstripping, inside mirrors, front seat assemblies, instruments, and cigarette lighters.

The short-block assemblies for both the gasoline and diesel engine, along with the transmissions, are shipped to the Westmoreland plant from West Germany. The major body stampings for the Rabbit come from a stamping plant in South Charleston, West Virginia, which was purchased by VWMOA from American Motors Corporation.

There are also some 1,800 firms in Pennsylvania itself that are supplying components to VWMOA.

For all the parts involved in the U. S. Rabbit program, VWMOA and its parent firm in West Germany established very high quality assurance standards in order to retain the German VW quality image expected by the American public. Exhibits 3 and 4 depict the parts network and distribution network.

Labor Resources

Human resource is very often the most important element in a production system. Initial projections anticipated that full production would run at 800 cars per day, which would require the hiring of approximately 4,000 skilled workers.

EXHIBIT 3 PARTS NETWORK

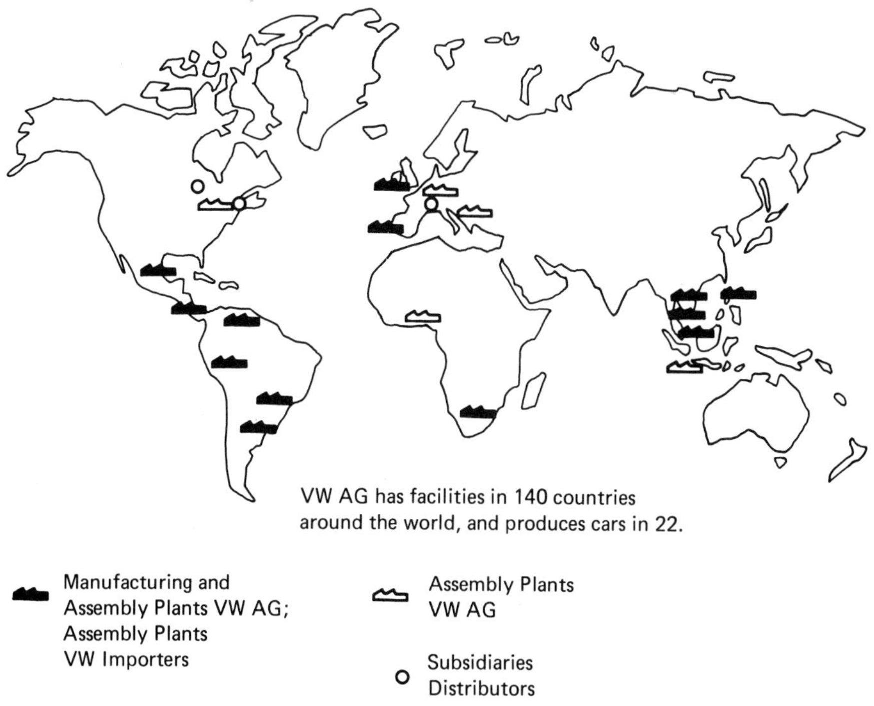

Source: Company publication.

EXHIBIT 4 THE U.S. DISTRIBUTION NETWORK

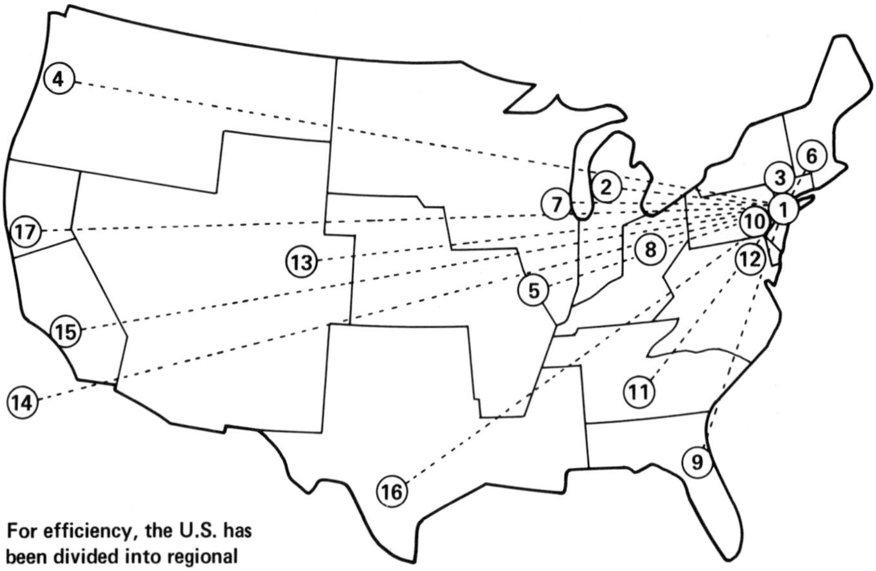

For efficiency, the U.S. has been divided into regional distribution organizations.

1. Volkswagen of America, Inc.
   Englewood Cliffs, New Jersey
2. Import Motors Limited, Inc.
   Grand Rapids, Michigan
3. World-Wide Volkswagen Corporation
   Orangeburg, New York
4. Riviera Motors, Inc.
   Hillsboro, Oregon
5. Volkswagen Mid-America, Inc.
   St. Louis, Missouri
6. Volkswagen of America, Inc.
   Wilmington, Massachusetts
7. Volkswagen of America, Inc.
   Deerfield, Illinois
8. Volkswagen of America, Inc.
   Dublin, Ohio
9. Volkswagen of America, Inc.
   Jacksonville, Florida
10. Volkswagen of America, Inc.
    Valley Forge, Pennsylvania
11. Volkswagen of America, Inc.
    Atlanta, Georgia
12. Volkswagen of America, Inc.
    Lanham, Maryland
13. Volkswagen of America, Inc.
    Englewood, Colorado
14. Volkswagen of America, Inc.
    Honolulu, Hawaii
15. Volkswagen of America, Inc.
    Culver City, California
16. Volkswagen of America, Inc.
    San Antonio, Texas
17. Volkswagen of America, Inc.
    Pleasanton, California

Source: Company publication.

Skilled labor was a surplus in Westmoreland County due to its high unemployment rate of 12 percent. In order to avoid a scramble for these VWMOA job opportunities within the county, the Pennsylvania Bureau of Employment Security (BES) offered to handle the preliminary job screening. The BES conducted a recruiting drive for Volkswagen that drew more than 40,000 applicants. Long traffic lines and inconvenience for thousands of applicants was reduced to a minimum through scheduling worked out by the BES. Although BES did all the screening, VWMOA did the actual hiring based on recommendations from the BES.

Training prior to the VW facility opening was conducted in cooperation with community colleges. Training upon completion of the facility was done by a program known as the MKD program (Medium Knocked Down). Under this program, between 1,000 and 2,000 cars that were operational models that were unfinished on the inside and even lacked seats and instrument panels were shipped from Germany to be completed during training in the U. S. facility.

A major factor in production strategy is undoubtedly personnel strategy. In addition to the production workers hired through BES, VW used other channels in staffing its personnel needs. Training and upper line management was a combination of contracted employees from German operations and Americans hired with previous auto industry experience. For example, Richard Cummins, VW production manager, is a former plant manager of a Chrysler's assembly plant. James McLernon, president of VW U. S., is a former General Motors executive. Richard Donaldson, VW general superintendent, is also a former General Motors executive. This strategy of attracting competitors' personnel goes against past promotion policies; however, it offers obvious advantages towards experience dealing specifically with U. S. assembly plant operations. Along with the top executives came a following of middle management and industry connections that would be instrumental in U. S. operations. Since VW eventually plans to acquire all Rabbit parts in the U. S., past dealings with U. S. parts suppliers by VW executives in their former positions will undoubtedly prove invaluable. To this experience of personnel from U.S. firms, 125 German employees were brought over on contract to help set up and train production personnel and management. Almost all of the 125 have now returned to Germany.

Also, the state of Pennsylvania had estimated a 10,000 to 15,000 job spin-off in related industries and by consumer spending throughout the state.

FINANCING

In July 1976, when the New Stanton plant location was chosen, the start-up costs were estimated to be about a $250 million cash outlay.

By mid-1978, actual expenditures totalled $300 million. However, the cash outlay required was much smaller than the projected $250 million. This happened mostly because of the state of Pennsylvania's role in helping VWMOA finance the project. The largest item in this project was the factory building and the land it is on, with a price tag of $40 million, part of which will be used to complete the assembly plant. The financing for this item was arranged through the state of Pennsylvania. The Pennsylvania Industrial Development Authority (PIDA), which was created in the mid-1950s to create jobs for the state's residents by providing low-interest loans to employers and manufacturers, guaranteed the loan to the Greater Greensburg Industrial Development Corporation (GGIDC), which does basically the same job as the PIDA but at a county level. The GGIDC in turn purchased the facilities and the land from Chrysler Corporation. The GGIDC then granted Volkswagen a thirty-year lease on the property. The lease calls for Volkswagen to pay interest only at 1.75 percent over the first twenty years and interest at 8.50 percent plus equal installments of principal over the remainder of the term. The loan was secured by a first lien on the property and a guaranty by Volkswagenwerk AG of Germany.

To further assist Volkswagen in financing completion of the facility, the Public School Employees' Retirement Fund and the State Employees' Retirement Fund agreed to loan the automobile maker $6 million for fifteen years at an interest rate of 8.5 percent. These loans were secured by an irrevocable letter of credit issued by a leading American bank.

The state of Pennsylvania arranged financing for access roads and railways into the plant area. In order to pay for the road construction, the state floated a $20 million highway bond. The state also spent $10 million for the construction of railroad facilities. In order to recoup that cost, a per-car toll for the use of the plant's rail access was levied.

Additional help came in the form of manpower training funds. The state contributed $585,000 and the local county governments $3.7 million. These monies came from the Federal Comprehensive Employment and Training Act. The local counties have dedicated their Federal manpower training funds exclusively to the training of people for Volkswagen.

Though Volkswagen did not specifically receive any tax breaks, such breaks did accrue to Volkswagen by virtue of the fact that GGIDC, a tax-exempt non-profit organization, owns the plant and the land on which it sits. Therefore, Volkswagen declared itself willing to make payments in lieu of property taxes in order to contribute its share of school district costs and local taxes. This was done in order to encourage the local people to look forward to having this plant. For the first two years, Volkswagen will pay 5 percent of what would be normal tax; for the ensuing three years they will pay 50 percent of normal tax; thereafter the full amount will be paid. This naturally decreased Volkswagen's operating costs for the first five years.

Another $250 million was lent to Volkswagen by various Pennsylvania financial institutions. $110 million was expended for various equipment and factory machinery. Part component purchases amounted to approximately $60 million. The port in Wilmington, Delaware had a price tag of $3.5 million. Part of this $250 million is still open and planned to be used for expansion, improvements, marketing, and so on.

The total project and set-up cost for producing an American-made Rabbit came to slightly more than $300 million.

In mid-1978, Volkswagen officials stated that they expect to pay off their loans and purchase the mortgages within the next five years.

PERFORMANCE AND OUTLOOK

On April 10, 1978, VW Westmoreland was dedicated during ceremonies inside the plant, which included actual completion of the first regular series production Rabbit ever assembled in the United States. The first car came off the line less than one year after crews began paving the plant's floor and only one and a half years after the final master agreement was signed.

With production up to 400 Rabbits daily on the first shift (it reached an output of 450 cars per day during December 1978 as a result of overtime work several days each week), VW Westmoreland started to build cars on a second shift on January 15, 1979. By January 30, 1979, the fifty-thousandth Rabbit came off the assembly line on its way to a dealership in Falmouth, Massachusetts. The first Deluxe Model Rabbit built at VW Westmoreland left the plant on February 7, 1979, enroute to a dealership in Lemon Grove, California. Earlier production had been of basic and custom models.

VW Westmoreland has two departments that look after quality, a high priority at the plant. One is called Manufacturing Quality Assurance. It deals with incoming vendor parts to make certain that they meet specifications; it performs dimension checks on press parts and subassemblies to ensure that they are built to correct tolerances and it also performs lab tests to make certain that the material properties comply with specifications, guaranteeing uniform and strong construction.

Manufacturing Quality Assurance also conducts emission tests to ascertain that the cars coming off assembly line comply with federal and State of California clean air standards, and performs tests to ensure compliance with Federal Motor Vehicle Safety Standards.

The other department concerned with Rabbit reliability is Quality Control. One of its functions is on line inspection. Inspectors in virtually every assembly area constantly monitor parts and subassemblies before they move onto the next work station. Also within the scope of Quality Control is a specifications section, which ensures that each car is built precisely to the design engineers' plans.

By mid-spring of 1979, VW Westmoreland's second shift was building Rabbits at the rate of 400 per day. At that time, the plant was producing cars at the rate of 200,000 per year, the goal set in 1976. Employment had reached 4,000 persons.

The plant serves a major market area containing nearly 70 percent of the nation's population, who live within a 500-mile radius and account for two-thirds of the country's income and more than half of its retail trade.

REFERENCES

American Metal Market/Metal Work News, "Volkswagen Selects U.S. Parts Suppliers for Engines of Its American Rabbit," Oct. 17, 1977.

Automotive Industries, "Volkswagen Westmoreland on Schedule," July 15, 1977.

Business Week, "Why VW Must Build Autos in the U. S.," Feb. 16, 1976.

Dun's Review, "The Great Rabbit Hunt," Sept. 1976.

Economic World, "Volkswagen's Rabbit Becomes an American Car," March 1978.

Governor's Press Office, Harrisburg-Pennsylvania, "Shapp Signs Final Master Agreement with Volkswagen Manufacturing Corporation of America," Sept. 15, 1976.

Time, "Beyond the Beetle," Feb. 2, 1976.

Time, "Back into Top Gear," March 15, 1976.

U. S. News and World Report, "Volkswagen Moves into Pennsylvania: Start of a Wholesale Migration?" Oct. 31, 1977.

PART IV

Strategic Management: Implementation and Recycling

Strategy making is the art of matching, calculating, and selecting; implementation is the process of unleashing organized, directional, and sustaining actions; and recycling is the process of adjusting and reformulating. A brilliantly conceived strategy would be an abstract idea if it inspired no action. A fully developed strategy could be rendered ineffective if it lacked capacity of adjusting and recycling.

In chapters 13 and 14, we will focus on implementation, dwelling upon strategy–structure–process, and tactical planning and execution, respectively. In chapter 15, we will discuss control and strategic adjustment and recycling. The control process of measuring overall performance and sensing changes, the mechanism of adaptation, and the process of adjusting and recycling ongoing strategy will be emphasized. These activities press the organization unswervingly toward the target in spite of anticipated or unexpected changes and innovations.

CHAPTER THIRTEEN

Strategy, Structure, Process and Human Resource Development

Implementation concerns the operational aspect of strategy management and initiates administrative actions of strategic and tactical types. Implementation is viewed by various authors as a management activity involving organization and execution,[1] a complex problem-solving process of group interaction,[2] and the combination of subactivities of organizational structure design and organizational process involving motivation and control.[3] In the context of this book, we will introduce a two-dimension theory of implementation: the horizontal dimension of the strategy–structure–process relationship; and the vertical dimension of strategies–tactics–action thrusts. The former provides the required congruence between internal response to environmental changes; the latter produces the desired vitality for total implementation. Human resource development involving human requirements and organization development, however, enhances the effectiveness of implementation.

The implementation of a company's strategy requires a keen appreciation of the relationship between strategy, structure, and process. We will study strategy as the driving force in effecting changes in a company's organizational structure and process. In studying the command structure and process, we propose to reaffirm the roles of the board of directors, the chief executive officers, and their staff. In particular, we consider human resource development as a constant preoccupation of top management. By studying short- and long-term management requirements, planning needed structural changes, and practicing organization renewal and development, management can correlate strategic choice to structural changes. However, implementation will not be complete without the dynamic and ceaseless tactical actions that ultimately ensure the success of strategy.

STRATEGY–STRUCTURE–PROCESS

The Relationship

Alfred D. Chandler, Jr., in his pioneering study of American industry's historical expansion,[4] establishes the notion that organizational structure is intimately related to a firm's strategy for expansion. The strategy of expansion in response to increase in volume, geographical expansion, and diversification required major modifications in structure. Chandler states: "A new strategy required a new, at least a refashioned, structure if the enlarged enterprise was to be operated efficiently. . . . Unless new structures are developed to meet new administrative needs which result from an expansion of a firm's activities into new areas, functions, or product lines, the technological, financial, and personnel economies of growth and size cannot be realized."[5] He traces the expansion of American business over a period of several decades, remarking in particular chapters on the accumulation of resources, the use of resources, the resultant continued growth, and finally, the rationalization of expanding resources. Those executives administering American industrial enterprises developed and adjusted strategies for business development and for mobilizing resources to coincide with the fluctuating market demand. The early formation of specialized departments, such as marketing, purchasing, and distribution, gave way to a centralized, functionally departmentalized administrative structure, and finally led to the adoption of multidivisionalized structures.

Two recent studies must be cited.[6] Both studies are expanded from Chandler's original work and summarized recent studies and suggested significant new findings. In their studies of three industries, Miles and Snow redefined the interplay. First, through strategic choice management perceives and enacts its environment; second, strategy shapes structure and process. Third, structure and process constrain strategy in that "an organization is seldom able to veer away substantially from its current course without major structure-process alterations."[7]

In the other study, Galbraith and Nathanson expanded the strategy–structure–process relationship to include human development, matters concerning personnel selection, training, and development. They delved further into the relationship by examining organizational form variations (such as decentralization), integration mechanisms (such as information sharing and coordination), and systems operations (such as resource allocation and rewarding), among others. Significantly, both studies found that a simple one-to-one relationship, such as structure follows strategy, is not totally correct. There are times when strategy follows structure. The real issue is that "the firm should match structure to its strategy, match all the components of the organization with another and match the strategy with the environment."[8]

Structural Progression

The strategy–structure–process relationship is dynamic by nature. Whenever the equilibrium is disturbed, changes begin to take place. One of the basic factors effecting changes is structural progression. Structural progression follows a normal corporate development model. Of the studies made on corporate development models, we choose to cite the three-stage development model.[9] The three stages of development include: (1) the small and simple organization of one unit or dominated by one person; (2) the transitional stage of functional departmentalization; and (3) the large and complex multiproduct, multidivision structure, which contains a general office to plan, coordinate, and allocate resources, and a number of operating divisions to carry on the actual operations of the ongoing business.

First, through each stage of development, structural changes are effected to reflect a distinct choice of strategy. Second, the management capacity and style is different, implying that the skill required to manage large organizations must grow with size, and that the style of management and character of the firm become unique during each stage of development. Third, there is the serious problem of transition, the process of recognizing symptoms of malfunction, designing structural changes, and executing changes.[10]

A company structured to implement strategies must consider the following propositions:

1. Organizational structure evolves around a company's strategy. Structure is designed to implement strategy. Structure provides the basic tool for accomplishing the organization's perceived purpose, objectives, and tasks to meet present needs and future designs.
2. Strategy–structure–process influence one another. The adaptive process facilitates business (choice of product/market domain), technology (choice of technologies for production and distribution), and administrative (system and administrative processes) changes.
3. Structural progression reflects corporate development needs for human resource development.
4. Organizational structure is dynamic and versatile. It is designed for gradual achievement of organizational readiness for future action and for smooth adaptation between stages of corporate development.
5. Congruence in strategy–structure–process is a goal in organization and management. Its attainment demands advanced planning and gradual adaptation.

Organizing for Strategic Actions

The design of organizational structure begins with a critical inquiry into the purpose, objectives, and tasks of the organization. An organization thrives when its purpose is embodied in its design; it fails when its structure is in conflict with its purpose. Thus, a governmental organization whose purpose is to administer public affairs to serve society for the public good, when structured solely on the basis of profit seeking and self-interest, is bound to fail. In this case, the central purpose of a public organization is misplaced, resources are misdirected and misused. On the other hand, a business firm is intended for economic performance; it is profit motivated and should be socially responsible. Its purpose as expressed in its self-conceived economic performance criteria and its considered view of social responsibility fundamentally shapes its strategy, thus its structure. In the words of Peter F. Drucker, "performance is the objective; economics is a restraint."[11]

Determining business objectives is the second step in structural design. Business objectives are the company's specific performance targets projected into the future. They are related to structural design in two ways: (1) business objectives reflect the firm's perception of its environment within which the company operates, and highlights the organizational capacity that a firm must develop; and (2) business objectives portray the organizational progression, thus the projected capacities that the company must develop.

In environmental analysis, management studies opportunities and threats. Emerging from the analysis are three critical factors of structural importance: (1) level of management capacity (for example, when confronting strong competition and frequent changes, an effective command/control mechanism is required); (2) the identification of crucial functions (when technology is the key to success, R&D function needs closest attention); and (3) the nature of risk management (when risk is high, financial management warrants strong emphasis). Likewise, the position audit reveals important information. For example, the identification of shortage of special skills, functional deficiencies, and the lack of behavioral concern can trigger organization modifications. Past and present performance evaluation that studies a company's basic weaknesses in management and resources, can result in large-scale changes in organization. Last, objective setting that considers the matching of external opportunities and threats with internal capacity establishes performance goals from which strategy is developed.

Task Definition

Task definition is a step to convert business objectives into concrete tasks. Strategically, business objectives must be broken down into functional targets and tasks. A 10 percent annual sales growth may mean the increase of sales at certain dollar value in product, territorial, and/or customer areas. It can dictate production increases within certain select units or the systematic development of new products by marketing, production, and engineering departments. The task breakdown, therefore, reflects the company's distinctive purpose and unique strategy.[12] Each vital function and its structure is subjected to a design study in light of strengths and weaknesses and future task specifications. In attacking deficiencies, organizational adjustment of responsibilities, realignment of units, personnel replacement, and the use of such methods as behavioral modification and organization development will be considered.[13] Thus, task breakdown is a meaningful criterion in determining how a function or department should be organized. In turn, the strategy–structure–process dictum progressively positions a firm for strategic action.

Organizing for Strategic Alternatives

A company revises its strategy in response to changing situations. A choice of strategy—growth, stability, or survival—calls for structural changes. In designing structural changes, one gives serious thought to three design considerations: centralization versus decentralization, structural variations, and planning and execution.

CENTRALIZATION VERSUS DECENTRALIZATION The centralization versus decentralization issue is a serious decision. As discussed in chapter 8, the decentralized structure is a form conducive to growth; a centralized form is preferred during stability and survival, other things being equal. In planning for decentralization during growth, advanced planning is imperative. The conversion should follow an evolutionary process. First, company growth is progressive, moving from one threshold of growth to the next. The process provides management with time to slowly evolve its centralized, functional form into a decentralized structure. Second, a decentralized organization calls for an increase in numbers of operating division general managers and/or group presidents. Time is needed to develop and recruit talented managers and to accommodate the new managers into an enlarged management team. Third, an enlarged organization calls for expanded capability of planning and control that is geometrically more difficult than the arithmetic increase in size. Time provides the test period for the newly created command/control structure and system. Indeed, time also provides a learning period for familiarizing management as well as operating personnel to the newly expanded business activity. Too often, acquisition-minded companies find themselves incapable of managing acquired operations, let alone of understanding the peculiarities and intricacies of the latter. During business contraction, when a centralized form is deemed desirable, the reversion from a decentralized form to a centralized structure follows the same steps, except that it is done for organizational contraction. Special caution should be given to planning and execution, focusing on minimizing adverse impact upon individuals and the organization.

STRUCTURAL VARIATIONS Under the three situations of growth, profit instability, and survival, organizational structure undergoes changes. The basic organizational form can be modified or completely revised each time. Weighing advantages and disadvantages of each of these forms aids in management decisions on design changes. Let us briefly review the various forms of organization. Structural variations take three basic forms: function; territory; and product or customer.[14] The functional structure, which divides a company's work by line function, is most prevalent in manufacturing organizations. A company that is geographically divided is likely to adopt a structure based on regional and district divisions. Banking and retail business generally adopt this type of organization. The selection of a product line or customer structure is common in large corporations in which product line or industrial identity gives the advantages of product/market concentration and profit accountability. General Motors divisions are grouped by product line—the Cadillac division, the Buick division, and so forth. For different reasons, GE's sector management is organized by industrial identity of consumer products and services, power systems, technical systems and materials, industrial products and components, and international operations.

Another widely used organization form is the matrix management, commonly referred to as project management.[15] A matrix structure has the unique feature of concentrated management; management resources are placed together under one organization, which answers to the customer for its performance responsibility. It is a hybrid form; function and product are of equal importance.[16] Government agencies such as the Departments of Defense and of Transportation have used project management for large contractual programs. Industries, such as aerospace, oil refining, and engineering construction, that manage large contracts also use matrix management. Generally, a matrix organization may be dictated by the customer offering a large contract.

A changing condition can force conversion of matrix organization to functional structure. The conversion of brand management into functional structure among food industries is a case in point.[17] Modification of structural variations can be introduced for improving efficiency, reducing costs, and responding to environmental changes. Its advanced planning is equally important.

PLANNING AND EXECUTION Planning and execution is the third issue to contend with when making structural changes under different situations. Because strategy deals with long-term changes and organizational responses, strategy is continuously evolving, and the organization moves gradually toward a series of

readiness. Structural changes are therefore made through advanced planning and progressive execution. Throughout the implementation, new or modified structural adjustments continue to reflect the progression. During the various stages of growth, for example, new and modified structures are designed and implemented. Moving towards a decentralized form, as noted before, requires advanced studies of structural variations, executive selection and development, and operating processes adjustments. When a warning signals pending changes in strategic situations—for example, the approach of the final phase of a growth period or the beginning of the instability phase—structural modification plans are formulated. During the transition period, centralized management is gradually installed: central planning and policy making is tightened, control and direction is redefined. As a company moves through the stability period, a series of organization plans are developed, either preparing the company for quick recovery or large-scale restructuring if survival is threatened.

EXECUTING CHANGES In executing organizational changes, special attention must be paid to the impact upon managerial behavior, coordination process, and timing of execution. Organizationally, the structure is designed to influence and control organizational behavior. By assigning responsibility and by establishing the framework for managerial action in decision making and interaction, structure controls managerial behavior.[18] In other words, when organizational changes are effected, a modified set of job specifications to reflect the revised authority, responsibility, and newly established relationship is mandatory.

By instituting new management systems to guide administrative action and coordination, management can create a competitive and aggressive attitude toward the external world and a cooperative and responsible attitude toward internal operations. A modified strategic planning system, a new product development system, or an overall performance control system to reflect changing behavior is each an efficient means to ensure quick transition to the newly structured organization. Finally, in effecting smooth conversion, timing is essential. A well-managed company will not alter its structure impulsively, nor will it change its basic system imprudently, lest poorly planned actions disturb organizational stability and cripple its long-term vitality. The central question remains that of how to institute change.[19] There have been two approaches: the evolutionary and revolutionary approaches. The evolutionary approach follows a prescribed practice of diagnosis, problem definition and evaluation, experimentation, execution, and postevaluation.[20] The other method is the execution of large-scale, company-wide structural changes. Whereas the former applies to all situations wherever time is sufficient to accomplish total planning, the latter operates in the initial phase of implementing stability and survival strategies. In both cases, forceful execution is necessary.

THE COMMAND STRUCTURE AND PROCESS

The overall management of company strategy falls in three areas: policy, strategy, and tactics of operational and technical nature. Formulation of overall company business policies rests in the hands of the board of directors and the CEO. Operating policies are the responsibility of chief executives and their respective area policy makers and the functional managers. Company strategy making, on the other hand, is the chief responsibility of the CEO, although the work is shared with group presidents, division general managers, and their staff. As a group, they manage the strategy.

These three areas of operations are referred to as the command structure; and its design and operational integration affect the overall management. In the design of an effective command structure, equal attention must be given to the three levels of command: the board, the general management, and their staff. As discussed in chapter 3, the board, in discharging its basic policy responsibilities, plays an important role in policy deliberation and approves corporate strategic plans. During implementation, the board leaves the implementation to the CEO. It exercises its power only to the extent of monitoring the progress of corporate strategies and initiating reformulation. However, the chairman of the board, with the assistance of the CEO, makes certain that board members remain vigorous, performing members of the overall command.

The Chief Executive Officer and Area Policy Makers

In his book, *The Concept of Corporate Strategy,* Kenneth R. Andrews emphasizes the function of general management in strategy making, and speaks of three qualities of a general manager.[21] First, the ideal general manager is viewed as the architect of strategy. To fulfill this role, he/she needs creativity, self-awareness, and sensitivity to society's expectations. Second, the general manager is an implementer of strategy. In that role, he/she supplies organizational leadership, integrates the conflicting interests that necessarily arise, promotes and defends strategy, and judges the results.[22] Third, the general manager is a personal leader. In providing that leadership, he/she is uniquely distinguished from all others. He/she achieves a leadership style, a pattern of personal behavior, and acquires a set of values that influences his/her company's character and social responsibility. Most definitely, the chief executive holds the key in strategic management. His/her decisions and determination increase chances of full implementation.

In areas of operating policies, chief executives at all operating levels insist that policy responsibilities in critical areas, such as marketing, finance, R&D, and production, are clearly established and that area policies are expressly stated in writing. Established operating policies eliminate the guesswork for decision makers. They should be selective to allow concentration on areas of importance and broad enough to provide room for discretion. Area policy makers (generally staff vice presidents), thus, formulate operating policies, control them, and coordinate actions in handling policy disputes and operating conflict; and they can be counted on to raise questions about policy and strategy. The relationship of policy and strategy is intimate. For that purpose alone, area policy makers are encouraged to advise and review functional strategies and coordinate their implementation. At the departmental level, operating policies are less formal and are administrative by nature. Functional managers and supervisors are responsible for setting specific guidelines, particularly in marketing and finance, where external contacts are frequent and misrepresentation can be damaging.

The Strategic Planning Staff and the Committee on Strategy

In performing that triple role, a chief executive draws support from the management team—the planning staff and the committee on strategy. The strategic planning staff serves a pivotal role. In implementation, the planning staff must be fully involved with ongoing strategies and maintains itself as a functional member in the command structure. It coordinates, monitors, and advises on recycling when reformulation of strategy is in order. It administers the committee work, raises strategic issues, and often takes on special assignments relating to strategic matters.

The committee on strategy reviews ongoing strategic actions, identifies and coordinates broad policies, studies strategic issues, and initiates adjustment and recycling. Although the committee is not a decision-making body, it is a mechanism for joint effort, team building, and group action.

The Command Process

In the final analysis, however, the efficacy of strategic management rests in the hands of the CEO. His/her dedication and management style accounts for much of the success of the company strategy. In recent years, there have been two approaches to the process of top management: the single CEO, and the team CEO.[23] In the first, more traditional method, the CEO's decision-making power is not shared. He/she delegates pieces of his/her function but never the integration of those pieces. The second, new method of the team approach in the chief executive office designates two or more executives—seldom more than four—to share the power with the CEO. Each executive acts as the CEO in a specific area of authority in which his/her decision is final, and integration is complete. Thus, in a two-person executive office, the CEO may be responsible for policy, strategy, and communication with the stockholders, the financial community, and the rest of the outside world. The other member of the office may be given the operating responsibility to ensure the success of the ongoing current business of the company. The advantage of the second approach is that it encourages delegated responsibility, greater efficiency, and speed. Naturally, there are serious limitations. The complex process of decision making involving two or more individuals can beget conflicts and indecision. The selection of responsible, talented, compatible people may be a Herculean task. Yet, because this method produces concentrated management essential to strategic implementation, it is an approach worth considering.

Strategic management must have a clearly defined process of command. First, activities of strategic planning, formulation, and implementation must not be disjointed. The command structure operates equally well throughout the three activities. Second, the command process is complemented by a control process, a responsive mechanism, and a self-adjusting process of recycling. Finally, the command flows in a vertically structured setting where its directives are converted into tactical actions throughout all levels of supervision.

HUMAN RESOURCE DEVELOPMENT

Developing human resources means planning for long-range personnel requirements, developing policies and systems to harness human potentials, and adapting management technology to consistently drive for organizational effectiveness. Long-range personnel development anticipates future managerial and critical personnel requirements and development. It is a natural extension of organization planning, through which critical functions are identified, positions and skills are categorized, and qualifications and brief job descriptions are developed. The tabulation and analysis of these requirements helps to indicate the critical needs to support the evolving future organizations. A growth company moving toward a divisionalized organization, for example, requires an increasing number of general managers, line managers of specialized skills, and staffs of various types. Similarly, the technically oriented company needs continual recruitment of advanced technical personnel. The identification, selection, and development within the organization and recruitment from without is a long and costly operation.[24]

The planning function, however, can be shared by the chief executive officers and the personnel department managers, who assume the primary responsibility for specifying requirements and aggressively pursuing personnel recruitment and development. The projection and development of long-range personnel requirements is often ambiguous, but it is extremely important to an organization's future. It is critical when considering the replacement of a CEO during restructuring, the need for competent general managers during growth, and the search for a top-notch chief financial officer during profit instability.

Reward System and Participative Decision Making

Human resources planning is the embodiment of human relations. For our discussion on strategic management, let us center our attention to two policy issues: the reward system and participative decision making.[25] The design of a reward system is important for two reasons: (1) a properly designed reward system accurately measures, evaluates, and rewards strategic performance of top executives; and (2) in its design, the criteria and methods of reward reflect the need of a strategic choice.[26] For example, a desired system rewards the executive for both long- and short-term performance. Both criteria and methods of reward vary. They can be determined in accordance with the strategic situation under consideration and the trade-off studies of the various methods involved.

The achievement of the company's objectives depends on the total participation of the organization, its managers and employees. In particular, strategic implementation requires the participation of all managers and employees. Participative decision making is necessary for two reasons. In the first place, decision making of strategic importance demands information exchange, joint deliberation, and the exploration of options. In the second place, participation improves decision making and control and, in turn, improves subordinates' satisfaction and morale.[27] However, in actual practice participation becomes complicated, too dependent upon the relationship of the participating individuals and the different perceptions. Studies have shown that for resource allocation, for example, the degree of participation differs between multidivisional firms and integrated, nondivisional firms. Managerial styles also affect participation. Staff studies can be prejudiced when information and analysis are tailored to the interest of top management.[28] Suffice it to say, participative decision making needs a favorable environment. Its creation requires careful development and management commitment.

Organization Development

The quest for improving management capability is a continuous and all-inclusive process. Business firms in general maintain good relationships with universities and research organizations, support university education programs, and operate in-house executive development programs. In addition, management technology literature continues to appear. Prominent writers, such as Herbert A.

Simon, Peter F. Drucker, and others, have made substantial contributions to the advancement of the management technology. New management hypotheses and methodologies have appeared and have been widely adopted. We focus here on organization development as a technique aimed at improving organizational effectiveness.

WHAT IS ORGANIZATION DEVELOPMENT? Developed initially from the pioneering work of Kurt Lewin and the varying techniques and skills in human resource development, organization development (OD) has made tremendous growth within the last twenty years. Of the many definitions given, the one prescribed by Wendell French is most concise. He defines *organization development* as "a long-range effort to improve the organization's problem-solving capabilities and its ability to cope with changes in its external environment, with the help of external or internal behavioral-scientist consultants, or change agents."[29] The primary objective of OD is the development of new ways of coping and dealing with organization revitalization problems. The emphasis is on improving the working relationships among the administrative, technical, and human systems as well as the way in which the total organization can relate to the external environment.[30]

Although a variety of OD approaches are currently being utilized, the majority of the techniques follow the action-research format of: (1) data gathering; (2) data feedback to relevant parties; (3) discussion and joint diagnosis; and (4) action planning and follow-up.[31] In effecting change, OD approaches rely principally on organizational influence and group processes. OD attempts to develop long-term organizational effectiveness through improvement in communication, openness, trust, risk taking, interpersonal relationships, teamwork, and intergroup collaboration.

APPLICATIONS OF OD TO POLICY AND STRATEGY Space limitations prevent us from discussing the various OD techniques that have actual or potential application to policy and strategy formulation and implementation. To give the reader an idea of the possibilities, however, we will very briefly describe the approaches and applications of survey feedback, the confrontation meeting, team building, intergroup relations development, managerial grid, and management by objectives (MBO).

Survey Feedback Survey feedback starts with gathering data about organizational procedures, the work situation, interpersonal relations, or any aspect of the organization that is of concern to the members, through the use of questionnaires or interviews. The data thus gathered is summarized, tabulated, and communicated back to the respondents. These then become the basis for discussing problems; exchanging ideas, interpretations, and perceptions; and pinpointing issues. Finally, action plans are formulated to deal with problems and issues of concern.

This technique should prove useful for the management team to highlight the members' concern about goals, policies, strategies, and plans. Paine and Naumes give an extensive description of the steps to be taken for applying this technique.[32]

The Confrontation Meeting The confrontation meeting developed by Beckhard[33] is a variation of the survey-feedback technique. The relevant data is gathered right at the meeting of the concerned parties rather than through questionnaires distributed prior to the meeting. The procedures essentially consist of the announcement of the goal of the meeting, meeting of small groups, summarization of data gathered in each group, presentation and sharing of data by group representatives, drawing up action plans, and follow-up. This technique should serve as a powerful tool for quickly assessing the organizational capability, gauging reaction to changes, and enhancing commitment to new conditions, such as after introduction of a newly structured organization, management system, or mergers.

Team Building The collective competence and knowledge of a management or any work group would be wasted if the members did not function well together. Hence, there is a need to examine and improve the working relationships among group members in order to create an atmosphere in which members can freely make their contribution to the task at hand. Team building, which consists of a group meeting for setting goals and priorities, examining the way the group works, and reviewing the working relationships among members, is designed to accomplish this.[34] This technique is useful for improving the effectiveness of committees, task groups, and project teams.

Intergroup Relations Development Central to the concern of the CEO is the effective working relationship among diverse groups, committees, departments, and divisions. Whenever groups interface, conflict and misunderstanding can arise. Typical problems include conflict and disagreement between corporate and divisional offices, line and staff personnel, union and management, and among various functional departments. Managing group conflict techniques are fully described by Blake and Mouton.[35]

Managerial Grid Also developed by Blake and Mouton is the managerial grid method.[36] A six-phase approach is utilized, which includes: orientation seminar; work-team development; intergroup development; production of organizational blueprint; implementation of organizational blueprint; and stabilization. This approach is designed to improve organizational effectiveness, whether dealing with strategic or lesser problems.

Management by Objectives Although scholars and practitioners are not fully in agreement with whether management by objectives belongs to the field of OD, MBO is widely used. In essence, it is an approach to organizational planning and control with the added objective of harmonizing personal, departmental, and organizational goals by increasing communication and shared perception, joint goal setting and action planning.[37] MBO is useful for strategic implementation, tactical execution, and appraisal of results.

SUMMARY

A fully developed strategy needs organizational support to make it effective. The design of a sound organizational structure that correctly reflects the corporate choice of strategies is at the heart of strategic management. A sound structure cannot be fully operational without the complement of supporting systems and processes. The command structure, however, is the central organ to formulate policies and strategies, and to manage their implementation. A viable command structure ensures the full participation of the board, the chief executives, the planning staff, and the committee. As an organizational entity, they manage the total process of strategy making. Furthermore, strategy management demands advanced planning and action toward gradually advancing the company's management capacity in areas of human development and management technologies. In this regard, we emphasize the application of organization development. We view organization development as offering a myriad of techniques to facilitate revitalization and strategy making.

NOTES

1. William H. Newman and James P. Logan, *Strategy, Policy and Central Management* (Cincinnati, Ohio: South Western Publishing, 1971), pp. 9–11.
2. Frank T. Paine and William Naumes, *Organization Strategy and Policy,* 2nd ed. (Philadelphia, Pa.: Saunders, 1978), pp. 238–41.
3. C. Roland Christensen, Kenneth R. Andrews, and Joseph L. Bower, *Business Policy: Text and Cases* (Homewood, Ill.: Irwin, 1978), p. 674.
4. *Strategy and Structure: A Chapter in the History of Industrial Enterprises* (Cambridge, Mass.: MIT Press, 1962).
5. Ibid., pp. 15–16.
6. Raymond E. Miles and Charles C. Snow, *Organizational Strategy, Structure, and Process* (New York: McGraw-Hill, 1978); and Jay R. Galbraith and Daniel A. Nathanson, *Strategy Implementation: The Role of Structure and Process* (St. Paul, Minnesota: West Publishing, 1978). For an excellent discussion, see Christensen, Andrews, and Bower, *Business Policy,* pp. 593–602, 661–77.
7. Miles and Snow, *Organizational Strategy, Structure, and Process,* p. 8.
8. Galbraith and Nathanson, *Strategy Implementation,* pp. 142–43.
9. For examples, Bruce R. Scott, "Stages of Corporate Development" (working paper, Harvard Business School, 1970); Leonard Wrigley, "Divisional Autonomy and Diversification" (Ph.D. dissertation, Harvard Business School, 1970); and Richard P. Remmelt, *Strategy, Structure, and Economic Performance* (Cambridge, Mass.: Graduate School of Business Administration, Harvard University, 1974).
10. Hugo E. R. Uyterhoeven, Robert W. Ackerman, and John W. Rosenblum, *Strategy and Organization: Text and Cases in General Management* (Homewood, Ill.: Irwin, 1973), extensively discuss the management of transition, pp. 86–92.
11. *Management: Tasks, Responsibilities, Practices* (New York: Harper and Row, 1974), pp. 40–41.
12. Ibid., pp. 40–42. Also, Christensen, Andrews, and Bower suggest four criteria in implementation: strategy and organizational structure, subdivision on task responsibility, coordination of divided responsibility, and effective design of information system, in *Business Policy,* pp. 677–82.
13. For an extensive discussion on group interaction including the use of problem-solving conference; for example, see Paine and Naumes, *Organization Strategy and Policy,* pp. 238–64.
14. For example, see Harold Koontz and Cyril O'Donnell, *Management* (New York: McGraw-Hill, 1976), chap. 14.
15. For example, see Charles C. Martin, *Project Management: How to Make It Work* (New York: AMACOM, 1976).
16. For this broad view, see Galbraith and Nathanson, *Strategy Implementation,* pp. 71–74.

17. *Business Week,* June 1973, pp. 58–66. For a discussion, see Joseph A. Morein, ''Shift from Brand to Product Line Marketing,'' *Harvard Business Review,* September–October 1975, pp. 57–64.
18. Charles R. Ferguson suggested structure as a means of defining and controlling organizational behavior in his proposed concept of auditing management revolving on strategy. *Measuring Corporate Strategy* (Homewood, Ill.: Dow Jones-Irwin, 1974), pp. 18–43.
19. For example, see Edwin B. Flippo and Gary M. Munsinger, *Management* (Boston: Allyn and Bacon, 1975), chap. 18, esp. pp. 474–87. Also, for a fine empirical study, see Larry E. Greiner, ''Pattern of Organization Change,'' *Harvard Business Review,* May-June 1967, pp. 19–32.
20. Greiner prescribed a six-step process: pressure of top management, intervention at the top, diagnosis of problem areas, invention of new solution, experimentation of new solution, and reinforcement for positive results. Ibid.
21. Homewood, Ill.: Dow Jones-Irwin, 1974, pp. 226–38.
22. Uyterhoeven provides an expansive treatment on the general manager's role as organization builder. He focuses on the management of corporate development toward diversification. Of special interest are the two chapters on general management at the division and corporate levels. Uyterhoeven, Ackerman, and Rosenblum, *Strategy and Organization,* pp. 71–134.
23. For a discussion of a company's experience (TRW Inc.), see J. David Wright, ''The Team Concept for the Chief Executive Office,'' in *The Chief Executive's Handbook,* ed. John D. Glover and Gerald A. Simon (Homewood, Ill.: Dow Jones-Irwin, 1976), pp. 134–44.
24. For an industry practice, see Walter Wickstrom, *Manpower Planning: Evolving Systems* (New York: Conference Board, 1971). Techniques are explained in Angela Bowey, *A Guide to Manpower Planning* (London: Macmillan, 1974).
25. Personnel policies embrace a number of broad topics. They may include policies of promotion, compensation, reward, separation, and retirement affecting strategic decision makers.
26. Galbraith and Nathanson summarized a number of studies and suggest a linkage between compensation policy and strategy. *Strategy Implementation,* pp. 81–85.
27. Studies reported by R. E. Miller in ''Human Relations and Human Resources,'' *Harvard Business Review,* July–August 1965. Also, for increasing trends in management requirement planning, see James W. Walker, ''Human Resources Planning: Managerial Concerns and Practices,'' *Harvard Business Review,* May–June 1976, pp. 55–59.
28. Studies summarized by Galbraith and Nathanson in *Strategy Implementation,* pp. 77–80.
29. ''Organization Development Objectives, Assumptions and Strategies,'' *California Management Review,* Winter 1969, pp. 23–34.
30. Newton Margulies and Anthony Raia, *Organizational Development: Value, Process, and Technology* (New York: McGraw-Hill, 1972), p. 5.
31. Ibid.
32. Paine and Naumes, *Organizational Strategy and Policy,* pp. 156–92.
33. Richard Beckhard, ''The Confrontation Meeting,'' *Harvard Business Review,* March–April 1967, pp. 149–55.
34. See Edgar F. Huse, *Organization Development and Change* (St. Paul, Minnesota: West Publishing, 1975) pp. 230–38.

35. R. R. Blake, H. A. Shepard, and J. S. Mouton, *Managing Intergroup Conflict in Industry* (Foundation for Research in Human Behavior, 1964).
36. Robert R. Blake and Jane S. Mouton, ''An Overview of the Grid,'' *Training and Development Journal,* May 1975, pp. 29–37.
37. Huse, *Organization Development,* pp. 183–94.

CHAPTER FOURTEEN

Tactical Planning and Execution

Tactical planning and execution is an important linkage in the implementation of strategy. In the context of our discussion, tactics link strategy and action together to form the vertical dimension of implementation. In chapter 1, we defined *tactics* as an organized but ceaseless stream of specific actions designed to execute strategic decisions. Tactics, as distinguished from strategy, are formulated at the supervisory level by individuals responsible for selecting the appropriate action to solve operating problems. Tactics are operational, more people and force oriented than strategy, and are directed at short-term actions. Strategy and tactics must be synchronized. Neither can be independently effective without the other. Tactics are fluid, highly dynamic, but are equally innovative in approach.

In this chapter, we focus on tactical planning and execution. Three topics will be discussed: the line organization's role in the management of functional strategies; management of tactical operations; and tactical actions concerning the development of action plans and tactical control.

THE MANAGEMENT OF FUNCTIONAL STRATEGIES

Line Management and Implementation

Line organization refers to functional departments whose operations have direct responsibility for accomplishing the primary objectives of the enterprise. In a manufacturing company, departments such as marketing, production, engineering, and finance can be regarded as line organizations.[1] They play a substantial part in the formulation and execution of company strategy. In formulating company strategy, they participate in the deliberation of division or group objectives, strategies, and resource allocation. In execution, they formulate functional strategies in their respective areas and direct tactical execution. Without functional strategies, tactical planning is impossible, and tactical actions are directionless. Thus, total participation of line managers in formulating company strategies, and involving supervisory personnel in their development, is basic to tactical planning.

Managing Functional Strategies

Serving as the link between company strategy and tactical actions, functional strategies substantiate the former and guide the latter. It is in this context that we consider managing functional strategies as part of tactics. In developing functional strategies, each functional head takes the lead. He/she provides input to the general manager and seeks advice from department personnel as to the realism of objectives and the practicality of courses of action affecting the department. In particular, he/she encourages them to raise strategic issues, those critical matters affecting the making and implementing of strategies, and to participate in the development of component strategies to guide tactical actions. In execution, each functional head organizes and motivates his/her people in the direction dictated by the strategy. He/she maintains a balanced focus upon departmental goals. Gains in one area may incur losses in other areas, leading to imbalance and conflicts within the department. For example, overemphasis on immediate gains can cause long-term losses. Thus, the logical desire to increase sales volume can result in the imbalance of large sales in existing accounts with little improvement in new account sales because it takes more time and effort to develop new account sales.

Additionally, the functional head coaches his/her people in tactical planning, and insists on the development and use of action plans to direct and control critical actions. The degree of subordinates' participation in tactical planning is one of judgment of the manager and depends on the nature of the activity. Last, the functional head coordinates departmental actions with those of other functional managers, making sure that company-wide programs are given full support and that his/her activities cause no undue effects on other employees. A salesperson, for example, can influence product design or improve production efficiency when he/she feeds back product information to an engineering department, or if he/she increases large-order sales to maintain longer production runs. When actions at functional levels are guided by well-coordinated functional strategy and tactical plans, actions are coordinated and the intended impact of company action upon the outside world is assured.

Short- and Long-Range Programming

Line organizations manage departmental activities and ensure their coordination with other functional departments in achieving company-established objectives. Of special importance to tactical planning is the management of program and project activities. Programs and projects cover major, critical activities that require highly concentrated management. The commercialization of a new product by the marketing department, the construction of a new plant affecting production, or a cash-rebuilding activity managed by the finance department can be designated as programs. Programs can involve activities limited to a single department or dispersed among several departments. They can be short-range programs or long-range programs with a life span beyond two years.

Programming, the art of tactical planning, must: (1) clearly define all tasks and break down subtasks to the lowest operating level; (2) sequentially lay out activities and identify performing units at each level of operations; and (3) rigidly specify the time of accomplishment for each activity.[2] It is usually accomplished under stringent restrictions on performance specifications (tasks), completion schedule (time), and budgetary limitations (costs). Within these restrictions, the program manager plans, directs, and controls the program. During the planning stage, he/she subdivides the task, formulates the budgets, identifies any incompatibility among program activities, and constructs the timetable. In programming, he/she follows a six-step process:[3]

1. Divides the total operations necessary to achieve objectives into parts (tasks), thus concentrating attention on one task at a time. Subdivision of tasks may be continued for several levels down the organization to interrelate actions and to stipulate accountabilities.
2. Notes the necessary sequence and the relationship between each of these tasks. Unless the relationships are recognized and watched closely, individual tasks may cause program inefficiency and delay.
3. Decides who is to be responsible for doing each task. This includes performing units, responsible personnel, and individuals specially assigned to the program.
4. Decides how each task will be done and the resources that will be needed. Program resources include people, materials and supplies, facilities, and budgets.
5. Estimates the time required for each task, indicating the date or the hour when the task can begin and the time required to complete the operation, once it is started.
6. Assigns definite dates (hours) when each task is to take place. A fixed date at the end generally governs the schedule, although it is wise to make allowances for schedule slippage. Further, schedule incompatibilities must be accommodated and bottlenecks eliminated.

During execution, the program manager directs the operation through policies, directives, and personal leadership that motivates and inspires people into action. Because tactical actions are subject to counteractions from various sources, managerial choice of approaches and assessing of impact about certain actions is necessary. However, because tactical actions also involve ceaseless administrative and human action, group action to secure coordinated effort is equally important. Thus, effective program management demands a well-defined management process to ensure the free and timely flow of performance, schedule, budgetary, and administrative information for direction and control.

Managing Long-Range Programs

Long-term programming is a type of tactical planning extending the programming period for longer than a two-year span. It develops a long-range action plan that states intermediate objectives and proffers a series of short-range plans for their achievement. R&D programs are often long range; capital improvement, acquisition and merger, or pollution control activities are other long-term examples. Long-range programming is designed to realize three advantages:[4] (1) it forces long-range actions to start promptly and facilitates progressive planning, moving from short-range to intermediate to long-range planning; (2) it identifies intermediate goals and establishes decision thresholds thus preparing executives administratively and psychologically to initiate changes and replanning; and (3) it ensures that actions having long-term impact are fully coordinated.

Long-range programming serves as the basis for tactical planning and action. It guides organizational growth in spite of unexpected events until it reaches full program development. A venture management program developing long-range ventures starts with a small group of individuals appointed for their enterprising talent and technical capability. The group grows steadily and is guided by the short-range and intermediate program goals. A long-range research program is normally started the same way.[5] It can become large and complex, its predetermined course can change along the way, or it may be cancelled when the situation warrants it. In their initiation, long-range programs are generally directed by a central group; and in their execution, they are managed by a single program/project, but require coordination with participating departments. During program transition from one stage of development to the next, liaison between departments is essential. A long-range new product development program may move from research to development, to production, and ultimately to marketing. Operating departments should give close attention to directing and guiding the program toward its long-range objectives and managing short-range activities within the established constraints.

Resource Allocation and Management

Within the framework of corporate planning and implementation, functional managers study and submit resource requirements and manage allocated resources. Resource management requires managers to allocate people, facilities and equipment, and administrative expenses for profit contribution.[6]

PERSONNEL AND FACILITIES PLANNING Departmental personnel planning is the first and foremost task of resource management.[7] The personnel plan specifies human resource requirements to meet departmental goals. It consists of a personnel projection and a human resource development plan. The projection specifies the number and types of new and existing personnel. The personnel development plan outlines those actions, such as motivation and incentive programs, executive development programs, career advancement, and employee performance appraisals, that will ultimately create a climate favorable to personnel development. Whereas a well-designed incentive system outlines methods and actions to inspire people's contribution, other motivation techniques channel individual talents to fit the organization's needs. Personnel development, on the other hand, focuses on individual desires and goals for career development to adjust the organization to its people. An effective manager, thus, studies organizational needs in terms of human resources to achieve a balance of task and people.

Facilities and equipment planning is particularly important to production and engineering departments. The production department continuously reviews its plant and equipment requirements and seeks to improve production methods and create cost saving. A central planning group in the production department generally assembles resource requirements data from units within the department and prepares future plans and capital budgets for company approval. Line units, however, concentrate on short-term requirements and manage allocated resources. In an R&D department, facilities and equipment can become a large expenditure, especially when exotic equipment and special facilities are required. R&D requirements are of two types: long-term and short-term. Long-term requirements are regarded as capital expenses, which undergo a process of capital budget review and approval. Short-term requirements, however, demand the manager's close attention. In planning and managing R&D resources, managers are advised to note the three difficulties listed below and to devise means to overcome them:[8]

1. The total resources available to the R&D management needs to be relatively stable over a period of time. Their sudden or wide change can affect morale because the performance of the engineering staff depends on available facilities and equipment.
2. Facilities and equipment are fixed costs that affect profit contribution.
3. Each project absorbs a different portion of the resources. Their cost allocation must be correctly computed, even though their precise forecast is difficult.

BUDGETS Budgeting is the formulation of plans in numerical terms for a given future period. Budgets reveal administrative plans in terms of costs to be incurred and state anticipated results. By preparing budgets, managers are forced to allocate resources to financially responsible units, to coordinate departmental activities, and to measure performance against budgetary standards. Because departmental budgets are administrative by nature and short-term in character, budgeting must be closely synchronized with strategic planning. In budgeting, functional managers must take direct charge and consult key departmental personnel for input and advice. A self-imposed budget functions better than the one that is externally assigned. Budgets are of two types: (1) the centrally developed budget, such as the manufacturing cost budget, the sales expense budget, or the general and administrative expense budget; and (2) the department-submitted administrative budgets. Thus, management attention is divided between the allocations provided by its own department's budget, and the constraints placed upon it by centrally developed budgets.[9]

PPBS AND ZERO-BASE BUDGETING Aside from the traditional methods of fixed and variable budgeting—the latter showing budgets at different levels based on volume differences—the Planning, Programming, Budgeting Systems (PPBS) and the zero-base budgeting merit special note.[10] Both are useful for program budgeting. PPBS calls for budgeting by mission rather than by organizational units and line items. Budgeting by mission focuses on tasks and scheduled commitment of funds. It also provides means to measure results and allows considering alternative ways of accomplishing a given task. Thus, a new product development, a venture project, or an advertising campaign is broken down to tasks in terms of dollars and time frame. PPBS is usually associated with defense budgeting and weapon systems programming. Since its introduction in the mid-1960s, it has been widely used in government organizations. Industrial application is equally widespread.

Zero-base budgeting is a technique focusing on functional budgeting by combining a group of programs into function. Thus, the marketing department's budget is broken into programs rather than into line items. By stating each program budget from base zero, it allows calculating expenses afresh, thus avoiding the use of previous budgets as a point of reference. In doing so, line managers are forced to propose budgets from a new set of objectives and criteria. Zero-base budgeting is widely used in public and private organizations. Its principal advantage lies in the fact that the technique steers budgeting away from bureaucratic and formalistic approaches.

MANAGEMENT OF TACTICAL OPERATIONS

Tactical Planning

Successful management depends on policies, strategies, and tactics. Policies define the company's mission and objectives to guide the company along the desired course and set forth operational guidelines that ensure its smooth progression. Strategy delineates courses of action and means of attack to meet varying situational needs and secure the company's long-range objectives. It is, however, the tactical execution at all levels that carries out the directional and organized activities. Tactics work in a narrowed scope of operation (the execution of a sales activity or an action to correct cost deviations); prescribe certain interpersonal relations (the joint effort among department personnel or interaction between a salesperson and customer); and are subject to the dynamics of administrative activities under the restriction of time. Let us emphasize: strategy concentrates on resources and functions; tactics focus on people and actions. Tactics are thus the art of directing and activating.[11]

However, we know that before any such successful execution can take place, tactical planning must occur. Tactical planning must: (1) identify the basic cause of a problem and determine methods of attack; (2) lay out key activities in a sequential fashion; (3) assign and coordinate personnel; and (4) plan actions to neutralize administrative obstacles and personnel resistance. Tactical planning follows a process similar to that of strategy making. In assessing environmental factors, tactical planning emphasizes people and problems. In position auditing, the analysis of strengths and weaknesses focuses on the assumed perception of adversaries and on their likely responses once the action is taken. In establishing tactical objectives, planners concentrate on defining a series of objectives, their sequential relationships, and flexibilities in arrangement. In considering the feasibility of tactical actions, attention is given to timing, impact, and the choice of correct tactics.

GUIDELINES FOR TACTICAL PLANNING Tactical planning, working within the framework of strategy is, of course, subject to certain guidelines. First, tactics are submeans of implementation. As such, a set of subobjectives are structured to guide tactical actions. Each tactical action is intended to achieve certain objectives. Let us cite tactical planning of a sales campaign as an example. Once a major customer area is identified in a sales strategy, a series of subobjectives are delineated. The activities for penetrating that market may include the use of planned presentations by company executives and sales personnel, special product announcements, and programmed sales visits over a long period of time.

Second, tactical actions are restricted by resources and time constraints. Using the sales campaign as an example again, a sales campaign to generate a specific amount of sales is programmed in a series of promotional activities. Each activity is specified for a given time span so that all culminate on a final date of the forecasted sales. Each promotional means is utilized to coincide with the sales activity. A conditional forecast in anticipation of customer and competitor's counteractions will govern the decision on how each tactical move will be actually carried out. Third, tactical planning takes into consideration the people: those customers and competitors involved in the tactical encounters. A salesperson studies the decision-making process of the customer organization and defines the decision makers' needs and extent of authority. The sales plan thus describes the tactical situation, appraises the decision-makers' behavior, and plots counteractions on the part of the salesperson. In essence, tactical planning applies to all managerial and supervisory activities of strategic importance.[12] It directly affects the implementation of functional strategies.

TACTICS AND PEOPLE Sound tactics are designed to create an invigorating climate that encourages people to do their best.[13] Such a stimulating climate is free of obstacles from excessive policies and procedures and constraints. A healthy climate encourages people to act responsibly and creatively and to adapt to changes of events. Capitalizing on individuals' capacities and emphasizing team effort and joint accountability are sound tactics. To mobilize individual contribution, a skillful tactician believes that all people can achieve more if trust exists in the organization and if individual initiative is encouraged.[14] First, people will achieve more if the results of work rather than the activity itself are clearly defined. An understanding of the purpose of the job other than the detailed description of the execution encourages initiative. Second, providing at the beginning the information and means necessary for accomplishing work, giving timely encouragement and consistent follow-up attention during execution, and extending proper recognition and rewards at the completion of the job are good practices. Third, there is the need for an incentive system that compensates quality work, balanced results, and team accomplishment. The system must be fairly executed and personally rewarding.

To focus on team effort and joint accountability, management considers achieving organizational goals through proper delegation and recognizing joint accountability through sharing results essential to tactical execution.[15] Excessive competition among employees that gives recognition only to star performers, stress put on one activity over another, or stressing immediate results over long-term advantages are all tactics of expediency that produce more harm than good. Joint accountability makes the whole team responsible and assigns individual accountability in accordance with the person's accomplishments or influence affecting the outcome.

Tactical Execution

Tactical action is focused on the first-level execution, where actions take place and where the initial results are secured.[16] In the marketing department, it is the sales force and its immediate supervisors, including supporting units, who account for sales results. In the production department, it is the production workers and their immediate supervisors who are responsible for production efficiency and productivity. First-level execution thus requires that supervisors be provided with means to solve problems at the working level without undue interference from above. First, tactical planning must be practiced at all levels of supervision. People tend to be much more committed to a result if they have a hand in its planning. R&D performance, for example, can be greatly improved when project managers and engineers are intimately involved in planning their work. The dictated projects and rigidly controlled projects from the top can inhibit initiative and involvement.

Second, operational problems are better solved at their source. This requires a delegation of authority downward. True authority, not what is written on the job description, is sensed by the employees. A plant manager does not feel free to handle union relations if he or she must clear all matters with the personnel department. Authority can be built from the bottom up if competent individuals are encouraged to take actions to solve problems as they occur and if policies and control are properly executed at the appropriate supervisory levels. Third, staff assistance must be given to the supervisory levels where needs exist. Staff personnel must consult line, and their identity with line must be complete. One of the demanding tasks of executives is their ability to use staff efficiently, and to manage line-staff conflicts. This cardinal requisite applies equally to supervisory personnel.

Guidelines for Tactical Execution

Above all, tactical execution demands calculated deliberation. A supervisor must keep in mind the impact of his/her actions, correctly gauging reactions of his/her opponents, and continuously devising means to minimize negative reactions and to remove administrative and personnel obstacles. A good tactician pays close attention to the more important rules listed below.[17]

TIMING Timing is a critical factor in execution. A prompt move to "strike while the iron is hot" can exert dramatic impact. Conversely, a delayed approach that assumes "time is a great healer" may be desirable when immediate confrontation is considered harmful to the cause and when later moves may be stronger and more receptive.

INTENSITY A tactical move can be intense or gradual. A "concentrated offensive" may be necessary when a fast, massive action can produce dramatic results. A sales activity can be maneuvered to a climax when massive action is imperative. Conversely, a "foot in the door" tactic favors a smooth and subdued approach to ensure initial penetration and avoid outright rejection.

JOINT ACTION Sometimes, a coordinated action accomplished by joining hands with other departments and allied forces may secure easier results than acting alone. The tactics that seek "strength in unity" and "you scratch my back, and I will scratch yours" can be employed prudently to secure results otherwise not possible.

CHOOSING THE CORRECT TACTICS Tactics do not advocate exploitive means or devious approaches. Tactical choices are many. The choice and the application, however, are largely intuitive, judgmental, and personal. The correct choice is made by carefully evaluating the people involved, the situation, the urgency of objectives, the timing, the means available, and a number of other factors.

MAINTAINING ALERTNESS AND DYNAMICS OF ACTION Operational encounters are continuous and fluid. An artful tactician remains alert at all times, accurately sensing the impact of his/her actions, assessing new, evolving situations, and continuously exploring counteractions to negative obstacles and to keep the activity moving in the right direction. Equally important is the maintenance of the momentum of the action once it is begun. An action that sustains a constant flow of activities is the very key to tactical execution.

TACTICAL ACTIONS

Action Plans

Action plans as guide to tactical actions are developed at a lower level of operations. In practice, however, action plans are the missing link in strategic management.[18] The difficulties can be traced to three causes: (1) company objectives and strategy can lose their meanings when communicated down through the organization; (2) a poorly developed, less articulated strategy can cause problems in converting strategy into actions; and (3) supervisors at lower levels are inclined to assume impulsive actions, often disparate and nondirectional. Yet, action plans are essential to the implementation of tactics. Action plans convert tactics to actions. They force supervisors and performing units to focus on organizational goals and their achievements. Organizational goals, when correctly and fully communicated, produce coordinated actions and motivational effects. Because organizational actions are so many, so diverse, and involve so many people and units, individual and group conflicts can result. Action plans, when practiced in all units, tend to tie human and administrative actions together, thus reducing conflicts.

An action plan is a statement of objectives tasks (activity) and the logical step-by-step flow of future actions expressed in terms of what is to be accomplished, by whom, and when.[19] Action plans are unit operating plans developed by the supervisors of the performing units to direct critical activities and operations of a special nature. They range from a salesperson's work plan, sales supervisors' marketing plan, to a production manager's planning of weekly and monthly activities. Their formulation follows the steps in tactical planning discussed in the preceding sections. The plans must be personally meaningful to the individual and to the units responsible for the activity, and they must be versatile and flexible. They should be briefly written. They will continuously undergo changes; actions will be achieved, altered, or abandoned. Tactical objectives and plans are kept current to reflect changes in objectives, strategies, and tactics. The rule of involving key personnel in planning and execution applies equally to action planning. The format of the plan is much simplified to allow easy implementation. Each performing unit develops its own plan defining task objectives and describing activity flow, which includes types of activity, date of completion, and responsibility assignment (see figure 14.1).

Action planning cannot be treated as a routine exercise, giving the impression that people are planning but not acting. Nor can it be reduced to paper shuffling, so that people are busy producing paper, but not performance. Action planning is judged by its real value in involving people and units. So long as it remains informal in procedure and true in substance, action planning will provide the vital link for strategy making. In turn, it will assure full execution at the lowest level where actions really begin. Having achieved action planning, managers and supervisors jointly devise the control mechanism to allow feedback on performance and trends to keep the organization from moving away from its intended course.

FIGURE 14.1 A SIMPLIFIED ACTION PLAN AT THE PERFORMING UNIT LEVEL

Department objectives:
Unit task objectives:
Responsible individual:

Target completion date:

Action Plan

Tasks/Subtasks*	Completion Date	Responsibility Assignment

Tactical Control

Like strategic actions, tactical actions are subject to controls. Without proper control, tactical actions can become directionless and wasteful. In exercising proper control over tactical actions at operating levels, the same principles of control apply. Thus, tactical control follows the same process of setting standards, measuring and comparing actual progress against plans and standards, taking corrective actions, and completing the feedback loop. As an illustration, let us cite tactical control over a sales activity.[20] In this case, the salesperson's territory marketing plan and work plan are the basis for tactical control. The marketing plan contains a salesperson's plan for the year, and the work plan is a complete write-up of planned activities for a week or a month. Sales supervisors use these plans for measuring monthly and weekly activities. When checking the work plan against weekly and monthly activity and expense reports, the supervisor measures the result against progress and early assumptions. Corrective actions are taken to redirect activities if necessary and assumptions are redefined or modified.

As in the case of strategic control, tactical control is meant to produce positive results, not the unwarranted rigidity in restricting an individual's initiative and drive. Tactical control is exercised on tactical-controlling points, on items of importance, and is directed at updating assumptions and plans.[21] It is consultative and flexible.

SUMMARY

Effective strategy management requires sound planning at all levels and involvement of people in all parts of the organization. Tactical planning and execution provide the needed intelligence and initiative among line organizations and performing units. Line management plays a vital role. It manages functional strategies, programs, and projects and directs unit activities. Programming of short- and long-range activities and tactical planning of departmental operations require the ability to relate departmental objectives to sequentially phased tasks and to inspire individuals to fully use their potential. Action plans are simplified, but dynamic by nature. Their real value lies in stimulating individuals to think and act tactically, consistently focusing their actions on people and results. Once tactical actions are properly carried out at the lower level where actions are, strategic implementation is assured, and strategy and tactics are working in unison.

NOTES

1. Although engineering is not ordinarily regarded as a line function, its principal role of product design and technological innovation in industries, such as aerospace, engineering construction, and pharmaceutical manufacturing, accords it a clear chain of command similar to that of a line function. For discussion, see Harold Koontz and Cyril O'Donnell, *Management,* pp. 332–35.
2. Programs are defined as significant, large, operational activities. They can also be regarded as a structural classification of activities in connection with budgetary planning. For a discussion on programming, see William H. Newman and James P. Logan, *Strategy, Policy, and Central Management* (Cincinnati, Ohio: South-Western Publishing, 1971), pp. 465–68.
3. Charles C. Martin, *Project Management: How to Make It Work* (New York: AMACOM, 1976), chaps. 4–6.
4. Newman and Logan, *Strategy, Policy, and Central Management,* pp. 472–74.
5. For a discussion on R&D Programs, see Brian C. Twiss, *Managing Technological Innovation* (London: Longman, 1974), pp. 222–28.
6. For an excellent discussion on resource allocation and management, see Charles R. Ferguson, *Measuring Corporate Strategy* (Homewood, Ill.: Dow Jones-Irwin, 1974), pp. 80–90.
7. Russell L. Ackoff, *A Concept of Corporate Planning* (New York: Wiley-Interscience, 1970), pp. 68–84.
8. Twiss, *Managing Technological Innovation,* pp. 196–201.
9. For examples, consult Carl L. Moore and Robert K. Jaedicke, *Managerial Accounting* (Cincinnati, Ohio: South-Western Publishing, 1972), chaps. 20, 21.
10. For PPBS, see Robert B. Buchele, *The Management of Business and Public Organizations* (New York: McGraw-Hill, 1977), pp. 64–68; for zero-base budgeting, see Robert Albanese, *Management Toward Accountability and Performance* (Homewood, Ill.: Irwin, 1978), pp. 118–19.
11. Management textbooks on directing include topics such as motivation, leadership, and communication. For example, see Koontz and O'Donnell, *Management,* pt. 4; and Edwin B. Flippo and Gary M. Munsinger, *Management* (Boston: Allyn and Bacon, 1975), pt. 4.
12. For sales planning, see Harper W. Boyd, Jr., and William F. Massy, *Marketing Management* (New York: Harcourt Brace Jovanovich, 1972), pp. 174–76; and for tactical planning in production, see Richard Tellier, *Operations Management: Fundamental Concepts and Methods* (New York: Harper and Row, 1978), pp. 178–209.
13. For an excellent treatment of management tactics, see Edward C. Schleh, *The Management Tactician: Executive Tactics for Getting Results* (New York: McGraw-Hill, 1974), esp. p. 3.
14. Ibid., chap. 13, esp. pp. 145–52.
15. Ibid., chaps. 2, 6, esp. pp. 59–68.
16. Ibid., chaps. 4, 7, 10.

17. For discussion, see Theo Haimann and Raymond L. Hilgert, *Supervision: Concepts and Practices of Management* (Cincinnati, Ohio: South-Western Publishing, 1972), pp. 148–50.

18. Action plans can be narrowly interpreted as plans of action at low level of supervision, or broadly interpreted to mean plans at all levels. Frank T. Paine and William Naumes, *Organizational Strategy and Policy,* 2nd ed. (Philadelphia, Pa.: Saunders, 1978), pp. 152–62.

19. William F. Christopher, *The Achieving Enterprise* (New York: AMACOM, 1974) pp. 102–5.

20. Philip Kotler, *Marketing Management: Analysis, Planning & Control* (Englewood Cliffs, N.J.: Prentice-Hall, 1976), pp. 396–400.

21. For discussion, see Haimann and Hilgert, *Supervision,* pp. 367–75.

CHAPTER FIFTEEN

Control and Recycling

Planning and controlling is a twin concept in management.[1] A firm cannot survive long without planning its future courses and responding to external changing forces. Nor can a firm sustain its business without effective control of its internal operations. A company's strategic assumptions evolve simultaneously with new information and coming events, and the validity of the strategy must be tested continuously against changing external forces and internal dynamics. Hence, strategy must be updated, adjusted, modified, and recycled whenever circumstances force replanning and regrouping.

There are three sections in this chapter: (1) strategic control, dealing with the essence of control, the control mechanism, and the information system; (2) responses, concerning sensing, adaptation, and strategies of responses; and (3) recycling, covering topics of reformulating and regrouping.

STRATEGIC CONTROL OF OVERALL PERFORMANCE

The Essence of Control

Control is a function assumed by all managers to measure the progress against objectives and plans, to place restrictions on undesirable actions, and to apply corrective measures to ensure efficient operations and obtain results. Like planning, organizing, staffing, and directing, control is essential to management at all levels. Managerial processes energize the organizational structure and produce results. Control related to the implementation of company strategy, however, focuses on the overall performance of a company, on the design of an information feedback system, and on the proper adjustments to changes. Control necessitates good planning, without which control is ineffective. As a navigational aid, control helps to steer the company on the correct course, to harmonize goals, and to stimulate enthusiasm and coordination. However, control must not inhibit individual initiative and freedom of action, which will cause widespread antagonism or impose bureaucratic rigidity.[2]

The Control Process

Management control involves four steps: (1) it stipulates a realistic and well-defined goal, plan, or standard; (2) it measures the actual performance by some mechanism sensitive to the areas prescribed in the plan; (3) by such measurement it can identify deviations of actual performances from defined standards; and (4) it can initiate corrective actions as required. Technically, these four elements are identified as characteristic (goal); sensor; comparator; and effector.[3] Figure 15.1 shows the interaction of the four steps in the control process.

In the control model shown in the figure, the concept of feedback lies at the heart of the process. Feedback supplies the information that provides readings on how well the organization is doing and gives advanced signals for formulating strategies of responses. In a strategic control system, the strategic plan specifies the performance characteristics to be controlled. In general, quantity, quality, time, cost, and direction are the five performance factors. Sensing and measuring the determined criteria depends on the creation of a system of measurement and distribution of information. Feedback enables the comparison of actuals against standards and the identification and analysis of deviations. It also facilitates analysis of external changes against original assumptions. These three processes culminate in management decision making to assure corrective actions and to determine strategic responses, which can be either positive or passive. For example, a positive response counteracts, and a passive signal triggers monitoring.

Design of Control System

In the design and operation of a strategic control system, the control model forms a base of reference. There are at least three other considerations requiring close attention. (1) The control system must meet requirements of the company as a whole. It is not limited to the traditional financial and accounting control. It operates in all areas and at all levels of management. The distinction of strategic control at company, group, and division levels, and operating control at functional and supervisory levels bespeaks the need for a hierarchical system of control that parallels the firm's decision making and the formal planning process. In other words, strategic and tactical planning is supported by strategic and tactical control. (2) The balanced concept of goal setting also applies to control. The application of multiple criteria expands the horizon of executive responsibility and ensures the

FIGURE 15.1 THE CONTROL MODEL

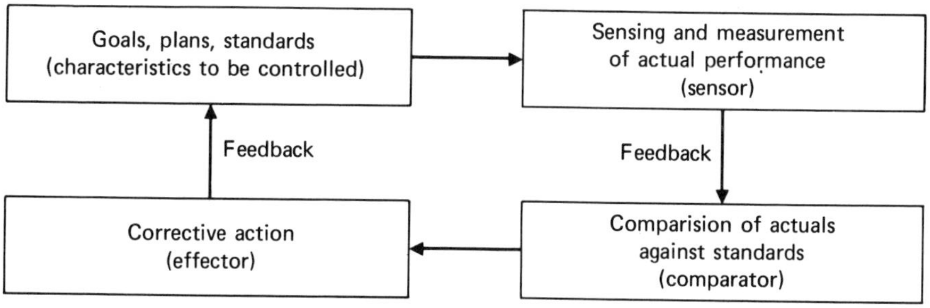

balance of subgoals. The fallacy of using a single criterion, such as the use of return on investment alone to determine compensation, promotion, and reassignment of managers, often leads to false planning and control.[4]

A single criterion can cause imbalance of goals and priority ranking. The emphasis on short-term profitability, for example, may cause managers to act contrary to long-term interest of the company as a whole. Too often, general managers are led to believe that their performance is measured on a yearly profitability basis, rather than by the long-term, multiple criteria measurement. Such practices generate more harm than good. First, general managers are likely to take expedient means to achieve immediate gains at the expense of future advantages. Second, they become disinterested in strategic planning, fearing that their tenure with the company will be short-lived if they do not show these gains. Third, their freedom of action is restricted. (3) A good control system places equal emphasis on formal (quantitative) and informal (behavioral) control, which is embedded in the value, interaction, and sentiment characterizing individual and group behavior.[5] When reinforced by an incentive and compensation system that rewards and sanctions individual and group actions, informal control can be made effective.

The Control Mechanism

The design and operation of control in a multidivision company, with several operating divisions serving diverse business interests, is both difficult and challenging. As overcontrol inhibits initiative, undercontrol tends to cause irresponsibility and business failure. Hence, proper control serves two purposes: to improve performance of managers' control function; and to institute a formal mechanism to ensure successful operations. Such a mechanism is composed of organizational control, internal control, and strategic control.

ORGANIZATIONAL CONTROL Within the corporate structure, organizational control over strategic matters is accomplished at general-management and functional levels. The combined policy, overall, administrative, and tactical control falls among the five units discussed in chapters 3 and 13. The policy control is assumed by the board of directors. The board holds periodic review on the ongoing strategy, questioning its validity, modification, and recycling. It conducts inquiries on critical strategic issues, and raises warning signals of policy concern.

The CEO and president exercise the overall strategic control. In that capacity, they jointly establish the control format and criteria, and oversee the strategic operations through a well-designed control system supported by a sensing-response mechanism to facilitate adjusting and recycling. They rely upon their policy vice presidents to monitor functional operations, develop operating policies, and effect coordination. They designate the planning staff to act as central control and use the committee on strategy or its nucleus to conduct periodic review of group and operating divisions' operations. Their communications with group and division general managers is constant and spontaneous. They hold scheduled review meetings to assess performance, adjustment, and responses to changing events and competitive counteractions.

The administrative control is performed by the planning staff. In that role, the planning staff manages the review meetings and coordinates overall implementation activities. It consults with policy executives and special staff on law and technology and other members of the committee on performance and coordination problems. The staff oversees the administrative aspect of the control system.

Last, line management performs the tactical control function relating to tactical execution and those critical short-term activities essential to long-range programs. Their input is communicated through the internal control system as well as the strategic control system via the company's integrated information system. As such, line managers are required to improve their control operations and take the initiative to correct deviations, adjust, and regroup whenever appropriate.[6]

INTERNAL CONTROL Internal control is an integral part of a firm's formal control system, exercising tactical control over line operations. Tactical control is different from strategic control, which focuses on monitoring changes affecting strategic assumptions and programs of strategic significance. There are five types of internal controls: (1) overall performance control; (2) policy control; (3) financial control; (4) budgetary control; and (5) operating control.[7]

Overall Performance Control A system of overall performance control measures performance of the enterprise and its large segments of operations. It provides a myriad of operating, financial, and resource data to measure and evaluate performance. It is the responsibility of the general managers and relies upon annual operating plans and strategic plans as bases for control.

Policy control Policy control is maintained through policies established by the board of directors, and policy executives at all general management and functional levels. Its application correctly reflects the intention of policy makers.

Financial control The measurement of a firm's financial activities covers all aspects of financial results: profitability; return on investment; cash; and assets management.

Budgetary Control One of the most widely recognized forms of managerial control is budgetary control. It controls departmental budgets and centrally prepared budgets relating to the total operation. Normally, budgets reflect cost and results.

Operating Control Operating control is a control used by line management to regulate departmental and program activities.[8] Production control and scheduling, personnel control, methods, standards, and action plans of operating units are such examples. Operating control is tactical by nature and is important to the implementation of strategy.

STRATEGIC CONTROL Strategic control complements the company's internal control by instituting special controls over strategic operations: the monitoring of external changes, the progress of strategic programs and actions, and the validation of ongoing strategies. Hence, strategic control is directed at (1) management visibility control; (2) strategic operations control; and (3) strategic change control.

First, management visibility control assures information flow of external and internal data and facilitates assessment of changing environmental variables. It supplies the broad viewpoint for management to appraise environmental factors, having impact on originally established assumptions and early formulated policy guidelines on product/market/business development. The control requires wide collection of pertinent data from two sources: (1) sources to reflect economic, sociopolitical, industrial, and technological changes; and (2) sources to reflect internal resources, technological, and organizational development. Information required for management visibility is a unique type requiring special design and treatment beyond the normal capacity of a management information system. Furthermore, its analysis and presentation pose another challenge. Environmental data of strategic nature is complex and is often quite deceptive. For example, economic forecasts come from many sources, and they often contradict each other. Technology data are difficult to collect and frequently are illusive. Needless to say, the same difficulties exist in the collection and interpretation of competitive and governmental data.

Second, strategic operations control concentrates on programs and action. We have consistently pointed out the importance of identifying and assigning responsibilities for managing strategic programs and preparatory actions. Strategic programs can include R&D programs crucial to the company's future development, new product/market programs spearheading a company's diversification, acquisition and merger programs critical to a company's growth strategy, or a divestiture program for restoring solvency, to cite a few. Strategic actions are ad hoc and short term. For example, a go-ahead decision for an R&D project having significant impact upon the company's future is an ad hoc decision. Its authorization to proceed is, however, a short-term action. Strategic action can include staff assignment of a general nature, such as studies on monitoring economic downturn, on major government policy changes, on anticipated major competitive thrusts, or on pending industry structural changes or price/cost increases. Strategic operations control can be established through periodic reporting or scheduled reviews.

Third, strategic change control provides a means to validate and adjust strategies. Strategy evolves with events. Its assumptions must be updated against evolving events, and its operations must be controlled to detect deviations. In the section on strategic adjustment and response, we will explain a sensing-adapting mechanism. Such a control subsystem is intended to institute strategic change control. Its use is essential to detect the trigger points for operating contingency plans and to determine the degree of strategic adjustments needed.

The Information System Strategic data are of a unique type. First, environmental information flows inward to the organization. Internal data of a large variety flow within the organizational structure—downward, upward, and laterally. External and internal data are correlated and converted into information formats meaningful to the needs of decision-makers. Second, strategic data are long range, and its intended use by general management is limited to certain organizations. Third, strategic data are selective, real-time, and of high quality. Fourth, an information system for strategy management conceives a broader perspective. It depends on the company's computerized Management Information System (MIS) for information generation, storage, and retrieval, but it relies on the personal information network of memos, individual initiatives, group action, and departmental synthesis for its versatility and completion. The design of the company's MIS to serve the needs of strategy management thus requires a new approach.

Strategy-Planning Information System Russell L. Ackoff's proposed approach to the design of an integrated management system for corporate planning is worth emphasizing.[9] The integrated system consists of three subsystems: (1) the decision-making subsystem; (2) the control subsystem; and (3) the management information system. Each subsystem follows different steps of design, but their developments are interrelated and mutually complementary. The design of a decision-making subsystem is a three-step process: (1) analyzing decision flow to identify decision centers and required type and quality; (2) modeling significant decisions to study decision parameters and optimize solutions; and (3) determining information requirements and criteria for information system design.

A decision-making subsystem is the foremost task in designing the overall system, and it takes into full consideration the organizational structure, position descriptions, performance specifications, and incentive systems for motivating managers to perform to their fullest potential. The control model governs the design of the control subsystem. Such a design identifies strategic control activities, information requirements, sources of data generation, control units, and the information flow that directs and ensures interaction among participating units. The combined design of the decision-making and control subsystems establishes information requirements for each phase of strategy management, making certain that the information subsystems can well serve the three phases simultaneously.

The design of the information subsystem is a large undertaking. In most companies, the information system is largely computerized and serves management for strategic and operations planning, controlling, and decision making. Recent disappointments in large computerized MISs, due to excessive enthusiasm, cost, and inherent weaknesses of large systems, dramatize the need for reappraisal of common design assumptions. Five common pitfalls are:[10]

1. Managers are overburdened with too much irrelevant information.
2. Information needs cannot be logically determined unless the design content is clearly understood and tested.
3. Information does not produce good decisions unless decision rules and feedback on performance are provided for.
4. Uncontrolled information flow among departments can lead to intense, unhealthy competition within the organization.
5. Managers must control the computer, and not be controlled by it.

A well-designed and efficiently operated information system undoubtedly plays a key role in strategy management. We have pointed out the computer-generated information explosion that unnecessarily burdens rather than streamlines the process. Condensations, syntheses, and analyses of data at all levels are means to reduce irrelevant information, and increase information usefulness. A constant flow of information and its efficient processing are ways to monitor the continuing validity of strategy and to stimulate adjustment and recycling. Because business strategy is continually evolving, its adequacy depends on a simply designed and extremely sensitive information system.

STRATEGIC ADJUSTMENT AND RESPONSE

The Tentative, Dynamic Nature of Strategy

As we have demonstrated, strategy making is an art of matching, calculating, and selecting, for which assumptions are made whose validity is verified by future events. Business strategy, thus, is inherently tentative about the approximation of its calculation and forecasts, and needs continuous fine tuning and adjustment. To be sure, the formal yearly formulation of company strategy defines the company's total perspective of purpose, mission, objectives, and courses of action. But strategy cannot and must not be made to change quickly and unwarrantedly. It will only evolve gradually and become increasingly purposeful when the company moves steadily but confidently along the basic direction that it chose to pursue. In essence, strategic adjustment and response caused by the continuous updating and development of fresh information and by changes in the dynamics of the contending forces are not only necessary, but imperative. After all, successful strategy operates for a long period of time. It cannot be regarded as static and absolute, subject only to the mechanical, yearly preparation as a ritual and rigidly interpreted once strategy is made. Indeed, strategic implementation can only be effective if a sensing and responding mechanism has been developed and put into operation to effect needed updating, adjustment, and response.

THE SENSING MECHANISM The sensing-adaptation-response mechanism works within the strategy-making framework. First, the five organizational units involved in strategy making continuously function as a working group. Each remains watchful of environmental changes, and each acts decisively in responding to changes. Second, the strategy-making process forges ahead; fresh data are collected and processed; controls are exercised; environmental signals are monitored; adaptation and adjustments are made simultaneously. Third, the sensing mechanism operates in a feedback information network that can trigger the group into action.

In strategy making, sensing signals of changes is crucial. Correct and early sensing reduces surprises and increases time for response. Signals can be external or internal. External signals are strategically significant, less predictable, and their impact more difficult to ascertain. For example, a signal of an approaching economic recession is very significant to a company's strategy: its start, intensity, and duration is difficult to predict; and its impact upon the company's employment and losses are impossible to gauge at first. So are the signals of a technological breakthrough, a sudden competitive action, and, indeed, changes in government policies and regulations. Internal signals are less significant because internal changes are gradual, short, and are controllable. To a greater degree, knowledge of internal changes is available and thus forecast of the impact is possible.

SENSING STRONG OR WEAK SIGNALS Additionally, signals can be strong or weak, clear or ambiguous. A strong signal has three characteristics: the signal content is complete and clear, the response time is short, and the response options are limited. A strong, surprising signal is sudden, urgent, and unfamiliar. Such surprises often generate discontinuity as with a sudden appearance of an opportunity or a threat whose impact could mean increase in profits or large losses. The 1973 energy crisis and the sudden threat of the 1974–1975 recession were surprises to many firms.

A weak signal is one that precedes a strong signal, and its early detection and continuous monitoring is necessary. The early warning allows gradual response and affords time to achieve a position of readiness for decisive and direct response at a later, more opportune time when the signal content is complete and the impact outcome is clear. Hence, the ability to detect a significant but weak signal, to monitor its characteristics and intensity, and to simultaneously plan gradual response is an important function of strategic management. This sensing mechanism triggered by the information system and acted upon by the vigilant strategic units, in particular the planning staff, can significantly increase the adaptability of strategy and reduce surprises whose effects can be severe.

THE ADAPTATION MECHANISM In his discussion on managing strategic surprises, Ansoff suggested various forms of response.[11] The mechanism derives from the progressive relationships between information content and state of knowledge. Each dimension represents a five-step progression from ambiguity (uncertainty) to clarity (certainty). Thus, information content progresses from early detection of a conviction that discontinuities are impending to the last stage that profit impact and consequences are computable. Correspondingly, the state of knowledge advances from a sense of threats/opportunities to the last stage of a certainty of outcome.

The continuing monitoring and gradually increasing readiness are central to the adaptation mechanism, which conducts threat/opportunity analysis to identify strategic issues and estimate the impact of each issue on the firm as a whole, and on each business unit separately. Throughout the monitoring stage, various adjustments are made when necessary. On the other hand, strategic adjustments are constantly made in response to signals and events of a familiar type. This will be a case when a company adjusts its functional strategies to meet a competitor's marketing challenge in introducing a new market approach, a new product, or a new pricing strategy, or to counteract a competitor's announcement of a new technology, a device, or a cost-saving production method. Such events are expected to occur occasionally, and, through prior experience, their impact is not too difficult to gauge, and the required responses are generally short term.

In order to manage the sensing-adaptation-response mechanism in both situations—discontinuity and normal changes—Ansoff proposed a strategic issue management system that includes four participating units: the planning staff; general management; task force; and operating units. The planning staff detects, tracks, and analyzes strategic issues; general management assigns specific issues for planning and execution; and task forces and operating units execute specific projects. An urgent and unfamiliar signal, once detected and ascertained, can be placed under the planning staff, a special staff, or a task force for monitoring and planning. A significant impending change in government policy and regulations on pollution control or safety regulations, for example, may require a task force to monitor its progression and estimate its impact. Early responses can be planned, which may require the company's participation in the government policy formulation process. A dynamic, long-term response posture may be adopted to direct a series of external actions and internal adjustment and preparedness.

Response Strategies

In executing dynamic response, there can be three modes: the normal mode, the ad hoc crash response mode, and the preplanned crisis mode. The normal response, following a routine, noncrisis approach, takes a longer time to complete. The ad hoc crash response realizes a time savings by speeding up the response process, and the preplanned crisis response specifies a gradual response that lowers the reponse time and increases the capacity for handling strategic surprises.[12]

Under the preplanned response, there can be three basic strategies: the awareness strategy; the flexibility strategy; and the direct response strategy. Each of these response strategies calls for reevaluation of external environment and internal preparedness. The awareness strategy calls for management to assume a position of sensing, monitoring, and planning in tracking and measuring signal content and determining its impact and of planning company's readiness to exert gradual and progressive responses. The flexibility strategy heightens the company's preparedness and ensures repositioning to external opportunities and threats. The direct response strategy launches the total, planned attack through redeployment of resources and, if necessary, a new course of action.

The flexibility strategy requires the quick repositioning to new products and new markets whenever the need arises; the direct response strategy demands an entrepreneurial risk-taking mode, when bold calculation forces a large commitment of resources and swift, major actions. In essence, to avoid strategic surprises, management must develop an ability to plan contingencies, to quickly apply counteractions, and above all, to develop a psychological readiness to face unfamiliar events.

RECYCLING—THE REMAKING OF STRATEGY

The Recycling Process

Company strategy is recycled formally every year during the time of annual planning, as described in chapter 3. During the annual updating, past and present strategies are analyzed. Their limitations are identified; planning premises are reestablished; and their total effectiveness evaluated. Reflecting the latest calculation and adjusting the company's perspective, the new strategy is formulated, and long-term objectives updated. During its subsequent implementation and prior to the next yearly revision, the ongoing strategy continuously undergoes reevaluation and adjustment. The need for recycling only occurs when the two aforementioned conditions exist. In such a case, the strategy-making process simply repeats itself. The five-step process, as discussed in chapter 3, reminds us that the process includes environmental analysis, internal assessment, objective setting, situation analysis, and the strategic plan. Recycling, however, is less formal and is quickly accomplished and implemented because it involves only those elements that are affected by the development of new strategy. In other words, the recycling does not follow the formal planning system, and its development can be partially completed.

The five organization units involved in strategy making are instrumental in initiating, recycling, and implementation. The respective roles of the five units remain the same as they are in the annual formulation. But the administration of the process is more expeditious and less formal. Resource reallocation, structural changes, and regrouping of functional activities are quickly accomplished. Certainly, implementation of the new strategy requires the same vigor and functional support. Functional strategies are thus recycled, and tactical planning and execution are reintroduced.

Reformulation and Regrouping

Reformulation is a process used when, under different conditions, a company's fundamental position is threatened and its basic assumptions are challenged. At this time, reformulation of strategies is necessary. It calls for the complete remaking of a strategy, or a part of it such as that which applies to a group or a division.[13] Let us discuss the three conditions forcing the reformulating, its management, and the anticipated problems and difficulties.

Under three different conditions, a company is forced to initiate strategic reformulation.

CONDITION 1 A company's position is threatened. This occurs when the company's strategic position undergoes major changes. The shift to an all-out growth strategy calls for reformulation. Sudden and impending decline in sales and earnings that forces the shift from growth to profit stability strategy is another situation. So is the adoption of survival strategy when business conditions worsen. During the growth syndrome in the late 1960s, we witnessed quick shift of corporate strategies to face adverse, changing business conditions. As we stated previously, the vicious cycle is a reality of modern business life. All companies will face at one time or another the changing business fortunes.

CONDITION 2 The company's basic assumptions are challenged. Under drastic environmental changes or internal adjustments, a company's major thrust in doing business is placed in jeopardy. The multiple threat of the fuel economy, auto safety, and customers' preference for small cars has forced the auto industry to reassess its assumptions, and thus their reformulation of strategies. The oil industry's early assumptions of a stabilized petroleum market, a large supply of resources, and indeed the shift to public resentment have long been challenged since the energy crisis. Exxon, Mobil Oil, and other oil companies are known to have engaged in serious attempts to reformulate their respective strategies. Internal changes, such as the arrival of a new management or as a result of large-scale mergers, are other situations requiring complete reformulation of corporate strategies.

CONDITION 3 Company position is jeopardized by surprises. Surprises can occur in many different ways. Sudden economic downturn, rapidly deteriorating market, technological breakthrough, and government action are examples of surprises. Under such situations, companies are forced to take drastic actions, thus they reformulate strategies to solve the immediate and future problems.

Among the many such companies experiencing strategic reformulation, Xerox Corp. is an excellent example. The company itself is a success story of a well-managed, rapidly growing giant in its industry. Its rise to $4 billion in sales in 1974 in only twenty years is rarely matched by other modern U.S. companies. However, due to a combination of factors, its fundamental, competitive position is threatened and its basic assumptions were challenged. Illustration capsule 20 sketches the causes for the reformulation and the management calculated responses still in implementation.

Management of Reformulation

Management of reformulation requires the same attention given to strategic planning and strategic formulation, except that it is carried out in urgency and intensity. To be sure, the nature and the scope of the change and timing of desired responses affect the manner and intensity of the reformulation process. In a desired situation, management gains its knowledge of oncoming changes through its control system and its sensing-adjusting-response mechanism. Through its adoption of a response strategy, management maintains a posture of preparedness, slowly moving from strategic planning to formulation. Under severe external and internal pressure, management has little time to scan and measure advanced signals. In such cases, drastic actions are necessary. In recycling, all of the five strategic units are involved. The prime responsibility, however, falls to the board of directors, the chairman/CEO/president, and planning staff.

Illustration Capsule 20

XEROX CORP.

Xerox Corp., once a little-known Rochester producer of industrial photographic goods, grossing only $15 million a year, has in only twenty years become a $4 billion giant with 85 percent of the market share. From 1964 through 1974, growth in earnings averaged 24 percent a year.

However, in 1975, the "perpetual money machine" slowed down. C. Peter McColough indicated that the company had gone through a major readjustment and is now beginning to move offensively again. In the first half of the seventies, growth was 15 percent per year. In the later half, McColough expected it to slow 8 percent or 9 percent. This slowdown could hurt Xerox in its head-on battle with IBM. The slowdown in copier demands and recession hurt Xerox in 1974. Also costing Xerox was the development of the 9200 duplicator, the 800 Electronic Typing System, and the $84.4 million write-off of the mainframe computer manufacturing.

Many actions have taken place in an effort to get the company growing again. A cost-cutting program has been put in place. In 1975, some 8,000 employees were laid off, not including the 4,000 laid off from the mainframe computer operation. However, 4,000 were added back to support the two new projects listed above.

Three copier rebuilding plants on the West Coast were consolidated into one, along with two in Illinois. Building plans for new headquarters and a new Dallas plant were shelved. Two purchasing offices in Rochester were combined and opened only three days a week. These actions have been a part of the readjustment to bring Xerox back to a growth position.

Competition is causing Xerox to adapt. While the plain paper copying industry grew 12 percent from mid-1974 to mid-1975, Xerox only grew 6 percent. To compete, Xerox, typically highest priced in the industry, cut its rental charges to 11 percent on January 1, 1975. A price war brought competitors such as IBM and Pitney Bowes down also.

Xerox's 9200 copier is making inroads against competitors, and McColough expected to have 5,000 installations in 1975, with revenues of $1 billion annually by 1980. This program is backed by 600 specially trained salesmen and 1,000 servicemen, which makes it very appealing. However, this operation was not expected to make a profit until late 1977.

Foreign markets represent a tremendous long-range growth opportunity for Xerox. Foreign operations accounted for 45 percent of Xerox's sales and earnings in 1975. Despite this growth potential, Rank Xerox (Xerox' 51 percent owned British operation) did even more poorly than its parent in 1974. This was attributed to increased costs, increased competition, inflation, and an $18 million write-off due to the mainframe computer failure.

Fuji Xerox is also having a tough time. Once dominating almost the entire market, in 1975 their share was down to 52 percent and sliding. Competitors again hurt Xerox.

Xerox entered the seventies in a strong position and will try to finish the decade that way. Although Xerox has an excellent management team, it still encounters difficulties in the mid-seventies. Competitive pressures, rapid technological advances, and the increasing tightness of the money situation were not anticipated soon enough.

Xerox has had to make major readjustments both in their daily operations and in long-range strategies. To help the planning effort, Xerox has established a Business Product and Development Group. Their job is to lead Xerox into the markets of tomorrow. The unit is highly concerned with acquiring companies that will extend Xerox's technological capabilities.

In the future, Xerox is adamant about expanding into the automated office systems market, and being more than just a copier manufacturer. The information demands of the future will be more intensive, and Xerox intends to have the technology and aggressiveness to meet them. Xerox has had to restrict its growth, trim the corporate fat, and change their strategies to retain their position in the market. Through the use of careful and thoughtful planning, Xerox is intending to put their company back onto the growth track.

Source: "Why Xerox's Money Machine Slows Down," *Business Week*, 5 April 1976, pp. 60–66.

One of the more difficult constraints in reformulating strategy is the success syndrome.[14] Company management bestowed with continual success is reluctant and insensitive to change and often acts too slowly to be effective. Another problem that can be expected is the need for concentrated attention and policy debate. Policy changes can result in controversies, conflict, and resignation of top management. Subsequently, drastic actions lead to personnel changes and organization disruptions. The company could use the process of regrouping. However, implementation of a reformulated strategy is more difficult. It requires a transitional period during which concepts and methods are discarded, new ones can be tried and accepted, and the newly structured organization placed in operation. In other words, regrouping is a long and difficult task requiring the recycling of the total implementing process once again.

SUMMARY

Linked with strategic planning and strategic formulation, strategic management, is the third phase of strategy making. Each phase of the process must function to its fullest extent, and the inadequacy of one will render the others partially ineffective. Implementation is guided by strategies and tactics, and is carried out by organizational units and people. It is thus administrative by nature, and it is forceful and continuous. In such a long and complex process, let us summarize a few of the more important aspects:

1. Business strategy shares a close relationship with organizational structure and process. They mutually react to one another. Strategy instigates structural and process changes; yet, structure and process place constraints on strategy.
2. Business objectives must be converted into tasks. Key tasks are time phased, sequentially programmed, and critically controlled.
3. The command structure of strategy management centers around the chief executive officers and their planning staffs. Management assumes a dynamic leadership, a natural management style, and an aggressive, direct approach.
4. Tactical execution revolves around the line management. It develops functional strategies to direct tactical planning and execution, and encourages the making of action plans to guide program/project and operation activities.
5. Planning and control is a dual, united concept. A well-designed control system parallels a good planning system throughout the organization.
6. The control model governs the design and operations of the control system. A sound strategic control system insists on overall performance control, balanced control, quantitative, and qualitative (behavioral) control.
7. The strategy management information system imposes unique demands on the company's Management Information System, which should be designed carefully and with ingenuity.
8. Strategic adjustment and response requires the design of a sensing-adaptative-response mechanism that can react to strong and weak signals and develop response strategies to enhance readiness.
9. Reformulation of strategy is a necessary process. Three conditions cause reformulation, which depends on effective control to sense changes and to recycle and regroup.

NOTES

1. Robert N. Anthony proposed a planning/control framework that combines strategic planning, management control, and operating control as an integrated system. *Planning and Control Systems: A Framework for Analysis* (Cambridge, Mass.: Harvard University, 1965).
2. Douglas McGregor, "Do Management Control Systems Achieve Their Purpose?" in *Business Policy and Strategy: Concepts and Readings,* ed. Daniel J. McCarthy, Robert J. Minichello, and Joseph R. Carran (Homewood, Ill.: Irwin, 1975), pp. 470–82.
3. Fremont E. Kast and James E. Rosenzweig, *Organization and Management: A System Approach* (New York: McGraw-Hill, 1974), pp. 408–73.
4. C. Roland Christensen, Kenneth R. Andrew and Joseph L. Bower, *Business Policy: Text and Cases* (Homewood, Ill.: Irwin, 1978), pp. 663–64.
5. Ibid., pp. 663–77.

6. Effective management requires all managers to be proficient in instituting and practicing adequate control techniques. Harold Koontz and Cyril O'Donnell, *Management* (New York: McGraw-Hill, 1976)., pp. 652–56.
7. For general discussion on control, see Koontz and O'Donnell, *Management,* pt. 6, and Theo Haimann and William G. Scott, *Management in the Modern Organization* (Boston: Houghton Mifflin, 1974) pt. 4.
8. Operating control deals with controls where a form of methods, standards, or plans exists.
9. *A Concept of Corporate Planning* (New York: Wiley-Interscience, 1970), pp. 119–26.
10. Ibid., pp. 113–19.
11. H. Igor Ansoff, "Managing Strategic Surprise by Response to Weak Signal," *California Management Review,* Winter 1975, pp. 21–33.
12. Ibid., pp. 26–30.
13. Thomas J. McNichols considers reformulation or recycling as a distinct phase in developing recovery strategy. His five-phase conceptual model includes formulation, implementation, organization, interpretation, and reformulation. *Policy Making and Executive Action* (New York: McGraw-Hill, 1978), pp. 581–94.
14. Ibid., pp. 590–91.

CASES FOR PART IV

22. GULF AND WESTERN INDUSTRIES, INC.
23. SEARS, ROEBUCK, AND CO.
24. AMTRAK
25. TITLE IV-D PROGRAM

GULF AND WESTERN INDUSTRIES, INC.

Gulf and Western Industries is a diversified corporation operating in several different business areas. It was one of the earlier examples of the conglomerate form. Unlike many other firms which started to diversify in the sixties and seventies, it is one of the few which still actively refers to itself as a conglomerate. The company does this at a time when other firms go to great lengths to disassociate themselves from what they feel is a term that has fallen into disrepute, particularly on Wall Street.

HISTORY

The Gulf and Western Company was originally incorporated as the Michigan Bumper Corporation, on November 8, 1934. The company's name was changed to Michigan Plating and Stamping Company on November 8, 1955, and again, to Gulf and Western Industries, on August 1, 1960. A fully owned subsidiary was incorporated in Delaware on April 18, 1967, and this was merged with the parent corporation on July 12, 1967.

The year 1958 was a milestone in the history of Gulf and Western. In that year, a new, vital and enthusiastic management team, headed by Charles G. Bluhdorn, appeared. The team provided many innovations, not the least of which were a new business approach and new capital. There was little doubt that the youthful Gulf and Western Industries had a bright future. The company had as its goal to serve the automobile after parts customer, wherever and whenever the opportunity arose. An effective action plan was developed which, despite formidable opposition and a complicated market, gave the company leadership in the field.

Prior to 1961, Gulf and Western had been primarily interested in growing within the automobile part field. Through a carefully worked out plan, they acquired many automobile parts manufacturing establishments. With the incorporation of the American Parts Company, in Houston, Texas, Gulf and Western Industries opened a new era of marketing and warehousing in the automobile after parts market. The American Parts System offered to the customer a viable alternative to the National Auto Parts Association (NAPA), their major competitor.

Prepared by Professor William Naumes of Temple University with the assistance of Kwame Ofinam.

Success has many contributory factors. In this instance, a great weight must be assigned to the fact that customers for automobile parts had been able to find in the American Parts System the satisfaction they had heretofore been denied. As the American Parts System took the market by storm, Gulf and Western Industries grew rapidly.

DIVERSIFICATION

In 1965 a major tactical move gave indication to the direction Charles G. Bluhdorn had decided to follow. Gulf and Western purchased, between September 10th and October 4th, 57.5 percent of New Jersey Zinc Company, merging on February 25, 1966. New Jersey Zinc's operational activities were continued by a 100 percent owned Delaware subsidiary with the same name. The tactical deviation of jumping from auto parts to zinc caused a great deal of amazement and even amusement to some in the business world. As *Forbes* quoted Bluhdorn: "When I bought New Jersey Zinc, everyone treated it like a joke. 'Look at what that crazy man has done now,' they said." In the first half of 1966, General Plastics, Incorporated of Kalamazoo, Michigan was acquired.

Having been relatively successful in these acquisitions, Gulf and Western began to flex its muscles. The company diversified into the leisure time business by merging with the Paramount Pictures Corporation of New York, on October 19, 1966. Again cynics and pessimists abounded; in the words of the chairman of the board:[2] "Eyeball to eyeball, I tell you this: they said, Paramount Pictures would bankrupt me." Instead of doleful ruin, the Gulf and Western 1972 Annual Report said,

> The unparalleled box-office success of Paramount Pictures Corporation's *The Godfather* helped the leisure time group achieve a record year in fiscal 1972. Sales reached $291 million compared with the previous record of $297 million set in fiscal 1971, when Paramount's *Love Story* was breaking box-office records. Operating income in fiscal 1972 rose to $31.2 million compared with $20.1 million the year before. (See Exhibit 1)

A wise corporation, like a wise human, never places all its eggs in one basket, however. Therefore, in 1967, management found it appropriate to diversify further by branching into pipes and wire, sugar, and mining, while delving still deeper into the leisure area. This was accomplished by purchasing all the stock of Taylor Forge and Pipe works, Incorporated, for $18 million; acquiring the business and assets of Collyer Insulated Wire Company; merging with South Puerto Rico Sugar Company; and acquiring the assets and business of Desilu Productions, Incorporated; while a Canadian subsidiary purchased 50 percent of the stock of Hedman Mines, Limited, on April 18, 1967.

In fiscal 1968, the Gulf and Western organization acquired sixteen motion picture photoplays. In addition, they invested in agricultural produce, metal works, tobacco, tools, publishing, and phonograph record companies. In this period they acquired a 98 percent interest in Scott-Mattson Farms, Inc., packer and processor of fruits and vegetables; the assets and business of Alloy-Flange and Fitting Corp. of New York; Resource Publications, Incorporated of Princeton, N.J., a publishing firm; and The Stax Records, Volt Records, and affiliates. They acquired, by merger, the

---

[2] *Forbes*, Sept. 15th, 1973, pg. 48.

EXHIBIT 1 OPERATING INCOME COMPARISONS

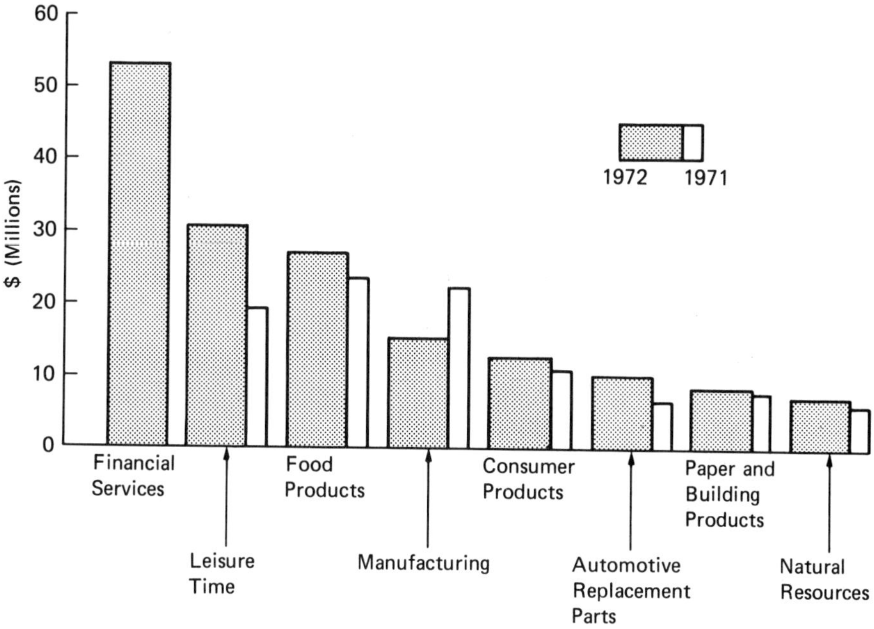

E. W. Bliss Company, a metal working machinery manufacturer; Consolidated Cigar Corporation, a tobacco product manufacturer; and Universal American Corporation, a tool and bearing manufacturer.

Gulf and Western took another major diversification turn in 1968. In June, 57 percent of the shares of the Providence Washington Insurance Company were obtained and, in September, transferred to the Associates Investment Company, 92 percent owned by Gulf and Western. This provided the base for a major move into the financial area.

By November, Associates owned 95 percent of Providence Washington. On July 1, 1969, by the merger of a 100 percent owned subsidiary with the Associates Investment Company, later called the Associates Corporation of North America, investment business was added to the perpetually broadening sphere of activities.

In December 1969, the wholly owned Consolidated Cigar Corporation acquired Roger's Incorporated, a manufacturer and importer of pipes, lighters, tobacco pouches and leather goods. In September 1971, Auto Pak Company Incorporated, maker of refuse compactors, was taken over, thus giving Gulf and Western entry into the sanitation field.

In the 1972 fiscal year, Camino Tours Incorporated, Fun in the Sun tours, and Hawaiian Polynesian tours were acquired. The three travel companies absorbed up to this point were linked together as the Gulf and Western Travel Corporation.

The company widened its international operations with a policy the 1972 Annual Report called "expanding abroad in partnership with foreign businessmen and

EXHIBIT 2 GULF & WESTERN INDUSTRIES, INC., FINANCIAL SUMMARY

Net Sales and Other Operating Revenues 1972 $ Millions	1972 % Total	1971 $ Millions	1971 % Total	*Operating Groups*	*Operating Income* 1972 $ Millions	1972 % Total	1971 $ Millions	1971 % Total
300	19	372	19	Financial Services	54.0	37	50.2	38
291	14	279	14	Leisure Time	31.2	21	20.1	15
100	5	84	4	Food Products	27.6	19	24.3	18
604	29	606	32	Manufacturing	15.8	11	21.2	16
187	9	179	9	Consumer Products	12.4	8	11.7	9
163	8	141	7	Automotive Replacement Parts	10.0	7	8.0	6
226	11	204	11	Paper and Building Products	8.6	6	8.5	7
102	5	77	4	Natural Resources	7.2	5	4.4	3
3*	—	4*	—	Corporate (including realty) and Intercompany Items	20.3*	14*	16.0*	12*
2,060	100	1,938	100					
390		372*		Less Financial Services Revenues				
1,670		1,566		As Reported in Earnings Statement	146.5	100	132.4	100

**Denotes deduction.*
Amounts for 1971 for certain groups have been restated to reflect the transfer of certain operations among groups.
Operating income represents earnings from operations before dividends and other income and before deduction of interest expense, minority interest and income taxes except that for Financial Services it is operating earnings before income taxes.

companies"; they acquired a 58.5 percent interest in John M. Henderson & Company Limited of Aberdeen, Scotland, an equipment supplier to petroleum, steel, machinery and coal industries, during fiscal 1972. Also, 20 percent of Fratelli Fabri Editori of Italy was taken, while the Gulf and Western Far Eastern Pacific Corporation was inaugurated to search for probable investments all over the Pacific area.

During the same period, Gulf and Western entered cable television and real estate. Athena Communications Corporation and a 50 percent interest in the Richards Group (real estate) provided the vehicles for these moves.

MADISON SQUARE GARDEN

Gulf and Western had acquired an 18 percent interest in Madison Square Gardens, over time, by October 1972. These purchases had been purely for investment purposes. At that time, the firm decided to increase its holdings in what until then had not been a very profitable operation. As reported in the *Wall Street Journal:*

> Gulf and Western's Madison Square Garden Holding lifted to 20 percent, may go higher. . . . Progress and growth motivate Charles G. Bluhdorn, the Chief Executive of Gulf and Western. He stated that he expects the Garden to "develop very actively its real estate holdings, and we'll help any way we know how and I am sure Mr. Wasserman [of Madison Square Garden] will help in any way he knows how." This is because the "greatest growth pools for real estate [are] in the U. S., with vast and unexplored opportunities which aren't [available] in Asia or Africa but right here in New York City, in Suffolk County, N. Y., and in Chicago."

As predicted, Bluhdorn's company offered to buy one million shares of the Garden at $7 which was extended till January 18, 1974, at 5 P.M. New York time. By January 25, 1974, according to *Moody's Industrial News Reports,* Gulf and Western "received approximately 380,000 shares of Madison Square Gardens common stock in response to its previously announced offer which expired January 18. Now the company has 1,350,000 common. That is 28 percent of outstanding shares."

It was noted that, by this move, Gulf and Western was able to include its share of Madison Square Garden's earnings on its Income Statement. Boosting the percentage of ownership over 20 percent allowed the company to show a return from the now-profitable holdings, despite the lack of a dividend payout from the Garden.

RELATED POLICIES

So far, the company has considered growth for both profits and size as prime objectives. When necessary and profitable, in the long or short run, divestitures do take place, however. For instance, the company registered its first significant sale of an asset in June, 1969, when Norma-Hoffman Bearings Company was sold. This was followed by the June 1970 disposition of the 50 percent interest in Paramount Studios, Incorporated, and the sale of 10 percent of A.P.S., Incorporated. Rocket Jet/AAD division was liquidated, and 49 percent interest in Universal Realty Corporation was sold. Between 1971 and 1972, Gulf and Western sold all interests (securities, 82.5 percent, common shares, 17.5 percent) in FBT Ban Corporation of Indiana, Incorporated; during the same time period, Amron Corporation, ETS Daniel Doyen S.A., and the four Belgian subsidiaries of the latter were sold.

Guided by the chairman's philosophy that "companies are not built in the courtrooms," Gulf and Western, with its marathon list of acquisitions, has had sur-

EXHIBIT 3 GULF & WESTERN INDUSTRIES INC. AND SUBSIDIARIES, FINANCIAL HIGHLIGHTS OF FIVE YEARS OF OPERATIONS

	Dollar Amounts, Except Per Share, in Thousands				
	1972	1971	1970	1969	1968
Operating Results—year ending July 31:					
Net sales and other operating revenues	$1,669,671	$1,566,327	$1,629,562	$1,563,564	$1,330,565
Net earnings from operations	69,601	55,252	49,825	50,982	67,732
Net earnings	69,411	55,576	44,771	72,050	70,366
Primary earnings per share:					
Net earnings from operations	3.31	2.61	2.26	2.15	3.00
Net earnings	3.30	2.63	2.00	3.15	3.13
Fully diluted earnings per share:					
Net earnings from operations	3.31	2.61	2.26	2.00	2.64
Net earnings	3.30	2.63	2.00	2.67	2.74
Depreciation and depletion	45,614	40,665	42,769	41,454	29,124

Financial Position—July 31:					
Working capital	$ 559,940	$ 478,426	$ 416,994	$ 576,510	$ 469,591
Net property, plant and equipment	607,394	584,922	552,622	525,059	518,215
Total assets	2,230,482	2,079,067	2,154,463	2,172,027	2,055,334
Shareholders' equity	673,833	621,682	580,346	590,066	537,874
Book value per common share	30.00	27.63	25.49	23.16	19.93
General Statistics:					
Number of shareholders:					
Common stock	45,000	51,000	54,000	51,000	43,000
Preferred stock	35,000	39,000	40,000	40,000	42,500
Capital expenditures	$ 81,767	$ 98,477	$ 86,676	$ 72,825	$ 61,587

The per share amounts have been adjusted for the stock dividends paid in fiscal years 1968 and 1969 and for the effect of the distribution to shareholders of record on July 18, 1969, of one share of stock of Transnation Development Corporation (formerly G&W Land and Development Corp.) for each 20 shares of the Company's common stock held.
Source: Gulf and Western Industries Annual Report, 1972.

prisingly smooth sailing, with exceptionally few courtroom battles. The company, however, tries to take good care of its stockholders' interest and does not "turn the other cheek," as its history has revealed. Almost a decade ago, at Grand Rapids, Michigan, during the takeover of an auto hardware producer, Crampton Manufacturing Company, a terrific proxy fight developed. Here, although Crampton's management supported the Gulf and Western move, the Sparton Corporation, also a parts manufacturer, which owned a large block of shares in Crampton, disagreed. When it was all over, Gulf and Western had the upper hand. The second litigation involved the Muskegon Piston Ring Company, on whose seven-man board Gulf and Western already had two seats, and whose management wanted to halt further expansion. The case was bitterly fought in the courts until Gulf and Western won. To avoid any bad name tags that could be damaging to future business, all interests were liquidated immediately. At the time, a major auto supplier's officer commented to *Business Week* about Gulf and Western being "overly aggressive—but I am not so sure that is bad." The Gulf and Western business empire remained relatively peaceful until the company quietly started to buy shares of the Great Atlantic and Pacific Tea Co. from March 1972 through January 1, 1973.

THE A & P INCIDENT

"On February 1," *Business Week* reported, "Gulf and Western filed a schedule 13D with the Securities Exchange Commission because its A & P holdings were near the minimum 5 percent holdings disclosure rule. The form disclosed that Gulf and Western had accumulated 1,046,000 shares of A & P common stock, or about 4.2 percent of the 24,875,224 shares outstanding. On the same morning, Bluhdorn announced a tender offer for 3.75 million shares at $20 a share." This began the herculean court battles with mighty A & P, who insisted that Gulf and Western was trying to take it over, but "a source close to Bluhdorn said, 'it would be premature and totally incorrect at this time to say that Gulf and Western is going after A & P. This is an investment where the downside risk is negligible and the opportunity to make money considerable.'" As the battle raged on, *Business Week* opined, "Bluhdorn's options would appear to be to back off by selling his 1.1-million shares, or to fight the case in court and then revive his tender offer should he win—an expensive gamble. If he sells out, it would be consistent with G & W's earlier behavior when it met opposition from incumbent managements: the conglomerate has retreated from initial investments it made in Grumman, Pan American, Alice-Chalmers, Sinclair, and Armour." True to form and principle (as *Newsweek* reported), "In an eventful board meeting at Gulf and Western Industries, directors of the big conglomerate voted to give up on its tender offer for 19 percent of the stock of the Great Atlantic and Pacific Tea Co. and return the shares tendered it."

It retained, however, the shares it had previously purchased. These shares, moreover, represented a "paper profit" for G & W.

SUBSIDIARIES

Grouping of Subsidiaries

In 1973, *Business Week* said that Gulf and Western, which since 1972 had been in the process of buying through its fully owned subsidiary, Associates First Capital Corporation, a big factoring concern, Talcott National Corporation of New York, "got a warning from the Justice Department that if it takes over Talcott National Corporation, it will have to shed Talcott's City Finance Co. subsidiary. The word from Washington came only three days before expiration of G & W's tender offer for Talcott shares. However, justice will let G & W keep Talcott's big factoring operation and other properties, including a tannery, a distributor of forklift truck parts, and a fire engine manufacturer."

One faculty that has made Bluhdorn so successful is his ability to move in the right direction at the right moment. In his words, "Timing is everything. You must move fast when an opportunity presents itself." The reverse, of course, applies when it is necessary to go slowly, deliberately and cautiously. By so doing, today Gulf and Western has the following major subsidiaries, all fully owned:

Abaco Farms, Ltd. (Bahamas)
Alloy Hyflo, Ltd.
Associates First Capital Corp. (non-consolidated)
Associates Corporation of North America
Bonney Forge International Ltd. (Scotland)
Bonney Forge Italia. S.P.S. (Italy)
Central Romana By-Products Co., Incorporated
Columbus Circle Investors Corporation
Consolidated Brands, Incorporated
Consolidated Cigar Corporation
Dawn Industries, Ltd.
E. W. Bliss Company
E. W. Bliss (Israel) Ltd.
Eagle Signal International, Incorporated
Enrico Manufacturing, Ltd.
Famous Music Corporation
Far East Leasing Company
Farmers Produce, Incorporated
Foxcraft Products Corporation
Guaranteed Parts Company, Incorporated
G & W Far East Pacific Corporation
Gulf & Western Americas Corporation
Gulf & Western Indonesia, Incorporated
Gulf & Western International Service Company
Gulf & Western B. V. (Netherlands)
Gulf & Western Precision Systems, Ltd. (Canada)
Gulf & Western Realty Corporation
Gulf & Western Systems Company
Inflax Data Systems, Incorporated

Islands Produce Ltd. (Bahamas)
Mal Tool & Engineering Corporation
New Jersey Zinc Company
Okeelanta Farms, Incorporated
Okeelanta Sugar Refinery, Incorporated
Orbit Tool and Die Corporation
Paramount Pictures Corporation
Plant Life Services Incorporated
Randco Incorporated
Scott-Mattson Farms, Incorporated
Sea Shipping, Incorporated
Sega Enterprises, Ltd. (Japan)
P. Sorensen Manufacturing Company, Incorporated
South Puerto Rico Sugar Corporation (Puerto Rico)
Stofin Company, Incorporated
Taylor Forge Company
Taylor Forge Company of Tenn
Taylor Forge Ltd (England)
T. F. Pipe Works of Canada Ltd.
Unicord Incorporated
Universal American Corporation

In addition, it owns substantial interests in the following companies, according to the 1974 *Directory of Corporate Affiliates:*

A.P.S. Incorporated	83 %
Athena Communications Corporation	17.9 %
Brown Company	57 %
Bulova Watch Company Incorporated	20 %
Cinema International Corporation N-V (Holland)	49 %
Famous Players Ltd.	51 %
Hedman Mines Ltd. (Ontario)	50 %
Madison Square Garden	28 %
Kayser-Roth Corporation	23.06%
Keebler Company	5.51%
Polly Bergen Company	53.5 %
Producciones Automotrices S. A. (Mexico)	80 %
Quebec Iron & Titanium Corporation	33⅓ %

Richards Group, Incorporated	50 %
Shattuck Denn Mining Corporation	48 %
Science Management Corporation	8 %
Skill Corporation	5 %
T. F. de Mexico, S. A. (Mexico)	51 %
W. T. C. Air Freight	8 %
Unnamed Dominican Finance Company	50 %
Unnamed French Group with 21 theatres	50 %

Gulf and Western is structurally organized into eight operating groups: Financial Services, Leisure Time, Food Products, Manufacturing, Consumer Products, Automotive Replacement Parts, Paper and Building Products, and Natural Resources; with each group are sub-operating-units thus:

GULF & WESTERN INDUSTRIES, INC.
1 Gulf & Western Plaza, New York, N.Y. 10023 GW—(NYSE)

1. *Auto Replacement Parts Group*
   A.P.S. Inc. Houston, Texas
   Units:
   American Parts System, Houston, Tex.
   American Welding & Industrial Sales
   Auto Body Parts Corp.
   Hendrie & Blothoff, Denver, Colo.
   Newport Supply Co.
   Warehousing Service, Inc.

2. *Consumer Products Group*
   Consolidated Cigar Corp. New York, N.Y.
   (a) Sub-Units:
      Anglo Dutch Co.
      Rogers Inc. Bridgeport, Conn.
      Simon Cigar Co.
      Suttiff Tobacco Co. Richmond, Va.
      N. V. Willem

3. *Financial Services Group*
   Associates First Capital Corp. South Bend, Ind.
   New York, N.Y.
   Sub-Units:
   Associates Corp. of North America, So. Bend, Ind.
   Auto Parts Finance Co. Inc.
   The Capital Life Insurance Co. Denver, Colo.
   Emmco Insurance Co. South Bend, Ind.
   Excel Insurance Co.
   Providence Washington Insurance, Co.
   Providence, R.I.

4. *Food Products Group*
   Gulf & Western Food Products Co. Vero Beach, Fla.
   Sub-Units:
   Gulf & Western Americas Corp.
   La Ramona Free Trade Zone
   La Ramona Hotel
   Scott-Mattson Farms, Ft. Pierce, Fla.
   South Puerto Rico Sugar Co.

5. *Leisure Time Group*
   Paramount Pictures, New York, N.Y.
   Sub-Units:
   Dot-records, Inc.
   Famous Music Co., New York, N.Y.
   G & W Travel Co.
   Paramount Pictures New York, N.Y. & Hollywood, Calif.
   Paramount Records
   UPITN

6. *Manufacturing Group*
   Gulf & Western Mfg. Co., New York, N.Y.
   (a) Sub-Units:
       E. W. Bliss Co., Grand Rapids, Mich.
       Bohn Aluminum & Brass Co., Detroit, Mich.
       Bonney Forge & Foundry, Allentown, Pa.
       Butterworth Mfg. Co., Bethayres, Pa.
       Collyer Insulated Wire Co., Lincoln, R.I.
       Daybrook-Ottwa Co., Bowling Green, Ohio
       Eagle Signal Co., Davenport, Iowa; Baraboo, Wis.
       Flinchbaugh Products, Red Lion, Pa.
       Gramewell Co., Newton, Mass.
       John M. Henderson Co.
       Klock Co., Manchester, Conn.
       Mackintosh-Kemphill, Pittsburgh & Midland, Tex.
       Mal Tool & Engineering Co. Manchester, Pa.
       Michigan Plating & Stamping Co. Grand Rapids, Mich.
       Morse Cutting Tools Co. New Bedford, Mass.
       Mt. Clemens Metal Products, Mancelona, Conn.
       North & Judd Mfg. Co. Middletown, Conn.
       O & S Bearing and Mfg. Co., Whitmore Lake, Mich.
       Plasta-Fiber Industries
       Van Norman Machine Co. Springfield, Mass.
       Wilcox Crittenden, Middletown, Conn.
       Young Spring & Wire Co., Detroit, Mich.

7. *Natural Resources Group*
   New Jersey Zinc, Bethlehem, Pa.
   Quebec Iron & Titanium
   Quebec Metal Powders
   Ray Resources
   Royal Asturienne

8. *Paper & Building Products Group*
Brown Co., Pasadena, California
Sub-Units:
Brown Co. Pasadena, Calif.
Livingston-Graham, El Monte, Calif.
Monarch Match Co. San Jose, Calif.
Shattuck Denn Mining
Sterling Pulp & Paper
Superior Match Co., Chicago, Ill.
Symons Corp., Des Plaines, Ill.

Finance

Each unit draws up its own financial statements, which are consolidated at the corporate level into the company's overall balance sheet, and earnings statements that attest to its consistent profitability and growth.

In this area Gulf and Western presents a good image to financial analysts, unlike other conglomerates. According to *Forbes,* "In its 1972 lines of business disclosure, Gulf and Western had the most specific and most comprehensive breakdown of divisional sales and earnings—Sales $1.7 billion, Operating income $146.5 million broken down eight ways on four year basis with additional breakdowns on depreciation, capital expenditures and Subunit Sales Volume in each of the eight areas." On the New York Stock Exchange, Wall Street had neglected the conglomerate stocks and in the spring of 1970, Gulf and Western sold for $10 per share. By the end of fiscal 1972 it had recovered at 34, and had a bright outlook by the middle of January 1973. *Forbes* said, "Gulf & Western (35) with a number of business areas doing extremely well, and profits outlook for fiscal 1973 at $3.75 a share."

TOP MANAGEMENT

Steering the affairs of the huge corporation are the officials.

Directors

C. G. Bluhdorn
J. H. Duncan
H. V. Zerbe
D. M. Judelson
Joel Dolkart
T. H. Neyland
Irwin Schloss
J. D. Barnette
W. W. Sherill
Judd Leighton
G. A. Smathers
D. F. Gaston
M. S. Davis
R. T. Abbott, Jr.
D. L. Fife
S. J. Stoberman
F. S. Levien

Officers

C. G. Bluhdorn, Chairman of the Board & Chief Executive
D. N. Judelson, President
D. F. Gaston, Executive Vice President

R. T. Abbott, Jr., Senior Vice President

M. S. Davis, Senior Vice President

G. H. Pitts, Senior Vice President

Joel Dolkart, General Counsel & Secretary

N. R. Forson, Vice President & Treasurer

W. M. Flatley, Contr.

Vice Presidents

N. J. Call
A. L. Carta
J. H. DeVries
R. L. Jones
E. W. Kelley
M. J. Lawlor
L. E. Levinson
G. A. Longtin
E. O. Falberg
G. V. Salvi
G. I. Ritthaler
F. V. Rogers
M. B. Hollander
R. B. Stearns, Jr.
J. J. Shaw

It is interesting to note the almost identical backgrounds of the two dynamic personalities behind the meteoric growth of the Gulf and Western Industries from a tiny company to a conglomerate giant.

Charles G. Bluhdorn

Charles G. Bluhdorn was born in 1926, emigrated to the United States from his native Vienna in 1942. After three hard years of holding a job and attending City College of New York-Evening Division, he interrupted his studies for military service with the United States Air Force from 1945 to 1946. After release from the Air Force, he pursued his studies at the City College of New York and Columbia University. At this time, he was a member of a coffee importing firm as well as being the treasurer of KSB Company of New York City, exporters of agricultural products. Immediately upon graduation in 1949 and until 1956, he became self-employed in commodity trading. Bluhdorn's keen interest in, and an uncanny perception of, profitable opportunities enabled him to recognize the Michigan Plating and Stamping Company as the vehicle that would rocket him to the zenith of American entrepreneurship. Today, from his permanent home in New York City, he sets the corporate policies, strategies, and actions of Gulf and Western as chairman of the board, chief executive officer and director. Simultaneously, he serves as chairman of the executive committee of the Madison Square Garden Corporation, as a member of the executive committee of Famous Players Limited, in Toronto, and as a trustee of the Trinity School in New York City and of the Freedoms Foundation, at Valley Forge in Pennsylvania.

John H. Duncan

The second personality is John H. Duncan, who was born in the United States in 1928. He graduated from the University of Texas in 1949, majoring in Business Administration. The following year he enlisted in the United States Air Force, serving as a commissioned officer in the Far East until 1953. After military service, he returned to Houston to become the vice-president of the family founded "Duncan Coffee Company," with a double responsibility for sales and marketing and heading the company's diversification program. During this period, he became acquainted with Charles G. Bluhdorn. Coca Cola bought the family business in 1958, and Duncan joined the young Gulf and Western as vice-president. In 1959, he became president, and in 1967, chairman of the executive committee and a director of the firm. He still holds these positions.

Present Position

Chairman Bluhdorn said that "people make companies." Therefore, companies with good management are bought and the personnel retained. How well this policy has worked and is working can be judged by his company's current position and performance over the years. *Fortune's* Directory of the 500 largest industrial corporations of May 1973 rated Gulf and Western seventy-eighth by assets. The May 15 ranking by market value placed Gulf and Western 315 in 1972, up from 351 in 1971, *on* a percentage change of 23.8 over 1971. *Forbes* twenty-fifth annual report on the largest 780 companies in America, which gives a better assessment on management performance, ranking by return on equity and total capital, price to earnings ratio, debt to equity, etc., places Gulf and Western 284 by growth, 189 by profitability and 606 by stock market (computed by five-year price change).

Generally, recessions are bad for the business community, and as to the position of Gulf and Western in a 1974 recession, Bluhdorn, the chairman, said:

> I can tell you exactly what would happen; movies? We have no *Godfather* to release early this fiscal year, but products for tv will be better. *Paper Moon* is doing very well. *Great Gatsby's* production costs have been kept under $6 million, and I have read the script for *Godfather II,* and it's sensational. Let me say for the first time to anyone: *The Great Gatsby* and *Godfather II* will both be as big as our two preceding blockbusters, *Love Story* and *Godfather I,* maybe bigger.
>
> Manufacturing? You think it will go down? I agree, but the man running it, Guy H. Pitts, does not, and it is showing a tremendous push now, much better than I expected.
>
> High interest means trouble for our finance company, Associates, but they will not fall down to where they were. They have been cutting overhead expenses and arrange for more long-term money. Financially, Associates is in beautiful shape. In this new fiscal year, it will do well, but not as well as last year.
>
> Let me take you through our commodity-based businesses candidly. We are based on the assumption that America can't control inflation. The government has created a catastrophic shortage in zinc and zinc oxides which should last at least five years. Sugar? We are sold out through 1975.

While predicting a better than the current $4 per share earning next year, he agreed that the $1 billion debt is a bother, adding, according to *Forbes,* "it's low interest and much of it is due at the end of the century. The last five years were damned tough. But we've got through them, and we'll be around for the next five."

Operating in all growth fields, G & W's future appears to be further growth, and keeping the chairman's references to "internal growth" in mind, the probability is that growth will be from within, though mergers and even outright takeovers must not be discounted. On stock market prices of conglomerates, Bluhdorn has high hopes and declares they are "the opportunity of the century!" (See Exhibit 2.)

EXHIBIT 4 GULF AND WESTERN INDUSTRIES, INCORPORATED, Consolidated Earnings, 9 Months to April 30

	1973	*1972*
Net Sales & Revs.	1,398,636,000[4]	1,995,632,000
October Quarter	439,000,000	363,000,000
January Quarter	453,599,000	384,910,000
April Quarter	506,037,000	447,722,000
Net before Taxes	83,812,000	63,211,000
Income Taxes	17,600,000	12,950,000
Extraordinary Credit	. . . .	500,000[2]
NET INCOME	66,212,000	50,761,000
Oct. Qtr.	20,213,000	16,970,000
Jan. Qtr.	21,939,000	16,711,000
Apr. Qtr.	24,060,000	17,080,000
Average no. Common Shares[5]	18,549,000	19,286,000
Earn. Common Share[1]	$3.35	$2.41[3]
Oct. Qtr.	0.98	0.81
Jan. Qtr.	1.10	0.79
Apr. Qtr.	1.27	0.81

1. *$2.93 (1972, $2.41) fully diluted.*
2. *Net gain on exchange of security of bank holding Co. Sub—for Co. debt, less, $7,100,000 prov. for losses on security disposed.*
3. *$2.39 before extra ord. credit.*
4. *Restated to exclude sale of business closed or disposed.*
5. *Incl. Com. equiv. shs.*

Source: Moody's Industrial Reports, *June 5, 1973.*

SEARS, ROEBUCK, AND COMPANY: AN AMERICAN INSTITUTION IN THE SEVENTIES

Sears, Roebuck, and Company, the nation's largest retailer, with record 1978 sales of almost $18 billion and earnings close to $1 billion, entered 1979 in a much more solid position financially than the company had had in the previous five years of operations. Since 1972, Sears pretax retail earnings had eroded from their historic 10 percent level to about 7 percent. Though it would be too early to say that Sears had turned the corner on its profit instability problems of the mid seventies, the early returns look highly favorable for the Chicago-based corporation.

While Sears' operations are still focused on general merchandise sales through its retailing outlets, it is also engaged in the property-liability and life insurance businesses through the wholly owned Allstate Insurance Company and its subsidiaries. Sears also owns Allstate Enterprises, Inc., which is part of the Allstate Group. By acquisition, Allstate Enterprises has put together a California savings and loan association that ranks as the eleventh largest in the country, and Homart Development Co., which develops and operates shopping centers.

The size of the Sears organization and its sprawling operations is staggering. Without question, it is the world's largest retailing corporation. The company and its consolidated subsidiaries distribute broad lines of goods through 3,727 selling locations, including 866 full-line stores and 1,473 independent sales merchants, in all 50 states, Puerto Rico, and Central America. In addition, Sears owns a 40 percent equity interest in Simpsons-Sears Limited, which is a large retailer of general merchandise in Canada. Numerous unconsolidated subsidiaries in South America make up a large part of Sears' international operations. During 1978, Sears and its domestic subsidiaries employed an average of 472,000 people.

The statistics generated by Sears are indeed impressive. And yet, despite the dominance of this mammoth company over the retail field and the enormous marketing and financial resources at its disposal, Sears suffered an unprecedented decline in earnings during the crucial years of 1974 through 1978. How did this

---

Prepared by Edward B. Beckerley and Reginald J. Brown, under the supervision of Dr. Y. N. Chang of California State University, Fullerton. (This case is prepared from published information. The company in no way participated in its preparation.)

happen? Why did this retail giant find itself in a dilemma of increasing sales yet declining profits, after two decades of steady, high-rate growth? It is necessary to first understand how Sears developed its present operational form and organizational structure.

SEARS: A HISTORY OF GROWTH

Early History

In 1886 Richard Sears founded the R. W. Sears Watch Company. He offered competitive prices by purchasing discontinued lines or the stock of bankrupt companies. In 1887 Sears hired a young watchmaker named Alvah Curtis Roebuck. On September 16, 1893, the firm became Sears, Roebuck, and Company. The name would remain long after Alvah Roebuck left the company.

In 1895 Julius Rosenwald and his brother-in-law, Aaron E. Nausbawm, joined the company, providing the capital and executive ability for the growth over the next decade. In fact, within five years Sears, Roebuck, and Company was able to surpass the dominant leader in the mail-order industry, Montgomery Wards.

Sears' market was rural America, with its general stores and busy farmers. The general store offered a limited stock of goods and had relatively high prices.[1] Sears' competitive prices and dream catalog were popular with the American farmer. The farmer could always have faith in Sears' products because they were assured with a guarantee.

The tremendous increase in sales brought expansion and encouraged vertical integration. When products could not be purchased at a suitable price an interest was often purchased in a factory that supplied these goods. By 1918 Sears had a financial investment in over thirty factories. Part ownership was important to Sears; it could guarantee a steady source of supply, and Sears could often increase the efficiency of the operation.

Richard Sears had organized a strongly centralized organization. Even after he retired, the same basic plan prevailed under Rosenwald. As Sears established branch mail-order houses, this brought about a gradual decentralization, which caused confusion, inefficiencies, and unnecessary competition in procurement of goods.

By 1924, Sears had worked out a centralized, functionally departmentalized structure for its mail-order business. Rosenwald, in consultation with the heads of the functional departments, set broad policies and procedures.

From Rural to Urban Market

In 1925, Rosenwald hired General Robert E. Wood directly from Montgomery Ward, where he had begun to advocate a new business strategy. Wood felt the United States was rapidly becoming an urban nation, and the automobile would allow rural customers to shop in urban areas. Since mail-order buyers were chiefly from rural areas, the ability to shop in an urban area would cause a decline in the mail-order business market. This awareness came from an odd passion Wood had for reading the *Statistical Abstract of the United States.* Other companies, such as J. C. Penny, were already exploiting the small-town market. Wood felt that Wards, with its established reputation and existing branch mail-order distribution houses, could be used as retail distribution points, and its highly developed purchasing organization should enter the retail market. Wards was not receptive.

Rosenwald was interested in Wood's retail ideas and invited Wood to join the Sears organization as vice-president, through which he eventually became president. Under his management, the creation of a nationwide chain moved rapidly. By the end of 1928 Sears had 246 stores, and in 1929 as many as 25 a week were opening.

Wood further decentralized the retail organization to make the branches more responsive to local situations. By 1948 Sears had reached its final basic decentralized structure. The manufacturing units and buying remained centralized. The stores and mail-order houses in the branch territories remained decentralized. The stores and mail-order houses in the branch territories had a wide range of goods to choose from. If the store manager wanted he could even do his own purchasing, though most took advantage of the merchandising support of the home office.

Wood approached the retail market by locating stores on the fringe of urban areas with populations of more than 100,000. He concentrated on hard goods such as hardware, guns, tools, and consumer durables like appliances. This strategy, and the organization it took to implement this strategy, served Sears until 1970.

Post-War Growth

After World War II, the increasing complexity of production and demands of the market forced Sears into large economy of scale, which began to make regional factories less attractive and caused a movement away from backward integration.

Sears could design its own products but lacked the technical capability necessary to be competitive with other suppliers. It was to Sears' advantage to have its suppliers sell their own national brands, because it forced the manufacturers to keep up their product development.[2]

The growth of Sears' retailing has been remarkable in both its scope and diversity. Aided by the rapidly growing credit economy of the 1950s and 1960s, Sears' sales and earnings increased an average of over 10 percent a year. Sales went from $3.7 billion in 1958 to $17.8 billion in 1978. Earnings went from $166 million in 1958 to $922 million in 1978.

In 1927, only 15 percent of all Sears' products were sold on credit. By 1978, 54.3 percent were sold on credit. In fact, one out of three adult Americans are Sears credit card holders. Prior to World War II, the retail division of Sears generated over 90 percent of Sears' income; in 1978 only 65 percent of the total income was supplied by retail. The Allstate Group's share of income was about 27 percent, while everything else accounted for the other 8 percent.

Sears' international operations have rapidly grown since 1947. Sales abroad in 1978 were $2.8 billion, with earnings of $72.5 million. Simpson-Sears, the Canadian subsidiary, has grown to 63 retail stores, 4 catalog merchandise centers, and 931 catalog sales offices. Sears' Latin America subsidiaries operate 12 fulltime stores, 23 medium-size stores, 21 hard-line stores, and 24 sales offices.

Sears turns out more than 15 million copies of its large catalog five times a year, to say nothing of its specialty and tabloid catalogs. This brings the total production of catalogs to 315 million a year, which makes Sears the largest publisher in the United States.[3]

One out of every 204 working people in the United States works for Sears now, and its sales represent currently about 1 percent of the GNP. Sears purchases from over 12,000 domestic suppliers, most of whom have been suppliers for many years. These purchases are made from forty-seven buying departments located in

Chicago and New York, and supported by regional offices in Atlanta, Dallas, and Los Angeles. Approximately 76 percent of the sources from which Sears purchases have no equity investment by Sears. Sources outside the U. S. accounted for 9 percent of all purchases during fiscal 1977.[4]

Up to the early 1970s, Sears' growth had been truly phenomenal; few people would have foreseen the slow period that Sears was about to enter.

SEARS 1974–78: PERIOD OF INSTABILITY

Identity Crisis

In the early seventies, Sears reached a major turning point in its corporate life. After over fifty years in the retail business, Sears had physically expanded to all the major market areas in the U. S. and was embarked on expanding its international operations. The question then became one of how to bring in higher profit from their already existing domestic stores. Sears chose at that time to replace many of its standard store items with higher-priced goods, the objective being that a bigger profit is obtained on more expensive items. Management quickly implemented this change and in the process began what would become Sears' most serious crisis since it was founded: a crisis of identity.

Almost immediately after Sears traded up out of the mass market and tried to appeal to higher income customers, it began to lose its sales and earnings momentum. Its stocks of high-priced Johnny Miller sportswear and costly womens wear went largely unsold. Instead the Sears' strategy alienated many of its traditional low-income customers and failed to attract new, more affluent customers simply because the Sears name had never before been associated with "upscale, fashion oriented" goods. This strategy also made Sears a sitting target for the big discount chain stores, who gladly welcomed many ex-Sears customers searching for lower prices. The effect of this new competition on Sears is discussed later.

In addition to the failure of the aforementioned strategy, Sears was struck by an even more severe blow: the American economy, aided by crushing inflation and the Arab oil embargo, plunged into its worse economic recession in the winter of 1974 since the Great Depression. This had a very severe effect on Sears' wholly-owned subsidiary, Allstate Insurance Company, which suffered underwriting losses of over $200 million in the first nine months of 1975. Yet for most merchants, the 1974–75 recession passed quickly into history as sales in late 1975 rebounded strongly. Sears, on the other hand, was still reporting dismal results: a shocking 24.8 percent drop in profits in 1974. Though many Sears managers continued to put the blame on the recession for the poor results, it became increasingly obvious that a drastic change in company strategy was needed. Unfortunately, once again Sears acted with too much haste and in the process confused both their customers and itself.

Reacting both to the failure of its previous strategy and the heated competition from discounters, Sears sharply slashed the prices on almost every item in the store, from a 20 percent price reduction on refrigerators to 15 percent on its "affluent" apparel. And this was just the beginning of a massive cost-cutting program that included layoffs of hundreds of employees and the installation of budget shops in most of its stores. To add to the confusion, Sears instituted a new bonus program for its store managers that tied the bonus to sales volume.

This disastrous program of price cutting and emphasis on sales-at-all-costs caused retail profits to dive further, even as sales increased an incredible $2.25 billion in 1977. Since both the "trading up" and "price slashing" strategies were created under the leadership of chairman Arthur Wood, his early retirement in 1977 in favor of the new chairman, Edward R. Telling, was not unexpected. Telling immediately set out to recapture the American middle class that Sears had lost. In an emotional message to Sears customers, staff, suppliers, and competitors, Telling outlined in 1978 his solution to the company's identity crisis: "Middle-class, homeowning families emerge as the targeted customers, and the renewed emphasis is on product service and value, the hallmarks of Sears' past successes."[5] Whether or not Sears rebounds from its problems under this sort of strategy is questionable in view of certain fundamental economic and demographic changes in American society following World War II and culminating in many ways in the seventies.

Economic and Demographic Changes

In the postwar period, most people, after the rationing of the war years, went on a spending spree almost unequaled in American history. Though buying by consumers always increases following wars, this period was unusual in that it was the beginning of the emergence of millions of people from the working class. Whereas their fathers had mainly been factory workers, most of the young men (and a few women!) were moving into more professional and managerial white-collar positions. Their main goal was to give their children the kind of life and luxury they never had.

However, these children, used to a life of luxury, now have a different attitude toward the use of their disposable income. No longer will they buy just anything. Consumerism is the order of the day. Combined with the continuing high inflation of the seventies, average shoppers have become much more conservative and value-oriented in their spending. No longer is Sears automatically the place where they shop, even though their parents may have been Sears customers.

Another problem for Sears has been the gradual shift of the American populace from the urban city centers to suburbs. Though Sears has also followed the consumer out to the suburbs to a large extent, by 1975, 35 percent of Sears' stores were still located in the inner-city neighborhoods and heavily industrialized areas. These same areas were composed to a large extent of blue-collar workers who found themselves unemployed during the 1974–75 recession. With food and energy costs sky-rocketing, it is no wonder that sales for Sears in these areas have declined sharply over the past decade. Meanwhile, their competitors are concentrated almost exclusively in the suburbs, and have mostly avoided the declining market in the cities. Recently, Sears created the Homart Development Company, with the job of developing shopping centers, in an effort to speed up Sears' movement to suburban market.

A third factor that has strongly affected Sears' market (and other merchants as well) is change in the population mix. The explosive population growth and large families of the 1950s are no longer present in these days of zero population growth and the two-children family. A greater percentage of the population is composed of older people who tend to put a smaller percentage of their dollar into retail goods. Even more important to merchants, older people tend to either rent or live in condominiums, and so do not need the home improvement products (a large part of the retail trade) connected with single family homes, as they did in the past. A fixed income does not allow the kind of rising consumption needed to sustain the thousands of retail merchants currently operating.

EXHIBIT 1

Summary of Operations (millions)	1978	1977
Net sales	$17,946	$17,224
Cost of sales, buying and occupancy expenses	11,318	11,152
Selling and administrative expenses	5,169	4,816
Pension plan expense	173	45
Operating income	1,286	1,211
Per cent of net sales	7.2	7.0
Equity in net income of—Allstate Group	466	417
—Other companies	101	57
Interest expense	(523)	(353)
Profit sharing contribution	(72)	(140)
Income taxes (current operations)	(343)	(356)
Net income	922	838
Per Share	2.86	2.62
Average shares outstanding	322.4	319.9
Dividends per share—regular	1.12	.93
—extra	.15	.15
Year-End Position (millions)		
Customer installment accounts	$ 6,627	$ 6,681
Inventories†	2,533	2,626
Property, plant and equipment (net)	2,619	2,535
Long-term debt	2,040	1,990
Retained income	6,262	5,750
Shareholders' equity	7,092	6,524
Shareholders' Investment (per share)		
Book value (year end)	$ 21.98	$ 20.27
Per cent return on average equity (excludes unrealized gains and losses on equity securities)	13.5	13.4
Market price common stock (high-low)	27–20	33–24
Closing price fiscal year end	21	25
Price/earnings ratios (high-low)	9–7	13–9
Miscellaneous Data		
Shareholders (Profit sharing fund counted as single shareholder)	326,086	286,773
Retail stores (excluding foreign corporations)—		
Number	866	862
Retail space (gross sq. ft. in millions)	114.0	112.0
Catalog merchandise distribution centers	14	14
Other selling facilities and independent catalog merchants	2,861	2,901
Capital additions (millions)	$ 324	$ 262
Depreciation (millions)	$ 209	$ 196

†The financial statements for the years subsequent to 1974 are not comparable to prior periods due to the adoption of the LIFO method of inventory valuation on February 1, 1975.

EXHIBIT 1 (Cont.)

1976	1975	1974	1973	1972	1971	1970
$14,950	$13,640	$13,101	$12,306	$10,991	$10,006	$9,251
9,384	8,523	8,180	7,548	6,700	6,060	5,605
4,276	3,927	3,819	3,500	3,177	2,897	2,677
33	27	23	19	15	13	8
1,257	1,163	1,079	1,239	1,099	1,036	961
8.4	8.5	8.2	10.1	10.0	10.4	10.4
210	76	168	203	170	140	102
43	53	38	52	38	25	23
(270)	(281)	(371)	(262)	(156)	(147)	(169)
(114)	(86)	(88)	(120)	(111)	(101)	(87)
(435)	(392)	(303)	(433)	(416)	(399)	(363)
694	522	495	675	627	557	468
2.18	1.65	1.57	2.15	2.01	1.80	1.52
317.8	316.1	314.9	314.3	312.9	309.8	308.6
.80	.80	.80	.75	.70	.675	.60
*	.125	.125	.125	.105	.075	.075
$ 5,752	$ 5,267	$ 5,048	$ 4,673	$ 4,268	$ 3,949	$3,794
2,215	1,878	1,979	1,879	1,642	1,429	1,308
2,488	2,441	2,342	2,099	1,835	1,550	1,366
1,706	1,471	1,239	1,126	1,061	841	776
5,257	4,817	4,588	4,384	3,984	3,608	3,282
5,921	5,287	4,736	4,929	4,761	4,199	3,733
$ 18.56	$16.67	$15.00	$15.66	$15.16	$13.48	$12.08
12.1	9.8	9.7	14.2	14.5	14.3	13.1
40–31	37–29	45–21	58–39	62–49	52–38	41–26
31	35	30	44	57	50	40
18–14	22–17	28–13	27–18	31–25	29–21	27–17
267,541	270,733	270,014	267,457	262,080	251,951	253,265
859	858	851	840	837	836	827
110.5	108.8	105.7	102.2	98.6	94.2	89.6
14	13	13	12	12	11	11
2,920	2,918	2,886	2,785	2,648	2,507	2,346
$ 235	$ 290	$ 415	$ 407	$ 357	$ 364	$ 273
$ 177	$ 172	$ 156	$ 134	$ 126	$ 112	$ 110

**Extra dividend of 15 cents per share paid in April, 1977 versus 12½ cents per share paid in January, 1976 (fiscal 1975).*

Source: Annual Report, 1978, *pp. 32–33*

As a consequence of these and other changes over the past thirty years, Sears has had to rethink its strategy in the important areas of management, marketing and merchandising, and finance. Most of these strategies were developed to coincide with the changes that Sears enacted in its operations during its period of instability, 1974–78.

Competition

The retail trade has long been a highly competitive business. In the mid-seventies, with the cost of food, housing, and energy taking an ever bigger share of family take-home income, competition for the consumer dollar became more severe. As discussed earlier, one reason Sears found it difficult to respond to the rapid changes in the marketplace was simply the enormous size of its operations. Consequently, Sears found itself caught between the big national discounters such as K-Mart Corporation and the more regional discounters like Dayton-Hudson Corporation's Target Stores Division. As consumers became increasingly price conscious, they left Sears and its high prices and frills and responded more to the discounters. A few remarks from consumers tell it all, as recorded by Gordon Weil in his book on Sears: "Said a woman in a Sears store in Connecticut, 'An average-income family can't afford to shop here anymore.' Meanwhile, a man in an Illinois K-Mart explained, 'Things are a few pennies cheaper here. Do I need any other reason?'"[6]

Not only did Sears have to contend with the big discounters, they were also confronted with a host of new specialty stores whose depth of product lines could not be matched by a full-line store like Sears. These specialty stores offered everything from apparel (The Gap, Casual Corner) and home electronics (Radio Shack) to sporting goods (Herman's World), furniture (Levitz, Wickes, RB) and toys (Toys R Us). "Sears can show customers three types of football helmets while we can show them forty," a marketing vice-president for Toys R Us was quoted as saying.[7] At this same time, many of Sears' long-time customers began shopping at the more prestigious department stores, such as Bloomingdales and Robinsons, because their higher personal income allowed them to afford more brand-name products and better service.

These and other developments put Sears at a competitive disadvantage. While other retailers were increasing sales by opening more stores at a fast clip (notably K-Mart and Penney's), Sears was expanding much more slowly and selectively, since it had covered most of the high-volume markets.

By the end of 1976, though Sears was still the dominant retailer, it was rapidly losing ground to K-Mart, whose sales grew from $3.8 billion in 1972 to $8.4 billion by 1976, and to J.C. Penney Company. After years of poor growth, J.C. Penney made a strong attempt to promote itself as a moderately-priced store and successfully attracted a number of Sears' apparel customers. In terms of selling space, by the end of 1975 Sears had 58 million square feet, Penney had 55 million square feet (opening 2.8 million square feet in 1975), and K-Mart, which added a staggering 8 million square feet in 1975, had reached 53 million square feet.

In some areas, Sears has conceded the product line to another competitor. For example, in freezers, Sears finds that Montgomery Ward is such an overwhelming competitor that Sears will sacrifice sales growth and/or market share to improve substantially the profitability of the freezer line.

Yet, it must be emphasized again that since Sears passed Montgomery Ward earlier in the century, its number-one position in the retail trade has never been in doubt. Sears still has nearly double the sales of K-Mart, its closest competitor and will probably retain this dominance well into the next decade. (See Exhibit 2 for competitive information.)

OPERATIONS

Management

In early 1976, Sears began to reform its organizational structure to help it meet the challenges of the discounters. The key to this reform was increased centralization, with the local store managers having less autonomy in setting prices and merchandise decisions. The similarity to K-Mart's structure is striking, in that its local people have very little discretion in their actions. Most prices on key Sears goods as well as what goods will be on store shelves are now determined under the centralized control in Chicago. The control starts with Telling and A. Dean Swift at the top of the Sears organization. Underneath them are five executive vice-presidents who supervise forty-seven group managers in the metropolitan areas and twelve zone managers in rural areas. Next come the store managers, and below them are the division managers who supervise a broad merchandise line in each store.

In 1974, then Sears chairman Arthur Wood began the first corporate planning department in Sears' history. By 1976 the department had six staffers, whose job was to coordinate the planning of the various operating departments and encourage long-range thinking. So far, nothing like a master plan has been developed, and this has led to some criticism. Some managers contend that there is too much duplication of planning for merchandising, distribution, and other areas. With no central focus, they say, Sears doesn't know where it is going and what market areas it should pursue.

Since taking over as chairman, Edward Telling, who for a long time was the link between the Chicago headquarters and the field executives, has tightened management control and seen that corporate directives are carried out in the five different Sears territories.

EXHIBIT 2 SEARS, ROEBUCK AND ITS LEADING COMPETITORS (1975)

	Sales (millions of dollars)	*Net Income (millions of dollars)*	*Percent of Sales*
Sears, Roebuck	$13,101.2	$511.4	3.9%
J. C. Penney	6,935.7	125.1	1.8%
K-Mart	5,612.1	104.8	1.9%
F. W. Woolworth	4,177.1	64.8	1.6%
Montgomery Ward	3,622.7	44.3	1.2%

Source: Business Week, *December 8, 1975, p. 52.*

Marketing and Merchandising

Sears has traditionally tried not to stock products associated closely with other manufacturers. This has been done because Sears' management has worried that those goods are not reflective of Sears' own style and characteristics, thus taking away some of the company's marketing advantage. However, this advantage was more illusory than real. Sears' reputation for top-quality electronic equipment and photographic supplies, for example, was minimal. Beginning in 1974, Sears started offering others' goods under their own names, such as Fisher and Koss stereo systems and Kodak camera supplies.

Sears also began taking a closer look at its myriad product lines. It is reducing the number of items in its product lines from 60,000 to about 35,000. This has helped ease some of Sears' inventory problems and alleviate confusion on the part of the customer. Sears also implemented a highly disciplined set of price guidelines to keep stores from selling too many promotionally priced goods. When Sears went on its price slashing binge in 1975–76, it also resorted to a lot of "cheap, silly promotional stunts," which further hurt Sears' reputation.

Keeping inventories at the right level had always been one of Sears' strong points. Understocking cost customers, and overstocking meant that prices would have to be cut sharply later to sell the merchandise. As Sears' sales growth declined, their inventories began to grow sufficiently large to hurt profit margins. In line with its increased centralization, Sears now requires its stores to carry a wider variety of goods and not to devote space to big inventories of certain items. This should result in a faster inventory turnover.

Sears is also emphasizing the traditional role of its 640 buyers in working with suppliers to develop unique products that are reasonably priced and high in quality. In fact Sears' whole merchandising strategy is strongly dependent upon its good relationship with its suppliers, such as Whirlpool and Kenmore.

In store planning, Sears was fairly cautious in opening new stores during the recession and afterwards. Store sizes were reduced by about 25 percent compared to a decade ago. While Sears has begun to open more stores in 1979 than in previous years, the number is still fewer than in the years just prior to the recession. This is due in part to keep a new store from taking away business from an old store. Exhibits 3 and 4 show the company's facilities and interests in certain manufacturers.

EXHIBIT 3 SEARS' FACILITIES AS OF JANUARY 31, 1979

Full-Line Department Stores	367
Medium-Size Department Stores (carrying extensive assortment of general merchandise)	373
Hard-Line Stores (carrying major household appliances, sporting goods and automotive supplies)	126
Catalog Merchandise Distribution Centers	14
Other Selling Facilities and Independent Catalog Merchants	2861
Major Retail Distribution Warehouses	92*
Service and Parts Center	211

**Plus 354 other warehouses serving individual stores.*
Source: Annual Report, 1978, *p. 19.*

EXHIBIT 4 COMPANIES IN WHICH SEARS HAS MORE THAN 20% EQUITY INTEREST

Allstate Insurance Company (wholly owned)
Allstate Enterprises, Inc. (wholly owned)
Homart Development Co. (wholly owned)
International Subsidiaries (78% to 100% owned)
Simpsons-Sears Limited (40.4% owned)
Roper Corporation (39.8% owned)
DeSoto, Inc. (31.3% owned)
Kellwood Company (22.4% owned)
Universal-Rundle Corp. (59.3% owned)

Source: Annual Report, 1978, *p. 20.*

Finance

In the mid seventies, Sears was already thinking seriously about moving outside the retailing and financial services areas. While the food processing, fast foods, agriculture, and oil areas have been mentioned, nothing has of yet come out of these proposals. Meanwhile, as Sears' stock plunged from a high of $120 per share in 1972 to about $20 per share in 1978, Sears stuck to its basically conservative financial policies, until recently. In 1978 and 1979, Sears began implementing what appeared to be a program aimed at increasing its financial flexibility and options.

In an interview recorded in the Sears 1978 Annual Report, Jack F. Kincannon, senior vice-president of finance, explains why the new, flexible program for financing was adopted: "Our objective is to reach a market in early 1980 which can provide a new source of funds for the company. We have a number of alternatives, including (1) shareholder approval to issue up to 50 million shares of preferred stock and an additional 100 million common shares, should the right opportunity arise. (2) Leveraged leases for a number of merchandise distribution centers being built over the next five years. We will continue to own the land and will benefit if there is eventual appreciation in the residual value of the properties. (3) Our two "offshore" financings completed recently which represent new sources in the world money markets. One was for $150 million in the Eurodollar market, the other was for $96 million in Japan."[8] Match this with the selling recently of $550 million consumer receivables (for the first time) and the repurchasing by Sears of its common shares on the open market and you get a picture of a broadening financial base for the retailer. Exhibits 5 and 6 provide business and financial data.

FUTURE OUTLOOK

Industry Outlook

For the retail trade as a whole, the future for the short term appears to be one of relatively moderate sales and earnings growth, probably averaging around 9 percent a year. With high inflation and record consumer debt, the economy appears more uncertain. Much of the predicted sales growth must be achieved in an environment of slow but steady growth in GNP, increased disposable income, and consumers' confidence in hard and soft goods.

EXHIBIT 5 RETAIL BUSINESS MIX

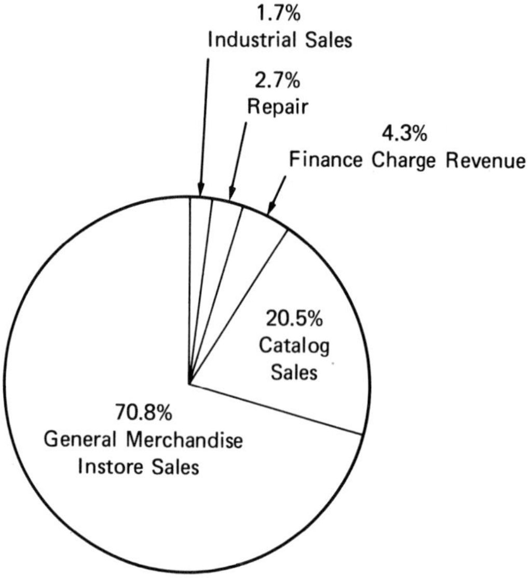

Percentages Indicating the Origin or Classification of Company Net Sales

	1978	1977
General merchandise sales (including catalog counter sales in stores of 10.8% and 11.4% and other catalog sales of 9.5% and 9.1%)	90.0%	91.3%
Industrial sales	1.9	1.7
Repair services	2.9	2.7
Finance charge revenues	5.2	4.3
Total net sales	100.0%	100.0%

Source: Annual Report, 1978, *p. 11.*

Since the bankruptcy of W. T. Grant, a number of retailers, such as K-Mart and J. C. Penney, are buying and renovating old Grant stores to suit their own operations. The number of retail stores in the nation is expected to continue to grow at a rapid pace, reflecting the anticipated economic growth of the nation.

Outlook for Sears

From management's viewpoint, Sears is expected to attain sales increases of 7 to 9 percent in 1979 and will follow the industry in this respect. After reducing inventories and controlling markdowns in 1978, Sears now plans to pursue an aggressive and sustained growth policy. Sears plans a 30 percent increase in the next five years in the number of active Sears credit accounts and will target its mailings to

EXHIBIT 6

Canada

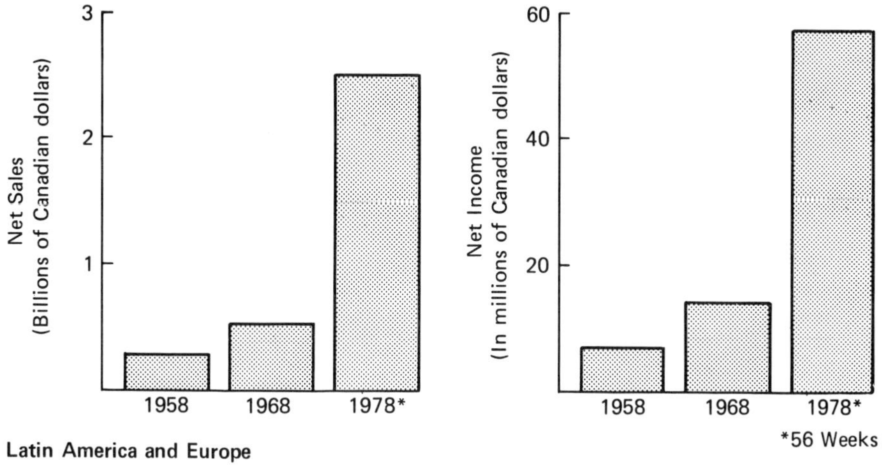

Latin America and Europe

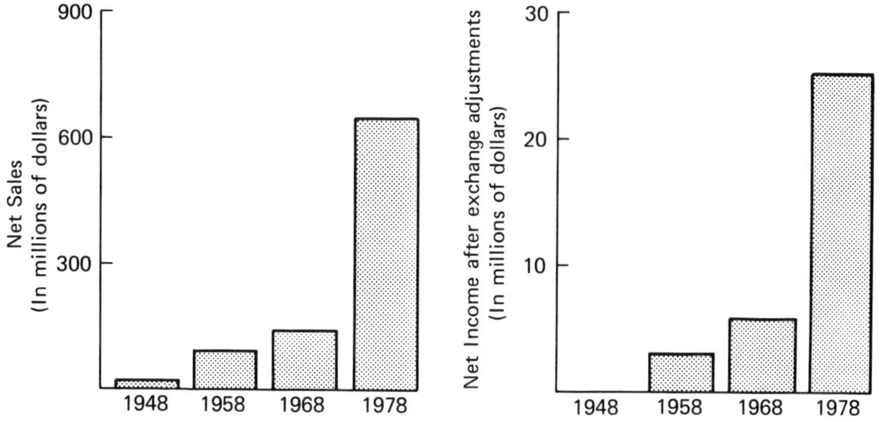

Source: Annual Report, 1978, *p. 12, 46.*

Sears-type customers. In the area of service, the number of service units will be increased sharply to build a stronger reputation for prompt and efficient service. New physical distribution concepts are in the planning stage to provide better delivery of all types of merchandise. An aggressive store expansion program is currently being implemented with many openings in new market areas. Finally, the company has made and will continue to make a series of financial steps that will give Sears much needed flexibility in the financing of its future growth.

Overall, Sears' management believes that the strategy of stressing "quality, service, and maintaining a competitive level of regular, everyday prices" will continue to attract consumers in the numbers needed to make sales and profits increase to the desired high level.

The opinions of institutional investors are somewhat more cautious. The current softness in the economy, they believe, poses special problems for Sears. Whether or not a full-blown recession develops, Sears could suffer declining sales on washers, refrigerators, and other big ticket durable goods upon which it is heavily dependent. Sears still is unable to move swiftly on changes in inventory and merchandising due to its unwieldy size—a problem for which Sears still has not found a satisfactory solution. By committing itself to selling staple goods, which are relatively unexciting to consumers, Sears may lose many of its customers.

Still, many investors profess confidence in the company's ability to re-establish a strong identity and a strong market. Sears has the driving momentum that comes from being the most powerful selling force in the world. In this sense, most observers are "bullish" on Sears' ability to solve its problems. It has adapted to change throughout its history; it's time to do so again.

NOTES

1. Alfred D. Chandler, *Strategy and Structure* (MIT Press, 1973), p. 228.
2. "Sears' Strategic About-Face," *Business Week,* Jan. 8, 1979, p. 81.
3. Ibid., pp. 80–81.
4. *Sears 10K Report,* Jan. 31, 1978.
5. "Sears' Strategic About-Face," p. 80.
6. Gordon L. Weil, *Sears, Roebuck, U. S. A.* (Harcourt, Brace, Jovanovich, 1979).
7. "Sears' Identity Crisis," *Business Week,* Dec. 8, 1975, p. 53.
8. *Sears Annual Report,* 1978, p. 9.

REFERENCES

Books

Chandler, Alfred D. Jr., *Strategy and Structure: Chapters in the History of the American Industrial Enterprise* (MIT Press, 1973).

Weil, Gordon L., *Sears, Roebuck, U.S.A.: The Great American Catalog Store and How It Grew* (Harcourt, Brace, Jovanovich, 1979).

Articles

Business Week, "Sears' Identity Crisis," December 8, 1975, pp. 52–58.

Business Week, "Sears' Cutbacks Chill Suppliers," October 30, 1978, p. 35.

Business Week, "Sears' Strategic About-Face," January 8, 1979, pp. 80–83.

Business Week, "Why Sears' Profits Tumbled," April 21, 1975, pp. 32–33.

Forbes, "Telling Changes," December 1, 1977.

Fortune, "How Sears Retailing Strategy Backfired," May 8, 1978, pp. 103–4.

Newsweek, "Yellow Brick Road," December 18, 1978, p. 60.

Time, "At the Top of the Tower," November 21, 1977, p. 80.

Other Sources

Sears Annual Report, 1955 and 1978.

Sears 10K Report, January 31, 1978.

Standard and Poor's Industry Survey, 1978.

Moody's Handbook, 1969 and 1978.

AMTRAK—EIGHT YEARS AFTER

On April 4, 1979 the California Department of Transportation held public meetings in the Los Angeles area to hear the public's view of the National Railroad Passenger corporation (Amtrak). These meetings were the result of the proposed legislation, by the United States Congress, to reduce Amtrak's route structure to one half of its present size. The reasons for these meetings were the continual losses incurred by Amtrak and the inefficiency of the services it provides.

SERVICE OR PROFIT?

Amtrak is a quasi-public corporation designed to serve the transportation needs of the public and to be a for-profit corporation. The original charter states, "The corporation shall be a for-profit corporation, the purpose of which shall be to provide intercity rail passenger service, employing innovative operating and marketing concepts."[1] However, the purpose of the corporation has never been fully realized. Amtrak has never made a profit on any line or any service. During this time the federal government has been appropriating funds to Amtrak to keep the company from default. This brings up the question of whether or not Amtrak is a government agency or a for-profit corporation. The Rail Passenger Service Act of 1970 has been revised many times in an attempt to justify the federal grant spending:

> *Amtrak Improvement Act of 1973* extended Amtrak's authority beyond the original two-year experimental stage.
>
> *The 1974 Act* expanded Amtrak's scope of responsibilities. It required Amtrak to directly perform its own maintenance and repairs, and directed Amtrak, the U. S. Railway Association, and the Secretary of Transportation to cooperate to improve service in certain sections of the country.
>
> *The Amtrak Improvement Act of 1975* authorized, for the first time, cash grants for capital improvements rather than federally guaranteed loans. It also

---

Prepared by C. James Hillquist, under the supervision of Dr. Y. N. Chang of California State University, Fullerton. Case prepared from published information; the company described in no way participated in its preparation.

directed Amtrak, the Secretary of Transportation, and the Interstate Commerce Commission to submit to Congress proposals setting forth criteria and procedures under which Amtrak would be authorized to add or discontinue routes.

The Amtrak Act of 1976 amended the Railroad Revitalization and Regulatory Reform Act to permit Amtrak to purchase several northeast corridor railroad lines.

The Amtrak Improvement Act of 1978 locked into law until October 1, 1979 all routes currently in the system. The "For profit" clause was modified by the act, and Amtrak is to be "operated and managed" as a for-profit corporation.[2] Additionally, the Department of Transportation was directed to evaluate the common stock ownership of Amtrak and present recommendations on retaining, retiring, or converting common stock held by private railroads. The act also authorized to operate commuter services under agreements with a state, regional or local transportation agency.

Although these revisions have given Amtrak new power and more federal money, the corporation has lost almost $2.5 billion in eight years of operation. (See Exhibit 1.) Amtrak is also required by the Department of Transportation (DOT) to open one new route a year. All of these new routes have been unprofitable. (See Exhibit 2.) These regulations in fact hamper Amtrak's goal to be profitable.

CAPITAL STRUCTURE

Amtrak's capital structure is different from business corporations because of the large amount of federal grants. But Amtrak does have common stock that is owned by railroads.

EXHIBIT 1 DEFICIT BY YEAR

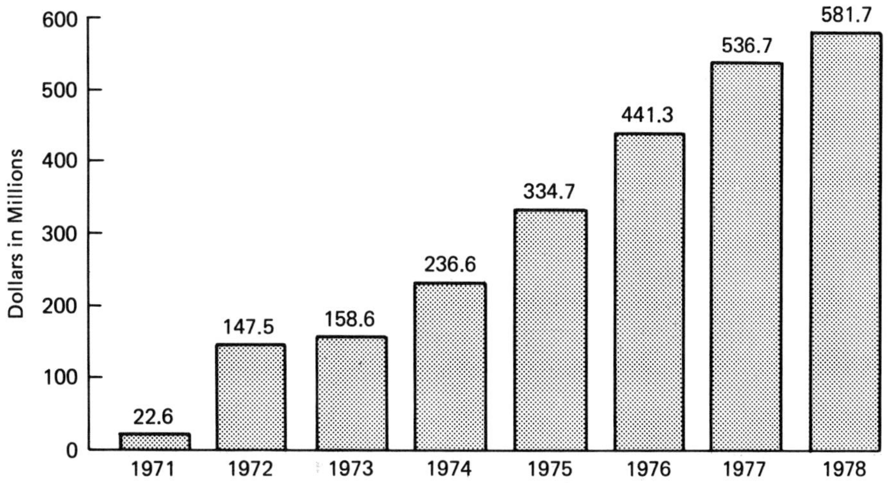

Source: Taken from Interstate Commerce Commission Reports, 1972–1978.

EXHIBIT 2 PAYMENTS BY U.S. GOVERNMENT VS. PAYMENTS BY PASSENGERS SELECTED AMTRAK ROUTES AND MARKETS

Route City Pairs	*Passenger Revenue Per RPM ($)*	*Operating Loss Per RPM 1/(4)*	*Ratio: Oper. Loss To Psgr. Rev. Col. (2)/Col. (1)*	*Local Coach Fare ($)*	*Oper. Loss Paid By U.S. Govt. ($) Col. (3) × Col. (4)*
Chicago-Dubuque	4.76	23.81	5.00		
Chicago-Dubuque				9.75	48.77
New Haven-Hart.-Spgfld.	8.33	45.00	5.40		
New Haven-Spgfld.				4.50	24.30
Washington-Cumberland	4.92	26.23	5.33		
Washington-Cumberland				9.50	50.65
San Francisco-Bakersfield	6.00	38.00	6.33		
San Francisco-Bakersfield				18.00	114.00
Florida-Chicago	4.37	20.00	4.57		
Florida-Chicago				74.00	338.67
Seattle-Vancouver	6.82	34.09	5.00		
Seattle-Vancouver				8.75	43.74

1. Represents revenues less expenses, the latter include allocations of corporate general expenses and interest.
Source: Columns 1 and 2: Amtrak 5 Year Plans, Sept. 1974 and August 1975. Column 4: Amtrak tariffs.

The federal funding to Amtrak is a multi-step process. Funds must be authorized by legislation originating in both House and Senate commerce committees. After the bills have been signed into law by the President, the money is then released to the Department of Transportation. These funds are apportioned to Amtrak on a quarterly basis for operating and capital expenses.

The purchase of common stock by the private railroads in the amount of $197 million was paid over three years as compensation for Amtrak assumption of rail passenger service. The fee was equivalent to one half of the railroad's passenger service operating losses of 1969. The funds were used by Amtrak to cover operating expenses.

OPERATIONS 1978

Amtrak's financial health during fiscal year 1978 continued the downward trend experienced since its inception, with expenses increasing and revenues remaining the same or even decreasing in some areas. While Amtrak is not expected to be the for-profit corporation envisioned by its most optimistic supporters, neither was it expected to become such a financial burden.

Following the same general financial patterns as in previous years, Amtrak's railway operating expenses rose in fiscal 1978 to nearly three times its revenues ($853.5 million to $313.0 million). The net loss of $581.7 million for fiscal year ending September 1978 brings the total deficit to $2.5 billion. Exhibit 4 shows condensed income statements for the last five years.

Fiscal year 1978 was also disappointing in terms of revenue. Despite an overall revenue increase of $1.7 million over fiscal 1977, passenger and related revenues actually declined. Exhibit 5 details the various types of revenues in the years 1976 to 1978. As can be seen, passenger and related revenues (e.g., baggage, sleeping cars, dining and buffet services) increased $25.5 million in fiscal year 1977 but decreased $3.8 million in 1978. The items contributing most to this decrease were sleeping cars ($1.5 million decrease) and dining and buffet ($1.4 million decrease). This reflects the decline in long distance train travel. Were it not for the increase in property rentals ($4.2 million), Amtrak would have had its first revenue decrease of the history of the company.

During fiscal 1978 Amtrak carried some 289,200 fewer riders than during 1977. Approximately 11,000 were lost in the northeast corridor, but that route showed an actual revenue increase of $8.0 million due to fare increases.[3] All other short distance routes carried 94,400 more riders in 1978 than in 1977 and accordingly recorded a $1.8 million revenue increase. The major decline of revenues were in the long-distance riders and a revenue decrease of $10.8 million. Special trains, while carrying more riders, showed a relating large loss in revenues when compared to 1977. This was the result of decreased fares.

MANAGEMENT DECISIONS AND POLICY MAKING

The policy making of Amtrak is one of many channels. In order for policies to be changed or eliminated the management of Amtrak must submit the plan to the Department of Transportation and to subcommittees of Congress. This process is one that takes months; thus Amtrak's plans are forced to have a long delay. Managerial decisions are also affected by government intervention. Such decisions as discontinuance of a high-loss line are strictly prohibited by the Rail Passenger Act of 1978. The government bureaucracy definitely contributes to Amtrak's inefficiency.

EXHIBIT 3

	1978	*1977*	*1976*	*1975*	*1974*
Stockholders' Equity					
Capital Stock Issued					
Common Stock $10 Par Value	$ 93,856,938	$ 93,856,938	$ 93,856,938	$ 93,856,938	$ 93,856,938
Paid in Surplus-Initial Capital from Railroads for which stock waived	102,263,415	102,263,415	102,922,189	102,922,189	103,238,223
Other Capital Surplus-Federal Grants	2,511,571,810	1,818,603,267	1,109,869,016	715,600,000	404,511,590
Other Capital Surplus-Contributions	102	102	102	102	102
Retained Income-Unappropriated-Operating Deficits	(2,487,131,042)	(1,905,479,415)	(1,368,805,761)	(927,463,213)	(589,440,803)
Total Stockholders' Equity	$ 220,561,223	$ 109,244,307	$ (62,157,516)	$ (15,083,984)	$ 12,166,050
Total Liabilities & Stockholders' Equity	$ 1,300,275,950	$ 1,023,286,255	$ 826,248,406	$ 454,358,012	$ 300,964,920

Source: Interstate Commerce Commission Reports, 1978, 1979.

EXHIBIT 4 CONDENSED INCOME STATEMENTS FOR FISCAL YEARS ENDED SEPTEMBER 30, 1974–1978 (In Thousands)

	1978	*1977*	*1976*	*1975*	*1974*
Railway Operating Revenues	$ 313,002	$ 311,272	$ 277,769	$ 246,247	$ 250,264
Railway Operating Expenses	853,450	803,435	679,966	554,761	465,001
Net Revenue From Rwy. Operations	(540,448)	(492,163)	(402,197)	(308,514)	(214,737)
Net Rental Income (Expense)	(3,695)	(4,119)	(6,017)	(5,798)	(7,778)
Other Income (Expense)	547	367	182	(331)	42
Fixed Charges	38,056	40,758	33,311	20,092	14,137
Net Income (Loss)	$(581,652)	$(536,673)	$(441,343)	$(334,735)	$(236,610)

The top management of Amtrak is also greatly influenced by government interference. The board of directors of Amtrak is directly under the power of Congress. In one case the board of directors was replaced when a couple of members of Congress were upset by a board action.

FACILITIES, EQUIPMENT, AND ROUTES

Amtrak's major facilities are tracks and stations. Most Amtrak trains run on tracks owned by other private rail corporations. Amtrak leases the right of way for the routes. This leasing is one main cause for the poor on-time performance. Amtrak trains are on time only 71.5 percent of the time.[4] The reason for this is that freight trains are not re-routed to allow the faster Amtrak trains to pass. The only exception to Amtrak's leasing of track is in the Northeast corridor. Here Amtrak owns the track and leases the right of way to freight carriers. The Northeast corridor has a near 100 percent on time record because Amtrak controls re-routing of freight carriers.

Although Amtrak reduced or eliminated service at many stations in 1978, it worked to improve the quality of service at others. In 1977 Amtrak had begun a two-phase station improvement program. Phase I had called for completion of station repairs by the end of fiscal 1978, while Phase II proposed a program to upgrade all stations. In part because of budget restrictions, Phase I was not completed as scheduled, but several Phase I programs were completed. Expenditures on station improvements (Phase I) during 1978 totaled $7.4 million. This is in contrast to the proposed $34.2 million expenditure needed to complete Phase I. Proposed station improvement program funding for 1979 was $3.7 million and Phase II was redirected to construct emergency repairs.

During the past year, 339 passenger complaints were received by Amtrak, complaining that Amtrak did not have sufficient equipment to meet normal travel demands. This type of complaint is a serious one because it is illegal for this shortage to occur.[5]

EXHIBIT 5 REVENUES FOR FISCAL YEARS ENDED SEPTEMBER 30, 1976–1978 (In Thousands)

	1978	*1977*	*1976*
Transportation Revenue			
Passenger Revenue	$246,142	$247,000	$232,028
Baggage	83	239	231
Sleeping Car	10,862	12,383	7,285
Parlor and Chair Car	2,918	2,835	836
Mail	10,134	10,567	7,980
Express	2,397	2,219	1,759
Other Passenger Train	7,741	6,112	7,317
Switching	18	25	21
Total Transportation Revenue	$280,295	$281,380	$257,457
Other			
Dining and Buffet	$ 20,172	$ 21,554	$ 18,094
Rents—Land, Buildings, Other	9,754	5,597	379
All Other	2,781	2,741	1,839
Total Other Revenue	$ 32,707	$ 29,892	$ 20,312
Total Revenue	$313,002	$311,272	$277,769

The number of passenger cars in Amtrak's fleet declined in 1978. Total cars owned in 1978 were 1,815 compared to 2,249 in 1977.

Delivery and service on western routes of 284 new bi-level passenger cars were scheduled to take place in late 1977. However, because of budget restrictions, Amtrak's new equipment would not arrive until mid-1979. The 1979 plan included the purchase of 355 new "low-level" cars in addition to the 284 cars already expected. But due to the delays in other car orders the possibility of obtaining these cars was low.

The next several years should see a steady reduction in size of Amtrak's fleet; it is scheduled to consist of only 1,632 passenger cars by 1982. Amtrak also expects that by that time its fleet will be entirely composed of all-electric equipment. Projected increases in ridership are expected to be accommodated by the increased carrying capacity of the new units.

Amtrak now has a route structure of 27,000 miles (Exhibit 6). This route structure covers the United States coast to coast. This may not be the case in the future. The Department of Transportation has recommended to Congress a restructured 18,950 mile system that would "serve the American traveling public well by providing daily service on all routes and substantially lowering the annual cost of maintaining Amtrak with federal subsidies".[6] This plan would cut the most unprofitable lines and replace those services with bus or comparable mass transportation.

Some routes have been teamed with bus service. For example, Bakersfield, California to Los Angeles. A passenger may now go to Los Angeles from San Francisco via Bakersfield. This service has reduced the deficit on the San Francisco-Bakersfield route.

EXHIBIT 6 AMTRAK INTERCITY RAIL PASSENGER ROUTES

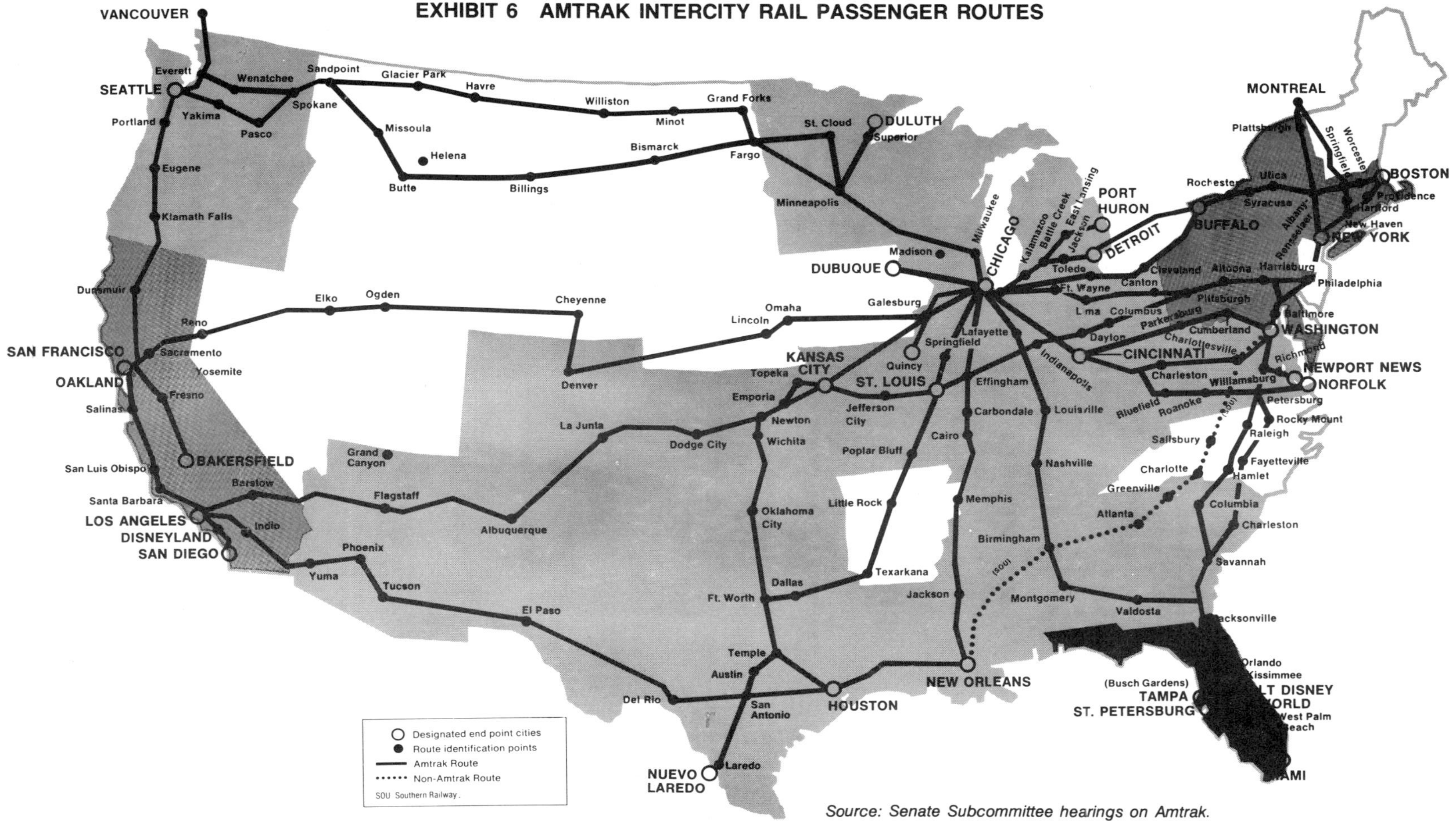

Source: Senate Subcommittee hearings on Amtrak.

THE NORTHEAST CORRIDOR

The major source of revenue from the entire route structure is the Northeast corridor (NEC). While the acquisition of the NEC has caused a considerable increase in Amtrak's overall expenses, its operations are much less costly than other Amtrak operations. Exhibit 7 shows a condensed statement of the NEC compared to the total Amtrak system.

During fiscal 1978, the entire NEC, including the Harrisburg-Philadelphia and New Haven-Springfield spurs as well as the NEC's Washington-Boston spine, generated 39 percent of total Amtrak revenues while only accounting for 31 percent of total expenses. The total NEC system cost $2.27 for each dollar of revenue while the total Amtrak system cost $2.85 for each dollar of revenue.

Of the NEC $86.4 million purchase price, 63 percent had been paid by the end of 1978. It was expected that the balance would be paid by fiscal year 1981. Congress has authorized $120 million to complete the purchase of the NEC. The NEC is also a priority in terms of improvement. At the end of 1978, a total of $267.8 million had been spent on the NEC to purchase and improve the service.

Amtrak is now considering a complete revitalization program on the NEC to reduce the time between Boston and New York to under 2 hours from the present scheduled time of 2 hours, 40 minutes. A system presently used in France is being considered to reduce the time of the trip.

EXHIBIT 7 CONDENSED STATEMENT OF NORTHEAST CORRIDOR FINANCIAL OPERATIONS FOR FISCAL YEAR 1978 (In Thousands)

	Total Amtrak System	*Total System Without NEC*	*Total NEC*	*NEC Spine (Washington-Boston)*
Revenue	$ 313,002	$ 191,295	$ 121,707	$ 115,123
Total Operating Expenses	830,504	573,007	257,497	235,784
Net Loss From Operations	$(517,502)	$(381,712)	$(135,790)	$(120,661)
Operating Cost Per Revenue Dollar (Actual)	2.65	3.00	2.12	2.05
Corporate Expenses	60,190	41,888	18,302	16,758
Total Expenses	890,694	614,895	275,799	252,542
Net Profit (Loss)	$(577,692)	$(423,600)	$(154,092)	$(137,419)
Percent of Loss	100%	73.3%	26.7%	23.8%
Total Cost Per Revenue Dollar (Actual)	$ 2.85	$ 3.21	$ 2.27	$ 2.19

Note: Figures do not include audit adjustments increasing total loss by $3.96 million.
Source: Interstate Commerce Commission Reports, 1978.

MARKETING

Amtrak's marketing efforts are directed toward attracting increasing numbers of passengers by expanding markets. To accomplish this, Amtrak has a passenger-related research program that attempts to obtain a profile of travel characteristics of all types of passengers (short or long distance). Amtrak is attempting to discover what is the best available market open to them so their promotion and advertising efforts can be directed to local, regional, or national levels.

Amtrak stresses the importance of a good, intensive advertising campaign to introduce new or improved equipment on its routes. Amtrak also recognized that increasing ridership does not necessarily mean profit, but an increase in passengers using the rail service may justify the need for Amtrak, even at a cost to the taxpayer.

Amtrak's marketing policy has been trying to offset the passenger decline. Passenger volume has dropped steadily since 1929. In 1929, rails carried 780,468,000 passengers, but in 1977 Amtrak carried only 19,000,000 passengers.[7] The reasons are limited rail coverage by Amtrak and the cost of time. Exhibit 8 shows rail is very expensive when compared to other forms of transportation.

FINANCE

Cash and Working Capital

Because Amtrak is continually short of operating capital, the company must obtain its quarterly allocation of federal grants early to meet operating costs. At the

EXHIBIT 8 TOTAL TRIP COST OF AMTRAK'S SERVICES, INCLUDING TIME VALUED AT $5 PER HOUR, EXCEEDS THAT OF ANY OTHER MODE OF COMMON CARRIER TRANSPORTATION

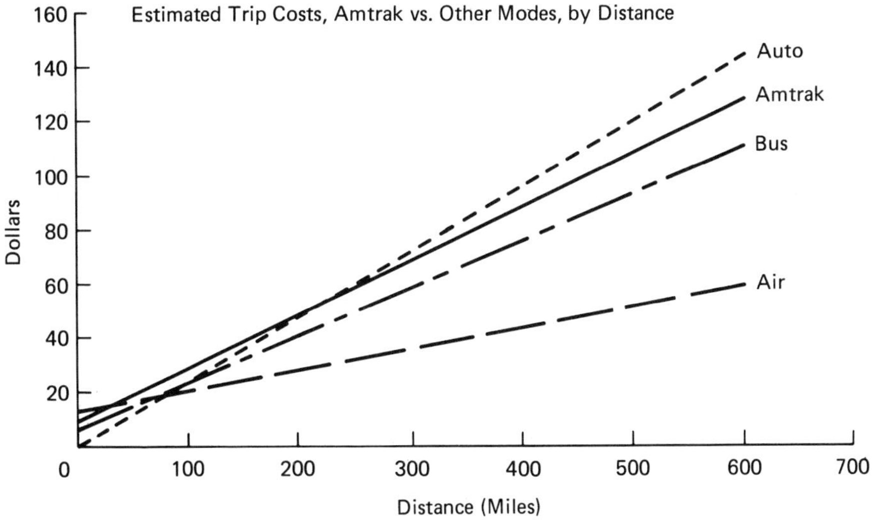

Source: Miller, "An Economic Policy Analysis of the Amtrak Program," (American Enterprise Institute for Public Policy Research, Washington, D.C. 1975) p. 157.

EXHIBIT 9 COMPARATIVE BALANCE SHEET SEPTEMBER 30, 1974–1978

	1978	*1977*	*1976*	*1975*	*1974*
Assets					
Current Assets					
Cash & Temporary Cash Investments	$ 5,639,240	$ 5,508,285	$ 14,643,639	$ 14,412,625	$ 6,798,335
Accounts Receivable	83,289,286	45,226,679	31,767,296	13,364,085	37,532,829
Materials and Supplies	64,601,080	59,863,541	43,039,675	19,713,436	7,543,970
Other Current Assets	1,066,811	1,151,817	728,748	636,697	1,392,591
Total Current Assets	154,596,417	111,750,322	90,179,358	48,126,843	53,267,725
Properties					
Passenger Cars & Locomotive-Net of Accumulated Depreciation	786,722,237	711,259,854	615,297,213	378,328,948	228,479,984
Roadway and Other-Net of Accumulated Depreciation	348,220,823	189,757,398	110,050,818	16,478,886	15,452,101
Total Properties	1,134,943,060	901,017,252	725,348,031	394,807,834	243,932,085
Other Assets and Deferred Charges	10,736,473	10,518,681	10,721,017	11,423,335	3,765,110
Total Assets	$ 1,300,275,950	$ 1,023,286,255	$ 826,248,406	$ 454,358,012	$ 300,964,920
Liabilities and Stockholders Equity					
Current Liabilities					
Notes Payable	$ 29,000,000	$ 20,060,000	-0-	$ 327,000,000	$ 180,000,000
Accounts Payable	138,120,657	117,672,073	126,745,162	47,923,619	27,465,639
Due to Bank	14,968,796	12,066,638	12,865,400	-0-	-0-
Equipment & Mortgage Obligations Current	17,757,841	17,525,995	12,755,765	3,988,572	4,989,541
Total Current Liabilities	$ 199,847,294	$ 167,324,706	$ 152,366,327	$ 378,912,191	$ 212,455,180

Long Term Debt					
Long Term Notes Payable	$ 472,184,000	$ 492,627,500	$ 533,300,000	$ -0-	$ -0-
Equipment Lease Obligations	102,536,982	120,009,366	127,170,145	88,247,540	71,691,951
Mortgages Payable	289,386,677	132,194,210	75,569,450	-0-	-0-
Total Long Term Debt	864,107,659	744,831,076	736,039,595	88,247,540	71,691,951
Other Liabilities and Deferred Credits	15,759,774	1,886,166	-0-	2,282,265	4,651,739
Total Liabilities	$ 1,079,714,727	$ 914,041,948	$ 888,405,922	$ 469,441,996	$ 288,798,870
Stockholders' Equity					
Capital Stock Issued					
Common Stock $10 Par Value	$ 93,856,938	$ 93,856,938	$ 93,856,938	$ 93,856,938	$ 93,856,938
Paid in Surplus-Initial Capital from Railroads for which stock waived	102,263,415	102,263,415	102,922,189	102,922,189	103,238,223
Other Capital Surplus-Federal Grants	2,511,571,810	1,818,603,267	1,109,869,016	715,600,000	404,511,590
Other Capital Surplus-Contributions	102	102	102	102	102
Retained Income-Unappropriated-Operating Deficits	(2,487,131,042)	(1,905,479,415)	(1,368,805,761)	(927,463,213)	(589,440,803)
Total Stockholders' Equity	$ 220,561,223	$ 109,244,307	$ (62,157,516)	$ (15,083,984)	$ 12,166,050
Total Liabilities & Stockholders' Equity	$ 1,300,275,950	$ 1,023,286,255	$ 826,248,406	$ 454,358,012	$ 300,964,920

Source: All financial statements taken from Interstate Commerce Commission Reports, 1978, 1979.

end of fiscal 1977, Amtrak was forced to hold checks it had written until the federal grants for the first quarter of 1978 were available. However, it was recognized by Congress that Amtrak would not be able to operate without additional grants, and a supplemental operating grant of $29 million was made available during September 1978, permitting the checks to be released and cashed.

As Amtrak's balance shows (Exhibit 9), Amtrak's cash balance on September 30, 1978 was $5.6 million. This balance was arrived by restating (thereby including in the balance) $15.0 million in checks that had been written but not yet cashed by creditors. This procedure allows Amtrak to operate on the float, minimizing interest payments on borrowed money.[8]

Long-Term Financing

Using federal grants, Amtrak has been reducing its long-term debt in all categories except mortgages payable relating to the Northeast corridor.

Capitalized lease obligations (Exhibit 10) are made up of leases for the rental and ultimate purchase of computer equipment. On September 30, 1978 Amtrak recorded $109 million in equipment debt. Since interest is included, the balance is shown as $159 million.

The long-term notes balance of $472 million are for equipment and are federally guaranteed loans. The total long-term debt is expected to increase due to improvements underway on the Northeast corridor.

COMPETITION

While common carriers of passengers have not been successful in wooing consumers away from their automobiles, it is important that Amtrak attract customers away from buses and airplanes. Evidence through 1977 showed that Amtrak has been unsuccessful. After reversing the long-term decline of rail share in the early seventies, rail share again is declining (Exhibit 11). Rail and bus generally have been losing some of their market share to airlines. The deregulation of the airline industry has resulted in fare decreases. Air ridership has increased, and most studies suggest that much of the increase in air volume has been at the expense of the rail and bus industry and not the automobile. If air fares continue to decrease, Amtrak's market share may go even lower.

EXHIBIT 10 SUMMARY OF LONG-TERM DEBT SEPTEMBER 30, 1978 (In Thousands)

Capitalized Leases (Including Interest)	$158,862
Northeast Corridor-Purchase	32,387
Northeast Corridor-Due U.S. Government	267,796
Los Angeles Commissary (Including Interest)	211
Long-Term Notes	472,184
Total	$931,440

EXHIBIT 11 PERSONAL CONSUMPTION EXPENDITURES OF INTERCITY PASSENGERS, BY MODE, AS A PERCENT OF PURCHASED INTERCITY TRANSPORTATION EXPENDITURES, 1967–1977

Year	*Rail*	*Air*	*Bus*
1967	11.1	65.2	19.2
1972	5.0	75.6	15.0
1973	5.2	76.4	13.9
1974	5.7	76.5	13.6
1975	5.5	77.6	13.0
1976	5.3	79.3	11.5
1977	4.9	80.3	10.7

Source: Department of Commerce.

THE FUTURE

Congress and others have expressed concern about the increasing financial deficits of Amtrak. Amtrak's 1977 five-year plan indicates that the federal government is now paying for Amtrak's capital expenses and about 60 percent of its operating expenses. The federal government will apparently continue to absorb Amtrak's deficits. The operating subsidy provided by Congress for fiscal year 1978 and the supplemental appropriation have been matters of considerable concern and controversy.

The controversy over Amtrak subsidies is likely to continue. Because Amtrak did not receive all of its 1978 budget request, the company sought and obtained a supplemental appropriation. In addition, the $510 million included in the President's budget for 1979 is much less than the $613 million the corporation's five-year plan said would be needed. According to the 1977 five-year plan, Congress can expect Amtrak's appropriation requests for operating expense to climb steadily each year. The projected subsidy for 1982 is $875.8 million. (See Exhibits 12–15).

As can be seen in Exhibit 15, the projected increase of passengers between 1977–1982 is 38 percent. This percentage is higher than the increase between 1973 and 1977. Thus the General Accounting Office of the United States considers the projections of Amtrak unrealistic. The five-year projection assumes that all routes currently in Amtrak's system remain unchanged and that there are no new routes needed.

POSSIBLE ENERGY CRISIS

Fuel consumption varies greatly between the different modes of transportation, and America's heavy reliance on the private automobile is the primary reason the nation may face a critical shortage in the years ahead.

The private auto accounts for 95 percent of all local passenger transportation

EXHIBIT 12 OPERATING GRANTS

	(millions)
Actual	
1971	[a] $ 40.0
1972	170.0
1973	9.1
1974	140.0
1975	276.0
1976	328.8
1976 transition	99.7
1977	482.6
Projected in plan	
1978	545.0
1979	613.0
1980	678.2
1981	765.0
1982	875.8

a. $197 million in railroad capital payments was also applied to operating expenses in fiscal years 1971–74.
Source: Amtrak's Five-Year Plan, March 6, 1978.

EXHIBIT 13 CAPITAL PROGRAM

	Guaranteed loan authority (millions)	*Direct capital grants* (millions)
	Actual	
1971 (initial funding)	$100.0	$ —
1972–73	100.0	—
1974	300.0	—
1975	400.0	—
1976	—	114.2
1976 transition	—	25.0
1977	—	93.1
	Projected in plan	
1978	—	134.8
1979	—	341.4
1980	—	293.4
1981	—	139.5
1982	—	144.4

Source: Amtrak's Five-Year Plan.

EXHIBIT 14 REVENUES

	(millions)
Actual	
1972	[a]$152.7
1973	177.3
1974	240.1
1975	246.5
1976	268.0
1976 transition	77.5
1977	306.7
Projected in plan	
1978	352.9
1979	403.3
1980	445.0
1981	505.7
1982	578.3

a. These figures were taken from Amtrak's financial statements and were not verified.
Source: Amtrak's Five-Year Plan.

EXHIBIT 15 PASSENGERS

	(millions)
Actual	
1973	14.5
1974	17.2
1975	16.1
1976	18.0
1977	19.2
Projected in plan	
1978	20.5
1979	21.3
1980	22.1
1981	24.2
1982	26.4

Source: Amtrak's Five-Year Plan.

and for 87 percent of all intercity passenger movement in the United States.[9] American cars and trucks alone use one-seventh of all the oil used in the world every day.[10] Presently the U. S. has only 6 percent of the world's total population but uses 35 percent of the total energy demand.[11]

There is a growing realization that public transportation must increasingly be used. This realization is based on reports of upcoming fuel shortages. Amtrak's value may grow as the public realizes that passenger trains are three to four times more energy efficient than automobiles.

A report issued by the U. S. Department of Transportation in 1974 showed that a railroad passenger train consisting of one locomotive and nine cars can move between 270 and 360 passengers per mile on a single gallon of fuel. The intercity bus also was found to rank high, with an efficiency factor equal to 282 passengers moved per mile on one gallon. The study found automobile factors to be much lower, varying from 112.5 for a subcompact auto to 72.0 for a luxury car. Commercial jet airlines ranked still lower, averaging 30 passengers transported per mile per gallon on a 250-mile flight to 60 passengers on a 1,000-mile flight using wide bodied jumbo jets.

To illustrate fuel savings further, a new eight-car Amfleet train can carry 550 passengers 100 miles on 200 gallons of diesel fuel. It would take 110 five-passenger autos and at least 726 gallons of gasoline to take the same number of people the same distance, based on fifteen miles per gallon.

Passenger trains can vary in size and, as cars are added, fuel efficiency increases appreciably. Also rail service provides the flexibility to add or subtract cars to custom fit the passenger load.

The automobile requires high-octane gasoline, the most expensive form of petroleum. Only the train offers the possibility of operating on electric power, which can be provided by means other than through oil generation. Today, more than half of Amtrak's passengers ride in a corridor between Washington and Boston that is electrified.

CONCLUSION

Though Amtrak has continually incurred large losses, it is providing a service that may become more useful. The decision now facing Congress is one that compares the possibility of increased ridership versus the reality of company deficits. The feedback received by the DOT may be the deciding factor concerning the future of Amtrak.

NOTES

1. U. S. Congress, *Rail Passenger Service Act of 1970* (U. S. Government Printing Office), 1970.
2. Interstate Commerce Commission, *Report to the President and the Congress on Amtrak, March 1978* (U. S. Government Printing Office, 1978).
3. *Ibid.*
4. Interstate Commerce Commission, *Report to the President and the Congress on Amtrak, March 1977* (U. S. Government Printing Office, 1977).
5. *Ibid.*
6. Department of Transportation, *A Reexamination of the Amtrak Route Structure, May 1978* (U. S. Government Printing Office, 1978).
7. Association of American Railroads *1978 Yearbook of Railroad Facts,* p. 30.
8. National Railroad Passenger Corporation, *1978 Annual Report.*
9. Senate subcommittee, *Amtrak Discontinuance Criteria* (U. S. Government Printing Office, February 3, 1976).
10. Institute of Strategic and International Studies, *Understanding the National Energy Dilemma.*
11. *Ibid.*

TITLE IV-D PROGRAM IN NEW YORK STATE: A CASE STUDY IN PROGRAM MANAGEMENT

A typical citizen reaction to governmental programs, especially those in the field of social services, is that "they cost a lot" or that they drain tax revenues to aid individuals who, in many cases, are undeserving or unproductive. This case will describe a program that is unique in social services by offering the possibility (and some will say the inevitability, if run correctly) of making money for government or at least of showing a profit in terms of recovering more than its own operating expenses in court-ordered child support payments. This program is the enforcement aspects of the Social Security Law of 1975, known commonly by its legislative classification, Title IV-D.

Title IV-D is a federal-state-local intergovernmental system for locating absent parents of families receiving Aid to Families with Dependent Children (ADC) payments and collecting court-ordered child support payments from them. In New York State, the program is operated by the Office of Child Support Enforcement, Department of Social Services, utilizing county social services departments as the direct implementing agents.

As an intergovernmental program, Title IV-D poses problems of management at each level of the federal system. For the purposes of our case, primary attention will be given to the problems of local management. Title IV-D is unique in some details which will be described below, but as an intergovernmental program, it has much in common with other human services programs. It is a highly specialized program that depends on adherence to federal and state-mandated guidelines to determine the proper organization, procedures, staffing, funding, and reporting for local IV-D units. Its management must be in the hands of a qualified expert in child support enforcement, a relatively new specialty, yet it must be coordinated with pre-existing agencies that overlap its goals of finding absent parents and collecting court-ordered child support payments. A good IV-D manager must not only run his own organization and operate within a social services department, but he or she

---

Prepared by Jeremy F. Plant under the supervision of Donald Axelrod, State University of New York at Albany, and William Wallace, Rensselaer Polytechnic Institute.

must be capable of negotiation and cooperation with family court judges, police, probation officials, and Title IV-A ADC specialists—and do this in a manner prescribed by federal and state guidelines.

The complexity of government hinders higher level officials, such as a county commissioner of social services, from fully understanding the requirements and problems of the various programs that are nominally under their control (and which may have staff and directors specifically recruited for, and paid by, the program). Put another way, new government programs like Title IV-D often are simply added to existing formal arrangements that may or may not be advantageous for the achievement of their program goals. As one might infer, such a system creates problems of management, which this case will illustrate. First it is necessary to sketch the basic outlines of the Title IV-D program.

TITLE IV-D: AN OVERVIEW

Title IV-D reflects the changing nature of ADC recipients nationwide since the ADC program was begun in 1939. At that time, death and disability of the father were the major causes for ADC eligibility. Since World War II the reason for eligibility has increasingly become the absence of the father. The absent-father figure has risen from 45.5 percent of ADC cases in 1948, to 66.7 percent in 1961, and 85 percent in 1975. Corresponding to this dramatic rise has been the percentage of recipients who are born out of wedlock: 11 percent in 1948, 24 percent in 1961, 35 percent in 1977. Illegitimacy creates the problem of determining paternity in order to set support payment levels, making such cases additionally troublesome.

Title IV-D was created in the belief that absent parents should be located and made to pay the court-ordered support for their children. Title IV-D was expected to collect at least as much money from these parents as it expended for staff, offices, and expenses. It was realistically expected to show a profit. To achieve effective enforcement, the program alters in some basic ways the overall ADC approach. It requires the establishment of a single organizational unit within the local welfare department concerned solely with child-support enforcement functions and supervised by an official reporting directly to the local social services commissioner. A major change from the past is in the assignment of support payments by the resident parent to the state/local social services department. In the past, child-support payments were ordered by Family Court to be paid directly to the family, with ADC payments dependent on the level of that support, which was counted as income. Now the government is in the position of the creditor. The ADC family signs over its support rights and then is assured of 100 percent funding, regardless of whether the absent parent actually pays the support that has been ordered.

While the core agency for the implementation of the Title IV-D program is the local Child Support Enforcement Agency, the program requires other agencies to become involved as well. The county IV-A agency* is required, for example, to process the applications for ADC assistance and to refer cases to the IV-D agency once assignments of rights and guarantee of cooperation by the ADC recipient have been granted. The IV-A and IV-D agencies are then required to communicate with each other concerning all changes in the status of absent parents of ADC families or any other information pertinent to the case that may arise.

---

*The IV-A unit is responsible for administering the ADC program, including determination of eligibility, disbursement of funds to eligible recipients, monitoring of ADC cases, and reporting to state and federal authorities.

The family court retains a central role in the IV-D program. Family court judges still have total discretion in awarding levels of support payments. The attitudes of the judges, the level of their workloads, and the interest of local law enforcement and probation agencies in enforcing court orders all help to determine the total levels of support returned to the government under the program. Probation departments perform the collection function.* Law enforcement agencies serve court orders and apprehend delinquent parents for nonsupport.

THE IV-D PROGRAM IN NEW YORK STATE

Implementing the IV-D program in New York State is the responsibility of the Office of Child Support Enforcement (OCSE), Department of Social Services (DSS). OCSE is divided into two sections: operations and legal staff. The operations staff is divided once more into geographical units: the metro unit, which handles operations in New York City and its suburbs, and the upstate unit, which is in charge of the remaining forty-eight county units. The upstate operations unit is located in Albany; the metro unit and the central and legal staff of OCSE are in the Harlem Office Building in New York City.

The basic mission of the operational staff of OCSE is to assist the local IV-D units in developing programs which comply with federal and state guidelines. Basic to this mission are the on-site visits by OCSE staff to examine local IV-D operations. Each year one or two OCSE child support specialists visit each county for two to three days and prepare a report on the county program, noting discrepancies from the Child Support Manual or non-compliance with state and federal regulations. A copy of the report is sent to the local commissioner of social services, who is expected to note the discrepancies and prepare a written response outlining steps he is taking to insure compliance. In the spring of 1977, all forty-eight counties were reviewed in a three-month period.

In its on-site reviews, OCSE concentrates on organizational and procedural questions. Especially stressed are the federal requirements that a separate IV-D unit be established, with its director reporting directly to the local commissioner; that all IV-D personnel (including the director) be engaged only in IV-D functions; that proper record keeping in the manner prescribed by federal statute be established; and that accounting procedures and reimbursement of collected support payments to the federal and state levels of government be administered by the local unit in accordance with established procedure. OCSE audits do not attempt to set quotas on collections and/or casework closings by a local unit; they tend to concentrate more on adherence to procedure than on measurements of performance or productivity.†

Within the guidelines, there is much latitude as to the level of staffing and the division of labor to be employed by the IV-D agency. Some IV-D agencies concentrate on *investigation:* finding the absent parent, either by utilization of the automated state and federal Parent Locator Systems (PLS) or through field investigation. (Many absent parents do not go far from their former residence and remain in the same community or general area.) Others concentrate on *clerical tasks:* efficient

---

*Changes in the state social services law adopted on June 23, 1977 transfer the overall responsibility for the support collection function from local probation departments to social services departments. However, the case examines the situation as it existed prior to June 1977.

†Changes in the state social services law now give the state DDS responsibility to determine an expected support collection level for each county, based on a complicated formula that takes into account task performance of the county unit, number of cases, and socio-economic factors.

processing of new cases and accounting and filing procedures mandated by the state guidelines. Others work on *enforcement:* making sure that absent parents are actually fulfilling their court-ordered payments. The task of enforcement requires that the IV-D unit work closely and effectively with the family court and probation department and other law enforcement agencies who serve family court orders, since IV-D investigators are not peace officers and cannot serve these functions without making special arrangements.

In the final analysis, the kind of IV-D program that a county in New York will have is largely a decision of the county political officials, who will determine funding and staffing levels in the county budget; of the local commissioner of social services, who will determine the priority within the welfare system given to IV-D and select the officials who will work under him on the program; and of the county IV-D coordinator, who will be able, as the specialist on IV-D, to work within the constraints of guidelines and politics to flesh out the particulars of the county program.

With this background in mind, let's take a look at the management decisions that must be made by a IV-D director in a typical (but fictional) medium-sized upstate New York county. After looking at the problems in Lincoln County, we'll consider what options are open to the IV-D director, what advantages and disadvantages of each course of action seem evident, and how exact the IV-D director—or any program manager—can be in determining estimates of costs/output quotients which may be required of him/her by politicians or bureaucratic superiors. First let's look at the IV-D program in Lincoln County.

THE SITUATION IN LINCOLN

Dr. John Anderson, Lincoln County social services commissioner, was not surprised at the findings of the OCSE review team (see Exhibit 1). He had known for the past year that the arrangements for Lincoln's IV-D program were somewhat makeshift but had had little help from the local board of supervisors in creating new positions for the IV-D unit. Jack Wells, his deputy, was the administrative brains in the department and had helped in setting up the bookkeeping, records, and initial assignments of personnel, but his time had had to be divided between IV-D and other assignments in the department. Wells had not had the time to sit down with the Sheriff, the probation director, or family court judges to explain the impact of the program on them, and the job of coordination had simply not been done. Wells' attempts to integrate IV-D tasks and personnel with those of the IV-A program blurred the distinctions between the two and did not square with the OCSE audit.

Even more fundamentally, Anderson himself did not know where the program should be heading. What goals should be set in terms of collections, number of cases to be closed, and net benefits to the county? The program needed a fulltime director, and Anderson decided that his first priority in changing the Lincoln program would be the hiring of a IV-D coordinator.

After advertising the position and letting the word out to friends around the state that the county was looking for such an individual, Anderson narrowed the choice down to two individuals: Joe Roberts and James Jones. Both men looked promising but differed widely in background and orientation. Roberts, 35, was a former investigator in the Lincoln County Sheriff's Department who was currently employed as an insurance claims adjustor. Jones, 32, was a case supervisor in the Lincoln IV-A unit, a ten-year employee of the Lincoln Social Services Department.

EXHIBIT I NEW YORK STATE DEPARTMENT OF SOCIAL SERVICES OFFICE OF CHILD SUPPORT ENFORCEMENT, REPORT OF INSPECTION/STAFF VISIT (LINCOLN COUNTY DSS CHILD SUPPORT ENFORCEMENT UNIT)

Purpose:	Period:	File Number:	Date of Report
Inspection	April 12–14, 1976	77-1-36	May 4, 1976

Reporting Unit:	County:
Upstate Operations	Lincoln

Reference:

Initial Inspection—1976

Summary:

1. There is no single organizational IV-D Unit.
2. The IV-D function is not under full-time supervision.
3. The IV-D supervisor is performing IV-A and other non-IV-D duties.
4. Referrals from IV-A to IV-D are not appropriate IV-D cases.
5. The IV-A to IV-D referral form does not contain all required information.
6. The IV-A Unit is not furnishing IV-D with all required documentation.
7. There is no separate IV-D case file.
8. IV-D files do not reflect current status of the case.
9. The Central Registry file is not separated into Known and Unknown sections.
10. Initial location investigations are not completed within 30 days.
11. The military is being contacted directly for location assistance.
12. No attempts are made to obtain voluntary resumption of support payments.
13. No efforts are made to determine parent's ability to support.
14. There is no adequate monitoring of support orders.

In addition, the following problem area recommendations are submitted:

1. IV-D case files should be established and maintained by the absent parent's last name.
2. A IV-D Unit should be established, designated The Child Support Enforcement Unit or the Office of Child Support Enforcement, and identified within the agency to LCDSS personnel and the general public.

Distribution:		
Commissioner, LCDSS	2	Reporting Staff: Janice Stevens, Sr. Child Support Specialist Gordon Harper, Sr. Child Support Specialist
Director, OCSE	1	
Systems	1	
Fiscal	1	
Local Agency Manpower	1	
File	1	Jeffrey G. Sterngold, Director, Upstate Operations, OCSE

Anderson chatted briefly with each candidate during the interviews and described the findings of the OCSE review. His question to each man was simple: given these deficiencies and a probable increase of no more than one or two staff positions, what could you do to improve Lincoln's IV-D program? Where would you start? Anderson realized that neither man was as yet an expert on all the details of the program, but each had some experience in related program areas and could be expected to have some views on what to do as IV-D coordinator.

Roberts was interviewed first. He had some definite opinions on the role of the IV-D unit. It was a mistake to see the IV-D program as a part of the welfare system, in his opinion. He saw it as part and parcel of the criminal justice system, dependent for its success on close dealings between IV-D and the enforcing agencies: family court; probation; and police agencies, especially the Sheriff's Department. As coordinator, Roberts would spend much of his time working to develop closer relations with these agencies and would appear himself in family court when needed to press for sound decisions on support judgments. Roberts recalled that family court warrants "were used to line the desk drawers" when he was in the Sheriff's Department; they were the lowest-priority enforcement item to be acted upon by the department. He would urge the commissioner to allow him some leeway in the use of his IV-D personnel to work with the law enforcement agencies to keep tabs on absent parents. In addition, he would use new staff positions to increase the clerical staff competence, since the success of his system required constant surveillance of records on payments to insure maximum dollar intake for the unit. His measure of productivity would be net cost. He did not "want to build an empire" of his own at IV-D but felt that a small staff, working closely with enforcement agencies, could clear the maximum "profit" for the unit. Investigations using either field work or the available state/federal automated locator systems, he felt, required a great deal of paperwork and staff time for limited ends. Solving the maximum number of cases would be secondary to "showing a profit."

Jones was familiar with the IV-D program by virtue of his work on IV-A. Jones made no attempt to conceal his feelings concerning the present state of the IV-D unit, which were apparently shared by much of the Social Services Department. He felt IV-D to be "floundering" because the assigned personnel did not see their role in the broader perspective of the welfare system. His criticism of IV-D was also managerial in tone: IV-D personnel needed to be directed more efficiently so that the maximum number of absent parents could be located. Jones felt that the Lincoln IV-D program could pay its own way or show a profit for the county through a combination of effective investigations and efficient administration. The major goal he set for the IV-D unit was to become a model of efficiency for the rest of the county Social Services Department. He had strong views on the program deficiencies noted by the state review team: he would clear up overlaps with the IV-A unit yet insist that each unit work closely with the other to process new ADC cases efficiently and smoothly. Managing the flow of paperwork required by the unit would be one of his chief problems, as well as determining the proper workload responsibility for the staff.

When informed by Anderson that new staff positions might be hard to come by, Jones voiced his hope that a new position could be created for research and analysis of county trends in ADC cases to develop such data as the characteristics shared by absent parents, the cases that tend to be "closed" (found—in Jones's

LINCOLN COUNTY IV-D ORGANIZATION

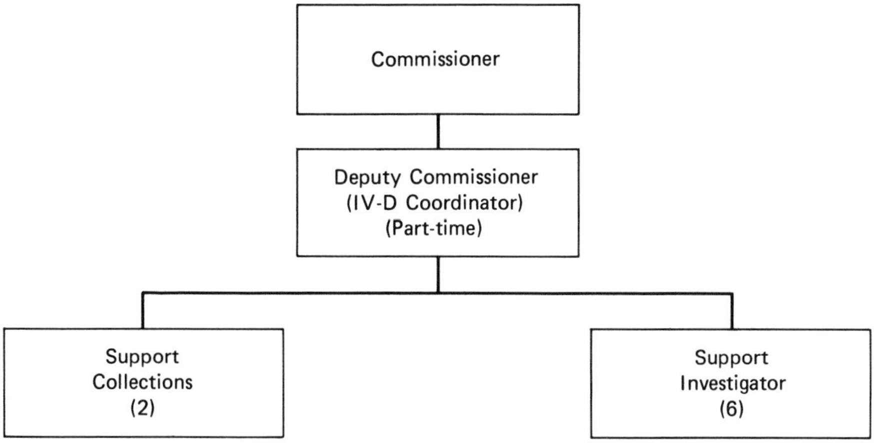

meaning of the word) and those which tend to remain open, and the levels of support ordered by the family court. To Jones, the IV-D program was a means of learning more about the entire ADC program. Investigation of each and every case as thoroughly as possible was the key to the success of the unit. His own role, he told Anderson, would have to be largely internal management: making certain that the staff worked smoothly, with an equitable distribution of cases, that guidelines were adhered to, and that proper filing and reporting procedures were established. In his view paperwork, in and of itself, was not the problem. The emphasis should be on staff understanding and acceptance of operating systems. When Anderson asked about external relationships, Jones wondered if he meant dealing with the IV-A unit, since to him these seemed to involve the greatest number of overlaps in case processing. Jones had little understanding of the overlaps between IV-D, the judicial system, and law enforcement agencies.

After much deliberation Anderson selected Jones and sent him the following letter.

July 1, 1976

Mr. James Jones
1 Main Street
Lincoln, New York

Dear Jim:

I am pleased to inform you that I am recommending your appointment as Coordinator, Child Support Enforcement Activities, Lincoln County Department of Social Services. I was very impressed with your appreciation of the current problems of the IV-D unit and your suggestions for possible ways to improve operations.

Once you get yourself settled in, let's meet and discuss some changes you think are needed to get the IV-D program rolling. I'd also like your help in drafting a letter to OCSE outlining the changes we'll be making to comply with their recent review.

Congratulations, and I look forward to working with you.

Sincerely,

John Anderson, D. S. W.
Commissioner

Shortly after his appointment, Jones sent the following memorandum to his staff:

Memorandum

TO: IV-D Staff
FROM: J. M. Jones
SUBJECT: Staff Meeting 7/8/77

I. I'm calling a "get acquainted" meeting for July 8, 1977, to discuss the IV-D program in Lincoln. I'm interested in getting your views on where we should be going and the best way of getting there. Please feel free to prepare questions for me on what options are open to us. I'm including some material I hastily put together (see Table 1) comparing our program in a number of important areas with those of some similar counties (in population) upstate. As you can see, we don't stack up too favorably.

II. I guess you know that there will be some changes taking place soon in our unit. I hope this meeting will establish some priorities we can all agree upon. I would especially like to know:

1. What indicators should be used to allocate and evaluate your work as investigators, i.e., number of locations made, total amount collected, and number of assigned cases?
2. What is the proper caseload per investigator? Currently it runs about 250 per investigator. I'm looking forward to getting your views as to the reasonableness of the workload.
3. What is the best organization for the unit? Should we organize on the basis of specialities or should we apportion cases in some equitable fashion and handle them from start to finish?

III. Of course, I'm depending on you to let me in on all the inside dope on IV-D I couldn't get across the hall. Feel free to air your pet gripes so we can get Lincoln up near the top for IV-D programs in New York.

EFFECTS OF THE STAFF MEETING

Not surprising to Jones, the morale of the investigators was low, and it showed at the staff meeting. Four of the six investigators had come to the IV-D unit from IV-A when the program began in 1975; they had no training or experience in investigative work. Two others were recent college graduates with no special training in investigations. The two support collectors had two-year college degrees; one from a local community college, in criminal justice, the other from a business school.

In the course of the meeting, Jones gathered that little specialization was evident in the operations of the unit. The six investigators divided up the caseload alphabetically and tried as best they could to keep up with their cases from start to finish. The two support collectors worked entirely on the enforcement of court-ordered payments. Al Smith, with the degree (and interest) in criminal justice, worked as liaison with the family court and tried to get enforcement of court orders in delinquent cases. Liz Golden monitored the flow of support funds and generally supervised the paperwork and accounting procedures.

Jones discussed the comparative figures on Lincoln's program vis-a-vis other counties and then opened the floor for "gripes." It didn't take much effort to get a wide-open discussion started:

> Our work is to find the absent parents, but when we do, we have no guarantee that they'll pay or that the court will try to make them.
>
> There's no way you can make money from these deadbeats. They're generally unproductive, and even if you find them, they don't have much to offer.
>
> The usefulness of the Parent Locator Service is more than offset by the paperwork reporting that is required on each request. What good are 1975 addresses and job information for finding a guy in 1977?
>
> You can't handle 300 cases at one time and do a thorough job. If we had the staff to handle 75 apiece, we could show a tremendous net gain in productivity.
>
> The IV-A people don't understand IV-D and don't want to do their required part in it. We have to handle the assignments and get information directly from the mothers, or we'll never get it.
>
> This is not a welfare program; it's law enforcement. Let's move over to the courthouse so we can keep in touch with enforcement. This program doesn't relate to social services.
>
> You can't collect from them until you find them.
>
> We're not appreciated by the rest of the people in the department.

Despite the criticisms, Jones came away from the meeting impressed with the possibilities of revitalizing the program on the basis of the enthusiasm that came out during the meeting. He called Anderson and got approval for organizing the staff into teams, with three investigators and one support collector per team. In addition to serving as a way of dividing the workload, the teams were each asked to come up with their own ideas on how best to orient the total Lincoln IV-D program. Jones was especially pleased to hear from Anderson that the county board had heard through the grapevine that the IV-D program might finally get off the ground. Anderson implied that, with the proper nurturing, this might lead to some additional staff for the program.

Jones spent much of the first few months gathering data on the IV-D program in Lincoln and comparing what he found there with data on other counties in New York State. If he were given even one additional staff position, he wanted to know the best way of utilizing it. In addition, he gave a good deal of thought to a policy problem that bothered him: should the success of IV-D be measured in cost/effectiveness terms or in terms of its mission, which presumably is to locate and secure legally-required payment from all absent parents of ADC families? The more he thought about it, the more the two criteria seemed incongruous. Paring the staff to a minimum might be the most cost-effective approach. Some absent parents would always remain close enough to be found without full-blown investigations, and

TABLE 1 COMPARISON OF IV-D PROGRAMS IN UPSTATE COUNTIES

County	*Caseload*	*Collections*	*Average number of cases receiving collections*	*Percent of cases receiving collections*	*Expenditures*	*Ratio Collections/ Expenditures*
Albany	3,197	$ 434,000	627	.20	$ 369,000	1.18:1
Broome	1,500	316,000	469	.31	99,000	3.19:1
Clinton	490	125,000	132	.27	61,000	2.05:1
Columbia	398	39,000	53	.13	51,000	1:1.31
Dutchess	2,494	220,000	602	.24	317,000	1:1.44
Rensselaer	1,495	306,000	300	.20	112,000	2.73:1
Schenectady	1,995	353,000	388	.19	105,000	3.36:1
Saratoga	940	247,000	259	.28	49,000	5.04:1
Lincoln	1,500	160,000	200	.13	110,000	1.45:1
Statewide, less NYC	115,220	9,923,000	17,868	.16	9,217,000	1:1

a small clerical/accounting staff might be all that would be needed to process voluntary payments and account for dollars. The totals would be small but the ratio impressive. Investigation was a costly enterprise, since there was no guarantee that once found the individual would pay or even that a reasonable support settlement would be required by the court.

On the other hand, it seemed to Jones that an increase in investigative staff would overcome the inertia in the Lincoln program. If the caseload were 75 to 100 rather than 250 per investigator, the results would be impressive, since the investigator would have no backlog of cases and could process new cases faster, get support collections earlier, and in addition maintain a follow-up capability for continuing cases. Jones was disturbed that many parents were found, reported missing again, and then refound in a seeming endless cycle. As he saw it, a caseload of 250 created communications problems between his investigators and the IV-A staff. Adding staff positions was the only approach that offered a feasible solution to those problems.

The staff concurred. Each team, working independently, stressed the addition of staff. The team idea was quite well received, but the teams differed in regard to the proper breakdown of cases. Team A argued that each team should get 50 percent of the cases and handle them to completion. Team B toyed with the idea of team specialization, with one team concentrating on initial processing and investigation, the other on follow-up work. The support collection function was felt by one individual (a support collector, not surprisingly) to be worthy of a "team" in itself, which would also work with the family court, probation, and police. Jones was pleased with the constructive tone of the suggestions and considered them carefully.

At the end of Jones' fourth month as coordinator, he assessed the changes in the statistical picture of the Lincoln program. They were as follows:

	Cases	Cases receiving collections	Percent receiving collections	Total collections
July	1,500	200	13	$160,000
October	1,600	320	20	185,000

Jones was pleased by the increase in cases resulting in collections, since he regarded this as the most important index of the program's effectiveness. However, he still compared Lincoln, with its small staff, to other counties in the hope of determining the effect that adding staff might have on collections. Statewide, the relationship of staff to collections was ambiguous, and no clear figures could be derived to point up the marginal utility of a new staff position in terms of the collections/expenditure ratio. Even the relatively small increase in locations had begun to tax the docket of family court, and the collections-to-locations ratio that Jones tabulated went down somewhat. More staff meant more locations, but it wouldn't necessarily mean a straight-line increase in collections as well.

Jones was troubled by the implications of the figures. He recognized only too well that his unit had little real control over the collection function, yet it would be evaluated in terms of total collections by outside analysts. He arranged to meet with

Steve Will, the county probation director, to talk over the problem of collections. Will was moderately knowledgeable about the IV-D program and very knowledgeable about one aspect of it: namely that the reimbursement by the federal government did not cover agencies like his that were involved in the program but not under the formal organizational heading of the IV-D program. Will mentioned his own understaffing problems to Jones and offered little hope for strenuous support of the IV-D program. Jones called Sheriff Roy Brown a short time later and again was told that "my boys are doing the best that can be done under the circumstances." Jones decided to continue these discussions with outside parties involved in enforcement on a more regular basis. He knew that, though they were outside his control, he could not afford to make enemies by leaning too hard on them for priority treatment. The pleas of overwork and understaffing, he knew, were well founded; he experienced them first-hand in his own unit.

A further external problem was the poor communications with IV-A people. Two of his investigators complained that IV-A staff were slow in assigning support rights and referring cases and were not cooperative when it came to sharing information that might be of some use to the investigators. For example, one investigator had followed up some leads on an absent father that had come through the PLS, and once he found the individual, he learned that a IV-A staffer had been given the same information at the time of assignment but had not transmitted it to him. Other complaints centered on the unwillingness or inability of the IV-A staff to require the active cooperation of the ADC recipient in IV-D investigations. Jones discussed the problem with the head of the IV-A office but expected little change. He remembered his own attitudes toward IV-D in the past. When he met the IV-A director, he was greeted by the question, "How does it feel to be a cop?"

All these issues came to a head when Jones received the following letter from Anderson:

Memorandum

TO: James Jones
FROM: John Anderson
SUBJECT: IV-D Budget

As you know, the time is fast approaching when our budget requests have to be developed and discussed with the Board of Supervisors. The IV-D budget is, quite frankly, a troublesome item to me. Don't get me wrong—the board is as impressed as I am with the measures you have taken to improve the morale and performance of your unit. This may actually be our problem. At least one board member (I think you know who he is) has told me that he expects Lincoln to top the state average for the collection/expenditure ratio. He said, "There's two types of people I don't much care for—welfare bureaucrats and welfare cheaters. If you have to have the first, they should be there to find the cheaters." Great, but it means I have to have some definite plans from you on how to incorporate new staff into your program.

Jim, let me give it to you straight. You're probably going to get two new positions at $12,000 apiece. In return the program is going to have to show a return of $3 for every dollar spent. What I need as soon as possible from you is a plan which shows how you propose to organize the unit with this expansion, the emphasis you are going to put on the various elements of the program, and a fairly accurate date when you might reach the 3/1 ration. Remember, this isn't a contract, but it's as close to one as you can get. You may want to spend some time discussing the problem with the Family Court judges and the probation people. I have confidence that you can reach the 3/1 figure and surpass it.

Give me a battle plan within a week or two. Good luck.

Jones began at once to plan Lincoln's IV-D program for the next year.

STUDENT ASSIGNMENT

Draft a response to the commissioner's memo that will also serve as an outline for the Lincoln IV-D program in the upcoming year.

PART V

Business Strategies in Special Situations

We have observed that strategy works well in difficult situations and in intense competition. In small-business operations, strategy holds special importance because strategy is a method with which the weak can overwhelm the strong. In international business, business strategy applies well in complex situations in which special features restrict actions and when unique competitive environment demands innovation.

In chapter 16, we hope to dispel the misconception that strategy is only applicable to large and medium-sized firms, and we argue for the notion that understanding the art of strategy making is a prerequisite for entrepreneur-managers. Given the severe future environment, strategy provides an indispensable tool with which small businesses can succeed and survive; strategy can reduce the high failure rate among small firms and minimize their vulnerability to business and financial errors. In chapter 17, we focus on the international environment and internal constraints—the political, legal, financial, cultural environment, and internal liabilities. We consider a well-nurtured outlook and a fully developed skill as the basis for developing international business strategy. In chapter 18, we provide a short summary of the text and a look at the future.

CHAPTER SIXTEEN

Business Strategy for Small Business Firms

In the United States, small business firms constitute 97 percent of the business community (9.4 million of the total 9.7 million business firms in 1972), accounting for one-half of private employment, 43 percent of business output, one-third of gross national product and over half of all invention and innovation.[1] Small businesses are a vital force in the U.S. economy, yet the failure rate among them is extremely high—78.6 percent of 1969 and 65.6 percent in 1975.[2] In an economy of future turbulence and austerity, small business firms will find financial capital scarce, competition fierce, and swift changes more difficult to accommodate. To survive and to aspire to become large and successful—the process that we have seen companies such as Ford, IBM, and Xerox go through—demands abundant imagination, brilliance, and intelligent thinking and action beyond the pioneering, determination, boldness, and unreserved enthusiasm of enterprising small business firms.

THE IMPORTANCE OF BUSINESS STRATEGY

Small Business Defined

At the outset, let us define *small business*. Under the Small Business Act of 1953, a *small business* is defined as "one which is independently owned and operated and is not dominant in its field of operations." Of course, size, in terms of the number of employees and dollar value of sales and measured on industry basis, is a distinct criterion. Thus, small manufacturers have an average employment not in excess of 250; wholesalers have annual sales of less than $5 million; and retail and service concerns have annual sales of not over $1 million.[3]

Entrepreneurship

A small business possesses certain special characteristics that differentiate it from medium and large corporations. Aside from independent ownership and small size, entrepreneurship is a feature of a small firm. Entrepreneurship represents independent ownership, risk taking, a keen desire for business venture, plus a unique style of management. A small firm thrives on a strong, enterprising, and often a one-person dominated leadership. The firm is driven by a single, identifiable purpose, although this purpose is ambiguous at times and too often inadequately defined. Decision making is greatly centralized; organizational structure is informal. Because of its smallness, it possesses great flexibility and the ability to quickly respond to immediate opportunities and threats, although such responses are frequently poorly directed and illogically developed. On the other hand, there is a greater employee identification with the firm because communication lines are shorter, and employee morale is generally higher.

Excessive managerial and financial difficulties are perhaps the most pronounced characteristic of a small firm. An entrepreneur is constantly concerned with the firm's capacity to survive. External threats include declining earnings and the disappearance of a market; but there is also the temptation to expand and grow, which can result in strengthening the firm's survival capability or can invite disaster. Internally, there is always the pressing demand of time: the time to overcome operational difficulties, stabilize organization and operation, and solve cash difficulties. The inherent limitations of financing threaten small business' very existence because there are limited sources of financing (equity finance is virtually nonexistent for small business), and short-term loans carry high interest rates. Perpetually, it seems that there is the lingering threat of insufficient earnings and cash shortages.

Causes of Business Failure and Prerequisites for Success

To expand our discussion on managerial and financial difficulties inherent in small firms, let us briefly review causes for business failure and the prerequisites for success. Of the many interrelated causes of failure, the single most important cause is the lack of management capability—the knowledge and skill that is required for effective management. According to Dun and Bradstreet analysis, management inexperience and incompetence account for 92.9 percent of the mistakes causing business failures. Of this, lack of experience in the line makes up 16.9 percent; lack of managerial experience, 13.7 percent; unbalanced, poorly rounded experience, 21.1 percent; and incompetence, 41.2 percent.[4]

MANAGEMENT INEXPERIENCE AND INCOMPETENCY Management inexperience and incompetence is a direct reflection of a lack of preparation and training. Too often, small business is initiated without advanced planning and thorough analysis of the business itself. An entrepreneur who lacks vision and perspective, who is incapable of developing the required management knowledge and skill, who is beset by personnel and financial difficulties, usually finds himself/herself unprepared to manage.

Typically, he/she has unreserved enthusiasm, but lacks direction and consistency. He/she possesses unbounded energy but finds it often misplaced and self-destructive in the long run. He/she excels in a narrow sphere of technical significance but is totally unaware of planning, controlling, and directing the total organization. Too often, he/she is negligent in financial management, failing to meet obligations and develop sources of finance. Thus, the resulting inability to counter competition, the lack of capital, heavy borrowing, poor accounting, premature expansion, and declining sales and earnings are visible indicators of a failing small firm.

REASONS FOR SUCCESS There can be at least three measurable sources of success: (1) the ability to identify and exploit genuine business opportunities; (2) the capacity to capitalize on small business firms' unique competitive advantages for business development; and (3) the consistent acquisition of managerial knowledge and skill.

A genuine business opportunity[5] is one in which a real need exists, which can either be stimulated or created, for the proposed goods or services that can be produced in sufficient volume with a price high enough to operate at a profit. An improved economic climate and increases in consumer purchasing power offer business opportunities. Consumer changes in taste and life style (an increase in leisure time, for example), technological development, geographical expansion of population centers, and the general trends requiring small business firms to serve large corporations—all these dynamic economic and social forces present innovative entrepreneurs with potentially genuine opportunities.

IDENTIFYING COMPETITIVE EDGE Most crucial, however, is the capacity to capitalize on the company's competitive edge. Small business firms must thoroughly assess the general advantages inherent in being small and must examine the particulars of each competitive situation. A small firm can uniquely serve certain markets in which larger corporations are reluctant to compete. Because of its flexibility and proximity to customers, a small firm can also serve certain customers' peculiar demands. In addition, in most industries, there are enough marginal operators whose inferior products, higher prices, and poor services invite new, successful competition.

Last, but most important, a successful entrepreneur consistently acquires and expands his/her managerial ability. Through the long and laborious period of preparation, the entrepreneur's managerial ability expands. As the chief executive officer, he/she learns the necessity for managing time, building a management team, and motivating people to assume delegated responsibilities.

Barriers to Planning

Small companies have been found to be deficient in planning of all types and are greatly handicapped in practicing strategy making. There is either a total absence of both or the partial practice of one without the other. Reasons are numerous; among them several stand out.[6]

1. The entrepreneur mode of management defies planning.
2. Lack of competent people, resources, and time, all subject to work pressure, renders planning inefficient and impractical.
3. The centripetal character of small firms rejects externalization, an orientation requiring firms to look to the outside world.
4. Planning deficiencies are found in small companies that have a propensity to become exploiters rather than creators of opportunity.

Constraints in Small Businesses

Aside from barriers to planning, there are the real constraints peculiar to small business firms. Unless they are correctly recognized and dealt with squarely, strategy thus developed will not be effective. These constraints can be stated as follows:

1. Unlike publicly held corporations, whose ownership and management are separated, small business combines ownership and management in the hands of the owner(s). Small firms are therefore often deprived of professional management. The owners' personal goals and business objectives are often vague and restrictive.
2. Small businesses have peculiar characteristics, which defy ordinary and textbook solutions. For example, in a large corporation, a president or a manager can be removed. In a small firm, the removal of the owner or a partner is improbable or impractical. Similarly, additional help can be hired, managers developed, and new functions added in large firms. However, in a small firm, overhead expenses restrict hiring and training, and financial constraints limit management options. Small firms must face these difficult realities in their search for solutions.
3. Small business is heavily restricted by its management lack of depth and by its preoccupation with survival. Management is reluctant to accept sound management practices and is impatient with solutions that take time to effect.

Barriers to planning and constraints are the realities of small firms. So are the high failure rate and large opportunities. Small-business strategy is designed to overcome difficulties and solve problems. In reality, business strategy is far more important to a small firm than a large one. A small firm is fragile and vulnerable. It cannot afford to make major mistakes, and it lacks sustaining power to recover. Strategy provides a solid foundation for survival, the ability to move swiftly once a genuine opportunity exists, and to consolidate quickly once anticipated threats become apparent.

A SIMPLIFIED APPROACH

In chapter 1, we defined strategy making as an activity embracing strategic planning, strategic formulation, and strategic management. Size does not alter the concept, nor its substance.[7] Size, however, decisively affects the method through which the process is performed. Bearing in mind the barriers and constraints, a simplified approach as discussed here will improve chances of developing and executing strategies in small firms.

Organizing and Administering Strategic Planning

Organizationally, there are five units involved in strategy making (see chapter 3). In a very small company, some of these units may not exist; for example, the board of directors, the planning staff, or the committee. Let us briefly review each of these functions and discuss alternate forms of organization to carry out these activities.

THE BOARD OF DIRECTORS In the absence of a board, it is desirable to have an advisory board composed of owners, a responsible consultant on general management, or a CPA. They can form a sounding board as well as an advisory body on strategy.

THE ENTREPRENEUR-PRESIDENT The president is the driving force behind the development and implementation of business strategy. In a small company, he/she is often the planner and strategist, but he/she must not involve himself/herself with the chore of information collection and preliminary analysis. He/she must remain the manager of the firm, not the operating officer, nor its planner. His/her chief task is to inspire others to think and act strategically and direct strategic operations.

THE PLANNING STAFF When cost benefits justify the establishment of a planning unit, it must be small. In the absence of a planning staff, the president can designate an individual, a senior associate, or a line manager to perform duties of a senior planner.

THE EXECUTIVE COMMITTEE Small firms must practice team building and stimulate group action. Whatever the name of the committee and whatever the format, the president must learn how to use committee work to expeditiously and purposefully assist in deliberating strategic decisions.

LINE MANAGEMENT Line management's participation is mandatory. Small companies are generally operations oriented, ''operating'' being their greatest skill. In companies whose marketing, technology, or financial functions are a constituent part of the operations, any one of the line managers can act as planning staff to the president. At the departmental level, functional strategies and tactical planning is a part of the strategic plan.

Administering Small-Business Planning

In administering planning in a small firm, we suggest three phases of activity. Each phase is shortened in duration and reduced in content, compared to the phases as discussed in chapter 3. Individual consultation is frequent, and a streamlined round-table approach is judiciously adopted.

INITIATION-GUIDELINE PHASE The president initiates the planning cycle by setting forth in writing his/her views on the company's operations, its tasks and problems, market trends, and near-term outlook. At scheduled meetings, a tentative set of company objectives is established, and the alternative levels of achievements and resource requirements are defined.

DEVELOPMENT-REVIEW PHASE During the critical development-review phase, individual consultation among managers and the president, conferences within each department, and a scheduled planning conference will be held to discuss the company's total approach and each department's plans of action.

APPROVAL-RELEASE PHASE Planning in small companies should focus on short-range goals. The immediate one-year plan receives the closest scrutiny, and a two-year extension is adequate for most small companies. In a small firm, there is only one plan. Physically, the plan is put in one document: the strategic portion concerning the company and the operating portion concentrating on the monthly and quarterly operating plans of line departments.

Strategic Planning and Formulation

In small firms, the five-step process discussed in chapter 4 is equally applicable. The process is restated here for small businesses.

ENVIRONMENTAL ANALYSIS The purpose of business environmental analysis is the identification of opportunities and threats. A genuine opportunity exists when it offers a definite competitive edge to small firms and when its attainment is within the reasonable limit of the firm's capacity. Potential threats can come from all directions: customers, competitors, suppliers, and creditors. Studies of the economic, sociopolitical, industrial, and technology forecasts are necessary, but they must be limited to those areas of true concern.

INTERNAL ASSESSMENT The purpose of internal assessment is to accurately assess the firm's capacity by identifying its strengths and weaknesses.[8] Management capability holds special importance to a small firm.[9] An entrepreneur must practice self-appraisal in examining his/her managerial ability, and the organization's effectiveness. Are responsibilities clearly assigned, authority delegated? Are important policies established? Are managers effective in planning and control, and are they skillful in handling human relations?

OBJECTIVE SETTING Objective setting not only forces management to occasionally question the firm's purpose and objectives, but it obliges owners to study their personal desires. The difference between making a living, building a thriving business for resale, or expanding ownership to become large, fundamentally dictates the thrust of strategy. Furthermore, the level of business objectives must be in concert with the firm's financial and management capabilities.

STRATEGIC GUIDELINES AND SITUATION STUDY We view formulating business strategy in two phases: the preliminary phase, and the formulation phase. In a small firm, actions taken in the preliminary phase prevent one-person domination by the entrepreneur-president. During the formulation phase, serious thoughts are given to strategic alternatives, course options, and resource development.

THE STRATEGIC PLAN Business strategy should be simple, versatile, and action oriented. It is simple because of the size of and the narrow options available to a small firm. It must be made versatile because ever-changing situations require mobility and flexibility to act. Strategy must also be action oriented, keeping the writing at a minimum but specifying actions in greater detail.

Strategic Management

The various aspects of strategic management discussed in part four of this text apply to small business operations. There are, however, a few points of special importance:

1. Organizing for tasks and strategic alternatives is the prime concern of small business firms. Structurally, departments are simply organized to pursue a specific strategy. Each department is assigned specific tasks and goals. The organization as a whole is guided by a simply stated objective, broken down by departmental tasks and a clearly defined program of action.
2. The central task of strategy making rests with the entrepreneur-president. In a small firm, the president is greatly limited by the lack of competent personnel. He/she generally works in a number of capacities and his/her time is largely consumed in a loosely organized fashion, lacking defined responsibilities, policies, and systems to direct efficient operations. In this situation, delegation is difficult, and management is chaotic and conflict-ridden.
3. Continual organization development is another prerequisite in strategic management. All small business firms are primarily concerned with advancing to a certain position of stability. A stabilized position reflects the size of a firm that has acquired appropriate economic power in the marketplace and that can resist major financial and organization disruptions. A stabilized position also shows the firm's readiness for pursuing aggressive growth. Hence, a small firm advances from one threshold to the next. Each threshold in turn poses management challenges. Such challenges present at least three tasks as important. First, the entrepreneur determines to advance his/her management knowledge and skill. Second, management makes concerted effort to extend the firm's total management capability. Third, the organization practices human resource development.

STRATEGIC ALTERNATIVES IN SMALL BUSINESS FIRMS

Basic Strategies

We have established that all business firms are required to solve growth, profit instability, and survival problems. In small firms, however, the search for stability is the single most pressing task; developing the capacity to survive is a constant concern. Growth, however, is a defensive measure during the early stages of development because well-guarded growth is in itself necessary to survival. Growth of a totally aggressive type is, on the other hand, not to be sought until stability has been achieved. We shall discuss the three strategic alternatives—stability, survival, and growth—and briefly discuss strategic considerations for initiating, operating, and expanding a business.

STABILITY STRATEGY A stability strategy is directed at achieving early stabilization of sales and profits and developing order and stability within the organization. A cardinal rule for small firms to observe is to move slowly and cautiously. Overoptimism and lack of conviction can result in overextending the company's position and a loss of resources and time. A constant shift of a company's position diverts its concentration from its primary market and slows down the process of securing a foothold in the prime area. Stability strategy thus calls for decisive actions in marketing, production, finance, and management areas.[10]

Marketing actions must be directed at quickly developing a firm's competitive position—the niche necessary to assure its early success—the customers' firm acceptance of the company's products and services, and the fortification of an established position in the marketplace. Once that niche or that competitive edge is identified, it must be fully exploited. For example, when a company chooses to compete on technological basis, technological development is crucial to its marketing effort. Production is a critical function in many small firms. Here, low-cost production and the ability to quickly respond to customers' schedule changes and to sustain losses during periods of low production are the strategic considerations.

One of the most deficient areas of small-business management is finance. A stabilized financial position begins with a good accounting system and is evidenced by its capacity to remain solvent, to develop limited sources of funds, and to practice profit planning and control.[11] Effective management to ensure orderly functioning of the organization and proper development and motivation of employees is, after all, the prerequisite of organizational stability. In meeting adverse situations of profit instability, the firm can resort to retrenchment, turnaround, and stabilization strategies to restore profit and achieve quick recovery.

SURVIVAL STRATEGY Survival strategy complements stability strategy in that management is constantly in search of means to increase the firm's capacity to survive. A fragile product/market position without a firm foothold in the marketplace constitutes a constant threat. The inability to obtain customers' genuine acceptance of the firm's products and services and to thwart competitors' encroachment can cause depressed sales. Above all, a firm's sustaining power in maintaining operations in good as well as bad times is a true test of its capacity to survive. Internally, liquidity is the key. A quick thrust into the marketplace, a decision to lease or purchase, make or buy, or a seemingly attractive growth opportunity that can overtax the firm's resources must be carefully evaluated.

A small firm must be especially vigilant against inventory buildup that is not easily converted into cash. It should make constant effort to prune unprofitable products, services, or customers, and scrutinize cost control practices and overhead expenses. Survival strategy makes certain that business decisions and company actions are taken in the interest of increasing the firm's capacity to survive, by insuring against property damage or theft, third-party liability, and death or disability, for example.

GROWTH STRATEGY Sound growth that produces profitability through time and expands the firm's survival capacity at any point in time is always a reasonable goal for a business firm. For a small company, growth strategy applies to all stages of development. During the early stages, growth is defensive by nature, purposefully instituted to enlarge the firm's capacity to survive and achieve early stability.[12] A defensive growth strategy is designed to seize immediate opportunities through a series of short-term, exploratory, and quick actions without undue commitment of the company's limited resources (financial and personnel) and restricted capacity (production, marketing, and management). A sudden appearance of a favorable, economic or marketing opportunity, a firm contractual possibility, or a special order for a production run are such opportunities.

Once stability is well-established and readiness position is in order, the company pursues aggressive growth strategy. Growth strategy takes a great amount of innovative thinking and good management. Readers are reminded of the pitfalls of the growth syndrome, the need for mastering the five subgrowth strategies, and the difficulties inherent in each stage of growth. At this point, let us add a note of caution. In recent years, capital formulation in general and venture capital in particular for small business expansion are difficult to obtain. A task force study prepared by the U.S. Small Business Administration revealed important data.[13] Referring to the chart developed by the task force (see figure 16.1), we can see that public financing is not available to a firm until it has reached a revenue level of $10 million. Costs for the private sources are so high that it is almost impossible to obtain funds. The chart also notes the varying lengths of time it takes for a firm to reach the different stages of growth.

Strategies in Initiating, Operating, and Expanding Businesses

There are special situations when strategy is important to small-business survival: at the time of initiation; during operations for reaching stability; and when expanding.

STRATEGIC CONSIDERATIONS IN INITIATING A BUSINESS[14] The success of a new business is fundamentally affected by decisions made during its formative years. A business founded on a solid base is offered a better chance of surviving. Early, sound decisions in initiating, organizing, and operating a business will decisively strengthen the initial growth. During these formative years, at least four decision areas require special attention.

The Decision for Self-Employment Most business people cite the desire for independence and higher income as major reasons for "going it alone." To succeed in a new business of one's own making, however, takes more than desire or aspiration. First, a business-person-to-be must truly understand the limitations of business ownership. Greater risks, irregular income, longer working hours, higher personal sacrifices, and a constant fear of failure are truly the hazards of small-business ownership.

Second, entrepreneurship calls for unique personality traits. An entrepreneur is a gambler and an achiever. He/she is decisive, versatile, and has the ability to communicate and direct others. Regarding these attributes, a soul-searching and objective self-analysis is necessary. A business person must perform honest self-appraisal. What are the hidden reasons for "going-it-alone"? What precisely is the business to be? What are his/her goals? What about his/her family's attitude toward the undertaking? And how is he/she rated against those limitations and attributes? Once the decision is positive, he/she should develop a plan to learn the business and acquire experience, diligently working through a preparatory period during which he/she achieves full readiness both mentally and physically.

The Method of Entry There are at least three ways of initiating a business:[15] (1) buying a going concern; (2) building from scratch; and (3) acquiring a franchise. The selection is one of convenience and economics. Buying a successful going concern appears least hazardous, but it can be complicated—misjudgment leading to buying a failing business, or securing one at an inflated price, for example. Starting a new business from scratch is convenient to an entrepreneur who has a new idea, new technology, or a genuine business opportunity, but it increases uncertainty of success. Franchising is also attractive. It is less risky, but is restrictive in operation and profits. In any case, a thorough analysis of the market potential and trends, product acceptance, competition, return on invest-

FIGURE 16.1 LIFE CYCLE OF A NEW ENTERPRISE MODEL OF A GROWING AND SUCCESSFUL COMPANY, 1975–1976 FINANCIAL MARKET CONDITIONS

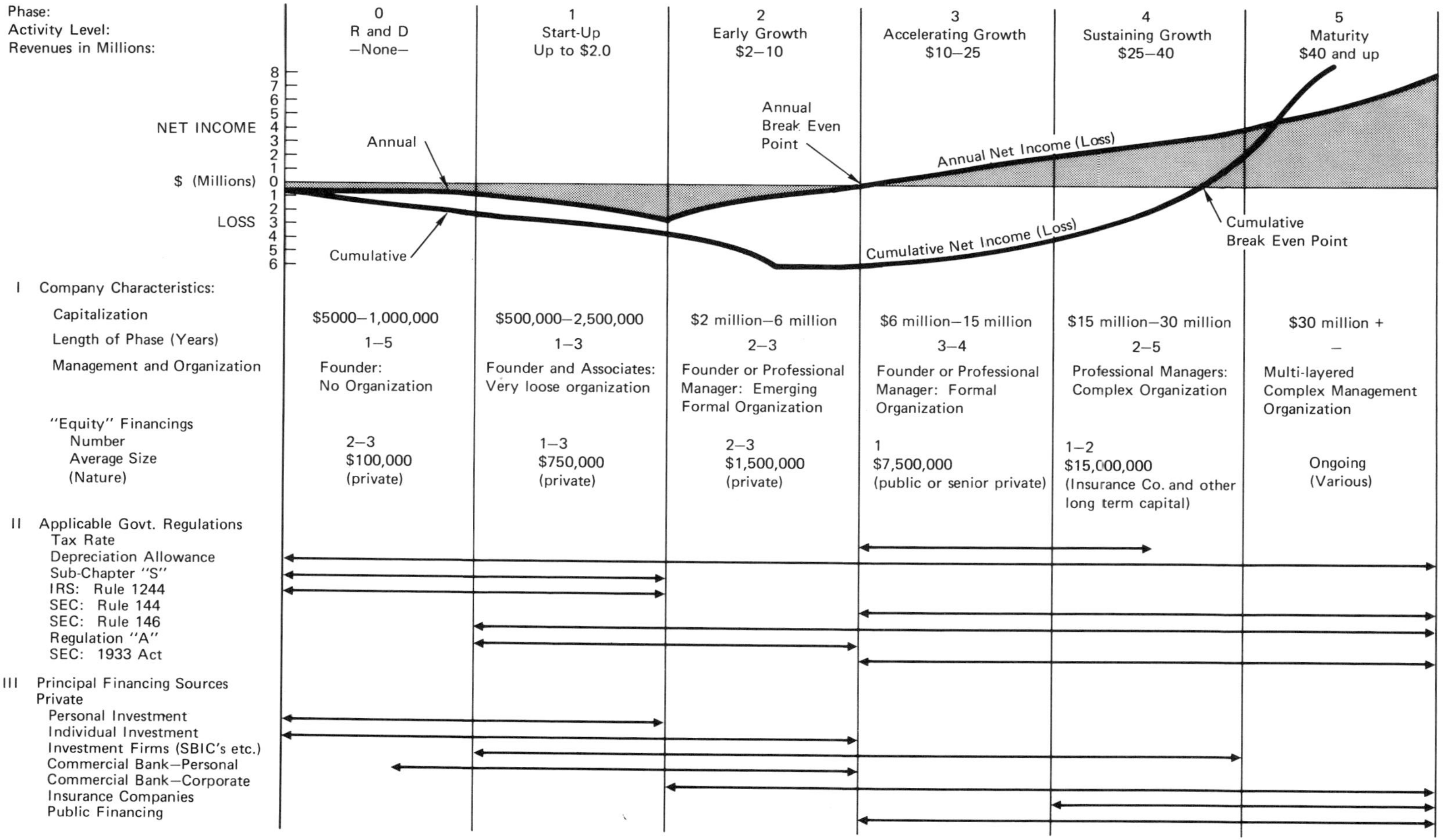

ment, risks, and probability of success and failure is absolutely essential for making comparisons before making the choice.

The Business Plan The business plan is a summation of the firm's strategy. It is not only necessary for obtaining funds, but it is also a blueprint to direct the systematic development of the business. A good business plan must give adequate treatment to the following points: (1) the legal form of the business, its principals, the name of the firm, and its capitalization; (2) specific business objectives; (3) sales forecasts and projection of sales, earnings, and cash; (4) location and physical facilities; (5) financial requirements and uses of funds projection; and (6) organization and management.

Financing the Business Financing the initial capital requirement—the total of owner's equity and borrowed funds plus accepted credits—calls for a comprehensive preparation of a business plan and the active search for sources and their development. Generally, the owner's equity plus that from family, friends, and associates constitutes about two-thirds of the total capital. Banks, prospective creditors, and other sources of financial assistance, the Small Business Administration, for example, provide the remaining third. Financial capital is used for purchase of fixed assets, for working capital, and for contingency funds to meet unexpected costs and expenses. Over- or undercapitalization caused by inaccurate and incomplete estimation of costs and expenses is symptomatic of poor financial planning and management and is the prime reason for early failure.[16]

STRATEGIC CONSIDERATIONS FOR OPERATING A BUSINESS The immediate objective of operating a new business is to enhance the firm's capacity and to stabilize its organization and operation. The key lies in management, especially in three areas: (1) the entrepreneur's managerial ability; (2) personnel development; and (3) the stabilization and improvement of the operation.

The Managerial Capability of the Entrepreneur The general expansion of the managerial capability of the entrepreneur begins with a conscientious effort to acquire knowledge and skill in management.[17] The entrepreneur must develop a small but viable organization, minimum in structure but precise enough to formulate those policies most essential to ensure a quick, flexible operation. He/she learns the art of strategy making, acquires skill to delegate, and cultivates a serious business attitude—a strong sense of obligations in meeting business commitments to customers, suppliers, and creditors.

Personnel Development Because small business firms are noted for their inability to draw well-trained, competent people and because they are labor-intensive, it is imperative that each company pay special attention to personnel management in general and to the development of managers in particular.[18] Two areas deserve special attention: team building and industrial relations. Team building is a task of the entrepreneur, who makes certain that a nucleus of a management team is formed by drawing from among associates the more dedicated and competent to share managing and decision making. Promotion from within, recruitment from without, training, and coaching are effective methods. The development of supervisory personnel and efficient handling of industrial relations dealing with employees' working conditions and general welfare increases their identity with the company and participation in operating decisions. Productivity and low-cost production can be achieved only if good personnel policies and procedures are followed.

Stabilization and Efficiency of the Operation The three functions that can greatly contribute to operational stability and efficiency are production, marketing, and finance. To achieve stability and efficiency in production, a company practices cost control, scheduling, and standardization of methods of operation. Management remains sensitive to all costs (direct and indirect, fixed and variable costs, material and labor). Scheduling directly affects cost and efficiency; good scheduling stabilizes operation and prevents excessive inventory. Standardization of production methods is an intermediate goal that requires concentrated industrial engineering and cost-accounting efforts.

Marketing operations are often difficult to bring up to a high degree of stabilization. At the minimum, though, basic marketing policies on product, pricing, and selling must be formulated. Control and training of sales forces also requires early concentration. Sales personnel should be properly motivated and compensated, but control over expenses, reporting, and selling activities affecting the general area of customer relations should be properly enforced.

Financial management in the early years is most crucial. The institution of a good accounting system in management of cash (timely collection and payment, for example), and the involvement of the financial department with all other operations on cost control and profit improvement are target areas. As discussed previously, a small business firm must not imitate large firms. Small firms should never build a high overhead that overtaxes their limited resources, nor formalize communication by the overuse of formal meetings and voluminous policies and procedures manuals, or overcentralize decision making at the top without encouraging participation from below. In a small business firm, low-level supervisors are truly the driving forces of the firm; their initiative must be nurtured and encouraged.

STRATEGIC CONSIDERATIONS FOR EXPANDING A BUSINESS During the years it takes to develop the firm's readiness for all-out growth, the company has significantly expanded its capacity in management and finance. However, in preparing for the all-out growth, the company must develop capabilities in at least three areas: (1) functional decentralization; (2) planning and control; and (3) growth strategy.

Functional Decentralization As the organization grows, the structure evolves from a simple functional form to a departmentalized organization, and finally to a divisionalized, decentralized operation. A small company may remain a departmentalized organization of varying forms for an extended time before it goes into the next stage of decentralized operation. Such a decentralized operation is organized either on a product/business basis or a geographical basis. It is composed of more or less autonomous divisions as profit centers, responsible for their respective performances on earnings and assets. Its basic concepts lie in initiative—the ability of operating divisions to move swiftly and responsibly without undue interference from the central headquarters.

Decentralization calls for gradual transformation, paying specific attention to excessive costs generally associated with divisionalized organization, and the availability of competent division managers and a strong central staff. When a company deems decentralization necessary to its overall strategy, it increases organizational formality in contrast to organizational flexibility, expands policies and procedural control, strengthens central staff, and accelerates executive development to ensure a large reservoir of competent managers at all levels.

Planning and Control By now, effective planning and control has been institutionalized—a competent staff, an efficient information system, and a well-tested operation with policies and procedures clearly established. Long-term strategic planning and short-term operating planning are formalized, and have been made an integral part of the operation. A management information system begins to take a definite form, and orientation toward the external world has been accelerated. Control over performance, policies, administration, and cost is effective. Limited but competent staff organization that provides policy-making and consultative assistance to the chief executive and line managers is well-entrenched in the organization. The firm has indeed reached a point of stability and a position of readiness for planning, directing, and controlling a larger, more complex organization.

Growth Strategy With an enlarged marketing/financial base and a determined management in a stabilized organization, the company has reached the threshold of large-scale expansion. Growth strategy is formulated to direct the operation. One of the pressing issues in pursuing growth strategy is how to determine the rate of growth: what are the annual increments in sales and earnings the company is capable of achieving, and what is the general path through which the growth rate can be sustained in the long run? The small company assumes a cautious approach. Of the four basic approaches discussed in chapter 8, market intensification through new product development and geographical expansion is a good basic approach. It protects the primary market in which the firm is competent and allows slow expansion into adjacent market areas.

Diversification offers a more aggressive approach, but it also invites higher risk. Acquisition and merger, though providing quick gains, is a grave step requiring larger resources and effective management. International business constitutes another option, but it poses greater difficulties and challenges. A small company pursues growth cautiously and progressively, realizing the difficulties and inherent dangers each stage of growth will bring to the company at each of the threshold stages—at $10 million, at $20 million, or at $40 million in annual sales. Approaching each threshold, the company broadens its marketing/financial base and conscientiously enlarges its organizational capability. Hence, growth is planned and controlled.

SUMMARY

In this chapter, we demonstrated that strategy making is essential to small-business success and that an entrepreneur-president can be an effective manager and a strategist at the same time. To substantiate our argument, we examined extensively all aspects of small-business management. First, we reviewed the role and the special character of a small firm and discussed causes of failure and the prerequisites for success. Those three sources of success serving as a basis for subsequent discussion are: (1) the ability to identify and exploit genuine business opportunities; (2) the capacity to capitalize on the small firm's unique competitive advantages; and (3) the consistent acquisition of management knowledge and skill.

Second, we portrayed the management style of the entrepreneur, noting risk-taking and boldness, general lack of managerial ability, and one-person domination leadership. We recognized difficulties in strategic planning, in organizing, and administering planning, and suggested methods to alleviate them.

Third, we studied strategic alternatives. By examining the basic strategic alternatives and considerations under the three situations of initiation, operation, and expansion of a business, we demonstrated the broad application of strategy to solve immediate and long-term problems.

Throughout the chapter, we focused on problems peculiar to the small firms—their causes and remedies and their implications for management and strategy. Small business firms play a vital economic and social role. Their long-term viability is certainly a concern of the economy as a whole.

NOTES

1. Statement of U.S. Senator Gaylord Nelson before the U.S. Senate Joint Economic Committee hearings, on *The Role of Small Business in the Economy—Tax and Financial Problems* (Washington, D.C.: U.S. Government Printing Office, 1976), p. 3.
2. Business failures of firms with liability size under $100,000 in *The Business Failure Record 1975* (New York: Dun & Bradstreet, 1976), p. 7. For standard textbooks on small-business management, see H. N. Broom and Justin G. Longenecker, *Small Business Management* (Cincinnati, Ohio: South-Western Publishing, 1976), and Clifford M. Baumback, Kenneth Lawyer, and Pearce C. Kelley, *How to Organize and Operate a Small Business* (Englewood Cliffs, N.J.: Prentice-Hall, 1973).
3. Statement of Louis F. Laun before U.S. Senate Joint Economic Committee hearings, on *The Role of Small Business,* p. 71.
4. *The Business Failure Record 1975,* p. 7.
5. Extensively discussed in Baumback, Lawyer, and Kelley, *How to Organize,* pp. 41–46.
6. For discussion, see Theodore Cohn and Roy A. Lindberg, *Survival and Growth: Management Strategies for the Small Firm* (New York: AMA, 1974), pp. 44–58.
7. Frank F. Gilmore, "Formulating Strategy in Small Companies," *Harvard Business Review,* May–June 1971, pp. 71–81.
8. A list of strengths and weaknesses common to small business in Theodore Cohn and Roy A. Lindberg, *Survival and Growth,* pp. 52–53. For financial analysis, see Richard Sanzo, *Ratio Analysis for Small Business* (Washington, D.C.: U.S. Small Business Administration, 1970).
9. Ibid., pp. 78–84, 91–188.
10. For an extensive discussion on marketing, production, finance, and other matters, see Theodore Cohn and Roy A. Lindberg, *Survival and Growth,* chaps. 6, 8, and 10.
11. For discussion on means to increase liquidity capacity, see John W. Ellis, "A Financial Planning Aid for the Small Businessman," *Journal of Small Business Management,* October 1975, pp. 19–28.
12. Survival and growth are mutually supporting, but growth must be secondary to survival. Growth that does not sustain or add to a firm's survival capacity is self-destructive. Cohn and Lindberg, *Survival and Growth,* p. 9.

13. Joint Economic Committee, U.S. Senate, *Joint Hearings on S.1726 Small Business Economic Policy and Advocacy Regulation Act of 1977* (Washington, D.C.: U.S. Government Printing Office, 1977), pp. 26–53. Also, Joint Economic Committee, *Hearings on Capital Formulation Part I* (Washington, D.C.: U.S. Government Printing Office, 1978).
14. Extensively discussed in Hans Schöllhammer and Arthur H. Kuriloff, *Entrepreneurship and Small Business Management* (New York: Wiley, 1979), pt. 1, pp. 1–177.
15. Discussed in textbooks, for example, Baumback, Lawyer, and Kelley, *How to Organize,* pt. 2; and Broom and Longenecker, *Small Business Management,* pt. C.
16. For a practitioner's point of view, see Gardiner G. Greene, *How to Start and Manage Your Own Business* (New York: New American Library, 1975), pp. 12–69. For financial considerations, see Jack Zwick, *A Handbook of Small Business Finance* (Washington, D.C.: U.S. Small Business Administration, 1975).
17. In a concise and forceful discussion, Theodore Cohn singled out externalization (the process of becoming aware of the outside world), rationalization (the process of adapting the organization to goals or purpose envisioned), and institutionalization (the process of formalization and definition of structural form) as the essential precepts in expanding a firm's capacity to cope with survival and growth. *Survival and Growth,* chaps. 3, 4, 5.
18. For example, see Broom and Longenecker, *Small Business Management,* chaps. 8, 9.

CHAPTER SEVENTEEN

International Business Strategy

In the previous chapter, we examined business strategy for small firms. In this chapter, we discuss business strategy in yet another situation—that of international business. The study of strategy in the international context is such a large area that there is not enough space in this book to give it a comprehensive treatment. Thus, we will not attempt to cover all the features of the internal and external environment of an international business nor discuss the various strategic alternatives. Instead, we will highlight the special considerations in planning, formulating, and managing international business strategies.

THE NATURE OF INTERNATIONAL BUSINESS

International business, also called multinational or transnational business, involves business transactions across national borders. Included are various activities in selling and buying products, licensing, and direct investments of various forms. In recent years, there has been a renewed trend for more firms to get involved in some form of international operations. In response to changing needs and conditions, the nature of overseas business involvement has expanded from predominantly export-import operations to other forms of activities. More recently, the joint venture and cooperative agreement between two or more organizations have become more widespread.

Within the context of business strategy, it is important to examine some of the factors that have encouraged firms to take the big step of going beyond the domestic market. As discussed in chapter 8, international business is a form of expansion and diversification.

In the first place, when a firm has abundant financial resources, production capacity, managerial talent, and skilled personnel, but finds the domestic market saturated, it considers the overseas market a route of expansion. Thus, foreign operations can absorb the extra capacity that would otherwise go to waste. Second, even without the urge to expand, overseas operations also serve as a means of diversification, not of product line but of geographical markets. Thus, overseas ventures, whether through exports or direct investment, help spread the economic risks across a wider number of markets.

Other benefits can also be derived. Well-selected exports serve as counter-cyclical markets for smoothing manufacturing operations and cash flow for firms engaged in highly seasonal products. Thus, a U.S. firm manufacturing skis and winter clothing could export to markets in South America during the low-activity summer months in the Northern Hemisphere.

Direct investment serves other purposes. One frequent reason for an exporting firm to go further by making a direct investment is to avoid tariffs and other trade barriers. This was particularly true of the establishment of manufacturing and marketing subsidiaries and affiliates in the European Economic Community (EEC) after its formation. With manufacturing and marketing facilities within the boundaries of the EEC, the firms avoided paying the high tariff and thus were able to compete favorably in those markets.

Overseas location also allows multinational firms access to lower resources and materials costs, giving them an advantage over their domestic counterparts in attaining greater efficiency in purchasing, manufacturing, and distribution. The search for raw materials is another incentive to search for overseas business, particularly those operating in resource-oriented industries such as oil, chemicals, metal, and rubber. By locating close to the sources, firms gain not only cost advantages but also greater assurance of getting regular supplies. In a world of dwindling resources, it is no surprise that there is growing entry of multinational companies into the resource-rich countries, such as Brazil, Malaysia, and the oil-producing countries.

STRATEGY FORMULATION IN THE INTERNATIONAL CONTEXT

Strategy formulation for operations confined to one's domestic market are difficult enough, but when the firm ventures beyond its national borders, the resulting process is considerably more complex. First, the multinational company (MNC) will have to compete with a wide array of foreign firms. Second, the MNC operates in different economic, legal, political, and cultural environments. Third, the evaluation and implementation of strategies involve calculations in a multitude of foreign currencies that vary in exchange rates and degrees of appreciation or depreciation. Last, there exists the complex relationships between the MNC and the host country in which a firm does business, on the one hand; and the MNC and the country where the firm resides, on the other hand. Both relationships are governed by international, public, and private laws of the countries concerned.

The process of formulating strategies still follows the basic format of evaluating environmental opportunities and threats, assessing resources and readiness, objective setting, and developing and selecting alternatives. Above all, the decision to go international must be consistent with the overall policy and strategy of the firm. Such a decision cannot be treated in isolation from the rest of the company's decisions.

These added factors in doing business abroad introduce a new set of complications. Hence, a firm must correctly assess environmental differences, market demand, and political risks; appraise internal qualifications and capabilities; and explore strategic alternatives. Let us discuss each of these in that order.

Environmental Differences

THE ECONOMY OF THE HOST COUNTRY The characteristics and trends of key economic factors of the host country are of utmost importance. They serve as bases for evaluating market size, costs, and profitability of strategic alternatives. In measuring the economic capacity of a country, the total GNP or the gross domestic product (GDP) are used. GDP is composed of the value of goods and services produced in a country regardless of the nationality of the supplier of labor or capital. The addition of factor income received from abroad and the subtraction of factor income paid abroad gives the GNP.[1] The level of GDP or GNP has been shown to correlate with the sales levels of various products or industries.[2] Hence, the MNC can assess the potential sales for a product line if given the level of expected growth of the national economy. The nature of the host country's infrastructure, that is, its roads, railways, ports, navigation facilities, and so forth, also affect the ease and costs of moving products and materials. The organization and structure of the markets influence the choice of product line and channels of distribution. The rate of inflation, unemployment, and balance of payments could lead to government policies that may limit the strategic alternatives of the MNC.

FOREIGN EXCHANGE One of the factors that complicates international business is that transactions have to be conducted in many currencies. This creates two complications. First, in buying and selling foreign currencies, the rates are subject to the forces of demand and supply. Second, each currency is also affected by the state of the economy of the country, the inflation rate, productive capacity, balance of payments, political decisions, and the evaluation of speculators, central banks, and money users. These fluctuations or gradual appreciation or depreciation of currency's exchange rate create both risks and opportunities for the MNC.

LEGAL AND POLITICAL FACTORS The system of law and policies governing business formation, acquisitions, selling, pricing, advertising, and competitive activities serves to constrain strategic options of an international company. There are also laws specifying guidelines for hiring, firing, promotion, employment ratios of foreigners to nationals, and dealing with unions. Furthermore, there are policies with respect to ownership. licensing, repatriation of profits, royalties, importing, and purchasing. The manager who "goes international" may find little similarity between the familiar laws and policies of his or her home country and those of foreign countries.

Another complicating factor is the love-hate relationship that usually exists between the government and nationals of the host country and the international firm. On the one hand, the host country accepts, if not encourages, the operation of foreign firms within its borders for the benefits gained through taxes, increased employment, economic growth, and assistance in the balance-of-payments situation. At the same time, there is concern about the power of the MNC over the local population, the dependence of the economy on the MNC, the loyalty of the MNC to its home country,[3] and the effect on the national character and traditions of the host country. Related to this is the risk of losing assets, sales, and profits as a result of political action. In addition, there is the possible emergence of militant, nationalistic groups that may put pressure on the host government to drive out the foreign investors, impose restrictive policies, or, in the extreme, harass foreign employees or destroy facilities.

Thus, it is essential that multinational companies considering direct investment study the guidelines provided by the host country in order to develop an effective investment and ownership strategy.

In an informative article on investment policies, Sachdev classified five different groups of policies on a continuum of varying restrictiveness.[4] On one extreme are the expropriatory policies of countries that feel that MNCs have overlooked the goals and needs of the host countries, thus, justifying, rightly or wrongly, their use of expropriation and confiscation as policy instruments. At the other extreme are countries with open-door policies that offer investment incentives, tariff protection for import substitution, relaxed investment codes, and lower corporate taxes. In between are regulatory policies, receptive policies, and promotional policies. Each situation calls for some variation in strategy.

CULTURAL ENVIRONMENT *Culture* is the set of social norms and responses that conditions a population's behavior.[5] It is a set of solutions and programmed approaches to particular situations that one generation hands down to the next. Cultures vary, so their effect on organized human activities, such as business, also varies, thereby creating wide diversity in business practices. Managers who grow up in one culture with little experience in another social setting would experience great difficulty and frustration in adjusting to different ways of conducting business.

Culture conditions preferences, attitudes, values, and perceptions. Thus, products that are highly desirable in the home market may have little appeal in their present form in another cultural environment. Marketing approaches have failed for lack of understanding of the prevalent social norms. For example, General Mills' advertisement of a breakfast cereal using a freckled, grinning child had great success in the United States, but failed to appeal to the British market, which is not as child oriented as that of the United States.[6] In Thailand, Warner Lambert used a well-known U.S. television commercial for Listerine that showed a boy and a girl who were overtly fond of each other, and one advising the other to use Listerine for bad breath. It flopped because such public portrayal of boy-girl relationships was objectionable to the Thais.[7]

Also closely linked to culture is language. Language reflects the culture, values, and perception of a people so that the connotations of a word cannot be fully grasped without an understanding of the social context from which it comes. Thus, American advertisers who routinely translated slogans from American English to other languages found that a lot was lost in the process. General Motors' "body by Fisher" came out "corpse by Fisher" in Flemish![8] Pepsi's "come alive with Pepsi" had problems in Germany because "come alive" in German meant "come back out of the grave."[9]

TRADE AGREEMENTS AMONG COUNTRIES After World War II, a number of countries formed alliances and made mutual cooperation agreements. These pacts might take the form of multilateral trade expansion on a nondiscriminatory basis, agreements for international income redistribution through trade agreements focusing on the economic relations of a particular geographic or political area, or agreements on the terms of trade of specific products or commodities.[10] One such agreement, the General Agreement on Tariffs and Trade (GATT), with over eighty member countries, was formed to attain a broad, multilateral, and relatively free system of trading, primarily through the reduction of tariffs. Other regional arrangements include the European Free Trade Association (EFTA) and the Council for Mutual Economic Cooperation (COMECON). These national groups have agreed to remove or reduce artificial restrictions on the movement of goods and commodities among the participating countries, with each country retaining its own tariffs, quotas, or other restrictions on trade with nonparticipating countries.

The most well-known regional integration is the European Economic Community (EEC), which, since 1973, has had nine members. The EEC members have agreed not only to reduce duties and other trade restrictions among member countries but also to have a common tariff against nonmember countries. This last proviso was a major factor in encouraging firms from nonmember countries, such as the United States, to locate some of their manufacturing and marketing facilities inside the EEC to avoid tariffs. Other regional agreements are found in South America, the Caribbean, Southeast Asia, Africa, and the Middle East.

Intercountry agreements have several implications for the MNC. First, competitive conditions change. Firms exporting to the country group have to surmount the trade barriers, while firms located within the boundaries of the group are spared these costs. Second, the markets, by being joined together, increase through trade creation and through more vigorous competition. Third, due to the bigger market area accessible, the firm operating within the boundaries can attain economies of scale that improve competitiveness. Fourth, integration movements generally incorporate policies that favor firms operating within the area over firms of other countries. Hence, in addition to the complex regulations of the host country, there are the numerous policies and guidelines imposed by the charter of the association of countries. These provide both constraints and advantages to the MNC.

PAYOFFS AND BRIBERY Although the constraints of payoffs and bribery relate more to political and cultural factors, we single these out for discussion because of the grave implications they have for the multinational companies. It is a fact that payoffs and bribery are common practice in international business. To better assess this phenomenon, it is important to identify two types of payoffs: the "lubrication" bribe and the "whitemail" bribe.[11] The lubrication bribe usually involves payment of a relatively small sum of money to make the employees of an organization, usually a government agency, do the work they are supposed to do. For example, payments are made to the customs officials to accelerate paperwork that allows the shipment of machinery, raw materials, or components from the docks to the plant. A gratuity is given to the clerk in an agency to find and process an application for a construction permit.

The whitemail bribe usually represents payments to high-ranking officials as a result of pressure exerted. For example, the chairman of United Brands paid $2.5 million to top officials of the government of Honduras in return for a $7.5 million reduction in the proposed tax on banana exports.[12]

Usually, MNCs do not fight against the occurrence of lubrication bribes, but rather accept them and treat them as part of regular operating costs. However, most firms favor resisting the pressure of whitemail bribery.

Assessing Market Demands

Assessment of national markets is an important step in strategy formulation. Four analytical techniques are noted.[13] One technique is the extrapolation of past demand patterns. For short periods of time, a straight-line projection may be sufficient; for longer periods, projection may be made based on the industrial growth patterns of comparable but more advanced countries.[14] Another technique makes use of income elasticities, which measure the relationship between the change in demand for a product and the change in income. A third method forecasts demand by analogy. For example, it if is assumed that Malaysia's development pattern is analogous to that of Venezuela, forecast of product consumption for Malaysia can be estimated from the observed pattern in Venezuela. The fourth technique uses regression analysis to correlate the demand for a particular product and some gross economic indicators for the chosen country.

Assessing Political Risks

In addition to facing economic risks of loss of sales, increasing costs, and declining profits, due to industry trends or competitors' moves, the MNC is also subject to risks that are the result of political change. Political risks exist (1) when discontinuities occur in the business environment; (2) when they are difficult to anticipate; and (3) when they result from political changes. To be considered a risk, the changes must significantly affect the profit or other goals of the MNC. Not all changes due to political action can be classified as "risk"; only those that are difficult to anticipate. An example would be the recent crisis in Iran, which not only brought destruction of property and curtailment of operations but also exposed the American personnel to threats, harassment, and physical harm.[15]

Although political risks are difficult to predict, it is nevertheless important that an assessment be made of the political situation of a country being considered as a market in order to have a more objective evaluation of the expected returns and costs before making a commitment. Schollhammer has proposed a quantitative approach for evaluating and predicting political risks.[16] His model attempts to infer the risk situation of a country by using quantifiable indicators of political unrest—protest demonstrations, riots, armed attacks, deaths from political violence, and government sanctions. Using data from sixty countries, the model was tested by analyzing the relationships between scores on political unrest variables and economic and political data. The conclusion was that the resulting scores and ratios can provide executives of MNCs with an indication of the comparative political risks in the investigated countries.

Internal Qualifications and Capabilities

Even though international business provides some attractive benefits, it is not suitable for every company. As with any other strategy under consideration, the firm has to assess and evaluate its capability to see if it has the resources for an effective multinational operation. In the following sections, we will discuss some of the recommended prerequisites for going overseas. We are not suggesting that the firm has to have these capabilities before venturing beyond the domestic market. We are saying only that its chances for success would be enhanced if it has or will develop these capabilities. These include: (1) technological lead; (2) strong trade name; (3) advantages of scale; (4) scanning capability;[17] (5) an outstanding product or service; and (6) an outstanding international executive.

TECHNOLOGICAL LEAD A firm with some innovative approaches or with a new product or process has an advantage that it could exploit in the international field. It is also likely that such a firm would have numerous contacts overseas. These could serve as the bases for entering and exploiting the overseas markets.

A STRONG TRADE NAME In various countries of the world, including the United States, foreign products may have greater appeal than the domestic ones. In many cases, foreign products may be attributed superior performances; in others, snob appeal gives the product a premium rating. Given these tendencies, the firm can market its products without too much promotional effort. A strong trade name also allows the firm the higher price and margin to cover the promotional and distribution costs.

ADVANTAGE OF SCALE In many cases, the major advantage of the firm lies primarily in its size. Bigness allows economies of scale denied smaller firms. The big firm also retains the advantage of its ability to marshal enormous financial, material, and human resources to launch an overseas venture. Besides, a large firm with its bigger financial base can weather a series of setbacks in the more risky foreign markets. This is not to say that only large firms survive in the international arena. On the contrary, a large number of small firms are successful in exporting and importing.

A SCANNING CAPABILITY When costs of production and distribution constitute an important aspect of a competitive situation, the ability of a firm to search the world for low-cost resources and production capabilities may take on greater importance when going international. Efficiency in the search process is important because presumably any firm can seek low-cost sites if it is ready to pay the price for the search.

AN OUTSTANDING PRODUCT OR SERVICE Gunnar Beeth, a consultant in international business, suggests that one of the major requirements for effectively pursuing the international market is an outstanding product or service.[18] Even with abundant resources and strong international connections, a firm will eventually fail if it does not possess a product or service that is outstandingly good or outstandingly competitive. Furthermore, in international business a product that is a little better usually has a better chance of success than a product that is a little less expensive. It would be prudent for the manager, before attempting to enter the international market, to determine whether the company's product or service is sufficiently outstanding to carry the cost of international business and whether the product or service is desired in the foreign markets in terms of local competition as well as in terms of unusual local tastes and preferences.

AN OUTSTANDING INTERNATIONAL EXECUTIVE Beeth further notes that another important prerequisite is having an outstanding international executive. Qualifications include the ability to understand, influence, and motivate people from different countries. An outstanding international executive is capable of developing a core of local executives and promoting genuine cooperation between executives from home and locally recruited managers. He/she is thus constantly concentrating on building a viable organization that is capable of adapting to local situations and developing functional capabilities in marketing (such as research and distribution), production, and R&D to meet local demands.

INTERNATIONAL BUSINESS STRATEGIES

Generally, a firm's involvement in overseas business develops in stages. For a start, exporting is favored because of its greater flexibility and lower risk. Another low-risk alternative is licensing. After the firm acquires more knowledge and experience about its foreign markets, it may make a longer-term commitment through direct investment. Under direct investment, several variations in degree of ownership and type of cooperation with other organizations are also possible. These alternatives will be discussed in this section.

Export Operations

Firms may engage in exports in order to lower unit costs of products. These firms include those that have high fixed or R&D costs, a domestic market too small to justify large-scale production, or an elastic demand curve that prevents raising prices sufficiently to cover costs.[19] Exports may also be a means of utilizing excess capacity.

Several strategic options are open to the firm in exporting. On one extreme, it could choose to handle all the vital functions, which include market research, sales promotion, credit investigation, collection, and shipping. It could also contract any or all of these functions to other firms or intermediaries between the firm and the importer. It could make use of an export management company, which provides a number of services from obtaining orders for its clients to selecting appropriate markets, distribution systems, and promotional campaigns.

Another possibility is to have another firm handle the exports through a "piggyback" arrangement. A firm that already has an extensive export department may be willing, for a fee, to handle additional complementary but noncompetitive products.

Still another possibility is to have agents and distributors handle the sales to another country. In a country such as Japan, with complex regulations and a cumbersome marketing system, the correct choice of distributor would be vital to gaining a foothold and ensuring long-term survival.[20]

Licensing

Licensing provides additional revenue sources with minimal added expenditure. It can serve as the means of building goodwill for the MNC's product. licensee's market, in return for royalties, usually based on the output or sales of the licensed product.[21] Aside from being an alternative to exporting or direct investment, a licensing agreement serves as an inexpensive way of exploring the receptivity of a country or region to a particular product.

Licensing provides additional revenue sources with minimal added expenditure. It can serve as the means of building goodwill for the MNC's product. Rather than risk having foreign firms steal the product or trademark, licensing prevents such actions while providing revenues. If reciprocal rights to new products or technology are included in the contract, licensing could serve as a low-cost source of innovation.

Sometimes, technology or products that are already obsolete in the home country or for which organizational interest has waned may still yield revenues through licensing in another less-developed country.

There are also disadvantages to licensing. The licensee may use the license only for furthering its own goals without regard for the development of the licensed product. The company may in a short time develop its competence so that it no longer needs the support of the licensor, but instead emerges as a competitor. There is also the difficulty of maintaining quality standards, the limited profit opportunities, and the high taxes levied on licensing royalties.

Acquisitions

One alternative in making a direct investment overseas would be to enter a market through an acquisition instead of starting a business from scratch. Acquisition is a means of obtaining productive facilities and establishing a major position in a country. Acquisition also allows the firm to rapidly acquire additional product lines, technology, marketing networks, distribution systems, managerial capability, and other assets.[22] Synergistic benefits may be derived when a company complements its strong product line with the distribution networks of the acquired company. In the complex problems of dealing with local government agencies, unions, distributors, and interest groups, an acquisition may quickly provide the necessary expertise through existing personnel. An acquisition may actually be less expensive than building a new subsidiary.

However, acquisitions are not without problems. In foreign countries, information about candidates for acquisition may be difficult to obtain, making an accurate evaluation almost an impossibility. Firms in a number of countries may be more secretive than the typical American firm. Acquisitions may also lead to less-modern facilities.

Joint Ventures

Instead of going it alone, the MNC may consider associating with other organizations through a form of ownership strategy known as the joint venture. The joint venture may be an association between the MNC and private local firms, local government agencies, or other foreign enterprises.

Joint ventures offer a number of advantages. They are a major way of raising local financing and reducing risks from devaluation and inflation. Because joint ventures require less investment than an acquisition or the start of a wholly owned subsidiary, they allow the MNC to spread its investments over a wider range of countries. Joint ventures are also quick ways of obtaining local management, which may be in short supply in various countries. The local partner may also provide sources of materials, marketing capability, contacts for gaining government approvals, local currency loans, tax incentives, and other benefits. Finally, the presence of the local partner may reduce the risk of expropriation, restrictive policies, and harassment by nationals.

Disadvantages of the joint venture include lower profitability, loss of control of the business entity, conflict with local managers, and having to share technology with the local partner. It must be noted, though, that in many countries the MNC has no choice but to take on a local partner if it wants to operate within the country.

Other Strategies

Undoubtedly, MNCs would favor entry into countries with favorable investment policies and shy away from those with expropriatory or restrictive policies. However, it must be realized that investment policies are only one of several factors considered in the investment decision. If other factors, such as the size of market, low labor and material costs, availability of other factors of production, and other benefits, are present, the MNC may still seriously weigh the possibility of doing business in such a country. Before taking such a risk, the MNC would invariably look for assurance from the host government that other factors in the investment climate will be made more favorable to counterbalance the investment risk. In recent years, more MNCs have responded to restrictive situations through the use of the management contract. In this case, the MNC serves not as the mobilizer or allocator of capital, but as a generator and seller of management capability.[23]

Recent growth in business with Eastern European countries has popularized other forms of joint industrial effort. These include:[24]

1. *Coproduction and specialization:* Both the Western and Eastern partners produce components for a final product to be assembled by one partner. Technology is usually supplied by one partner, and the product is usually marketed in each partner's respective market.
2. *Subcontracting:* The socialist partner manufactures the product according to the Western partner's specifications and delivers the product to the Western partner.
3. *Turnkey operation:* The Western partner sells plant, equipment, and technology to a socialist partner and is paid in the products of the newly created plant.

SUMMARY

International business is transacted in multiple languages, using various currencies, in different economic, legal, political, and cultural settings. Because of these varying factors, the planning, formulation, and management of international business strategies are considerably more complex than comparable strategies in the domestic market. The process is further complicated by the rapid and uneven changes in conditions and situations in various countries and regions.

Furthermore, international business is subject to political economic intricacies. As we have explained, international business is governed by multilateral and bilateral trade agreements and restrictions, the host government's laws and legislations, and policies and regulations of the parent countries. In every region or every nation, such restrictions are different. For example, one host nation may place greater restrictions on foreign investments and on trade activities than will another nation. The extent of regulations imposed by the parent countries may also differ in each case. However, international business, one of the oldest business institutions, offers such diverse opportunities that no company, large or small, can forgo serious consideration of entry. Indeed, the large U.S. trade deficit has once again caused the government to encourage business to go abroad. We have introduced another situation in which, as in small businesses, strategy has its fullest application.

NOTES

1. Stefan H. Robock, Kenneth Simmonds, and Jack Zwick, *International Business and Multinational Enterprises,* rev. ed. (Homewood, Ill.: Irwin, 1977), p. 349.
2. Ibid., pp. 380–81, 386–88.
3. Roy Blough, *International Business: Environment and Adaptation* (New York: McGraw-Hill, 1966), pp. 80–81.
4. Jagdish Sachdev, "Foreign Investment Policies of Developing Host Nations and Multinationals: Interactions and Accommodations," *Management International Review,* no. 2, 1978, pp. 33–43.
5. Robock, Simmonds, and Zwick, *International Business,* p. 309.
6. Edward A. McCreary, *The Americanization of Europe* (New York: Doubleday, 1964), p. 129, cited in David Ricks, Marilyn Fu, and Jeffrey Arpan, *International Business Blunders* (Columbus, Ohio: Grid, 1974), p. 13.
7. R. S. Diamond, "Managers Away from Home," *Fortune,* 15 August 1969, p. 56, cited in Ricks, Fu, and Arpan, *International Business Blunders,* p. 14.
8. Edward M. Mazze, "How to Push a Body Abroad Without Making It a Corpse," *Business Abroad,* 10 August 1964, p. 15, cited in Ricks, Fu, and Arpan, p. 11.
9. *Advertising Age,* 9 May 1966, p. 75, as cited in Ricks, Fu, and Arpan, p. 11.
10. Robock, Simmonds, and Zwick, *International Business,* pp. 127–39.
11. Peter Nehemkis, "Business Payoffs Abroad: Rhetoric and Reality," *California Management Review,* Winter 1975, p. 7.
12. Ibid., p. 10.
13. Robock, Simmonds, and Zwick, *International Business,* pp. 379–89.
14. See for example, graphs of "Typical Patterns of Growth in Manufacturing Industries," in Alfred Maizels, *Industrial Growth and World Trade* (Cambridge University Press, 1963), p. 55, as reproduced in Robock, Simmonds, and Zwick, *International Business,* p. 381.
15. David Tinnin, "The Americans Caught in Iran's Turmoil," *Fortune,* 31 December 1978, pp. 37–39.
16. Hans Schollhammer, "Identification, Evaluation and Prediction of Political Risks from an International Business Perspective," in Michel Ghertman and James Leontiades, eds., *European Research in International Business* (Hoorn, Netherlands: North-Holland Publishing, 1978), pp. 91–109.
17. Discussions on the first four items adapted from Raymond Vernon and Louis T. Wells, Jr., *Manager in the International Economy,* 3rd ed. (Englewood Cliffs, N.J.: Prentice-Hall, 1976), pp. 5–20.
18. *International Management Practices: An Insider's View* (New York: AMACOM, 1973), pp. 3–7.
19. John D. Daniels, Ernest W. Ogram, Jr., and Lee H. Radebaugh, *International Business: Environments and Operations* (Reading, Mass.: Addison-Wesley, 1976), pp. 371–75.
20. Pamela Sherrid, "Learning the Tricks of the Japan Trade," *Fortune,* 20 November 1978, pp. 68–70.
21. Endel J. Kilde, *International Business Enterprise,* 2nd ed. (Englewood Cliffs, N.J.: Prentice-Hall, 1973), p. 209–16.
22. William A. Dymsza, *Multinational Business Strategy* (New York: McGraw-Hill, 1972), pp. 177–206.

23. Sachdev, "Foreign Investment Policies," pp. 41–42.
24. James F. Pederson, "Joint Ventures in the Soviet Union: A Legal and Economic Perspective," *Harvard International Law Journal,* Spring 1975, p. 391, as cited in Ronald E. Hoyt, "East-West Trade Growth Potential for the 1980s," *Columbia Journal of World Business,* April 1978, p. 63.

CHAPTER EIGHTEEN

Conclusion

In this final chapter, we present a brief summary of the book and comment on future perspectives. At the beginning of this book, we suggested four objectives for the policy course: (1) reviewing and integrating prior studies; (2) developing skills to analyze and solve complex business problems; (3) learning a new discipline of strategy; and (4) relating classroom learning to business practices. We hope that with proper instruction and case analyses, these objectives are readily realized. Let us list a few major points:

1. Studying policy and strategy will continue to be a rewarding experience. Students are benefited by learning a new concept that expands their professional knowledge and skill and brings their classroom experience closer to the realities of the business world. As policy research expands, future research will narrow the scope and materially enrich the field, thus benefiting teaching and learning.
2. The business climate in the 1970s has shown dramatic changes. Rules of the business game are changing; so is the game. Strategy will redefine the way the game is played.
3. Strategy is not simply a process of analysis, goal setting, and choice. It is the art of matching, calculating, selecting, and managing. It centers on overcoming difficulties and constraints, developing and deploying limited resources, and organizing and managing enterprises in perspective.
4. All business firms confront at one time or another three basic situations—growth, stability, and survival—and thus the strategies for them are imperative. At the heart of their sound development is the penetrating assessment and collective judgment of the situations, problems, and the realistic choice of objectives and means of attaining them.
5. Effective strategic management requires a two-dimensional thrust: the horizontal succession of strategy-structure-process, and the vertical thrust of strategy-tactics-actions.

6. Strategy guides operating decisions of short- and long-term importance. It becomes operationally effective only when its assumptions are continuously updated according to the realities and when it can be adjusted, responsive, and recycled.

BUSINESS STRATEGY: THE STATE OF THE ART

For the past two decades, policy and strategy have been taught in business schools, and their application enthusiastically attempted in the business world. We have reviewed the challenging nature of policy teaching and research and traced the development of strategy in the business world.

Business strategy is still in its early development. Concepts are awaiting redefinition, and the art itself requires refinement because constraints of strategic thinking are often at odds with the impulsiveness for action so deeply rooted in the American business culture. Strategy making is an attitude, a method of thinking, and an art of management. It must be nurtured, practiced, and applied. We firmly believe that business firms, large or small, will rely upon business strategy to guide their development in the turbulent world, and that strategy will be the central thrust of future management. It will be no easy task.

BUSINESS STRATEGY: THE CENTRAL THRUST OF MANAGEMENT

In the early 1970s, we witnessed a sharp turn of events. The 1973–1974 energy crisis was a watershed that sharply marked the end of a growth-inspired past and the beginning of an uncertain future. During the past two decades, American industry's relentless pursuit of economic growth has produced an era of unprecedented output and material abundance. Toward the end of this growth era, even many successful large and small firms found themselves overextended, flabby, and feeble, totally unprepared to face the onslaught of a depressed economy and a multitude of severe challenges unknown in the past. Business failures skyrocketed; corporations quickly passed through the first two phases of growth and profit instability, and completed the vicious cycle with financial insolvency. The losses were enormous, and the injuries were fundamental, nearly wrecking the confidence of the American business community. Business executives vowed not to repeat the same mistakes.

Still, there is a heightened degree of economic and political uncertainty. The world economy continues to face difficulties. Fear of the scarcity of energy, material, and capital is real and present. Other concerns of rising inflation, government intervention, and ever-sharpening competition dominate the thought of modern business executives. They are in a serious search for a new, daring approach to management.

Business strategy offers an alternative. Business strategy conveys a deep meaning in economics and administrative science. Strategy attempts the deployment of minimum resources for maximum returns. It enhances decision making in developing, using, and investing resources of all types. Strategy focuses on achieving: how to exploit opportunities; counteract threats; and overcome competition. It causes a firm to acquire a dual orientation—an orientation that is external as well as internal. It centers on calculating, matching, risk taking, and is continually evolving and dynamic. Strategy galvanizes the energies of company management at all levels. It provides a direction and a focus for effort. It is the chief determinant of organizational structure, tasks, and required capacities. Indeed, strategy dominates actual management as well.

STRATEGY MAKING: A TOTAL CONCEPT AND A PRACTICAL APPROACH

We have noted that strategy making consists of strategic planning, strategic formulation, and strategic management. It is necessarily a total function: the lack of or deficiency in any one of these activities renders the entire process ineffective. Strategy making is a self-directed and organizationally supported function. Business strategy is proactive, not reactive; it affects the total organization, not just one part. A company that leaves its destiny to drift by chance, or a company that guides its operations with a weak strategy, has no assurance of consistent performance. Hence, sound strategy is made through a concentrated organizational effort, a methodology of substantive nature, and a way of intelligent thinking and action.

Strategic Planning

Strategic planning entails environmental analysis, internal assessment, and objective setting. Its purpose is to explore opportunities and threats (present and future), define strengths and weaknesses (past and projected), and postulate immediate and long-term objectives. In essence, strategic planning is confined to the basic design of a company's purpose, character, and business interest. It guides strategic formulation.

Strategic Formulation

By strategic formulation, the company explores courses of action, means of deploying resources, and formulates the strategic plan. It focuses on the development of its strategic posture, the proper identification of its central issues, and its strategic alternatives. It evaluates and selects objectives, explores and chooses alternatives, delineates courses of action, and seriously considers competitive countermoves, constraints, and contingencies. When corporate strategies fully express management's desired direction and program of action, the strategy is forceful, flexible, and sound.

Strategic Management

Strategic management is the third phase of strategy making; it is the management of the ongoing strategy. It requires competency of the entire company to move the organization along the course dictated by the strategic plan and to effect adjustment and recycling. Management must give full recognition to the evolving and dynamic nature of strategy. Old assumptions are tested and validated by fresh input, and new ones emerge. The dynamic exchange of actions among the contending forces—the customers, the competitors, and the government—is monitored, studied, and adjustments are made. Through the institution of strategic control and the mechanism of sensing-adapting-responding, company management maintains its comprehensive perspective and develops the ability to monitor and measure significant signals and to regroup when necessary.

We favor a practical approach to strategy making. Business strategy deals with practical matters—overcoming competition, and attaining economic advantages. It is concerned with people, organization, personal values, and economic resources of a firm. We place special emphasis on decision makers, those executives involved in strategy making—their roles, functions, and interaction—and the process of administering strategic planning. In formulating and managing strategy, we emphasize a new style of thinking and managing, and stress the linkage of strategy-tactics-action. Strategic concepts are subtle, their meanings practical. A creative strategist reduces complexity to simplicity, and applies theories to down-to-earth practices.

THE STRATEGISTS: THE CEO AND GENERAL MANAGERS

Throughout the book, we have expressed a firm belief that strategy making is a discipline and an attitude, and that the CEO and his/her general managers are strategists as well as managers. Their role is pivotal. Singularly and jointly, they are the architects and implementors of strategy and assume a role of personal leadership that moves their organization toward strategic actions. Their convictions, beliefs, and dedication to strategy making is key. The acquisition of this art, like that of management, is a lifetime pursuit. A strategist upholds a distinguishing style of leadership. He/she maintains, at all times, a total perspective (a dual concentration on present and future), a balanced approach (decisive, yet cautious), an economic view (the search for the optimal return), and a supreme administrative skill that inspires people. He/she alone assumes the responsibility for the organization's strategy. He/she consults, deliberates, and encourages his/her associates to develop a similar dedication to strategic thinking and action. But he/she alone decides on strategy.

Of course, strategy making is not the act of a single person. The CEO and the general managers actively seek assistance. In strategic planning, the CEO relies upon the planning staff to perform planning studies and analyses and coordinate the planning activity. In formulating strategy, the CEO relies upon the general managers to formulate their respective strategies, critiques their formulation, while also inviting the participation of senior associates and planning executives for consultative deliberation. Strategic formulation is, after all, a mental exercise, a challenge of one's capacity to think intuitively and rationally and to act intelligently and decisively. A seasoned strategist relies on consultative deliberation and occasionally engages in critical exchanges with an outsider (a member of the board or a consultant), to broaden personal views and to attain a certain objectivity in decision making. In strategic management, the CEO and the general managers inspire the organization to action, assume the overall control, and, most important, monitor signals of changes and assume appropriate actions. Let us repeat: strategy making is the prime responsibility of the CEO and the general managers. They are individually measured by their strategic performance. Their real task, then, is a determined act—that is, to expand their capacities for strategy making.

THE ENTREPRENEUR—STRATEGIST IN A SMALL BUSINESS FIRM

In this book, we have provided a full exposition on business strategy in small firms. We believe that business strategy is equally, if not more, important to a small firm than to a large one. But strategy making is more difficult for an entrepreneur-president. First, he/she must discard the myth that business strategy is only applicable to large and medium-sized firms. Second, he/she must accept the reality that the firm's vulnerability can only be lessened if he/she understands the essence of strategy making and practices it. The owner is in fact his/her own planner, strategist, and implementor. We have identified areas of deficiency, suggested a simplified approach to strategic planning, and discussed methods of formulating and managing strategies that are unique to small operations. However, the true test lies in the entrepreneur's own determination to become an effective manager and a successful strategist at the same time.

THE FUTURE MANAGER

Ever since the late 1960s, there has been a growing interest in the shape of the future. Future industrial societies are envisioned in radically different ways: one group foresees a doomsday economy characterized by the depletion of natural resources and ecological self-destruction; the other promises an industrial society distinguished by advanced technology and professionalism in policy and decision making.[1] Future organizations will be large but quite different in character. There will be more interdependence between public and private institutions; tasks and goals of the firm will be more technical, complicated, and unprogrammed; organizational structure will be less rigid; and workers' involvement, participation, and autonomy in their work will be increased.[2]

There will be crises and reorientations that will effect the transition from the present world of uncertainty to the realization of a postindustrial society, appearing around the year 2000. A task of this magnitude will challenge all modern executives. A technically led and growth society will accelerate change and intensify competition. A future organization of greater complexity and radically changed work ethics will demand new knowledge and skill. Business strategy will provide part of the answer because strategy produces economics, vision, and a sense of direction and conviction.

Our attempt to reduce the complex nature of strategy to practical terms has led us to concentrate on the essentials of strategy making. The infinite variations of strategic behavior are beyond imagination and thus await the practitioner's own discovery. We did not attempt to indulge in situational differences involving different industries and firms. Indeed, the secret of applying theories lies in the heart of the appliers.

NOTES

1. Daniel Bell, *The Coming of Post-Industrial Society* (New York: Basic Books, 1973); and Herman Kahn, ed., *The Future of the Corporation* (St. Paul, Minn.: Mason of Lipscomb Publishers, 1974).
2. Warren Bennis, *Beyond Bureaucracy: Essays and the Development and Evolution of Human Organization* (New York: McGraw-Hill, 1966); and Chris Argyris, *On Organizations of the Future* (Beverly Hills, Calif.: Sage Publications, 1973).

CASES FOR PART V

AMERICAN RECREATION CENTERS, INC.

American Recreation Centers, Inc. (ARC) operated a chain of sixteen bowling centers, an office building in Corona, and a shopping center in Hayward, all in California. Fourteen of the bowling centers were in the northern half of the state, and headquarters were in Sacramento.

In July 1975 Robert Feuchter, president and board chairman, proudly announced the fourth consecutive year of increased sales. Although net income was down $39,000, fiscal 1975 had ended with the second best profits in ARC's history. Concurrently, he announced the establishment of an ESOT (Employee Stock Ownership Trust) and revealed ARC's plans to open two new bowling centers in August.

Although Feuchter was enthusiastic about the future, he continued to be concerned about long-range planning, particularly in the areas of growth, diversification, and possible energy shortages. Since bowling was no longer a growth industry, he knew that profitable expansion depended upon careful selection of sites and innovations in operating efficiency. He also believed that some diversification probably was essential for long-term survival, even though ARC had, so far, been unable to find synergistic firms or services. ARC would have to plan for the possibility of energy shortages which might seriously affect bowling operations and profitability. Inflation, too, was of some concern, and ARC had recently begun to hedge against rising prices by acquiring underlying real properties at the time new centers were acquired.

Feuchter had joined ARC in 1959 as vice president under ARC's founder, Elliot Jones, Jr. A group of the shareholders became dissatisfied with Jones' performance in 1963 and instituted a proxy battle that resulted in electing four new directors to the then nine-member board. Profits had declined to almost zero, and little could be accomplished because of conflicts and arguments. Although a majority of the board at first supported Jones, other stockholders teamed with dissidents in 1964 to secure his resignation. Feuchter, who had been filling the void in general management, voluntarily resigned after Jones's dismissal.

A management consulting firm was brought in to "straighten out the firm's affairs," and one of their members became board chairman and chief executive

---

Prepared by Leete A. Thompson of California State University, Sacramento.

officer. In 1965, the consulting firm asked Feuchter to rejoin the firm as president and assume the general management duties he had performed in his former position as vice president. In Feuchter's words,

> I discussed the appointment with other directors and Mr. Jones. I was hopeful that Mr. Jones would be recalled by the directors, but they had voted him a separation payment and definitely would not reconsider the decision.
>
> No one else in the company seemed to have the ability, competence or desire to assume the duties. At a special meeting of the board on May 4, 1965, I was appointed president.
>
> Mr. Hamman stayed on as board chairman for one additional year. At that point, the consulting firm felt that their services were no longer needed fulltime, so Mr. Hamman resigned and the directors elected me chairman.

THE BOWLING INDUSTRY

The rapid growth in bowling that began in the 1950s can be attributed, in part, to its practicality as a participative sport. It provides vigorous exercise that can be started at an early age and continued into retirement. The necessary personal equipment is relatively inexpensive and long-lived. A bowling session does not require a great amount of time (as would golf) and, unlike outdoor sports, bowling is possible during evening hours, when most employees are free. Moreover, employers often pay all or part of a bowler's fees. In fact, more money probably is budgeted for employee bowling than for any other employee recreational activity. Employers tend to appreciate the fact that bowling is one of the few employee recreational activities for which supervision can be shifted outside the firm—virtually all scheduling and supervision of teams and leagues is taken care of by the bowling proprietor.

The number of regular bowlers rose from 22 million in 1958 to 30 million in 1961–62 when bowling activity suddenly reached its zenith. Thereafter, the approximately 3 percent annual decline in league bowlers (those who belong to teams that bowl regularly) was catastrophic to the industry. Bowling centers had been built in anticipation of a rapid growth rate, and many folded, unable to continue lease payments or installment payments on the heavy capital investments. By 1965, 10,750 bowling centers with 159,000 lanes remained, and these numbers had declined to 8,674 centers with 138,562 lanes by 1973. In California, the State Department of Human Resources and the Franchise Tax Board reported that the number of "bowling and billiard centers" (approximately 60 percent of them bowling alleys) fell from 735 in 1962 to 597 in 1970, and 537 by June 1973.

The chief suppliers of bowling and billiard equipment—Brunswick Corporation and AMF, Inc.—also suffered greatly in the 1960's. According to Standard and Poors "Industrial Surveys" Brunswick, which sold its bowling lanes and pinsetters, repossessed assets worth $17.7 million in 1966 and 1967. The firm even became an important competitor in operating bowling centers that they had repossessed. AMF, which leased its equipment to bowling centers, set aside $62.8 million to cover losses on receivables. Both firms began programs of diversification which reduced their dependence on bowling, and the efforts to diversify were spurred again in 1972 when the Japanese bowling boom leveled out. By 1973, only about 20 percent of AMF's revenues came from sales to the bowling industry.

Many of the bowling chains also decided to diversify. Charan Industries, which operated eleven bowling centers in the New York-New Jersey metropolitan area, increased its revenues nearly 58 percent by acquiring firms in the real estate and construction fields. Fair Lanes, Inc., a huge Baltimore-Washington area chain, continued to acquire bowling centers, but they diversified into commercial real estate development as well as into food and restaurant chains until bowling-related revenues constituted only 50 percent of sales. Great Lakes Recreation Co., a Detroit chain of eleven centers, diversified into motels, while Treadway Companies' acquisitions of motels, food distribution, and management services all but dwarfed their bowling center chain in size. Unfortunately, the chains did not find diversification to be as profitable as they had anticipated.

There was much speculation about the cause of bowling's top-out in the 1960s; perhaps it was only cyclical. League bowling had dropped off before, then it rose again. Certainly bowling had not lost its popularity with casual (non-league) bowlers. In 1974, it remained the second most popular participative sport (after swimming). Data summarized in the U. S. Department of Commerce's *Statistical Abstract of the U. S.* show that the number of people in the U. S. who bowled at least a few times a year rose from 30 million in 1961 to 43 million in 1974. League bowling also made a comeback after 1971. Membership in the American Bowling Congress, Women's Bowling Congress, and American Junior Bowling Congress together increased from 7.7 million persons in 1971 to 8.9 million persons by 1974. The number of women and junior Bowling Congress members rose steadily from about 35 percent of all Congress members in the 1960s to 49 percent.

On the other hand, bowling may have been a casualty of American affluence and the sport's traditional image as a blue-collar recreation. Membership in the American Bowling Congress dropped during the sixties, concurrent with increased disposable income per capita, and concurrent with the shift from blue collar to white collar or service employment of the labor force. Recreation expenditures increased relatively more for boats, camping equipment and golf than for bowling. The theory that regular bowling declines when people step up in income class seemed to be partially supported by a 1975 Louis Harris survey for the National Bowling Council. He found that among the more than 9 million league bowlers, 21 percent of those with family incomes of less than $10,000 per year bowled at least once a week, whereas only 17 percent of those with family incomes over $10,000 bowled that frequently. However, nearly one-third of all higher income families had casual bowlers (at least once a year), while only 21 percent of those families earning less than $9,999 bowled in 1974. Perhaps 1973–75 increases in league bowling reflected little more than consumers' reaction to the recession—a shift from expensive physical recreation to bowling.

Owners and managers of bowling centers continued to face such imponderables in 1975. Expansion of facilities or diversification out of bowling called for long-range forecasting of consumer behavior as well as evaluating the effects of inflation, fuel and energy shortages, and increased employment of women. Expansion of bowling facilities involved considerable risks because it incurred very high fixed costs for relatively long periods of time. A modern alley in a favorable urban location had a practical annual capacity of approximately 15,000 games per lane, but the break-even point might exceed 9,000 games per lane. Improved automation of services, while desirable, tended to raise the break-even point, so decisions to stake a firm's life on the future of bowling activity had to rest upon assumptions that the number of bowlers would increase and/or that the 24-hour load factor per lane could be improved in the long run. Women bowlers, who almost equalled men in numbers, had increased both the total market and the utilization of lanes during the formerly idle morning and early afternoon hours. Even so, bowling activity continued to be highly seasonal. Utilization of lanes tended to be high from September through May—the traditional winter league season—and low during the late spring and summer months. The seasonality continued despite summer leagues, tournaments and promotional specials employed by most operators during the off-season.

In 1975 approximately 85 percent of all bowling alleys in the U. S. were small, family-owned businesses. The typical owner was a member of the Bowling Proprietors Association of America, paying dues and attending meetings at both the state and national levels. Most of the twenty-five chains had dropped out rather than try to coordinate so many meetings. Furthermore they feared government anti-trust action if they participated in some proposed activities. In 1973 the chains, including ARC, formed the loosely-structured Multi-Unit Bowling Information Group without incorporation or by-laws. They scheduled three meetings per year to exchange information and discuss common problems.

THE BOARD OF DIRECTORS

ARC's board of directors had decreased in size over the years—from fifteen to nine, then to five members. A summary of the directors' backgrounds follows:

Robert Feuchter, President and Chairman, Board of Directors

-B.A. in business administration, University of California at Los Angeles, 1949

-Hughes Aircraft Co., Culver City, California—9 years: 8 years in finance, budgeting, cost control and data processing; 1 year as General Accounting Manager, Commercial Products Division

-American Recreation Centers—15 years: 5 years as vice president and director and assistant secretary; 3 years as president and director; 7 years as president and chairman of the board of directors.

Bruce C. Elliott, Vice President-Treasurer, Assistant Secretary, Director

-B.A. in business administration, University of California, 1947

-C.P.A., 1950

-Hugh J. Peat & Co., public accounting—2 years

-Self-employed C.P.A. practice in Monterey—7 years

-State of California, Legislative Audit Committee—2 years

-American Recreation Centers—16 years: 6 years as treasurer; 1 year as treasurer and assistant secretary; 9 years as treasurer, assistant secretary, and director.

John Chartz, Director

-B.S. in engineering, Santa Clara University, 1948

-Various firms as process engineer—3 years

-Dalmo-Victor, Belmont, California, major stockholder, vice president, and general manager—5 years

-Textron Corp., as manager, Dalmo-Victor Division—6 years

-Randtron Corp., Redwood City, California, vice president and major stockholder—12 years

-American Recreation Centers—15 years as director

-Major stockholder in two small firms manufacturing industrial rubber and fiberglass products

-Member of El Monte Investment Group.

C. Gervaise Davis III, Secretary and Director

-LL.D., Georgetown University, 1955

-Washington D.C. law firm—2 years

-San Francisco law firm—2 years

-Monterey law firm as partner—2 years

-Walker, Schroeder, Davis and Brehmer, a Monterey law firm, senior partner—13 years

-American Recreation Centers—10 years: 2 years as legal counsel; 3 years as assistant secretary and legal counsel; 5 years as secretary, legal counsel, and director.

Eliot Peck, Director

-B.S. in engineering, University of California, 1936

-U.S. Armed Services—5 years

-Various firms as a process engineer—10 years

-U. S. Steel, Pittsburg, California, senior staff engineer—25 years

-Member of El Monte Investment Group.

The board of directors, at Feuchter's urging, had adopted a policy of diversification into "other service industries" in his initial year as board chairman. ARC opened a luxury beauty salon in April 1968, and they continued to seek other appropriate diversifications after brief ventures into a landscape and nursery business and a sporting goods supply store. The directors also wanted to enter the physical security business, but they were unable to acquire "a going concern, with good management, at a reasonable price."

ARC's diversification policy in no way implied abandonment of bowling. In fact, the directors continued to favor purchasing centers from individual proprietors who were nearing retirement age, and in 1972, they approved a policy of adding at least one additional center each year. They also agreed with Feuchter that survival would require adoption of the latest innovations in bowling facilities. In this regard, they had approved the installation of ARC-developed fastball returns for all alleys.

Non-union salaried employees had been granted a profit-sharing and pension plan in 1971 to encourage their performance and, in 1975, the profit-sharing plan, covering 50 employees, was replaced with an Employees Stock Ownership Trust, which encompassed 190 of the 650 employees. The ESOT would use ARC's annual contributions to purchase ARC common stock. The board hoped that the employees, as owners, would be highly motivated.

In general, the board lacked sufficient time to plan for long-range needs, because two of its five members were harried executives, heavily involved in "crisis" decisions. Davis, the secretary and legal counsel, considered ARC to be only 40 percent of his client billings, and he devoted most of the twenty hours per week he spent with ARC to the solution of immediate problems. The board usually held six formal meetings a year, but their typical agenda was filled with practical, current matters such as operations problems in one or more centers, acquisition proposals, reviews of projects, or declarations of dividends.

Feuchter was convinced that the firm needed additional outside directors with broad experience and competence. He was particularly pleased with Chartz, with whom he consulted by telephone or on weekend social visits. However, directors were paid only $25 per meeting, and Feuchter did not feel that ARC could afford the relatively high premiums for director liability insurance.

ORGANIZATION AND MANAGEMENT

ARC employed approximately 650 people in 1975. President Feuchter, Vice President-Treasurer-Assistant Secretary Bruce Elliott, and Vice President of Sales and Marketing Paul Wagner were considered to be "key" officers. A chart of the organization is shown in Exhibit 1.

According to Elliott,

> Each of the bowling centers has a general manager. The general managers report on line authority direct to the president, and they are responsible for all operations and employees at the centers. However, a maintenance director, who also reports to the president, is responsible for equipment at all the alleys and has authority to hire mechanics for any center with the permission of its general manager. The arrangement has caused no serious problems.
>
> The financial and marketing divisions act as staff to the president. Every one of the staff officers and managers reports directly to the president. Theoretically, Mr. Feuchter has too many people—too wide a span of control—especially since he gets heavily involved in the details of the operations. However, with a company of this size, he doesn't have any alternative. Sometimes Mr. Feuchter starts a project but, due to pressing matters, delegates it to me or Mr. Wagner. Many times he will directly delegate a staff officer to handle a project dealing with operations.
>
> The general managers have leeway to do anything within reason at the centers. Nonmerchandise purchases up to $25 can be made without approval of the president. The key officers also have authority to do just about anything necessary related to operations. The president has never criticized or restrained any of us from taking as much authority as we needed or wanted to take.

Elliott observed that his duties seemed to vary considerably from day to day:

> Board meetings. . .take about 5 percent of my time. I have to travel occasionally to look at possible takeovers for expansion purposes, or to look at a company as a diversification opportunity. The assessment problem takes up a lot of my time. I am continually traveling to various counties to discuss property taxes with assessors. A running battle. . .continued conflict over the exorbitant property tax rates on the centers.
>
> I also work with the corporate general staff—the accountant, four bookkeepers and two women in the reception area who perform clerical and typing duties for all the officers. They all look to me for daily direction. By necessity, office management evolved to the

EXHIBIT 1 ORGANIZATION CHART, AMERICAN RECREATION CENTERS, INC.

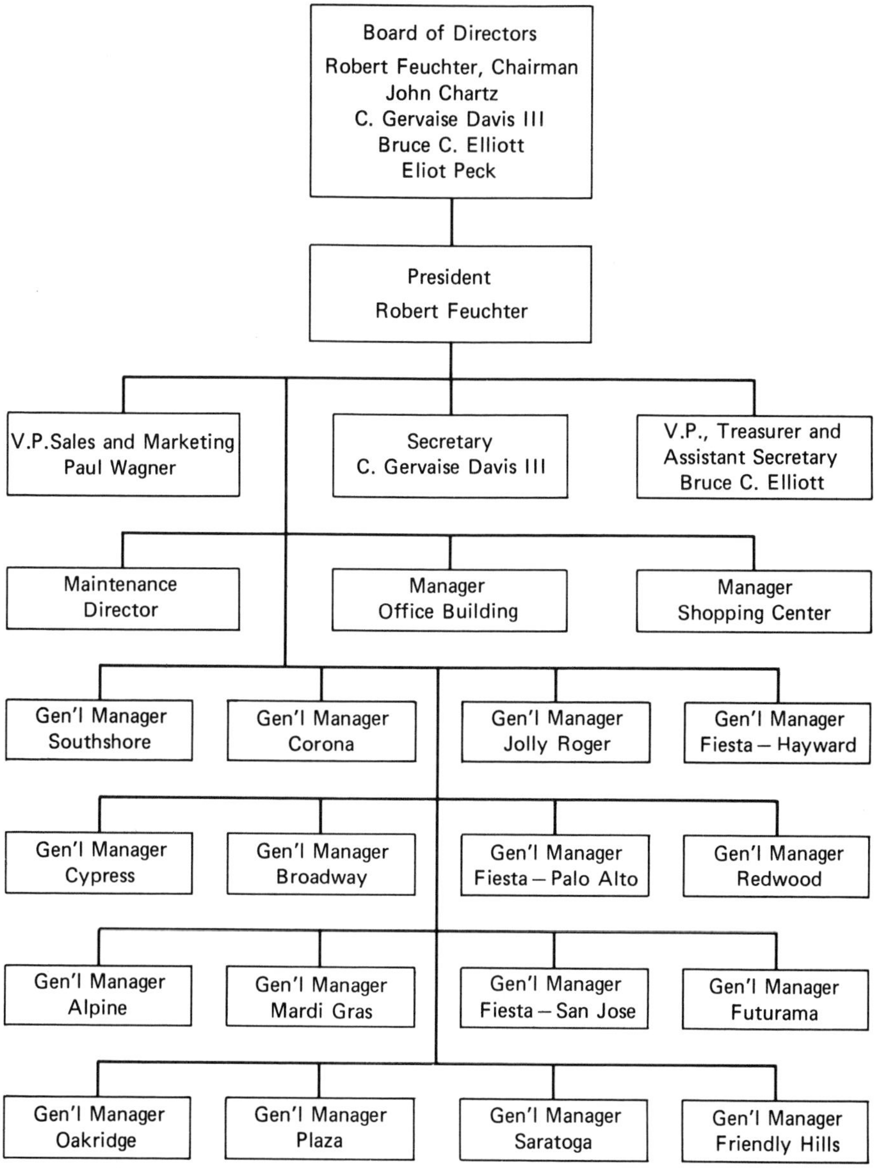

treasurer. I delegated some office management to the accountant, but it's not officially set up that way.

The vice president for sales and marketing, Wagner, discussed the organization and management at ARC in somewhat different terms.

> I don't have any staff assigned directly to me, either at headquarters or the centers. Each center is staffed with two promotion specialists reporting to the managers. It's their responsibility to carry out ARC's marketing policies, but the policies are not written down in a manual. I consider the sales staff to include the center managers, assistant managers, promotional specialists and sales counter personnel. Counter salesmen are the important marketing element.
>
> My key responsibilities include coordination of the program between the centers and training personnel to perform the various marketing functions. I don't get directly involved in performing marketing tasks. There are some problems in getting things done, since the sales force reports direct to the managers, who report to the president. I don't feel, however, that the organizational structure poses any major weaknesses.

Wagner disclosed that he devoted six to ten hours weekly to training sales personnel. Also, some time was spent recruiting new employees or selecting employees to move up to assistant manager or manager positions. On the average, the remainder of his week was taken up in sales management activities. However, during promotional campaigns each season, he tended to be fully occupied in the role of advertising director.

Feuchter viewed the organization and management of ARC more as a problem of staffing. He observed that

> A center's managers have to be carefully selected because it is the key management position. A manager has to be very reliable. . .a person I can trust and have confidence in, because the centers are too decentralized to keep on top of their performance. . .Legally, we're a holding company. A few centers have to maintain a separate identity because of old provisions on the acquisition contracts. But practically, we're one.
>
> I occasionally make a mistake in choosing a manager, and I've had to "deep six" a few in the past years who didn't work out. A couple couldn't get along with the officers or customers. Others got dictatorial with employees. You can't order employees around these days—you have to utilize more subtle methods.
>
> It's our policy to promote managers from the ranks of the centers' sales staffs. Educational level is generally high school. Sales people start working on the sales counter and, then, if they show the aptitude, are given a promotional specialist position. We generally want employees in these positions who like to bowl themselves and enjoy long hours of work at the centers. Assistant managers are in charge of the evening bowling. If they show promise performing in that capacity, some additional duties are delegated to them.

OPERATIONS

ARC attempted to purchase, build, or expand bowling centers only in areas where the population growth trend and competition were favorable. They also tried to drop centers which failed to show sufficient profit. For example, a contract to manage the Sea Bowl in Pacifica, California was dropped for this reason in 1969. In 1975, they were negotiating the sale of another disappointing center—the Jolly Roger Lanes in Grass Valley, California.

Most of the areas in which ARC competed continued to enjoy a favorable population trend, but there was some question about the growth rate in Whittier (see

Exhibit 2). One of the difficulties in judging favorable population trends is that pockets of change exist in each city, county, or standard metropolitan area. Corona (population 28,000) and Whittier (population 73,000) locations, for example, were pockets in huge population districts. From the bowling center manager's point of view, the number of people within easy commuting distance is important. One firm, Bowl America, Inc., a large chain in the southeastern U. S., was reported by *Barron's* to believe that a successful center must have 2,000 people within a 3-mile radius for each lane. It seemed obvious that many of the standard metropolitan

EXHIBIT 2 POPULATION IN ARC'S OPERATING LOCATIONS 1970–75

	Population—Standard Metropolitan Area Census Estimated (000s)*					
Bowling Center Location	1970	1971	1972	1973	1974	1975
Alameda	1,081	1,091	1,101	1,111	1,098	1,100
Mel's Southshore (40 lanes)						
Corona	1,380	1,425	1,467	1,505	1,530	1,572
Corona Bowl (24 lanes)						
Grass Valley	21	n.a.	n.a.	n.a.	n.a.	n.a.
Jolly Roger Lanes (12 lanes)						
Hayward	1,081	1,091	1,101	1,111	1,098	1,100
Fiesta Lanes (40 lanes)						
Monterey	250	253	256	258	263	266
Cypress Bowl (24 lanes)						
Oakland	1,081	1,091	1,101	1,111	1,098	1,100
Broadway Bowl (40 lanes)						
Palo Alto	557	559	562	564	575	577
Fiesta Lanes (32 lanes)						
Redwood City	557	559	562	564	575	577
Mel's Redwood Bowl (40 lanes)						
Sacramento	816	836	857	875	885	902
Alpine Alley (40 lanes)						
Mardi Gras Lanes (40 lanes)						
San Jose	1,090	1,123	1,157	1,190	1,189	1,209
Fiesta Lanes (40 lanes)						
Futurama Bowl (42 lanes)						
Oakridge Lanes (38 lanes)						
Plaza Lanes (40 lanes)						
Saratoga Lanes (32 lanes)						
Whittier	7,037	6,999	6,958	6,945	6,956	6,948
Friendly Hills Lanes (32 lanes)						
California Metropolitan Areas	18,800	19,019	19,230	19,441	20,216	20,406

**Alameda County (Alameda, Hayward and Oakland); San Diego County (Corona); Nevada County (Grass Valley); San Mateo County (Palo Alto and Redwood City); Sacramento-Placer-Yolo Counties (Sacramento); Santa Clara County (San Jose); and Los Angeles-Long Beach (Whittier). Estimates 1971–75 from United California Bank's "Annual Forecasts."*

areas had bowling center competitors who shared patrons in over-lapping radii of 3 miles. Competitive factors, such as traffic density, price structures and service, then were critical. The Whittier center might well overcome other disadvantages because it was considered to be "the prestige bowl in its market." Strong competitors often were able to draw patrons from a considerable distance. The sparse population in Nevada County was one important reason for sale of the Jolly Roger Lanes in Grass Valley.

Wagner discussed ARC operations in considerable detail. He said that locations were specifically decided on to take advantage of market demand in an area. Population growth trends and lack of bowling facilities in the specific area indicated the best locations. When asked whether ARC was operating at full capacity, he replied,

> Room for any volume increase during peak hours would exist in only two or three bowls. During the day and early morning hours they have a substantial number of lanes open. Housewives' leagues have improved this. Regular league times start at 6 p.m. Agreements for price and reservations are entered into with the teams in May and September. The agreements aren't really binding on the teams. Bowling captains have been known to sign up for more than one league at the same time and then cancel.

He indicated that business slowed down severely during the last of April and first of September, when leagues were formed. Also, leagues did not play between Christmas and New Year's. In reply to a question about promotional efforts, Wagner explained that promotional programs covering all locations were conducted several times a year. Campaigns before the start of a new league season stimulated business during slack periods and attracted new teams. During holiday weeks, they promoted student play by special low rates per line, and in the newer facilities, special holiday fun packages on New Year's Eve included dancing, food, liquor, and bowling for one ticket price. . ."They have the run of the entire place."

He believed that direct sales were the most effective promotional method:

> Repeat business from league teams must be solicited by the promotional staff, counter salesmen, and managers—by phone or direct contact. New league business comes from direct contact with employee "reps" or businesses with recreational programs. Promotional brochures are mailed out at random. We spend $10,000 or $15,000 a year on TV, radio and newspaper media advertising—mainly to promote open play on holidays or during the slack, off-season. It's hard to give a dollar amount, because broadcast stations do a lot of trading and bartering. For example, time can be purchased with free bowling tickets; then broadcasters use these to put together an advertising campaign for another client.

In response to a question about ARC's marketing research, Wagner answered that the firm had no formal marketing research program: "Attempts to promote new demand evolved over years. Brunswick and AMF assist bowl operators by providing training materials, seminars and classroom instruction for sales people and managers. Also they supply data on marketing trends and industry developments."

Billiard rooms, coffee shops, and cocktail lounges were included in most of the centers. Beer, wine, and mixed drink sales were natural, and relatively profitable, adjuncts to bowling. Food service also was complementary, but ARC had not always found it to be profitable. A 1969–70 attempt to solve the problem by leasing all food service operations was aborted when the contractor suffered heavy losses. In 1971,

ARC took over what appeared to be the most profitable food centers and leased facilities in the other centers to experienced food service firms. Losses continued, so additional food operations were leased out in 1974. Billiard parlors were quite profitable, when patronized, because desk clerks could handle the play as part of their regular duties, but patronage had dwindled as more home tables were purchased. Revenues from billiards dropped $70,000 in fiscal 1969 alone. According to Feuchter: "Billiard activities have become a minor part of our business." By 1975, various coin-operated games were enticing patrons (particularly teenagers) in increasing numbers to most bowling centers.

Pricing was, of course, a significant factor in marketing ARC's bowling services. While the policy according to Wagner, was to "set rates as high as possible without hurting demand," price competition was conceded to be a problem from time to time. League agreements seldom called for discounts, although ARC did pioneer in giving players who belonged to leagues at any of their centers substantial discounts on open play, during non-prime hours. Wagner explained that "It was first tried as a promotion gimmick to attract league teams to the centers. It has become very popular. Some competitors question the logic of discounted rates, but it has resulted in much more casual play by league members."

ARC always tried to raise prices enough to offset increased labor costs. Union contracts covering all employees below assistant managers were renegotiated every two years, usually with an across-the-board hike. Contracts generally included cost-of-living escalation clauses which tended to raise wages between contracts. Mr. Wagner explained that ARC followed a policy of raising prices in 5-cent and 10-cent increments to a level that would at least provide enough income to offset the increased wages for the contract period. Some competitors adjusted prices more frequently, he said, "but our prices can't be too far out of line. It's easy to monitor, because prices are posted by all operators, and feedback is fast from regular bowlers."

FINANCES

At the end of fiscal 1975, ARC's 293,469 shares of common stock were widely distributed among northern California investors and were being traded in regional over-the-counter markets at about 7½ bid and 8 asked. Major stockholders included the three key officers (approximately 10 percent), outside directors (8 to 9 percent), former convertible debenture holders, and a federally-qualified Employee Stock Ownership Trust (ESOT). The ESOT encompassed all 190 of the firm's non-union employees and would increase employees' future share of ownership much beyond the present 25 percent. It also could provide ARC with immediate cash if it borrowed money to purchase ARC stock. In 1975, $175,000 was allocated to the ESOT—52,000 in stock @ 8 per share, and $123,000 to buy ARC stock in the open market.

ARC's financial statements for 1965 through 1975 are shown in Exhibits 3, 4, and 5.

Elliott took a certain amount of pride in the firm's presentation of financial data, although he volunteered that ARC's auditing firm had questioned excluding the current portion of long-term debt shown on the books; yet the liability was just as real as a twenty-year note for $800,000. A lease usually required minimum rental plus taxes, insurance and additional rentals based on sales volume above a minimum. In the past, ARC had been unable to sell some unprofitable centers, he said, because potential buyers refused commitment to existing long-term leases. The company would be much better off now if they had purchased facilities, he said; unfortunately, they didn't have the money at that time.

EXHIBIT 3 AMERICAN RECREATION CENTERS, INC., CONSOLIDATED STATEMENT OF INCOME, FISCAL YEAR ENDING LAST WEEK IN MAY (000s)

Revenues	*1965*	*1966*	*1967*
Bowling	$2,692	$2,576	$2,956
Restaurant	1,480	1,485	1,754
Bar	1,132	1,240	1,425
Accessories, billiards, & misc.	377	350	325
Total Revenues	$5,681	$5,651	$6,460
Operating Costs			
Operating, General & Administrative Expense**			
Cost of goods sold	1,800	1,754	2,017
Salaries, wages, & other payroll cost	2,199	2,247	2,589
Rents	649	673	806
Depreciation & amortization	467	468	480
Administrative salaries & related	117	102	122
Other administrative expenses	127	103	87
Total	5,359	5,347	6,101
Net income before interest & extraordinary items	323	304	359
Interest	305	284	266
Extraordinary (income) or expense			
Net Income Before Taxes	17	20	93
Provision for estimated income taxes	6	6	40
Net Income	$ 11	$ 14	$ 53

***General and administrative expenses not reported separately after 1971.*

It should be mentioned that even though ARC did not show its long-term lease obligations as liabilities, a footnote on each balance sheet did list the minimum commitments for the five years following, and showed the decrease in net income which would have resulted from capitalizing the leases. In 1975, the footnote indicated that assumed depreciation over the forty-year useful lives and interest related to capitalization of the twelve existing leases, expiring 1982 to 2009, would have been $1,064,000 in 1974 and $981,000 in 1975, resulting in a net income decrease of $48,000 in 1974 and $39,000 in 1975.

Elliot was very dubious about the value of using financial ratios in connection with ARC. In his words: "They are certainly of interest to analysts and investors or lenders, but they aren't of any real importance in managing the company."

ARC's equity base had increased but Feuchter favored still wider sale and distribution of the stock. Toward this end he had supported the board's decision to grant stock options to key officers, and stock dividends of 4 percent in each of the past four years. In 1974, ARC became a member of the Committee of Publicly

EXHIBIT 3 (Cont.)

1968	*1969*	*1970*	*1971*	*1972*	*1973*	*1974*	*1975*
$3,224	$3,277	$3,256	$3,461	$3,823	$4,266	$5,192	$ 5,731
1,839	1,419	1,051	224*	419	772	1,385	1,860
1,644	1,537	1,475	1,516	1,625	1,854	2,343	2,550
272	199	171	170	307	328	374	348
$6,979	$6,432	$5,953	$5,371	$6,174	$7,220	$9,294	$10,489
				5,172	6,101	7,797	8,957
2,192	1,866	1,649	1,307				
2,873	2,637	2,402	2,005				
914	901	905	937				
485	482	470	475	466	446	426	436
116	148	149	129				
92	90	94	148				
6,672	6,124	5,669	5,001	5,638	6,547	8,223	9,393
307	308	284	370	536	673	1,071	1,096
236	205	204	174	174	173	193	270
(27)	(11)	(33)	(35)				
98	126	113	231	362	500	878	826
48	51	46	115	182	255	430	417
$ 50	$ 63	$ 67	$ 116	$ 180	$ 245	$ 448	$ 409

**Most food service centers taken over by private contractor in 1971; ARC reclaimed some in 1972 and leased others in 1973–75.*

Owned Companies, a national organization dedicated to attracting more stock ownership. Additional employee ownership was encouraged when, in 1966, ARC adopted a stock purchase plan for employees in which the company added 50 cents to each employee dollar of stock purchase within certain limits. The ESOT, implemented in 1975, was another move in this direction.

Restructuring the long-term debt and improving the firm's liquidity had been significant goals for the president since he took office. In 1965, long-term debt consisted of:

Installment contracts	$ 665,584
Secured notes, payable monthly installments	2,321,727
7% & 8% unsecured subordinated notes	269,898
Other unsecured notes	82,967
Total	$3,340,176

EXHIBIT 4 AMERICAN RECREATION CENTERS, INC., CONSOLIDATED BALANCE SHEET, FISCAL YEAR ENDING LAST WEEK IN MAY (000s)

Assets	*1965*	*1966*	*1967*
Current Assets			
Cash	$ 89	$ 93	$ 112
Marketable securities, at cost			99
Accounts receivable, less allowance for doubtful accounts	71	30	47
Inventories	81	61	71
Prepaid insurance, taxes, rent and other expenses	127	157	130
Total Current Assets	368	341	459
Fixed Assets & Leaseholds, at cost			
Land and buildings	103	103	104
Machinery and equipment	5,890	6,005	6,084
Leaseholds & leasehold improvements	1,840	1,854	1,869
Total	7,833	7,962	8,057
Less accumulated depreciation and amortization	2,277	2,737	3,218
Total Fixed Assets	5,556	5,225	4,839
Other Assets and Deferred Expenses			
Debenture purchase fund	16	34	38
Deposits, liquor licenses & misc. deferred expenses	252	216	182
Unamortized long-term debt discount and expenses	120	97	77
Total Other Assets & Deferred Exp.	388	347	297
Total Assets	$6,312	$5,913	$5,595
Liabilities & Stockholders' Equity			
Liabilities			
Current Liabilities			
Accounts payable	$ 242	$ 269	$ 320
Accrued taxes and expenses	179	209	257
Income taxes payable			
Notes payable to bank	59	37	17
Dividends payable			
Total Current, exclusive of current portion of long-term debt	480	515	594
Long-Term Debt	4,218	3,763	3,273
Current Portion of Long-Term Debt	459	410	336
Income Taxes Deferred to Future Years	251	258	298
Total Liabilities	$4,949	$4,536	$4,165
Stockholders' Equity			
Capital Stock (no par, $2.50 stated value)	$ 539	$ 539	$ 539
Capital in Excess of Stated Share Value	517	517	517
Retained Earnings	307	321	374
Total Stockholders' Equity	1,363	1,377	1,430
Total Liabilities and Net Worth	$6,312	$5,913	$5,595

EXHIBIT 4 (Cont.)

1968	*1969*	*1970*	*1971*	*1972*	*1973*	*1974*	*1975*
$ 73	$ 175	$ 120	$ 104	$ 29	$ 88	$ 26	$ 59
138	76	234	357	350	100	495	552
85	87	52	45	52	63	77	106
69	53	44	42	51	98	100	94
174	191	174	179	196	277	328	396
539	582	624	727	678	626	1,026	1,207
104	179	205	205	1,578	1,762	2,651	3,285
6,169	6,411	6,469	6,511	6,704	6,808	7,385	7,495
1,899	1,907	1,933	1,967	2,023	2,123	2,157	2,236
8,172	8,497	8,607	8,683	10,305	10,693	12,193	13,016
3,676	4,165	4,610	5,085	5,517	5,961	6,362	6,793
4,496	4,332	3,997	3,598	4,788	4,732	5,831	6,223
34	33	34	36				
235	212	155	227	302	245	253	298
66	51	37	21				
335	296	226	284	302	245	253	298
$5,370	$5,210	$4,847	$4,609	$5,769	$5,603	$7,110	$7,728
$ 235	$ 269	$ 241	$ 221	$ 311	$ 385	$ 533	$ 681
282	211	165	170	196	233	303	329
	26	23	114	156	224	236	159
5	7	7	9	6	7	9	12
522	513	436	514	669	849	1,081	1,181
3,027	2,772	2,393	1,991	2,833	2,271	3,162	3,340
378	324	310	325	510	410	474	428
346	411	420	420	396	349	305	286
$3,895	$3,696	$3,249	$2,925	$3,898	$3,469	$4,548	$4,807
$ 539	$ 558	$ 589	$ 601	$ 623	$ 668	$ 707	$ 734
518	520	520	517	562	633	681	714
418	436	489	566	685	833	1,174	1,473
1,475	1,514	1,598	1,684	1,870	2,134	2,562	2,921
$5,370	$5,210	$4,847	$4,609	$5,768	$5,603	$7,110	$7,728

EXHIBIT 5 AMERICAN RECREATION CENTERS, INC. SOURCE AND APPLICATION OF FUNDS FISCAL YEAR ENDING LAST WEEK IN MAY (000s)

Source of Funds Operations	*1965*	*1966*	*1967*	*1968*	*1969*	*1970*	*1971*	*1972*	*1973*	*1974*	*1975*
Net income	$ 11	$ 14	$ 53	$ 50	$ 63	$ 67	$116	$ 180	$ 245	$ 448	$ 409
Depreciation & amortization	469	469	482	488	489	476	478	466	446	427	436
Other miscellaneous charges	27	12	6	14							
Increase (decrease) in deferred income taxes	6	7	40	48	11	9		(23)	(48)	(44)	(19)
Funds Provided from Operations	513	502	581	600	563	552	594	623	643	831	826
Proceeds from addn'l long-term debt			23	176	214	72	236	1,334	260	1,349	634
Issue of capital stock or exercise of stock options					21	31	10	35	2	13	3
Other sources	187	138	126		39	71	(56)		57	39	(40)
Total Funds Provided	$700	$640	$730	$776	$837	$726	$784	$1,992	$ 962	$2,232	$1,423
Application of Funds											
Retirement of long-term debt	$536	$505	$464	$421	$470	$451	$638	$ 491	$ 776	$ 459	$ 456
Payment of short-term debt	61	22	21								
Additions to fixed assets & leaseholds	103	109	95	145	325	142	82	1,659	390	1,572	833
Increase of other assets & def. chgs.		4	150	53				15			
Purchase of treasury stock							20	6	2	3	7
Dividends declared				5	12	14	19	24	25	31	45
Total	700	640	730	624	807	607	759	2,195	1,193	2,065	1,341
Net increase (decrease) in working capital, exclusive of current portion of long-term debt				151	30	119	25	(203)	(231)	167	82
Total Funds Used	$700	$640	$730	$776	$837	$726	$784	$1,992	$ 962	$2,232	$1,423

Service on the long-term debt, including interest, sinking fund payments, redemptions, and installment payments promised to be in excess of $900,000 in 1966. In addition, leases on nine of the ten centers would require payments of $660,000. It seemed unlikely that cash flow would be sufficient even to retire the maturing debt. However, by dint of hard work and bargaining, installment contracts for purchase of bowling lanes and pin setters were renegotiated to extend the terms; Series B convertible debentures were exchanged for promissory notes payable in monthly installments over ten years, and sinking fund payments were suspended for 1966. Estimated debt maturity for 1967 was thereby reduced from $745,826 to $409,970. Fixed charges were increased but ARC was able to survive.

Long-term debt continued to be reduced until 1972, when relatively large long-term secured note issues were used to purchase two bowling centers. All debentures were retired July 1, 1973. Installment contracts were reduced gradually until the fall of 1973, when additional contracts for equipment were assumed. By May 28, 1975, ARC's long-term debt consisted of the following:

Installment contracts—3½% to 7% interest	$2,183,318
7% debentures, due 9/30/72	304,500
Series A, 6% convertible debentures, due 7/1/73	870,000
Series B, 6% convertible debentures, due 7/1/73	437,500
6% notes, due 6/15/68 or before	378,256
Total	$4,173,574

Debt service and other fixed charges were still high in 1975. Notes and installment contracts of $474,000 and $367,000 would fall due in 1976 and 1977, interest costs had risen, and payments on non-cancellable leases were expected to be $930,000 in 1976 and $961,000 in 1977. However, cash flow would be relatively high. In addition to the great improvement in debt structure since 1965, profits had risen from $11,000 to $409,000, cash dividends had been paid since 1968, the stock was selling at a bid price of 7½ versus $2.03 in 1970, all lanes had been modernized, and ARC had acquired six more bowling centers, the Southgate Shopping Center in Hayward, and an office building adjoining the Corona Bowl near San Diego. Birdcage Lanes, in Sacramento's newest shopping center, and Northridge Lanes in Los Angeles County's San Fernando Valley—both brand new—were scheduled to open in August 1975.

THE FUTURE

Wagner saw a profitable future for the bowling industry. He felt that ARC's place lay in bowling and related services, and that the company had never had much success with ventures into other fields. It was ARC's policy, until about 1971, he said, to contain expansion within northern California. "The president probably did this due to lack of capital and adequate personnel necessary to branch over a wide geographical area. Now with business improving and some capital available. . .he would consider expanding into neighboring states. Occasionally, a national firm has voiced consolidating overtures, but none of the offers to date has been worth consideration."

Wagner emphasized that: "The president is solely responsible for handling the diversification program, looking primarily for a service-oriented business, not involving manufacture of a product, and manageable by the ARC team." As for himself, he said, "My goals include providing the best possible marketing training for development of the sales staff. I am primarily concerned with developing a good sales management training program to improve management of existing centers and enable the company to expand when opportunities arise." Another of his goals, he said, was "to find ways to maximize utilization of the lanes. This is the primary job of the sales and marketing staff."

Marketing policies, Wagner observed, were "formulated jointly by the key officers, based on inputs from the general managers and other sales staff in the centers." With regard to the board, he said, "I am not aware of any marketing policies specifically established by the board of directors."

Elliott said that his only goal was to maximize profits. He seemed to feel that efficiency of operations was the only way to profits, and he commented in some detail about the systems for controlling cash, payrolls, and inventories with budgets and daily or weekly feedback on expense and sales items from each center. One bar to efficiency, he thought, was the seasonality of bowling, which seemed always to result in losses during the first two quarters of a fiscal year. He was not sure that a long-term budget would be fruitful in planning, nor was he sure that additional outside directors would be of great value—"that is Mr. Feuchter's idea." In this regard, he said that the inability to obtain liability insurance from a reputable company to protect directors against stockholder court-actions had been the stumbling block. In his view, "the company is too small . . . the better insurance underwriters want companies with substantial equity investments. Possibly the insurance would be written by a specialty insurance company . . . I don't know what it would cost."

Feuchter appeared to be more concerned than other executives and directors about formulating goals and policies for the future. Although he obviously was pleased with the progress made since 1971, he continued to believe that the firm should have additional outside directors—men less concerned with ARC's day-to-day operations. At one time, he said, they had invited a potential outside director—a professor from Santa Clara—to sit in on a couple of meetings, but the man was much too theoretical. Feuchter insisted that any goals or plans must be pragmatic. In his words:

> I don't think general goals have any real meaning or any realistic application to management of a company's operations. I have read with interest some elaborate goals stated in recent annual reports of companies . . . wordy goals related to ecology and environmental factors sound good to investors, but it's doubtful whether managers are really sincere in what is being proposed.
>
> I could probably come up with a fancy society-related goal stating that ARC is interested in promoting wholesome recreation for the family. It would be true . . . about 40,000 persons use the facilities weekly for recreation and most of these customers are, of course, family members.
>
> But I don't see where stating such goals would add any real significance to our operations. In general, I don't feel that the effort of formulating intangible concepts is worthwhile to ARC or any other organization for practical day-to-day operations.

He said that ARC had not established formal goals and policies and had not found a need to write down the ones key officers had practiced over the years.

> I have my goals, and one of them is to gain growth for the company—both internally and by expansion. Diversification policies will be continued in the future. . .Internally, profit margins must be widened still more to attract investors. The existing centers have substantial potential for unit sales expansion during weekdays until 6 p.m. and on weekends. Also, I'm not sure that employees are used efficiently in the centers. It may be that the company has outgrown the organization, but I hate to add overhead.

Feuchter indicated that he had just about given up on diversification when he saw the experience of competitors in their ventures outside the bowling industry. "For the time being," he said, "the energy problem is more pressing. Will the government say that bowling is an 'essential industry' if electricity is rationed, or will they limit the maximum hours we can stay open during a day?"

FOURWINDS MARINA

Jack Keltner had just completed his first day as general manager of the Fourwinds Marina. It was mid-August and although the marina's slip rentals ran until October 30, business took a dramatic downturn after Labor Day. Jack knew that it would be unwise to change the way current operations were being run in the three weeks remaining in the season, but he also knew that before the following spring he would have to move decisively to implement some of the changes which he had been considering. Major changes would be required if Fourwinds Marina was to survive.

In his previous job as Fourwinds' controller, Keltner had been intimately involved in the operation of Fourwinds Marina. He believed, at a minimum, that the following changes should be made over the next 12-month period:

1. Add 80 slips of E, F, and G docks and put in underwater supports on these docks to deter breakage from storms. Cost: \$250,000–300,000. Annual profits if all slips are rented: \$74,000+.
2. Add a second girl to assist the present secretary-receptionist-bookkeeper. Savings: \$300+ per month, provided the Indianapolis office is closed.
3. Reorganize the parts department and put in a new inventory system. Cost: \$30,000. Savings: \$2,500–\$3,000 per year.
4. Keep the boat and motor inventory low. Boat inventory as of mid-August was approximately \$125,000. It had been over \$300,000.
5. Reduce the work force through attrition if a vacated job can be assumed by someone remaining on the staff.
6. Outfit E, F, and G docks for winter storage using an improved and more extensive bubbling system. Profits to be generated: uncertain and difficult to estimate.
7. Light and heat the storage building so that repair work can be done at night

Prepared by Professors W. Harvey Hegarty of Indiana University and Harry Kelsey, Jr., of Wake Forest University.

and in the winter. Cost: $12,000, which can probably be paid for from the profits in two winters of operation.

Keltner had no experience in marina management, but was considered a hard worker willing to take on tremendous challenges. He had joined the Taggart Corporation after four years as a CPA at Ernst and Ernst, one of the "Big Eight" accounting firms. Functioning as controller of Taggart Corporation, which owned Fourwinds Marina and Inn of the Fourwinds on Lake Monroe, he found that a tremendous volume of work was demanded, necessitating late hours at the office and a briefcase full of work to take home with him most evenings. Keltner lived in a small community near Fourwinds Marina and had to commute frequently to the home office of the Taggart Corporation in Indianapolis, an hour and a half drive from Lake Monroe. Keltner stated that he hoped to shift all of his work to Lake Monroe, site of the marina and inn as soon as possible. In his view, handling the accounting for the marina, the inn, and other Taggart Corporation interests could be done just as effectively at the Marina. The inn and the marina comprised 90 percent of the business of the corporation.

Much of the explanation for Keltner's heavy work load lay in the fact that there had been virtually no accounting system when he first joined Taggart. He had, however, set up six profit centers for the marina and was now generating monthly accounting reports.

Keltner believed each of the seven changes he had in mind would add to the effectiveness and profitability of the marina operation and that was his prime concern. The operation of the inn was under control of another general manager and, further, was operated as a separate corporate entity. Keltner was responsible only for the accounting procedures of the Inn of the Fourwinds.

As he turned over the structure, background, and development of the inn and the marina, Keltner realized that his new role as general manager of Fourwinds Marina, when added on to his job as controller of the Taggart Corporation, presented an imposing challenge. Managing the marina was a full-time, seven-day-a-week job, particularly during the season. The questions uppermost in his mind were: (1) What would be the full plan he would present to Taggart to turn the operation around and make it profitable? and (2) How would the plan be funded? The financial statements of the marina presented a glum picture (see Exhibits 1 and 2), but Keltner had good data available to analyze revenue and costs on almost every segment of Fourwinds' operations. Moreover, there was the knowledge he had gleaned working with the past general managers and observing the operation of the marina.

THE PREVIOUS GENERAL MANAGER

The day the previous general manager resigned, Jack Keltner was called in by Sandy Taggart, president of the Taggart Corporation. Keltner was informed that Leon McLaughlin had just submitted his resignation as general manager of the marina—apparently because McLaughlin and Taggart had disagreed on some compensation McLaughlin felt was due him. Part of the disagreement concerned McLaughlin's wife who had been hired to work in the parts department and had spent little time there due to an illness. Taggart had wasted no time in hiring Keltner as McLaughlin's replacement.

McLaughlin had been the fifth general manager in the five years that the marina had been in operation. He had had 15 years of marine experience before being hired to manage the Fourwinds Marina. His experience, however, consisted of

EXHIBIT 1 FOURWINDS MARINA INCOME STATEMENT, FISCAL YEAR ENDING MARCH 31, 1974

Revenue:		
Sale of new boats	$774,352	
Sale of used boats	179,645	
Sale of rental boats	17,051	
Total Sales		$971,048
Other income:		
Service and repair	$128,687	
Gasoline and oil	81,329	
Ship store	91,214	
Slip rental	174,808	
Winter storage	32,177	
Boat rental	99,895	
Other Income		608,110
Total Income		$1,579,158
Expenses:		
Fixed Costs:		
Cost of boats	$798,123	
Cost of repair equipment	56,698	
Ship store costs	64,405	
Cost of gasoline	51,882	
Boat rental costs	8,951	
Total Fixed Costs		980,059
Operating Expenses:		
Wages and salaries	$228,154	
Taxes	23,725	
Building rent	58,116	
Equipment rent	8,975	
Utilities	18,716	
Insurance	25,000	
Interest on loans	209,310	
Advertising	30,150	
Legal expense	19,450	
Bad debt expense	8,731	
Miscellaneous	39,994	
Total Operating Expenses		670,321
Total Costs		1,650,380
Operating Loss		$ 71,222
Depreciation		122,340
Total Loss*		$ 193,562

**This represents the total operating loss of the Fourwinds Marina in the fiscal year ending March 31, 1974. Fourwinds sold a subsidiary in 1973–a boat sales firm in Indianapolis—on which a loss of $275,580 was written off.*

EXHIBIT 2 FOURWINDS MARINA BALANCE SHEET, MARCH 31, 1974

Assets			*Liabilities*	
Current Assets:			Current Liabilities:	
Cash	31,858		Accounts payable	89,433
Accounts receivable	70,632		Intercompany payables	467,091
New boats	199,029		Accrued salary expense	8,905
Used boats	60,747		Accrued interest expense	20,383
Parts	53,295		Accrued tax expense	43,719
Ship store	2,741		Accrued lease expense	36,190
Gas/oil	2,626		Prepaid dock rental	178,466
Total Current Assets	$ 420,928	Less	Boat deposits	4,288
Fixed Assets:		Depreciation	Current bank notes	177,600
Buoys and docks	984,265	315,450	Mortgage (current)	982,900
Permanent buildings	201,975	17,882	Note payable to floor plan	225,550
Office furniture	3,260	704	Note on rental houseboats	71,625
Houseboats	139,135	15,631	Notes to stockholders	515,150
Work boats	40,805	7,987	Dealer reserve liability	13,925
Equipment	72,420	38,742	Total Current Liabilities	$2,835,225
	$1,441,860	$396,396	Long-term note on houseboats	117,675
Net Fixed Assets	$1,045,464		Common stock—1,000 shares at	
Other Assets:			par value $1 per share	1,000
Prepaid expense	2,940		Retained earnings deficit	(990,105)
Deferred interest expense	25,321		Loss during year ending	
	$ 28,261		March 31, 1974*	(469,142)
Total Assets	$1,494,653		Total Liabilities and Net Worth	$1,494,653

Loss during year ending March 31, 1974 is composed of an operating loss of $71,222 plus depreciation of $122,340, and a write-off loss of a solid subsidiary of $275,580.

selling and servicing boats and motors in Evansville, Indiana, and was not in marina management. McLaughlin had taken pride in running a "tight ship" and had often said that the marina had an excellent chance in turning around after some lean times. McLaughlin had found it fairly easy to keep Fourwinds staffed because the resort atmosphere was so attractive, and his goal had been to have the majority of the staff employed on a full-time, year-round basis. Even though the marina was closed from November until April there was a considerable amount of repair work on boats needed during those months. McLaughlin was told when hired that he had a blank check to get Fourwinds shaped up and profitable; this promise, however, was later rescinded.

McLaughlin and his wife had a mobile home near the marina, but had maintained a permanent residence in Evansville. For the most part, McLaughlin had put in six full days a week, but he had usually not worked at all on Sundays, believing that he was entitled to one day per week off. In general, McLaughlin had proved to be an effective organizer; his biggest managerial weakness was in the area of employee and customer relations.

TAGGART CORPORATION

The other principal investors involved in the Taggart Corporation besides A. L. "Sandy" Taggart, III were William Brennan, president of one of the state's largest commercial and industrial real estate firms and Richard DeMars, president of Guepel-DeMars, Inc., the firm that designed both the marina and the inn.

Sandy Taggart was a well-known Indianapolis businessman and chairman of the board of Colonial Baking Company. Colonial was one of the larger bakeries serving the Indianapolis metropolitan area and surrounding counties. He did his undergraduate work at Princeton and completed Harvard's Advanced Management Program in 1967. He was an easy-going man and did not appear to be upset by problems. He maintained his office at the Taggart Corporation in Indianapolis but tried to get to Fourwinds at least once every week. He kept in daily contact with Leon McLaughlin and continued to do the same with Keltner. He enjoyed being a part of the daily decision making and problem solving that went on at the marina and felt that he needed to be aware of all decisions, due to the corporation's weak financial position. Taggart believed that Fourwinds' current problems stemmed from a lack of knowledge of the marina business and a lack of experienced general managers when operations were begun some six years ago. Taggart acknowledged that a lack of expertise in maintaining accurate cost data and in cost control had plagued Fourwinds Marina, but he was pleased with Keltner's progress in correcting these problems.

LOCATION AND SETTING

The Fourwinds Marina and the Inn of the Fourwinds were located on Lake Monroe, the largest lake in Indiana. The lake is a 10,700-acre manmade reservoir developed by the US Army Corps of Engineers in conjunction with and under the jurisdiction of the Indiana Department of Natural Resources. With the surrounding public lands (accounting for some 80 percent of the 150-mile shoreline) the total acreage is 26,000. It is a multipurpose project designed to provide flood control, recreation, water supply, and flow augmentation benefits to the people of Indiana. Lake Monroe is located in the southwestern quadrant of the state, about nine miles or a 15-minute drive southwest of Bloomington, Indiana, home of Indiana University, and a 90-minute drive from Indianapolis (see Exhibit 3). The Indianapolis metropoli-

EXHIBIT 3

Metropolitan Area	*County*	*Population*	*Miles from Lake Monroe*
Indianapolis	Marion	1,144,000	70
Terre Haute	Vigo	173,000	80
Louisville, Ky.	below Floyd	893,000	115
Evansville	Posey	289,000	127

tan area had a 1974 population of over 1 million people; estimated spendable income was about $3.5 billion annually. A recent *Fortune* survey indicated that the Indianapolis area was considered a desirable site for future expansion by many of the nation's top industrial leaders.

Indianapolis is located at a crossroads of the national interstate highway system; more interstate highways converge at Indianapolis than any other point in the United States. Its recently enlarged airport could accommodate any of the jet aircraft currently in operation; the city was served by most of the major airlines. In 1973, the per capita effective buying income in Indianapolis was $4,264, which contrasted with $3,779 for the United States as a whole; almost half of the Indianapolis area households had annual incomes of $10,000 and above. While approximately 75 percent of the customers of Fourwinds Marina came from the Indianapolis area, it was estimated that a total potential market of some 2.9 million inhabitants resided within a 100-mile radius of Lake Monroe.

Although both Fourwinds Marina and the Inn of the Fourwinds were owned by Taggart Corporation, they were operated as distinct entities. Being adjacent to one another on Lake Monroe, they cooperated in promoting business for each other. The inn occupied some 71,000 square feet on 30 acres of land. It was designed to blend into a beautifully wooded landscape and was constructed of rustic and natural building materials. The inn catered to a broad segment of the population, with double-occupancy rooms ranging in price from $21 to $33. The inn had 150 guest rooms (singles, doubles, and suites), together with meeting rooms for convention and sales meetings. The largest meeting room could seat 300 for dining and 350 for conferences. Recreation facilities included an indoor-outdoor swimming pool, tennis courts, sauna, whirlpool bath, and a recreation room with pool tables and other games. The inn had two dining rooms and a cocktail lounge. Although the inn was open year-round, its business was heavily concentrated in the summer months.

The Inn of the Fourwinds was the first lodge of its nature built on state property by private funds. By virtue of the size of its food service facilities (in excess of $100,000 per annum), it qualified under Indiana State Law for a license to serve alcoholic beverages on Sunday. The Indiana Department of Natural Resources exercised control over the room rates charged at the inn; this was part of the agreement between the state of Indiana and Taggart Corporation.

The Pointe, located three miles from the marina in 348 acres of lakefront property, was a luxury condominium development designed to meet the housing needs of both primary and secondary home buyers. Seventy units were under construction. Twenty of these had already been sold and down payments had been received on 80 more. These condominiums ranged in price from $25,000 to

$90,000, with an average price of $60,000. Approval had been secured for the construction of 1,900 living units over a seven-year period. The development had a completed 18-hole golf course. Swimming pools and tennis courts were under construction. The Pointe was a multimillion dollar development by Indun Realty, Inc., Lake Monroe Corporation, and Reywood, Inc.; Indun Realty was a wholly owned subsidiary of Indiana National Corp., parent firm of Indiana National Bank, the state's largest fiduciary institution.

FACILITIES AT FOURWINDS MARINA

The Fourwinds Marina occupied four acres of land and was one of the most extensive and complete marinas of its type in the United States. Its facilities consisted of boat docks, a salesroom for boats and marine equipment, an indoor boat storage facility, and a marine repair shop.

As shown in Exhibit 4, the marina had seven docks projecting out from a main connecting dock that ran parallel to the shore line. The seven parallel docks extended out from 330 to 600 feet into the lake at right angles to the connecting dock. The center dock housed a large building containing a grocery store, snack bar, and rest rooms, together with a section of docks used as mooring for rental boats. At the end of the dock was an office for boat rental, five gasoline pumps, and pumping facilities for removing waste from the houseboats and larger cruisers.

The three docks to the right of the center dock (facing toward the lake) were designated as docks A, B, and C and were designed for mooring smaller boats—runabouts, fishing boats, and small sailboats. A bait shop was on A dock. A, B, and C slips were not always fully rented. The three docks to the left were the prime slips (docks E, F, G); these were designed for berthing houseboats and larger cruisers. Docks E, F, and G were the marina's most profitable slips and stayed fully rented; as of mid-August there was a waiting list to get into these slips.

Fourwinds Marina had a total of 460 rentable slips priced from $205–$775 for uncovered slips and $295–$1,125 for covered slips per season (April 1–October 30). Seventy-five percent of all the slips were under roof and being in the more desirable location tended to be rented first. Electric service was provided to all slips, and the slips on E and F docks had water and trash removal provided at no extra cost. To the left of the prime slips were 162 buoys, renting for $150 per season. This rental included shuttle boat service to and from the moored craft. The rental buoys were not considered to be very profitable. Not only did the buoys shift and break loose occasionally but the dock staff went to considerable time and trouble to retrieve boats that broke loose at night or during storms.

TERMS OF THE LEASE WITH THE STATE OF INDIANA

The 34 acres of land on which the Fourwinds complex was located was leased to Taggart Corporation by the state of Indiana. In 1968, a prospectus was distributed by the Indiana Department of Natural Resources asking for bids on a motel and marina on the selected site. Only one other bidder qualified of the eight to ten bids submitted. The proposal submitted by Taggart Corporation was accepted primarily because of the economic strength of the individuals who composed the group and secondarily because of the favorable content of the bid.

The prospectus specified a minimum rental for the land of $10,000. Taggart Corporation offered in its bid a guarantee of $2,000 against the first $100,000 in marina sales and income and 4 percent of all income over that amount. For the inn,

EXHIBIT 4 PHYSICAL LAYOUT FOURWINDS MARINA

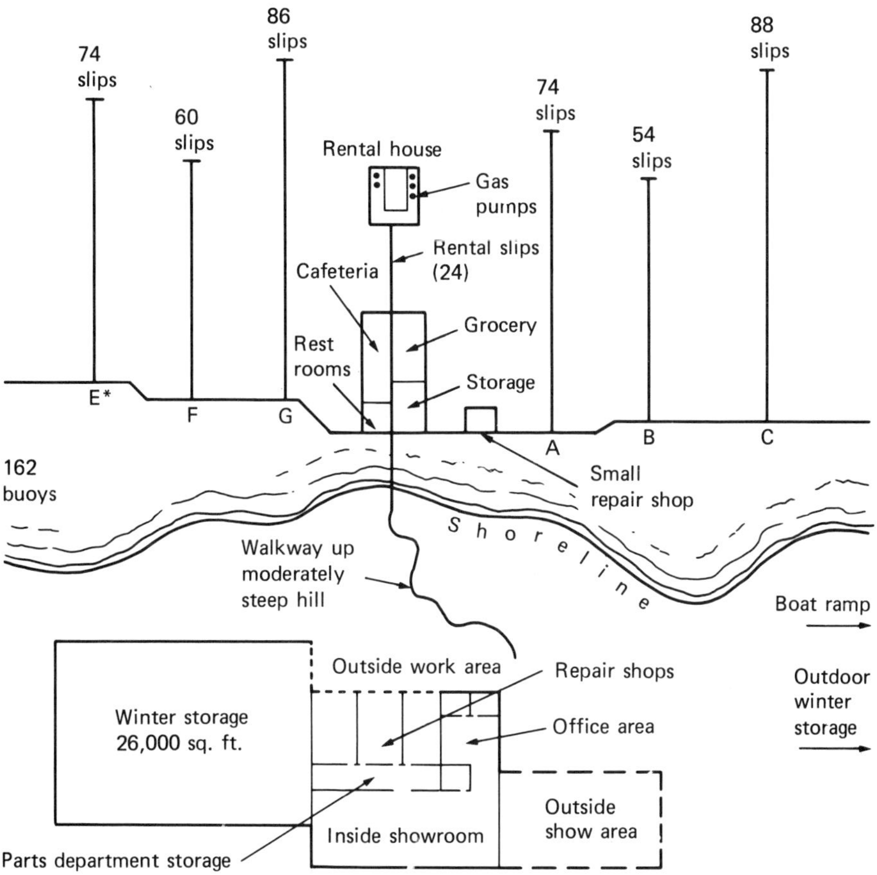

**E, F, and G range from 15 × 34 feet to 18 × 50 feet. About two thirds of these slips are covered.*
†A, B, and C slips range from 9 × 18 feet to 12 × 32 feet. Over 80 percent of these slips are covered.

Taggart guaranteed $8,000 against the first $400,000 of income plus 4 percent of all room sales and 2 percent of all food and beverage sales over that amount. It was stipulated that the Indiana Department of Natural Resources would exercise control over the prices of room rates at the Inn of the Fourwinds and slip rentals at the marina; Taggart Corporation was free to price the other services and products as it saw fit.

An initial lease of 37 years was granted to Taggart with two options of 30 years each. At the termination of the contract, all physical property reverted to the state of Indiana and the personal property went to Taggart. The entire dock structure was floating and was considered under the personal property category.

Prior to tendering a bid, members of Taggart Corporation visited similar facilities at Lake of the Ozarks, Lake Hamilton in Hot Springs, and the Kentucky Lakes operations. They received a considerable amount of information from the Kentucky Lakes management.

Construction of the initial phase of the marina began in May 1969 and the first 100 slips were opened in August under a speeded up construction schedule. The inn had its formal opening in November 1972.

MARINA OPERATIONS

Slip Rental

Reservations for slips had to be made by November 15 of each year or else the slip was subject to rental on a first come basis. Ordinarily all slips were rented for the year. The rental period ran from April 1 through October 30. Rental varied from $205 to $1,125, depending on the size of the slip and whether it was covered. Because the marina was located on state property, the Indiana Department of Natural Resources had the right of final approval over the rates which Fourwinds charged on slip rental.

Buoy Rental

One hundred and sixty-two buoys were rented for the same April 1–October 30 season at a rate of $150. Shuttle boat service for transporting boat owners to and from their craft moored at the buoy area was operative 24 hours a day. It was not a scheduled service, but operated as the demand occurred. This required the primary use of a runabout and driver. The charge for the service was included in the buoy rental fee for the season. As long as the buoy field was in existence, it was felt that the shuttle service had to be operated on a 24-hour basis during the season.

Boat Storage—Winter

Experience at Fourwinds showed that it was more expensive to remove a boat from the water and store it than to allow it to remain moored at the dock all winter. The main inside storage building was not heated or lighted; this precluded doing repair work in this building. An investment of about $12,000 would cover the cost of lighting and spot heating to overcome this drawback. When boats were stored, they were not queued according to those needing repair and those not needing service. As a result, time was lost in rearranging boats to get to those on which work was to be performed. The storage facility was not utilized in the summer months. Keltner was considering whether to install lights in the winter storage facility so as to give the marina an inside display area for the used boats which it sold; the used boats currently were stored and displayed on a lot outside the main display area for new boats.

Presently the rates for winter storage were:
100 percent of base rate ....Inside storage.
70 percent of base rate .... Bubbled area of covered slips.
60 percent of base rate .... Bubbled area of open slips.
50 percent of base rate .... Open storage areas out of water.

The base rate for storing a boat depended on its size. Boats 6-feet wide were stored at a charge of $7 per foot of length; an 8-foot wide boat carried a charge of $10 per running foot. Hence, a boat 6-feet wide and 15-feet long would have a base rate of

$90; a boat 8-feet wide and 20-feet long would carry a base rate of $200. The base rate did not include charges (approximately $75) for removing the boat from the water and moving it to either inside or outside storage areas.

Last winter, the inside storage facility was filled to capacity. One hundred boats were stored at an average base rate charge of $150 to $165. The marina had experienced some problems with vandalism on boats stored in the more remote areas of the uncovered, out-of-water storage area; however, the marina claimed no responsibility for loss, theft, or damage.

Boat and Motor Rental

The marina's rental equipment was up to date and well maintained; it consisted of:

15 houseboats—rental Monday to Friday $300
Friday to Monday $300

10 pontoon boats—hourly rental $20 for 3 hours
$35 for 6 hours

6 runabouts for skiing—$15–20 per hour
12 fishing boats—$12 for 6 hours
$18 for 12 hours

Maximum hourly rental was 13 hours per day during the week and 15 hours per day on Saturday and Sunday (the rental rate did not include gasoline).

It was not uncommon to have all 15 houseboats fully rented from Memorial Day weekend through Labor Day weekend. Pontoons were about 50 percent rented during the week. Utilization of runabouts was 50 percent, while fishing boats were rented approximately 40 percent of the available time. The man who operated the boat and motor rental for Fourwinds had a one-third interest in all of the boat rental equipment; the Marina owned the balance. Funds for the purchase of the equipment were contributed on the same one-third to two-thirds ratio. Net profits after payment of expenses, maintenance, depreciation, and so on were split according to the ownership ratio. The area utilized by the rental area could be converted to slips in the $500 range as a possible alternate use for the dock space. Rental income after expenses, but before interest and depreciation, had been slightly less than $20,000 the preceding season.

Small Boat Repair Shop

A small boat repair shop was located between C and D docks. It was well outfitted with mechanical equipment and had a small hoist for removing small boats from the water for repair at the docks. However, the shop was currently closed because a qualified mechanic could not be found to operate the facility on a seasonal basis.

Grocery Store

The grocery store at the marina was subleased to another party at $500 per month. The leasee was doing a profitable business and charged prices similar to those which might be expected at a seasonal recreation facility.

Snack Bar

The snack bar was operated by the Inn of the Fourwinds and returned a 5 percent commission to the marina on food sales. Currently, Keltner felt that the manager of the snack bar was not doing a reliable job in operating the unit. Keltner had found the snack bar closed on several occasions for no apparent reason. Food offered for sale included hot sandwiches, pizza, snack food, soft drinks, milk, and coffee. The snack bar's prices were at the high end of the range for such items but Fourwinds' customers had expressed satisfaction with the quality.

Gasoline Sales

Five gasoline pumps were located around the perimeter of the end of the center dock. They were manned 13 hours per day, from 7 a.m. to 8 p.m., seven days a week. The pumps for the removal of waste from the houseboats and other large craft were located in this same area. It took an average of five minutes to pump out the waste and the marina made no charge for this service. The marina's gasoline pumps were the only ones available on Lake Monroe.

Boat and Boat Accessory Salesroom

A glass enclosed showroom occupying approximately 1,500 square feet of floor space was located at the main entrance to the marina property. Major boat lines such as Trojan Yacht, Kingscraft, Burnscraft, Harris Flote Bote, and Signa, as well as Evinrude motors, were offered for sale. In addition, quality lines of marine accessories were available. The salesroom building also housed the executive offices of the marina and the repair and maintenance shops. Attached to the building was the indoor winter storage area for boats. Last year, total boat sales were approximately $971,048. The marina's boat inventory had been reduced from last year's $300,000; recently, some boat lines had been dropped so that more emphasis could be placed on those which offered higher profit on sales.

Fourwinds Marina was the only sales outlet in Indiana that stocked larger boats. They were also the only facility in Indiana with large slips to accommodate these boats. With E, F, and G docks filled and a waiting list to get in, selling the larger, more profitable boats had become nearly impossible.

ASPECTS OF THE MARINA'S DOCK OPERATIONS

Dock Construction

The entire dock section at Fourwinds was of modular floating construction and had an expected life of 20–30 years, if properly maintained. Built in smaller sections that could be bolted together, the construction featured a steel framework, with poured concrete surfaces for walking upon and Styrofoam panels in the side for buoyancy. In the event of damage to a section, a side could be replaced easily, eliminating repair of the entire segment of dock. Electrical conduits and water pipes were inside the actual dock units. The major damage to the Styrofoam dock segments came from ducks chewing out pieces of the foam to make nests and from gasoline spillage that literally "ate" the Styrofoam. An antigas coating was used to minimize the damage from gasoline spillage. Damage from boats to the dock was minimal. A maze of cables underneath the dock sections had to be kept at the proper tension to prevent the dock from buckling and breaking up. Three people were involved in dock maintenance. Original cost of the entire dock and buoy system was $984,265.

EXHIBIT 5 ORGANIZATION CHART

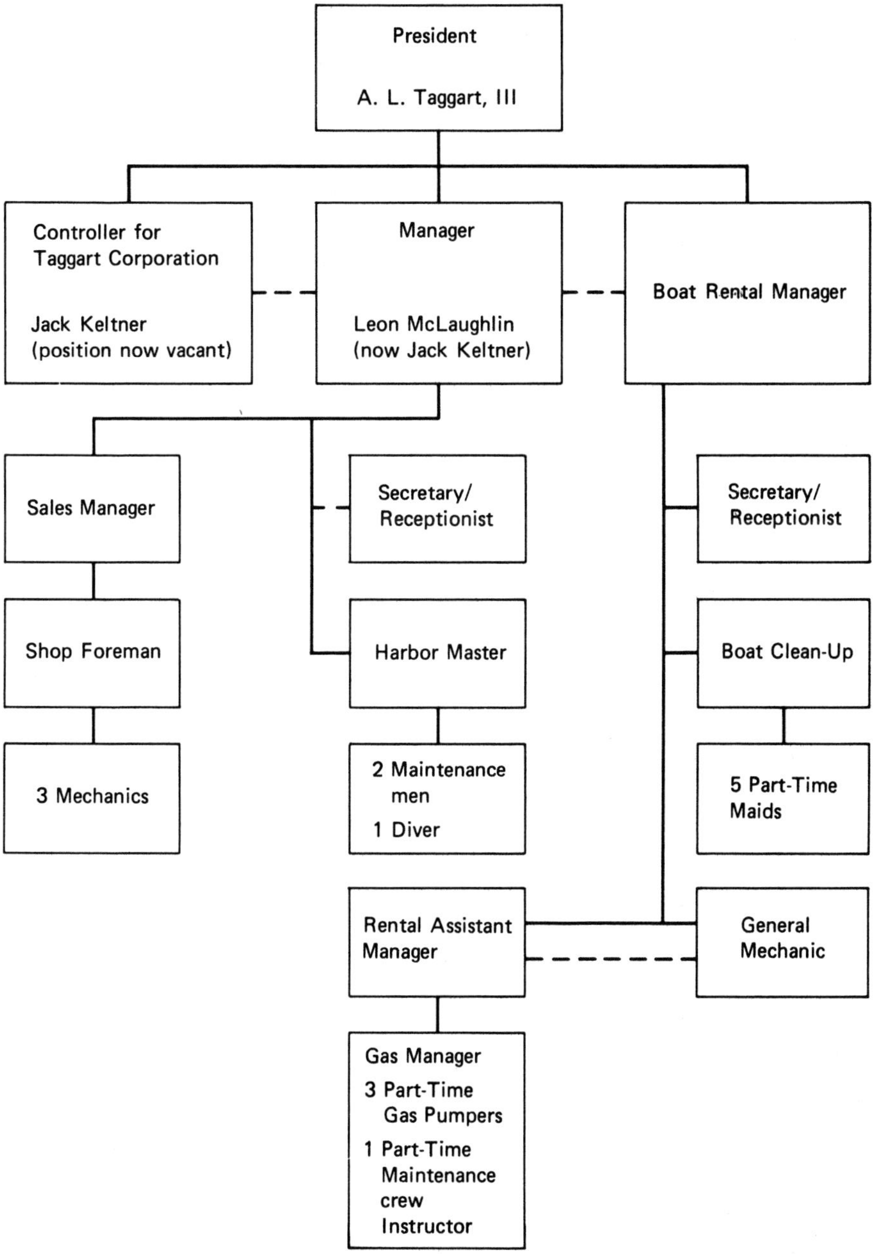

Winter Storage

Winter storage tends to be a problem at a marina which is located in an area where a freeze-over of the water occurs. Nonetheless, it is generally better for the boat if it can remain in the water. Water affords better and more even support to the hull. By leaving the craft in the water, possible damage from hoists used to lift boats and move them to dry storage is avoided. These factors, however, are not common knowledge to boat owners and require an educational program.

To protect boats left in the water during the winter season, Fourwinds Marina had installed a bubbling system. The system, simple in concept, consisted of hoses that were weighted and dropped to the bottom of the lake around the individual docks and along a perimeter line surrounding the entire dock area. Fractional horsepower motors operated compressors that pumped air into the submerged hose. The air escaping through tiny holes in the hose forced warmer water at the bottom of the lake up to the top, preventing the surface from freezing and melting any ice that might have formed before the compressors were started. The lines inside the dock areas protected the boats from being damaged by ice formations, while the perimeter line prevented major damage to the entire dock area from a pressure ridge that might build up and be jammed against the dock and boats in high wind.

A policy of the marina prohibited any employee from driving any of the customer's boats. Maintaining a duplicate set of keys for each boat and the cost of the insurance to cover the employee were the prime reasons for this policy. This meant, however, that when boats were moved in the absence of their owners they had to be towed, thereby creating some possibility of damage to the boats during towing. Towing of boats occurred mainly during the off-season period for reasons of dock repair, storms, or cold weather conditions.

STRATEGIES TO ACHIEVE GROWTH OBJECTIVES FOR A COLLEGIATE BASKETBALL PROGRAM

Frank Broyles, atheltic director at the University of Arkansas, sat in his office one summer day, contemplating some strategies for the growth of the University's basketball program. He had just had a conference with Eddie Sutton, the head basketball coach, and Wilson Matthews, assistant athletic director, regarding the Razorback basketball program.

Broyles remembered that a little over a year ago Lanny Van Eman, former basketball coach for the Razorbacks, had resigned. During Van Eman's reign as basketball coach, he had compiled a 39–65 win-loss record, but during that time Van Eman had made basketball an exciting sport for the fans with his "runnin' Razorback" offensive displays. However, for the past twenty years the basketball program at the University of Arkansas had merely existed. It had never been really promoted like the football program. Its budget was skimpy at best. The facilities for playing were below par. Fan interest was never really high. And as a result, the U of A's basketball team had won only one Southwest Conference Championship (tied with SMU in 1958) during the past twenty-five years.

When Van Eman resigned, Broyles met with the Athletic Committee of the university board of trustees the next day. Together they discussed the future of the basketball program. Broyles remembered vividly the commitment he had received from the board of trustees to put the basketball program in full gear. The program was to grow—in fan attendance, in facilities, in budget, in coaching and player talent, and whatever it took to field a team that would be competitive with teams not only in the SWC but also on a national scale.

Broyles recognized that to grow the U of A had to have a winning tradition in basketball, just as it had a winning tradition in football during the past twenty years. His first step was to hire a basketball coach who had a winning tradition. After lengthy interviews with several prospects, he finally hired Eddie Sutton, basketball coach at Creighton, an independent school in Omaha.

Sutton's win-loss record as a college coach was a respectable 73 percent. The previous five-year record at Arkansas was a 35 percent win-loss. If, somehow

---

Prepared by Robert D. Hay, University of Arkansas.

or another, Sutton could turn that record around, Broyles thought that his first strategy of hiring a quality coach would be instrumental in the growth of the basketball program.

Sutton was a believer in the Henry Iba school of playing defensive basketball. However, Sutton was also a strategist himself in developing what he called a patient offense. This strategy had won twenty-three games for Creighton and a chance to win the NCAA playoff the year before he was hired at Arkansas as the highest paid coach in the Southwest Conference. He pledged to Broyles that he would turn the basketball program around. Most of the fans scoffed, some forgot about it, while a few believed that he could do it.

Sutton hired Gene Keady, 80 percent win-loss record, head coach of Hutchinson Junior College, to be one of his assistant coaches. The other was Pat Foster, assistant coach under Van Eman. Together the three of them, with Tom Skipper, graduate assistant, performed their recruiting efforts.

After teaching defensive basketball with hard-nosed discipline (something lacking in the U of A's basketball teams during the past years), the first year's team had a 3–4 win-loss record at Christmas time. Then the Sutton philosophy began to take shape. The Razorbacks filled Barnhill Fieldhouse (capacity 5,200) for their opener against Texas Tech, the traditional powerhouse of the SWC. They played Texas A&M with a packed house before regional television and won in overtime. Sutton's team during his first year generated fan interest to its highest peak in several years. Their 17–9 record represented the most wins by an Arkansas team in seventeen years. Their 11–3 record in conference play gave them a second-place tie with the most conference wins since 1943 for an Arkansas team. Sutton was named SWC basketball coach of the year.

Now that the basketball season was over, some additional plans had to be made to reach the growth objectives laid out by Broyles and the board of trustees. Therefore, an informal three-man strategy committee was formed to discuss and formulate the growth strategies for the basketball program.

The old strategy was summarized by Orville Henry, sportswriter for the *Arkansas Gazette,* as follows: You cannot make any money in basketball. Therefore, just budget so much money, turn your head, and hope that losses can be held to a minimum. The new philosophy was to be: You can have a first-rate basketball program anywhere in the collegiate field if (1) you hire a man who knows what to do, and (2) you provide him with the facilities and support required to win. If you are going to spend money, why not go first class, get the people involved, and make money.

One of the first strategies considered by the three men (Broyles, Sutton, and Matthews) concerned itself with basketball facilities. Barnhill Fieldhouse had a seating capacity of 5,200. The court sat on a mounting in a dirt-filled facility which was used for football, baseball, and track during inclement weather. The building was twenty years old but was losing its attractiveness. Somehow or another, a facility was needed to hold bigger crowds. How much seating capacity should it have? How much would it cost? How would it be financed? Should it be a multi-purpose building? Should Barnhill be renovated or should a new building be proposed? What is the relationship between winning and attendance and seating capacity?

Information was gathered from other schools regarding their win-loss percentage and attendance figures. (See Table 1.)

TABLE 1

University	*Five-Year Average % of Games won*	*Five-Year Average Yearly Attendance*
Oral Roberts	84%	102,000
Texas Tech	65	97,000
Hutchinson Juco	81	85,000
Creighton	64	77,000
Baylor	61	74,000
Texas	50	63,000
Texas A&M	55	55,000
Southern Methodist	48	48,000
Texas Christian	48	44,000
Tulane	40	39,000
Rice	37	39,000
Arkansas	34	39,000
Mac Murray	24	5,000
Okla City Univ.	65	22,000
Univ.-Nebraska-Omaha	57	13,000

TABLE 2

University	*Yearly Attendance*	*Gymnasium Seating Capacity*	*Gymnasium Quality*	*Parking Facilities*
ORU	102,000	10,750	Good[a]	Good
Texas Tech	97,000	10,000	Good	Good
Hutch Juco	85,000	7,500	Good	Good
Creighton	77,000	9,800	Good	Good
Baylor	74,000	10,000	Good	Good
Texas	63,000	7,800	Poor[b]	Poor
Texas A&M	55,000	7,500	Fair	Poor
SMU	48,000	9,000	Good	Good
TCU	44,000	7,200	Good	Good
Tulane	39,000	5,000	Poor	Poor
Rice	39,000	5,000	Fair	Good
Arkansas	39,000	5,200	Poor	Poor
Mac Murray	5,000	1,100	Poor	Fair
OCU	22,000	3,400	Good	Poor
UNO	13,000	4,000	Good	Fair

a. From judgments made by the interviewees
b. A new facility is being built

TABLE 3

University	*Yearly Attendance*	*General Admission*	*Reserve Seats*	*Number of Season Tickets sold*	*Faculty and Students*
ORU	102,000	$1.50	$2.00-$3.00	4500	F 17.50; S 1.25-1.50
Texas Tech	97,000	2.00	3.50	3500	F 1.00; S 1.00
Hutch Juco	85,000	1.50	2.00	2500	F free; S free
Creighton	77,000	2.00	3.50	2000	F ½; S .50
Baylor	74,000	2.00	3.50	1400	F free; S free
Texas	63,000	2.00	3.00	0	F free; S free
Texas A&M	55,000	2.00	3.00	750	F free; S free
SMU	48,000	3.00	3.00	1000	F free; S free
TCU	44,000	2.00	3.00	500	F free; S free
Tulane	39,000	2.50	4.00	200	F 1.00; S free
Rice	39,000	2.00	2.50	100	F Nom.; S free
Arkansas	39,000	1.50	3.00	300	F ½; S free
Mac Murray	5,000	1.00	1.00	25	F free; S free
OCU	22,000	2.00	2.50	400	F free; S free
UNO	13,000	2.50	2.50	160	F free; S free

An estimate was received from local architects and building construction companies that suggested that to renovate Barnhill Fieldhouse, it would cost about $400 a seat. Further information was obtained regarding facilities at other schools. (See Table 2.)

As far as financing of any new facilities, the three men devised a tentative strategy regarding the sources of capital: (1) raise money from the Razorback Fund, a private source from supporters of the U of A athletic program; (2) get a "grant" from the state legislature; (3) float a bond issue; and (4) if any deficit exists, use money from the football program.

Discussion continued among the three men regarding ticket policies. Should prices be competitive with other schools? Should we price at the market, or below the market? What about prices for faculty and students?

What should we do about selling season tickets?

Information was gathered from different schools concerning ticket policies and prices. (See Table 3.)

Financial data for the various schools interviewed was difficult to come by. There were only two schools who made a yearly profit from basketball—Texas Tech and Hutchinson Junior College. The financial data estimates were as shown in Table 4.

"Do you think that we have a large enough market area to draw from to increase our attendance?" was a question the three men constantly asked. The U of A's basketball crowds averaged around 3,000 people—two-third, students and one-third non-students. For thirteen home games the average yearly attendance was about 39,000 for the past five years. Very few people attended who lived more than 10 miles from the university. However, if the drawing power could be extended to a 50-mile radius, a potential population of 200,000 could be reasonably estimated (a four-county rural area). Further information revealed the information shown in Table 5.

The University of Arkansas had no major competition from college teams. The closest team was Tulsa, 125 miles away. However, the university is located in Fayetteville, with a population of 35,000.

TABLE 4

University	*Net Profit (net loss)*	*University*	*Net Profit (net loss)*
Texas Tech	$ 25,000	Arkansas	(100,000)
Hutch Juco	14,000	OCU	(105,000)
SMU	Breakeven	Tulane	(150,000)
Mac Murray	(21,000)	TCU	(loss)
UNO	(26,000)	Rice	(loss)
Creighton	(30,000)	Texas	??
Baylor	(50,000)	ORU	??
Texas A&M	(60,000)		

TABLE 5

University	Yearly Attendance	Population of Market Area	% of Customers Student	Non-Student	Radius of Drawing Power	No. of Competing Teams
ORU	102,000	350,000	20%	80%	40 mi	1
Texas Tech	97,000	250,000	50	50	50	0
Hutch Juco	85,000	100,000	20	80	25	0
Creighton	77,000	500,000	20	80	25	3
Baylor	74,000	160,000	60	40	25	0
Texas	63,000	400,000	75	25	30	5
Texas A&M	55,000	75,000	66	34	10	0
SMU	48,000	1,500,000	50	50	30	5
TCU	44,000	1,500,000	34	66	50	6
Tulane	39,000	1,200,000	60	40	50	3
Rice	39,000	1,200,000	60	40	15	4
Arkansas	39,000	200,000	66	34	50	0
Mac Murray	5,000	35,000	90	10	20	1
OCU	22,000	500,000	25	75	15	8
UNO	13,000	500,000	80	20	20	3

Promotion of basketball in Razorback country was handled by nine radio stations who were connected into a university-sponsored sports network. The Razorbacks had been on regional TV about ten times during the last five years. No actual promotion was ever made to sell season tickets, of which about 300 were sold each year to interested fans. Arkansas is really known as a football state. As a result, not much basketball coverage was given to basketball via the newspapers. Further information is provided in Table 6.

There was constant discussion among the three as to whether the Razorbacks should play two or three basketball games in Little Rock, 200 miles away. The meetings usually centered around the question of whether the university should try to get the support of central, eastern, and southern Arkansas fans for their basketball program, as well as their football program (at least four games of football were played in little Rock each year and three games in Fayetteville). Two years before, the Razorbacks played two games in Little Rock. The crowds were very sparse and the project was a financial failure. A year before, another attempt was made to play basketball in Little Rock. The results were the same—small crowds and financial losses.

As Broyles pondered the situation, he wondered about what strategies to follow to achieve the growth obejectives that he had presented to the board of trustees.

TABLE 6

University	*Yearly Average Attendance*	*Number of Radio outlets*	*Number of Times on TV (Five Years)*	*Number of Stars on Team (Five Years)*
ORU	102,000	1	7	2
Texas Tech	97,000	6	10	6
Hutch Juco	85,000	2	0	20
Creighton	77,000	2	10	1
Baylor	74,000	2	10	6
Texas	63,000	1	13	2
Texas A&M	55,000	3	12	3
SMU	48,000	1	10	1
TCU	44,000	2	11	2
Tulane	39,000	0	1	0
Arkansas	39,000	9	10	1
Rice	39,000	1	10	1
Mac Murray	5,000	0	0	0
OCU	22,000	0	1	2
UNO	13,000	1	0	0

AMPAK INTERNATIONAL, LTD.

In June 1975, Robert Williams, the manager of the International Division of Rally Dawson Sports was seriously considering the possibility of opening a new subsidiary somewhere in the Middle or Near East. The countries that had come up for review included India, Pakistan, Syria, Egypt, and Israel. Due to the current political instability and the unpredictable economic policies of the various governments under consideration, the Middle Eastern countries had been placed on a list labelled as "potential future investment areas—not for present action." Further, due to recent government nationalization policies in India, that country had been classified as similar to the Middle East. As a result, the focus had been turned to Pakistan. After extensive field research and several visits by the members of Rally Dawson Sports' international staff, the company had negotiated a tentative agreement calling for a joint venture with Hamid Sports, Ltd., a local corporation. It was this tentative agreement that Williams was considering.

Rally Dawson Sports, headquartered in Houston, Texas, had been in the sporting goods business for twenty-two years. It had two manufacturing outlets, one located near Houston and the second one in Waco. The company's gross sales for 1974–75 were over $29 million (see Exhibits 1 and 2 for financial statements of the company). Though there had been a short period of instability (1968–69), a steady growth of profits had been experienced since 1970 when a new management took over the operations.

A Pakistani site would be the third international location for Rally Dawson. In 1962, the company had moved to Spain and formed Compania Catalan de Desportes S.A., a manufacturing subsidiary. Rally Dawson's experience with the Spanish concern was very encouraging and in 1969 Bert Philips, the president of Rally Dawson, recommended Italy as the second international site. It took about eight months for the operations to start in Bologna, Italy.

Rally Dawson produced many types of sports goods used both by professionals and amateurs. Its major distribution channels led to retail sporting goods stores and to department store chains. It also sold directly to professional sports teams and to some major universities.

Prepared by Professor David Springate of Southern Methodist University with the help of Amir Niazi.

EXHIBIT 1 INCOME STATEMENT FOR RALLY DAWSON SPORTS FOR 1974 (Dollars in Thousands)

Sales	$29,503
Cost of Sales	14,203
Gross Profit	
	$15,300
Sales Salaries	802
Advertising	398
Delivery and freight	1,034
Depreciation	246
Office Salaries	300
Business taxes and licenses	65
Rent expense, office space	200
Miscellaneous	162
Interest	105
	$ 3,312
Net Profit before taxes	11,988
Income taxes	5,754
Net Profit	$ 6,233

EXHIBIT 2 BALANCE SHEET FOR RALLY DAWSON SPORTS, DEC. 31, 1974 (Dollars in Thousands)

Current Assets		*Current Liabilities*	
Cash	$ 2,100	Bank Advances	$ 730
Marketable Securities (at Cost)	500	Unearned fees	120
Accounts Receivable	2,500	Accounts Payable	1,400
Notes Receivable	650	Accrued Salaries	50
Inventory	3,100	Accrued Liability	700
Prepaid Expenses	700	Income Taxes	5,754
	$ 9,550		
		Long-Term Liabilities	
		Bonds (due 1980)	400
Fixed Assets		*Shareholders Account*	
At Cost	$ 4,550	Capital Stock	$ 4,500
Accumulated Depreciation	250	Retained Earnings	950
Land	450		
		Total Liabilities	$14,800
	$ 5,250		
Total Assets	$14,800		

LINK WITH HAMID SPORTS COMPANY

Some of the reasons that prompted Rally Dawson to consider venturing abroad again in 1974 were:

1. To jump tariff and import barriers and regulations. These sometimes included local content regulations or requirements that local exports be made in order to receive an import license.
2. To reduce or eliminate high transportation costs involved in serving Near and Middle-Eastern markets.
3. To obtain or use local materials available at a lower cost.
4. To obtain incentives (usually tax breaks) offered by the host governments.
5. To participate in the rapid market expansion in the Middle and Near-East.
6. To continue a strategy that called for the combination of Rally Dawson's advanced technology, reputation and managerial know-how with low-cost production inputs such as labor, capital and raw materials available in some countries abroad.
7. To diversify product lines and to some extent shield the company from cyclical developments in the American and European economies.

The primary reason for selecting Pakistan as a suitable location for investment stemmed from the facts that labor costs were extremely low and that suitable raw materials were available within the country at relatively inexpensive rates. In addition, Pakistani sporting goods had established a reputation of being long-lasting products of quality.

Williams had, however, not been in favor of joint ventures in the past. In the initial stages of the investigation, he advocated establishment of a manufacturing subsidiary solely owned by Rally Dawson. Although it was legally possible to establish in a manner such that Rally Dawson would have no Pakistani partners, a practical perspective made the joint venture more desirable. The government of Pakistan encouraged private foreign investments where local entrepreneurs were given opportunity to gain know-how and to exercise some ownership control. With a local partner foreign investors found the investment approval process expedited. Subsequent government red-tape was also reduced.

Once Rally Dawson began to consider Pakistan as one of the probable areas for investment, it contacted the Pakistani Trade Office in Washington, D. C. The Trade Office maintained an active list of qualified Pakistani businessmen who would be interested in any joint-venture opportunities. The company was introduced to its proposed partner, Hamid Sports Company, through the Trade Office.

The Pakistani counterpart in the proposed joint venture had been in business for eighteen years. Located in Sailkot (about 900 miles from Karachi) Hamid was the third largest producer of sports goods in Pakistan. Sixty percent of the annual sales for its fiscal year 1974–75 were in domestic markets and 40 percent were exports. Most of the export sales were centered in the Middle East (Syria, Libya, and Egypt) with these countries each constituting 30 percent of the exports. The remaining 10 percent was divided between Thailand and Ceylon. Total gross sales for Hamid for the fiscal year 1974–75 were almost $10 million. (See Exhibits 3 and 4 for recent income statement and balance sheet information for Hamid.) The Izmir Hamid family

EXHIBIT 3 INCOME STATEMENT FOR HAMID SPORTS COMPANY FOR 1974 (Dollars in Thousands)*

Sales	$9,700
Cost of Sales	4,850
Gross Profit	4,850
Selling Expenses	
Salaries & Commission	200
Advertising	100
Delivery & Freight	210
Automobile	40
Depreciation	178
	$ 728
Administrative Expenses	
Salaries	$ 105
Printing & Postage	50
Telephone & Telegraph	24
Business Taxes & Licenses	88
Sundry	63
Interest	25
	1,083
Net Profit before taxes	$3,039
Income taxes	$1,793
Net Profit	$1,246

**Translated from rupees to dollars*

held 80 percent ownership interest in Hamid Sports. The residual 20 percent was divided among three other prominent families in Pakistan.

The management of Hamid Sports had not been able to keep up with current and timely strategies for maximizing the overall efficiency of production. This was due to the limited resources available in the country and the prohibitive cost of sending its managers abroad on a regular basis to attend management development programs. For this reason Hamid Sports was looking at the proposed joint Pakistan-U. S. investment as an opportunity to benefit from fresh technological and business management inputs. The venture would lead to expansion of Hamid's facilities in Pakistan. Hopefully it would also lead to the capture of larger portions of the domestic market and parts of the export markets of Western Europe, the U. S., and Canada. Hamid had wanted to expand sales into the latter areas for some time.

To date Hamid Sports had specialized in field hockey, cricket, soccer, badminton, and tennis equipment. The joint venture would also enable Hamid to introduce new product lines and help produce products for golf, skiing, football, and baseball which would have a market potential in Western Europe and North America.

EXHIBIT 4 BALANCE SHEET FOR HAMID SPORTS COMPANY FOR 1974 (Dollars in Thousands)*

Current Assets		*Current Liabilities*	
Cash	$ 750	Bank Advances	$ 400
Accounts Receivable	1,500	Accounts Payable	520
Inventory	1,600	Accrued Liability	275
Prepaid Expenses	400	Income Taxes	2,260
Total Current Assets	$4,250	Long Term Debt	—
		Shareholders' Advances	—
Fixed Assets			
Cost	$1,900	Capital Stock	2,500
Less: Depreciation	178	Retained Earnings	372,800
Total Fixed Assets	2,078	Total Liabilities	$ 6,328
Total Assets	$6,328		

**Translated from rupees to dollars*

PROPOSED JOINT VENTURE

The joint venture, if consummated, would be called Ampak International, Ltd. It was to be a closely held corporation. The ownership would be 60 percent American (Rally Dawson) and 40 percent Pakistani (Hamid). The total initial capital investment was proposed to be the equivalent of $5 million.

The site for the proposed plant was selected when two representatives of Rally Dawson visited Pakistan in March 1975. It was to be in Kotri, approximately 90 miles from Karachi. The latter was the largest seaport and the business center of the nation. In terms of availability of labor, Kotri had the reputation of having a substantial supply of unskilled, semi-skilled and skilled labor. Kotri was a highly industrialized area and locating the plant there was expected to be beneficial both in terms of communication facilities and labor. Another advantage compared to interior locations was the transportation cost saving. The port was relatively close to Kotri.

The investment proposal was put together in March 1975. It was decided that Rally Dawson would raise most of the capital needed for importing the machinery and initial start-up capital needs. Hamid was assigned the chief responsibility of raising the local capital, custom duties on imported machinery, land and the actual structure of the plant. In the initial proposal, it was suggested that the plant would have 500 workers working two shifts of eight hours each. The two shifts will enable Ampak to deduct a greater depreciation expense and also accomplish a higher level of production.

Machinery required was to be imported from the U. S. It was expected to have a higher level of efficiency and be more effective than equipment already in operation in Pakistan. Though Ampak was to be a labor-intensive project, a technologically sophisticated plant would go a long way toward increasing profits.

Managers of the two firms that would form the proposed joint venture had suggested a list of products to be produced by Ampak International, Ltd. The list was a result of a market research done by a four-member team, consisting of two international staff executives from Rally Dawson and two members of Hamid's International task force. There was a possibility that in the final analysis, some of the products mentioned on the following list, put together in May 1975, would be dropped.

1. Tennis equipment (for Western Europe, Canada, and the U. S.)
2. Cricket equipment (for Pakistan, the U. K., and a small market in the Middle East)
3. Golf equipment (for Western Europe and the U. S.)
4. Soccer equipment (for Pakistan, Western Europe, and the Middle East)
5. Baseball equipment (for the U. S. and possibly to Japan)
6. Skiing equipment (for Switzerland, Austria, and most of Scandinavia)
7. Football equipment (for the U. S. and possibly for Canada)
8. Badminton equipment (for Thailand, Malaysia, Indonesia, Ceylon, and Pakistan)
9. Field hockey equipment (for Western Europe, the Middle East, and Pakistan)

Although the products mentioned above were varied, it was considered feasible that a large manufacturing outlet could handle the production complexities. Many of the raw materials used to produce these products were common. In addition, not all items would be produced initially.

It was proposed to have the plant begin operations within one year. The tentative plan was that Ampak would issue 500,000 shares of common stock with a $10 (equivalent) par value. Rally Dawson Sports would exchange its machinery and start-up capital for 300,000 shares of Ampak's newly issued stock. Its total contribution would thus be $3,000,000. Hamid would buy the rest of the shares.

Hamid Sports had assets it could use in the Muslim Commercial Bank in the amount of $1,400,000. It was planning to raise the remaining $600,000 through the Pakistan Industrial Development Bank. The terms of the tentatively negotiated loan were $600,000 for six years at 10½ percent. It was to be secured by Hamid's plant and equipment in Sailkot.

The proposed breakdown of the initial $5 million capital of Ampak was:

Land	$ 200,000
Plant	1,000,000
Equipment	950,000
Start-up Capital	2,600,000
Market Research	75,000
Customs fees and initial administration (until plant operational)	375,000
	$5,000,000

MANAGERS

Staffing of Ampak was one of the major concerns for Rally Dawson. The general manager for the operations was to be Howard Adams. His present assignment was operations manager for the Spanish subsidiary. Prior to this he had been manufacturing manager for Dow Chemical in Brazil.

The administrative manager, Aamir Kohn, was selected from Hamid as he possessed skills which would be conducive to the local operations. As most of the skilled and semi-skilled labor would be Pakistani, fluency in the language and cultural empathy were important ingredients for this job.

The controller was to be a person who had extensive experience in the area of international accounting. Joe Sutton, previously associated with Clark Equipment Company, had been on Rally Dawson's staff for the last nine months and was very familiar with the company's international accounting practices.

The chief engineer, Khurshid Rakahmi was a Pakistani who had worked in Pakistan with a sporting goods enterprise for the last eight years.

Some of the factors behind the selection of the U. S. managers were technical competence, managerial skills, cultural empathy, diplomatic skills, personal motives, emotional stability, and business background.

An additional task was the finding of a person to serve as a liaison between Ampak and the Pakistani government. The importance of developing a good working relationship was felt to be crucial in Pakistan, a developing nation. The final choice was a Pakistani who had an MBA from the Harvard Business School and a LLD (Law Degree) from the University of Panjals (a local university). He had worked for the Department of Commerce of Pakistan for four years. Prior to this he was associated with Procter and Gamble in New York City and in various Western European locations.

STRATEGY IN THE EVENT OF FAILURE

In the event that the new venture failed the proposed plan was to dispose of the assets and pay off the creditors first. If the sale of all the assets was not adequate to cover the funds needed to pay off the creditors, the two groups involved would then pay their share of the debt according to ownership interest. The government of Pakistan had no restrictions on foreign investors taking out the liquidation funds as long as all debts were paid and local stockholders were fairly treated.

Another situation that might arise was where the new plant did not turn out to be as profitable as anticipated. It was expected that if the plant barely broke even after two years Ampak would be dissolved. However, it was expected that Rally Dawson Sports would invest in another manner (a new joint venture or a new subsidiary of Rally Dawson Sports with some local capital participation) instead of transferring its remaining liquid funds back to the U. S. In this way, newly gained market knowledge and awareness of the economy and the area would not be wasted, but utilized in a constructive fashion.

FUNDING SOURCES AND PROFITS

The major factor that led Rally Dawson Sports to resort to external sources of funding and not use the local Pakistani banks was the national government's hesitation. In discussions with government officials it became obvious the government was well aware of the fact that Rally Dawson Sports had other alternatives for raising capital, especially in the U. S. Officials stated that it would be more feasible for the Pakistani banks to finance the local working capital needs. In this way they would not have to dip into their foreign exchange earnings for machinery purchases outside Pakistan.

With reference to taking out profits, Williams knew that the Pakistani government allowed foreign investors to take out profits to the extent of the initial investment and any subsequent additions to capital. In other words, Rally Dawson Sports would be able to take out profits up to a $3 million limit plus half of any cumulative earnings. Such transactions would be coordinated by the State Bank of Pakistan, which assigned various remittance accounts to different commercial banks around the country.

INVESTMENT CONSIDERATIONS

There were several advantages that led Williams and the International team at Rally Dawson to look favorably on the proposed joint venture.

a. A joint venture would protect the U. S. investment against nationalization. There was, of course, no guarantee that the government would not nationalize but the fact that a local interest would be involved could normally be expected to deter government take-over.

b. The interest rate offered by the Pakistan Industrial Development Bank to Hamid Sports was substantially lower than what Rally Dawson could get from the First National City Bank in Pakistan if it financed all the Pakistan venture itself (10½ percent as opposed to 12¾ percent).

c. A joint venture would reduce the capital requirements of Rally Dawson. The manufacturing subsidiary in Spain, Catalan de Desportes S. A., had a critical need for additional capital equipment and the Spanish economy was currently experiencing an unusual period of credit squeeze. This fact had resulted in Rally Dawson being forced to resort to external sources of financing, namely the Import-Export Bank. With the lower capital requirements of a joint venture, such risks would be reduced.

d. The international staff at Rally Dawson had no prior exposure to the Near East. Williams felt that by going into a joint venture they would rapidly acquire needed skills and know-how of the local market place. Also, Williams knew that Hamid Sports had an effective distribution system which would facilitate the distribution of products put out by the new plant.

On the other hand, Williams had some reservations about the financing arrangements that meant that all of Rally Dawson's needed capital would have to be exported to Pakistan. He knew that the PIDB had made an exception earlier in a similar case for John Deere Corporation and had granted the firm a loan. John Deere had gone into a joint venture with a local enterprise and PIDB helped John Deere by financing one-third of the company's investment share. (John Deere had a 60 percent ownership interest in the fertilizer plant.) When asked, the bank responded that fertilizer was critical to the agricultural production of Pakistan and it had made an exception because that was a direct contribution to the national goal of self-sufficiency in food.

PROJECT EVALUATION BY RALLY DAWSON SPORTS

Rally Dawson Sports usually looked for a five-year payback period. Williams also knew he could think of a project's rate of return on investment as that rate that would discount all the amounts received as income or as repayment of principal

EXHIBIT 5 PROFITABILITY CALCULATION OF MR. WILLIAMS

Estimated Rates (X)	*Probability of Occurrence (P)*	*Weighted Values of the Estimated Rates P•X*	*Deviation of Rates from Mean* $(X - \overline{X})$	*Deviation Squared* $(X - \overline{X})^2$	*Variance* $(X - \overline{X})^2 \cdot P$	*Standard Deviation (Square root of Variance)*
(1)	(2)	(3)	(4)	(5)	(6)	(7)
18%	.1	1.8	+8	64	6.4	
14%	.2	2.8	+4	16	3.2	
10%	.4	4.0	0	0	0	
6%	.2	1.2	−4	16	3.2	
2%	.1	0.2	−8	64	6.4	
	1.0	$\overline{X} = 10.0$			19.2	
					$s^2 = 19.2/5 = 3.84$	1.96

The standard deviation of a series of numbers may be written:

$$s = \sqrt{\frac{\sum (X - \overline{X})^2}{N}}$$

to an amount equal the cost of the investment. But he felt payback to be a better measure of risk.

Williams felt that no one could know at the time an investment was made what rate of return would actually be realized. But some measures could be made. Rally Dawson Sports had tried in the past to measure risk by a probability distribution of estimated rates of return on its investments. In one attempt he had gone so far as to estimate annual returns for the joint venture. This is shown in Exhibit 5. The probability measurement chart shown could be used to measure statistically Rally Dawson Sports estimate of risk. Calculations of the variance and the standard deviation of the distribution were possible. Exhibits 6, 7, and 8 show additional projected financial statements for the joint venture that Williams had shown up. At this point they were not yet considered to be final projections.

EXHIBIT 6 PROJECTED STATEMENT OF ANNUAL COST OF SALES FOR JOINT VENTURE (1976–80) (Dollars in Thousands)*

	1976	*1977*	*1978*	*1979*	*1980*
Inventory (beg. of year)	$ 500	$1,100	$1,830	$2,440	$2,134
Material purchases	600	800	1,000	600	650
Direct Labor	200	350	400	375	360
Factory Overhead:					
Fuel	50	55	60	60	65
Insurance	115	115	115	120	120
Utilities	40	45	50	50	55
Maint. and Repair	30	35	60	50	50
Property taxes	200	200	200	200	200
Trucks	30	20	15	25	20
Employee Benefits	60	60	60	60	60
Depreciation	175	150	150	150	150
	$2,000	$2,930	$3,940	$4,134	$3,864
Less:					
Inventory (end of year)	$1,100	$1,830	$2,440	$2,134	$ 864
Cost of Sales	$ 900	$1,100	$1,500	$2,000	$3,000

**Translated from rupees to dollars*

EXHIBIT 7 PROJECTED STATEMENT OF ANNUAL EARNINGS FOR JOINT VENTURE (1976–80) (Dollars in Thousands)*

	1976	*1977*	*1978*	*1979*	*1980*
Sales	$1,800	$2,300	$3,000	$4,000	$5,500
Cost of Sales	900	1,100	1,500	2,000	3,000
Gross Profit	900	1,300	1,500	2,000	2,500

Selling Expenses					
Sal. and Comm.	185	200	225	275	300
Advertising	40	50	75	100	150
Delivery and Freight	45	55	65	85	125
Automobile	30	10	8	15	25
Depreciation	175	150	150	150	150
	$ 475	$ 465	$ 523	$ 625	$ 750
Admn. Expenses					
Salaries	$ 120	$ 115	$ 120	$ 130	$ 150
Profess. fees	80	110	70	50	40
Printing and Postage	25	30	22	25	30
Telep. & Telegraph	30	40	35	45	50
Taxes and licenses	100	120	130	150	175
Sundry	35	20	35	40	60
Interest	24	30	24	24	24
	$ 414	$ 455	$ 920	$ 464	$ 529
	$ 889	$ 920	$ 959	$1,089	$1,279
Net Profit before taxes	$ 11	$ 380	$ 541	$ 911	$1,221
Income taxes	6	228	324	546	732
Net Profit	$ 4	$ 152	$ 217	$ 364	$ 488

**Translated from rupees to dollars*

EXHIBIT 8 PROJECTED STATEMENT OF ANNUAL CASH FLOWS FOR JOINT VENTURE (1976–80) (Dollars in Thousands)*

	1976	*1977*	*1978*	*1979*	*1980*
Cash Receipts	$1,600	$2,400	$3,000	$4,000	$4,500
PIDC Loan	200	100	200	——	——
Bank Advances	300	100	200	——	——
	$2,100	$2,600	$3,400	$4,000	$4,500
Cash Disbursements					
Raw material Purchases	$ 600	$ 800	$1,000	$ 600	$ 650
Direct Labor	200	350	400	375	360
Factory Overhead	700	680	710	715	720
Selling Expenses	475	465	523	625	750
Admn. Expenses	414	455	436	464	529
Income taxes	6	228	324	546	732
Plant addition	——	——	20	——	——
Long Term Debt Repayment	——	——	——	——	——
Bank repayment	24	48	48	60	60
	$2,419	$3,026	$3,461	$3,385	$3,801
Cash over (short)	$ (319)	$ (426)	$ (61)	$ 615	$ 699
Cash balance (begin.)	800	481	55	6	609
Cash balance (end)	$ 481	$ 55	$ (6)	$ 609	$1,308

**Translated from rupees to dollars*

PAUL MUELLER COMPANY

Paul Mueller Company is a manufacturing organization with approximately 600 employees working in the design, production, and sale of a diversified line of standard and custom-made stainless steel equipment. Its products are used for cooling, heating, storing, or conveying products in the dairy, brewery, winery, food processing, chemical, and pharmaceutical industries. Principal products include bulk-milk cooler tanks, beer storage tanks, beer fermenting tanks, cookers, mixers, blenders, carbonaters, washers, pasteurizers, chemical tanks, transfer surfaces, tank heads, and conveyors.

The *Thomas Register of American Manufacturers* lists the company under the heading "food and meat processing equipment." Moody's *Industrial Manual* codes the firm under both "machinery" and "plant equipment." The company is a member of the National Association of Food and Dairy Equipment Manufacturers. On the other hand, its bulk milk coolers are shipped under Brussels' nomenclature "refrigerators and refrigerating equipment." Likewise, Schedule B nomenclature refers to them as "commercial-type refrigerators and freezers."

Mueller's competitors are many because of the company's broad product mix. However, for a given product line such as bulk-milk coolers, its principal competitors can be identified. For example, approximately 90 percent of all domestic bulk-milk cooler sales are made by the Paul Mueller Company, Zero Manufacturing Company, Whirlpool Corporation, Van Vetter, Dairy Kool, Girton, and the C. P. Division of St. Regis Paper Company.

COMPANY BACKGROUND

Paul Mueller was incorporated in 1946. By the end of 1971 its total assets had risen to $14.5 million. Sales in 1971 had grown to a record high of $19.3 million. Direct export sales were being made in Central America, South America, the Caribbean, Europe, Africa, the Near East, and the Pacific. A wholly owned Canadian facility had been purchased in 1967, and a joint venture established in 1968 in the

Prepared by Professor C. E. Ferguson, Jr., University of Alabama and L. Dandurand, University of Nevada-Las Vegas.

Netherlands was operating at capacity. In addition, plans were being formulated to expand facilities of the joint venture while direct export sales had risen to approximately $900,000. Assets of the Canadian subsidiary represented about 9 percent of total consolidated assets and Mueller's recognized share of the joint-venture income amounted to about $245,000 before taxes, or approximately 6 percent of total net income before taxes.

Paul Mueller attributes his company's success "largely to the reputation it has established by producing the highest quality stainless steel products available" (1971 Annual Report). The company's reputation is based on craftsmanship, and craftsmanship is a function of facilities, personnel, and pride. Its plant facilities include standard and customized machines designed for cutting, forming, machining, welding, finishing, and testing. It also has storage, materials handling, and shipping facilities, including overhead cranes, trucks, and railroad sidings.

The firm's employees include skilled welders, machinists, engineers, salesmen, accountants, and management. Most of them have worked at Mueller's for several years and are proud of their achievements.

An active research and development program is stressed, and it has developed such products as Mueller Temp-Plate Heat Transfer Surface or "Temp-Plate," Mueller-Matic Automatic Washing Systems or "Mueller-Matic," and HiPer Form Refrigerant Control System or "HiPerForm." Furthermore, customized machinery is designed and constructed for the firm's own use. In addition, the program has developed a set of trademarks, patents, and licenses.

A prime goal or long-term objective of the Paul Mueller Company is to maximize returns on its stockholders' equity. To do this it has defined its sales territory to be worldwide.

The company desires an image of quality, and although it would produce a wide range of items for any industry, it maintains an emphasis on stainless steel products for selected processing industries such as dairy, food, and beverage. The firm wants to grow through expansion of its product lines, increased sales of existing items, and international expansion. During this growth process, bulk milk coolers remain at the center of attention because of their dependability in providing revenue and profit.

PRODUCT LINE

Mueller's has become one of the world's largest manufacturers of farm-type bulk milk coolers. This position was attained in large measure due to its reputation, craftsmanship, and aggressiveness. However, the Mueller "TempPlate," which was developed and patented by Mueller's, provides the firm with a competitive advantage.

Heat transfer is a critical characteristic of bulk milk tanks. Some competitors utilize an "icebank" approach, where ice water is circulated around the tank in between the inner and outer walls. Others use coils similar to domestic refrigerators. Mueller's however, utilizes a heat-transfer plate. This plate is constructed by spot-welding the center portion two sheets of stainless steel, and welding the edges. A gas is then forced between the sheets which causes them to separate and form "passageways." This product then becomes the inner wall of a bulk milk tank. One side of this surface comes into actual contact with the milk. The surface covers the entire bottom of the tank and parts of the sides; therefore, most of the milk comes into immediate contact with the cooling surface. The refrigerant is then pumped

TABLE 1 PAUL MUELLER COMPANY AND SUBSIDIARIES FIVE-YEAR SUMMARY OF OPERATIONS

	1975	*1974*	*1973*	*1972*	*1971*
Net Sales	$32,154,314	$35,396,364	$27,521,304	$25,832,229	$19,296,612
Cost of Sales	22,869,253	28,168,765	20,784,013	18,683,295	13,644,447
Gross Profit	9,285,061	7,227,599	6,737,291	7,148,934	5,652,165
Selling, General and Administrative Expenses	4,043,479	3,977,730	3,349,137	3,000,223	2,664,562
Operating Income	5,241,582	3,249,869	3,388,154	4,148,711	2,987,603
Other Income (Expense):					
Interest Expense	(161,499)	(161,564)	(31,080)	(5,604)	(15,978)
Other, Net	137,877	127,918	45,972	173,533	142,912
	(23,622)	(33,646)	14,892	167,929	126,934
Income Before Provision for Income Taxes	5,217,960	3,216,223	3,403,046	4,316,640	3,114,537
Provision for Income Taxes:					
Currently Payable	2,390,000	1,354,000	1,599,000	2,067,000	1,557,000
Deferred, Net	41,000	80,000	49,000	(19,000)	—
	2,431,000	1,434,000	1,648,000	2,048,000	1,557,000
Income Before Equity in Earnings of Joint Venture	2,786,960	1,782,223	1,755,046	2,268,640	1,557,537
Equity in Earnings of Joint Venture, Net of U.S. Tax Provision	82,880	501,143	388,231	198,254	146,969
Net Income	2,869,840	2,283,366	2,143,277	2,466,894	1,704,506
Other Statistics—Consolidated					
Earnings Per Common Share	2.25	1.78	1.67	1.92	1.31
Weighted Average Shares Outstanding	1,277,609	1,283,575	1,286,242	1,286,242	1,300,187
Cash Dividends Declared Per Share of Common Stock	.62	.585	.52	.4576	.44
Stock Dividends Declared on Common Stock	—	10%	10%	—	—
Shareholders Equity (Net Worth)	16,943,000	14,908,000	13,445,000	11,905,000	9,982,000
Working Capital	10,759,000	7,782,000	7,963,000	7,770,000	6,047,000
Book Value Per Share of Common Stock	13.26	11.61	10.45	9.26	7.68
Capital Expenditures	401,000	1,097,000	1,680,000	768,000	223,000
Average Number of Employees	784	963	802	701	582

through the "Temp-Plate" cooling the milk. Turbulence, created by forcing the refrigerant through the surface, also speeds the cooling process. This heat surface is sold as a separate product, and also becomes a component of other products where rapid cooling is desired.

Several bulk-milk tank lines are available, and each line has several items. For example, the Model "O" series contains eighteen listed sizes ranging from 300 gallons to 5,000 gallons. In addition, unusual sizes can be custom made. Product units can be self-contained, or remote (when compressor and condensor are separated from the tank). Accessories such as the "Mueller-Matic" automatic washing system can be purchased with the tank. Consequently, although a given dealer may be carrying only the bulk-milk cooler line, there are a wide assortment of product items to offer the consumer.

DISTRIBUTION NETWORK

Domestically, the firm distributes nationwide through its company salesmen and independent dealers. The salesmen are located throughout the U. S. and call on dealers. They are responsible to the bulk-milk cooler sales manager at the home office. The firm also has a processing equipment sales manager at the home office responsible for other lines. Dealers include such businesses as farm implement agencies and cooperatives.

Except for Europe and Canada, international sales are the responsibility of the international sales manager. He performs the same role on the international scene that the Mueller salesmen fulfill in the domestic market. He contacts, arranges contracts, and maintains continuing relationships with dealers in foreign markets. The Canadian market is organized similarly to that of the U. S. However, the European market is somewhat different.

European sales are made by dealers but contracts are arranged by Mueller Europa—the Netherlands joint venture. In addition, a subsidiary of the foreign partner has an exclusive contract with Mueller Europa covering the Benelux market. The international distribution system of Paul Mueller Company is shown in Figure 1.

Physical distribution of international sales depends upon the item sold. Bulk coolers are manufactured in the U. S., the Netherlands, and Canada. Bulk coolers are heavy and bulky. To the extent possible they are shipped from the nearest source by rail, barge, and ship. Trucks are also to be used as necessary.

LANDED PRICE

Price as a competitive tool plays a less important role than product in the bulk-milk cooler line. Certainly, price is important and will be weighed against other factors by the industrial purchaser. Moreover, high tariffs and an inflexible pricing structure often restrict sales in a given foreign market. However, the buyer is usually looking for a quality product at a "reasonable" price.

Prices vary considerably for a given product line. For example, the model "O" series contains list prices ranging from $2,598 to $17,000. These prices correspond to sizes ranging from 300 to 5,000 gallons respectively.

International dealers receive a 45 percent discount off list. This enables them to adjust their selling prices in accordance with local conditions and their own requirements. For example, they in turn could sell for list less 10 percent.

Mueller's grants different discounts for its washer system and replacement parts and accessories. These discounts are 50 percent and 43 percent respectively.

FIGURE 1

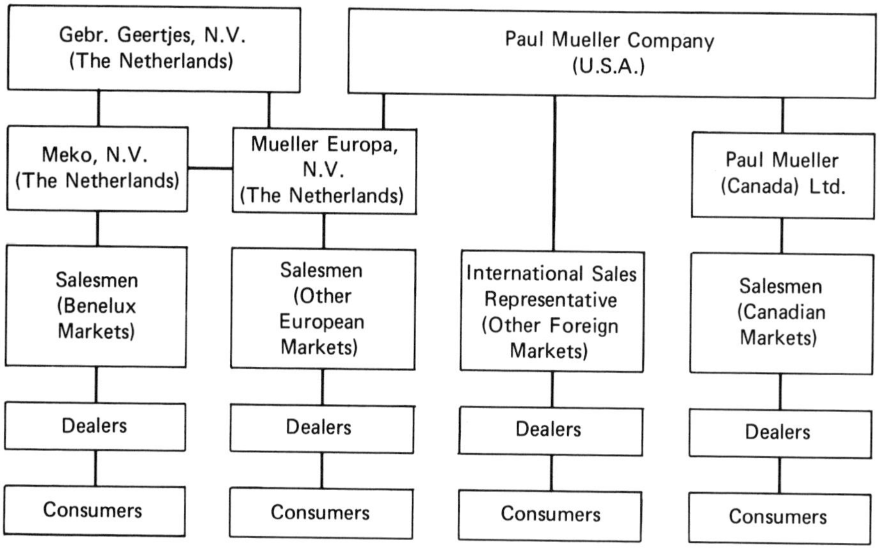

All prices are F.O.B. Springfield regardless of the quantity involved. Naturally, these prices would not apply to the Canadian or the Netherlands operations. Mueller's would include cost, marine insurance, domestic inland freight, ocean freight, and documentation and handling charges of a freight forwarder. In many cases the C.I.F. value would be used as a basis for applying the importation tariff. If the importer lived inland from the port of entry, the firm could also assist in estimating tariffs and foreign inland freight charges to determine a pro-forma landed cost at point of destination.

Payment terms are usually on the basis of a confirmed, irrevocable letter of credit in U. S. dollars. In some cases, specific arrangements could be made with the credit department. International purchases do not qualify for the Volume Purchase Refund Plan or the Cooperative Advertising Program. Finally, the firm does not charge extra for meeting specific electrical requirements or for preparing slatted-type crating for shipment. On the other hand, an extra charge is made for preparation of solid-type, export boxing.

INTERNATIONAL PROMOTION

International promotion consists mainly of brochures and personal salesmanship. Each dealer has a manual referring to the Mueller Company, prices, parts, warranties, instructions, and specifications. Some of the information has been translated. For example, the Latin American dealer receives a "Manual de Ventas" regarding Mueller's "enfriadores de leche." Likewise, some of the brochures have been translated. One brochure is entitled "El Método Mueller." In this case the brochure is a literal translation maintaining pictures and layout of the U. S. or English version. Occasionally, ads are placed in the international media similar to Mueller's domestic ads appearing in the *Dairy Review.* However, even in the domestic market, the primary promotional emphasis is placed on personal salesmanship.

The Paul Mueller Company is subject to most of the problems affecting its competition such as increasing prices of stainless steel and labor. Its strength lies in craftsmanship, research and development, patented products, and management. It does not appear to enjoy relative advantages in its distribution system, its pricing, or its promotion. Its bulk-milk cooler lines could experience increasing difficulty in maintaining overall competitiveness in certain foreign markets as those markets or nearby markets establish facilities and develop technical capability either through domestic or international investment. Paul Mueller currently has a good organization and enjoys a product advantage, but that may not suffice to sustain it. If it wants to continue to grow and prosper, it may be required to establish more direct investments, and to parallel this process with the development of an effective distribution system. This appears to be especially relevant to the Brazilian market in particular and the LAFTA market in general.

TABLE 2 PAUL MUELLER COMPANY AND SUBSIDIARIES CONSOLIDATED BALANCE SHEET, December 31, 1975 and 1974

Assets Current Assets	*1975*	*1974*
Cash (Note 5)	$ 435,865	$ 168,844
Marketable securities, at cost, which approximates market	2,400,000	—
Notes receivable, current maturities	522,374	303,732
Accounts receivable, less reserve of $61,450 in 1975 and $54,262 in 1974 for doubtful accounts (Note 1)	3,934,640	5,620,805
Inventories, at the lower of cost (last-in, first-out) or market	7,489,996	12,084,060
Prepayments	102,824	84,369
Total Current Assets	$14,885,699	$18,261,810
Notes Receivable, less current maturities	389,477	891,409
Equity in Underlying Net Assets of Joint Venture (Note 1)	1,095,329	1,206,931
Other Assets	147,278	143,349
Property, Plant and Equipment, at cost (Note 1):		
Land and land improvements	1,172,787	1,126,147
Buildings	3,987,587	3,995,795
Shop equipment	4,535,358	4,308,177
Transportation, office and other equipment	541,247	489,435
Construction in progress	14,480	53,315
	10,251,459	9,972,869
Less—Accumulated depreciation	5,180,126	4,641,536
	5,071,333	5,331,333
	21,589,116	25,834,832

Liabilities Current Liabilities		
Notes payable to banks (Note 5)	—	4,000,000
Accounts payable	1,123,106	2,563,618
Accrued expenses—		
Federal and state income taxes	937,424	10,030
Payrolls and vacations	948,241	1,052,387
Other	256,677	165,176
Advance billings	861,590	2,688,375
Total Current Liabilities	4,127,038	10,479,586
Deferred Income Taxes (Note 4)	495,000	418,000
Interest-Free Forgivable Loan of Canadian Subsidiary	24,475	29,370
Shareholders' Investment:		
Common stock, par value $1 per share— Authorized 3,000,000 shares Issued 1,342,325 shares	1,342,325	1,342,325
Paid-in surplus	4,306,728	4,301,833
Retained earnings	11,872,797	9,795,467
	17,521,850	15,439,625
Less—Treasury stock 68,883 shares in 1975 and 64,083 shares in 1974, at cost	579,247	531,749
	16,942,603	14,907,876
	21,589,116	25,834,832

THE DAIRY INDUSTRY

Demand Factors

In 1971, the Paul Mueller entity reported net earnings of $1.7 million for its stockholders. This figure represented a return on shareholders' equity exceeding 18 percent after taxes. A substantial proportion of the return was associated with bulk milk tanks, and a substantial proportion of bulk milk tanks was associated with foreign markets.

Prosperity can be short-lived. Perceived needs and ways to meet them can change rapidly. A bulk milk tank is not immune to this danger of obsolescence. Therefore, a progressive organization attempts to predict changing needs, and ways of fulfilling those needs. Likewise to forecast behavior, management needs to understand the total environment. In this way predictive models will be able to cope with the dynamics of the international marketplace.

To understand the problem of environment one must analyze the product itself, i.e., its characteristics, the target market, the supplier industry, and the user industry. A bulk milk cooler is designed to rapidly cool milk, and to keep it cool. Milk is a very perishable product. It is an excellent culture for bacterial growth. Milk which is rapidly cooled and kept cool will inhibit bacterial growth. The ultimate consumer demands "fresh" milk.

TABLE 3 PAUL MUELLER COMPANY AND SUBSIDIARIES, SALES DATA BY PRODUCT CATEGORY (In Thousands of Dollars)

	1975		*1974*		*1973*		*1972*		*1971*	
	Sales	Percent of total sales	Sales	Percent of total sales	Sales	Percent of total sales	Sales	Percent of total sales	Sales	Percent of total sales
Farm Milk Coolers	$ 9,791	30%	$14,230	40%	$14,405	52%	$14,736	57%	$11,268	58%
Food Processing Equipment	6,874	21%	4,072	11%	3,166	12%	2,667	10%	2,615	14%
Beverage Equipment	6,471	20%	10,502	30%	5,168	19%	5,214	20%	3,437	18%
Industrial Equipment	7,230	23%	3,473	10%	3,114	11%	1,927	8%	1,249	6%
Construction Products	1,788	6%	3,119	9%	1,668	6%	1,288	5%	728	4%
Total	32,154	100%	35,396	100%	27,521	100%	25,832	100%	19,297	100%

There are many factors influencing the sale of milk. Some of these include governmental regulations on sanitary levels, cultural patterns, industry promotion, education, standard of living, substitutes, and cost. Milk kept at 5°–10° above freezing may extend the retail shelf life by one to two weeks while maintaining taste and meeting sanitary regulations. Certainly, this affects cost, and therefore, competitiveness with "substitutes."

Cost of the product to the ultimate consumer is also affected by "bulk" handling methods at different links in the channel. The reduced cost of bulk handling affects not only "fluid" milk, but also "manufacturing" milk which is converted into cheese, powdered milk, and other dairy products. Therefore, in order to properly evaluate links in the derived demand/needs chain, one should start by analyzing the ultimate consumer of all products derived from milk. Working backwards, one could continue to use this same approach until reaching the initial point of production, i.e., the dairy farm. Eventually, utilizing this derived approach, and building conclusions based on the information gathered into the model, one can begin to predict the effects on the sales of bulk milk coolers due to changes in the problem environment.

When the changeover to bulk milk coolers began in the U. S. about 1955, a substantial proportion of American household consumers had already installed domestic refrigerators and were demanding inexpensive quality milk. Likewise, an infrastructure capable of supporting a more efficient milk supply system had been established. In other words, when the Paul Mueller Company entered the market, the ultimate consumer was demanding products which required the intermediate use of the bulk milk coolers. In addition, the necessary roads, electric power, transportation equipment, and supporting technology were available.

Brazil: A Potential Market?

It was thought that the Brazilian consumer would also demand products requiring the bulk milk cooler. In a rapidly changing society, it is expected that over the long-run there will be an increasing demand for the final products and hence, bulk milk tanks. Another product might meet these needs, however with good projections and a strong research and development and marketing program, it seems reasonable to assume increasing demand for bulk milk tanks in the Brazilian market.

The acceptance of a changeover to bulk milk tanks is closely related to level of economic development. The changeover to bulk milk tanks is closely related to level of economic development. The changeover can be perceived as a result of and a contribution to economic development. In a market such as Brazil, which can be considered an underdeveloped market, it may be desirable or necessary to "create" demand. One approach would be to concentrate on a "key" link in the channel such as the processor, i.e., the creamery or processing plant. This was the approach used in the U.S. However, in the U.S. market the demand and infrastructure were already available.

BRAZIL

Brazil is located in the southern half of the western hemisphere. It occupies substantial portions of the northern, central, and eastern parts of South America, or approximately one-half of the total land area of the subcontinent. With its 3.3 million square miles of land, it is the fifth largest country in the world. It has 4.5 thousand miles of coastline fronting the Atlantic Ocean. By 1970, its population had exceeded 92 million persons, making it the eighth most populous nation in the world.

The country has extensive mineral resources: iron ore, coal, petroleum, uranium, gold, manganese, tungsten, bauxite, nickel, quartz, lead, zinc, diamonds, and silver. Its forest area covers about 1.4 million square miles, and is rich in timber, fruits, resins, fibers, and waxes. Most of Brazil's land is located in the tropical zone roughly on lines paralleling Belem and Rio de Janeiro. South of Rio de Janeiro/Sao Paulo is the temperate zone. Arable land is found mainly in the south. The country has an extensive river system, much of it potentially capable of providing hydroelectric power.

Although, to a large extent Brazil is self-sufficient, it is still considered an underdeveloped country, and it must import certain materials and industrial products. Also, it suffers from many of the problems affecting other underdeveloped countries, such as: few rich and many poor, sophisticated cities and backward rural areas, dependence on a one crop economy, political instability, lack of capital, lack of infrastructure, and lack of technological skills. However, in the last fifteen years the country has experienced remarkable industrial development.

Concentrating mainly on the southern region around Rio de Janeiro and Sao Paulo, the country has been able to attain self-sufficiency in many lines of manufactured goods and appliances for industrial, agricultural, and domestic use. In addition, Brazil has increased its ability to export finished goods, thereby eliminating its traditional reliance on either sugar, gold, rubber, or coffee to earn foreign exchange.

Brazilian culture has also been influenced by the importation of Negro slaves from Africa, and the immigration of Italians, Portuguese, Spaniards, Germans, Japanese, and others. Unlike other Latin American countries such as Mexico, Peru and Guatemala, the Indians of Brazil had never reached a level of civilization comparable to that of the Aztecs, Incas, or Mayas. Therefore, the Indian contribution to the Brazilian culture is relatively minor, and explains a major difference between Brazil and many other Latin American countries. All of these influences in a new physical/social environment have made the Brazilian a unique individual.

Recent Developments

Education has experienced a significant improvement. By the mid 1960s the country had over 4,000 secondary schools with about 1.5 million students. The secondary school system had developed programs relating to commercial, agriculture, and other specialities. In addition, there were thirty-seven universities in the country, and a substantial number of students were studying in foreign countries for advanced degrees.

Other elements of the infrastructure also remain underdeveloped. However, telephone and telegraph service is improving, especially in and between the larger cities. Although the postal services, railroads, and shipping sectors have not kept pace with development, the country has an extensive network of domestic air services and regular international connections are maintained. Hydroelectric power is being increased, and road construction in the interior is being improved and extended. Likewise, a National Housing Plan was put into effect in 1964, and programs are underway relating to medical facilities, water supplies, and irradication of certain diseases such as malaria, yellow fever, and typhoid.

Current Conditions and Trends

Real growth rate in the last four years, 1968–71, has equalled or surpassed 9 percent per annum. In 1971, it was estimated that Brazil would export $3 billion worth of goods and services. Of this figure, manufactured goods would account for 20 percent. In the mid 1960s these goods represented only 5 percent of the total. Coffee which had represented about 50 percent of the total at that time was now down to about 33⅓ percent.

Brazil, under the direction of a "right-wing" military/technocratic government, with the apparent approval of the majority of Brazilians, is experiencing relative stability, low wages, an expanding domestic market, abundant raw materials supplies, and a base to supply LAFTA as well as other foreign markets. These and other conditions seem to indicate that the Brazilian market will continue to expand and offer opportunities to domestic and international businesses.

The Brazilian government has announced that its import policy will be aimed at promoting industrial efficiency and the elimination of excessive protection which keeps prices high to the consumer. It has also stressed balanced growth between the government and private sectors where the private sector includes foreign enterprise.

President Medici's 1971–73 Development Program focuses priority on education and health, agriculture and agricultural marketing, development of science and technology, and strengthening of nationally-owned private industry.

Antonio Delfim Neto, the current finance minister, has built on the policies of Roberto Campos, the former minister of planning and economic spokesman. These policies encourage private enterprise and government intervention. Delfim has instituted an innovation called a "mini-devaluation" or crawling parity, designed to manage a high rate of inflation. Delfim's policies are backed by the current Minister of Planning, Joao Paulo dos Reis Velloso, an economist who graduated from Yale.

Delfim has stated: "We have chosen the capitalist system of development. We believe over the long-run in complete liberalization. We have Brazilian solutions to Brazilian problems."

Based on these policies and past experience, the country has developed the modern corporation, a banking system and a viable stock market. Confidence in Brazil's future is increasing. Wealthy and middle-class Brazilians are investing in Brazil, as are European, Japanese, and U. S. firms. Even "flight" capital from Chile is being invested in the country.

Although official terror still exists, terrorist activity has diminished, there is little organized political opposition, and the majority seems content with expectations of rising prosperity.

Eximbank Chairman Henry Kearns believes that Brazil's size, resources, and self-confidence encourage the belief in continuing stability. In a report published in *Commerce Today* (September 6, 1971), Kearn indicated that Brazil has honored her obligations, has exhibited friendliness to U. S. businessmen, and has encouraged foreign involvement in her economy.

Agriculture in Particular

Regarding agriculture in particular, Kearn stressed that agriculture remains the base of the Brazilian economy, that it is receiving increased attention and government priority, that Brazil is determined to call upon new technology, equipment, and assistance from abroad, that expenditures of $50 million to $100 million were expected to be made annually, and that the U. S. was well-suited to supply the advanced technology and equipment needed.

In addition, the Bank of America reported it had estimated that the agriculture sector would grow about 11 percent in 1971, and of this, farming activities would expand by 19 percent, and cattle raising by 4.8 percent.

Furthermore, the Pan American Union, in its American Republic Series, reports that more than 30 percent of the livestock in Latin America is raised in Brazil; that in the rolling prairies of Rio Grande do Sul, one finds fine herds of Hereford and Polled Angus, and that the Ministry of Agriculture is importing purebreds which are sold to farmers for upgrading of native stock.

American Products

An American firm planning to enter the Brazilian refrigeration market should expect to encounter a monopolistic, competitive type environment. This competition would derive from European and other American exporters, as well as local production.

A given American firm such as the Paul Mueller Company, in addition to its relative product advantage over its American competitors, should enjoy some of the Latin American preference shown for American products. Reasons explaining this preference include: (1) high quality; (2) dependability; (3) reasonable delivery time; and (4) availability of replacement parts. In addition, many Latin Americans prefer to do business with American businessmen because they perceive them to be straightforward, fair, and dependable.

On the other hand, Latin American importers have indicated that American firms have lost sales because: (1) they did not provide reasonable or comparative credit terms; (2) they did not furnish technical information in Spanish; and (3) they delayed in answering correspondence and bid quotations. It would seem, that with a little additional effort and perhaps utilization of Export-Import Bank programs, these problems could be overcome.

Production and Trade

Brazilian gross national product over the past four years has grown at approximately 9 percent per year. In 1971 GNP growth was estimated at 11.3 percent. In 1970, although the country experienced an inflation rate of 19 percent, real growth was 9 percent, and the GNP had grown to $35 billion. Furthermore, by the beginning of 1972, GNP had exceeded $40 billion and was expected to continue rising. Although quite small in comparison with the U. S.' $1 trillion economy, and considering that 60 percent of the population earns less than $40 per month and that 1 percent of the population receives 30 percent of the income, Brazil, especially in its larger cities and surrounding areas in the southeastern part of the country, seems to represent a substantial market for refrigeration products.

By 1970, Brazilian exports had increased to $2.7 billion from $1.6 billion in 1965. Likewise, imports had grown to $2.8 billion from $1.1 billion. Table 4 shows current import and export trends.

A heavy influx of investment funds from the U. S., Europe, and Japan offset any trade deficits and provide Brazil with a strengthening international liquidity position. For example, the country's position changed from $.5 billion in 1965 to $1.6 billion in 1971. Table 5 shows Brazil's liquidity trends.

During this time, and considering the several "mini" devaluations each year, the cruzeiro/dollar exchange rate has gone from Cr. 2,220.0/$1.00 (old cruzeiros) to approximatelay Cr. 5,620/$1.00 (new cruzeiros) in December 1971. The exchange rate are shown in Table 6.

TABLE 4 BRAZILIAN EXPORTS AND IMPORTS 1965 TO 1970

Year	*Exports (Billions of $)*	*Imports (C.I.F.) (Billions of $)*
1970	2.7	2.8
1969	2.3	2.3
1968	1.9	2.1
1967	1.7	1.7
1966	1.7	1.5
1965	1.6	1.1

TABLE 5 BRAZILIAN INTERNATIONAL LIQUIDITY

Year	*International Liquidity (Billions of $)*
1971	1.6
1970	1.2
1969	.7
1968	.3
1967	.2
1966	.4
1965	.5

TABLE 6 U.S. AND BRAZILIAN EXCHANGE RATES

Year	*Cruzeiros per U.S. $*
1971	5.620
1970	4.950
1969	4.350
1968	3.830
1967	2.715
1966	2,220.0*
1965	2,220.0

**On February 13, 1967, one new cruzeiro = 1,000 old cruzeiros.*

The U. S. remains Brazil's major trading partner, although its share of both imports and exports has been declining in recent years. On the other hand, trade between Brazil and other LAFTA countries, especially Argentina has grown. As of 1970, LAFTA accounted for 60–70 percent of Brazilian-manufactured exports. Consequently, the U. S. exporter must be aware of the changing structure of competition, the growth of local capacity, and the possible need or opportunity to establish production capability in the Brazilian market. Brazil's trading pattern in 1970 can be seen in Table 7.

Import Constraints

Brazilian imports are subject to import regulations. Generally, import licenses are not required. However, importers must obtain a *guia de importacao* (import certificate) from the Foreign Trade Department of the Banco de Brasil (Cateira de

TABLE 7 BRAZILIAN TRADING PATTERN FOR 1970

Country or Group	*Percent of Brazil's Imports*	*Percent of Brazil's Exports*
U.S.	27.9	27.4
EEC	23.8	29.2
LAFTA	14.2	10.8
Other European	12.8	13.5
Others	21.3	19.1

Comercio Exterior-CACEX) which is valid for 180 days. The "guia" must be presented to customs in order to have the product released.

Used equipment may be imported provided that it is in good condition, is not obsolete, and cannot be obtained from local producers.

If payment is desired via a letter of credit, the "guia" must be obtained, and foreign exchange must be secured prior to issuance of the credit. The "guia" may be issued in any convertible currency. Usually, it must be obtained prior to shipment.

Currency or foreign exchange can be obtained from any bank authorized to deal in foreign exchange. In purchasing foreign exchange, the importer must close an exchange contract, spot or future delivery. Payments before shipment or prior to the arrival of shipping documents require permission from GECAM (Gerencia de Operacoes de Cambio), the Foreign Exchange Department of Banco Central. Time Drafts can be paid prior to maturity provided a discount is granted.

Chase Manhattan collection experience for sight drafts drawn on Brazilian importers indicates that 32 percent were paid in four weeks and 53 percent in five to ten weeks. Time drafts were 74 percent and 11 percent respectively. Morgan Guaranty Trust reported a combined payment experience of 61 percent for under thirty days, and 29 percent for thirty-one to sixty days. Collection charges for documentary drafts payable abroad for all Brazilian cities for a draft of any amount were applied at a rate of ⅛ percent with a minimum of $2.50.

The exporter to Brazil is required to furnish a set of documents including the following: (1) full set of clean on board bill of lading; (2) signed commercial invoice; (3) marine insurance policy; and (4) statement regarding unused portion of L/C shipments. Regarding marine insurance, under Resolution No. 3171, marine insurance for shipments to Brazil must be placed with insurance companies there. For the placing of insurance abroad, prior permission must be obtained from the Instituto de Resseguros do Brasil.

Credit terms up to 180 days from date of shipment are automatically permissible for all imports. Credit terms exceeding 180 days and up to 360 days require prior approval by CACEX. Imports exceeding 360 days require approval from Banco Central prior to obtaining a "guia." Down payments for shipments on credit terms exceeding 360 days may not exceed 20 percent. The interest rate may not exceed the prevailing rate that was in effect in the financial market of the country in whose currency the transaction was carried out on the date of the "guia."

Import duties are currently relatively high for refrigeration imports into Brazil. Using Brussels Nomenclature 84.15 (Refrigerators and refrigerating equipment, electrical and others), whereas the EEC, Columbia, and the U. S. apply C.I.F. tariff rates of 13 percent, 50 percent, and 13¾ percent respectively, Brazil applies a combined rate of approximately 205 percent. Since the rate for the category of products for which national producers have obtained a measure of production is 16–64 percent, the bulk milk cooler, as well as display cases and walk-in coolers, approximates the range of rates applied to the category of luxury and nonessential goods. For the long-run, at least, this seems inconsistent with the nature of the product. Consequently, although current exports of this product to Brazil may be hindered by this high tariff, previous discussions have demonstrated several economic/environmental factors influencing changes in the Brazilian economy, from which it can be inferred that there will be a tendency for rates to become more reasonable.

AUTHOR INDEX

SUBJECT INDEX